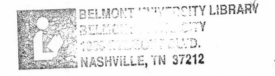

VICTORIAN LITERATURE AND CULTURE

Volume 24

ADVISORY BOARD

VICTORIAN LITERATURE AND CULTURE

Volume 24

EDITORS

JOHN MAYNARD
ADRIENNE AUSLANDER MUNICH

AMS PRESS
1996

ISSN 1060-1503

Series ISBN 0-404-64200-4

Vol. 24 ISBN 0-404-64224-1

Library of Congress Catalog Card Number: 73-80684

For current subscription information or back orders for volumes 19-23, write to AMS Press, Inc., 56 East 13th Street, New York, NY 10003-4686, USA.

VICTORIAN LITERATURE AND CULTURE is a publication of the Browning Institute, Inc., a nonprofit organization. It is published through the generous support of New York University, the State University of New York at Stony Brook, and the University of North Dakota. The editors gratefully acknowledge our indebtedness to our editorial assistants Corinne Abate, Megan E. Abbott, Maria Jerinic, and Traci Marie Kelly.

Manuscripts and editorial correspondence can be addressed to either editor: Adrienne Munich, Department of English, SUNY/Stony Brook, Stony Brook, NY 11794 (516 632 9176; fax: 516 632 5729);
John Maynard, Department of English, NYU, 19 University Pl., Rm. 235, N.Y., NY 10003 (212 998 8835; fax: 212 995 4019).

Please submit two copies of manuscripts; articles should be double-spaced throughout and follow the new MLA style (with a list of Works Cited at the conclusion.) Chapters of books submitted for the *Works in Progress* section may follow the author's chosen style in the book project.

Correspondence concerning review essays should be addressed to Winifred Hughes, 50 Wheatsheaf Lane, Princeton, NY 08540 (609 921 1489).

Suggestions for reprints of Victorian materials, texts or illustrations, should be addressed to Jeffrey Spear, Department of English, NYU, 19 University Pl., Rm. 200, N.Y., NY 10003 (212 998 8820; fax: 212 995 4019).

Visit the *VICTORIAN LITERATURE AND CULTURE* web site: http://www.nyu.edu/gsas/dept/english/journal/victorian/

All AMS Books are printed on acid-free paper that meets the guidelines for performance and durability of the Committee on Production Guidelines for Book Longevity of the Council on Library Resources.

Manufactured in the United States of America

CONTENTS

SPECIAL EFFECTS

WORKS IN PROGRESS

REVIEW ESSAYS

BROWNING BIBLIOGRAPHY

ILLUSTRATIONS

Following page 80

THE *MEMSAHIB* AND THE ENDS OF EMPIRE: FEMININE DESIRE IN FLORA ANNIE STEEL'S *ON THE FACE OF THE WATERS*

By Jennifer L. Otsuki

RECENT FEMINIST SCHOLARSHIP has focused on the figure of the *memsahib* and her role in the construction and maintenance of the British empire. Jenny Sharpe suggests that *memsahib* is a ''class restrictive term of address meaning 'lady master,' which was used for the wives of high-ranking civil servants and officers'' (91). The honorific character of the term may well have been guarded carefully within the Anglo-Indian community as a measure of ever finer gradations of rank, but there is no indication that Indians made such rigorous class distinctions in their use of the term. Earlier historical accounts of colonialism have largely effaced the participation of women in the empire, and in the few places where she has been allowed to appear, it is usually as the cause of the bitter racial and social divisiveness of colonial society. The *memsahib* is invariably identified as the figure who most actively enforces the terms of this segregation. ''Few women have been described so negatively as the British *memsahib,* referred to in one recent history as 'the most noxious figure in the annals of British imperialism''' (Gartrell 165). Feminist historians and critics have attempted to reconstruct the political and social complexity of the European woman's position in colonialism, exploring her involuntary absorption into the symbolic political and racial structure of empire as well as her complicity in the processes of imperial expansion and consolidation. The vilification of the *memsahib* is symptomatic of the palpable contradiction running through the ideological structure of empire, which grants her racial privilege, but denies her the free enjoyment of mastery.

The contradictory position of the *memsahib* can be summed up by juxtaposing two accounts of the figure, both taken from former members of the Raj, but given from opposing perspectives — an opposition that is tellingly divided along gendered lines. John Morris evaluates the *memsahib*'s contribution to the structure of British empire in the following terms:

> Most of them started out as perfectly reasonable, decent English girls . . . and many of them in the course of time developed into what I can only describe as the most awful old harridans. And I think they were very largely responsible for the break-up of relations between the British and the Indians. In the early days, before the Englishwoman went out to India at all, British officers spent much of their time with Indians, got to know them better, got to know the language well and so on, whereas once the Englishwoman started to arrive in India she expected her husband to spend his time with her. She couldn't communicate with anybody except her cook who knew a few words of English, so she was forced to rely almost solely upon her husband for amusement and company. I don't think she realized what a menace she was. (Allen 176–77)

Vere Birdwood, a member of a distinguished Anglo-Indian family whose association with empire dates back to 1765, offers a faithful echo of Morris's depiction of Englishwomen, but with this crucial difference: she links the image of feminine insularity to the ideological structure of the empire. She observes that English brides

> never entirely integrated with India and this was terribly important as far as the whole ethos of the Raj was concerned. The men were very closely integrated but not their wives. We were in India, we were looked after by Indian servants and we met a great many Indians, and some of us undoubtedly made a very close study of India and Indian customs, but once you stepped inside the home you were back in Cheltenham or Bath. We brought with us in our home lives almost exact replicas of the sort of life that upper middle class people lived in England. (Allen 72)

Where he finds guilt, she finds ethos. The exclusiveness that he identifies with the collapse and end of empire, she identifies with its ideological and cultural origins. As Birdwood indicates, the social isolation of the *memsahib* was essential to the "whole ethos of the Raj." Her insularity is the very condition which makes possible the recreation of the highly ritualized social life of Home (that is, English domestic culture), which is precisely what she has been imported from England to accomplish.

Historically, the social interactions between the races decreased with the increase in the number of European women in India.[2] The *memsahib*'s complete failure "to integrate" with the surrounding native culture — an intractability which it is important to note that Birdwood, like Morris, does not associate with her male counterparts — is converted into the topos of feminine guilt. The decay of relationships between colonizer and colonized is laid directly at the feet of the *memsahib,* whose increasing numbers only make more glaringly apparent the lack of social interchange between European and Indian societies. The twin images of feminine insularity and feminine guilt become an endlessly repeated theme in the imperial narratives of the period. Forster strikes the familiar note when he declares in *A Passage to India* that

> it is possible to keep in with Indians and Englishmen, but he who would also keep in with Englishwomen must drop the Indians. The two wouldn't combine. Useless to blame either party, useless to blame them for blaming one another. It just was so, and one had to choose. (65–66)

The image of masculine intimacy with the native male will be examined at greater length. It is invoked here to underscore the failure of the *memsahib* and the Indian to "combine." The relationship is encased in futility, and Forster's apparent plea for tolerance towards these traditional combatants only succeeds in extracting the entire relationship from any causal history which would allow for a sustained analysis of the social breakdown. He defers to the image of a timeless, irrational, inevitable incompatibility. The *memsahib* is accused of an "intransigent ethnocentrisim" which has led "scholars of Indian colonial history to conclude that British women were largely responsible for maintaining social distance between the rulers and the ruled" (Chaudhuri 232).

But domestic life in the colonies imposed its own peculiar conditions and constraints, which require particular examination. It was essential that the colonial world achieve a decisive reconnection with European social forms as part of its mission of cultural aggrandizement. But the colonial reproduction of English life had a distinct tendency to harden into ritual and icon, in large part because it was too remote from its point of reference (England) to risk an autonomous process of development. The authorizing context of Home was too far removed to exercise reliable checks or adjustments to the adaptation of social forms in the colonies. How could the colonist guarantee that the adaptation would not become decay and de-evolution, the result of the insidious influence of the Indian climate and lifestyle? The rituals of daily life were required to take on a static, timeless character very different from their English counterpart, and nowhere was this tendency more apparent than in the role reserved for women. The burden of cultural authenticity, always a subject of intense anxiety in the remote regions of empire, rested on the efforts of white women to construct a racially and symbolically pure imitation of English life. But it was an image of England that belonged to what Homi Bhabha refers to as the "patriotic, atavistic temporality of Traditionalism" (Bhabha 300).

This tradition of the domestic icon reaches a crisis in the novels of the late Victorian period, both those set in England and those in the colonial world. The works of Forster, Flora Annie Steel, and Olive Schreiner incorporate the sense of this crisis in their representations of the *memsahib.* The colonial conflict in *A Passage to India* originates in a problem of gender identity, triggered by the modern sensibilities of Adela Quested, a newcomer from what Forster describes as "feminist England." Her first encounter with the alien geography of India produces a disorientation which jolts her out of the confines of the classic trope she has come to India to fulfill: the traditional courtship and marriage plot of domestic fiction. But she fails to comprehend the extent to which individual identity and desire, masculine or feminine, but especially feminine, have been extinguished on behalf of ethnic and national community. The weight of the imperial order attempts to contain her within the limits of the symbolic identity white women are required to fulfill in the colonial structure. Adela, as the figure of the feminist *memsahib,* is caught between opposing political agendas: her attempt to establish an autonomous feminine identity is relentlessly reinscribed into the atavistic reductiveness of the colonial structure.

In the opposition between native and colonizer, or between the colonies and Europe, the *memsahib* represents a middle term in which the contradictions of the colonial equation are revealed. From the perspective of contemporary "feminist England," they appeared to be symbols of the oppressed, women trapped in the patriarchal forms of past generations, representing the anti-progressive, anachronistic, mythic residue of an epoch which English feminism had already surpassed. But from the native perspective, the *memsahibs* symbolized the entire network of colonial oppression, the privileged vehicles through which the native's daily social subjugation and humiliation were to be achieved. She is bracketed with the Englishman and his authority by virtue of her racial privilege and the practical social power (or powerlessness) that racial identity produces in the colonial context. This double perception creates a particularly complicated situation for colonial novels of the late Victorian period: when feminine desire becomes a restless, unbounded force attempting to attach itself to newly defined objects which necessitate redefinitions of the meaning and function of domestic culture, the threat to the ideological coherence of empire is immeasurable.

Flora Annie Steel was a popular essayist and novelist, whose *Complete Indian Housekeeper and Cook* (1888) served as a handbook for the uninitiated Englishwoman making her first trip to India. Her extensive Indian writings (including many novels and short stories set in India, several histories of the country, and an autobiography detailing her years in India as the wife of a civil engineer) established her reputation among her contemporaries as an authority on both Indian and Anglo-Indian life, prompting Maude Diver to compare her in admiring terms to Kipling.[3] Steel's contribution to the rhetoric of empire is her adroit, complex, always-ideologically-engaged manipulation of the most common racial and sexual stereotypes surrounding both the Indian character and the image of the *memsahib.* Steel's Indian writings offer a kind of case study of colonialist typologies. She combines the iconic images of racial and sexual identity, forcing them to brush up against each other in ways which allow them to illuminate imperial discourse beyond the conceptual boundaries of simply stereotypes —

without withdrawing her own belief in their continuing viability in the narrative of empire.

Her first and most famous novel, *On the Face of the Waters* (1896), is structured by a double plot, detailing on the one hand the political unrest which culminates in the Sepoy Revolt of 1857 and the siege of Delhi, and on the other hand, the failure of English domesticity, centering upon an Englishman's abandonment of his marital and familial obligations. Both plots converge in their mutual attempt to define the primary function and symbolism of the English patriarch, in his double incarnation as imperial father. Each plot vies to answer definitively and exclusively which relationship will define the primary terms of his paternity: the biological and cultural ties of a patrilinear inheritance, descending in untainted racial purity from father to son, or the figuratively paternal yet erotically charged relationship between English officer and native soldier. The conflict between domestic and military duty is an ongoing dilemma of empire, but Steel thematizes the conflict as a sexual rivalry between the *memsahib* and the native, thereby exposing the homoerotic structure of imperial patriarchy. The *memsahib's* position in the imperial triangle makes her a rival to the other masculine figures, and it is this accession to masculine forms of privilege and position that links Steel's representation of the *memsahib* to the contemporary feminist challenges to both English and colonial domestic culture. The Englishwoman enters this rivalry in the name of the domestic, but it is a domesticity that has undergone significant reorganization, in which active feminine desire plays a complex and subversive role. Within a colonial context, it is necessary to create a privileged symbolic position for white women, which reinforces both cultural and racial difference. The problem is to sustain this difference without at the same time endowing the *memsahib* with practical political authority, which would undermine the connection to a tradition of privatization of the feminine in the domestic realm. Steel submits the figure of the *memsahib* to a disciplinary process that will allow for the ideological recuperation of domestic culture: in *On the Face of the Waters,* the rehabilitation of the domestic is a necessary parallel to the reestablishment of British control of India. The imperial objective cannot be severed from the domestic, but they are never fully reconcilable. It is the *memsahib* who will bear the responsibility for these contradictory impulses. Steel takes the internal contradiction in the logic of empire as the central problem of the Sepoy Revolt, providing one of the most sustained and revealing accounts of the role white women were obliged to play in the formation of imperial discourse.

* * *

JUST BEFORE THE OUTBREAK of the Sepoy Revolt, Charles Morecomb, a British officer in *On the Face of the Waters,* insists that it is useless to attempt to differentiate between cause and effect in India, since both are "incomprehensible." The scene is the Residency of Delhi, whose gardens present a startlingly precise replica of an English park. The only incongruity in this perfectly sculpted reproduction is the sight of a Mohamedan tomb attached to the house. The scene is a palimpsest, with the history of one conqueror of the Indian terrain peering through that of another. The English occupants have long ago converted the tomb into a house, replacing the gravestone with a dining table. But the transfiguration has not been without its incidents: when the local residents' protest to government produces no response, the Englishman who occupies the house and the government agent who sanctioned the purchase are assassinated. When Morecomb's startled female listener asks if there could be a "connection" between one history and another, he assures her that there can be no causal linkage between scattered instances of disorder, disturbance, burning, etc., because none of these events can be traced to anything like a systematic and generalized resistance to British rule. For "in India, Mrs. Erlton, it is foolish to try and settle which comes first, the owl or the egg. You can't differentiate cause and effect when both are incomprehensible" (148; bk. 2, ch. 5).

Morecombe invokes a familiar motif from the orientalist's rhetoric of India, one that stresses the inexhaustible mystery and irrationality of the east. India represents a geography and a people finally resistant to European efforts at modernization. The elusive character of India sanctions the civilizer's unspoken despair, while providing the apparently inescapable necessity for his continuing colonial presence. The West finds a rationale for the abandonment of rationality in its own conceptualization of its relationship to native culture, pointing to the alternately impervious or incorrigible Indian character as the all encompassing "cause" for the collapse in ordered analysis. Any British responsibility for the failure of order is inconceivable, not because it is impossible in fact but because it functions outside the field of inquiry established by this dual stance of energy and despair.

Another familiar stereotype of empire is juxtaposed to this distinctly masculine shrug of the shoulders, one that joins the irrationality of India to the incoherence of the feminine. The collapse of logical causality produced by the clash of cultures abruptly yields to an image of an exclusively feminine guilt, which places the failure of understanding between British and Indian *men* at the doorstop of the women, both English and Indian. The cashiered officer Jim Douglas observes bitterly that

> all women were alike in this, that they saw the whole world through the medium of their sex; and that was at the bottom of all the mischief. Delhi had been lost to save women; the trouble had begun to please them. . . . (286; bk. 4, ch. 1)

In effect, a clear, sustained analysis of cause and effect is replaced by the image of feminine "mischief," code for the more inclusive image of feminine desire.

Feminine sexuality emerges here as a mechanically appetitive force, manifesting itself as a self-aggrandizing, totalizing drive, which can be seen as the destructive feminine equivalent of a patriarchal imperialism. The reference to the "loss of Delhi" makes clear that feminine desire has managed to obtrude itself into the imperial order, deranging and dispossessing the arrangements and possessions of men.

Yet what is the actual relationship of the feminine to the Sepoy Revolt, according to Steel? As Rebecca Saunders observes, "Incredibly, in Steel's version of the mutiny, it is the taunts of harlots that spur the sepoys to violence" (313). The Indian prostitutes outside the military cantonments at Meerut are "instructed" to inflame the sepoys with the cry "We of the bazaar kiss no cowards!" Steel comments that with this taunt, the "word had been spoken. Nothing so very soul-stirring after all. No consideration of caste or religion, patriotism or ambition. Only a taunt from a pair of painted lips" (191; bk. 2, ch. 7). The triggering event of the war is an image of subversive feminine sexuality. A double history is erased by this gesture. The imperial record of aggressive westernization — which in colonial terms is at once the vehicle, goal, and ideal embodiment of post-enlightenment rationality, as well as the justification for the west's intrusion into the east — suddenly disappears. At the same time, the coalescence of Indian resentment towards the colonial government's ever more coercive interference in Indian cultural and religious practice is completely dismissed. The political coherence of an emergent Indian nationalism is blocked before it even takes shape. Steel's invocation of the Indian prostitutes forces feminine desire to enter into the imperial chain of signs, substituting itself for the quintessentially western and masculine image of rationality. In the narrative of colonial order, a patriarchal British empire's responsibility is deflected onto two figures, the inscrutable East and an appetitive womanhood. The principle of feminine guilt is created by converting an efficient or proximate cause into a formal one. The accidental becomes the essential as the narrative performs precisely the frustration of logical distinctions upon which a western metaphysics depends. Masculine history is metonymically supplanted by the image of feminine guilt.

The novel begins with the image of a dysfunctional marriage, revealing the hidden corruption and instability within the colonial order's privileged inner circle. Kate Erlton, the English heroine of the novel, is a neglected and embittered wife who imagines her relationship to the alien terrain and society around her strictly in terms of her failed relationship to her husband. She embodies the entire catalogue of the *memsahib's* most typical attributes: the racial and social insularity, and the intensely nostalgic, melancholic relationship to English tradition. For Kate, "[the] cult of home was a religion . . . and if a visitor remarked that anything in her environment was reminiscent of the old country, she rejoiced to have given another exile what was to her as the shadow of a rock in a thirsty land'' (23; bk. 1, ch. 2). She believes her life has been maimed by her separation from her young son. But Kate herself has arranged the boy's early departure to England, early even by the strictest colonial standards, where the separation of families was the norm. She sends him to England not because she feels the threat of the Indian climate but primarily as a means of separating him from the influence of his father. The conventional image of the fragmented Anglo-Indian family, alienated from itself because of the insidious influence of India, is reversed: the real danger comes not from the foreign climate or enervating native influences but from corruption within the English patriarchal order itself. The son is an exact physical replica of the father, and Kate's greatest fear lies in that uncanny resemblance. A feminine critique of English domesticity becomes coextensive with a critique of the colonial father.

Kate's outward situation conforms to the conventional image of the *memsahib.* Though she appears to be passive and unresisting in the face of her husband's neglect and her own isolated, disengaged social position, she is in fact the one responsible for perpetuating the appearance of conventional propriety, which Erlton's increasingly scandalous public behavior threatens to undermine. His casual infidelities are easily ignored, but when he is suspected of cheating on a bet, minor betrayals of the male-female bond are escalated to a violation of masculine codes of honor. This necessitates Kate's intrusion into the primary exchanges between men: she enters into secret negotiations with the ex-lieutenent Jim Douglas not for Erlton's sake, as she is quick to assert, but in the name of her son. Externally, she shores up the traditional position of an errant, ineffectual patriarch; internally, she usurps his authority by re-routing the exchange of identity between father and son through feminine formulations of the ideal masculine character, reconfiguring the terms of what should have been an exclusively masculine inheritance. The threat of feminine usurpation is supposed to be muted by the image of maternity: Kate's machinations are not intended to be self-interested because she works for the benefit of her child. But the desire of the domestic female has been thwarted, and she appears as an aggrieved, suffering figure that exposes the emptiness of the domestic icon. The individual man is always capable of failure, and the women dependent upon him are quick to see and act upon the vacancy created by his impotence. The structure of authority remains patriarchal, but effective power shifts constantly between male and female positions.[4]

It becomes clear that feminine desire is split in this novel between traditionally polarized forms: sexuality and domesticity. It is only a small step to identify the expression of opposing types of feminine desire with opposing racial models of the feminine character. This is the strategy Steel adopts throughout her many novels, particularly in a 1905 history, where these divergent images of feminine desire become the basis of an extended comparison between the English and Indian ideals of womanhood. Steel concludes that

> it is between the women of England and the women of India that the solution of the problem "How to rule and be ruled" lies. The one great unalterable split between East and West is in their relative Ideals of Perfect Womanhood. Let, then, the sister subjects take heed to their ways; let them remember that all give and no take is quite as demoralizing to both parties as the converse. (Steel and Menpes, 203; ch. 18)

How does the question of colonial rule become enmeshed with the figure of a woman to such a degree that both the formulation and the resolution of the basic antagonisms imbedded in the colonial relationship are to be examined through the same vehicle: the figure of woman? The opposition between the respective "ideals of perfect womanhood" defines the "great, unalterable split between East and West." The essentially divided relationship between women (*memsahibs* and Indian women) becomes the metaphoric vehicle for the divisiveness of the cultures generally. Steel does not posit a monolithic, universalized image of Woman but rather opposing culturally-and historically-specific metaphors, locked into a struggle whose arena is the entire colonial stage. The colonial structure necessitates the intrusion of one ideal upon the other, in the form of an unforgiving critique: "perfection" is an exclusive proposition, and the contending images of femininity can only exacerbate imperialism's inescapable dynamic of imposition and subordination. More importantly, "Woman" becomes the figure through which the basic antagonisms of the colonial relationship become *narratable.* "She" is the central nexus where racial, political, social, and gendered oppositions intersect and achieve the coherence of a systematically organized meaning. For "Woman" is not simply the primary site of convergence for colonial issues; "she" becomes the metaphorical vehicle which transforms the contiguities of events surrounding the Revolt into a causally ordered, teleological narrative.

Morecomb's denial of rationality is actually the abandonment of historical narrative. Steel restores the possibility of imperial storytelling through the image of feminine guilt. The entire network of colonial rivalries operates through the elaboration of this common figure. Rational narrative is replaced by mythic, master narrative organized around perpetually recurring metaphoric paradigms.

> In the West we formulate as our ideal woman a human being of equal rights with man; mistress of her own sex, as he is master of his; therefore free to use that sex as she chooses. Mother *in posse,* she has *in esse* a right to refuse motherhood. She has therefore the right to go down to the grave still withholding from the world its immortality, still denying to it vast possibilities. . . . In the East this is not so. The ideal there, is of a human being who is not the equal of man; who cannot be so, since the man and the woman together make the perfect human being to whose guardianship is entrusted the immortality of the race. . . . That is one point of divergence. The next shows even greater cleavage. The Western woman is taught that she has the right to monopolise the whole body and soul of a man. She can demand his love — that mysterious something over and above duty, over and

> above mere sexual attraction or friendship, which is the sole sanctifier of marriage. She proclaims that unless she can find divine love, marriage is no marriage; it asserts that she may love whom she chooses, provided the sexual relationship with her husband remains unimpaired. . . . The ideal Eastern woman knows nothing of monopoly or love. The sole sanctifier of her union with a man is the resulting child; the sole tie, the tie of fatherhood and motherhood. . . . Marriage to her, as to her husband, is no personal pleasure: it is a duty to the unborn. . . . (Steel and Menpes 157–58; ch. 14)

The Eastern woman is subject to a literalizing confinement to sexual reproduction. For her, essence and potential are indistinguishable and exhaustive. Her circumscription within the physical defines her signifying function and the limits of her value within a system of social exchange. Of course, to assign to the Indian woman the status of the "literal" is already to situate her as a sign of a particular kind: the opposition between the literal and symbolic invokes the traditional dependence of the feminine subject or essence on the body. But it is clear that in Steel's formulations, the Indian woman's task of physical reproduction is a trope of stagnation, the sign of non-progressive history. She is required to act as the eternal site of human origin, but she never emerges as a subject in her own right. Steel takes the imperial commonplace of Eastern eroticism and identifies it as the necessary outgrowth of the Indian ideal of womanhood. Where reproduction is paramount, the sexual relation takes on the greatest importance and is translated into her fiction as the Indian woman's "eternal cult of purely physical passion, their eternal struggle for perfect purity and constancy, not of the soul, but the body, their worship alike of sex and He who made it. . . ." (*Face* 80; bk. 1, ch 6). Though both Western and Eastern women are figures defined by a powerful eros, the Indian woman is circumscribed not only by her physicality but by her own obsession with it. She appears as the totalized object of desires over which she has no personal control.[5]

Steel's invocation of this most common of stereotypes surrounding Indian sexuality is presented as a dispassionate analysis of cultural norms. But even within the canon of colonial narratives, the image of the sexualized eastern woman is also used as the vehicle for a certain imperial self-reflection and critique. Jim Douglas views the extreme circumscription of his Indian mistress's life as established within the Indian woman's "cult of purely physical passion" (80; bk. 1, ch. 6). Zora has lived on a rooftop in Delhi since the day he purchased her from a "house of ill repute" (28; bk. 1, ch. 3) at the age of twelve or thirteen. Douglas himself is a cashiered British officer whose military career is destroyed when he intervenes between his former commanding officer and the man's wife. The husband strikes the wife, but in order to preserve her own reputation in open court, she allows Douglas to take full responsibility for assaulting a superior officer. Typically, his alienation from the intensely masculine world of the regiment, and with it, normative Anglo-Indian culture, is caused by feminine mischief. In the middle of the siege, the British hero of Delhi, General Nicholson, intuits the inevitable cause of Douglas's disgrace: "What was it? A woman, I expect" (394; bk. 5, ch. 2). Douglas's rooftop idyl is motivated by a "restless, reckless determination to show himself that he had no regrets for the society which had dispensed with his . . ." (28; bk. 1, ch. 3). This rooftop image will return later, not as the sign of alienation and distance but of cultural realignment. For the present, Zora is dying of an unnamed, enervating disease, the "slow decline" that seems to strike so many "secluded women." But she continues to regard her life with a bemused contentment. The anger is the Englishman's alone: "Before God! it had been unfair; this idyl on the housetops. The world had held no more for her save her passion for him, pure in its very perfection. That she had been content made it worse, not better . . ." (37–38; bk. 1, ch. 3). Douglas's frustration is perfectly unself-reflective. The colonizing male does not account for his own intrusion into the economic configuration of Zora's life or for the way her sexual labor has merely shifted form indiscriminate service in a brothel to exclusive service of an Englishman. He has purchased her as he would have "bought a horse, or a flower-pot, or anything else to make life pleasanter to him" (28; bk. 1, ch. 3). He sees Zora's self-constriction as the product of her own racial and cultural inheritance, exacerbated by the Indian woman's irretrievable lack of imagination. Her "absolute content[ment]" is to be read as a personal and racial limit. He is only relieved that she will die before either of them grows weary of their "idyl."

In *European Women and the Second British Empire,* Margaret Strobel argues that

> concubinage entailed physical proximity and intimacy in a context of inequality. . . . The fact that such a structurally unequal relationship has been taken as evidence of closeness between the two communities indicates how little understanding there was and is of gender and power in the dynamics of colonialism. Only if one ignores the element of subordination in a concubinage relationship can it be read as closeness. (6).

The myth of intimacy between colonizer and colonized, fostered by situations of concubinage, was a dominant topos throughout the empire. Such situations were supposed to improve relationships between colonizer and colonized in the case of the colonizing men but not in the case of the colonizing women. In her role as mistress of a household, the English woman also engaged in situations of intimacy with Indian servants, but this daily contact failed to produce authentic personal relationships. The *memsahib*'s intrusion into the system of servitude and concubinage between western males and the native classes was seen as creating distance and hierarchy where there had once been intimacy and affection. Steel employs this stereotype in depicting Kate Erlton's complete isolation within the midst of her Indian household. Kate unwittingly draws a pattern for an English style collar on what turns out to be an incendiary political pamphlet entitled "The Sword is the Key of Heaven." The paper urges Indian men to revolution. But to Kate, the Persian writing appears as no more than a "broad line of black curves and square dots" (23; bk. 1, ch. 2).

By contrast, Jim Douglas demonstrates a particular talent for generating relationships of intense and highly eroticized loyalty with his native subordinates. Attached to Zora's household is a sepoy named Soma, an Indian soldier formerly under Douglas's command who continues to offer him fealty. Soma's twin sister Tara acts as a serving maid to Douglas's Indian mistress, a role she takes on after Douglas "saves" her from becoming *suttee* at the age of sixteen. Together, Soma and Tara form a permanent and passionately-devoted retinue to their white master, despite the burgeoning nationalism of the Revolt. Douglas's impulsive chivalry confers upon Tara both salvation and social disgrace. Like the earlier rescue of Zora, Tara's salvation at the hands of the progressive Englishman is double-edged. Douglas regards his intervention as a simple instance of what Gayatri Spivak calls the "white man saving brown women from brown men" (121). But when the Englishman "drag[s] the sixteen year old widow from the very flames" (*Face* 30; bk. 1, ch. 3), he also deprives her of the status of *sati,* or holy woman. As a failed *sati,* Tara becomes an outcast who must enter the service of the Englishman's mistress rather than live "the life of a dog, which was all that was left to her among her own people" (31). Soma will no longer touch the hand of his twin, for it has been made "unclean" (31). As Jenny Sharpe argues, Tara's relationship to the figure of *sati* is equivocal: Tara represents herself as a "deferred *sati*" (107), clinging stubbornly to the image of her eventual self-immolation but requiring this moment of spiritual transcendence to wait upon a completely undefined period of "indebtedness" to the man who has obtruded himself between her and her ideal destiny. For whom is Tara to be *sati?* For her long-dead husband or for the Englishman who has apparently substituted himself as the recipient of her acts of feminine self-sacrifice? Tara's period of deferred *sati* is expressed as menial service to the women who enter into romantic relationships with Douglas, to Zora and to Kate Erlton. After Zora's death, Tara again prepares herself to embrace *suttee* by shaving off her hair, a gesture of symbolic and material self-mutilation which prefigures the moment of self-immolation. But Douglas interferes a second time, this time claiming a lock of Tara's shorn hair and threatening to advertise it as a "love token." Initially, Douglas regards the whole episode as a mock epic rape of the lock, a "childish cantrip" (78; bk. 1, ch. 6) that exploits Tara's irrational superstition for her own good. But by claiming the lock as a "love token," he reinscribes Tara as a sexual being whose spiritual purification (eligibility to become *sati*) depends now on the man who holds the lock hostage. The Englishman inserts himself into the ritual marriage drama not in the sanitized form of an impersonal and salutary imperial intervention but as a rival actor in an erotic relationship.

The symbolic value of the eroticized lock transforms parody into colonial allegory in which the white Master replaces the forgotten Indian husband. Tara's capacity for self-sacrifice is transferred to the Englishman.

The rooftop has been a scene of double exile, both for Tara and for Douglas: life as a widow is existence without communal context, while Douglas's failed military career deprives him of the cultural rationale which could make his continuing interventions in Tara's life coherent. Ambivalent about his relationship to the precepts of western humanism, Douglas's gestures of chivalry pivot uncontrollably towards female debasement. The colonial allegory sketched by the relationship between these two culturally alienated figures establishes the possibility of equivalence between Indian and English males, and though the Indian female's role remains subordinate throughout, the prospect of a cross-cultural substitution is at stake. Douglas has obtruded himself into an allegory capable of subverting the traditional hierarchy between the narratives of the colonizer and those of the colonized. It is not until he redefines his efforts to save Tara as co-extensive with saving Kate Erlton — in other words, it is not until "saving brown women from brown men" becomes the vehicle for saving "Englishwomen and children" from brown men — that an appropriate narrative hierarchy is re-established. At the height of the siege of Delhi, Douglas will install Kate on another rooftop, with Tara again in attendance. Knowing of Tara's unspoken passion, he relies on her to guard the Englishwoman whom he presents as his "wife."

The Western male's discovery of total sexual devotion is a motif repeated throughout the colonial canon. In Steel's last novel, *The Law of the Threshold,* she repeats the dramatic configuration of *On the Face of the Waters* by creating another triangle in which an Indian and an English woman are rivals for the attentions of the same Englishman, and in both cases the Indian woman's passionate self-effacement leads to her death. The sacrifice of the native woman prepares the way for the English marriages which end both novels. Kipling employs a variant of the theme in "Georgie Porgie" and "Lispeth," where the native woman finds herself supplanted by a nameless, generic English "Bride." In Tara's case, the native woman is made not only to witness her displacement but also to serve the usurper. The image of the eastern romance is not simply a topos of masculine adventure: the journey into the exotic unknown in search of treasure, fame, and power tends to be metaphorized by the emergence of the Eastern woman who personifies the uncontainable desires that have initiated the wandering or quest motif in the first place. The desire for markets, conquest, and empire coalesces through the intersection of romance in its generic incarnation as a quest narrative with the image of the eroticized native woman. She is more than the sexual counterpart of the luxuriance and abundance which have drawn the adventurer to the East. She becomes the personification of desires too vigorous, too expansive to be contained by domestic resources or possibilities.

She is the image of the illimitable, self-aggrandizing appetite underlying the imperial expansion outward beyond traditional boundaries. Sexual desire can never be legitimately identified with the domesticated feminine ideal of the West; for though Western women may be the receptacles of masculine desire, that desire finds no sympathetic connection with the sexless image of the domestic female. The eroticized native concretizes imperial desire, creating a convergence between the military, the commercial, and the sexual.

A certain equipoise is generated among the various significations of the imperial romance, but this balance is finally threatened by the very figure that makes it possible. The western male's sexual involvement is always understood as a form of "going native," an abandonment, however temporary, of the primary imperial objectives of the quest narrative. The collapse of romance into the sexualized image of the native woman provides the "Western male not simply with a fantasy projection of prohibited satisfactions but the discovery of a sexual equal, a mirror image of his own passion, operating through the figure of a gendered other. In Conrad's *Lord Jim,* Marlow describes Jim's history as a romance, more specifically a "love story," and meditates on the specular relationship between the Eurasian, Jewel, and the young Englishman:

> She had learned a good bit of English from Jim, and she spoke it most amusingly, with his own clipping, boyish intonation. . . . She lived so completely in his contemplation that she had acquired something of his outward aspect, something that recalled him in her movements, in the way she stretched her arm, turned her head, directed her glances. Her vigilant affection had an intensity that made it almost perceptible to the senses; it seemed actually to exist in the ambient matter of space, to envelop him like a peculiar fragrance, to dwell in the sunshine like a tremulous, subdued, impassioned note. . . . (Conrad 251)

But the "love story" must be subordinated to the more compelling relationship Jim forges with an ideal of heroic masculine identity. As with most quest narratives which posit a journey into the alien, the Eastern romance finds its culmination in motifs of self-discovery and self-identification. Far from a passive receptacle, the native woman serves as the ceaseless confirmation of the Western male's own immeasurable desirability. This liaison provides both the justification of the imperial presence — domination is what the native desires — and the signal for its inevitable termination. Empire cannot be established simply as a relationship between the conqueror and the conquered. The structure of empire demands the reinscription of the domestic terrain and culture. The Eastern romance must always find a conclusion, either in the death of the adventurer (his permanent incorporation into the structure of native life) or the abandonment of the woman. David Quint argues that "the romance episode . . . resists fitting into the teleological scheme of epic. . . . [T]he romance narrative bears a subversive relationship to the epic plot line from which it diverges, for it indicates the possibility of perspectives, however incoherent they may ultimately be, upon the epic victors' single minded history'' (15). To the extent that the ideal of empire succeeds in reasserting its priority, the specular relationship between epic adventurer and native woman will always be interrupted by the image of the West. As *Lord Jim*'s Jewel observes, ''You always leave us — for your own ends. . . . He could not see me anymore — he was made blind and deaf and without pity, as you all are. . . . He went away from me as if I had been worse than death. He fled as if driven by some accursed thing he had heard or seen in his sleep'' (261–62). The native woman disappears into a dream, while the Western adventurer embarks on his inevitable return. Even within the fictional canon devoted to empire, the Eastern romance is code for the exploitation of native women.

STEEL'S UNCRITICAL INVOCATION of the trope of exploitation has important consequences for her own delineation of the Western ideal of womanhood. Feminine desire is the defining force for both Western and oriental models, but the polarity that emerges between them derives its energy from a colonial inflection. It is no accident that ''equality,'' an apparent levelling of political and social privileges between the sexes, is defined specifically as sexual freedom. Steel declares that for the Western woman, the reproductive potential does not define an essence, only a possibility. She claims a startling degree of freedom for Western women over what is traditionally the disputed site of control between the sexes, the female body and its reproductive capacity — a freedom so startling as to be unrecognizable by her contemporaries as a description of actual historical conditions. Steel's rhetoric clearly reflects feminist issues of the 1890s and pre-World War I period. Susan Kent observes that a woman's right to control sexual access to her own body was for many feminists the ''core of their movement'' (112). In the 1891 *Motherhood: A Book for Every Woman,* Dr. Alice Ker argues that ''In the marriage relation, the choice of time and frequency is the right of the woman, by reason of the periodicity which characterises her being, and the violation of this law injures not only herself, physically and morally, but also her husband and her children'' (qtd. in Kent 113). But for Steel to declare that control over sexual access and reproduction not only lies exclusively with the individual woman but that the principle has been incorporated into the normative culture's view of ideal womanhood is to suggest that English society had come to embrace this crucial feminist precept as early as 1905. Clearly such an assertion exaggerates the historical position of British feminism of this period — or indeed of the present, where questions of choice are still debated. What then motivates this extraordinary assumption of sexual freedom for the Western woman?

The axes defining difference are never stable but are situated and resituated according to relationships of power. For Steel and her contemporaries, within a comparatively homogeneous racial image of the West the critical boundary divides male and female. Within this bracketing, the concept of feminine sexual freedom is exactly the question to be debated. When the primary axes intersect on the cultural or imperial level, the terms of opposition shift, relocating not along opposing gender lines but between one woman and another. Steel's inflated claim of western feminine autonomy derives more from the comparison to Eastern women than from any traceable historical reality. Feminine sexual freedom is aligned with modernity and enlightenment, becoming a marker of cultural value. The progressiveness of the West increases in direct proportion to the equally cumulative sense of Eastern degeneracy. A cultural comparison structures feminine difference, and for Steel, the dominant modality of cultural comparison is colonialism not anthropology. Within the tradition of colonialist rhetoric, the condition of Indian women is invoked as a measure of the backwardness and decadence of Indian society. In his *History of British India,* James Mill argues that

> The condition of women is one of the most remarkable circumstances in the manners of nations. Among rude people, the women are generally degraded; among civilized people they are exalted. . . . The history of uncultivated nations uniformly represents the women as in a state of abject slavery. . . . As society refines upon its enjoyments, and advances into that state of civilization, in which the qualities of the mind are ranked above the qualities of the body, the condition of the weaker sex is gradually improved, till they associate on equal terms with the men. . . . (1: 445–46)

Steel's claims about the autonomy of Western women must be positioned within a larger tradition of colonial discourse: the image of the Englishwoman's intellectual and spiritual freedom is supposed to be evidence of Western cultural superiority. But this representation of feminine sexuality was designed to act as a subordinate trope within the larger semiotic network of empire.[6] Steel is one of the few imperialist writers who examines the implications of this trope as it pivots uneasily between a colonial world under attack by Indian nationalism and an image of contemporary England where the ideology of separate spheres is being challenged by the feminism of the late Victorian period. If the *memsahib* appropriates this colonialist trope not on behalf of empire but in the name of feminine identity, what are the consequences for colonialism's reproduction of British culture? In other words, what are the consequences for the *memsahib*'s relationship to the domestic icon?

Feminine difference engenders a subtle hierarchy between Indian and English women, inevitably paralleling masculine relationships of colonial power. In Steel's autobiography, the *memsahib* takes direct possession of this cultural advantage, wielding social authority in her own person, and not simply through her association with masculine power. But in Steel's fiction, the hierarchical relationship between Indian and English women is more complex and requires a mediating figure that offers itself as a common object of desire for both groups of women — the Englishman in his role as the white Master.

The Western woman is driven by desire, but it is a desire no longer circumscribed by the image of maternity. This opening up of female desire makes possible a theoretically endless series of self-configurations. In effect, the ideal Western woman is no longer constrained by any predetermined sense of the *essential* feminine character. Inevitably, she will be predisposed in certain directions by the dictates of normative culture — the region in which Steel locates the *memsahib's* ''search'' for self-identity remains the domestic. This indeterminacy sets in motion a powerful confrontation between the traditional function and status of domesticity in the reproduction of national culture as opposed to the *memsahib*'s newly forged freedom. But even as Steel articulates the principle of feminine freedom (in the passage quoted earlier), she delimits it for the married woman by reserving the sanctity of the ''unimpaired sexual relationship'' to the husband. Sex is isolated, sacralized, and finally displaced by the image of ''divine love.'' Sex is sublated, and as an untouchable and increasingly disembodied icon of marital propriety, it paradoxically acts as the license for the emergence of an ever more expansive feminine desire. As long as this desire remains nonsexual, it is allowed to grow more powerful. Steel's ''ideal woman'' seeks to establish a monopoly over her object. The irony of Steel's formulation is that the vehicle for achieving this monopoly is marriage, the traditional social form for viewing feminine identity as a construct dependent upon male agency. Feminine desire floats ambiguously, provisionally in a ''romantic'' attachment to a man, but one who may or may not be a husband. The search for *''spiritual* affinities'' becomes the overriding feminine quest.

The image of an alternative colonial romance is emerging, but this is a specifically feminine one. As with the masculine version, a myth of sexual equality drives this new, Western, feminine romance, culminating again in an image of ''affinity'' or specularity between the questing subject and its other. The romance of the *memsahib* is built upon the comparison with a sexualized and thus irremediably primitive, *native* other. At the level of rhetorical formation, Steel requires the figure of the Eastern woman to perform a kind of sexual labor on behalf of the Western woman. For the latter, a gap has opened between the feminine body and subjectivity, and it is in this space that the Western woman's symbolic self-constitution takes place. Feminine desire and feminine identity become continuous, one the conceptual, *form-giving* basis through which the other is engendered. Identity is not coincident with the body any more than desire is linked to sex. What material form feminine desire takes and how it is elaborated will establish the track of the Western woman's semiotic history.

Following Levi-Strauss, Catherine Clément argues that the feminine relationship to cultural signifying practices depends upon woman's confinement to a primitive condition which will serve as the ground of masculine language:

> Levi-Strauss finds the two axes of exchange that make men's cultural law: the exchange of words, the exchange of women. The exchange of words — language;

> the exchange of women — exogamy. Their development, however, is not the same: language perfects itself to the detriment of the information that it carries and progressively separates itself from the wealth of the original meaning. It "entropies," having been destined to inevitable degeneration, to an apocalypse of language. . . . The exchange of women, on the other hand, has kept its original value, for women are both sign and value, sign and producer of sign. . . . [W]oman is in a primitive state; she is the incarnation of origin. . . . Ultimately one might even think, as we know, that the woman must remain in childhood, in the original primitive state, to rescue human exchange from an imminent catastrophe owing to the progressive and inescapable entropy of language. Words have been able to circulate too much, to lose their information, to strip themselves of their sense. At least let women stay as they were in the beginning, talking little but causing men's talk. . . . (Cixous and Clément 28)

In this passage, Clément describes the traditionally masculine domination and control of language. But any model of a universal feminine relationship to language or the symbolic order will fail to consider the ways in which women are differentiated by race and culture: these highly specific historical forces also define the feminine access to the system of social circulation. Clément argues that the "perfection of language" is always based on a process of erosion or entropy in which "language perfects itself to the detriment of the information that it carries and progressively separates itself from the wealth of its original meaning." In "White Mythology," Derrida describes this process in terms of usury, comparing the circulation of a word to the circulation of a coin, whose original surface value delimits the possibilities of exchange. The gradual but inevitable erasure of this surface value is understood by Derrida as the accession of infinite possibilities of exchange, since "value" is no longer imprinted as a permanent measure on the face of the coin. When subjectivity is mediated through the individual's relationship to language, entry into the system of social circulation can be seen as a virtually infinite increase in the possibilities for self-configuration. But the erosion that produces the possibilities of Derrida's unbounded signification is also understood as Clément's "apocalypse of language." Access to this linguistic freedom is traditionally split along gendered lines. A figural economy is erected in which masculine induction into the realm of the symbolic, which in Derridean terms is also a domain of potential freedom, depends on a counter movement of literalization of feminine.

In Steel's colonial history, we can see this gendered figural economy at work. The theoretical difference between the two models of ideal womanhood is treated as a linguistic difference or as opposing relationships to cultural signifying practices. The split confers a virtually indeterminate figurative potential upon the Western woman. Feminine desire undergoes a process of idealization in the name of "romantic monopoly," and this metaphorization produces a highly recognizable image linking British womanhood with sexual frigidity. Nancy Paxton argues that Steel reflects a "gynephobia" that is "intensified" by her position as a "memsahib in the patriarchal structure of the Raj" (Paxton 165). Englishwomen who mistake feminine freedom with sexual license introduce the same destructive dynamic into Anglo-Indian society that Steel sees at work in Indian society.[7] When Kate receives a letter from her husband asking for a divorce, the extent to which this process of idealization has obscured the sexual tie becomes evident to her for the first time. The loss of direct access to the female body is now experienced by the woman herself. The signifying indeterminacy/freedom which creates the hierarchical difference between Western femininity and the primitive, originary sexuality of the Indian woman shifts from a neutral condition to one of feminine self-alienation.

Freedom and self-alienation combined, however, create the Western woman's metaphoric status. They are also the markers of her modernity, and thus of her cultural superiority. The Western female subject is already figurative in the sense that she cannot locate a literal base. The gap that has opened between the feminine body and subjectivity is pure signifying potential, and it is this open figurality that allows her to be incorporated into the central narrative of the white master. The Western woman is not confined to the literal; her domain is that of a symbolic monopoly which coincides with what Clément identifies as the traditional masculine relationship to language. The *memsahib* enters the domain of cultural signs not as a subordinate figure to the male but as a rival. She is taken up into a colonial discourse where the hierarchies between physical/spiritual, literal/figurative, sign/signified are preserved but not as a relationship between genders. Hierarchical difference is mounted now on the dichotomy between one racially marked woman and another.

For the *memsahib,* the fundamental relationship between English men and women is not based on a model of feminine self-abnegation; it is based on monopoly. Theoretically, Western women can achieve self-definition through any terms they choose, but Steel ironically redirects the process of feminine identity formation through the traditional vehicle, the domestic marriage plot. She argues that for the Western woman, marriage creates the basis for virtually unlimited claims upon the man, even to a complete domination of his mental and emotional energies. An Indian woman in Steel's *The Law of the Threshold* describes the Englishwoman as "hedged in by hundreds and hundreds and hundreds of years of self-repression" (198). But it is from this history of repression that Western feminine desire takes both its form and its energy. The wealth of the female body is lost in the birth of a symbolic feminine subject. Kate Erlton's fanatical devotion to the "cult of home" has the external appearance of exemplary conventionality. But the domestic space has become for her the locus of

emotion, the refinement, the *fin-fleur* of sentiment. Briefly, what made her happy; what gave her satisfaction. It was only, then, a question of different forms of enjoyment (i.e. the opposing preferences of husband and wife); the one as purely

> selfish as the other. More so, in a way, for it claimed more and carried the grievance of denial into every detail of life. . . . She had asked for a purely selfish gratification of the mind. . . . (223; bk. 3, ch. 3)

Feminine desire becomes a desire for totalization driven by an impossible ideal of feminized romance. The vehicle of this romance is the domestic, the privileged image of national culture and empire. The history of the eighteenth- and nineteenth-century novel in England can be seen as a consolidation of the domestic into a national and imperial icon. Kate Erlton's "cult of home" is a variant of this theme, and her "grievance" against her husband is his continual refusal to participate in it. Erlton insists upon retaining free movement between public and private, or between masculine and feminine domains, asserting the traditional mobility of the male. The irony of Steel's romantic *memsahib* is that she has no desire to be released from the ideological confinement of the domestic space. Rather, she wishes to extend its authority — constituted as a feminine field of containment — to include the Master.

* * *

THROUGH THIS IMAGE OF a gendered monopoly, feminine guilt converges with the system of colonial rule. The problem lies in the inevitable rivalry that opens up between *memsahibs* and native soldiers as each struggles to achieve a monopoly or sole possession of their common "Master," the Englishman. In effect, the two become rival figures for defining the function and symbolic significance of empire — as either the reproduction of British culture through the importation of English domesticity or the perpetual erotics of military domination and physical violence. One cannot be accomplished without the other. Military domination cannot function for long without the moral cover of something like a civilizing mission, and vice versa. The totalizing desire of the *memsahib* supplies the energy for a gender crossing or violation which finally allows the now symbolic female to enter into the homoerotic structure of desire binding together the white master and the Sepoy.

In Steel's *On the Faces of the Waters,* the initial British response to the Sepoy uprising is sharply divided between mutually exclusive impulses, to protect the "women and children" or to restore order among the Sepoys. Attention and energy are disastrously split between these two images of colonial rule, setting up the basic conflict for the novel's split plot. The attempt to regain physical control over native soldiers bewildered by the void in leadership — by the Master's sudden, inexplicable abandoning of his role — is juxtaposed with a tale of domestic rejuvenation. This second plot repeats on the person level the generalized dilemma of the Englishman during the Revolt, focusing on the relationship between Jim Douglas and Kate Erlton. Douglas's path crosses Kate Erlton's during the outbreak of violence in Meerut. From that moment on, his sole objective is to "save the life of a woman," ironically repeating his former chivalric deeds on behalf of Indian women. In the process, he recreates his fractured relationship to the military order. When General Nicolson offers Douglas a place on his own personal staff, he is unable to accept it; his dishonored past intervenes, as does his present obligation to "save Kate" (395; bk. 5, ch. 2). When Delhi falls to the native insurgents, Douglas installs Kate on a rooftop and disguises her as the wife of an Indian merchant by staining her skin with dye and dressing her in Zora's old robes and jewels. Douglas himself acts the merchant's part, having learned to imitate Indian postures and attitudes by living with a troupe of jugglers and actors.[8] But by protecting Kate, he is prevented from participating in the military operations which alone can effect his recuperation within the masculine sphere.

The tension between the two plots of the novel is a confrontation between the colonial and domestic narratives. It acts out the violent collision between the two images of romance that have been developed thus far, one masculine, the other feminine. Note that in the masculine version of the imperial romance, the native emerges as the ideally satisfying object because "she" achieves a kind of specularity in relationship to the Western male — "she" reproduces for him the fantasy of illimitable desire and his illimitable desirability. The sexualized native woman is a literalization and thus is a certain betrayal of the equipoise between libido, commercialism, and empire. When desire is reduced to the image of a single eroticized figure, the other signifying layers are threatened. But what Steel's novel reveals is that there is nothing essential about the gender of the sexualized native figure. This need not be a heterosexual romance — quite the opposite, since it is only in the discovery of "her" specular potential that "she" achieves the full possibilities of her seductiveness. Western desire, male or female, is the impulse to dominate. The native male becomes interchangeable with the female. Perhaps Steel's most original contribution to the literature of empire is that she has made the two central native characters in this novel twins, a brother and sister, Soma and Tara, linked absolutely in their impassioned devotion to Jim Douglas, their common master. They are magnificent physical specimens, exquisitely matched and virtually interchangeable in the "extraordinary likeness between them in face and figure. . . . It would have been difficult to give the palm to either for superior height or beauty; and in their perfection of form they might have stood as models of the mythical race-founders whose names they bore" (29; bk. 1, ch. 3). The image of the Indian woman gives way to the erotically charged engagement between white master and native soldier. In the confusion of the first rebellion at Meerut, Soma, the male twin, stands irresolute between the British officers and the rebels, "waiting for the master to come" (196; bk. 3, ch. 1). Steel suggests that Soma's hesitation was typical of the initial sepoy reaction to the uprising. He stands "aloof from it voluntarily, waiting, with a certain callousness, to see if the master would come, or if folk said true when they declared that his time was past, his day done. Where was he? He should have come hours ago, irresistible, overwhelming . . ." (197). Soma along with hundreds of other insurgents converge upon Delhi to wait for the return of the Master in the familiar, beloved form of the avenger. "The masters were not going to fight at Meerut then, and he must try Delhi" (199).

The necessity of incorporating the *memsahib,* the white woman, into the imperial dynamic is the need to restore the heterosexual image of empire. The self-contained sufficiency of direct physical engagement between native and western males is juxtaposed to the necessity of rechanneling that violent physical energy into the protection of the women and children. This then becomes the paradigmatic form of feminine guilt; the intrusion of the white woman distracts the Master from regaining ascendancy over the native male. The whole figure of empire is jeopardized by her presence, but her intrusion is necessary for the empire to achieve normalization in the form of a domestic, heterosexual ethic. She makes her claim upon the Master in the name of the "cult of home."

The rejuvenation of the domestic order takes place on a Delhi rooftop as a repetition of the earlier Indian idyl, but this time with an English woman. Kate will be joined by a young English boy, another refugee being hidden by a faithful Indian nursemaid. Together they will complete the configuration of a domestic setting, despite the immersion in Indian cultural forms, costumes, and ritual practices. The *memsahib* finally achieves, in effect, her romantic monopoly, absorbing the imagination and practical attention of the Master. The double image of empire is now dominated by a female figure, but one that cannot be abandoned, as could the native other. The white female subject has entered the symbolic structure of empire and imperial desire, and she cannot be ejected from it. Her physicality does not function as an image of sexual fulfillment for the white male: Kate and Douglas only mimic their parts as husband and wife. Importantly, the white woman does not emerge as an object of sexual desire for the native male in this novel. The spectre of rape is remarkably muted: it is retained for its continuing rhetorical function, but there are no scenes of actual sexual assault upon Englishwomen. English and Eurasian women and children are killed in the palace at Delhi by Indians, but the violence is not directed at female sexuality because there is a more important erotic scenario at stake. The Englishman stands between the sepoy and the *memsahib.* They becomes rivals over him, redirecting all erotic tension through that central figure.

Douglas and Kate are the two English characters who have been most estranged from the conflicted image of imperial and domestic culture: Douglas through his court-martial and subsequent native idyl, and Kate through her disastrous marriage. Their symbolic realignment with empire is achieved through a process of cultural hybridization in which an exchange of properties between eastern and western feminine ideals occurs. In Steel's original comparison between Indian and English women, she suggests that such a transaction is the only possible answer to the problem of colonial rule: "it is between the women of England and the women of India that the solution of the problem 'How to rule and be ruled' lies. . . ." Let, then, the sister subjects take heed to their ways; let them remember that all give and no take is quite as demoralising to both parties as the converse" (Steele and Menpes 203; ch. 8). But the benefits of this exchange appear to be reserved exclusively for the rejuvenation of English domesticity. While waiting out the siege, Kate takes to "amusing herself once more by making her corner of the East as much like the West as possible . . ." (294; bk. 4, ch. 2). The Englishwoman's "cult of home" replaces the Indian woman's "cult of passion": superimposed upon the image of that previous idyl is a scene of English domesticity in which Douglas reluctantly but helplessly participates:

> Here he was looking at a woman who was not his wife, a child who was not his child, and feeling vaguely that they were as much a part of his life as if they were. . . . As he sat . . . watching the pretty picture which Kate, in Zora's jewels, made with the be-tinseled . . . child, he thought of his relief when years before he had looked at a still little morsel lying in Zora's veil. Had it been brutal of him? Would that dead baby have grown into a Sonny? Or was it because Sonny's skin was really white beneath the stain that he thought of him as something to be proud of possessing; of a boy who would go to school and be fagged and flogged and inherit familiar virtues and vices instead of strange ones? . . . [He reflected] on the mystery of fatherhood and motherhood, which had nothing to do with that pure idyl of romantic passion on the terraced roof at Lucknow, yet which seemed to touch him here, where there was not even love. (357; bk. 4, ch. 6)

For Douglas, racial and cultural realignment occurs through this fiction of domestic life in which he plays a part that seems far more real than his eight years with an Indian mistress. It is the very interpenetration of the two images and the two histories that produces his profound sense of reintegration.

But even as Kate revels in the restoration of domesticity with an attentive and captive male, she is also immersed in the costumes and ritual forms of Indian domestic life. The monotony of her rooftop existence is shared primarily with Tara, whose material labor on behalf of the "mem" is an expression of her intense passion for the white Master. Unable to resist the counter-influence of her Indian surroundings, Kate begins to learn the language, caught in a contradictory attempt to normalize the abnormality of life under siege by reflecting both Indian and English forms of domesticity. Douglas dismisses her appetite for Indian grammar as a sign of female triviality because "in truth his nerves were all jangled and out of tune with the desire to get away from this strange shadow of a past idyll; to leave all womanhood behind and fall to fighting manfully" (294; bk. 4, ch. 2). Because he is himself caught up in the internal contradiction of empire irresolvably split between violence and the eternal reproduction of domestic culture, Douglas is unable to measure the effects of this process of feminine hybridization. But the "exchange" between Eastern and Western feminine ideals becomes the disciplinary vehicle for realigning western feminine desire with imperial ideology. Kate is forced to question her own claims not only upon Douglas but upon any Englishman. Her simple presence in Delhi prevents the military apostate from recuperating a legitimate military identity. "Saving a woman . . . counts as nothing" to Douglas, compared to that elusive chance at reinstatement in the world of men. Kate embraces the Indian woman's custom of self-abnegation and, finally, of self-immolation, vowing to become *suttee* for Douglas by disappearing from her rooftop hiding place. If she disappears, nothing will stand between him and his "chance" (465; bk. 5, ch. 6).

Kate's promise to become *suttee* forces the unspoken rivalry with Tara into the open, for now the Englishwoman attempts to encroach upon a feminine ideal Tara has claimed as her own. Tara resolves to prevent Kate from assuming a religious and sexual identity she believes is reserved for Indian women: "she had no right to do it! . . . It is foolishness! The mems cannot be *suttee*. . . . I will not have it" (399–401; bk. 5, ch. 2). Tara's only display of territorialism (the Indian woman's approximation to the *memsahib*'s demands for "monopoly") is not based on an extension into the world but upon the contraction of death. Indian feminine territory is defined by the ever diminishing, self-consuming space of the funeral pyre. Tara fashions an alternative disguise for Kate, as a "Hindoo lady under a vow of silence and solitude," concealing her in a garden retreat devoted to "old Anunda, the Swami" (401). Here, the Englishwoman completes the process of exchange, immersing herself in the Indian feminine ideal through an epiphany of desirelessness: "She was losing hold of life. . . . Yes! she was losing her grip on this world without gaining, without even desiring, a hold on the next" (412; bk. 5, ch. 3). The *memsahib* loses even her desire for control. Once Tara has successfully spirited Kate out of the city, she reclaims her lock of hair and, in a "mad exultation" (406; bk. 5, ch. 6), finally throws herself from one of the many burning buildings that accompany the British army's triumphant re-entry into Delhi.

Jenny Sharpe argues that Steel reasserts the terms of racial difference between the two women by representing the domestic (Western) individual as "superior" to the Hindu *suttee* because her actions continue to be the expression of free will. Sharpe traces the late nineteenth-century debate which questioned whether the *sati* could really be understood as a *voluntary* suicide. Can the subjectivity of the *sati* be read in terms of the "free will of the individual" (107)? Contemporary English and Hindu reformers argued that the woman does not choose death so much as she rejects the suffering and oppression of the widow's life. *Suttee* becomes a form of release, since social degradation and ostracism are the destiny of women who attempt to forego the ritual. But, Sharpe argues, Steel allows Kate to enter and leave the "space of *suttee*" with will intact: "The free will of the domestic individual is demonstrated through a reverse tropological move in which the English woman occupies the space of the Hindu widow'' (108). The rhetorical strategy is well observed, but Sharpe fails to recognize the extent to which the Englishwoman's own volitional status is transfigured by her participation in this chiasmic exchange. Moreover, Steel actually envisions the ideal shape of such an exchange in her essays on Indian culture, where she insists that ''the Western woman has quite as much to learn from the Eastern woman as the Eastern has from the Western'' (Steel and Menpes, 165; ch. 14). Steel regards the self-effacing tendencies of the oriental ideal as a salutary and necessary discipline for the Western woman, whose relentless desire for a sublated romantic monopoly threatens to undermine domestic culture. ''Like a shuttlecock [the Western woman] bandies, and is bandied over the network of sex which constitutes modern society, claiming a point here, repudiating it there, clinging to the bat of marital faithfulness with one hand, with the other wielding the doctrine of spiritual affinities, until it is no wonder that the Divorce Court is full!'' (160; ch. 14). It is through their common desire for Douglas that both Kate and Tara define the terms of a symbolic *suttee,* converting feminine will into supplements of masculine imperial desire. Kate must sacrifice her own desire for domestic monopoly to the violent erotics of an imperial romance in which women play no direct part. In the process of revitalizing domesticity, Kate learns self-renunciation. She becomes alienated from her desire in the moment of its achievement. Once in possession, she seeks renunciation.

But Kate cannot release Douglas through any action or word of her own because the whole system of gendered social relationships is compulsory. Her decision to renounce his protection circulates within the coercive logic of this system and is no more the exercise of free will than Tara's ''willingness'' to serve Douglas's various women. Douglas himself is a hostage of the rooftop, bound to maintain the rhetorical position of the ''women and children'' in the rationale for violence against the natives.[9] But his domestic captivity frees men like Erlton to act out the desire to go on ''hacking and hewing for ever and ever'' (327; bk. 4, ch. 4). Erlton is killed during the Siege, winning the Victoria Cross, while Douglas misses his chance at redemption. Kate's gesture of renunciation is returned to her by the intransigence of the structure of imperial desire. At the end of the novel, she sums up a situation of mutual regret and frustration: ''You had your chance of saving a woman . . . and you saved her. It isn't much, I suppose. It counts as nothing to you. Why should it? But to me — . . . Why didn't you let them kill me, and then go away? . . . It would have been better than saving me to remember always that I stood in your way. . . .'' (465; bk. 5, ch. 6)

But with the newly recuperated image of English domestic life, built again upon the self-alienation of feminine desire, Douglas and Kate return to Europe where they will literalize their rooftop union with a Scottish wedding. The colonial stage does not benefit from this supposed transformation within the ruling class. The site of its completion is Europe, not India, where the return of a recuperated domestic icon has interesting implications for the novel of the late Victorian period. During the late 1880s and '90s, the sufficiency of domestic life is challenged by the emergence of a restless feminine subject. The traditional split between the domestic and public spheres comes to be seen as the enforced privatization of women, because confinement to the domestic realm prevents direct feminine participation in the economic and political arena. The domestic is no longer seen as the "natural" sphere for the expansion of the feminine character but as a delimitation and exclusion of women from the material sources of social authority. When Steel identifies the domestic as the intrusive vehicle of (white) feminine power and thus a curtailment of both masculine freedom and desire, she reverses the attack on domestic culture mounted by many of her contemporaries.

Steel's work employs other important inversions of the image of colonial life. India itself is usually held responsible for the breakdown of English marriage in the colonies. The climate, the splitting up of the Anglo-Indian family, and the peculiar conditions of colonial life generally were seen as placing intolerable strains upon the Anglo-Indian community. But Kate's marriage to Hubert Erlton fails because of fundamental tensions in the relationship between English men and English women. Historically, India has served as the unacknowledged supplement to English domestic life, providing it with the economic basis for maintaining a class-inflected image of genteel leisure. But the public exchange between the colonies and the European metropolis was always seen as occurring at the expense of English domestic culture: the price of Kipling's "white man's burden" was a sustained attack upon Anglo-Indian marriage, and nowhere is this colonial topos more powerfully represented than in Kipling's many short stories about marital infidelity in the Anglo-Indian community. When domestic culture is transported to the colonial world and is made to confront the sources of its own material conditions of existence, it seems to crumble as cultural icon. *On the Face of the Waters* employs the colonies to rehabilitate the still privileged but wavering image of English domestic culture. The colonies now fuel the recovery of a social image that England, through its novelistic tradition, is in the process of rejecting. The relationship between the colonial world and Europe is inverted: the colonies become the stage for regenerating the terms of cultural authenticity, providing an arena for the enactment of cultural values and disciplines that are increasingly anachronistic from the perspective of the metropolis. John McClure argues that in "Kipling's fiction, Europeans rediscover in India the joys of life in an earlier time, the age of medieval chivalry so celebrated by Victorian poets and essayists. As rulers of the subject peoples, they enjoy a lordly and heroic status that sets them above their decadent European kin" (98). But the revitalization of the domestic sphere and with it a traditional image of

British culture is represented in Steel's fiction as a disciplinary process directed at the inevitably guilty intrusions of the *memsahib*.

Brandeis University

NOTES

1. See Chaudhuri and Strobel for a useful recent collection of studies of Englishwomen with a substantial section on late nineteenth-century British feminism's relationship to imperialism, including Paxton's analysis of Steel's autobiography; and see Callan and Ardener for studies of various types of colonial or "incorporated" wives. Barr and Fowler offer histories of the *memsahib*, with particular focus on the "lady-*sahibs*," or Englishwomen of the upper classes; Strobel and Macmillan both provide historical accounts of the various types of *memsahibs*, including missionaries, travellers, reformers, and unusual or "eccentric" women who clearly broke with the conventional types; Sangari and Vaid offer studies of Indian women during the colonial period; Borthwick studies native reform movements focusing on women's issues; and Sharpe examines the image of rape in colonial rhetoric.
2. See Strobel, 1–15.
3. In *An Englishwoman in India*, Diver refers to "the magic pen of a Kipling or a Mrs. Steel" (4). Diver particularly admired Steel's role in "advancing" the education of Indian women. See also Paxton's account of Steel's autobiography, *The Garden of Fidelity, Being the Autobiography of Flora Annie Steel, 1847–1929*.
4. This narrative of feminine intervention in the structure of masculine authority has a well-established tradition in Kipling's short stories, particularly the series entitled "Under the Deodar Trees," where ambitious, intellectually-restless and politically-astute women undertake to shape the public careers of callow, undeveloped young men. Though the women work through male vehicles, the professional success of the men becomes a piece of feminine artwork.
5. In *History of British India*, James Mill locates the origin of this figure of Indian woman's sexual obsessions in Hindu society and writings.

   > "In Halhed's Code of Gentoo Laws, the character of women is depicted in terms which, were they not strong evidence to an important point, delicacy would forbid to be transcribed: "A woman," says the law, "is never satisfied with sensual pleasures no more than fire is satisfied with burning fuel. . . . Such women examine not beauty, nor pay attention to age; whether their lover be handsome or ugly, they think it enough that he is a man, and pursue their pleasures." (1: 450 note 2)

   Horace Wilson, the editor of the 1848 edition of the *History*, carries on an ongoing refutation of Mill's representation of the Hindu character, observing in the preface that "Of the proofs which may be discovered in Mr. Mill's history for the operation of preconceived opinions, in confining a vigorous and active understanding to a partial and one-sided view of a great question, no instance is more remarkable than the unrelenting pertinacity with which he labours to establish the barbarism of the Hindus" (1: 7).
6. The debates over the legal and social position of Indian women invited a complex intersection of opposing ideological interests: both colonialists eager to extend British influence and native reformers and/or nationalists equally intent upon resisting

British intrusions into Indian cultural life, used women's issues as a battleground. Joanna Liddle and Rama Joshi point to the "nine major laws liberalising women's legal position in British India, including those forbidding female infanticide, sati, and child marriage, and those raising the age of consent, allowing widow remarriage and improving women's inheritance rights" (26). Lata Mani provides a powerful analysis of how the debate over *sati* divided between the "civilizing claims" of colonial rule and the counter debate over the Indian woman's status as a symbol of traditional culture. See also Spivak and Sharpe for analyses of the *"sati."*

7. Many of Kipling's early short stories about life in Simla as well as in the more isolated stations focus on the marital infidelities of Anglo-Indian couples. So frequent is this image in his fiction that in the preface to "Under the Deodar Trees," he comments that "it may be as well to try to assure the ill-formed that India is not entirely inhabited by men and women playing tennis with the Seventh Commandment . . ." (391).
8. Rebecca Saunders compares Douglas's apprenticeship to the Indian jugglers to the espionage plot in *Kim.* Douglas, like Kim, learns to imitate Indian types in order to become a British spy (322).
9. Sharpe correctly argues that Steel is divided between establishing the Englishwoman's capacity for independence and retaining the rhetorical advantages of the image of feminine victimization at the hands of native insurgents. But any reading of the western female's autonomy must take into account the extent to which protection and maintenance of the Englishwoman shifts from Englishman to Indian woman: Sharpe insists that "the energy of Steel's narration goes into demonstrating that Englishwomen need neither protection nor saving:" (101). But Kate's secret life in Delhi depends in every particular on Tara's services. When she is left alone and it seems that a drunken courtier is about to burst in upon her hiding place, Kate slides down the roof and throws herself on the mercy of a female neighbor she has never seen before, the Princess Farkhoonda. Like Tara, the Princess conceals Kate, but only at the expense of her own love interests. The survival of the *memsahib* is transferred to Indian women, who acknowledge no bond of common interest or perspective with the foreign interloper. The image of the western female's independence is built upon the self-annhilating labor of Indian women.

WORKS CITED

Allen, Charles. *Plain Tales from the Raj: Images of British Indian in the Twentieth Century.* New York: St. Martin's P, 1975.

Barr, Pat. *The Memsahibs: The Women of Victorian India.* London: Seckor and Warburg, 1976.

Bhabha, Homi. "DissemiNation: time, narrative, and the margins of the modern nation." *Nation and Narration.* Ed. Homi Bhabha. Suffolk: Routledge, 1990. 291-322.

Borthwick, Meredith. *The Changing Role of Women in Bengal, 1849-1905.* Princeton: Princeton UP, 1984.

Broe, Mary Lynn, and Angela Ingram, eds. *Women's Writing in Exile.* Durham: U of North Carolina P, 1989.

Callan, Hillary, and Shirley Ardener, eds. *The Incorporated Wife.* Worcester: Croom Helm, 1984.

Chaudhuri, Nupur, and Margaret Strobel, eds. *Western Woman and Imperialism: Complicity and Resistance.* Bloomington: Indiana UP, 1992

Chaudhuri, Nupur. "Shawls, Jewelry, Curry, and Rice in Victorian Britain." Chaudhuri and Strobel, 213-46.
Cixous, Hèléne, and Catherine Clément. *The Newly Born Woman.* Minneapolis: U of Minnesota P, 1986.
Conrad, Joseph. *Lord Jim.* Ed. Robert Hampson. London: Penguin, 1989.
Derrida, Jacques. "White Mythology." *Margins of Philosophy.* Trans. Alan Bass. Chicago: U Chicago P, 1982.
Diver, Maud. *The Englishwoman in India.* Edinburgh and London: Blackwood, 1909.
Forster, E. M. *A Passage to India.* New York: Harcourt Brace Jovanovich, 1984.
Fowler, Marian. *Below the Peacock Fan: First Ladies of the Raj.* Markham: Viking, 1987.
Gartrell, Beverly, "Colonial Wives: Villains or Victims?" Callan and Ardener, 165-85.
Kent, Susan. *Sex and Suffrage in Britain, 1960–1914.* Princeton: Princeton UP, 1987.
Kipling, Rudyard. *Kim.* Ed. Edward Said. Suffolk. Penguin, 1989.
———. *Plain Tales from the Hills.* Ed. Andrew Rutherford. Oxford: Oxford UP, 1992.
———. "Under the Deodar Trees." *Wee Willie Winkie.* Ed. Hugh Haughton. Suffolk: Penguin, 1989.
Liddle, Joanna, and Rama Joshi, eds. *Daughters of Independence: Gender, Caste and Class in India.* Avon: Zed Books Kali for Women, 1986.
McClure, John A. *Kipling and Conrad: The Colonial Fiction.* Cambridge: Harvard UP, 1981.
MacMillan, Margaret. *Women of the Raj.* London: Thames and Hudson, 1988.
Mani, Lata. "Contentious Traditions: The Debate on Sati in Colonial India." Sangari and Vaid, 88–126.
Mill, James. *History of British India.* 10 vols. London: James Madden, 1848.
Paxton, Nancy L. "Complicity and Resistance in the Writings of Flora Annie Steel and Annie Besant." Chaudhuri and Strobel, 158–76.
Quint, David. "Epic and Empire." *Comparative Literature* 41 (1989); 1-32.
Sangari, Kumkum, and Sudesh Vaid, eds. *Recasting Women: Essays in Colonial History.* Delhi: Kali for Women, 1989.
Saunders, Rebecca. "Gender, Colonialism, and Exile: Flora Annie Steel and Sara Jeannette Duncan in India." Broe and Ingram, 304–24.
Schreiner, Olive. *The Story of an African Farm.* London: Penguin, 1986.
Sharpe, Jenny. *Allegories of Empire: The Figure of Woman in the Colonial Text.* Minneapolis: U of Minnesota P, 1993.
Spivak, Gayatri C. "Can the Subaltern Speak? Speculations on Widow-Sacrifice." *Wedge* 7/8 (1985): 120–30.
Steel, Flora Annie. *The Garden of Fidelity, Being the Autobiography of Flora Annie Steel, 1847–1929.* London: Macmillan, 1929.
———. *The Law of the Threshold.* New York: Macmillan, 1924.
———. *On the Face of the Waters.* New York: Macmillan, 1897.
Steel, Flora Annie, and Grace Gardiner. *The Complete Indian Housekeeper and Cook.* London: Heinemann, 1898.
Steel, Flora Annie, and Mortimer Menpes. *India.* London: Adam & Charles Black, 1905.
Strobel, Margaret. *European Women and the Second British Empire.* Bloomington: Indiana UP, 1991.
Wilson, Horace. Preface. *History of British India.* By James Mill. Ed. Horace Wilson. London: James Madden, 1848.

PASSING AND THE MODERN PERSONA IN KIPLING'S ETHNOGRAPHER FICTION

By John McBratney

THE TERM "PASSING" usually refers to the experience of light-skinned African-Americans who seek "to cross, or 'pass,' the color line undetected" into the white community (Madigan 524). Such crossings were widely depicted by early twentieth-century African-American authors such as Charles W. Chesnutt, James Weldon Johnson, and Nella Larsen. But passing, in the more general sense of "be[ing] held or accepted as a member of a religious or ethnic group other than one's own" (*OED*), was a theme in nineteenth- and early twentieth-century British literature as well.[1] Indeed, passing can be viewed as typical of new ways of negotiating cultural difference in the modern period. In an effort to widen the context in which modern passing is seen, I offer this study of Rudyard Kipling's "ethnographer" fiction, in which Anglo-Indian[2] ethnographers seek, by way of Indian disguise, to pass as native.

Kipling, like the African-American writers mentioned above, wrote at a time of transition in the thinking about culture, when pre-modernist notions of race were gradually giving way to modernist conceptions of culture that, in a spirit of relativism, challenged received ideas about racial essence and hierarchy. In the second half of the nineteenth century, many Western social scientists believed in the Darwinian idea that the peoples of the world were evolving along a single track defined by the recent economic and political ascendancy of the Northern European races over those of Asia, Africa, and Australasia.[3] However, despite their faith in the unilinear evolution of races (according to which the world's less progressive peoples might theoretically one day hope to achieve the civilization of the more highly developed), many of these scientists continued to believe in the earlier and wholely contrary notion that every racial "type" possessed an essence that persisted largely unchanged through time.[4] This essence was thought to link certain measurable physical attributes to less easily measured moral and intellectual capacities.[5] According to contemporary notions of hereditary transmission, this linkage remained intact from generation to generation and, thus, guaranteed the fixity of racial type.

Seen in this light, each race was thought to be more or less predisposed to success or failure in the struggle for existence. The varied fortunes of the world's races seemed to reflect the varied fitness of the racial type. Current racial performance appeared to augur well or ill for the future. While Europeans and Americans might enjoy continued pre-eminence in the world, non-Western peoples, it seemed, had to resign themselves to little or no advance, or even to extinction. Tennyson summed up the notion of differential capacities for progress in "Locksley Hall" (1842): "Better fifty years of Europe than a cycle of Cathay" (2: 130). Convinced of the permanence of these differences, social scientists came to arrange the peoples of the world in a hierarchy of more or less immutable racial types — with the "civilized" Europeans at the top; the "savage" Tierra del Fuegans, Australian aborigines, South African Bushmen, and Andaman Islanders at the bottom; and the "barbaric" or "semi-civilized" races in between.

At the turn of the century, however, anthropologists like Franz Boas and Bronislaw Malinowski came to challenge the nineteenth-century consensus about race. Where racial type had once been considered the sole determinant of culture,[6] a range of factors, including history and environment, was now felt to influence cultural practice. Boas in particular cast doubt on the very notion of racial essence. He came to see it as a reification imposed on the diversity of individual human beings rather than a quality inherent in any human group (Stocking, *Race* 183, 194). With the shift from an essentialist to a nominalist definition of race, racial identity came to be viewed as an entity that cultures constructed or manipulated to govern inter-group relations (Banton, *Idea* 110).

As the idea of racial type came under challenge, the concept of racial stratification was also seen as increasingly untenable. If there was no fixed racial essence, there was no necessary permanence to the ranking of races. The arrangement of "dearer" races atop the "cheaper" ones might reflect the vicissitudes of history rather than the inevitable expression of racial essences. The Anglo-Saxons might be the racial front-runners today, but there was no guarantee that they would enjoy supremacy tomorrow. Taking the history of the Anglo-Saxon as the standard against which all other racial histories had to be measured might lead to false comparisons. Indeed, the very act of racial comparison was called into question. If no single narrative could account for the diverse histories of the world's societies, each society then had to be judged on its own terms, independent of the values and achievements of another society.

With this argument, the whole meaning of culture began to shift.[7] Where "culture" had previously referred to a set of particular humanist values (Arnold's "sweetness and light") possessed by only a few Western or Westernized societies, it now came to mean the body of socially constitutive beliefs and practices possessed by *every* society, regardless of the degree of its resemblance to the Western model. Where culture had once been spoken of in the singular, as a quality that peoples had more or less of, it now came to be used in the plural, as an aspect equally characteristic of all peoples. Where societies had once been studied by the "comparative method" to determine their rung on the evolutionary ladder,[8] they were now analyzed as separate cultures, which had to be seen, first and foremost, as individual wholes.[9] According to Malinowski, students of culture had to "grasp the native's point of view, his relation to life, and realize *his* vision of *his* world" (qtd. in Stocking, "Ethnographer's" 106). With this understanding, anthropologists saw (or at least thought they saw) not only the worth of individual cultures but the relativity of all cultural values.[10] With the growing legitimacy of cultural relativism, the notion that racial types might be ranked according to a single scale fell into increasing disfavor.

Cultural relativism, then, ushered in a radical revision of traditional notions of racial essence and stratification. The present-day ethnographer James Clifford has called this paradigm shift the advent of "the ethnographic" (93). According to him, with the coming of this moment in about 1900, the nature of identity in culture was redefined. Individual identity was thought, in the nineteenth century, to fall along a cultural gradient culminating in the ideal of the highly cultivated middle-class European. Subjectivity in the ethnographic age, however, "enact[ed]," in Clifford's words, a "process of fictional self-fashioning in relative systems of culture and language" (110). The idea of a self regulated ineluctably by an innate racial essence gave way to the concept of a flexible, self-invented cultural persona. The notion of a racial hierarchy was supplanted by the idea that the self might fashion itself out of a range of ethnic identities unranked as high or low. Cultural identity came to be thought of as a dynamic entity continually reconstructed by the individual actor on a stage governed by multiple, relative, non-privileged cultural scripts.

Despite the gradual success of the new paradigm, modern ethnographic thinking by no means put an end to the influence of earlier views of race. Notions of racial essence and stratification persisted, and in some cases gained strength. The literature that treated the phenomenon of passing reflected this tension in conceptualizations of race. In the fiction of Chesnutt, Johnson, and Larsen,[11] for example, the attempt to pass testifies both to the ability of blacks to invent new ethnic identities in a post-Civil War period of increasing black self-determination and to the power of a white racism, barely diminished by its supposed defeat during the War, to punish those blacks who tried to pass. Kipling's fiction about ethnographers is also concerned with the ambiguous experience of those who seek to fashion themselves anew in an era of competing understandings of culture. Although he promoted nineteenth-century notions of racial privilege unapologetically in works like "The White Man's Burden," in other writings he presented a more modern view of culture which implicitly questioned the idea of white supremacy. Several British characters in his Indian fiction are, like their counterparts in early twentieth-century African-American literature, driven by a need to shape their identity unencumbered by traditional notions of racial difference. They are finally quite different from their counterparts in Chesnutt, Johnson, and Larsen, yet they resemble those African-American characters in their use of masking devices to pass. By considering those figures who cross the racial bar in Kipling's ethnographer fiction, I hope to provide a fuller understanding of the link between passing and the self-invented persona in an ethnographic age.

I

IN THE LATTER HALF of the nineteenth century, British readers saw the proliferation of a new kind of literature: "ethnographic" fiction (Street 96). In response to the growth of anthropology as a legitimate scientific enterprise, R. M. Ballantyne, G. A. Henty, H. Rider Haggard, Robert Louis Stevenson, Rudyard Kipling, and others sought to render the foreign settings of their fiction with an anthropological verisimilitude. Although this new literature was often avowedly romantic in its rejection of the perceived tawdriness of naturalism, it nonetheless sought to ground the romantic in an ethnographic realism. Disguise received a particular emphasis in this new genre. The romance had always featured masquerade as a prominent aspect. The quester who entered *terra incognita* often went in disguise out of both a need to secure safety in traveling and a desire to experiment with alternative identities. But with the transfiguration of the romance in ethnographic fiction, disguise was treated with a new self-consciousness. During a period of greater ethnographic sophistication, disguise became a matter of mastering — of decoding, imitating, and controlling — aspects of another culture.

Kipling's "ethnographer" fiction illuminates particularly well the uses of disguise. In focusing on ethnographers themselves, it calls attention to the shifts they use, including masquerade, to gain ethnographic information.[12] In their variety, Kipling's amateur ethnographers reflect the diversity of Anglo-Indians — military officers, civil servants, political agents, doctors, clergyman, and policemen — dedicated to the gathering of ethnographic detail. Taken together, his ethnographer writings evoke, with a richness unparalleled in Anglo-Indian fiction, the vitality and earnestness of early Anglo-Indian anthropology, which began with the work of Dr. Francis Hamilton Buchanan in the early 1800s and culminated in the Imperial Gazetteers of the late nineteenth and early twentieth centuries directed by William Wilson Hunter, Denzil Ibbetson, and H. H. Risley.[13] To assess the nature of Kipling's fictional ethnographers, I would like to focus on the representative figures of Strickland, a policeman who appears throughout Kipling's Indian fiction,[14] and on the apprentice spy Kim. For both these figures, their forays into Indian life involve the donning of disguises in an attempt to pass as Indian, a practice that has important consequences for the ethnographic rethinking of identity and culture.

II

KIPLING INTRODUCES STRICKLAND in the short story "Miss Youghal's Sais." Strickland's habit as a police detective is to enter the Indian bazaar under the anonymity of disguise to uncover evidence against criminals.[15] But his real delight in life does not rest in the capture of horse thieves and murderers; it lies instead in "going Fantee" (32), or going native — in passing as a mullah, a fakir, or other figure from his repertoire of Indian roles. The list of his dramatic accomplishments is drolly impressive:

> He was initiated into the *Sat Bhai* at Allahabad once, when he was on leave; he knew the Lizzard-Song [sic] of the Sansis, and the *Hálli-Hukk* dance, which is a religious *can-can* of a startling kind. When a man knows who dance the *Hálli-Hukk,* and how, and when, and where, he knows something to be proud of. He has gone deeper than the skin. (32)

Strickland's success depends on an ability to decipher what the narrator elsewhere calls the "marks" and "signs" (39) of the Indian underworld. This decoding of indigenous sign systems informs an *en*coding of these signs in his own performative self. These performances take him "deeper than [his white] skin," into a realm of racial indeterminacy that troubles his peers.

To upstanding Britons, Strickland "was a doubtful sort of a man [whom they] passed by on the other side" (31). Even the Anglo-Indian narrator, who is a friend of Strickland, finds the idea of going native one "which, of course, no man with any sense believes in" (32). Because of his peers' uneasiness, Strickland has been barred from professional advancement toward a position at Simla, the elite hill-station and hot-season home of the Government. Anglo-Indian reservations are two-fold.

First, Strickland's methods are dangerous. Experience in "the Great Game," the decades-long struggle between Russia and Britain over control of Central Asia, had taught the Government the hazards of sending British spies disguised as Asians across the Indian border to bring back geographical, political, and ethnographic information. The difficulties incurred by such early players of the Game as Charles Christie, Henry and Eldrid Pottinger, Arthur Conolly, and Alexander Burnes convinced officials that it was more safe and effective to send Indians in disguise whenever agents needed to travel into Afghanistan or Turkestan (Hopkirk, *Great* 5). The dangers of masquerade could be just as serious for agents inside India. Strickland, got up as an Indian *sais,* or groom, nearly loses his life when the wife of a fellow-groom falls in love with him and then, in a fit of unrequited passion, tries to poison him with arsenic. Another amateur ethnographer, Trejago in "Beyond the Pale," brings terrible punishment upon his beloved and himself when, dressed in a *boorka,* he approaches her room to make love: she has her hands cut off, and he is knifed in the groin.

But the more serious ground for objection to disguise has to do with the nature of British imperial identity. In an empire in which the colonized far outnumbered the colonizer, the British had to govern by prestige rather than force. They had to project a spectacle of power based upon sets of signs that clearly demarcated the ruler from the ruled. One of these semiotic registers was the Anglo-Indian uniform: military dress for the soldier and a carefully assembled outfit, including solar topi, for the civilian. Many of Kipling's Indian tales stress the importance of uniform in the maintenance of a sturdy British identity. In "The Madness of Private Ortheris," the title character proves his temporary insanity by exchanging his uniform for mufti and recovers his wits only after another swap returns him to his original outfit. For Britons who served in India, the uniform signified their place in the Raj and guaranteed the integrity of the Raj itself.

Going about in native dress, thus, seriously violated the official sartorial code. The violation held whether the disguise failed or succeeded. If it failed (that is, were penetrated by an Indian spectator), loss of face might result. If the disguise succeeded, the consequences might be even more dire, for such success might raise unsettling questions about the nature of imperial identity. From the Anglo-Indian standpoint, successful passing by one of its own called attention to the boundary where Indian garb met Anglo-Indian skin. This border area could be seen, figuratively, as the element within which the masquerader moved. Where, in this arena, did the Indian end and the Anglo-Indian begin? One could not be sure, for passing opened up a gap between skin and clothing that confounded the distinction between white and brown, colonizer and colonized. The specter it raised was not the turning of a white man into a brown or into some blending of the two, but the breaching of a space between colors that defied color-coding.

In a work that has deep implications for the study of passing, Marjorie Garber argues that transvestism produces along gender lines a "third term" between the terms of male and female. But this third category, she explains,

> is *not* a *term.* Much less is it a *sex,* certainly not an instantiated "blurred" sex as signified by a term like "androgyne" or "hermaphrodite". . . . The "third" is a mode of articulation, a way of describing a space of possibility. Three puts in question the idea of one: of identity, self-sufficiency, self-knowledge. (11)

Strickland's cross-dressing produces in terms of ethnicity what Garber speaks of in regard to gender. In going "deeper than the skin," he embodies a third entity that, by resisting incorporation into a unitary Indian or British identity, upsets the logic of racial categorization altogether. This resistance affords him the piquant pleasure of not being pigeonholed. Before duped Indian spectators, he knows he is not the Indian they take him for. And before his disapproving compatriots, he knows he is seen neither as a "temporary" Indian nor a masquerading Briton. Either of these images would reassure his peers, since either would confirm his essential Britishness. Instead, he defies essentialist logic. He confronts his fellows with a perplexing absence of established racial identity, a selfhood so slippery it eludes the binarism of white and brown. The advantages of this indeterminacy are profound. Released from the imprisoning gaze of those who would see him as either Indian or Anglo-Indian, Strickland enjoys a freedom of identity remarkable in a land of hierarchy.

Both Indian and Anglo-Indian societies were strongly stratified in the nineteenth century. Hindus ranked their members by caste at birth, and Anglo-Indians ordered theirs by a combination of class and professional distinctions enshrined in the Warrant of Precedence. Both communities were equally quick to exclude those persons who did not belong. Under these circumstances, there was little crossing from one society to the other: Britons were automatically *mlechas,* or outcasts, in Hindu society; and, except for servants, Indians were barred from regular British social life. Perhaps the most egregious instance of British cliquishness was the Anglo-Indian club, where Britons gathered after work to drink, read, chat, play tennis and bridge, and otherwise relax in a world off-limits to Indians.[16] Although the barrier between Indian and Briton was a complex compound of differences in custom, religion, class, and race, the appeal to race, to the obvious difference in skin color, was the easiest means of marking the cultural divide.

Given the importance of color, the magnitude of Strickland's transgression, and of his freedom, is clear. By going deeper than skin color, he puts pressure upon the single point of Indo-British interaction that most sensitively registers the whole difficulty of relations between colonizer and colonized. By pressing upon that point, he calls into question the most salient aspects of the racial ideology upon which the Raj is founded. In his playing off of Anglo-Indian against Indian identity, he mocks the racial essentialism that gives the Briton a clear sense of selfhood. And by subverting the binarism of brown and white, he collapses the hierarchy of color to which Anglo-Indian political authority is pinned. For himself, he achieves a freedom beyond race as great as his trespass is large. In his noncomformity, he has taken as his model the "one man [in India] who can pass for Hindu or Mahomedan, hide-dresser or priest, as he pleases" ("Miss Youghal" 31). The phrase "as he pleases" captures the moral and psychological license that Strickland seeks, and gains, by cheerfully ignoring the demands of conventional racial sentiment. The liberties he has taken and won seem of the completest kind.

Strickland's freedom lasts only so long, however. His game ends when he falls afoul of the very Anglo-Indian society whose strictures he had tried to ignore. His troubles begin when he falls in love with Miss Youghal, a recent arrival with her parents at the station where Strickland lives. Mr. and Mrs. Youghal disapprove of their daughter's suitor because of his strange "ways and works" (33) and forbid the lovers to meet. Strickland circumvents their ban by posing as Miss Youghal's *sais.* Although his donning of this mask seems congruent with his other charades, it in fact represents a significant departure. Where he had formerly gone native as an end in itself, he now does so as a means to an end. He has adopted what Garber calls "cross-dressing for success" (51) — here success in love. He has ceased to be the third term and has become an Englishman acting as an Indian, as is clear to Miss Youghal, who is in on his game. The two continue their clandestine courtship until Strickland, having exploded in anger at a general who flirts with his beloved, blows his cover. The good-natured general finds the masquerade charming and rides off to reconcile the Youghal parents to the lovers. In a response that recalls the mad Otheris, Strickland cries out for "decent clothes" (38). His days of delight in racial indecipherability are clearly over. Mr. and Mrs. Youghal consent to the lovers' marriage as long as Strickland promises to "drop his old ways, and stick to Departmental routine" (39). Strickland, for the most part, abides by this contract; as a result, "He is forgetting the slang, and the beggar's cant, and the marks, and the signs, and the drift of the under-currents, which, if a man would master, he must always continue to learn" (39). The narrator, who has been privy to his friend's disguise, ends by noting ironically that, despite Strickland's loss, "he fills in his Departmental returns beautifully" (39).

In his subsequent appearances in Kipling, Strickland lacks the freedom and range of his earlier liminal self. The now respectable official finds that his ethnographic capacities, atrophied by disuse, have become a target of mockery. In "To Be Filed for Reference," MacIntosh Jellaludin, an Oxonian who has married an Indian woman, converted to Islam, and gone even deeper than Strickland into Indian culture, calls the policeman "ignorant West and East" (346). In "The Son of His Father," his obtuseness is even more harshly ridiculed. When Beshakl, Strickland's groom, brings home his master's mare in battered condition, he complains that a gang of dacoits has robbed him and beaten the horse. The now police chief turns much of the government of northwestern India upside down to round up the criminals. Only Strickland's servants and his son Adam know the truth: that having lost all his money to drink, Beshakl had hired out his master's horse to an abusive wood-cutter to recoup his losses. While the police chief had sat god-like in a hill-station office trying to track the robbers, Adam, a juvenile version of his once-skillful father, had roamed the servants' quarters picking up gossip. Strickland is upstaged by his own son and, in an even more galling irony, hoodwinked by a groom, a figure he had formerly impersonated. Where he had once been indifferent to the prospect of high position in the Government, he now resides regularly at Simla. He laments his imprisonment within a system of precedence to which he had previously been oblivious: "[he] used to say, sometimes, that he envied the convicts in the jail. They had no position to keep up, and the ball and chain that the worst of them wore was only a few pounds' weight of iron" (292). His decision to turn conventional has curtailed his freedom to pass as an Indian. He has ceased to embody the ethnic third term.

III

IF STRICKLAND HAS LOST his ethnic liminality, his son has inherited it. Anglo-Indian children in Kipling are often blessed with an uncanny ability to float between British and Indian worlds. Kipling — who was born in Bombay, spoke Hindustani as his first language, and in his early years glided freely between his parents' Anglo-Indian house and the servants' quarters — was himself such a charmed child. He fictionalized this hybrid figure most successfully in the eponymous hero of *Kim.* Like Strickland, Kim is an Anglo-Indian on the margins of respectable society. Kim's marginal status derives from his orphaned condition and his Irish descent. A liminal figure, he, like Strickland, has become comfortable moving among Indians. He finds great joy going abroad in native disguise to gather and transmit intelligence. He begins as a young rake's go-between and graduates to apprentice in the Indian Survey — work which blends together cadastral, ethnographic, and political investigations as part of the Great Game. Again like Strickland, his pleasure lies not in the success of his missions but in the game itself — in the manipulations of identity that, in defiance of conventional ethnic categories, free the individual from the tyranny of racial essence and hierarchy. Even more than Strickland, Kim delights in foiling efforts to pin down his identity. When his mentor Mahbub Ali struggles to define him on his Asiatic side, Kim teases, "What am I? Mussalman, Hindu, Jain, or Buddhist? That is a hard nut" (234). The "hard nut" is precisely that riddle of selfhood that Strickland, in his prime, had posed to his peers. By embodying this riddle, Kim enjoys a fluidity of identity and a range of motion even greater than Strickland's.

Mahbub Ali is not the only father figure whom Kim fools. Abdul JanMohamed has asserted that *Kim* concerns the "prolonged and unnatural recovery of the paternal function" (79). The novel is not so much about a boy in search of his paternity as about a child pursued by father-surrogates who seek to adopt him, mold him to their ends, and thereby tame his wildly polymorphous selfhood. But in the face of these adults, Kim remains, until the end, slyly resistant to their demands and protective of his protean ability to pass as another. His resolve is reflected in the excerpt from "The Two-Sided Man" that heads chapter 8:

> Something I owe to the soil that grew —
>   More to the life that fed —
> But most to Allah Who gave me two
>   Separate sides to my head.
>
> I would go without shirts or shoes,
>   Friends, tobacco or bread
> Sooner than for an instant lose
>   Either side of my head. (214)

Kim's father-figures break down into two kinds, each appealing to a separate side of his nature. Those players of the Great Game like Mahbub Ali, Colonel Creighton, Lurgan Sahib, and Hurree Chunder Mookerjee enlist him in their spy ring. The Buddhist Teshoo Lama, on the other hand, adopts him as his *chela,* or disciple, in his search for the sacred River of the Arrow. The two types represent not only different careers but, in the tradition of Indian philosophy, divergent epistemologies. The players of the Game move in a sensuous world; the lama seeks, in a spirit of Buddhist non-attachment, to escape the world. These rival philosophies place their special demands on Kim's sense of his own subjectivity. Where the players of the Game try to tailor Kim's costume changes to fit their ends of intelligence gathering, the lama seeks to render the youth's shape-shifting moot. Where Colonel Creighton would like Kim to subordinate his pleasure in cross-dressing to his duties as a British spy, Teshoo Lama wants him to transcend the delights of ethnic self-fashioning entirely. Kim, like Strickland, frets under the trammels these authority figures seek to impose. To him, the regimented world of Anglo-India is especially cramping. Once again, the uniform is a primary locus of conflict: Kim hates the "horrible stuff suit" (158) of the soldier boy into which he is at first thrust and longs to wear the loose-fitting Indian clothes to which he is accustomed.

Kim tries to preserve his chameleon nature by achieving a rapprochement between the Game and the Search. This balancing act culminates in Kim's journey with the lama into the Himalayan foothills, in which he helps both his master in his quest for the River as well as Hurree in foiling a Russian and a French spy who have sneaked into India. This attempt at reconciliation, however, proves disastrous: the Russian tears the lama's mandala; a fight ensues; the lama, as a result, weakens; and Kim falls sick. The two paths, the profane business of spying and the spiritual search for wisdom, are revealed to be fundamentally in conflict. Kim's ethnic identity is seen as similarly divided. Under the terms of the Great Game, he is, though disguised as an Indian, essentially British. With Teshoo Lama, he is, though vaguely Indian, remote from his British side. As his selfhood is subjected to increasing polarization, he finds it more and more difficult to maintain the non-dual state of the ethnic third term. As a youth just shy of adulthood, he is placed under greater and greater pressure, particularly by those who play the Game, to declare his full allegiance to the British half of his ethnic make-up. Kim's illness at the end is symptomatic of the deepening tension in his ethnic condition.

The novel ends ambiguously. Kim awakens from his sickness to feel "the wheels of his being lock up anew on the world without" (462). This moment of re-engagement with the material world contrasts with the lama's flash of enlightenment upon falling into the River of the Arrow, which allows him to float, in non-attachment, above the very earth Kim has rejoined. In affirmation of Kim's reintegration into the world, Hurree and Mahbub express their expectation that Kim will later join them in espionage. Yet other signs point to a very different future for the youth. The lama's memory of his still worldly disciple brings him back from nirvana to work *Bodhisattva*-like for the salvation of his charge. The lama, moreover, remains the most loving and beloved of Kim's father figures. The last words of the novel are his — a signal, it seems, of Kim's future as a Buddhist seeker after the Truth. Kim himself offers no clear sign of *his* sense of his fate, whether it lie with the Game or the Search. His silence at the end seems to imply his unwillingness, still, to settle on one future or one ethnic identity over the other. In this, we are meant to be consoled. If by the end of the novel Kim's polymorphous self-fashioning has been curbed, he has not yet been boxed into a single future or an exclusive ethnicity.

IV

IN KIM, KIPLING FOUND an apparently foolproof method for preserving ethnic indeterminacy. By continually delaying the moment at which he must choose either an Indian or British identity, the narrative postpones indefinitely the cracking of the "hard nut" of ethnic ambiguity that Strickland's life-story enacts. Kim is, in Garber's term, "the changeling" (92), a figure whose economy is a continual changing or exchanging of ethnicities, a boy who is always "on [his] way to becoming" (85) but who never finally arrives at a fixed adult identity. But Kipling ensures this freedom for Kim at a price. By suspending the action of the novel just short of Kim's choice of a single career, Kipling stretches the fantasy of his liberty to the point of thinnest credibility. Given Kim's return to the world and his deafness throughout the novel to the lama's spiritual message, it is hard not to see him as poised, if not committed, to pursuing a future in the Great Game. Assuming this, it is hard not to suppose that his powers of impersonation will, like Strickland's, decline with official promotion.

The cases of Strickland and Kim point up the limited conditions within which Kipling could represent passing. In their defiance of conventional ethnic definitions, the young Strickland and the boyish Kim mock the central myth of progress that shaped the Victorian conception of the self. Against the prevalent understanding that all Western identity unfolded along the single, rising line traced by a training in European culture, their cross-dressings represent a sly divagation from that path — not a "reeling back" into the Indian "beast" but an evasion of all stories of progress or regress. They frame, in place of the nineteenth-century Bildungsroman, the narrative of a new selfhood, one that involves the free negotiation of different cultural systems across the gap that these differences define. Their impression management implicitly challenges nineteenth-century assumptions of racial essence and hierarchy. In this sense, they inhabit Clifford's ethnographic moment.

Yet Kipling's characters can remain in this moment only as long as they preserve a child's or a child-like resistance to the respectable adult world's calls to conformity. There is something willfully adolescent in Strickland's fantasies of plunging deeper than the skin; and there is, in Kim, a good deal of Peter Pan. Both figures represent an ethnographic version of a motif that runs through much Victorian literature: the child who refuses to grow up. This figure, particularly as represented by the orphan, embodied most completely a Victorian society's desire to escape its own ideology of lock-step progress. Kipling's child represents a particular form of the late Romantic rebellion against the "Shades of the prison-house" of adult being — a rebellion fought on the new ground of the ethnographic, in the no-man's land between relative cultures, and in the refuge of "exotic" Oriental disguise.

The fragility of this refuge is clear. The skeptic in Kipling was aware of the fantastical nature of Romantic escape. He knew that, realistically, boys must grow into men to do a man's proper work. He also knew that, in order for such labor to be proper, it had to be worthy of the "race" (understood in its most conventional sense) to which the worker belonged. "The White Man's Burden" says all this. But nostalgic for the joys of childhood, Kipling found it difficult to trade these delights for the burdens of empire. That difficulty is felt in the ambiguous tones of the narrator of "Miss Youghal's Sais," who at once mocks Strickland's eccentric cross-dressing and satirizes his ultimate conformity. It is also suggested by the unstable mood of the ending of *Kim,* with its desire to preserve Kim's protean identity and, conversely, its implication that his identity has already been shaped in preparation for the Great Game. Given this ambivalence, Kipling keeps alive the possibility of indeterminate selfhood by carefully narrowing the range of conditions within which it can unfold. He accomplishes this narrowing in two ways: by creating enclosed theaters of ethnic performance and by excluding all but the Anglo-Indian from acting out a plurally ethnic persona.

Consider, first, the isolation of theaters of ethnic self-dramatization. As I have suggested, Kipling permits passing only within imaginative realms cordoned off from the "real world" of Anglo-India. These are sealed off in time and space — temporally, because they represent hiatuses in a person's maturation into a workaday adult, and spatially because they lie at the margins of proper society, the Indian underworld in Strickland's case and the open road in Kim's. But what sets these enclaves off most definitively is their theatricality. This quality begins in disguise and extends to pose. In his description of Strickland's *Háli-Hukk* dance, the narrator's tongue-in-cheek tone captures the staginess of Strickland's achievement. Likewise, when Kim taunts Mahbub Ali about his amorphous Asian identity, he has an actor's self-consciousness about his effect on an audience.[17] This self-consciousness is characteristic of the ethnographic moment as Clifford describes it: "ethnographic discourse . . . works in this double manner. Though it portrays other selves as culturally constituted, it also fashions an identity authorized to represent, to interpret, even to believe — *but always with some irony* — the truths of discrepant worlds'' (94; emphasis added). This irony is the sign of dramatic distance. By treating the ''truths'' of rival Indian and British worlds ironically, Strickland and Kim stake out for themselves a stage between cultures on which they can perform their indeterminate ethnicity.

Elsewhere, I have called these spaces ''felicitous'' because they grant to their occupants a happiness in self-authenticity largely free of the constraints of race and caste (278). As Clifford suggests, however, this happiness is a value found not in the transcendence of culture but in the pitting of one culture's constraints against another's. Indeed, for the individual who seeks a Romantic autonomy beyond ''the iron cage'' of modern life, these charmed circles are in part constituted by the very modernity they are ostensibly free of. This imbrication does not empty them of meaning; rather, it produces a worth that is self-consciously bracketed, or that is, as Chris Bongie has suggested in his work on exoticism, deliberately ''rhetorical'' (23). Kipling is, at some level, aware of the rhetorical nature of his felicitous enclaves, but to quote Bongie again, he ''engag[es] in a renewed, and strategic, dreaming of what [he] know[s] to be no more (but no less) than a dream'' (23).[18] By setting these dream-spaces apart from a world of hard-and-fast ethnic difference, he is able to conserve the illusion of independence. By giving felicitous spaces the fiction of separability from the real world of Anglo-India, he can clear a stage upon which passing becomes a means to enact a multifaceted persona.

Kipling also preserves the power of passing by excluding all but the Anglo-Indian from the benefits it confers. Another way of putting this is that no Indian is allowed to masquerade successfully as an Englishman. He depicts two groups of Indians who wish to be seen as Anglicized: the middle-class, English-speaking, and English-imitating Bengali, often referred to pejoratively as ''the *baboo*''; and the Eurasian, the person of mixed British and Indian descent. Toward both groups, Kipling is openly disapproving. In such stories as ''Without Benefit of Clergy,'' ''The Head of the District,'' and ''The Enlightenments of Pagett, M.P.,'' the Bengali who seeks to emulate his British ''superiors'' is presented as effete, sycophantic, craven, socially disruptive, and politically seditious. The ''brown-skinned Englishman'' is viewed above all as spurious, a would-be arriviste whose aspirations to speak, dress, act, and govern like an Englishman betray his ''innate'' inferiority at a moment of crisis. Eurasians are depicted with little more sympathy. In ''His Last Chance in Life'' and ''Kidnapped,'' biracial characters are inevitably victimized by their ''taint'' of black blood. Although they may wish to pass as pure-blooded whites, they manage to transcend the impurity of their mixed lineage for only a moment. In the end they, like Michele D'Cruze of ''His Last Chance in Life,'' break down and find ''the White drop in [their] veins dying out'' (91). The efforts of both *baboos* and Eurasians to pass only prove their unworthiness to be anything but Indians. In depicting them in this way, Kipling was pandering to the coarsest racial stereotypes.[19]

Only the Anglo-Indian, then, has the power and the privilege to impersonate another successfully. Unlike the Bengali or the Eurasian who wishes to assimilate into English culture, neither Strickland nor Kim wants such absorption into the Indian. They seek to avoid the fate of those Britons who go native without the will or opportunity to return to their British identity; these figures are, in Kipling, always contemptible. Instead, both pass safely as Indians within the scope of the third term. The Bengali and the Eurasian, contrarily, rarely want to enact the part of the changeling. The pleasures of that performance are too rarified for one bent on real social gains.[20] *Baboos* or Eurasians who try to pass are intent on crossing for success, in Garber's sense. Invariably, they fail, for their deceptions are always exposed.[21] Thus, while Kipling's Anglo-Indians may pass "down," Indians may not pass "up." Britons, like Strickland and Kim, may augment or transform their racial capital through the changeling's exchange of identities; however, Bengalis and Eurasians, seeking to gain a racial and social cachet, are made to feel their abasement all the more by their failure to assume a British identity.

For Kipling, then, disguising oneself successfully as another is a freedom reserved only for Anglo-Indians — and only within the cordoned-off theaters of ethnic performance. Taken together, these two strategies for limiting the practice of passing point up the riddle of Kipling's role in the new understanding of ethnicity inaugurated by the ethnographic. If the enclosure of spaces of ethnic self-fashioning celebrates the advent of the ethnographic, the barring of Indians from these same realms squarely opposes the relativism of the new ethnography. Kipling comes down, paradoxically, on both sides of the paradigm shift marked by the innovations of Boas and Malinowski. As such, he awkwardly straddles the modernist ideological divide instead of boldly crossing over it.

Where does the emphasis fall finally for Kipling: on the guardian of old ways of defining race or on the pioneer of new means of constructing ethnicity? I think it lies with the conservative, for in Kipling the cultural relativism ushered in by the ethnographic is relevant only to that culture that is socially, politically, and economically dominant to begin with, and then only within realms that do not really threaten that dominance. A genuine, full-blown relativism, in which the negotiation of cultural power would be truly dialogic and in which both the Briton and Indian would be equal actors in a theatre of self-invention with real consequences for the political status quo, is impossible for Kipling to envision, for it threatens too baldly the racial hierarchy upon which the empire depends.

This is not to suggest that Kipling's notion of passing, albeit restricted, did not disturb the Raj's self-perception. Ironically, the staunchest literary advocate of empire was also the first writer to betray the artifice of the imperial actor and, thus, expose "the illusion of [imperial] permanence" (Hutchins). But by restricting this actor to the theatrical spaces of the third term, Kipling kept at bay the doubts about the legitimacy of empire this figure connoted. Indeed, one can see the Anglo-Indian who passes as a figure "containing" cultural anxiety in both senses of the word — at once embodying *and* limiting the spread of British ruling-class fears. Although Kipling was acutely receptive to the revisionist energies of the ethnographic, as a loyal proponent of empire he had to hedge this receptivity carefully. Only those figures, like Strickland and Kim, whose fidelity to their racial kin is finally clear, are allowed the brief happiness of passing as Indian and, thereby, fashioning, for a time, their own personae out of the plural cultures of India.

John Carroll University

NOTES

1. In the British case, the increased treatment of passing coincides with the expansion of the British Empire and those phenomena associated with it: travel, espionage, exploration, Orientalist scholarship, and archaelogical and ethnological study, to name just a few. In his preface to *An Account of the Manners and Customs of the Modern Egyptians* (1836), Edward William Lane describes how he passed as a Muslim to enter a mosque (Said 160). By disguising himself as an Indian Muslim doctor, Sir Richard Burton was able to make the pilgrimage to Mecca, as told in his 1893 *Personal Narrative of a Pilgrimage to al-Madinah and Meccah* (Said 195). In *The Seven Pillars of Wisdom* (1935), T.E. Lawrence records his experience in the Middle East during World War I as a British political agent posing as an Arab.
2. As I use the term here and throughout the essay, "Anglo-Indian" means what Kipling and his readers would have understood by it: a Briton who resides in India. In the 1911 census, "Anglo-Indian" was used for the first time officially to designate persons of mixed British and Indian parentage (Lewis 127, n. 2). To avoid confusion, I use the pre-1911 term "Eurasians" to refer to these persons.
3. For a discussion of the effect of evolutionary theory on thinking about race, see Burrow 98 and Penniman 152.
4. For commentary on the persistence of racial typology in a period of evolutionary thought, see Banton, *Idea* 8; Banton, *Racial* 5, 46-47; Biddis 16-17, 19; Lorimer 144-49; Stepan 83-86, 110; Stocking, *Race* 42-68; and Stocking, *Victorian* 182.
5. For commentary on racial linkage, see Biddis 11 and Stepan 86.
6. Robert Knox, the leading British proponent of the theory of racial types, asserted, "Race is everything: literature, science, art — in a word, civilization, depends on it" (v). Sidonia in Disraeli's *Tancred* expressed his racial views with equal absoluteness: "All is race; there is no other truth" (1: 191). For commentary on the idea of racial determinism, see Banton, *Idea* 33, 100; Biddis 12; and Bolt 9.
7. For much of the following analysis of culture, I rely on Clifford 92-95 and Stocking, *Race* 195–233.
8. For a discussion of the comparative method, see Burrow 87, 155, and Stocking, *Race* 80.
9. For commentary on cultures as integrated wholes, see Stocking, *Race* 155-56.
10. In *The Mind of Primitive Man* (1911), in which he described his stay among the Inuit of Cumberland Sound, Boas declared passionately his conviction of the need to think about culture relativistically:

> Is it not a beautiful custom that these "savages" suffer all deprivation in common, but in happy times when someone has brought back booty from the hunt, all join in eating and drinking? I often ask myself what advantages our "good society" possesses over that of the "savages." The more I see of their customs, the more I realize that we have no right to look down on them. . . . As a thinking person, for me the most important result of this trip lies in the strengthening of my point of view that the idea of a "cultured" individual is merely relative and that a person's worth should be judged by his *Herzenbildung*. This quality is present or absent here among the Eskimo, just as among us. (qtd. in Stocking, *Race* 148)

11. Charles W. Chesnutt (1858–1932), a teacher, newspaperman, lawyer, and writer, was called "the first American Negro novelist" (F. C. S.). James Weldon Johnson (1871–1938) was a lawyer, diplomat, songwriter, and poet; he published one novel, *The Autobiography of an Ex-Colored Man,* which dealt with the problem of passing. Nella Larsen (1893-1963), a writer of the Harlem Renaissance, wrote two novels: *Quicksand* and *Passing*. All three authors wrote with unprecedented sensitivity about the plight of African-Americans of mixed race who sought to pass as white.
12. The term "ethnographer" is something of a misnomer. Kipling commonly referred to ethnologists rather than ethnographers, ethnology being the comparative study of cultures and ethnography the study of "the culture of a single tribe or society" (Driver 178-79). In using the term "ethnologist," he reflected current scientific practice, which was predominantly comparative in kind. I have used the anachronism "ethnographer" in reference to Kipling's protagonists for simplicity's sake.

    Kipling's ethnographers are not to be confused with modern-day professional ethnographers, whose history begins with Boas and Malinowski (Stocking, "Ethnographer's"). Kipling's students of culture are servants of the Raj who do their ethnography on the side. They belong to the period before Boas and Malinowski when anthropology required the cooperation of two different kinds of practitioners: the amateur who gathered data in the field and the armchair ethnologist, often teaching in a university, who arranged the data in meaningful patterns. Kipling's ethnographers more closely resemble the former than the latter figure. Boas's and Malinowski's ground-breaking contribution to anthropology was to combine the two figures in the work of a single participant-observer.
13. Kipling seems to have been intimately knowledgeable about mid- to late-nineteenth century Anglo-Indian ethnography. He certainly read Anglo-Indian histories that drew upon ethnology. In an 11 March 1896 letter to an unidentified recipient, he recommended Sir William Wilson Hunter's *Annals of Rural Bengal* (1868–72) as an introduction to the state of the British empire in India (Pinney 2: 235). He also seems to have known several Anglo-Indian ethnologists personally, as his 5 September 1889 letter to Edmonia Hill indicates. There, he describes a meeting with Captain John Gregory Bourke, an American soldier and ethnologist of southwestern Native American tribes: "I unloaded little scraps of Indian folk lore; found he had been corresponding with some men in India that I knew (so small is this big world of ours), put him on the track of other men who would ethnologically be of use to him and altogether had a very delightful time . . ." (Pinney 1: 337). (I have been unable to identify who these other, ethnologically useful men were.) *Kim* represents the most full and direct fictional embodiment of his familiarity with Anglo-Indian anthropology. Historians have linked the spy-cum-ethnographer network of the novel with the secret school for explorers at Dehra Dun founded in 1862 by Captain Thomas

Montgomerie to train native agents ("the Pundits," as they were called) in the gathering of political and military information in Central Asia. Hurree Chunder Mookerjee, Kim's Bengali associate, appears to have been modeled after the agent Sarat Chandra Das (Edwardes 127; Hopkirk, *Trespassers* 27; Mason 91), while Colonel Creighton, the head of the novel's spy ring, resembles Montgomerie himself (Hopkirk, *Trespassers* 27).

14. Strickland appears in "Miss Youghal's Sais," "The Bronckhorst Divorce Case," "To Be Filed for Reference," "The Mark of the Beast," "The Return of Imray," "The Son of His Father," and *Kim.*
15. Strickland illustrates the powerful connection between detection and ethnography. The detective thrives in solving the "mysteries" of foreign cultures. Conversely, as the French anthropologist Marcel Griaule has pointed out, the ethnographer must also be involved in detection: "The role of the person sniffing out social facts is often comparable to that of a detective or examining magistrate. The fact is the crime, the interlocutor the guilty party; all the society's members are accomplices" (qtd. in Clifford 73).
16. After World War I, the color-bar in Anglo-Indian clubs began to fall (Allen 103). George Orwell's *Burmese Days* concerns such a change. Flory's suicide is prompted by his failure to help his friend Dr. Veraswami enlist as a rightful member of the Kyauktada Club.
17. Kipling calls attention repeatedly to Kim's dramatic talents. He is seen as the consummate magpie, capable of mimicking the tones and gestures of a wide range of social types. At Lurgan Sahib's school for spies, he delights in the games of "dressing-up" in costume so crucial to intelligence work: "a demon in Kim woke up and sang with joy as he put on the changing dresses, and changed speech and gesture therewith" (260). Kipling's depiction of Kim at these moments falls in with the nineteenth-century stereotype of the Irish as a people of dramatic gifts. In *The History of England,* Macaulay observed: "The Irish . . . were distinguished by qualities which tend to make men interesting rather than prosperous. . . . Alone among the nations of Northern Europe they had the susceptibility, the vivacity, the natural turn for acting and rhetoric which are indigenous on the shores of the Mediterranean Sea" (qtd. in Curtis 77). Here as elsewhere, Kipling's handling of the Irish aspect of Kim's selfhood cobbles together concession to received racial views and experimentation with new, unorthodox ways of conceiving ethnicity. It is because Kipling sees Kim in essence as Irish that he can endow him with an actor's capacity to play with essentialist definitions of race. No wonder, as I will show, it is so hard to place Kipling in the history of shifting attitudes toward race.
18. Bongie has written that Kim represents "Kipling's awareness of the impossibility of that 'authentic experience' that he nonetheless continued to desire" (22). I would agree.
19. Robert Knox wrote, "I saw two . . . young persons — Brahmins I think they were, or of that race, who were educated lately in London by the India Company at a heavy expense, merely by way of experiment. The result will, simply, I think, amount to nothing. . . . They wore, if I recollect right, their native dress, showing that on their return to India they would once more sink into the vast gulf of non-progression" (247-48). Both Knox and Kipling repeat a commonplace of nineteenth-century racism: that any attempt by a "lower" race to rise results finally in its falling back to its original place in the racial hierarchy.
20. Hurree Chunder Mookerjee is an exception, but his case is too complex to study fully here. Briefly, he is self-conscious about playing the *baboo* in ways that no

other Bengali is in Kipling. By manipulating the cliché of the *baboo,* that is, by assuming and departing from the stereotype at will, he is able to achieve a freedom from prejudice and a scope of being unprecedented in turn-of-the-century depictions of Bengalis.

21. In this, they resemble the would-be "passers" in African-American fiction. Although light-skinned blacks, like Rena in Chesnutt's *The House behind the Cedars* and Clare in Larsen's *Passing,* are viewed much more sensitively and sympathetically than their counterparts in Kipling, they share the fate of the Bengali and the Eurasian: the destruction of their hopes of rising socially. The mixed-race narrator in Johnson's *The Autobiography of an Ex-Colored Man* represents an interesting exception in the African-American tradition, perhaps because he is a man. However, although he passes successfully, his good fortune — in the form of a white wife, family, and wealth — brings him little real happiness. Having chosen a white identity, he is debarred from participating in the black struggle for freedom. In this, he concludes, "I have sold my birthright for a mess of pottage" (511).

WORKS CITED

Allen, Charles, ed. *Plain Tales from the Raj: Images of British India in the Twentieth Century.* New York: St. Martin's, 1975.

Banton, Michael. *The Idea of Race.* Boulder, CO: Westview, 1977.

———. *Racial and Ethnic Competition.* Cambridge: Cambridge UP, 1983.

Biddis, Michael D. Introduction. *Images of Race.* Ed. Michael D. Biddis. New York: Holmes, 1979. 11–35.

Bolt, Christine. *Victorian Attitudes to Race.* London: Routledge, 1971.

Bongie, Chris. *Exotic Memories: Literature, Colonialism, and the* Fin de Siècle. Stanford: Stanford UP, 1991.

Burrow, J. W. *Evolution and Society: A Study in Victorian Social Theory.* Cambridge: Cambridge UP, 1966.

Chesnutt, Charles W. *The House behind the Cedars.* 1900. Ridgewood, NJ: Gregg, 1968.

Clifford, James. *The Predicament of Culture: Twentieth-Century Ethnography, Literature, and Art.* Cambridge, MA: Harvard UP, 1988.

Curtis, L. P., Jr. *Anglo-Saxons and Celts: A Study of Anti-Irish Prejudice in Victorian England.* Bridgeport, CT: Conference on British Studies at the University of Bridgeport, 1968.

Disraeli, Benjamin. *Tancred, or the New Crusade.* 1847. 2 vols. New York: Dunne, 1904.

Driver, Harold E. "Ethnology." *International Encyclopedia of the Social Sciences.* 1972.

Edwardes, Michael. *Playing the Great Game: A Victorian Cold War.* London: Hamilton, 1975.

Garber, Marjorie. *Vested Interests: Cross-dressing and Cultural Anxiety.* New York: Routledge, 1992.

Hopkirk, Peter. *The Great Game: The Struggle for Empire in Central Asia.* New York: Kodansha, 1992.

———. *Trespassers on the Roof of the World: The Secret Exploration of Tibet.* Los Angeles: Tarcher, 1982.

Hutchins, Francis G. *The Illusion of Permanence: British Imperialism in India.* Princeton: Princeton UP, 1967.

JanMohamed, Abdul R. "The Economy of Manichean Allegory: The Function of Racial Difference in Colonialist Literature." *Critical Inquiry* 12 (1985): 59–87.

Johnson, James Weldon. *The Autobiography of an Ex-Colored Man.* 1912; rpt. 1927. *Three Negro Classics.* New York: Avon, 1965. 391–511.

Kipling, Rudyard. "Beyond the Pale." 1888. In *Plain Tales from the Hills. Writings* 1: 189–98.

———. "The Bronckhorst Divorce Case." 1888. In *Plain Tales. Writings* 1: 264–72.

———. "The Enlightenments of Pagett, M.P." 1890. In *In Black and White. Writings* 4: 340-86.

———. "The Head of the District." 1890. In *In Black and White. Writings* 4: 168–203.

———. "His Last Chance in Life." 1887. In *Plain Tales. Writings* 1: 84-92.

———. "Kidnapped." 1887. In *Plain Tales. Writings* 1: 142–49.

———. *Kim.* 1900-01. *Writings* 19.

———. "The Madness of Private Otheris." 1888. In *Soldiers Three and Military Tales, Part I. Writings* 2:19–31.

———. "The Mark of the Beast." 1890. In *The Phantom Rickshaw and Other Stories. Writings* 5: 170–91.

———. "Miss Youghal's Sais." 1887. In *Plain Tales. Writings* 1: 31–39.

———. "The Return of Imray." 1891. In *Phantom Rickshaw. Writings* 5: 284–303.

———. "The Son of His Father." 1893. In *The Day's Work, Part I. Writings* 13: 277–310.

———. "To Be Filed for Reference." 1888. In *Plain Tales. Writings* 1: 338–50.

———. "The White Man's Burden." 1899. In *Complete Verse.* New York: Anchor, 1940. 321–23.

———. "Without Benefit of Clergy." 1890. In *In Black and White. Writings* 4: 101–38.

———. *The Writings in Prose and Verse of Rudyard Kipling.* Outward Bound Ed. 36 vols. New York: Scribner's, 1897–1937.

Knox, Robert. *The Races of Men: A Philosophical Enquiry into the Influences of Race over the Destinies of Nations.* 1850. London: Renshaw, 1862.

Larsen, Nella. *Passing.* 1929. Quicksand *and* Passing. Ed. Deborah E. McDowell. New Brunswick, NJ: Rutgers UP, 1986.

Lewis, Robin J. *E. M. Forster's Passages to India.* New York: Columbia UP, 1979.

Lorimer, Douglas. *Colour, Class and the Victorians: English Attitudes to the Negro in the Mid-Nineteenth Century.* Leicester: Leicester UP, 1978.

Madigan, Mark J. "Miscegenation and 'The Dicta of Race and Class': The Rhinelander Case and Nella Larsen's *Passing.*" *Modern Fiction Studies* 36 (1990): 523–29.

Mason, Kenneth. *Abode of Snow: A History of Himalayan Exploration and Mountaineering from Earliest Times to the Ascent of Everest.* London: Diadem, 1987.

McBratney, John. "Imperial Subjects, Imperial Space in Kipling's *Jungle Book.*" *Victorian Studies* 35 (1992): 277–93.

Orwell, George. *Burmese Days.* San Diego: Harvest-Harcourt, 1934.

"Passing." *Oxford English Dictionary.* 1989 ed.

Pinney, Thomas, ed. *The Letters of Rudyard Kipling.* 3 vols. Iowa City: U of Iowa P, 1990–96.

Penniman, T. K. *A Hundred Years of Anthropology.* New York: Macmillan, 1936.

S., F. C. Preface. *The House behind the Cedars.* By Charles W. Chesnutt. N. pag. 6

Said, Edward W. *Orientalism.* New York: Vintage-Random, 1978.

Stepan, Nancy. *The Idea of Race in Science: Great Britain, 1880–1960.* Hamden, CT: Archon, 1982.

Stocking, George W., Jr. "The Ethnographer's Magic: Fieldwork in British Anthropology from Tylor to Malinowski." *Observers Observed: Essays on Ethnographic Fieldwork.* Ed. George W. Stocking, Jr. Madison: U of Wisconsin P, 1983. 70–120.

———. *Race, Culture, and Evolution: Essays in the History of Anthropology.* New York: Free, 1968.

———. *Victorian Anthropology.* New York: Free, 1987.

Street, Brian. "Reading the Novels of Empire: Race and Ideology in the Classic 'Tale of Adventure'." *The Black Presence in English Literature.* Ed. David Dabydeen. Manchester: Manchester UP, 1985. 95–111.

Tennyson, Alfred. *The Poems of Tennyson.* Ed. Christopher Ricks. 2nd ed. 3 vols. Berkeley: U of California P, 1987.

VICTORIAN MILITARY PAINTING AND THE CONSTRUCTION OF MASCULINITY

By Joseph A. Kestner

IN *BE A MAN! MALES in Modern Society,* Peter Stearns observes that "for men, the nineteenth century, effectively launched and ended by major wars, was a militant, indeed military century. A greater percentage of European men served in the military, even in peacetime, than ever before" (68). This militarism was part of what Stearns denominates as the "self-conscious assertiveness about nineteenth-century masculinity" (78) manifested in myriad dimensions of the culture. The great number of campaigns cited by Brian Bond (*Victorian Military Campaigns*) and by Byron Farwell (*Queen Victoria's Little Wars*) demonstrated the degree to which warfare dominated Victorian consciousness and contributed to the formation of ideologies of masculinity, constructing paradigms of activity, aggression, dominance, endurance, heroism, comradeship, patriotism, and power. These constructions advanced racist, sexist, and classist agendas. As Norman Vance argues in *Sinews of the Spirit,* "the alliance of manliness with imperialism . . . represents an extension of the mid-Victorian combination of manliness and patriotism" (195).

Constructing Masculinity

MICHEL FOUCAULT OBSERVES in *The History of Sexuality: An Introduction:* "The arrangement that has sustained [sexuality] . . . has been linked from the outset with an intensification of the body — with its exploitation as an object of knowledge and an element in relations of power" (107). Victorian imperial battle painting represents the intensification of the male body as the site for negotiating masculinity through empowering political, economic, and racist programs: thus *Machtpolitik* intersects with formation of ideologies of masculinity. Some of the elements negotiated in such iconography include the following: rites of initiation and investiture; the heroic male body; comradeship; the inscription of the heroic code, or *andreia* (which in Greek means both manliness and courage); the reification of racist theories of polygenesis; the constructed isomorphism of masculinity and patriotism, as Vance has suggested; the construction of women and non-Caucasians as Other (thus infantilized or marginalized or regarded as atavistic); the classist depiction of men in the ranks; the ambiguities of the wounded male body in representations of veterans. As the nineteenth century advanced, battle iconography assumed a particularly significant function in the construction of masculinity because of the introduction of inexpensive processes for mass-market reproductions — and thus circulation — of images. Thus, those affected by such painting were not solely the observers of Royal Academy exhibitions or readers of illustrated guidebooks (e.g., *Royal Academy Pictures, Academy Notes*) or reviews: these images were circulated through all social ranks and in non-artistic locales.[1]

This construction of masculinity through representations of imperial battle campaigns, however, is intensely conflicted in its negotiation of *andreia.* Stearns observes:

> Masculinity is not simply a position of power that puts men in comfortable positions of control. . . . If we understand masculinity as a constant contradictory struggle rather than just the privileged position within a power disequilibrium, we come closer to a full definition of gender studies. (108)

The representation of Victorian imperial campaigns, therefore, not only advances codes of *andreia* but also interrogates those codes. Kaja Silverman in *Male Subjectivity at the Margins* contends that the "dominant fiction calls upon the male subject to see himself . . . only through the mediation of images of an unimpaired masculinity . . . by believing in the commensurability of penis and phallus, actual and symbolic father" (42). Victorian imperial iconography, from one perspective, would appear to necessitate the premise of the commensurability of penis and phallus, of possession of the penis with automatic inscription into the symbolic order and the Law of the Father. However, as Serge Leclaire notes, "The possession of the penis, which is highly cathected, serves as a screen denying the fundamental character of castration. Man comes to believe that he has not been castrated" (46). Silverman and Leclaire suggest new strategies for assessment of imperial battle imagery. Representations of "victories" are posited on the assumption of the commensurability of penis with phallus: depictions of battles such as Kandahar [1 September 1880, Second Afghan War], Ulundi [4 July 1879, Zulu War], or Omdurman [2 September 1898, Egyptian Campaign] reinforce the dominant fiction, as Silverman observes:

> The phallus/penis equation is promoted by the dominant fiction, and sustained by collective belief. . . . The dominant fiction offers a seemingly infinite supply of phallic sounds and images within which the male subject can find "himself." . . .

> It is imperative that belief in the penis/phallus equation be fortified . . . for it represents the most vulnerable component of the dominant fiction. (44–45, 47)

An entire range of imperial campaign imagery, however, exposes the fact that this dominant fiction depends upon a *méconnaissance,* "the misrecognition upon which masculinity is founded" (Silverman 42). In particular, war as historical trauma implodes this equation, as Silverman contends:

> History may manifest itself in so traumatic and unassimilable a guise that it temporarily dislocates penis from phallus, or renders null and void the other elements of the dominant fiction. . . .
>
> The male subject's aspirations to mastery and sufficiency are undermined . . . by the traumatically unassimilable nature of certain historical events . . . [which dramatizes] the vulnerability of conventional masculinity and the larger dominant fiction to . . . "historical trauma[,]" . . . a historically precipitated but psychoanalytically specific disruption, with ramifications extending far beyond the individual psyche. (47, 52, 53, 55)

Historical trauma, such as defeat in battle, exposes the *méconnaissance* upon which traditional masculine codes of power, aggression, superiority, activity, and difference are posited. During the nineteenth century, several defeats particularly exposed this misrecognition: Gundamuck [January 1842, First Afghan War], Isandhlwana [22 January 1879, Zulu War], Majuba Hill [26–27 February 1881, First Boer War], El Teb [9 February 1884, Sudanese War], and Khartoum [26 January 1885, Sudanese War]. Such battles, disrupting the equation of penis and phallus, contest the symbolic masculine order since, as Silverman notes, "masculinity is particularly vulnerable to the unbinding effects of the death drive because of its ideological alignment with mastery" (61). Silverman emphasizes

> the centrality of the discourse of war to the construction of conventional masculinity . . . how pivotal that discourse is to the consolidation of the penis/phallus equation. . . . However, although the discourse of war works not only to solicit civilian belief in the dominant fiction, but to shape the subjective experience of battle, it does not always manage to fortify the soldier against an introverted death drive. (62)

So strong is the desire to enforce the equation of penis with phallus that battle imagery may extrapolate an incident from a defeat, as with Richard Caton Woodville's *Maiwand: Saving the Guns,* in an attempt to deny the misrecognition. Of interest too are representations of "near defeats" which barely maintain the dominant fiction, such as Lady Elizabeth Butler's depiction of Rorke's Drift [22 January 1879, Zulu War] or Godfrey D. Giles's two representations of the battle of Tamai [13 March 1884, Sudanese War]. Rorke's Drift and Tamai expose the precarious nature of "the construction of conventional masculinity" observed by Silverman. If paintings of military defeats acknowledge the incommensurability of phallus and penis, those extrapolating a victorious moment or commemorating a near defeat (e.g., Tamai) attempt to recuperate and reaffirm a desperate commensurability. An examination of a range of battle paintings demonstrates the complexity of the construction of masculinity in representations of military campaigns.

Constructing Victory

THE PURPOSE OF SUCH iconography is to advance the code of andreia (manliness/courage) in an empowering politicized and intensely gendered image. In particular, the male body becomes the signifier of an empowered masculinity which, in the special example of imperial iconography, can become the signifier of cultural Caucasian superiority as well, a race-inflected discourse of East/West relations. Thomas Jones Barker's *The Relief of Lucknow, 1857,* finished in 1859, represents the generals Colin Campbell, James Outram, and Henry Havelock in November 1857 after they have relieved the garrison. In Barker's construction, the male rescue reaffirms the heroism of the incident without depicting the extensive and arduous combat that led to the reunion of the three men. Of the more than sixty figures represented in the painting, many are portraits of military officers, constituting a gallery of Victorian military heroism. In particular, several of the main figures were assimilated as heroes of chivalry by their compatriots. J. A. Froude wrote on 3 December 1857: ''We had been doubting, too, whether heroism was not a thing of the past: and what knight of the Round Table beat Havelock . . . ?'' To Lord Curzon, the same assimilation was true of Outram, ''that generous and gallant spirit, the mirror of chivalry'' (Girouard 220).

The cultural differences of the masculinities presented are significant. On the far left, a group of Indian natives quarrels over plunder; in the foreground right crouches a native servant; while on the right is a native bheesty, or water carrier: natives are shown as venal or servile. The Caucasian forces, on the other hand, are ennobled, as with the wounded soldier of the 23rd placed strategically adjacent to the plunderers, or the sunstruck 93rd Highlander on the right of the canvas juxtaposed to the native water carrier. The city of Lucknow, distinguished by the Tombs of the King and Queen on the left, the Chuter Munzil Palace in the center, and the Residency and Motee Mahul Tower on the right, is transformed into an almost celestial city in the soft morning light. Barker conveys a sense of cultural difference in this powerful image of Caucasian male rescue during the Indian Mutiny. Signs of fighting are kept to a minimum, as around the Red Gate, to emphasize the ennobling nature of the British presence in India.

Woodville's *Kandahar* (1881) depicts the 92nd Highlanders storming the village of Gundi Mullah Sahibdad during the Second Afghan War on 1 September 1880. Ayub Khan and his army were defeated with the loss of 2,000 men while the British lost ''less than 250 men killed or wounded'' (''Fine Victorian Pictures'', lot #100). Woodville completed this canvas in eight months, and the motive may well have been to reaffirm the symbolic masculine code after the defeat at Maiwand on 27 July during the same campaign. The officers on leaping mounts derive from David's image of Bonaparte at Saint-Bernard, while the humanitarianism of the Westerners is indicated by the Red Cross supplies on the extreme left. Although the Gurkhas accompanied and assisted the Highlanders on this expedition, Woodville emphasizes the role of the Highlanders in scaling the height of the village. Woodville's canvas of Kandahar may be usefully compared to that by Vereker Hamilton of the same incident. Hamilton, unlike Woodville, shows the Highlanders in a dramatic charge just prior to entering the village, deploying the motion of the kilts to dramatize the charge. Rather than showing the troops dispersed in the narrow passages of the village, Hamilton shows them coming in line, using the angled bayonet in the foreground to emphasize the thrust of the Highlanders' line. Subtle details contribute to this heroism: note the manner in which the clasped rifle forms a cross with the protruding bayonet, signifying the Christian force behind imperialism, and a bagpipe is silhouetted farther down the line.

The victory at Ulundi on 4 July 1879 during the Zulu War compensated for the catastrophic defeat of British forces at Isandhlwana the previous January. At Ulundi 5,000 British troops defeated 20,000 Zulus, with British losses only 15 killed and 78 wounded. B. Fayel's depiction of the battle shows the 17th Lancers who have "charged out of the square to deliver the final blow." While unquestionably a victory, Ulundi represented the triumph of artillery over ineffective native weaponry, for "not one [Zulu] got within 30 yards of the British lines. A hail of lead from rifles and Gatling machine guns scythed down wave after wave of screaming warriors" (Sears 229). Fayel's representation, therefore, elides the British technical superiority by emphasizing the subsequent charge of the Lancers.

The battle of Omdurman on 2 September 1898, the climax of the reconquest of the Sudan by Kitchener, constituted the last great victory for British forces during the century. Here 50,000 dervishes under the Khalifa were defeated by Egyptian and British forces 23,000 strong. Robert Kelly's *Flight of the Khalifa, Omdurman, 1898,* completed in 1899, shows the Khalifa in flight before the British forces, reaffirming British military — and racial — superiority. Kelly's painting of this flight masks the stunning daring of the dervishes, as recorded by Steevens:

> And the enemy? No white troops would have faced that torrent of death for five minutes, but the Baggara and the blacks came on. The torrent swept into them and hurled them down in whole companies. You saw a rigid line gather itself up and rush on evenly; then before a shrapnel shell or a Maxim the line suddenly quivered and stopped. The line was yet unbroken, but it was quite still. But other lines gathered up again, again, and yet again; they went down, and yet others rushed on. . . . It was the last day of Mahdism, and the greatest. They could never get near, and they refused to hold back. By now the ground before us was all white with dead men's drapery. . . . It was not a battle, but an execution. (264)

Steevens's account of the battle does not ignore the ferocity and tenacity of the Dervish forces, although Kelly's canvas focuses on the aftermath of the dervish onslaught to camouflage this aspect of the battle of Omdurman.

The event at Omdurman most remembered, however, is the famous charge of the 21st Lancers, in which the young Winston Churchill participated, commemorated in canvases by Woodville and George D. Rowlandson. Actually undertaken "contrary to orders" and "mainly prompted by the desire of its commander Lt. Colonel Rowland Hill, to gain battle honours for his Regiment" (Christopher Wood 244–45), the charge was in reality a foolhardy rush into an ambush laid by Osman Digna, for what appeared to be about 200 to 300 dervishes in a *khor* turned out to be thousands hidden in a depression in the desert. The motive to prove masculinity was acute in this instance, because the Lancers was a "regiment given the unofficial motto 'Thou shalt not kill' by the rest of the army, because they possessed no battle honours" (Wilkinson-Latham 35). Steevens recorded the incident as follows:

> The trumpets sang out the order, the troops glided into squadrons, and, four squadrons in line, the 21st Lancers swung into their first charge.
>
> Knee to knee they swept on till they were but 200 yards from the enemy. Then suddenly — then in a flash — they saw the trap. Between them and the 300 there yawned suddenly a deep ravine; out of the ravine there sprang instantly a cloud of dark heads and a brandished lightning of swords, and a thunder of savage voices. . . . It had succeeded. Three thousand, if there was one, to a short four hundred; but it was too late to check now. Must go through with it now! The blunders of British cavalry are the fertile seed of British glory. (272–73)

Rowlandson's canvas accurately depicts the furious charge the Lancers had to undertake once they grasped the situation, but the rashness of the event is reconfigured into masculinizing heroism. By leaving much of the left side of the canvas blank with the *khor,* Rowlandson accentuates the thrust of the Lancers, beset by the dervishes beneath their mounts. Woodville's *The Charge of the 21st Lancers at Omdurman,* painted in 1898, shows the defile into which the Lancers charged, but the heroism is reinforced through the portraiture: Colonel Martin "without drawn sword or revolver" is pointing at the right of the canvas, while "the officer on the grey, centre, may represent Captain Kenna, who was awarded the Victoria Cross" (Barthorp 164). Woodville's depiction appears to draw its detail from Steevens:

> The colonel at their head, riding straight through everything without sword or revolver drawn, found his horse on its head, and the swords swooping about his own. He got the charger up again, and rode on straight, unarmed, through everything. The squadrons followed him down the fall. Horses plunged, blundered, recovered, fell; dervishes on the ground lay for the hamstringing cut. . . . [E]verybody went on straight, through everything. (273)

Steevens opined:

> Our men were perfect, but the Dervishes were superb — beyond perfection. It was their largest, best, and bravest army that ever fought against us for Mahdism, and it died worthily of the huge empire that Mahdism won and kept so long. (282)

To Steevens the dervishes were "death-enamoured desperadoes" (283) and the total battle "a most appalling slaughter" (285). Churchill recorded in a dispatch for the *Morning Post:*

> They were about twelve deep. It was undoubtedly a complete surprise for us. What followed probably astonished them as much. I do not myself believe they ever expected the cavalry to come on. The Lancers acknowledged the unexpected sight only by an increase of pace. A desire to have the necessary momentum to drive through so solid a line animated each man. But the whole affair was a matter of seconds. (Macdonald 114–16)

Churchill's assessment essentially limns the heroism of the charge, which Steevens proceeded to criticise as one of "three distinct mistakes" (292) in the battle of Omdurman.

Steevens recognized all the ambiguity of the event, noting that the War Office itself could not outright condemn what the public so ignorantly hailed as a triumph:

> Of these [mistakes] the charge of the 21st Lancers was the most flagrant. It is perhaps an unfortunate consequence of the modern development of war-correspondence, and the general influence of popular feeling on every branch of our Government, that what the street applauds the War Office is compelled at least to condone. The populace has glorified the charge of the 21st for its indisputable heroism; the War Office will hardly be able to condemn it for its equally indisputable folly. That being so, it is the less invidious to say that the charge was a gross blunder. For cavalry to charge unbroken infantry, of unknown strength, over unknown ground, within a mile of their own advancing infantry, was as grave a tactical crime as cavalry could possibly commit. . . . The charge implied disregard, or at least inversion, of [their] orders. . . . As it was, the British cavalry in the charge itself suffered far heavier loss than it inflicted. And by its loss in horses it practically put itself out of action for the rest of the day, when it ought to have saved itself for the pursuit. Thereby it contributed as much as any one cause to the escape of the Khalifa. (292–93)

For the *Times,* the *Illustrated London News,* and the *Annual Register,* however, the emphasis was on the heroism of the charge (Stearn 120–21). The charge of the 21st Lancers illustrated the manner in which masculinizing heroism was constructed to reinforce the dominant ideology even out of tactical blunders and vainglorious mistakes.

Constructing Survival

IF VICTORIES SUCH as those at Kandahar, Ulundi, and Omdurman reinforced the dominant fiction of masculinity, other engagements when represented, even if ultimately yielding victory, could not be so easily accommodated into the dominant fiction. The defense of Rorke's Drift, 22 January 1879, during the Zulu War is one example of such an incident, in which 139 men confronted an attack by 4,000 Zulus; after twelve hours of fighting, the Zulus were routed. "For this action 11 Victoria Crosses were awarded, the highest number for a single engagement" (Spencer-Smith and Usherwood 78); Lady Butler included portraits of all the VC awardees in her canvas commemorating the fight. However, as Spencer-Smith noted (79), Butler could not have been unaware of her husband's outrage at the Zulu War, embodied in his 1880 essay "The Zulus." He observes that "nothing is more natural than that" the Zulus should "war against us" "from being . . . subject to frequent instances of manifest injustice" (*Far Out* 178). Thus, the canvas is conflicted about white superiority even as it celebrates VC victors.

The battle of Rorke's Drift was particularly renowned for representing an astounding military action by British forces on the day and evening of the disaster at Isandhlwana; this victory became a means of effacing the memory of the Zulu victory earlier in the day. In *The Defence of Rorke's Drift,* finished in 1880, Butler used men from the 24th Regiment who had returned from South Africa. "The viewpoint is roughly west to east, and the foreground figures hold the barricade opposite the front of the hospital, with the storehouse in the background" (Knight 113). Butler depicts John Chard and Gonville Bromhead in the center of the canvas, with a number of other VC winners portrayed: Fred Hitch with bandaged shoulder carrying ammunition,, on right; the surgeon Reynolds holding a wounded man; Schiess of the Natal Native Contingent shouting from the barricade. William Butler, however, could not conceive of the Zulus as savages waging capricious attacks on whites. He noted that the press had led the public to a "frenzy of hostility against black kings as a principle," adding:

> While the black king's dealings towards us are weighed and measured by the strictest code of civilised law and usage existing between modern states, our relations toward him are exempted from similar test rules, and the answer is ever ready for those who would preach the doctrine of a universal justice between man and man, of the impossibility of applying to savage communities the rules and maxims of ordinary life. (*Far Out* 176–77)

This abuse of blacks, Butler contends, "produce[s] in the native mind a deep and widespread feeling of antagonism and resentment which every now and again finds expression in open conflict" (178). The ending of slavery, Butler asserts, has not effaced the wrongs done by whites: "All these long centuries of crime are still unpaid for. The slaves set free by us fifty years ago were not a thousandth part of those we had enslaved. . . . Notwithstanding the wide gulf which we fancy lies between us and this black man, he is singularly like us. . . . [H]e does not die out before us" (189–90). The fact that Lady Butler completed her canvas of Rorke's Drift the same year William Butler denounced the treatment of the Zulus indicates the nature of the race-inflected nature of her subject and its celebration of a white masculinity her husband abhorred as one of the worst consequences of Britain's involvement in the scramble for Africa. The Zulu chief Cetshwayo, when he learned of his tribe's casualties at Isandhlwana and at Rorke's Drift, stated: "An assegai has been plunged into the belly of the Zulu nation" (McBride 22).

The most conspicuous precedent for the transformation of the charge of the 21st Lancers at Omdurman from a blunder to an achievement was the Charge of the Light Brigade at Balaclava, 25 October 1854, where a British force of 661 was reduced to 195 in twenty minutes, painted most notably by Woodville and by Lady Butler following the famous commemorative poem by Tennyson. Butler's *Balaclava* was exhibited in 1876 and proved controversial for its central figure, a dazed and possibly deranged participant climbing out of the valley with bloody sword. Scenes of pathos limn the sacrifice entailed in this rashly heroic action, especially the sergeant of the 17th Regiment holding the corpse of trumpeter and the slain lancer to the right of the pathway. The exhaustion of defeat, sacrifice, and despair are reflected in the collapsing figures in the middle distance. In Butler's *Balaclava*, the code of andreia is intensely compromised as the only victory appears to be survival, a tension and disequilibrium introduced into the dominant fiction particularly by the figure of the dazed hussar. In contrast to Butler's depiction, Woodville's several representations differ considerably. In his 1894 *Charge of the Light Brigade*, Woodville shows "horses completely airborne or crashing before exploding shells [to suggest] speed and violent activity. . . . The artist chose to depict the action's most appealing moment, before the Light Brigade disintegrated" (Lalumia 147). In this conception, Lord Cardigan leads the 17th Lancers into the valley, with no suggestion of the dismay recorded in Butler's *Balaclava.* In his 1897 *The Relief of the Light Brigade*, Woodville shows the British forces at the end of the charge, assailing the Russian artillery at the end of the valley. Woodville's two canvases, showing the commencement of the action and the best version of its conclusion, emphasize the heroism of the magnificent blunder. Woodville's final image of the Charge of the Light Brigade, *All That Was Left of Them*, however, shows the roll call after the troops emerged from the valley. Clearly inspired by Butler's 1876 canvas, the Lancers form a line as the remnants of the regiment exit the valley, a riderless horse signifying the fate of many. Woodville's "Brigade trilogy" thus presents an image of the action counter to that of the stunned despair of Butler's representation.

Although it is a matter of disagreement among scholars the extent to which Butler favored the man in the ranks over the officer class, Woodville was strongly attracted to the depiction of officers, as the presence of Cardigan in *The Charge of the Light Brigade* indicates. A similar emphasis appears in his 1884 canvas *The Guards at Tel-el-Kebir*, painted at the request of Queen Victoria, who wanted her son, the Duke of Connaught, included in an heroic moment of the most famous battle of the 1882 Egyptian War. In Woodville's canvas, the Duke, seated on a grey mount, is shown at the head of the Guards Brigade as it awaits the results of an attack by the 1st Division. Danger is signalled by the shell burst at the top left of the canvas. Connected with the Egyptian frontier is John Evan Hodgson's image of two soldiers toasting the Queen in the Egyptian desert, *"The Queen, God Bless Her!"*, exhibited in 1885. As Casteras notes, the image represents "a chauvinistic, private moment" on the part of the two soldiers, "who relax amid the pyramids and think of their nation's power and of their monarch" (*Virtue Rewarded* 21). Since news of the defeat of General Gordon reached London in February 1885, the canvas may allude to the Sudanese War as well, evoking such battles as Tamai (13 March 1884) or Abu Klea (17 January 1885). Both the Woodville and the Hodgson images juxtapose the resourceful British against the natives of the continent. The fact that Victoria wished her son commemorated as a hero, and that the same impulse applies to the distinctly non-aristocratic soldiers in Hodgson, demonstrates the manner in which masculinzing heroism transcended class differentiation.

Although the battle of Tamai on 13 March 1884 resulted in a British victory, the English troops barely survived against the dervishes, whose breaking of a British square was memorialized in Kipling's "Fuzzy-Wuzzy" of 1890. Godfrey Douglas Giles completed two canvases of the Battle of Tamai in 1885, representing two different moments of the battle. One *The Battle of Tamai* depicts "the Dervishes issuing from a deep ravine in which they had concealed themselves" (Spencer-Smith and Usherwood 174), Osman Digna's Hadendoa "attacking Graham's leading square" (Barthorp 90). For Hichberger this *The Battle of Tamai* contains a Caucasian-empowering racist agenda:

> Giles was reworking a familiar formula for the implication of racial inferiority. By emphasising and caricaturing the features of the Dervishes, he was able to make them look ridiculous. . . . The Dervishes, in the foreground, are crouching among the rocks. The state of mind and moral qualities implied by the postures are obvious; standing straight equals bravery and crouching cowardice. . . . In the foreground . . . blood pours from the head of a dying Dervish. (*Images* 112–13)

The battle had been fought in two brigade squares, one of which had been temporarily broken by the dervishes and was only relieved when the second square moved up in support. In *The Battle of Tamai*, the reformed 2nd Brigade advances to recover the abandoned guns of the Naval Brigade. Giles juxtaposes the captured Gatling gun with the figure of a Dervish in the pose of the Deposition in the left foreground, destabilizing the image by suggesting that British heroism rested on superior artillery rather than innate andreia. The second 1885 *The Battle of Tamai* depicts an earlier moment of the battle, the interior of the British square as the Hadendoa attack. Hichberger notes that in this canvas "the British wounded are depicted by polite formula, a shoulder or head neatly bandaged or a dead body lying behind a bush. The Dervishes evidently died with less dignity. . . . [T]o have shown British soldiers in pain would have offended the audience and suggested that the Dervishes were a worthy foe" (*Images* 113). Indeed, on the left of the canvas one British soldier thrusts a bayonet down a man's neck, with the bloody end protruding, while the same man is being stabbed by another British soldier. Kipling's poem pays grudging respect to the blacks who broke the British square, and both paintings by Giles, which record a bare survival rather than a resounding victory, contain an element of this disequilibrium of the masculine code. If the Dervishes in *The Battle of Tamai* have vestiges of atavistic behavior (e.g., crouching, "unclothed"), they nevertheless also manifest an alternative form of andreia which was capable of disrupting the British square.[2]

If Giles was hesitant to display the full threat of the dervishes at Tamai, William Barnes Wollen was the opposite in his *Battle of Abu Klea* (17 January 1885) of the next key battle of the Sudan campaign following Tamai. Wollen depicts the Mahdists breaking into the "left rear corner of the square against the Heavy Camel Regiment" (Barthorp 106). It would appear that Wollen's canvas is a bluntly truthful response to Giles's elisions in representing Tamai: Mahdists as well as British are standing; in the center a Mahdist and a trooper are lying on top of each other. "The British square was broken at one corner, owing to the jamming of a Gardner gun" (Harbottle 9). The savage hand-to-hand fighting in the center, as well as the black warrior dragging himself to help his comrade, show the precarious nature of a battle that lasted all of ten minutes. Churchill was to call Abu Klea "the most savage and bloody action ever fought in the Sudan by British troops" (*Battle of Abu Klea*, National Army Museum placard). Wollen demonstrates that without superior artillery, British superiority was highly questionable in such a contest, even though British forces were ultimately victorious at Abu Klea. It is particularly striking that Wollen should have selected the breaking of the square to represent the one maneuver most calculated to destablize the code of andreia.

Even in depictions of wars not involving colonial subjects, the masculine code could be interrogated in various manners. For example, Butler's canvases of the battles of the Alma and of Inkerman evoke highly tense and even conflicted assessments of the heroic paradigm. The least ambiguous of these is *The Colours:*

Advance of the Scots Guards at the Alma of 1899, showing Captain Lloyd Lindsay advancing the colors at the famous engagement of 20 September 1854. Lindsay's action is credited with bringing order to the line of the regiment after a fierce Russian onslaught had thrown it into disarray. His example won him a VC for valor. The battle of Inkerman (5 November 1854), however, evoked from Butler much more conflicted responses. In the famous *The Roll Call* of 1874, the batallion of the Grenadier Guards is "in formation after a winter action in the Crimea" (Lalumia 138), often construed to be Inkerman. Its innovations are noted by Lalumia:

> The artist eschewed two premises of academic doctrine pertinent to history painting on the grand scale: that fact must yield to artistic license in the creation of inspiring martial imagery on canvas, and that the most instructive subjects portray the patriotic actions of a single, high-ranking personage. . . . She depicted the common soldiers' exhaustion and suffering to the exclusion of war's glorious trappings and without reference to the commanders of the army. (139)

Butler emphasizes the tragic aftermath of a battle action, the calculation of the "Butcher's Bill" of dead and wounded after an engagement. Butler had read Alexander Kinglake's *The Invasion of the Crimea* and, as Hichberger observes, accepted that author's belief "that the aristocrats who commanded the army had failed their country and that only the heroism of the ordinary soldiers had won the war" (76). Of particular significance, as Spencer-Smith and Usherwood note, is that details indicate the engagement has been victorious: "the upright standards, the fleeing enemy soldiers on the distant hillside and the single Russian helmet lying in the blood-spattered snow in the foreground" (58). Its structure in a line rather than in the more traditional pyramidal format suggests its democratizing sympathies. The varied responses of the soldiers — compassion, grief, dismay, contemplation — individualize the men of the ranks in a stirring image emphasizing the tragic aftermath of victory. Details such as the short flags, the older man reaching to pat the hand of his young comrade, and the soldier reaching to see if his prone comrade is wounded or dead evoke this conflicted nature of masculinity *in extremis*. *The Return from Inkerman* of 1877, showing "remnants of the Guards Brigade and the red-coated 20th Regiment" (Lalumia 144), emphasizes Butler's focus on the ranks, for this engagement was widely known as the "Soldier's Battle" because of the "courage and determination of the men through hours of chaotic fighting" (Spencer-Smith and Usherwood 66). Spencer-Smith and Usherwood observe that details such as "spent shot, pieces of leather and the blood-stained shako on the road in the foreground, echo the terrible cost of the fighting while the low rain clouds and the line of black birds following the column add a sombre, symbolic intensity" (67).

Recuperating Defeat

THE CONSTRUCTION OF MASCULINITY is most conflicted, of course, in the representation of defeat or of the *topos* of the ''last stand.'' As Silverman notes, the historical trauma of war can disrupt conventional masculine codes and the equating of penis with phallus. Representations of defeats either recognize the incommensurability or, in the process of heroizing the defeat, attempt to recuperate the commensurability of penis and phallus necessary for instantiation of the masculine. It is possible that canvases of defeats are involved in an intricate process whereby ''the historical trauma of the war had to be registered before it could be bound'' (64), that is, the recognition of incommensurability is the move that permits the reinstantiation of commensurability: the ''temporary disintegration'' (65), at least for the nineteenth century, did not lead to the repudiation of the dominant fiction.

Again it is Wollen with his unique and strange sensibility who confronts this temporary disintegration. *The Last Stand of the 44th at Gundamuck, 1842*, exhibited 1898, shows a dozen of the eighty men of the Regiment who were surrounded and annihilated. Bloodied, ragged, exhausted, and encircled by bodies of dead comrades, the remnants of the retreat from Kabul prepare for death. The heroic attempt to form a ''defensive four-square drill formation, a device which demonstrated their discipline in the face of death'' (Hichberger 101) is emphasized by the bleak landscape and the ''jumbled angles of the weapons'' (Spencer-Smith and Usherwood 175). Of all images of the nineteenth century involving beseiged masculinity, Wollen's of Gundamuck is the most harrowing: Afghans are coming up on right and left and, even though the Afghan standard bearer on the left has been shot, the fate of the men in the pass of Jugdulluk is left in no doubt. Small details, such as the soldier in the foreground getting cartridges out of his dead comrade's box (with #44 on it), register poignant commentary. Nevertheless, British heroism is reinstantiated by the bleak yet sublime landscape and by the evocation of Rembrandt's *Night Watch* in the image of the standing soldiers.

The inspiration for Wollen's canvas is undoubtedly Charles E. Fripp's terrifying 1885 *The Last Stand at Isandlhula* (now called *The Battle of Isandhlwana*), 22 January 1879 during the Zulu War, an encounter in which 1,200 British troops were annihilated by 20,000 Zulus. The Zulus had ''slipped unseen into a ravine near the Isandhlwana camp'' (Sears 226) while Lord Chelmsford led half his troops to verify the existence of Zulus in the foothills of the mountain. Chelmsford's miscalculation, however, was not the cause of the disaster: after successfully repelling the initial charges of the Zulus, the regiment discovered it was without additional cartridges. Bureaucratic confusion prevented a resupply, which the Zulus recognized and exploited. In Fripp's representation, the troops are forming a small square. Spencer-Smith and Usherwood say, ''The contrast between the attitudes of the British infantry and the Zulus suggests a civilised superiority in the former, despite their being outnumbered by 'savage' hordes'' (173–74). Fripp's painting has elements of sentimentality absent from Wollen's *Gundamuck*, such as the wounded sergeant extending his arm toward the drummer boy, a means of ''demonstrating the 'cowardly' conduct of the Zulus in killing him'' (Hichberger *Images* 102). It is scarcely surprising that reviewers preferred Giles's *The Battle of Tamai* (Spencer-Smith and Usherwood 173), especially as Giles's canvas guardedly reaffirmed the dominant fiction and Fripp's decidedly did not. The savagery of the last moments is conveyed by numerous details: the soldier holding up a cartridge at the feet of the bloodied sergeant; the exulting Zulu at the extreme right background; the soldier to his left about to be stabbed; the equally exultant Zulu on the extreme left. While the presence of the Regimental Colors is artistic license, it serves to limn the topos of the last moment. Droogleever points out ''the absence of an officer'' in the canvas, which may suggest a conscious critique that the ''backbone of the British army was its non-coms'' (5). If so, Fripp's *Isandhlwana* of 1885 pursues the emphasis of Butler on the heroism of the rank and file. Most haunting is the face of the veteran adjacent to the drummer boy: a man who has seen it all now sees the end. Fripp's painting, showing the alternative of victorious black masculinity, sabotages the white dominant fiction by such devices.

Salvaging the dominant fiction in the wake of defeat is the project of Woodville's *Maiwand: Saving the Guns* of 1882, representing a glimmer of heroism at the battle of 27 July 1880 during the Second Afghan War, which pitted 3,300 British troops against 35,000 Afghan warriors. Woodville concentrates on C Battery of the Royal Horse Artillery withdrawing as the enemy pursue. Despite the fact that Maiwand concerned a defeat, Woodville constructs the canvas — with its upraised whips, its charging steeds, and its officer pointing forward — as a moment of heroic recovery of the dominant fiction, despite the bloodied head of the cavalryman on the right, the body being sustained to his left, and the bandaged head of the rider in the center middle. Butler grasped at a similar remnant of valor during the same retreat in her 1905 *Rescue of Wounded: Afghanistan*, which represents men rescuing comrades from the ruthless cruelty of Afghans, who were notorious for their treatment of captured soldiers. By emphasizing the wasteland of the Afghan landscape, Butler elevates the heroism of the comradeship. As in Wollen's *Last Stand at Gundamuck*, the landscape of Afghanistan itself constitutes the gauge of the obstacles encountered in an attempt to uphold the masculine codes.

Thomas J. Barker's *Major General Williams and His Staff Leaving Kars 28 November 1855* [*The Capitulation of Kars*], completed c. 1860, represents the functioning of the dominant fiction in defeat. The description at the National Army Museum indicates the thrust of the canvas:

> In 1855 A Russian army sent into the Caucasus drove Turkish forces into Armenia. Major General William Fenwick Williams, British commissioner with the Turkish army, organised the defence of Kars. When the city fell after a spirited resistance, the Russians allowed Williams to march out with the honours of war.

The painting is dominated by the castle of Kars in the right distance, and shows Williams, flanked by Captain Teesdale, Lt. Col. Lake, and others, exiting the defeated city. On the left, Dr. Sandwith, accompanied by a Kurdish chief, draws attention to the city and to Williams. The political nature of the defeat is marked by the Turkish officer breaking his sword as he emerges from below, right. As Harrington notes: "What was important in their eyes was that British soldiers had displayed courage against all odds in the wake of government blunderings for failing to send out reinforcements sooner" ("Defence" 23). A reviewer of William Simpson's version of the event claimed the heroism as equally applicable to Barker's canvas: "[Kars] is one of those defeats of ours which, like Corunna, is better than the victories of other nations" (Harrington, "Defence" 25). The location of suffering women in the foreground draws upon Delacroix's *Massacre of the Innocents at Chios* of 1824. The *Athenaeum* thus commended Barker's canvas for "English endurance and Saxon stubbornness" (28).

The Celtic Subject

A PARTICULARLY IMPORTANT group of military paintings represents Celts in Victorian battle imagery, another of the representations revealing the dominant cultural fiction's false equation of penis with phallus. The Irish and Scots in such canvases constitute "the colonized in the colonies" in imperial battle subject art, where soldiers from groups which have lost independence (the Act of Union 1707 in the case of Scotland, the 1800 Act in the case of Ireland) fight to maintain British hegemony over other colonized groups. The depiction of the Highland soldier, in particular, was extremely popular among battle painters, for his picturesque dress in the kilt, the accompanying bagpiping (a key motif in itself at Dargai), and renowned courage made him particularly attractive in this iconographic construction. No image from the nineteenth century so encapsulates this conflicted equation as Elizabeth Butler's 1879 RA exhibit *Listed for the Connaught Rangers: Recruiting in Ireland*, representing a "sergeant, private, and two drummer boys" with two Irish recruits (Spencer-Smith and Usherwood 74) in the 1870s. The canvas is striking in her work for the prominence of the landscape and for the ruined cottage at the picture's left. For Butler, "the civilian peasant dress form[ed] the centre of interest" (*Far Out* 75).

First visiting Ireland in 1878, at the time of her marriage to William Butler, the artist recorded her response to the ruined country:

> The village was deserted in the awful famine year of '47, some of the inhabitants creeping away in fruitless search for work and food, to die further afield, others

> simply sinking down on the home sod that could give them nothing but the grave. (Hichberger *Images* 129)

During the agricultural disasters of the 1830s and 1840s, many Scottish and Irish peasants had been forced to enlist in the army to avoid starvation and unemployment. As Spiers says, "In 1830 and 1840, over half of the non-commissioned officers and men came from Scotland and Ireland" (48). In 1878, the year in which Butler painted *Listed for the Connaught Rangers*, her husband William Butler, an ardent nationalist and friend of Parnell, wrote his essay "A Plea for the Peasant," in which he indicted the British government for forcing Irish men to enlist because of the gross brutality of British policy in Ireland. Although over fifty percent of NCOs and rankers came from Ireland and Scotland in the 1830s, and although their proportion decreased as the century progressed, the Irish contingent still "kept pace with Ireland's share of the United Kingdom population" (Skelley 286), albeit the Scottish did not. William Butler's indictment of 1878 is therefore directed at pervasive discriminatory policies of the British government which transcend but still affect the military.

The private soldier, Butler wrote, was "thrown to our service by the hazard of his social condition, that social condition being poverty or disgrace" (*Far Out* 284), concealing "the great secret that the cradle of an army is the cottage of the peasant" (288; on recruiting, see Skelley chapter 5). About the victories in the Napoleonic Wars or the Crimea or the colonial campaigns, Butler asserts "that it was only through the assistance of our Celtic peasants, Irish and Scotch, that our armies were able to achieve victory" (291). Recruits were automatically commodified since "recruiting officials received a fee for every man they enlisted" (Skelley 240), already a manifestation of *méconnaissance.*

About these Scottish and Irish troopers, Butler asks, "Were they men on whom the nation had lavished the benefits of civil law, the blessings of good government, the privilege of a free falth? Alas! the answer must be, No" (300). He continues:

> This poor Celt found voice and strength and space, at last, upon these Spanish battle-fields. Room for the hunted peasant! . . . While abroad over the earth Highlanders were thus first in assault and last in retreat, their lowly homes in far-away glens were being dragged down . . . by the cold malignity of a civilised law. . . . A dreadful famine came to aid the cause of peasant clearers in Ireland. It became easier to throw down a cottage while its inmates were weakened by hunger; the Irish peasant could be starved into the capitulation of the hovel which, fully potato fed, he would have resisted to the death. Yet that long period of peace had its military glories, and Celtic blood had freely flowed to extend the boundaries of our Indian Empire. (300–01, 302, 305–06)

Listed for the Connaught Rangers therefore demonstrates Silverman's contention about "the centrality of the discourse of war to the construction of conventional masculinity . . . how pivotal that discourse is to the consolidation of the penis/phallus equation. . . . However, although the discourse of war works not only to solicit civilian belief in the dominant fiction, but to shape the subjective experience of battle, it does not always manage to fortify the soldier against an introverted death drive'' (62).

In Lady Butler's canvas, the juxtaposition of ruined cottage with remote mountain and especially the contrast of the two recruits, one looking back with regret on the historical circumstances which have driven him to enlist, present the conflicted construction of masculinity present in the Celtic subject in battle iconography. This incommensurability was given particular point in the 1860s and 1870s when Scottish regiments were posted in Ireland to counter Fenian revolt. It must be noted also that the Connaught Rangers evoke the horrendous severity of the treatment of Connaught during the Elizabethan period and later under Cromwell, who according to a contemporary forced ''native Irish'' into the region, ''turned loose to starve in a ruined country'' (Woodham-Smith 111). Butler constructs not only contemporary but distant history in the canvas.

It was, however, Scottish troops which drew the focus of Victorian battle artists, especially because of their exotic dress — from mid-century the kilt — and their haunting bagpipe music. Scotland by the nineteenth century had undergone a metamorphosis in the public imagination from a variety of events, among them the visit of George IV to Edinburgh in 1822; the Eglinton tournament in 1839; the impact of Sir Walter Scott's novels; the visit of Queen Victoria there in 1842; her purchase of Balmoral in 1847; and her close relationship with Napoleon III's wife, Eugenie, who had a Scottish grandfather (see Wood, *Scottish Soldier* 76; Hichberger 108–09). More overt political events were the formation of the National Association for the Vindication of Scottish Rights in 1853, the creation of a Secretary for Scotland in 1885, and the growing cult of Mary Queen of Scots from the 1850s onward (see *The Queen's Image*, passim; Strong 162–63; Trevor-Roper; Hanham).

Butler painted a number of canvases of Scottish regiments but nearly always in the context of global rather than small/colonial/imperial wars. Representing the sacrifice of Scottish rankers for British military supremacy makes these canvases conflicted constructions of masculinity. In a canvas such as *Scotland for Ever!* (1881), showing the Scots Greys at Waterloo in the famous charge of the Union Brigade, the representation of what appears a victory (only two men are shown shot) is in fact equivocal: although Sergeant Ewart managed to capture the French eagle, ''a counter-attack by French cavalry while [the Greys] were returning from this mad-cap venture led to their being cut to pieces and reduced to little more than a squadron in number'' (Spencer-Smith and Usherwood 82), in Stephen Wood's terms a ''Pyrrhic achievement'' (50).

Butler's 1895 exhibit *The Dawn of Waterloo* shows the Irish members of the Scots Greys at reveille prior to the charge in *Scotland for Ever!*, but again this representation of Celts is intensely conflicted if one recalls William Butler's 1878 essay. The very colonized circumstance of the Scottish and Irish troopers explodes the penis/phallus equation. A similarly conflicted circumstance appears in *The Colours: Advance of the Scots Guards at the Alma* of 1899 and especially in *A Lament in the Desert: Cameron Highlanders 1885*, painted only in 1925.

In the latter, set during the Sudanese War of 1883–85, the colonized Scots bury one of their own in the campaign against the dervishes or what Kipling in 1890 called the Fuzzie-Wuzzies. In his 1880 essay "The Zulus," in which he attacks the British government for its abuse of this nation, William Butler had said that "nothing is more natural" than that blacks should revolt against British white occupation and conquest. As has been previously noted, Butler had defiantly declared that blacks were singularly like the British themselves. In *A Lament in the Desert*, Scottish troopers, themselves driven to enlist because of the Highland Clearances and other abuses, become the oppressed oppressing the oppressed. As in Kipling's *The Light that Failed*, the desert in Butler's canvas becomes a vast, democratizing levelling-ground of the races.

One of the greatest battle artists of the nineteenth century was the Scottish painter Robert Gibb, whose works epitomize the conflicted nature of masculinity in his subjects: Scots in global and colonial wars. In his most famous canvas, *The Thin Red Line* of 1881, Gibb depicts the 93rd (Sutherland) Highlanders receiving the charge of Russian cavalry at Balaclava on 25 October 1854, an "action immortalized by William Howard Russell's phrase 'that thin red streak topped with a line of steel' " (Spencer-Smith and Usherwood 171). If Gibb's title remained indelibly one of the paradigmatic signifiers of masculinity for the remainder of the century, it was to Alexander Kinglake's *Invasion of the Crimea* that Gibb owed his inspiration, in particular the following sections which construct Scottish masculinity as imperial model:

> The 93rd Highlanders, now augmented to a strength of about 550 men, . . . were drawn up in a line two deep, upon that rising ground in front of the village of Kadikoi which was afterward called the "Dunrobin" or "Sutherland" hillock. . . . When these horsemen [the Russian cavalry] were within about a thousand yards of him, [Sir Colin] Campbell gave a brisk order to his little body of men on foot, directing them at once to advance, and again, crown the top of the hillock. . . . At the critical moment, two batallions of Turkish troops turned and fled, leaving Campbell's small force of Highlanders to face the enemy. [Campbell] could not help seeing how much was to depend upon the steadfastness of the few hundred men who remained with him on the hill. . . . He rode down the line and said, "Remember, there is no retreat from here, men! You must die where you stand!" The men cheerily answered his appeal saying, "Aye, aye, Sir Colin; we'll do that." (Harrington, "The Man" 589–90)

Kinglake's account already contained the elements requisite for the construction of the legend: the desertion by the Turks, the small force, the line, the "last stand'' or ''backs to the wall'' *topos*. Although it is disputed whether there were two or four lines of troops, Gibb selects the former to emphasize the heroism of the rankers. *The Thin Red Line*, which in the diversity of faces of the Scottish soldiers derives from Butler's line in *The Roll Call*, is noteworthy for elements that became signatures of Gibb's style, especially his preference for infantry rather than cavalry, which lends his constructions a restraint alien to the work of Woodville or even Butler, who used the charging horse as a means of injecting dynamism into the canvas. Gibb, in contrast, concentrates on the psychologically-tense situation of the combatants, here reflected in the diversity of responses to the Russian charge, which has brought down one hussar. The canvas also heroizes Colin Campbell, one of the few men who rose from the ranks to become one of the greatest military commanders of the nineteenth century. Another signature of Gibb's technique is to emphasize the line rather than represent soldiers in the defensive square, which was the usual formation to repel cavalry. In fact, the Russians withdrew after two volleys were fired because they thought the line of Highlanders had to be supported, which was not true.

The same line formation appears in *Alma: Forward the 42nd* of 1889, showing Sir Colin Campbell leading the Black Watch to scale the Russian fortifications. A Russian officer recorded later: ''This was the most extraordinary thing to us, as we had never before seen troops fight in lines two deep'' (Harrington, ''The Man'' 590). The Scots at the Alma, according to Kinglake, were living embodiments of Victorian masculinity:

> These young soldiers, distinguished to the vulgar eye by their tall stature, their tartan uniforms, and the plumes of their Highland bonnets, were yet more marked in the eyes of those who know what soldiers are by the warlike carriage of the men, and their strong lithesome, resolute step. (Harrington, ''The Man'' 590)

In Gibb's canvas, the 42nd (Highland) Regiment advances ''in double formation towards the seemingly impregnable Russian positions on the slopes about the south bank of the River Alma'' (*Alma*). Kinglake again provided Gibb with the operative text:

> When Sir Colin rode up to the Corps which awaited his signal, he only gave two words, ''Forward 42nd'' and ''as a steed that knows its rider'' the great heart of the batallion bounded proudly to his touch — smoothly, easily, swiftly, the Black Watch seemed to glide up the hill. (*Alma*)

Gibb emphasizes the heroism of Campbell, who directs the advance with his sword in front of his troops. The battle of the Alma is particularly conflicted in its results because, while successful in itself, the British and French did not pursue the retreating Russians, who ''headed, unmolested, towards Sevastopol. . . . Sevastopol at that time was poorly fortified, and if an attack had followed this Allied victory, the port would have very likely fallen and the Crimean War could well have ended then'' (Woosnam-Savage 3).

Gibb's final Crimean canvas, *Saving the Colours: The Guards at Inkerman* (painted 1894–98; exhibited 1900), concentrates on the heroism of Lt. H. W. Verschoyle of the Guards, who carries the flag of the regiment after the engagement at Inkerman, a group the *Art Journal* called a ''band of heroes'' (Gilbert 28), albeit not a Celtic regiment. The Duke of Cambridge is shown on the right welcoming the victorious survivors. Bonnets on the ends of bayonets celebrate the victory. Because Gibb is not painting a line here, it is the interaction among the participants, rather than their forward-looking gazes in *The Thin Red Line* and *The Alma*, that is noteworthy: one man has his eyes on the colors; another looks with concern at Verschoyle, whose head is bandaged under his bonnet; the drummer boy in the left corner focuses his blue eyes on the heroic action. The battle honor CORUNNA (16 January 1809) is under the Union Jack, evoking a heroic encounter of the Peninsular War. In this interaction of the participants, Gibb signals the importance of comradeship, an element of the masculine code particularly significant in *Saving the Colours*.

Gibb's images of comrades are among the most famous in battle art. In the 1885 *Letters from Home*, two men sit in a cold tent exchanging confidences about domestic circumstances recorded in their letters. In his first battle picture, the 1878 *Comrades*, Gibb made comradeship the basis of the painting, showing ''a young soldier, dying amid a snowstorm'' during the Crimea (Gilbert 27). The emphasis on comradeship is crucial for the maintenance of the dominant fiction, as Silverman argues:

> The fiction of a phallic masculinity generally remains intact only for the duration of the war. As long as the soldier remains on the battlefield, he is fortified to some degree by his comrades; the ''binding'' which can no longer take place at the level of the ego occurs instead at the level of the group. (63)

Gibb's three soldiers of the Black Watch have left their column as one of their number has collapsed in the snow. Gibb constructs a military Pietà as the dying confidences are exchanged. As Lalumia observes, ''*Comrades* demonstrated that Lady Butler's anti-heroic conception of battle did not represent a phenomenon unique to'' her (145), for Gibb shows the ordinary ranker capable of extreme loyalty in combat. John Luard's *The Welcome Arrival* of 1857 is set in the Crimea and shows as its central figure his brother Major Richard Luard of the 77th Regiment. The comradeship of the canvas is linked by the sharing of a gift box, ''a newly opened crate of preserved foods and tobacco from England'' (Lalumia 102). The figure on the right may be a self-portrait of the artist. Of particular interest is the great number of wood engravings on the walls of the small hut, signifying the manner in which representations of the events themselves unite the comrades, one of whom appears to study a miniature.

The comradeship of Scottish forces is important in two of the most famous representations of the Gordon Highlanders scaling the heights at Dargai on 20 October 1897 during the Tirah Expeditionary Force campaign against the Afridis in northwest India. In Gibb's *The Dargai* of 1909, again a famous command was the germ of the action: "Colonel Mathias commanding the Gordons said to his men, 'Highlanders, the General says the position must be taken at all costs. The Gordons will take it' " (Harrington, "The Man" 593). Gibb, like Wollen, uses the landscape to suggest the brutal circumstances in which the charge occurred, during which the regiment lost three officers and thirty men. The rough terrain magnifies the achievement. Woodville's *The Storming of Dargai Heights* of 1898 deploys landscape for the same purposes, but it also includes the most famous element of the charge, Piper George Findlater continuing to play even though both his legs were wounded. Woodville foregrounds him to link the anecdote with the canvas, unlike Gibb, who chooses to ignore this element of the legend of Dargai. Findlater's action is a supreme marker of comradeship, but Gibb's representation emphasizes sheer bravery. The motif of the "charge up a height" which unites Gibb's *Dargai* with his *Alma*, draws a correlation between Scottish Highlanders and terrain that yields a powerful psychological nexus of masculine defiance. This imagery of Scots abroad eliminates the stigma of their ethnicity which would be felt in England: the penis/phallus equation abroad could be maintained as ethnicity was subsumed into racial superiority and national identity.

The Scots as heroic rescuers is a focus of Joseph Noel Paton's *In Memoriam* of 1858, which has a history both combat- and race-inflected. As the picture exists today, it represents a group of English women, one of whom holds a Bible, praying for divine intervention at the moment that Highlanders enter to effect their rescue during the Indian Mutiny, probably a scene at Cawnpore. As Hichberger observes, Paton constructs his figures in a manner "reminiscent of Christian martyrdom scenes . . . in the tradition of High Art representations of saints" (175). When first exhibited, the picture had in fact depicted a group "of maddened Sepoys, hot after blood," according to the *Times* (*The Raj* 241). In its original version, the canvas aroused fervid controversy. The *Illustrated London News* declared the subject was "too revolting for further description" (15 May 1858, 498), although the *Critic* regarded the canvas as one "to solemnly meditate. We feel it almost a profanation to hang this picture in a show-room, it should have a chapel to itself" (15 May 1858, 235). The picture was engraved not with murderous Sepoys but with the revised Highlanders, demonstrating — and circulating — the idea of British Caucasian superiority over the lustful dark natives. Hichberger says, "the depiction of ladies in the power of black soldiers was deeply offensive" (175) and for Paton ultimately intolerable. A canvas that contested the heroic code of white male militarism by *not* showing a rescue —

and thereby exposing the incommensurability of the penis/phallus equation — was reconfigured to affirm that equation.

This incommensurability, however, is not camouflaged in Frank Holl's *A Deserter* of 1874, in which Highlanders have caught a deserter/laborer, his "heavy, split boots and ragged attire . . . in obvious contrast to the brilliant red clothing of the Highlanders" (Casteras, *Virtue Rewarded* 51). When one considers William Butler's essay on the factors driving men to enlist — famine, the Clearances, unemployment, starvation (the last signalled by the loaf in the man's hand) — the issues of class, ethnicity, and imperialism are conjoined, especially since in the 1870s the recruit would be destined for a colonial campaign. Particularly because of its setting, questions of incommensurability and the misrecognition underlying the dominant fiction also conflict Robert G. Hutchinson's *Under Orders* of 1883, depicting the Black Watch in a barrack room of Edinburgh Castle prior to embarking for the Egyptian War which led to Tel-el-Kebir. Hutchinson shows the families gathered with their individual loved ones, with elderly relatives counselling the young soldiers. In the background of the painting, a reproduction of John Everett Millais's *Cherry Ripe* symbolizes the reason why the troops are fighting: to preserve white womanhood. Thus the canvas has a strange affiliation with Paton's *In Memoriam*, as Scots become defenders of Caucasian racial superiority whether that be in Africa or India.

This racial superiority, emphasized by the ethnicity of the Scot, appears in George Joy's *The Last Stand of General Gordon* of 1893, commemorating the death of Gordon at Khartoum on 26 January 1885, when the Sudanese capital fell to the Mahdi's forces. Although born in Woolwich, Gordon's Scottish heritage is frequently cited by commentators, including William Butler, who in *The Campaign of the Cataracts* described Gordon at his death as "the solitary figure of the great Celtic soldier" (84). Surmounting blacks for the last time, Gordon epitomizes the Scot caught at the very moment exposing the *méconnaissance* upon which the dominant fiction of the commensurability of penis and phallus rests. In this representation, the Celt in Victorian battle imagery, himself colonized, confronts another Other in the form of an alternative, non-Caucasian masculinity. In *The River War*, Churchill had speculated that Gordon "saw himself facing that savage circle with a fanatacism equal to, and a courage greater than, their own" when he confronted these "wild, harlequin figures" (qtd. in Johnson 285). Churchill assimilates Gordon to racist myths of blacks (especially Sudanese with their patched jibbahs) as savage clowns, and even Gordon admitted that "one black face looked like another to him" (Johnson 301). Johnson notes that a "saint cult" (304) was built around the figure of the Celtic Gordon, the motive of which was to justify the imperial idea:

> The vast majority of Gordon literature is important not for the study of Sudanese history but . . . for the study of western psychology, more particularly the psychology behind British imperial sentiment. . . . A man without imperfection, [Gordon] justified the winning of an empire by men of more mortal stature. (307)

Thus, this ultimate example of Celtic valor constructs white masculinity in imperial contexts. Richard Caton Woodville's *The Gordon Memorial Service at Khartoum* of 1899, painted expressly for the Queen, is the iconographic memorial to this construction of Gordon. The Catholic, Anglican, Presbyterian, and Methodist chaplains are shown before the ruins of the palace. Steevens recorded the event as follows:

> Thus with Maxim-Nordenfeldt and Bible we buried Gordon after the manner of his race. . . . [He] was an Englishman doing his duty, alone and at the instant peril of his life. . . . We came with a sigh of shame: we went away with a sigh of relief. . . . We left Gordon alone again — but alone in majesty under the conquering ensign of his own people. (314–16)

Steevens observes: "the vindication of our self-respect was the great treasure we won at Khartoum, and it was worth the price we paid for it" (318).

For Steevens, the imperial conquest was justified by the nature of the natives. In the conclusion to his book, he reveals he accepts the white western construction of African masculinity as something Other and inferior:

> Take the native Egyptian official even to-day. No words can express his ineptitude, his laziness, his helplessness, his dread of responsibility, his maddening red-tape formalism. . . . To put Egyptians, corrupt, lazy, timid, often rank cowards, to rule the Sudan, would be to invite another Mahdi as soon as the country had grown up enough to make him formidable.
>
> The Sudan must be ruled by military law strong enough to be feared, administered by British officers just enough to be respected. . . . [The Sudan] is not a country; it has nothing that makes a country. Some brutish institutions it has, and some bloodthirsty chivalry. But is it not a country: it has neither nationality, nor history, nor arts, nor even natural features. . . . Its people are naked and dirty, ignorant and besotted. It is a quarter of a continent of sheer squalor. . . . The Sudan is a God-accursed wilderness. (321–25)

The most startling passage in Steevens's record, however, is its famous penultimate paragraph, in which he sets a savage norm of masculinity from the Sudan campaign and the Gordon relief expedition:

> Perhaps to Englishmen — half-savage still on the pinnacle of their civilisation — the very charm of the land lies in its empty barbarism. There is space in the Sudan. There is the fine, purified desert air, and the long stretching gallops over its sand. There are the things at the very back of life, and no other to posture in front of them, — hunger and thirst to assuage, distance to win through, pain to bear, life to defend, and death to face. You have gone back to the spring water of your infancy. You are a savage again. . . . You are unprejudiced, simple, free. You are a naked man, facing naked nature.
>
> I do not believe that any of us who come home whole will think, from our easy-chairs, unkindly of the Sudan. (325–26)

Here the norms of masculinity are exposed to be savage and liberating simultaneously. Elements of both *Heart of Darkness* and *The Light that Failed* are suggested in Steevens's paean to masculinity in the desert.

The Veteran

THE ATTEMPT TO REASSERT the dominant fiction of masculinity is most difficult in the representation of the wounded male body, particularly in the case of the returned veteran. It is striking that representations of veterans from imperial campaigns were relatively few after mid-century. Silverman offers an explanation of this anomaly:

> Once removed from the battlefront, the traumatized veteran no longer enjoys the support of his comrades-in-arms. All that stands between him and the abyss is the paternal imago, within which he can no longer recognize himself. For the society to which he returns, moreover, he represents a sorry travesty of "our fighting men and boys," a living proof of the incommensurability of penis and phallus. (63)

Hichberger notes that forty paintings of veterans were exhibited at the Royal Academy between 1815 and 1914, eighteen of which involved Chelsea pensioners (*Images* 141). This small number is not surprising if one considers that the wounded body of the male becomes the signifier not of masculinity but of the Other, the resourceless, passive, non-aggressive paradigm associated with the feminine or the colonized. Few of these veteran depictions were of imperial war campaigns. Rather, the best known involve the Crimea. In Joseph Noel Paton's *Home: The Return from the Crimea*, exhibited in 1859, a corporal in the Scots Fusilier Guards is embraced by his kneeling wife as his aged mother hovers over him. He has lost his left arm and is still bandaged about the head. As Christopher Lloyd notes, "the painting can . . . be interpreted as an implied criticism of the war," the "anti-heroic sentiments" of which disturbed reviewers (202). There can be no doubt that to observers the wounded and incapacitated male body exposed the fragility of the penis/phallus equation. The disabled veteran, in fact, guaranteed that the prevailing order was *not* sabotaged. Hichberger notes that disabled veterans were depicted "to minimise any sense of physical threat from the veterans and to make them into recognizably suitable cases for pity" ("Old Soldiers" 63). Hichberger observes that the public feared "the dangers of radicals 'subverting' soldiers and veterans" (62). Located in a domestic setting, and disabled as well, "the veteran of the Crimea became an unthreatening patriot" (55). In C. M. Hodges's *Home Sweet Home* of c. 1890, a corporal of the 11th Hussars is shown home on leave, an image much in contrast to the broken veteran of Paton's *Home*. Here the domestic setting, the attentive wife, the loyal dog, the table laden with food, and the clean surroundings reveal the situation of a man unwounded and thus still within the dominant fiction.

The best known representation of the veteran of an imperial campaign is Henry Nelson O'Neil's *Home Again, 1858*, exhibited in 1859. As Spencer-Smith observes, the canvas represents a range of types of veterans returning from the Indian Mutiny. While most of the returnees are happily received by wife or mother, (as in O'Neil's smaller 1859 version [Figure 16]), "a highlander of the 93rd (Highlanders) with his arm round his daughter looks away in distress from the letter that he has just read. The words 'deceive . . . wife . . . who loved you' can just be traced" (30). This detail is especially trenchant, suggesting that the wife rejects the man as sexual partner, provider, and guide, clearly recognizing his new marginalized status. The *Athenaeum* in its review (30 April 1859, 587) indicted the falsity of O'Neil's optimistic construction: "The crowding down of relatives and friends to greet [the veteran] on the land, is too generally a myth. . . . [B]roken health and penury, to be endured in obscurity, are all that remain." The disabled veteran was too evident a marker of the disintegration of the dominant fiction of masculinity.

The social realist artists of the Victorian period were especially aware of this disintegration as marked by the veteran. In Thomas Faed's *From Hand to Mouth* of 1879, a veteran, accompanied by his son and daughter, stands in front of a shop counter reaching for money to pay for the goods on the counter before the suspicious shop proprietor. A pointed contrast with the well-dressed woman on the left emphasizes the plight of the veteran, the feared image of the unemployed, poor, migrant, dispossessed male. Here Faed records the total collapse of the dominant fiction. Treuherz argues: "Unemployment had caused them to enlist, but after discharge only a few were entitled to pensions and most were thrown onto the casual labour market. Unskilled, they became beggars or vagrants" (45). In the long line of the dispossessed in Luke Fildes's *Applicants for Admission to a Casual Ward* of 1874, a veteran leaning on a crutch appears to the far right of the canvas. Probably a survivor of the Crimea, he is a terrifying remnant of the campaign. Hichberger notes that the only review to record his presence called him a "professional beggar," suggesting he was a fraud (*Images* 148). The destitute nature of the man exposes the falsity of the dominant fiction and the devaluation of the male body once it has been wounded and impoverished. Since the casual ward was the last step before the workhouse, the veteran's plight is acute, linked as he is with an unemployed mechanic, a drunkard, a stowaway, and various outcast women.

Two other social-realist artists, Frank Holl and Hubert von Herkomer, also were attracted to the veteran. In his *Home from the Front* of 1881, Holl depicts soldiers of the McKenzie Highlanders returning from one of the wars of the late 1870s, such as the Second Afghan War. Unlike the situation of the veterans in

Faed's or Fildes's canvases, the welcoming citizenry accord the veteran acceptance and status in a civic ceremony, even when he may be wounded. Wives, sweethearts, and drummer boys enliven the canvas and camouflage the much more certain social neglect experienced by most veterans. In Herkomer's *The Last Muster* of 1875, a group of veterans is shown in the Royal Hospital Chelsea attending a service in the Chapel, during which the man at the end of the second row has died. His friend reaches to take his pulse. As Edwards notes, "the inmates of the Chelsea Hospital were seasoned war veterans who qualified for residence because of their indigence" (92). The flags hanging over the group evoke glories long forgotten by an ungrateful public.

The plight of a veterans's family after his death is signified by the neglect the public accorded his widow and family. In Thomas Brooks's *Relenting* of 1855, "a landlord and his agent prepare to evict a widow and her children from their garret chambers. From the portrait on the wall, the black-edged letter behind its frame, and the sword hanging nearby, it is apparent that the husband was a soldier, killed perhaps in the Crimea" (Casteras, *The Substance or the Shadow* 63). As Casteras notes, details such as the curtainless windows, the meager room furnishings, and the medicine bottles alluding to the illness of the eldest daughter denote a situation of the poverty all too often awaiting both the veteran and his family. In *Relenting*, the callous neglect of the veteran is transferred to his survivors, representing the unwillingness of the culture to deal with those exposing the falsity of the dominant fiction.

Painted in 1898, the veteran in C. M. Hodges's *Of Balaclava and '54*, narrating the tale of the Charge of the Light Brigade in the Crimea, transmits the masculine code to a young ranker, who listens respectfully. Unlike the veterans of *The Last Muster* with their broken masculinity, this veteran conveys to a later generation the empowering ideology of the dominant fiction. *Of Balaclava and '54* thus epitomizes the construction of masculinity in Victorian military painting.

John Springhall contends that battle artists

> supplied the British public on a regular basis with the visual imagery for the great imperial events of their times. Popular art was thus instrumental in defining the public image of warfare in Victorian Britain [especially through] popularised reproductions [in which could] be found all the qualities — hero worship, sensational glory, adventure and the sporting spirit [— through which] the age of imperialism saw itself. (68–69)

Lalumia asserts that in the 1880s and 1890s there was a "contemporary mood of confidence in the army's invincibility" (148). Imperial battle iconography, however, suggests that such attitudes were not universal. In fact, with the exception of the representations of indisputable victories, battle painting interrogated as much as it constructed the dominant fiction of masculinity, particularly because as MacKenzie observes such imagery revealed the connection "between imperialism and sexual separation'' (179). The all-male world of imperial battle imagery is the extreme example of the intensification of the male body, which became a site for negotiation and contestation of masculinity.

Battle Art and Masculinity

THIS CONTESTATION WAS stimulated by the debate about battle art itself, which included a pacifist critique that such imagery was marked by misrepresentation and reticence. Roger Stearn notes:

> Decorous selection and omission was the norm in pre-1914 portrayal of war, in the illustrated press as at the Royal Academy. Yet while its practitioners saw it as proper and beneficial, to their pacifist critics it was deliberate lying, the hiding of the real horror of war. While battle painting was accepted by the art establishment and popular with the public, a minority of critics condemned it, asserting that its subject and necessity of omission invalidated it as true art. (187, 125)

Two responses to this criticism may be in order. First, all art is necessarily selective and reticent by the very nature of its exclusion of material in construction of the canvas. Even more significantly, the pacifist critique overlooked the degree to which the role of the soldier and the nature of combat were in fact represented with considerable fidelity. Stearn observes, ''[battle artists] portrayed death and wounds, but in a style that omitted the horror, mutilation, disfigurement, suffering and agony, and showed relatively few British dead'' (20). He adds: ''Victorian battle painting followed self-censoring conventions: no ugliness or squalor; minimised, conventionalised wounds; few British dying or dead; and no cruelty, horror or agony'' (116). Such statements, however, contain only a fragment of truth. On the contrary, it is the case that squalor, agony, cruelty, and horror are not absent or omitted from military painting, for example, Fripp's *Isandhlwana* or Butler's *The Roll Call* or *Inkerman*. Gibb's *Saving the Colours* is memorable for its squalor, mud, torn and dirty uniforms, and bandaged heads; Wollen's *Gundamuck* epitomizes the horror of the ''last stand.'' In fact, the battle artist, by showing wounding, death, abandonment, stabbing, or collapse in a few carefully calculated details of a canvas increased its horror by this very selectivity, which caused such incidents to emerge from the mass with startling clarity and indelible precision. To indict military art for falsification overlooks the extraordinary advantage gained by artistic selection and construction.

Military painting, by the very nature of its enterprise, transcends the mere glorification of hero-worship and adventure. The fact that artists could focus on defeats such as Gundamuck or Isandhlwana or marginal victories like Tamai demonstrates their willingness to examine masculinities beyond the comfortable formulations possible if one only painted unqualified victories or attended to superficial heroics. The extent of the suffering depicted by Butler, Fripp, Giles,

Wollen, and other artists reveals that the model of Woodville's dashing manner was far from common. The very de-emphasis on the officer class in much of this painting represents not the adulation of but the dethroning of Carlylean-inspired hero-worship and its attendant glorifications. For this very reason, military painting becomes a prime site for the negotiation of masculinity in its conflicted composition. The circulation of such images is also key to their value as sites of such negotiation. Stearn notes: ''They were extensively disseminated through a variety of media including periodicals, prints, postcards, advertisements, encyclopedias, popular histories and textbooks. They complemented and reinforced the writings of the war correspondents, and contributed to increased popular imperialism and support for imperial wars and to the increased popularity of the army'' (128). The versions of masculinity thus circulated meant that they constituted a common discourse about its formation throughout the culture.

Klaus Theweleit describes in *Male Fantasies* the basis for this negotiation of masculinity in military painting: for the male ''the army, high culture, race, nation — all of these appear to function as . . . extensions of himself'' (2: 84). Representations of disasters such as *Gundamuck* or *Isandhlwana*, or of cliff-hanging conquests like *Rorke's Drift* or *Tamai*, or of disabled veterans depict the conflicted and fragile nature of the dominant fiction, even as representations of victory, as at Ulundi or Omdurman, exhibit the tense triumph of artillery as much as they exhibit andreia. The iconography of imperial campaigns constructs an ideology ''central to the maintenance of classic masculinity . . . through the alignment of [the phallus] with the male sexual organ,'' as Silverman contends (16). Battle iconography, however, under the press of historical trauma, could prove transgressive and expose the *méconnaissance* upon which the dominant fiction rests. For artists of imperial campaigns, the potential for disintegration of masculinity constituted the ultimate challenging conflict. The nineteenth century, so marked by the presence of wars large and small, deployed military art to interrogate as much as to construct a masculinity taut from the press of history and conflicted by such elements as race, social Darwinism, ethnicity, and wounding. For these reasons, masculinity in military iconography becomes decisive in an investigation of the construction of maleness during the era.

University of Tulsa

NOTES

The author wishes to acknowledge gratefully his Fellowship from the Anne S. K. Brown Military Collection, Brown University, which enabled him to complete the research for this essay. In particular, he is indebted to the Curator of the Collection, Peter Harrington, for invaluable information and assistance during the time of his residence at Brown.

Sections of this essay were delivered at the American Conference for Irish Studies, the Interdisciplinary Nineteenth-Century Studies Conference, and the Northeast Victorian

Studies Association during 1993; to the organizers of these conferences, the author expresses his gratitude for their assistance and collegiality.

Jenny Spencer-Smith, Keeper of Fine Art at the National Army Museum in London, provided much important assistance to the author during his research at that institution, for which he is most grateful.

1. Nearly all the paintings discussed in this essay are included in the "Catalogue of Oil Paintings" at the conclusion of Peter Harrington's *British Artists and War: The Face of Battle in Paintings and Prints, 1700–1914* (313–343). Harrington's alphabetical listing of artists includes all their known works, with dimensions and current location if known. Most of the canvases discussed in this essay are reproduced in Harrington's book, including the works of Butler, Woodville, Giles, Wollen, Fripp, Gibb, Joy, Kelly, and Barker.

2. Hichberger (*Images*) identifies one of these 1885 canvases as *An Incident at the Battle of Tamai*, which is in fact the title of a third canvas about the battle, exhibited in 1887; this canvas is in a private collection. I am grateful to Peter Harrington for this information.

WORKS CITED

Alma: Forward the 42nd. Unpublished file account. Glasgow: Glasgow Art Gallery.

Barthorp, Michael. *War on the Nile*. London: Blandford P, 1984.

The Battle of Abu Klea. Placard. London: National Army Museum.

Bond, Brian, ed. *Victorian Military Campaigns*. London: Hutchinson, 1967.

Butler, William F. *The Campaign of the Cataracts*. London: Sampson Low, 1887.

———. *Far Out: Rovings Retold.* London: Isbister, 1881.

Casteras, Susan P. *The Substance or the Shadow.* New Haven: Yale Center for British Art, 1982.

———. *Virtue Rewarded.* Louisville: Speed Art Museum, 1988.

Droogleever, R. W. F. "Charles Fripp and 'The Battle of Isandhlwana.'" *Soldiers of the Queen* 70 (September 1992): 5.

Edwards, Lee. "Hubert von Herkomer: 'Sympathy for the old and for suffering mankind.'" *Hard Times*. London: Lund Humphries, 1987. 90–103.

Farwell, Byron. *Queen Victoria's Little Wars*. New York: Norton, 1973.

"Fine Victorian Pictures." London: Christie's (23 October 1987).

Foucault, Michel. *The History of Sexuality: An Introduction*. New York: Vintage, 1990.

Gilbert, W. Matthews. "Robert Gibb." *Art Journal* (1897): 25–28.

Girouard, Mark. *The Return to Camelot*. New Haven: Yale UP, 1981.

Hanham, H. J. "Mid-Century Scottish Nationalism: Romantic and Radical." *Ideas and Institutions of Victorian Britain*. Ed. Robert Robson. London: Bell, 1967. 143–79.

Harbottle, T. B. *Dictionary of Battles*. New York: Van Norstrand, 1971.

Harrington, Peter. *British Artists and War: The Face of Battle in Paintings and Prints, 1700–1914.* London: Greenhill Books, 1993.

———. "The Defence of Kars." *Journal of the Society for Army Historical Research* 69 (Spring 1991): 22–28.

———. "The Man Who Painted *The Thin Red Line.*" *Scots Magazine* 130 (March 1989): 587–95.

Hichberger, Joan. *Images of the Army*. Manchester: Manchester UP, 1988.

Hichberger, Joan W. M. "Old Soldiers." *Patriotism*. Vol. 3. Ed. Raphael Samuel. London: Routledge, 1989.

Johnson, D. H. "The Death of Gordon: A Victorian Myth." *Journal of Imperial and Commonwealth History* 10 (May 1982): 285–310.

Knight, Ian J. *Zulu*. London: Windrow & Greene, 1992.
Lalumia, Matthew. *Realism and Politics in Victorian Art of the Crimean War*. Ann Arbor,MI: UMI Research P, 1984.
Leclaire, Serge. "Sexuality: A Fact of Discourse." *Homosexualities and French Literature*. Ed. George Stambolian. Ithaca: Cornell UP, 1979. 42–55.
Lloyd, Christopher, ed. *The Queen's Pictures*. London: National Gallery, 1991.
Macdonald, John. *Great Battles of the World*. New York: Macmillan, 1984.
MacKenzie, John M. "The Imperial Pioneer and Hunter and the British Masculine Stereotype in late Victorian and Edwardian Times." *Manliness and Morality*. Ed. J. A. Mangan and James Walvin. New York: St. Martin's P, 1987. 176–98.
McBride, Angus. *The Zulu War*. London: Osprey, 1976.
The Queen's Image. Ed. Helen Smailes. Edinburgh: Scottish National Portrait Gallery, 1987.
The Raj. Ed. C. A. Bayly. London: National Portrait Gallery, 1990.
Reader, W. J. *"At Duty's Call": A Study in Obsolete Patriotism*. Manchester: Manchester UP, 1988.
Sears, Stephen W., ed. *The Horizon History of the British Empire*. New York: McGraw Hill, 1973.
Silverman, Kaja. *Male Subjectivity at the Margins*. New York: Routledge, 1992.
Skelley, Alan Ramsay. *The Victorian Army at Home*. Montreal: Queen's UP, 1977.
Spencer-Smith, Jenny. "Henry Nelson O'Neil's *Home Again*." *National Army Museum Year Book* 1 (1991): 29–30.
Spencer-Smith, Jenny, and Paul Usherwood. *Lady Butler: Battle Artist*. London: Alan Sutton/National Army Museum, 1987.
Spiers, Edward M. *The Army and Society 1815–1914*. London: Longman, 1980.
Springhall, John. " 'Up Guards and at Them!': British Imperialism and Popular Art, 1880–1914." *Imperialism and Popular Culture*. Ed. John M. MacKenzie. Manchester: Manchester UP, 1986. 49–72.
Stearn, Roger T. "War Images and Image Makers in the Victorian Era." Diss. King's College, University of London, 1987.
Stearns, Peter N. *Be a Man! Males in Modern Society*. 2nd ed. New York: Holmes and Meier, 1990.
Steevens, G.W. *With Kitchener to Khartum*. 1898. London: Greenhill Books, 1990.
Strong, Roy. *Recreating the Past: British History and the Victorian Painter*. London: Thames and Hudson, 1978.
Theweleit, Klaus. *Male Fantasies*. Vol. 2. Minneapolis: U of Minnesota P, 1989.
Treuherz, Julian. *Hard Times*. London: Lund Humphries, 1987.
Trevor-Roper, Hugh. "The Invention of Tradition: The Highland Tradition of Scotland." *The Invention of Tradition*. Ed. Eric Hobsbawm and Terence Ranger. Cambridge: Cambridge UP, 1983.
Vance. Norman. *The Sinews of the Spirit*. Cambridge: Cambridge UP, 1985.
Wilkinson-Latham, C. "The Defence of Rorke's Drift." *Tradition 55 (1970):* 6–8.
Wood, Christopher. *Victorian Panorama*. London: Faber and Faber, 1976.
Wood, Stephen. *The Scottish Soldier*. Manchester: Archive Publications, 1987.
Woodham-Smith, Cecil. *The Reason Why*. London: Constable, 1953.
Woosnam-Savage, Robert C. "Gibb's *Alma*." Glasgow: Glasgow Art Gallery, n.d.

1. Richard Caton Woodville, *Kandahar*, 1881. 52 × 73. Christie's London.

2. Richard Caton Woodville, *The Charge of the 21st Lancers at Omdurman*, 1898. 60 × 98. Board of Trustees of the National Museums and Galleries on Merseyside (Walker Art Gallery, Liverpool).

3. Elizabeth Thompson, Lady Butler, *The Defence of Rorke's Drift*, 1880. 47 × 83. Royal Collection Enterprises Ltd.

4. John Evan Hodgson, *"The Queen, God Bless Her!"*, 1880. 26 × 36. The FORBES Magazine Collection, New York, all rights reserved.

5. Godfrey Douglas Giles, *The Battle of Tamai*, 1885. 41 × 72. Regimental Trustees of the York and Lancaster Regiment.

6. Elizabeth Thompson, Lady Butler, *The Roll Call*, 1874. 36 × 72. Royal Collection Enterprises Ltd.

7. William Barnes Wollen, *The Last Stand of the 44th at Gundamuck, 1842*, 1898. 26 × 48. The Trustees of the Essex Regiment Association, The Royal Anglian Regiment.

8. Richard Caton Woodville, *Maiwand: Saving the Guns*, 1882. 51 × 78. Board of Trustees of the National Museum and Galleries on Merseyside (Walker Art Gallery, Liverpool).

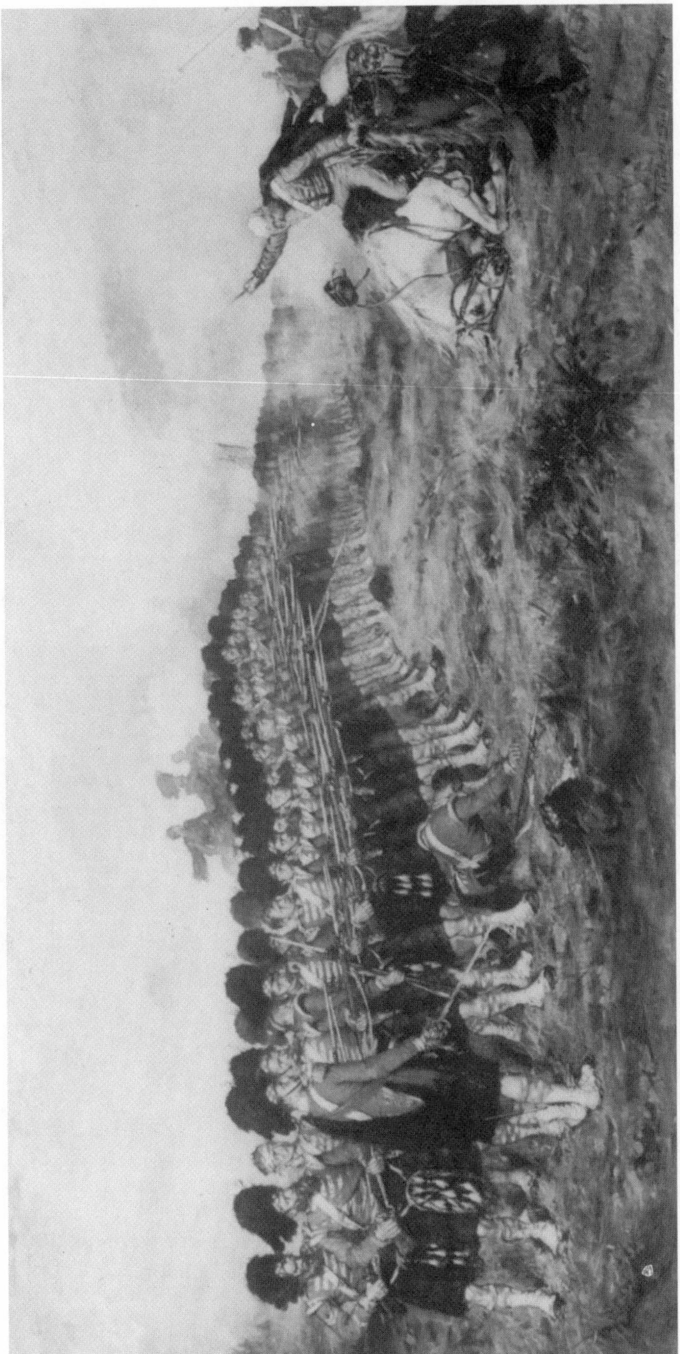

9. Robert Gibb, *The Thin Red Line*, 1881. 42 × 83. By permission of United Distillers, Edinburgh, Scotland.

10. Robert Gibb, *Saving the Colours: The Guards at Inkerman,* 1900. 110 × 71. Naval and Military Club, London.

11. Robert Gibb, *The Dargai*, 1909. 61 × 91. Sotheby's, London.

12. Frank Holl, *A Deserter*, 1874. 36 × 53. The FORBES Magazine Collection, New York, all rights reserved.

13. George Joy, *The Last Stand of General Gordon*, 1893. 120 × 84. Leeds City Art Galleries.

14. Richard Caton Woodville, *The Gordon Memorial Service at Khartoum*, 1899. 52 × 78. Royal Collection Enterprises Ltd.

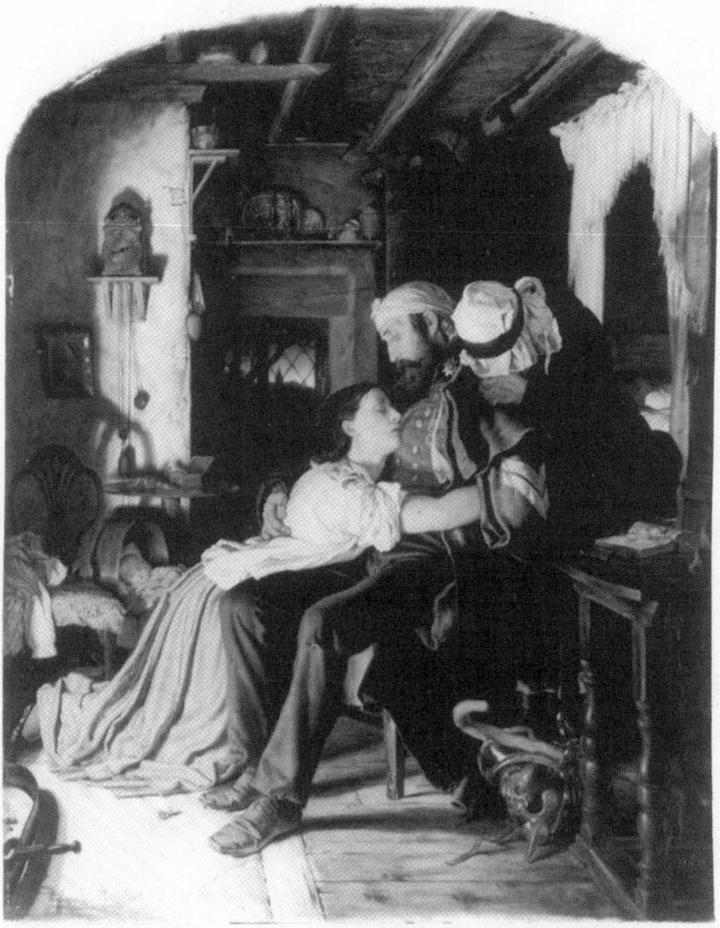

15. Joseph Noel Paton, *Home: The Return from the Crimea,* 1859. 27 × 22. Royal Collection Enterprises Ltd.

16. Henry Nelson O'Neil, *Home Again, 1858,* 1859. 20 × 34. The FORBES Magazine Collection, New York, all rights reserved.

17. Hubert von Herkomer, *The Last Muster,* 1875. 82 × 62. Board of Trustees of the National Museums and Galleries on Merseyside (Lady Lever Gallery, Port Sunlight).

PRISONS OF SUBJECTIVITY: OSCAR WILDE'S *DE PROFUNDIS,* AN AUTOBIOGRAPHY OF ESCAPE

By Jane Wood

> You knew what my Art was to me, the great primal note by which I had revealed, first myself to myself, and then myself to the world; the real passion of my life; the love to which all other loves were as marsh-water to red wine, or the glow-worm of the marsh to the magic mirror of the moon.

OSCAR WILDE'S PRISON LETTER to Lord Alfred Douglas is much more than the lover's complaint that its opening remarks would seem to suggest. Written between January and March 1897 towards the end of Wilde's two-year sentence, this lengthy epistle — later published as *De Profundis* — fabricates its author's escape from tragic subjection to constitute a new self-presence out of exile and loss. Its generic status has exercised the minds of critics ever since Wilde's detailed instructions were made explicit — both in respect of the form and content of the letter and of its subsequent destiny — in his correspondence with Robert Ross in April 1897.[1] From Wilde's instructions to Ross, particularly with regard to the copying and distribution of the letter, it seems clear that its author always anticipated that this most private of utterances would one day reach a far wider audience.[2] Ostensibly a love letter, it attempts to bridge separation by recalling the past, reworking the experience of bitterness and pain, and then shaping a future around hope and joy.[3] At the same time, the letter is self-evidently a public statement whose objective is an ameliorative and self-validating one for an artist struggling against what he perceives to be a divisive and philistine ideological machine. That Wilde considers his work a literary autobiography suggests a consciousness of its status as artifice. If it is to be understood as having a generic affiliation with unforced autobiographies, *De Profundis* is similarly a reinvention, a retrospective fashioning of a self to present to the world, and is, at least — in this sense, a fiction. It works not only to externalize an internal crisis but, paradoxically, to embody an awareness of epoch and articulate an individual life which both registers and resists the cultural specifics in which it is framed. Public image and private pain are as complexly related in this text as are the questions of authenticity and artifice which this dual dimension constantly raises.

At the risk of re-knotting the strands which critics more usually attempt to disentangle, I suggest that the multiform nature of this letter, and the internally-paradoxical nature of its content, are part of its strength in serving its author's purpose. In this paper I will briefly realign the arguments for a conventional confinement narrative and for a non-conventional spiritual autobiography, and then I will explore the ways in which diversity, ambiguity, and mutability are deployed throughout this text as strategies of resistance to an imprisonment that is at once literal and metaphorical. Escape from that imprisonment, I shall argue, is achieved by writing a self that is no longer the victim of its own history, but one that is an endlessly re-creatable object in it.

As a self-narrativization, *De Profundis* responds to a crisis in which the confident assertions of the aesthetic ideal espoused in earlier writings are re-examined in the light of the terrible reality of incarceration. Motivated by the experience of solitary confinement, it mounts a defence against an increasingly threatening loss of mental equilibrium for its writer. As Frank Kermode has shown of other prison narratives, language becomes the vital tool in the preservation of sanity, for its versatility enables the fashioning of new contingencies and new measures of self-awareness when familiar spatial and temporal reference points have been removed (see ch. 6). Regenia Gagnier argues that Wilde's letter is astonishingly similar to other prison writings in the way that its erratic and often hyperbolic flights of imagination are ''act[s] of resistance against insanity and against the material matrix of prison space and time, that is, confined, segmented space and timelessness'' (335). But in Gagnier's materialist reading of the text, imagination is itself shaped and determined by the regimented ordering of the prison day. Since the world outside the prison walls, she argues, is reconstituted according to the ''terms and cycles of imprisonment'' (344). But in Gagnier's materialist reading of the text, imagination is itself shaped and determined by the regimented ordering of the prison day. Since the world outside the prison walls, she argues, is reconstituted according to the ''terms and cycles of imprisonment'' (344), far from transcending the spatial and temporal conditions, Wilde's writing is framed within and by them. If this seems at first to be a reductive reading, which precludes the possibility of prison narratives being anything other than self-serving labors with no value or relevance beyond the fact of confinement, Gagnier goes on to allow that the ''productive labor'' of writing confers upon the prisoner the resilience to counter the dehumanizing effects of the system (348:49). By constructing an imaginative fiction of a past and future self, Wilde spans the timeless, featureless isolation of the prison cell and introduces into a stark and brutalizing environment a self-protective and humanizing one.

To consider Wilde's writing in terms of an act of resistance to an authority working to punish, silence, and suppress accords with Foucauldan ideas of the operations of power within cultural organization. Michel Foucault has theorized the way that nineteenth-century science, and medical science particularly, in its obsession with the body as a site of knowledge, observed, labelled, and classified the individual subject into categories of health or pathology, normality or deviancy, according to culturally-inscribed and often unscientific ideas of the normative (Foucault, 1981). Science therefore sanctioned many ready-made social and moral beliefs, and it provided the means by which identity could be turned into a weapon and used against those individuals whom orthodoxy perceived to be transgressors. To avoid the imprisonment of blanket assumptions about essential nature which underpin such simplistic categorization, Wilde's self-writing must seek a way of demonstrating that the work of the artist, and the manner and mode in which that work is communicated, is quite separate from the "nature" of the man.

In ideological terms, the sliding together of what Ed Cohen has called the "representation of homoerotic desire" in Wilde's pre-prison writing and his private preference and practice is a sophistical leap which permitted a Victorian middle-class judiciary to formulate a category of deviance.[4] From there, the state could authorize and define "legitimate male sexual practices (defining them as 'healthy,' 'natural,' or 'true') by proscribing expressions of male experience that transgressed these limits" (Cohen, "Writing" 805, 801). It is in this way that, to recall Foucauldian terms, the "homosexual" was discursively produced. With his high-camp profile rendering his position especially vulnerable, Wilde strives to maintain a dual self-perception which confers a freedom on the artist even as the man is bound in chains. Tensions already suffusing the autobiographical writing — between public image and private pain, between artistic detachment from the soulless technologies of socio-political organization and real, inescapable bondage to those technologies — are exacerbated by the problem of affirming a homoerotic ideal while resisting the essentializing assumptions bearing upon homosexual "identity."

In my view, it is this sustained negotiation between the dual entities of the artist and the man that is fundamental to Wilde's fashioning of a comic other to the tragic self. Haunted with a sense of tragic destiny, which is as tantalizing as it is terrifying, *De Profundis* time and again invokes tragic events to enable the author imaginatively to empathize with the tragic role and at the same time maintain a critical detachment from it. Where Jay Losey has pointed up similarities (and indeed direct allusions) between Wilde's *De Profundis* and Dante's *Commedia* to articulate an affinity between two tragic poets condemned to their respective forms of exile, I am suggesting that the empathy cannot be charted along a simple mimetic course. Although Losey's theory of the "artist in exile" is crucial to my reading of Wilde's text, my reservations are with the claims for the letter's status as a spiritual autobiography predicted upon conversion. Importantly for Losey, Wilde is transformed through suffering to a state of reconciliation, "the traditional form of spiritual autobiography" (443). It seems to me that the assumption of a linear, progressive narrative, whose mid-point is confession, sets too much store on authenticity.

To the degree that one can with any confidence speak of authenticity in respect of expressions of spiritual conversion, which are by definition retrospective constructions, Wilde's "confessions" are ever mindful of a desired public image and of maintaining an intellectual and artistic supremacy which is quite inconsistent with their avowals of humility and remorse. Importantly though, this qualification should not be read so much as a critique of the text's limitations as it is a recognition of its complexity. Giving expression to torment is a necessary unburdening which enables a measure of liberation. However, as a confessional autobiography, Wilde's letter serves only an expedient need. It is my view that, although Wilde adopts the paradigms of spiritual autobiography as a strategy for self-validation, his final remark — "[h]ow far I am away from the true temper of soul, this letter in its changing, uncertain moods, its scorn and bitterness, its aspirations and its failure to realise those aspirations, shows you quite clearly" (158) — explicitly exposes both the strategy and its inadequacy. The state of contrition and final redemption to which confessional narrative aspires remains in this work illusory.

Critics of *De Profundis,* in pursuit of a text of spiritual transformation have seized upon Wilde's adoption of the topos of the Fortunate Fall to substantiate a reading whereby the prison experience marks the turning point between death and resurrection.[5] Wilde's affirmation of Christ as the supreme figure of the Romantic Imagination permits him, through a complicity of interpretive practice, to discard an old way of life and embrace a new. Public scandal and private tragedy can then be transvalued by means of "Suffering" into self-knowledge. While such a reading represents an important contribution to the text's analysis, its reliance upon typological continuity begs questions of transformation and truth. Taking the Romance narrative of loss, self-discovery, and resurrection as a starting point, William Buckler modifies the "fortunate fall" theme in *De Profundis* so as to reject its simple continuity and make way for the supreme role of the artist in remaking himself in accordance with his own version of history (104-05). Rightly then, arguments for the authenticity of a declared spiritual enlightenment and conversion are called into question when the text is read as a work of art rather than a chronicle of a life. That said, I would want to challenge Buckler's conclusion that the "end" of art is self-realization. On the contrary, I shall be arguing that art is, for Wilde, the means of its endless deferral. Self-realization is not something that is incrementally arrived at but is throughout this work continually being made and lost, brought into being only to be forced into compromise or retreat. Even if we desist from reference to Wilde's post-prison experience, there remains the instability of the text itself. Coherence and continuity are conventions with which this form of expression is for the most part unconcerned.

Ambiguity and paradox are vital to this text's resistance to a single, coherent version of selfhood. Wilde's identification with Christ is inspirational in its provision of a romantic, individualist counter-measure to a contemporary scientific positivism and its suspicion of any modes of being that elude easy categorization into uniform structures.[6] The Romance quest to liberate the authentic and sincere self is appropriated as a strategy, an elegant gesture of defiant assertiveness which works to sustain both the aestheticized world of the artist and the psychological stability of the man. Or, put another way: "By counterposing realism and romance Wilde kept a positive past and created a possible future" and at the same time maintained "the individual voice of the silenced" to rail at the system designed to depersonalize and suppress it (Gagnier 348). Bearing these ideas of suspension and deferral in mind, it can be argued that Wilde moves out of the Romantic notion of deep subjectivity and towards a concept of social self-fashioning. Where Buckler argues that "depth of insight" and intense meditation upon the "inner spirit" to reveal the "truth of oneself" become the motivating theme of *De Profundis*" (100), I am arguing that Wilde had no such finite and absolute goal which, if realized, would leave no room for maneuver or change.[7] His task as I see it in *De Profundis* is to resist the centrality of the imprisoned self, to vacate the subjective role and fabricate, instead, elevation into a sphere of existence which is unfettered by a defining essentialism.

The overriding imperative for Wilde is to dissociate himself from the ideology which has pronounced him guilty by definition. He effects this severance, I argue, by writing himself out of tragedy and towards comedy. More precisely, Wilde detaches himself from the inevitable evolution of tragedy towards degeneration and annihilation to occupy a realm where endless possibilities for regeneration may be encountered. From tormented victim, whose perception of his situation is that of the tragic hero, Wilde works through self-conscious melancholia and martyrdom towards resurrection. But this is not the resurrection which characterizes the "end" of traditional spiritual autobiography, whereby the subject, though transformed, is absolved and re-inserted into the linear, progressive official culture. Instead, it is Wilde's purpose to validate ambivalence, diversity, and otherness as a conscious strategy of resistance to Victorian orthodoxy. Nonetheless, his starting point is despair and disillusionment:

> I thought life was going to be a brilliant comedy, and that you were to be one of many graceful figures in it. I found it to be a revolting and repellent tragedy, and that the sinister occasion of the great catastrophe, sinister in its concentration of aim and intensity of narrowed will-power, was yourself, stripped of that mask of

> joy and pleasure by which you, no less than I, had been deceived and led astray. (66-67)

Perceiving Douglas to be "the true author of the hideous tragedy" (72) in whose tangled plot he has become enmeshed, Wilde faces the task of extricating himself from the chain of destruction by which "Nemesis has crushed us both like flies" (87). Mitigation of tragedy's tyranny by the benign forces of comedy is of course as old as the *Oresteia* trilogy of Aeschylus. But, while *De Profundis* does achieve something of a cathartic release through the purgation of hatred and despair, the transmutation has for Wilde a more politically-enabling significance.

His maneuver works to resist the narrative of determinism which holds sway in classical tragedy and according to which the tragic protagonist's chosen course of action unwittingly precipitates the very catastrophe he seeks to avert. Wilde's predicament is engendered by an ambivalence towards the conventions of tragic form. Enchanted by the nobility of the genre and its power to evoke the pity and terror of the spectator, he longs to participate in its splendor but at the same time wishes to seize control of the plot, so that, by deferring indefinitely the moment of resolution, he may prolong the exquisite torment of its anticipation. To submit to an already-prescribed model of experience would mean to surrender to the "nature" of the tragic hero, which is perceived, within the terms of that model, to be constitutionally flawed. So for Wilde to persist in the subjective position as the "hero of his own history" would be a capitulation to the ideology which has circumscribed and determined that history. By dissenting, Wilde attempts to transcend the "prison" of essentialism and declare a freedom to fabricate his own beginnings, ends, and concords. Such *cris de coeur* as "Out of my nature has come wild despair" (96) and "I have to get it all out of myself" (98) are not, I suggest, so much soundings of the depths of subjectivity as the voiding of the remnants of the material realities which shackle him to the particular and the predictable.

And it is by extension that Wilde arrives at the postulation "Only that is spiritual which makes its own form" (99). Preoccupation with the materiality of self comes to be seen as imprisonment in established form, able only to articulate the solipsism of the tragic protagonist. Elevation from solitary confinement requires the transmutation of sense experience into mystical significance. "There is not a single degradation of the body," he writes, "which I must not try and make into a spiritualising of the soul" (99). From this moment, Wilde makes surprisingly little reference to the appalling realities of prison life. The exceptions, to which I shall refer later, are viewed from an altered perspective. Before the crisis of *De Profundis,* Wilde had explored the theory of self-division and posited a hypothesis which envisaged the possibility that the creative power of the imagination could escape the limitations of physicality to reside within the sphere of an aesthetic ideal. *The Picture of Dorian Gray* communicates this proposition with the self-confidence of one who revelled in the perversity of paradox:

> Soul and body, body and soul — how mysterious they were! There was animalism in the soul, and the body had its moments of spirituality. The senses could refine, and the intellect could degrade. Who could say where the fleshly impulse ceased, or the psychical impulse began? How shallow were the arbitrary definitions of ordinary psychologists! (58; ch. 4)

Crossing the boundaries between body and soul, *The Picture of Dorian Gray* calls into question these "arbitrary definitions," to move in what Wilde is later to call "a free sphere of ideal existences" (*De Profundis* 158). "Characters," unrestricted by the expectations of genre, that is to say, by the realist novel's requirement of progressive continuity and coherence, represent attitudes or modes of being in a dialogue between the dichotomies of ethics and aesthetics, life and art, flesh and spirit. Wilde himself is alleged to have explained, "Basil Hallward is what I think I am: Lord Henry what the world thinks me: Dorian is what I would like to be — in other ages, perhaps" (Ellmann 301). It has been argued that "the several symbolic persons" the artist creates are "all variations on one person, that person being at some level himself" (Buckler 96). This may be true, but in the context of my argument, there is a more subversive significance in that this prismatic refraction of self begins to threaten the notion of psychic wholeness upon which the ethical framework of society is structured.[8] In the hedonistic pre-trial days, Wilde's assumption of a multi-dimensional selfhood is an imaginative ploy which seeks to elude categorization according to unified models of prescribed or deviant behavior.

When the public arena has been ignominiously exchanged for the private cell, those former days when "I treated Art as the supreme reality, and life as a mere mode of fiction" (95) are revisited as "an elegy for lost greatness" (Ellman 482). Aestheticism is no longer the creed which inspired Dorian Gray to raise sensual experience from the sordid ritual of the struggle for survival into a "mystical philosophy" (*Dorian Gray* 125; ch. 10) but a position which must be defended against a ruthless orthodoxy. It is my argument that Wilde's conceptualization of an aesthetic of self which is other than and separate from the material self, provides a theoretical framework around which his autobiography is imaginatively constructed. Prompted by and vital to the carceral experience, it is the act of writing itself which becomes the vehicle for transcending the limits of matter and for creating a domain where the artist, if not the man, is free. Only by testing "the gaiety of language," writes Kermode, is the prisoner, paradoxically, free — free to devise "endless plots on reality" in order to escape "the architecture of our own cells" (156, 164–65).

With the mobility and versatility of nuance, slippage, and ambiguity, language is empowered to destabilize the inflexible tenets of a culture which values only the fixity of fact. In the hands of the imaginative writer, fact dissolves into metaphor, a discursive tool which undermines the anti-metaphysical positivism of contemporary scientific and philosophic disciplines and exposes the precariousness of its premises. Drawing an analogy between the multiformity of Wilde's self-image and the multifariousness of contemporary science's theory of natural selection through random variation,[9] Andrew Morris presents their respective diversities, unpredictabilities, and aberrant manifestations as the reason why both were perceived as threats to social and moral stability at the end of the century. Morris argues that the "dynamic of diversity" which was both a prerequisite for natural selection and essential to Wilde's aesthetic profile was anathema to an ideology which valued certainty, control, and conformity (519, 539). Viewed from this negative stance, it is only a short distance from diversity to perversity and relegation to the margins of society. Once again, it is by means of language that Wilde turns the fact of relegation and marginalization into a dynamic of positive advantage.

For Jonathan Dollimore, the linguistic gymnastics of Wilde's play with paradox, his inversions and aphorisms, are perverse strategies, the working tools, as it were, of a dynamic of diversity which powerfully undermined the stable binary models in which social and sexual difference are held. In general terms, Dollimore's claim is that the familiar dichotomies (we might, for the purposes of this essay include life and art, flesh and spirit, truth and falsity for instance) are powerfully enduring and necessarily hierarchical models which support established social, political, and moral relations. More specifically, Wilde's distortions and inversions displace these binaries from their mutually-defining but unequal poles and, in so doing, challenge the meanings and assumptions invested in them (64–68).[10] This theory of a linguistic strategy for disrupting the categories of cultural organization lends weight, moreover, to my argument for Wilde's escape from his tragic subjection. By disturbing the complacent traditions of dominant/subordinate relation, Wilde, Dollimore writes, subverts not only "a deeply conservative authenticity and the deep subjectivity on which it is premissed" (65) but also "the essentialist categories of identity which kept morality in place" (68). Testing "the gaiety of language," for the writer of *De Profundis,* becomes a less playful and more frantic exercise, but one which assists a textualized self to escape from the self that is confined.

The textualized self, figured in the diaphanous, mannered aesthete, the "Lord Henry" in Wilde, is freer to devise, "endless plots on reality," in Kermode's words, than is the confined self, represented as the wretched victim of a consuming passion. But Wilde's self-indulgent if scarcely surprising re-examinations of misery are indicative of a desire to ascribe positive value to both modes of experience. Accordingly, his exploration of his role of "wretched victim" is rescued from despair by the sense of nobility he confers upon himself as he allies himself with his forerunners in the genre of tragedy. His "Symphony of

Sorrow'' orchestrates itself, ''passing through its rhythmically-linked movements to its certain resolution, with that inevitableness that in Art characterises the treatment of every great theme'' (55). In this grand narrative, Douglas is merely the instrument of Doom, ''a puppet worked by some secret and unseen hand to bring terrible events to a terrible issue'' (64). More alarmingly, he enacts his own willful rebellion against the forces of destiny, diverting the plot like his Satanic antecedents who ''twist the ordered issue of vicissitude to suit some whim or appetite of their own'' (65). Although Wilde concedes that the dilemma of free will and determinism is the ''eternal paradox of human life,'' he develops, extends, explores, and manipulates paradox itself in an attempt to defer the moment of realization. For, in the discourse of tragedy, realization is the climactic moment, an anagnorisis which signals the slide towards unavoidable catastrophe. With this in mind, the recurring aphorism ''[w]hatever is realised is right'' is revealed as doubly ambiguous. On one level, it looks forward to Douglas's contrition and the assuagement of Wilde's own torment as a consequence. On another, it holds the very possibility of realization in abeyance. More problematically again, the undertow of doom running through this text, made palpable in these reiterations, is not simply a reinforcement of tragic destiny in the traditional sense, but it rather constitutes a self-pleasuring meditative discourse on the perilous. Aspirations for a resolution in the mode of comedy barely conceal an almost masochistic desire for self-destruction and for the epic finality which that would accord.

Paradox and contradiction, as I have already noted, are vital to the presentation throughout *De Profundis* of the dichotomies of flesh and spirit, love and hate, ethics and aesthetics, life and art, tragedy and comedy, not as fixed oppositions but as negotiable relations in an open-ended and ambivalent discourse. The discussion of Hate and Love continues to work at the paradox by offering Douglas the opportunity to re-examine fixed attitudes and opinions as flexible and mutable ideas.[11] Initially, Hate and Love are conceptualized as the polarities which define their separate spheres. Their personification, however, elevates them from labels of states of emotion to the status of agents, respectively, of tragic destiny and its placation, working within a mutually-referential field of relativity and not as absolute opposites. Tragedy and comedy are not to be understood here in the conventional, classical sense as sequential, but as alternative perspectives in coextensive discourses.

Appropriately, it is Douglas's hatred of his father which is recorded as perpetuating the ''terrible legacy'' (51) of familial philistinism. Between them, Douglas and Queensberry have dragged Wilde's name and reputation into the sewers and contaminated him with their ''hereditary disease'' (73). Envisaging his fall in terms of classical tragedy's concern with the fall of a great and noble family, Wilde attempts firstly to draw the perpetrator towards realization of his responsibility. ''Have you imagination enough,'' he asks, ''to see what a fearful tragedy it was for me to have come across your family?'' Further, ''[w]hat a tragedy it would have been for anyone at all, who had a great position, a great name, anything of importance to lose?'' (136). But then, self-protectively, he takes refuge in a disjunction between their respective spheres. Although tragedy has reduced Wilde's family honor to ignominy and shame, the genre itself is invoked as the means of restoring a measure of dignity and honor by registering the event among the grand narratives in the history of fallen might. The occasion of his denunciation in court is proclaimed equal to ''a thing out of Tacitus, like a passage in Dante, like one of Savonarola's indictments of the Popes at Rome'' (145). Such self-aggrandizement is calculated to insure against the slide into oblivion of his retrospectively-ennobled past. With the assurance that his suffering will not now have been without meaning, Wilde recovers from misrepresentation in the past and can go on to envision a future time beyond crisis.

To set such store on legitimating his past within the context of an official literary history might seem on one level inconsistent with Wilde's politics of perversity. Alternatively, his intention, I suggest, is not to emphasize for posterity the degradation of the fallen man but rather the enormity of the loss to art. In contrast, therefore, to this reclaimed greatness, Douglas's life is reduced to one of transience and inconsequentiality. As a representative ''specimen of a very modern type,'' his ''little life of little whims'' is too insignificant to impinge upon the world beyond ''its own little sphere'' (146) and will founder, Wilde predicts, on the ''high stage in History'' (147). Mediocrity and ''shallowness'' are perceived to be the signs of approaching modernity and are declared undeserving of the permanence accorded to more illustrious lives.

Problematically though, when Wilde attempts to bridge the gulf between them, a gulf which he has both widened and deepened, with the regenerative power of Love and forgiveness, he can find no language with which to apprehend the joy he believes they once shared. There is, it seems, no secular register to transcend tragic closure. In its absence, Wilde appropriates the language of Christian worship, repeating responses with labored reverence (75–76) and interceding in the miracle of the Eucharist. But the promised communion of souls ''that might bring balm to the bruised heart, and peace to the soul in pain'' is denied, and the Host is returned to bitter bread and brackish water (94). In spite of, or perhaps because of, this failure of spiritual exchange, it is within this discourse that Wilde seeks to procure his apotheosis.[12] Christ is recognized as a fellow sufferer for whom, no less than for Wilde, the ''chief war was against the Philistines'' (122). Accordingly, Wilde uses the vocabulary of Christ's teaching on Humility, Humanity, Spirit, and Love ostensibly for the purpose of edification, but in effect he presses it into the service of his own dissident philosophy. ''I see a far more intimate and immediate connection,'' he writes, ''between the true life of Christ and the true life of the artist'' (109). In what one critic has called the ''aestheticising of Christ'' (Kohl 284), Wilde envisages the supreme individualist, the anti-traditionalist, who reached out beyond the rule of law (of secular law at least) to draw attention to the anomalies of social organization and to those individuals who are the exceptions rather than the rule. Neatly, Wilde turns Christ's legendary sympathy and compassion for outcasts and sinners into a validation of difference.[13] Equally exceptional and equally non-conformist, Christ and the artist are alike in valuing priest and pariah, prostitute and poet.

On the strength of this alleged authority of divine sanction, Wilde finds the means of challenging the indictment which has classified his dissident individuality under the more readily definable legal parameters of incitement to corruption and perversity. The radical nature of his identification with Christ's romantic imagination works counter to late Victorian associations of artistic genius with decadence and degeneracy.[14] Perversity, he now claims, is, as Christ recognized, the only right response to a bigoted and philistine regime. Justifying his past within these terms, he asserts unapologetically "that my life had been full of perverse pleasures and strange passions" (144). His point is that this affirmation neither implies a pathology of perversion nor defines an essential nature which identifies absolutely. Clearly, the difficulty for Wilde in sustaining this somewhat precarious position is to secure a place for passion and pleasure within a rationale which readily encompasses difference. It is for this reason that I argue that Wilde is not seeking to reject sensuality and sexuality in favor of the purification which traditionally follows from spiritual enlightenment as in the mode of confessional autobiography, but rather to ascribe to them positive value.

In *The Picture of Dorian Gray,* Wilde sought to validate a way of life which set a high value on the pleasures of the senses. We might usefully return to that text for an articulation of a model of perverse ideality. In Lord Henry's vision of perfection, sensuality and sexuality do not signal depravity but are perceived to be the vital forces which breathed life into an ideal of masculinity, setting a standard which has held sway since classical and through Renaissance times. Of course, it is this same idea of the body's invasion and permeation by homoerotic energies that was, both at the time and since, read as a veiled narrative of homosexual reference.[15] Speaking for a world-weary fin de siècle Decadence, Lord Henry, the embodiment of the vital force which breathed life into Dorian Gray, muses on the errors of repression. Self-denial enervates and devitalizes and is guaranteed, he remarks, to make the soul grow "sick with longing for the things it has forbidden to itself, with desire for what its monstrous laws have made monstrous and unlawful" (18; ch. 2). Encouraged by this sanction, Dorian justifies his self-indulgence in a dissident philosophy:

> But it appeared to Dorian Gray that the true nature of the sense had never been understood, and that they had remained savage and animal merely because the world had sought to starve them into submission or to kill them by pain, instead of aiming at making them elements of a new spirituality, of which a fine instinct for beauty was to be the dominant characteristic. (130; ch. 11)

On the basis of this redefinition, the delights of bodily sensation are incorporated into Lord Henry's concept of hedonism, and Dorian is provided with a creed which releases him from a mortifying asceticism. While writing in prison, Wilde never relinquishes his belief in the positive value of sense experience. Although he admits to a naivety in failing to recognize how the less imaginative and sensitive might choose to interpret his pleasure principle, he cannot allow himself to slip into an apologia if he is to validate perversity and passion in a system designed to circumscribe and control them.

Originally titled *Epistola: in Carcere et Vinculis,* the letter nonetheless communicates a despairing finality, a seeming acceptance of the subjugation which social organization has imposed and fails to intimate the radical nature of Wilde's resistance to that imposition. As an "Autobiography of Escape," *De Profundis* does more than fabricate a triumph of Romance over Realism in order to transcend the prison walls. It transmutes deviancy into a positive strategy. The startling assertion "What the paradox was to me in the sphere of thought, perversity became to me in the sphere of passion" (96) undermines the binary organization of culture by refusing to be confined by the labels which polarize and imprison. Instead, Wilde effects a self-bifurcation which enables the writing self to begin to regard the material self as object.

"To become the spectator of one's own life . . . is to escape the suffering of life," promised Lord Henry Wotton (*Dorian Gray* 110; ch. 9). In the crisis of *De Profundis,* Wilde resurrects this casual and inchoate proposition to fashion a domain where the self that writes looks askance at the self that suffers. What the writing self now sees is no longer a protagonist of a great tragedy or comedy but a grotesquely parodic figure suspended in an uncanny conjunction of opposites. The disjunction between the writer's idea of himself as the urbane and witty artist and entertainer and the image projected by the trial journalists' obsession with reading only the immediate spectacle of the body is nowhere more apparent than in the recollection of the humiliating scene on the platform of Clapham Junction, as the prisoner was being transported to Reading gaol:[16]

> Everything about my tragedy has been hideous, mean, repellent, lacking in style. Our very dress makes us grotesques. We are the zanies of sorrow. We are clowns whose hearts are broken. We are specially designed to appeal to the sense of humour. On November 13th 1895 I was brought down here from London. From two o'clock till half-past two on that day I had to stand on the centre platform of Clapham Junction in convict dress and handcuffed, for the world to look at. I had been taken out of the Hospital Ward without a moment's notice being given to me. Of all possible objects I was the most grotesque. When people saw me they laughed. (129)

This is not so much a world upside-down as a world skewed out of focus. Despite the gap which has opened up between the images of self and other, the spectacle of the tragic victim has merged, it would seem, with the image of the artist as performer and entertainer. An iconoclastic modern age has produced a scenario which occupies an indeterminate space between the polarities of genre with the result that both forms are reduced to attenuated versions of their classical models. Cast in this scenario, the grotesque is a representation, an absurdity "specially designed" for the consumer of the image and is not a reflection of nature. For Wilde, the sickness and panic in society which has brought about this travesty is the inevitable consequence when a shifting value system turns around and mocks at its predecessor. "I used to say," he laments, "I thought I could bear a real tragedy if it came to me with purple pall and a mask of noble sorrow, but that the dreadful thing about modernity was that it put Tragedy into the raiment of Comedy, so that the great realities seemed commonplace or grotesque or lacking in style" (129). To speak of "the great realities" in tones of reverence denotes at least a shift in emphasis if not a contradiction. For, are these not the very criteria of tradition which Wilde has previously sought to unsettle? Bewildered by the shifting verities and values, Wilde responds to travesty and ridicule by translating an indeterminate status into a positive ambivalence.

Turning to the archetypal figure of tragic vacillation and delay, Wilde finds a prototype for artful resistance to a tyranny of categorization; at the same time, he is wary of the pitfalls of indecision. For Hamlet;

> madness is a mere mask for the hiding of weakness. In the making of mows and jests he sees a chance of delay. He keeps playing with action, as an artist plays with a theory. He makes himself the spy of his proper actions, and listening to his own words knows them to be but "words, words, words." Instead of trying to be the hero of his own history, he seeks to be the spectator of his own tragedy. He disbelieves in everything, including himself, and yet his doubt helps him not, as it comes not from scepticism but from a divided will. (148)

Ambivalence is both powerfully enabling and potentially eclipsing, and Wilde is mindful to draw a distinction between positive ambivalence and ruinous indecision. Hamlet's vacillation, according to Wilde's reconceptualization, fails to save him because of his persistence in the mutual exclusivity of the alternatives before him. Wilde, on the other hand, claims an omniscient view which overrides the necessity for such a final choice. His scepticism creates the space for infinite delay and is, therefore, his safeguard against (en)closure and the acceleration towards obliteration.

Having rationalized himself into this tertium quid, Wilde inhabits a realm in which all states of being have equal validity. In Art at least, if not in Ethics, he argues, contraries are both true. Thus, he can now claim "to truth itself I gave what is false no less than what is true as its rightful province, and showed that the false and the true are merely forms of intellectual existence. I treated Art as the supreme reality, and life as a mere mode of fiction" (95). Within this ontological exercise, truth and falsity become relational distinctions and not measures of absolutes. Similarly, in the sphere of textualized selfhood, the truth of self lies wherever the writer should choose to locate it. "A thing *is,*" Wilde concludes, "according to the mode in which one looks at it" (158). Arriving at this happy mutability, he escapes the "is" of essential being, but only to argue himself into the displaced domain of the spectator, a remove which merely exchanges one kind of prison for another. With the detachment of the writing self, he has become, like Dorian Gray's picture, his own voyeur and no longer originates action but participates vicariously in it. Wilde's fabricated self may well represent a triumph of Art over life. But for one who was proud to stand "in symbolic relations to the art and culture of my age" (95), it is at the same time a reaffirmation of alienation.

Poised between his rebuttal of subjective depth and psychic wholeness, and his disapprobation of their attenuated offspring, the "shallowness" of modernity, Wilde's freedom of ambivalence begins to atrophy into an intellectual impasse. When cast back into a now cruelly indifferent world outside the prison walls, the artful mechanisms of inversion, displacement, and deferral, which have worked to elude fixity in the material and the essential, cannot then be called upon to revitalize the shattered body and the stricken soul. Having relinquished the role of the subject of tragedy, the maker "of mows and jests"[17] is transfixed by his own mirror's gaze, able to mock the captive self but remaining captivated and forever in its thrall. It is a final paradox that when the man is made free, the artist is bound in chains.

University of Leeds

NOTES

1. Losey identifies some of the main arguments advanced by critics as to the letter's status (440). Wilde's instructions to Ross can be examined in letters (512–14).
2. Raby notes Wilde's anticipation in this regard (133).
3. In his biography of Wilde, Ellmann claims that *De Profundis* is first and foremost a love letter (483).
4. For a discussion of the way in which Wilde's "immoral" writing was used to testify to his homosexual practice, see Ellmann's account of the trials (409–49).
5. For example, see Philip K. Cohen (238).
6. Kohl presents a much fuller discussion of nineteenth-century attitudes to the Christian story and its re-interpretation in a contemporary historical context. It is unsurprising, Kohl argues, that Wilde recognized in the "charismatic figure" of Christ an artist and a man who might serve as a model for his own situation (284–89).
7. My argument also writes against Dollimore's reading of the text as a "renunciation of [Wilde's] transgressive aesthetic and a reaffirmation of tradition as focused in the depth model of identity" (95).
8. In a differently focused, but not incompatible argument, Goodman has recently remarked that Wilde's self-multiplication is indicative of an extravagant narcissism, which, in the hideous reality of public exposure, can no longer be sustained overtly

and, instead, is mediated through a series of masks. These masks are the tools of theatrical deception and are adopted by Wilde "to compensate for his narcissistic injury," and to present to a public audience a semblance of a re-unified and coherent identity (Goodman).

9. Most particularly as advanced by Darwin in *The Origin of Species By Means of Natural Selection* (1859), although evolutionary ideas of irreversible development had been current for decades.
10. Dollimore draws on the work of Derrida in order to represent the binary construct as theoretically unstable (and therefore vulnerable to displacement) but "pernicious . . . in practice" (where its terms may be used to establish a hierarchical relationship which then validates subjection and disempowerment) (64–65).
11. The upper-case emphases are Wilde's.
12. In his play, *Saint Oscar,* Eagleton presents Wilde's flights of imagination in a very literal sense. The character Oscar is seen to mount the cross and to assume the attitude of the crucified Christ as depicted in religious iconography.
13. Gagnier has also noted Wilde's assertion that Christ was not interested in reform for reform's sake, that is, in conformity to the secular law, but in the value and virtue of individualism expressed as exception (346).
14. For a fuller discussion of Wilde's validation of diversity in a culture which increasingly viewed artistic creativity as a sign and symptom of decadence and degeneracy, see Morris (520–29).
15. These ideas are dealt with in much greater detail by Ed Cohen ("Writing" 805).
16. The somatization of the unrepresentable and unspeakable on to legible signs on the body of the "criminal" has been examined by Ed Cohen in his discussion of the homophobic reporting of Wilde's trials (*Talk* 181–87).
17. See above and *De Profundis* 148.

WORKS CITED

Buckler, William E. "Oscar Wilde's Aesthetic of the Self: Art as Imaginative Self-Realization. *De Profundis.*" *Biography — An Interdisciplinary Quarterly* 12.2 (1989): 95–115.

Cohen, Ed. "Writing Gone Wilde: Homoerotic Desire in the Closet of Representation." *PMLA* 102.5 (October 1987): 801–13.

———. *Talk on the Wilde Side: Toward a Genealogy of a Discourse on Male Sexualities.* London: Routledge, 1993.

Cohen, Philip K. *The Moral Vision of Oscar Wilde.* New Jersey: Associated U P, 1978.

Dollimore, Jonathan. *Sexual Dissidence: Augustine to Wilde, Freud to Foucault.* Oxford: Clarendon P, 1991.

Eagleton, Terry. *Saint Oscar.* Perf. Londonderry, Northern Ireland. 25 Sept. 1989. Channel 4 Television; 12 Jan. 1991.

Ellmann, Richard. *Oscar Wilde.* London: Hamish Hamilton, 1987.

Foucault, Michel. *The History of Sexuality: An Introduction.* Trans. Robert Hurley. 1978. London: Pelican, 1981.

Gagnier, Regenia. "*De Profundis* as Epistola: in Carcere et Vinculis: A Materialist Reading of Oscar Wilde's Autobiography." *Criticism* 26. 4 (1984): 334–54.

Goodman, Lawrence. "How Psychoanalytic Theory Enables a Re-evaluation of Wilde, Aestheticism and the 1890s." Victorian Literature, Contemporary Theory Conf. University of Luton 1–3 July 1994.

Kermode, Frank. *The Sense of An Ending: Studies in the Theory of Fiction.* London: Oxford UP, 1967.

Kohl, Norbert. *Oscar Wilde: The Works of a Conformist Rebel.* Trans. David Henry Wilson. Cambridge: Cambridge UP, 1989.

Losey, Jay. "The Aesthetics of Exile: Wilde Transforming Dante in *Intentions* and *De Profundis.*" *English Literature in Transition, 1880–1920* 36. 4 (1993): 429–50.

Morris, Andrew R. "Oscar Wilde and the Eclipse of Darwinism: Aestheticism, Degeneration, and Moral Reaction in Late-Victorian Ideology." *Studies in History and Philosophy of Science* 24. 4 (1993): 513–40.

Raby, Peter. *Oscar Wilde.* Cambridge: Cambridge UP, 1988.

Wilde, Oscar. *De Profundis.* Ed. Isobel Murray. *The Soul of Man and Prison Writings.* Oxford: Oxford UP, 1990.

———. *The Letters.* Ed. Rupert Hart-Davis. London: Rupert Hart-Davis Ltd., 1962.

———. *The Picture of Dorian Gray.* Ed. Isobel Murray. Oxford: Oxford UP, 1981.

WILDE'S *INTENTIONS* AND THE SIMULATION OF MEANING

By Nick Frankel

> Every discourse is threatened with this sudden reversibility, absorbed into its own signs without a trace of meaning — Baudrillard
>
> You should say what you mean — Lewis Carroll

MODERN SCHOLARSHIP TAKES WILDE'S *Intentions* very seriously; and, although *Intentions* still only rarely gets discussed under that title, two of the four pieces that go to make up the work are now generally regarded as among the most significant critical or theoretical statements of the modern period.[1] In *Critical Theory Since Plato* (1971), for instance, Hazard Adams complained that "The narcissistic wittiness of Wilde, combined with the Arnoldian desire of some readers for 'high seriousness,' has caused Wilde's critical work not to be taken seriously enough." He decided to anthologize Wilde's "The Decay of Lying," he tells us, because beneath its "impertinent transvaluations . . . lie important theoretical implications" (672). In 1988 Zhang Longxi made a similar complaint, arguing that "as a most articulate and serious aesthetician . . . [Wilde] has very seldom, until quite recently, been taken seriously" (87). Longxi went on to compare Wilde with, among others, Northrop Frye, William K. Wimsatt and Monroe C. Beardsley, Edward Said, Harold Bloom, and Geoffrey Hartman, adding that "the graceful style of his writing . . . gives him an indisputable advantage over some of our contemporary critics whose a-bit-too-French French discourse can hardly ever match the ease and brilliance of Wilde's not-too-French French gestures" (101). In seeing Wilde as a forerunner of modern critical theory, Longxi was doing no more than expanding on Richard Ellmann's 1966 remark that "Wilde laid the basis for many critical positions that are still debated in much the same terms, and which we like to attribute to more ponderous names" (x). Ellmann had gone on to compare Wilde with Frye, Barthes, and Nietzsche in particular; more recently Ian Small added Charles Morris and Umberto Eco to the list (see Small 50–56).

This canonization of Wilde as a critical thinker accompanied the rise of critical theory itself and dates from 1969, the year in which Ellmann published *The Artist as Critic,* his much-consulted edition of what his subtitle calls "The Critical Writings of Oscar Wilde." Ellmann's collection set the terms according to which *Intentions* got read over the ensuing years, and even today his prefatory essay, "The Critic as Artist as Wilde," remains probably the best discussion of Wilde as a critical thinker — and certainly the most cited. Yet even more than the prefatory essay itself, which had first appeared (separately) in 1966 and had been republished several times already, it was probably the reversal of Wilde's own terms in the collection's title that, more than anything, canonized Wilde as one of the great critics. For Ellmann, this would have been a particularly just, if belated, restoration of Wilde to the critics' pantheon, since it was precisely Wilde's own glorification of the greatness of criticism that Ellmann singled out as grounds for canonizing him: "Wilde was one of the first to see that the exaltation of the artist required a concomitant exaltation of the critic. . . . If this sounds like T. S. Eliot admonishing Matthew Arnold, Wilde had expressed it, also as an admonition to Arnold, almost thirty years before" (ix).

It should not surprise us that Arnold's name crops up so centrally here. Thanks in part to Arnold's own mini-renaissance in the 1960s, "The Critic as Artist" had by 1969 begun to be seen primarily as a theoretical engagement with Arnold about the place of criticism. Nor should it surprise us, therefore, that Ellmann should have seen *Intentions* as a "formal book of criticism" (xix) or that he should have been drawn to "The Critic as Artist" in particular ("the most ambitious of the essays" [xxi]) — notwithstanding the fact that Wilde had dropped the dialogue's original Arnoldian title on publishing it in *Intentions* as if wanting to dissociate it from Arnold as such (see n. 9). In certain respects, indeed, and not merely those respects in which Arnold gets *named*, Arnold seems to hover over Wilde's canonization like some kind of presiding angel. Ellmann's reading of "The Critic as Artist," for instance, depends on seeing the dialogue as a kind of Bloomian overthrow of Arnoldian principles through the rigorous application of Paterian ones:

> Wilde rounded on Arnold by asserting that the aim of criticism is to see the object as it really is not . . . he wishes to free critics from subordination, to grant them a larger share in the production of literature . . . "The highest criticism," according to Wilde, "is the record of one's own soul." More closely he explained that the critic must have all literature in his mind and see particular works in that perspective rather than in isolation. Thus he, and we as well, "Shall be able to realise, not merely our own lives, but the collective spirit of the race, and so make ourselves absolutely modern, in the true meaning of the word modernity." (xii)

What is immediately striking here is that Ellmann's reading is as thoroughly Arnoldian in spirit as it is counter-Arnoldian in content, and that it leaves certain

Arnoldian principles intact even as it claims to be demolishing them. As a result, it manages to succeed in turning a work purportedly about "the importance of doing nothing" into one about the importance of doing earnest criticism; and it drains Wilde's dialogue of its irony or excess even as it transforms it into a "formal [work] of criticism" or "formulation . . . of aesthetic ideas" (xxi). Indeed, Ellmann does not even recognize here that "The Critic as Artist" is a dialogue (he consistently refers to it as an "essay"); his reading depends upon equating Wilde with the more apparently philosophic of his two imaginary interlocutors, Gilbert, at the same time as it depends on forgetting that the more philosophic is at the same time the least "earnest." Finally, of course, in clinging so closely to what he thinks Wilde is saying, Ellmann is forced to collapse three voices (his own, Wilde's, Gilbert's) into one and to contradict exactly what he claims to be Wilde's point ("to see the object as it really is not," "to free critics from subordination," and so forth).[2] By taking Wilde so seriously, in other words, Ellmann makes a mockery of him.

Ellmann's reading of "The Critic as Artist" demonstrates what is most problematic about the "serious" readings of *Intentions* I began by mentioning. Like Adams, Ellmann rejects the "distractions" of Wilde's prose in order to show how "important" Wilde's "critical work" really is.

But what happens to Adams's and Ellmann's "serious" conception of Wilde's critical writings once we stop thinking of those writings as *criticism*? Answering this question, I suggest, immediately brings back into account what we traditionally think of as matters of style (paradoxicality, wit, self-consciousness, and so forth), dismissed so peremptorily by Adams as "narcissistic" and "impertinent." At the same time, it brings back what is most distinctively "aesthetic" about *Intentions,* insofar as the readings I have been discussing ignore one of aestheticism's central dicta, that "In matters of grave importance, style, not sincerity, is the vital thing." But as Gwendolen's paradox itself suggests, "style" is finally an inadequate category for understanding the practice embodied in Wilde's writing. Jonathan Dollimore has argued that Wilde's paradoxes generally parody and subvert the very oppositions that they appear to enforce (see Dollimore 14–17, 103–30). And as Mikhail Bakhtin has suggested, insofar as we think of the practice of writing in terms of an imagined dichotomy between style and content, we work to the exclusion of historical actualities. In Bakhtin's ungainly but important formulation, "stylistics locks every stylistic phenomenon into the monologic context of a given self-sufficient and hermetic utterance, imprisoning it, as it were, in the dungeon of a single context" (274).

My question, then, is not designed finally to advance a purely stylistic analysis of *Intentions* so much as to expose the extent to which the stylistic and the sincere collapse in on one another. More particularly, it is designed to suggest that the "serious" approach to *Intentions* misconceives the *actual* character of literary texts, a misconception which generates in turn still further misconceptions about both the meaning of Wilde's work and the attitude adopted in that work towards questions of meaning. These misunderstandings stem basically from the fact that critics do not generally take sufficient care to distinguish *Intentions* as such from the particular essays and dialogues *contained in Intentions.* They misconceive the status of meaning "in" *Intentions,* in other words, because they are not sufficiently attentive to the meaningful status "of" *Intentions.* For the title alone suggests that *Intentions* cannot be equated simply with the sum of its parts. If we want to understand the problem of meaning posed "in" the work, we must begin by treating *Intentions* as a distinct historical event in its own right.

ANDRÉ GIDE SAID THAT Wilde's first concern was to amuse: "Of his wisdom or indeed his folly, he uttered only what he believed his hearer would relish" (3). Gide's remark is a useful place to begin answering the problems posed by *Intentions* for it points to the failure of the "serious" approach I have been describing, as well as suggesting a valuable alternative. Specifically, it suggests that the "serious" approach cannot account for the sheer *pleasure* of reading Wilde's work. (*Intentions* is no different from *The Importance of Being Earnest* in this respect. It works just as strenuously to produce laughter and hermeneutic desire in its readers — in fact, so strenuously as to make the activity of its production seem effortless or invisible.) In locating pleasure as the key principle, moreover, Gide's remark suggests that meaning is an effect *produced by,* not inherent within, the work itself. It thereby points to the particular *economy* of meaning governing Wilde's work. That is to say, within an economy of pleasure, Wilde's text may be the occasion for the work's meaning, but it is not in itself the site of that meaning. Meaning is the effect of an exchange between text and reader, and it is to be located, strictly speaking, in the act of reading.

Gide's remark also suggests that pleasure stands opposed to "wisdom" in the Wildean economy. This dialectic particularly interested the French philosopher Georges Bataille, whose notion of *nonproductive expenditure* or *loss* can be of tremendous help to our understanding of *Intentions.* Bataille argues that the principles which conventionally govern the production of meaning (which he calls principles of "classical utility") work to the exclusion of valuing what is pleasurable:

> [O]n the whole, any general judgment of social activity implies the principle that an individual effort, in order to be valid, must be reducible to the fundamental necessities of production and conservation. Pleasure, whether art, permissible debauchery, or play, is definitively reduced, in the intellectual representations *in circulation,* to a concession; in other words it is reduced to a diversion whose role is subsidiary. (117)

Bataille would see pleasure as the very basis of human activity, not just of art and play. But for our purposes his remarks are valuable simply for articulating in economic terms that rejection of "narcissistic style" we noticed in the arguments of Adams and Ellmann. "Meaning," in their accounts of *Intentions,* gets confined to what is of rational use — it is governed by a capitalist hermeneutic of useful productivity — and thus overlooks the very thing that distinguishes *Intentions* from the "earnest" Victorianisms that surround it. "Serious" readers like Adams and Ellmann cannot value pleasure's place in *Intentions* because, as opposed to "wisdom" — or indeed to "folly" — pleasure represents what Bataille would call an "object of free expenditure," an "insubordinate characterization" which, like materiality itself, "is not the condition for anything else" (129).

Gide and Bataille point the way, then, towards a reading of *Intentions* that sees meaning, far from residing "in" the text itself, to be a function of the text's defiance of our attempts to see meaning "in" it. But this is not to suggest that *Intentions* is simply a work of pure "nonsense." For what makes this new level of meaning particularly hard to pin down (and especially pleasurable therefore) is how thoroughly *Intentions* masquerades as a work that "possesses" or contains its own meanings — how thoroughly it *simulates* a work that conceptualizes "meaning" in the conventional sense (i.e., "immanent meaning"). So, though the work's real meaning lies in how seriously it takes pleasure as its objective and in how consistently it defies other kinds of productive activity, *Intentions* nonetheless seems at first to operate according to all the conventional codes.

The Distinction I Have been drawing so far between pleasure and "meaning" bears an obvious relation to the traditional question in Wilde scholarship about what kind of coherence, if any, *Intentions* achieves. Among the varying opinions, two views can be said to preponderate. On the one hand, as Herbert Sussman has suggested, the work has little intellectual coherence — indeed it challenges intellectual coherence as such — and is best approaches as art: "the reduction of Wilde's critical writing to coherent system is distorting because the central principle of these works is the questioning and the redefinition of intellectual activity itself" (109). On the other hand, *Intentions* is seen as a coherent set of aesthetic ideas, albeit derived heavily from a range of other "thinkers" whose extent has not yet been fully fathomed. This is still the dominant critical tradition; it began as soon as Wilde's works were published, and it received massive impetus from Ernst Bendz's 1914 *The Influence of Pater and Matthew Arnold on the Prose Writings of Oscar Wilde* (a monumental work in early Wilde scholarship). It continues today in Helfand and Smith's *Oscar Wilde's Oxford Notebooks: A Portrait of Mind in the Making* (1989): "Wilde's aestheticism, usually thought of as derived from Pater, Arnold, Ruskin, and the French decadent poets, is . . . a synthesis of Hegelian idealism and Spencerian evolutionary theory. . . . *Intentions,* Wilde's collected major criticism, represents the fullest statement and development of his synthesis'' (vii–ix).

Now deciding whether or not *Intentions* is a work of bona fide ''thought'' is crucial for our understanding of its meaning. Is *Intentions* an expression of what Helfand and Smith call ''mind,'' or is it what Sussman (after Wilde) calls a work of ''art''? We can settle this question by returning to the notion of a masquerade or *simulation* of meaning. For both these views of *Intentions* assume that language must be read ''seriously'' in the ways I earlier found problematic. They both assume, then, that *Intentions* must be read according to a clear distinction between art and thought — much as Adams assumed a choice between style and content. But *Intentions* makes such clear-cut dichotomies hard to sustain, as we have already seen (the work could in fact be defined as a sustained attack on such binaristic thinking). Far more than opposing art to thought, it seems fairer to say, *Intentions* makes an artwork *out of* thought; it turns the serious pursuit of meaning into an object of pleasure and adopts the language of dogmatic truth, borrowed chiefly from art criticism and theory, only to turn it away from its truth-claims and into an object of spectacle. Masquerading as the truth, perhaps the only thing *Intentions* is really serious about is the perfect simulation of ''mind'' or thought.

If *Intentions* merely simulates ''mind,'' we should reconsider too the discussion of plagiarism that has dogged the work since Whistler first raised the charge in the 1880s. Did Wilde absorb his predecessors in a thoroughly ''original'' manner, this discussion asks — that is to say, was he merely ''influenced'' by them or did he plagiarize from them? Both arguments assume that Wilde's language functions as the conveyor of certain immanent meanings or ideas — in structuralist terms, that signifiers denote (or should denote) uncomplicated signifieds. To this degree, both arguments fail to see that Wilde preempts and undermines the very notion of plagiarism through his attachment to the sign in itself (*not* the signified) as the locus of value, as if language itself were being turned into the object of spectacle. They assume that Wilde is ''serious,'' that he ''means what he says,'' to adapt the March Hare's useful phrase. But if Wilde's language *masquerades* as the language of ideas, it becomes impossible to hold Wilde to notions of ''plagiarism'' and ''influence'' since his language makes no truth-claims as such and only *acts* as if it does.

The traditional discussion of plagiarism adheres deeply to certain vested notions of ''meaning,'' then, and is a good illustration of my earlier remark that the meaningful status of *Intentions* gets misunderstood through misconceptions about the status of meaning ''in'' *Intentions.* It also returns us to the idea that *Intentions*'s — significance lies in its *actual* rather than its assumed ontological character — in what it *does* rather than what it *is*. In what follows, I demonstrate these ideas more fully, in the process arriving at what I hope is a clearer idea of *Intentions* as a distinct historical event. My discussion dwells in particular on the figure of James McNeill Whistler because, besides being one of the chief sources of the plagiarism charge itself, Whistler is central both to the historical meaning of *Intentions* and to the work's attitude to meaning as such, for Wilde's appropriations of Whistler demonstrate perfectly what I have been calling a simulation of meaning. As is well known, Wilde and Whistler had, prior to *Intentions*'s publication in 1891, been feuding for years over the position of dominance in the discourse of Aestheticism. What is less well understood is that *Intentions* performed the act of silencing Whistler. Most importantly of all, then, as well as demonstrating the work's attitude to meaning, my discussion locates the work's significance a performative act. It is to Whistler, then, that we must turn.

One of the most famous passages from *Intentions,* towards the end of "The Decay of Lying," holds that nature is nothing but an imitation of art, that "things are because we see them, and what we see, and how we see it, depends on the Arts that have influenced us" (40). It is a stunning passage, a *pièce de résistance* that is at once audacious and yet consistent with the logic of the essay as a whole, highly "artificial" yet apparently "serious" or meaningful. In some ways, it is the highpoint of "The Decay of Lying" if not of Aestheticism generally.

What is less well known is that the passage did not appear in the first published version of "The Decay of Lying" (in *Nineteenth Century,* January 1889), and that, as Ian Small has pointed out, Wilde's addition of it to his copy-text prior to the republication of the dialogue in *Intentions* constitutes (with one notable exception) the single largest addition he ever made to any of his works.[3] Just as little known is that the passage's arguments, and some of its exempla, are drawn heavily from Wilde's arch-antagonist James McNeill Whistler, that the passage even makes a number of oblique references to Whistler, and that it was introduced in direct response to Whistler's claim, made previous to its insertion, that ideas and phrases used by Wilde in the first version of "The Decay of Lying" were plagiarized from himself. These facts have an obvious bearing on the matter in question: examining how this passage silences Whistler's objections can tell us a great deal about what, or how, the passage means — about whether or not we should take it seriously.

The key to such a project lies in yet another citation from Whistler. In the first published version of "The Decay of Lying," as indeed in all subsequent versions, Vivian criticizes the practice of the modern realistic novelist by using the arch phrase, "He has not even the courage of other people's ideas, but insists on going directly to life for everything" (*Intentions* 8). When Whistler read this (first) version of "The Decay of Lying" late in 1889 (or rather when he read an account of it in a mischievous article that had recently appeared in the *Sun* newspaper, where Wilde was discussed as a plagiarist [see *Letters* 251 n. 1]) he recognized the first part of this phrase as one he had publicly used against Wilde himself three years earlier. No doubt he also recognized the idea of the phrase as a whole — that art and life have nothing to do with one another — as one that he had himself done much to popularize, partly through his resistance to realist conventions in painting, and partly through his notorious and widely-disseminated lecture *Ten O'Clock* (delivered 1885, published 1888).[4] Whistler had used the first part of the phrase late in 1886 in a letter to the committee of a National Art Exhibition. In this letter, Whistler had objected to Wilde's proposed candidacy for the committee with the comment "What has Oscar in common with Art? except that he dines at our tables and picks from our platters the plums for the pudding he peddles in the provinces. . . . Oscar — with no more sense of a picture than the fit of a coat, has the courage of the opinions . . . of others!" (164).[5] As was his wont, Whistler had sent copies of this letter to Wilde and to *The World,* where it had been duly published on 17 November 1886.

When Whistler read "The Decay of Lying" late in 1889, therefore, he once again took to the letters columns to resuscitate his charge that Wilde had plagiarized him. The timing was opportune: plagiarism was a hot issue, and an article had recently appeared on the topic in Henry Labouchere's magazine *Truth.* Whistler's letter duly appeared in *Truth,* then, on 2 January 1890. It began:

> Most Valiant *Truth* — Among your ruthless exposures of the shams of today, nothing, I confess, have I enjoyed with keener relish than your late tilt at that arch-imposter and pest of the period — the all-pervading plagiarist! . . . How was it that, in your list of culprits, you omitted that fattest of offenders — our own Oscar? . . . [I]n an article in the *Nineteenth Century* on the "Decay of Lying," Mr. Wilde has deliberately and incautiously incorporated, "without a word of comment," a portion of the well-remembered letter in which, after admitting his rare appreciation and amazing memory, I acknowledge that "Oscar has the courage of the opinions . . . of others!" (Whistler 236–37)

But, as Whistler was well aware, what was striking was not that Wilde had plagiarized a phrase from Whistler, but that Wilde had plagiarized a phrase Whistler had used to describe Wilde's very tendency to plagiarism. (In a letter to Wilde, published jointly with Whistler's letter to *Truth,* Whistler described this as "stealing your own scalp!" [Whistler 238]). Wilde's answer to the charge of plagiarism raised in 1886, then, was to plagiarize the charge, and thereby to so transform it that it no longer remained a charge to plagiarism as such. We know, in fact, from Wilde's reply to Whistler's 1890 letter, published in *Truth* the following week, that Wilde refused to accept that one could "own" ideas: as he (somewhat cryptically) put it, "as for borrowing Mr. Whistler's ideas about art, the only thoroughly original ideas I have ever heard him express have had reference to his own superiority over painters greater than himself" (*Letters* 254; Whistler 239).

What emerges from this exchange is that Wilde had written his answer to Whistler into the text of the first version of "The Decay of Lying." Rather than deny what Whistler had written about him in 1886, Wilde had answered Whistler by so thoroughly accepting what Whistler had written as to use it, boldly and openly, for the basis of a new idea, thus calling attention to the premises of the charge — putting it *sous rature,* as Derrida would say — and transforming it in the process. This is precisely what Vivian (though not Whistler) means by "having the courage of other people's ideas."

But that is not the end of the matter. As he had already done once before, Wilde responded to Whistler's 1890 letter by once again incorporating Whistler into the text of "The Decay of Lying," a far more significant response than his reply to *Truth.* However, he did not quote Whistler directly. Instead he wrote the passage concerning nature's imitation of art which I described earlier as the high point of the dialogue. But he drew so cunningly from Whistler this time that the latter could never decisively claim the basic idea as his own, even though it bore, or had appropriated, Whistler's aura. Consequently, as Vivian's argument develops, Whistler gets both invoked and erased, praised and eclipsed, finally rendered silent, if not abolished from his very own art. We can see this process enacted in the series of questions with which Vivian commences his argument:

> Where, if not from the Impressionists, do we get those wonderful brown fogs that come creeping down our streets, blurring the lamps and changing the houses into monstrous shadows? To whom, if not to them and their master, do we owe the lovely silver mists that brood over our river, and turn to faint forms of fading grace curved bridge and swaying barge? The extraordinary change that has taken place in the climate of London during the last ten years is entirely due to this particular school of Art. You smile. (*Intentions* 40)

In fact "this particular school of Art" is not the "Impressionists." As anybody with a familiarity of late-nineteenth-century painting knows, and as Cyril's smile may acknowledge, the Impressionists did not paint (or at least had not yet painted) what Vivian is describing.[6] Whistler, on the other hand, whom Wilde had once called the first artist in Europe, *had* painted these scenes — in fact he owed his reputation to them — and Vivian is specifically describing Whistler's Nocturnes.[7] Moreover, "the last ten years" refers exactly to the period of Whistler's ascendancy on the English art scene, following the debacle of his libel trail against Ruskin in 1878 and the triumphant restoration of his reputation thanks to his Venice etchings (1881). However, to say that Vivian merely "describes" Whistler's Nocturnes is to understate the case, for Wilde had been trying to replicate Whistler's Nocturnes verbally since at least 1881. Wilde had increasingly felt himself in competition with Whistler throughout the 1880s and so he had increasingly sought to outdo in words what Whistler had done in paint, a process that required that he copy Whistler and yet somehow eclipse him at the same time (see Borelius). But even this is to understate the complexity of the duplication process enacted by Vivian's questions, for Whistler himself had attempted to replicate his Nocturnes in prose in his 1885 *Ten O'Clock* lecture. The resulting passage had already acquired considerable fame by the time Wilde revised "The Decay of Lying":

> And when the evening mist clothes the riverside with poetry, as with a veil, and the poor buildings lose themselves in the dim sky, and the tall buildings become campanili, and the warehouses are palaces in the night, and the whole city hangs in the heavens, and fairy-land is before us — then the wayfarer hastens home. (Whistler 144)

Vivian's questions in "The Decay of Lying" specifically attempt to outdo this passage from Whistler's *Ten O'Clock* — and one must notice in this respect that Vivian's questions maintain a laconic self-consciousness even as they try to evoke the nocturnal "mood" achieved by Whistler.

Vivian's questions invoke/eclipse Whistler in other ways too. Wilde knew, for instance, that nothing could arouse Whistler's ire more readily than to be bracketed as one of the Impressionists. Probably for this very reason then, as Birgit Borelius has pointed out, Wilde consciously used the term "one of the Impressionists" to refer to Whistler and yet to avoid reference to Whistler (a contradiction that Wilde strove for) even where it can be clearly discerned that he had Whistler alone in mind (see Borelius 35–40). The word "master" functions similarly; it was (and is) a word commonly used to refer to great painters, and one much used by Whistler to refer to himself. Wilde could be fairly sure that Whistler would read it as addressed to himself yet also be sure of greater uncertainty in the public's mind as to whether Whistler was "intended" or not.

Now I have used the example of Vivian's questions so far principally to show how this passage responds to Whistler's 1890 letter by both reinvoking Whistler's art and erasing Whistler himself. This is a process very similar to Wilde's earlier "invisible" quotation of Whistler, a process indubitably more complex than that simplistically implied by the term "plagiarism" if only to the degree that it is activated by a desire to be read by the very person whose ideas are being so self-consciously invoked. Unlike plagiarism as we traditionally think of it, "plagiarism" in Wilde calls (Whistler's) attention to itself.

But the so-called plagiarism of Whistler in *Intentions* highlights a crucial point about what, or more accurately *how, Intentions* means. First, it shows that Wilde conceptualizes at least two kinds of reader for the work, whom we might for convenience's sake call "Whistler" and "others." For "Whistler," *Intentions* "means" intensely — it is thoroughly imbued with clear significance — because he thinks he sees himself referred to in it, just as he thinks that it is written in direct response to himself. To "others," on the other hand, it is not at all clear what *Intentions* means, or at least whether or not Wilde intends Whistler to be the point of reference. If it "means" anything, it "means" what Whistler had meant in 1885, only more wittily.[8] Second, the ideas and phrases cited from Whistler are somehow evacuated of their sense or turned against themselves even as they seem to convey clearly communicable ideas. That is to say, the language used by Wilde continually calls attention both to itself and to the conditions of its own production — or as Arthur Symons aptly put it when reviewing *Intentions* in 1891, Wilde "can be admirable even when his eloquence reminds us of the eloquent writing of others. He is conscious of the charm of graceful echoes, and is always original in his quotations" (94).

Symons's comment is invaluable for its sense of how Wilde's language always tends to disappear behind itself — in structuralist terms, its tendency towards "an incessant sliding of the signified under the signifier" (Lacan 154). But the comment is equally useful for its sense of the *pleasure* this gives to a reader, as if confirming Gide's understanding of the relation between pleasure and meaning. The remark seems especially resonant in the postmodern era, of course; it can usefully be compared with Jean Baudrillard's comments about *seduction*, for instance, which rearticulate in poststructuralist terms Symons's own insight into the complex relation between language, meaning, and pleasure. "Seduction," Baudrillard writes,

> appears to all orthodoxies as malefice and artifice, a black magic for the deviation of all truths, an exaltation of the malicious use of signs, a conspiracy of signs. Every discourse is threatened with this sudden reversibility, absorbed into its own signs without a trace of meaning. . . . Seduction takes from discourse its sense and turns it from its truth. It is, therefore, contrary to the psychoanalytic distinction between manifest and latent discourses. For the latent discourse turns the manifest not *from* its truth, but *towards* its truth. . . . In seduction, by contrast, it is the manifest discourse — discourse at its most superficial — that turns back on the deeper order . . . in order to invalidate it, substituting the charm and illusion of appearances. These appearances are not in the least frivolous, but occasions for a game and its stakes, and a passion for deviation — the seduction of the signs themselves being more important than the emergence of any truth — which interpretation neglects and destroys in its search for hidden meanings. This is why interpretation is what, par excellence, is opposed to seduction, and why it is the least seductive of discourses. (*Seduction* 2, 53–54)

The relevance of what Baudrillard describes semiotically here for the study of Wilde can hardly be overstated. Whether or not one agrees with Baudrillard that "every discourse is threatened with this sudden reversibility" (and Wilde, for one, surely would), there can be no question that the mechanism described by Baudrillard applies exactly to the process enacted by Wilde's invocation of Whistler. Wilde, as we have seen, turns Whistler's ideas and phrases against themselves ("takes from discourse its sense and turns it from its truth"). As a result, not just Whistler's ideas but Whistler *himself* gets "absorbed into his own signs." What Whistler calls "plagiarism," then, is what Baudrillard calls "an exaltation of the malicious use of signs" or "a passion for deviation" — in both cases, the excess produced is greater than "the emergence of any truth."

But Baudrillard's comments also get to the heart of the problems inherent in the "serious" reading of *Intentions* with which I began. For to theorize *Intentions* in terms of seduction is to see that, rather than "conveying" meaning that is latent in Wilde's language, *Intentions* simulates meaning in order to turn meaning against itself ("turns back on the deeper order"). That is to say, *Intentions* works not to produce meaning in the traditional sense but to *deplete* itself of meaning. It woos us, but it never delivers what it promises.

Baudrillard would say that *all* discourse "collapses under the weight of its own signs" (*Seduction* 58) and what is remarkable about *Intentions,* therefore, is not the structure but the visibility of its seduction. That this is in fact the case can be demonstrated by showing how thoroughly and how visibly *Intentions* appropriates all signs of Whistler. So far, of course, I have demonstrated this appropriation at a purely local level, namely in two passages from "The Decay of Lying." But at this point it becomes necessary to see how completely the first edition demands to be read under the sign of Whistler, citing Whistler not so much at its deepest level but at its most superficial — most conspicuously, at the level of typography and book design.

Birgit Borelius has already done a great deal to demonstrate the centrality of Whistler to our understanding of *Intentions,* and it is difficult to object to her conclusion that "Wilde published *Intentions* as a collection partly with the object of defeating his antagonist" (36). She argues that "The Critic as Artist" was Wilde's response to Whistler's systematic attacks on his critics (including Wilde) throughout the late 1870s and 1880s and, more particularly, that it evolved from "The Butterfly's Boswell," Wilde's 1887 review of a biography of Whistler by Walter Dowdeswell;[9] and she compares the texts of "The Decay of Lying" and *Ten O'Clock* in order to conclude that "*Ten O'Clock* is the basis of the whole of Wilde's argument in 'The Decay of Lying' " (33). Borelius's argument, as these two examples demonstrate, depends on uncovering Whistler's presence "in" Wilde's texts. But the clearest evidence of Whistler's presence — which is also evidence of his disappearance — is bibliographic and is not to be found "in" Wilde's texts so much as on their "surface." To see such evidence, however, we first need to see the importance to Wilde of the 1890 publication of Whistler's *The Gentle Art of Making Enemies* since there is considerable reason for supposing (a) that Whistler published it in response to Wilde's 1889 essays, especially "The Decay of Lying," and (b) that its publication caused Wilde great embarrassment and, together with the furor in *Truth* over "The Decay of Lying," prompted Wilde to publish *Intentions* in 1891. (The revised version of *The Gentle Art* [1892] may in turn have been prompted by *Intentions.*)

Whistler's *The Gentle Art* is in fact central to Wilde's *Intentions.*[10] The design of the first edition of *Intentions* thoroughly parodies the typography and design of *The Gentle Art.*[11] Arguably, the crude vegetable motif on the front cover of *Intentions'* first edition is a parody of Whistler's famous butterfly motif, located in approximately the same position on the front cover of *The Gentle Art.* Less arguably, the layout of *Intentions'* title-page (see fig. 1) copies the radical layout of Whistler's cover and title-pages, with their emphasis on luxurious blank spaces (see fig. 2). It also copies Whistler in its use of italicized capitals for the place of publication, dramatically located on the far left of the page. In fact all of the preliminaries to *Intentions* parody *The Gentle Art,* especially the page on which "All Rights Reserved" is printed.[12] In the case of *Intentions,* the words occupy an entire page to themselves; moreover, they are printed in italics, and are set far to the right, about two-thirds of the way down the page. This is precisely the format of the copyright page in *The Gentle Art* too, though the words are slightly different in Whistler's case.[13] In both cases, what recent changes in international law had seemed to impose as a legal requirement has been grasped as an opportunity to reconceptualize the page as a primarily *visual* field.

The same kind of parody is evident for the title-pages of each of Wilde's essays. In each case, the subtitle is set to the extreme right, far lower down the page than the main title, and a far smaller font has been chosen than that used for the essay's main title (see fig. 3). In these respects, the practice of Wilde/Ricketts (see n. 11) follows that of Whistler, whose title-pages bore two main distinctive features: a fondness for setting "secondary" information like subtitles and dedications asymmetrically — far to the right and low down the page — and a predilection for varying font sizes so as to achieve striking visual effects (see figs. 2 and 4).

In all of these cases, the same dual process that we saw in "The Decay of Lying" is at work. On the one hand, *Intentions* reconstitutes as a visual field what we would otherwise conceptualize as a verbal one. In this respect, *Intentions* merely imitates *The Gentle Art.* At the same time, however — as would be apparent to most readers of the 1891 edition — Wilde's book mocks exactly this tendency in *The Gentle Art,* partly through the explicitness and visibility of its imitation. In mocking *The Gentle Art*'s pretensions to painterliness, we might say, *Intentions* itself manages to be both painterly and antipainterly, appropriating the aura and power of Whistler's signs even while maintaining an ironic and derisive distance from them. This dual impulse to surpass and displace Whistler, visualized here simply in typographic terms, makes yet more sense when we recall that for several years Wilde and Whistler had been engaged in a public war over the respective merits of the painter and the writer. As Borelius has shown, this war consisted in each of them not merely outdoing but actively appropriating the other's art (see esp. 35–40). This "appropriation effect" had been part of the rationale for Whistler's *Ten O'Clock*; here it is the rationale for evacuating the "painterly" text of its painterliness.

Something similar to this "appropriation-effect" can be seen in the subtitles Wilde gave to his essays when he republished them in *Intentions*. Each subtitle parodies not only Whistler's typography but his acutely self-conscious manner of naming his paintings. Wilde's "A Note on Illusion," "A Study in Green," and "An Observation" (subtitles respectively to "The Truth of Masks," "Pen, Pencil and Poison," and "The Decay of Lying") allude, then, to Whistler's *A Note in Red, A Harmony in Green,* and to the mannered abstraction of his famous "Arrangements" and Nocturnes.[14]

The typographic design and subtitles for *Intentions,* therefore, are the visible instantiations of Wilde's relations to Whistler. To account for those relations in terms of "influence" or "plagiarism," however, is to miss both their visibility[15] and Wilde's tendency to turn Whistler's words into pure sign-value — into what Symons means by a *consciousness* of "The charm of graceful echoes." Baudrillard would say that Wilde's appropriations of Whistler are governed by an "excessive transparency" (*Simulations* 50) or "a thrill of vertiginous and phoney exactitude" (*Simulations* 50) — that Wilde duplicates Whistler so perfectly as to make him disappear. As a result "it is possible that the very memory of the original . . . will fade in the minds of future generations, but from now on there is no longer any difference. The duplication is sufficient to render both artificial" (*Simulations* 50).

Wilde's simulation of Whistler is so excessively exact, then, that Whistler's meanings get visibly "seduced" or drained of their content. But it is not just the book's typographic design that brings visibility to bear on Wilde's simulation; our attention also gets called to the fact by *Intentions*'s title, for what are "intentions" if not perfect simulations of some projected object or purpose ("meaning") that is not fully present?[16] That is to say, "intentions" are by definition "simulations" because they feign to possess what they do not in fact have — much as a Chopin prelude, or for that matter an *intonazione,* fakes being a preface to a larger musical text that does not exist. Intentions always simulate what they "tend" towards, and they must therefore always remain unfulfilled to remain "intentional." Pragmatically speaking, they are *statements* of intention — promises — rhetorical texts that display a real consciousness only of themselves. This description holds abundantly true for Wilde's *Intentions* which, for all it pretensions to immanent meaning, finally forces detailed bibliographic matters onto our attention, as if the book itself were determined to be read at the most material and visual level. Precisely to *see* those matters, then, is to see that *Intentions* represents the simulation, not the expression, of thought — thought turned into visual spectacle or a work of art.

One question remains: if we grant that *Intentions* is less interested in thought per se than in turning thought into spectacular simulation, what does this have to do with the questions of seriousness and pleasure with which I began? This question is best answered historically, by examining the reaction to *Intentions* of Wilde's close friend Richard Le Gallienne, who reviewed the book in the *Academy* shortly after its publication. But I want to approach Le Gallienne's review with the help of Roland Barthes, whose now slightly out-of-fashion notion of "the pleasure of the text" is premised, like Le Gallienne's review, on the idea of meaning's loss.

Barthes puts the matter as follows: "what pleasure wants is the site of a loss, the seam, the cut, the deflation, the *dissolve*" (7). Barthes's comment applies perfectly to works like *Intentions* that ultimately visualize language as a "pure materiality" (7) even as they seem to offer "a *comfortable* practice of reading" (14) premised on notions of "pure representation" (56). Barthes calls such works "texts of bliss" (14) since they offer their readers what he calls the enticement of "two edges": "an obedient, conformist, plagiarizing edge . . . and *another edge* . . . which is never anything but the site of its effect: the place where the death of language is glimpsed" (6). Like the "portion of a body where the garment gapes . . . the intermittence of skin flashing between two articles of clothing," says Barthes, the gap created between the two "edges" is the site of pleasure: "it is this flash . . . which seduces, or rather: the staging of an appearance-as-disappearance" (9–10).

The pleasure of the text, then, is the pleasure that comes from the contradiction between the appearance of language-as-representation and the fact of language-as-controlled-performance:

> never has pleasure been better offered to the reader — if at least he appreciates controlled discontinuities, faked conformities, and indirect destructions . . . a pleasure of performance . . . [whose] feat is to sustain the *mimesis* of language (language imitating itself), the source of immense pleasures, in a fashion so *radically* ambiguous (ambiguous to the root) that the text never succumbs to the good conscience (and bad faith) of parody (of castrating laughter, of the "comical that makes us laugh"). (9)

Barthes's theory of textual pleasure puts us in a position to be able to read Le Gallienne, whose reading of *Intentions* can be seen to repeat in *actual* terms what Barthes has suggested in theory:

> There will be many who, as the phrase is, take him seriously; but let me assure them that Mr. Wilde is not of the number. It all depends what one means by the phrase; for I, for one, take Mr. Wilde very seriously as a creator of work which gives me much and various new pleasure; he is so absolutely alive at every point, so intensely practical — if only people could see it — and therefore so refreshingly unsentimental . . . and he often writes prose that one loves to say over for the mere

> pleasure of the ear — his own literary touchstone. The artistic temperament should delight in him; for the serious in the pursuit of literary pleasure he is as serious as every new joy must be; it is only in the domain of thought where it is rather funny to see him taken with such an open mouth. Not that Mr. Wilde is not a thinker, and a very subtle one too; but it is rather, so to say, as a damascener of thought, than a forger of it, that he is to be regarded. (99)

Le Gallienne's remarks clearly exemplify Barthes's comment in *The Pleasure of the Text* that "what pleasure suspends is the *signified* value . . . That is the pleasure of the text: value shifted to the sumptuous rank of the signifier" (65). Le Gallienne's pleasure, in other words, results from his refusal to "take Wilde seriously." Much like Barthes, he conceptualizes *Intentions* as a textual "body" ("absolutely alive at every point, so intensely practical") whose meaning lies in its capacity to work on the reader's body ("prose that one loves to say over for the mere pleasure of the ear — his own literary touchstone"). Indeed, for Le Gallienne, *Intentions* is a "decorative" artifact ("damascened thought") that seems to project its own desire onto the reader — much as for Barthes the text of bliss "reveal[s] itself in the form of a body, split into fetish objects . . . [whose] whole effort consists in materializing the pleasure of the text, in making the text *an object of pleasure*" (56–58). Effectively, Le Gallienne is depicting Baudrillard's "seduction" from a reader's point of view.

But, it will be objected, Le Gallienne's was not a typical response to *Intentions,* even in 1891. It represents instead what we might call the extreme "Aesthetic" response. After all, like Arthur Symons, Le Gallienne was a key figure in the production of Aestheticist discourse as well as (at this time) a personal friend of Wilde. One might even go so far as to say that, culturally speaking, men like Le Gallienne and Symons were *invented* by Wilde (Nelson tells us that Le Gallienne's "hero-worship of Oscar Wilde knew no bounds," that Le Gallienne was "devoted" to Wilde [19, 16]). By the same token, Wilde in his turn owed much to Le Gallienne. Shortly after his review of *Intentions,* for instance, Le Gallienne was to be instrumental (in his capacity as publisher's reader) in bringing Wilde to the Bodley Head Press, where the latter was to succeed in finding an outlet for his most controversial work. As far as Le Gallienne's review is concerned then, *who* wrote was as important as *what* was written.

These objections are much to the point, for the socially specific character of Le Gallienne's reading is the key to the politics of pleasure in *Intentions* and a good instance of what Regenia Gagnier has called Wilde's "private art-as-seduction" (45). If Gagnier is right, Wilde employed his writing (or at least his *prose* writing) to seduce men like Le Gallienne and "to create an audience of intimates" (46) while simultaneously bewildering a broader "mass" audience with the spectacle of meaning's loss (or what Gagnier calls "public diversion-as-critique" [46]). The role of pleasure in this economy becomes clear, then, if we situate Le Gallienne's "pleasured" reading of *Intentions* in the context of his friendship with Wilde, a friendship acted out through the written word. Shortly before Le Gallienne's *Intentions* review, for instance, Wilde had written to Le Gallienne that ''Friendship and love like ours need not meetings'' (*Letters* 277), implying that such friendship and love could be more than adequately sublimated in the acts of reading and writing one another. Indeed, the very letter in which Wilde made this remark, where he expressed his pleasure in Le Gallienne's just-published book on Meredith in terms strikingly similar to those Le Gallienne would use about *Intentions,* may be taken as an act of such friendship and love.

For Le Gallienne and Wilde, then, the pleasures of the text are distinctly erotic acts. And there can be little doubt that such pleasures were finally a function of broader anti-homosexual prohibitions: as D. A. Miller puts it in his commentary on Barthes, ''If pleasure . . . is obliged for its expression to become — how unpromisingly! — a pleasure 'of the text,' the text is free to develop in the process a sexuality so accommodatingly perverse that only the boldest bad faith could think it had anything in common with the censorious notion of 'the pleasure of reading' '' (27). Were the glimpse of Le Gallienne's body in his review of *Intentions* not sufficient in itself, proof of the eros of textual pleasure is furnished finally by the following sonnet, sent by Le Gallienne to Wilde in 1889, where it constitutes the principal theme:

As one, the secret lover of a queen,
Watches her move within the people's eye,
Hears their poor chatter as she passes by,
And smiles to think of what his eyes have seen;
The little room where Love did ''shut them in,''
The fragrant couch whereon they twain did lie,
And rests his hand where on his heart doth die
A bruisèd daffodil of last night's sin.

So, Oscar, as I read your tale once more
Here where a thousand eyes may read it too,
I smile your own sweet ''secret smile'' at those
Who deem the outer petals of the rose
The rose's heart — I who through grace of you
Have known it for my own so long before.

(rpt. in *Letters* 242 n.2)

For Le Gallienne, the pleasure of reading Wilde's ''tale'' (Wilde had sent Le Gallienne a MS draft of ''The Birthday of the Infanta'') *is* the tale's meaning. Moreover, the tale wears its meaning on its sleeve: the irony for Le Gallienne is that ''those / Who deem the outer petals of the rose / The rose's heart'' search for a truth that is self-evident. Finally, of course, such pleasurable ironies are what divides Wilde's readers into knowers and fools, along the lines suggested by Gagnier (and a good example of what Wilde meant when he said that "The Decay of Lying" was "written only for artistic temperaments" [*Letters* 237].) Like the typographic design of *Intentions* or its carnation-green silk cloth cover,[17] "the outer petals of the rose" simulate a depth that they do not have. They are what Wilde would have called "a sphinx without a secret." Le Gallienne's pleasure derives, then, both from his understanding that "the outer petals of the rose" are all that can be publicly known and from watching others deem them "the rose's heart." While he silently smiles at those who "go beneath the surface . . . at their own peril," he knows that there is *only* surface — that the "outer petals" are, in both senses of the word, an *act.* His pleasure derives from his knowledge, embodied in his sonnet itself, that words are forms of practice, not necessarily expressions of a deeper truth.

I CONCLUDE WITH A PARABLE that rehearses in miniature the recent history of *Intentions* criticism and which, for that reason, provides a useful summary of the issues I have been raising.

At the beginning of *Simulations,* Baudrillard speculates on the fate of those iconoclasts, still with us today,

> whose rage to destroy images rose precisely because they sensed [the] omnipotence of simulacra, this facility they have of effacing God from the consciousness of men, and the overwhelming destructive truth they suggest: that ultimately there has never been any God, that only the simulacrum exists, indeed that God himself has only ever been his own simulacrum. (8)

But then Baudrillard reverses in his tracks:

> the converse can also be said, namely that the iconolaters [that is, the lovers, not the haters, of idols] were the most modern and adventurous minds, since underneath the idea of the apparition of God in the mirror of his images, they already enacted his death and his disappearance in the epiphany of his representations. (9)

Maybe the iconolaters already knew, speculates Baudrillard, that their idols, so despised by the iconoclasts, "no longer represented anything and that they were purely a game, but that this was precisely the greatest game." If so, they must have known in advance that "it is dangerous to unmask images, since they dissimulate the fact that there is nothing behind them" (9).

The "serious" readers I began by discussing share much in common with Baudrillard's iconoclasts; believing in the true Word, they want to demolish the false idol of Wilde's "style" in order to restore self-apparent meaning to its rightful throne. But in seeking for that meaning, they doom themselves to a search whose object is ever and infinitely receding from view, and thus they succeed only in establishing the false idol of their own meanings instead.

To iconolaters like Le Gallienne, on the other hand, there is nothing but "style" or the "game" — except, of course, that without an "earnest" position from whence to judge what constitutes "style," for them the term is meaningless. Indeed, the iconolaters see no truths in words as such. As far as they are concerned, far from representing immanent truths, words are deeds that wear the mask of Truth. To them, the meaning of meaning is that it is just an act.

By overthrowing the traditional concept of meaning, then, we align ourselves with the iconolaters and recognize the actual character of Wilde's *Intentions.* I have been arguing that the principal act accomplished by *Intentions* was the silencing of Whistler, an act which further historical analysis might demonstrate reified the discourse of Aestheticism (previously contested terrain) and left the field to Wilde. My approach, however, has been to argue that Wilde accomplished this act by simulating Whistler's meanings, a process I characterize as adopting Whistler's signs while abolishing Whistler's sense. That process gets carried out and can be seen — as it is in the nature of simulation to be seen — at the work's surface, chiefly in terms of typography and book design. In the act of simulation lies the key to Wilde's relations with a whole range of precursors besides Whistler, about the merits of which critics have long been undecided because of their commitment to the notions of "plagiarism" and "influence." My discussion has not pursued these theoretical implications, however, preferring to explore the local historical consequences of Wilde's actions. For Wilde to practice the art of simulation, then, opened up dramatic possibilities for a certain hermeneutic confusion among his readers, a confusion Wilde exploited in order to gather around himself intimates like Le Gallienne. To the latter, Wilde's *Intentions* flaunted a materiality to be relished — the work demanded to be read with the body (i.e., phenomenologically) in terms of a "pleasure of the text." To other, more serious readers, the work remains a site of confusion since they take Wilde's simulations to be representations of the Truth.

One problem remains, however: does not the logic of my own argument contradict the substance of that argument, insofar as it claims to reveal (a) truth about the work? If "every discourse is threatened with this sudden reversibility, absorbed into its own signs without a trace of meaning," cannot the logic of simulation be applied to my own argument? If my argument has done its work properly, I suggest, it too will possess a certain transparency. At the very least, it will have succeeded in throwing its own limits into view and opening itself up to obvious objections. After all, "there is no such thing as a universal truth. A Truth in art is that whose contradictory is also true" (*Intentions* 258). There are some things about which we cannot be too serious.

Virginia Commonwealth University

NOTES

My thanks to Jerome McGann, Susan Barstow, Herbert F. Tucker, Michael Uebel, Ashley Dawson, and my *VLC* editors for helpful and constructive criticism of earlier versions of this paper.

1. *Intentions* is the name Wilde gave to the collection of essays and dialogues he published through Osgood, McIlvaine and Co. in 1891. It consisted of "The Decay of Lying," "The Truth of Masks," "Pen, Pencil and Poison," and "The Critic as Artist." All of these pieces had been published previously but were heavily revised for republication in *Intentions.*
2. Ellmann's error was anticipated by Le Gallienne in 1891:

> One must not forget that the form is dialogue, and therefore dramatic. Otherwise, we may be inclined to resent some of Gilbert's information, besides missing the subtle pleasure of watching a young innocent soul undergoing initiation. It was for that — among other things — that Mr. Wilde wrote these two "colloquies" . . . not to tell us that creation is as essential a part of criticism as criticism is of creation. (97)

3. The exception is his addition of entire chapters to *The Picture of Dorian Gray.*
4. For example, Whistler had said in *Ten O'Clock,*

> To say . . . that Nature is to be taken as she is, is to say to the player, that he may sit on the piano. That Nature is always right, is an assertion, artistically, as untrue, as it is one whose truth is universally taken for granted. Nature is very rarely right, to such an extent even, that it might almost be said that Nature is usually wrong. . . . How dutifully the casual in Nature is accepted as sublime, may be gathered from the unlimited admiration daily produced by a very foolish sunset. (143–44)

5. This was not the first time Whistler had charged Wilde with plagiarism. See, for example, his telegram to Wilde of 15 February 1882, published in the *World* on that date (Whistler 74).
6. It is easy today to miss the specificity of the kind of painting Vivian describes, largely thanks to the fame acquired by Monet's great series of Thames paintings. But these were not accomplished till 1902–03. Before this time, Whistler's reputation as the painter of the Thames went unrivalled.
7. See, for example, the following Nocturnes by Whistler: *Nocturne: Blue and Silver — Chelsea, Nocturne: Battersea Bridge, Nocturne: Blue and Gold — Old Battersea Bridge, Nocturne: Grey and Gold — Chelsea Snow, Nocturne: Grey and Silver, Nocturne: Black and Gold — The Rag Shop, Chelsea, Nocturne: Silver and Opal — Chelsea,* and *A Shop* (not strictly a Nocturne). By praising Whistler's Nocturnes specifically, Wilde took a position in the debate on aesthetics precipitated by Ruskin's contemptuous dismissal of Whistler in 1878.
8. My argument here is indebted to McGann's discussions of the ways Byron used his poems to construct/manipulate particular audiences.

9. Borelius's argument explains why Wilde dropped the dialogue's original Arnoldian title ("The True Function and Value of Criticism") on publishing it in *Intentions* and gave it its present Whistlerian title.
10. I refer to the first legally published edition of *The Gentle Art of Making Enemies* (over the printing of which Whistler assumed almost total control; published by Heinemann in London, 1890) not the important, slightly earlier, suppressed and pirated edition (also published 1890) issued abortively by F. Stokes of New York and Delabrosse of Paris, a few copies of which escaped Whistler's court injunctions and still survive today. For a discussion of the complex events leading up to the publication of the Heinemann edition, see Weintraub.
11. Wilde himself was likely to have exerted considerable influence over the design of *Intentions.* Barber and Nelson have demonstrated that Wilde, like many writers of the 1890s, took a deep interest in the design of his books — in fact so deep an interest that the word "design" may insufficiently reflect the importance Wilde attached both to book production generally and to the surfaces of his books (covers, illustrations, typography, paper, etc.) in particular. Consequently the designer of *Intentions* was hand-picked by Wilde — his protegé Charles Ricketts, who, either alone or together with his partner Charles Shannon, went on to design all of Wilde's subsequent books except *Salomé.* One might add that Wilde's publishers were as interested in these things as Wilde himself. Barber notes, for instance, that "Osgood and McIlvaine [publishers of *Intentions*] were interested in binding and typography and determined to back new ventures in these fields" (325). It appears from comments made on their books by the *Publishers Circular* soon after *Intentions* came out — not concerning *Intentions* exclusively, but nonetheless a good criticism of Wilde's book — that Osgood McIlvaine owed their reputation to such innovations:

    > The title pages are studies, verging sometimes rather closely on the fantastic, but sometimes also things of beauty which will no doubt continue to be joys for ever. A book is doubly a book when printer and binder do their work well, and, so far, slovenly would be the last word of which a reader would think in connection with any of Messrs. Osgood's books. To handle them is quite a delight, and to hold a volume with pleasure is to be prepossessed in favour of its contents. Appearances go for a good deal in literature as in life. (*Publishers Circular,* 13 Jun. 1891, p. 631; qtd. in Barber 325.)

12. In gauging this page's effect, we need to remember that in 1891 these words "struck" harder than they would today. Their appearance on English books in 1891 effectively signalled the completion of the long struggle for the regularization of international copyright arrangements and the passage of the American Copyright Act. After 1891, Wilde often devoted an entire page to (sometimes elaborate) copyright statements, frequently emphasizing the fact of their importance in correspondence with his publishers. See *Letters* 365.
13. This difference can be accounted for simply by the year's gap between the two books. By the time *Intentions* was published in 1891, international copyright arrangements between the United States and Britain had become far more codified than in 1890.
14. See "The Red Rag" (126–28) for Whistler's discussion of this naming process.
15. Bendz perceived this visibility in 1914 when he wrote that Wilde's influences "often lie bare to the eye, and in the majority of cases are easily traceable . . . [O]f all recent writers . . . [Wilde is] the one most liable to influences. . . . Probably very few writers

of equal rank did to the same extent conjoin a quite feminine instinct of adaptability and imitation with an original and virile mould of mind. While imitating others, he remained true to himself (11, 19). Bendz's comments on the multiplicity of such imitations suggest that one might extend my remarks on Wilde's "seduction" of Whistler to those other writers about whom Symons said Wilde was "conscious of the charm of graceful echoes." As Bendz puts it, "the list of those to whom in one way or another Wilde was indebted, is practically inexhaustible, and must remain so" (18–19). Bendz's implicit recognition here that Wilde's duplications were *excessive* (that the list of debts must remain "inexhaustible") is particularly relevent to my argument, for Bendz seems to be saying that Wilde duplicated other writers so perfectly that he effaces all trace of them — indeed, that we cannot know *who* he imitates, so much as *that* he imitates. Needless to say, this comes close to my own (Baudrillardian) description of the process as one of simulation.

16. The idea of "simulation" is conveyed too by the binding of the first edition of *Intentions,* with its evocative fakery of an "aesthetic" script. Some see this script as a mime of Blake, others as a mime of Rossetti (who had in turn mimed Blake; see Barber). But the controversy over just "whose" script Wilde's binding echoes is itself a perfect demonstration of what I have been calling simulation, for it demonstrates what Baudrillard calls that fading of the original to a point where "there is no longer any difference." That is to say, the binding's script works by making its "original" seem as artificial as itself; it does to Rossetti/Blake what matters of typography and design do to Whistler.
17. In 1894 Ada Leverson had a copy of *Intentions* specially bound for Wilde as a gift. Wilde remarked: "It is more green than the original even" (*Letters* 373, n. 2).

WORKS CITED

Adams, Hazard, *Critical Theory Since Plato.* New York: Harcourt Brace Jovanovich, 1971.

Bakhtin, Mikhail. *The Dialogic Imagination.* Ed. Michael Holquist, trans. Caryl Emerson and Michael Holquist. Austin: U of Texas P, 1981.

Barber, Giles. "Rossetti, Ricketts, and Some English Publishers' Bindings of the Nineties." *The Library* 5th ser. 25 (1970): 314–30.

Barthes, Roland. *The Pleasure of the Text.* Trans. Richard Miller. New York: Hill and Wang, 1975.

Bataille, Georges. "The Notion of Expenditure." *Visions of Excess: Selected Writings 1927–1939.* Ed. Allan Stoekl, trans. Allan Stoekl, with Carl R. Lovitt and David M. Leslie Jr. Minneapolis: U of Minnesota P, 1985. 116–29.

Baudrillard, Jean. *Seduction.* Trans. Brian Singer. New York: St. Martin's Press, 1990.

———. *Simulations.* Trans. Paul Foss, Paul Patton, and Philip Beitchman. New York: Semiotext(e), 1983.

Bendz, Ernst. *The Influence of Pater and Matthew Arnold on the Prose Writings of Oscar Wilde.* Gothenburg: Wettergren and Kerber, 1914.

Borelius, Birgit. "Oscar Wilde, Whistler and Colours." *Scripta Minora* 3 (1966–67): 1–62.

Dollimore, Jonathan. *Sexual Dissidence.* Oxford: Oxford UP, 1990.

Ellmann, Richard. "The Critic as Artist as Wilde." *The Artist as Critic: Critical Writings of Oscar Wilde.* Ed. Richard Ellmann. New York: Vintage, 1970. ix–xxviii.

Gagnier, Regenia. *Idylls of the Marketplace: Oscar Wilde and the Victorian Public.* Palo Alto: Stanford UP, 1986.

Gide, André. *Oscar Wilde.* Trans. Bernard Frechtman. New York: Philosophical Library, 1940.

Helfand, Michael S., and Philip E. Smith, *Oscar Wilde's Oxford Notebooks: A Portrait of Mind in the Making.* Oxford: Oxford UP, 1989.

Lacan, Jacques. *Ecrits.* Trans. Alan Sheridan. New York: Norton, 1977.

Le Gallienne, Richard. Signed rev. of Oscar Wilde's *Intentions, Academy,* 4 July 1891; rpt. in *Oscar Wilde: The Critical Heritage.* Ed. Karl Beckson. New York: Barnes and Noble, 1970. 97–102.

Longxi, Zhang. "The Critical Legacy of Oscar Wilde." *Texas Studies in Literature and Language* 30 (1988): 87–103.

McGann, Jerome J. "Byron and 'The Truth in Masquerade' " *Rereading Byron,* ed. Alice Levine and Robert N. Keene. New York: Garland, 1993. 1–19.

Miller, D. A. *Bringing Out Roland Barthes.* Berkeley: U of California P, 1992.

Nelson, James G. *The Early Nineties: A View From the Bodley Head.* Cambridge: Harvard UP, 1971.

Small, Ian. "Semiotics and Oscar Wilde's Accounts of Art." *British Journal of Aesthetics.* 25 (1985): 50–56.

Sussman, Herbert. "Criticism as Art: Form in Oscar Wilde's Critical Writings." *Studies in Philology* 70 (1973): 108–22.

[Symons, Arthur]. Unsigned rev. of *Intentions, The Speaker,* 4 July 1891; rpt. in *Oscar Wilde: The Critical Heritage.* Ed. Karl Beckson. New York: Barnes and Noble, 1970. 94–96.

Weintraub, Stanley. "Collecting the Quarrels: Whistler and The Gentle Art of Making Enemies." *Twilight of Dawn: Studies in English Literature in Transition.* Ed. O. M. Brack, Jr. Tucson: U of Arizona P, 1987. 34–44.

Whistler, James M. *The Gentle Art of Making Enemies.* London: Heinemann, 1890.

Wilde, Oscar. *Intentions.* London: Osgood, McIlvaine, 1891.

———. *The Letters of Oscar Wilde.* Ed. Rupert Hart-Davis. New York: Harcourt Brace, 1962.

A WORD KEPT BACK IN *THE TURN OF THE SCREW*

By Allan Lloyd Smith

I

AS SUCCESSIVE CRITICS HAVE discovered to their cost, *The Turn of the Screw* challenges and even defies interpretation. Shoshana Felman has observed that the naive will see ghosts, but the sophisticated will be suspicious of the governess and so repeat her mistake: "the invitation to undertake a reading of the text is perforce an invitation to *repeat* the text, to enter into its labyrinth of mirrors" (190). In that labyrinth, it is indeed uncanny how critics have been led into hallucinatory readings, on occasion even inventing their own ghosts, as if those provided by the text were not enough, demonstrating the way in which the unreadability of the text provokes extreme positions in the reader[1]. Something is being very decisively not said, and our apprehension of it causes peculiar tricks of vision. The most skillful interpreters seem to trip up, even at the points where their eyes are most open. Felman, for example, while correcting Edmund Wilson's reductive Freudianism in the episode involving Flora's play with pieces of wood, nevertheless manages to leave out of her account, that is, to not see, some important material that gives substance to Miss Jessel's apparition (parentheses in James's text indicate Felman's omissions):

> [Flora] had picked up a small flat piece of wood, which happened to have in it a *little hole* that had evidently suggested to her the *idea of sticking in another fragment* that might *figure as a mast* and *make the thing a boat*. This second morsel, as I watched her, she was very markedly and intently attempting to *tighten in its place.* (. . .)(170)

Felman omits the next part: "My apprehension of what she was doing sustained me so that after some seconds I felt I was ready for more. Then I again shifted my eyes — I faced what I had to face." Then comes the chapter break — again omitted by Felman — and chapter 7 begins (Felman's omission in square brackets; italics for "know" and "we" are James's, and for "they" are Felman's):

> I got hold of Mrs. Grose as soon after this as I could . . . [and I can give no intelligible account of how I fought out the interval. Yet] I still hear myself cry as I fairly threw myself into her arms: "*They know* — it's too monstrous: they know, they know!" (. . .) "And what on earth — ? [I felt her incredulity as she held me.]"Why, all that *we* know — and heaven knows what else beside!" (170)

The implication of the omitted parts is on the whole "apparitionist," giving more weight to the notion "Flora saw." But because Felman wants to pursue the question of phallicism, the mast[er] as a *"key to meaning, a master-signifier"* (171), the question of the ghost of Miss Jessel is subordinated, exorcised.

Felman says, in admitting the difficulties of interpretation: "In its efforts to master literature, psychoanalysis — like Oedipus and like the Master — can thus but blind itself: blind itself in order to deny its own castration, in order not to see, and not to read, literature's subversion of the very possibility of psychoanalytic mastery." To take up the position of mastery is to take up the place of the Uncle, the place "precisely, of the textual *blind spot* . . . [to occupy] a spot *within* the very blindness one seeks to demystify, that one is *in* the madness, that one is always, necessarily, *in* literature" (199). Flora's innocent game, becoming a topos for psychoanalytical mastery, becomes enmeshed in a never-ending series of registrations of phallicism, so that (as John Carlos Rowe observes) any effort to interpretatively master *The Turn of the Screw* is only a displacement of the Uncle's power, producing "displaced images of his repressive authority, his authority as repression and censorship. Any allegorical reading of the hidden sexual or moral drama that governs the narrative serves to hide his mastery from view, to ascribe responsibility to another agent, who is always in the Uncle's secret service" (143).

But equally, we may argue, such Freudian, Lacanian, or even simply political and legal abstractions encourage us not to look too closely at what has evidently been happening at Bly. Here I would like to borrow a reading technique from Eve Kosofsky Sedgwick, who says of another James story ("The Beast in the Jungle") that it "seems to make a strong implicit claim of 'universal' applicability through heterosexual symmetries, but . . . is most movingly subject to a change of gestalt and of visible saliencies as soon as an assumed heterosexual male norm is at all interrogated" (195). The interrogation that I have in mind is of the assumed heterosexual adult norm, within which the positioning of the author as male must inevitably figure.

At the very center of the narrative we have the figure of a little girl inserting and tightening a piece of wood into a hole in another piece of wood. I discussed this episode in an earlier study of the uncanny (*Uncanny* 116) but now retrace this crucial material in order to correct my own misreading or negative hallucination of what the episode — linked so deeply even to the title of the story — is actually about. My previous reading argued that our attention is wrongly directed by critics like Felman to phallicism, to the boat and the mast[er], to the effect that the *female* ghost is erased, the "woman in black, pale and dreadful — with such an air also, and such a face! — on the other side of the lake," who "only fixed" the child, with "such awful eyes." This I read as the dreaded return of female sexuality, as the Medusa, who "fixes" what she looks upon, a mirror-image of the governess, who later sobs, "I don't save or *shield* them" (33 italics added). But now I think it has to be read not as allegory, nor as the sexually frustrated neurotic vision of the governess (whatever remains of truth in that understanding will appear later), but rather as symptom; we must ask what it is that Flora is telling through her actions. Her gesture allusively represents the act of sexual penetration. It may be correct, ultimately, to refer this episode to a patriarchal structure informed by phallicism, a series of relays of authority from the "Master" through Quint or the hysteria of the governess. But surely it is appropriate first to recognize the enactment for what it immediately is: something done *by* Flora, representing something done *to* Flora.

In redirecting our attention as readers to the meaning of Flora's game I do not of course assume that Flora (or Miles, or the governess) is anything but a literary representation, a figure without any life outside the realm of the text. The text exists fully only in its reading, it is created by the reader in that process. But, on the other hand, the author of the text uses both literary and materialist conventions to determine the reading effect.[2] Literary characters are coded to point to a hypothetical continuous existence, a past of their own, and the codifications may be complex or even contradictory in certain respects. Where the character's hidden past is the focus of the text's hermeneutic drive, it is reasonable to explore all the various signals that determine our reception of what that experience might be. While we may accept, with Andrzej Warminski, that attempts to historicize reading may wind up as not being "historical" at all in any genuine sense, because they omit the only *real* history involved, the history of the reading, and thus become allegory, it is not open to us either to accept the story as a fable that makes *any* historical reading impossible.[3]

Miles is expelled from school (the "little horrid unclean school-world"), for reasons too improper to be spelled out by the headmaster ("stupid sordid headmasters," 19; ch. 4). The governess's reaction is that he must have been "an injury to the others," a risk of corrupting, she sarcastically adds, "his poor little innocent mates" (II; ch. 2). On hearing the news, Mrs. Grose gives a look of comprehension but then "visibly, with a quick blankness, seemed to try to take it back" (10; ch. 2). Miles himself says, eventually, that it was because he "said things" (86; ch. 24).[4] What "things" then, we may ask, would cause a child's dismissal from an English school? Only those "things" which other children should not (could not) know. One of the more ingenious interpretations of this problem is Jane Nardin's: she argues that Miles has revealed intimate knowledge of an illicit love affair between a "base menial" and a "lady." Quint and Jessel (who she opines were in love but were prevented from marrying for class reasons). "If Miles loved Quint and Miss Jessel and sympathized with their love for each other, then perhaps what he did at school was simply to discuss their relationship and his feelings about it with his closest friends" (138). It is not *impossible* that Miles was expelled for talking about an affair between his governess and a valet; it is merely unlikely. Gossip like that would be conventional in an upper-class English school. Talk which indicated graphic personal knowledge of homosexual practices between a child and an adult, however, would certainly have been seen as corrupting, particularly so since this was *the* great area of difficulty in the English public schools. In reviewing Nardin's argument, another phrase of Sedgwick's about "The Beast in the Jungle" seems apposite: "The denial that the secret has a content — the assertion that its content is precisely a lack — is a stylish and 'satisfying' Jamesian formal gesture. The apparent gap of meaning that it points to is, however, far from being a genuinely empty one; it is no sooner asserted as a gap than filled to a plenitude with the most orthodox of ethical enforcements" (201).

According to Nardin, in "secretly voicing egalitarian sentiments about Quint and Miss Jessell, Miles would have been striking at his school's raison d'être: the preparation of status-conscious gentlemen to fit their places in a stratified society" (138). Thus the cause of Miles's expulsion was really his innocence in speaking indiscreetly of rank and sex. The dichotomy between his "seeming sweetness and his disgrace at school can thus be resolved without having recourse to theories of deep deceit or demonic possession" (139). But of course the alternative is *not* between deep deceit and demonic possession. If Miles speaks of what he knows, to those he "liked," he is not practicing "deep deceit" or being wicked any more than any abused child who becomes complicit in the activities practiced upon him or her by the adult. This seems to me the fatal mistake of critics of *The Turn of the Screw:* to believe that the complicit child is guilty, or wicked, instead of perceiving the affair from the child's point of view. For that matter, "demonic possession" is really a very apt description of the situation of such a child, whose behavior may cause others to see "ghosts," *the ghosts of the actions of the abuser.* Nardin comes nearer to this point of view when she says that "the ghosts are the logical offspring of the governess' attempt to understand a complex human situation in terms of a cultural tradition incapable of yielding real insight," that is, her religious moral training, which cannot comprehend that Miles may have committed a serious offence and yet not be a complete reprobate (139). She does not, however, have a satisfactory explanation of the processes whereby this seeing of ghosts comes about. It is my contention that the hallucinations are provoked by the symptomatic behavior of the children and Mrs. Grose. This assertion is made more comprehensible by Nicolas Abraham and Maria Torok's psychoanalytical work on "the phantom," which "offers a new way to interpret the behavior of fictional characters and some insight into how texts made enigmatic, if not illegible, by the mute presence of secrets may be explained'' (Rashkin 37).

II

''What haunts are not the dead, but the gaps left within us by the secrets of others.'' Nicolas Abraham, ''Notes on the Phantom'' (287)

NICOLAS ABRAHAM AND Maria Torok's theory of the phantom proposes a radical departure from the universalizing tendency of psychoanalysis, with powerful implications for the study of the uncanny in literature. Abraham and Torok argue that it is not axiomatic that childhood development proceeds in predetermined ways, nor that any particular even is traumatic for all individuals. Instead they stress that the process of individuation is ''potentially nonlinear, and that in certain cases it is constituted by specific influences *outside* the individual's immediate or lived experience'' (Rashkin 32).[5] The process begins with the child's differentiation from the mother (a process which is never completed), within which the infant ''[w]ith no conscious or unconscious of its own other than the mother's . . . perceives the mother's words, gestures, and physical attributes without distinguishing between the mother's conscious and unconscious intent or charge.'' The maternal unconscious, communicated without having been spoken, ''resides as a silent presence within the newly formed unconscious of the child. As the child matures, it will add its own repressions — produced by its own lived experiences — to this central core'' (Rashkin 34). There is no preprogrammed sequence of drives and repressions as in Freud's formulation of developmental stages, nor any single and privileged drive and repression, such as is represented by the phallus in Lacan's formulation. But since every mother is herself the child of another mother, there is a genealogical inheritance of the unconscious. ''We are all the psychic products of our infinitely regressive family histories'' (Rashkin 35). Abraham and Torok as practicing psychoanalysts inevitably focused most closely on family dynamics, but at this point we may stress the openness of their model to *cultural* determinants as well as more strictly personal ones: the child is absorbing a cultural inheritance incorporating certain secrets, absences, or silences. The ''phantom'' is Abraham and Torok's designation of the unknowing awareness of another's secret which ''introduces, via the concept of 'transgenerational haunting,' a novel perspective on the potential configurations of psychic history and on their role in pathogenic processes and symptom formation'' (37). According to Abraham,

> The phantom is a formation of the unconscious that has never been conscious — for good reason. It passes — in a way yet to be determined — from the parent's unconscious into the child's. Clearly, the phantom has a function different from dynamic repression. The phantom's periodic and compulsive return lies beyond the scope of symptom-formation in the sense of a return of the repressed; it works

> like a ventriloquist, like a stranger within the subject's own mental topography. (289–90)

Abraham and Torok's theory suggests that characters in literary texts "may be construed as cryptic poetic entities whose words and actions can be heard to tell the secret history generating their existence" (Rashkin 50). The implications for literary study of the uncanny are of course considerable. Esther Rashkin argues that:

> the linguistic elements of the text are considered to be incomplete and need to be joined with their missing complements, whose traces are hidden in the text. The reading of these traces and the union of meshing complements enables the interpreter to perceive or conjecture a drama or dramas concealed within a character's history. . . . This does not mean that a character's past is conceived to be real, or that it is afforded a status different from the character's "present." [This means] understanding that the text calls upon the reader to expand its apparent parameters to include invisible scenarios whose traces are symbolically and perhaps cryptonymically inscribed within it. Although predating the events of the text, these unelaborated dramas have no reality outside the limits of the text. . . . Approaching these texts with conceptual and interpretive tools such as anasemic analysis, symbol, cryptonymy, and the phantom can offer new insights into the problems of textual production, the genesis and motivation of narrative, and the connections between structures of repetition and concealment, inscription and signification. (50–51)

Some of these terms require further explanation. *"Anasemic analysis"* is the name given by Abraham and Torok to the process of discovering why a particular event has been experienced as traumatic and concealed as a secret. It consists of a constant movement "back up toward" (Greek: *ana*) earlier sources of signification *(semia)* that lie beyond perception. "Anasemia allows them to construe an individual's existence as constituted by the constant creation of symbols in response to traumas. It enables them to read these symbols — and thus the individual's life — as a series of telltale symptoms that tacitly speak of their founding silence beyond perception" (Rashkin 50). The symbols in question are not understood precisely as literary symbols would be but are instead fragments or broken halves of a missing whole which need to be reconnected to their absent complements. The symbol plays the role of a relay in a functional circuit: it is not a question of a one-to-one correspondence but something that functions dynamically in relation to objects. But it is not a question of asking what the symbols of the text mean, but rather: "How and with what does something symbolize? What constitutes the text's symbolic operation?" (Rashkin 48).

"Cryptonymy" is Abraham and Torok's term for establishing a signifying process, a theory of readability. In "Towards a Cryptonymy of Literature" Nicholas Rand explains:

> A theory of readability does not define the act of reading but rather attempts to create avenues for reading where previously there were none. More radically, it demonstrates that interpretation is possible even in the face of obvious obstruction. Such a theory is primarily concerned with converting obstructions into guides to understanding. (li–lii)

Words, as carriers of veiled lexical relationships, can be cryptonyms, words that hide. Through synonyms, for example, reference may be made to an unstated term which is concealed within the sequence, a word which should appear but does not. This is not far from Freud's reading techniques and has resemblance to the Lacanian process of interpretation. Where it differs is that Abraham and Torok avoid any standardized decoding, such as Freud practiced (rather at odds with his own theory) in his interpretation of dreams, and do not (like Lacan) pursue the chain of signification inexorably to a final reading of a signifying lack. ''In a cryptonymic reading,'' Rashkin explains, ''we may stop at a signifier if we can determine what it hides, how it hides it, and what drama might be linked to its process of hiding'' (45). In contradiction to the idea of a signifying chain as composed of a potentially infinite sequence of empty signifiers, ''the signified is not secondary'' according to Abraham (qtd. in Rashkin 45). Rashkin sees the difference here primarily in the notion that the bar or sign of repression can itself be made into an object of investigation.

In relation to the uncanny, the most obviously promising of these terms and procedures is the notion of *the phantom.* Abraham argues in ''Notes on the Phantom'' that ''what haunts are not the dead, but the gaps left within us by the secrets of others'' and ''what comes back to haunt are the tombs of others (287, 288). This concept of the phantom enables Abraham and Torok to postulate how influences *outside* an individual's lived experience can determine psychic development. It does this by linking certain states of mental disarray to the concealment of a secret rather than to that individual's unconscious understood as a repository of repressed wishes. The phantom is a formation outside any developmental view of human behavior. ''It holds the individual within a group dynamic constituted by a specific familial *(and sometimes extrafamilial)* topology that prevents the individual from living life as her or his own'' (Rashkin 40; emphasis added). A possibility suggested by the italicized phrase above is to consider the unspeakable (or at any rate unspoken) secret or secrets in a larger cultural sense; everything that is denied within the culture, and yet remains the truth; as in Schelling's definition of the uncanny, everything ''that ought to have remained secret and hidden but has come to light.''[6] In this model, the author, like contemporary readers, could be unaware of the secret that nevertheless shaped characters' actions or their fictional destinies. We could then usefully speak of ''the phantom'' at points where the character's actions, the narrator's comments, or the structures of plot are contradictory in terms of authorially postulated conditions but *are* consonant with other unspoken determinants. Perhaps such an extension is illegitimate in terms of Abraham and Torok's own practice, but their idea of an "unknown knowledge" that can be transmitted through a family line or community seems a very promising way to explain the psychological effect of something appearing to be familiar but strange at the same time, as in Freud's celebrated definition of the uncanny.[7]

III

> "*. . . there was a word Mrs. Grose had kept back.*" (*Turn of the Screw*, ch. 6)

RIGHT FROM THE BEGINNING, when she is so unmistakably relieved to welcome the governess, Mrs. Grose's discourse and reactions are often expressive of something else: "She had told me, bit by bit, under pressure, a great deal; but a small shifty spot on the wrong side of it all still sometimes brushed my brow like the wing of a bat; . . . I felt the importance of giving the last jerk to the curtain" (35; ch. 8). The governess believes that she is bolder, more imaginative, and more willing to face — whatever it may prove to be — than Mrs. Grose, her ignorant and unlettered assistant. But Mrs. Grose, nearer to the grosser aspects of life, as her name implies (nearer perhaps even to a sense of "gross indecency"?), is likely to know *some* things that the governess, the Austenish youngest daughter of a Hampshire vicar, whose reading did not even extend to eighteenth-century novels and whose sexual experience can be reasonably assumed to be negligible, would not. So a macabre comedy ensues when the two are at cross purposes over Miss Jessel, who has obviously been abused by Quint: Mrs. Grose says, "And afterwards I imagined — and I still imagine. And what I imagine is dreadful." "Not so dreadful as what *I* do," replies the governess, thinking of her own supernatural horrors (33; ch. 7). Or again, in talking of Flora's relation to Miss Jessel, Mrs. Grose tries "a grim joke. 'Perhaps she likes it!' " (32; ch. 2), which links with the governess's remark on the next page, regarding Miss Jessel, "It must have been also what *she* wished!" (33; ch. 7). Most suggestively of all, in terms of Abraham and Torok's theories of the cryptonym, "[T]here was a word Mrs. Grose had kept back" (27; ch. 6). Indeed there was, although arguably Mrs. Grose knows what it is little more than does the governess. These suggestive absences in Mrs. Grose's discourse open the door for the governess's hallucinations to begin when she misunderstands the latter's comment "He seems to like us young and pretty!":

> "Oh, he *did*," Mrs. Grose assented: "it was the way he liked every one!" She had no sooner spoken indeed than she caught herself up. "I mean, that's *his* way — the master's."
> I was struck. "But of whom did you speak first?"

> She looked blank, but she coloured. "Why of him."
> "Of the master?"
> "Of who else?"
> There was so obviously no one else that the next moment I had lost my impression of her having accidentally said more than she meant. (12; ch. 2)

It would be impossible to list all of the misconstructions entailed by the governess's comparative ignorance of what was, after all, not talked of in her society (or even, I shall argue later, James's). I will simply instance the exchange: "But now that you've guessed." [Mrs. Grose:] "Ah I haven't guessed! . . . How can I if *you* don't imagine?" (22; ch. 5), or the episode in which the Governess sees in Mrs. Grose's face "the delayed dawn of an idea I myself had not given her and that was as yet quite obscure to me" (23; ch. 5). These enigmatic traces of "something else," the brush of the bat's wing, become the fabric that sustains the apparitions seen by the Governess, even to the extent that "It was as if now in my friend's own eyes Miss Jessel had again appeared" (33; ch. 7).

Mrs. Grose tells the governess that Quint and Miss Jessel were infamous, and that he "did what he wished . . . [w]ith them all" (33; ch. 7). In the following passage we see how the implications of child sexual abuse can become subtly apparent in Mrs. Grose's discourse but are completely missed by the governess. The two are talking about the period when Miles and Quint had been perpetually together:

> ". . . he [Miles] denied certain occasions."
> "What occasions?"
> "When they had been about together quite as if Quint were his tutor — and a very grand one — and Miss Jessel only for the little lady. When he had gone off with the fellow, I mean, and spent hours with him."
> [There is a discrepancy here between the notion of Quint behaving as a "grand tutor" and Miles "going off with the fellow" which implies less respectable activities. The governess however misses this nuance:]
> ". . . I see. He lied."
> "Oh!" Mrs Grose mumbled. This was a suggestion that it didn't matter. [Mrs. Grose sees her companion going in the wrong direction and adds to it by saying that Miss Jessel didn't mind and didn't forbid him, thus reinforcing the theme of collusion between Quint and Jessel in exploiting the children.]
> I consider. "Did he put that to you as a justification?"
> At this she dropped again. "No, he never spoke of it."
> "Never mentioned her in connection with Quint?"
> She saw, visibly flushing, where I was coming out.
> "Well, he didn't show anything. He denied," she repeated; "he denied."
> Lord, how I pressed her now! "So that you could see he knew what was between the two wretches?" [i.e., their scandalous heterosexual relationship]
> "I don't know — I don't know!" the poor woman wailed
> [unable to articulate what she did know — or suspect]

> "You do know, you dear thing," I replied; "only you haven't my dreadful boldness of mind, and you keep back, out of timidity and modesty and delicacy, even the impression that in the past, when you had, without my aid, to flounder about in silence, most of all made you miserable. But I shall get it out of you yet! There was something in the boy that suggested to you," I continued, "his covering and concealing their relation."
>
> [which Mrs. Grose could take to imply the relation between Miles and Quint].
>
> "Oh he couldn't prevent —"
>
> "Your learning the truth? I dare say! But heavens," I fell, with vehemence, a-thinking, "what it shows that they must, to that extent, have succeeded in making of him!"
>
> "Ah nothing that's not nice *now!*" Mrs. Grose lugubriously pleaded. (36–37; ch. 8)

Among the symptoms of child abuse, the display of unexpected knowledge, as well as the compulsive reenactment of sexual scenarios in symbolic terms, is commonplace. Flora's "appalling" language points to the same conclusion, as does Mile's sexual precosity in his "saying things" at the school; his unexpected maturity in his dealings with the governess in the areas of implicitly sexual behavior is a further clear marker of the experience of abuse. The behavior of the children contains certain systemic lacunae: the fact, for example, that "*Never,* by a slip of the tongue, have they so much as alluded to either of their old friends" [Quint and Jessel] (48); their angelic manner versus sexual precocity; Miles's excellent behavior contrasted with his expulsion. This absence causes the governess to imaginatively "fill in" the vacant spaces. A nice example of the process comes when the governess expresses through prurient innuendo her intuition of the children's potential for abuse: "They were like those cherubs of the anecdote who had — morally at any rate — nothing to whack!" (17; ch. 4). She goes on to discuss Miles's baffling lack of a past in terms that show how her cognition is vexed and thwarted: "I remember feeling with Miles in especial as if he had, as it were, nothing to call even an infinitesimal history. . . . He had never for a second suffered. I took this as a direct disproof of his having really been chastised. If he had been wicked he would have 'caught' it, and I should have found the trace, should have felt the wound and the dishonour. I could reconstitute nothing at all, and he was, therefore an angel. He never spoke of his school . . . " (19; ch. 4). "Nothing to whack," "nothing at all" to "reconstitute": we are reminded of the governess's decision, in response to the letter from school, to say "Nothing at all" (14; ch. 3). But this nothing is a something, to have caused Miles's dismissal, and there is clearly *something* that causes the children's unnatural behavior, leaving such marks as make the governess see "a queerness in the traceable increase of their own demonstrations [of beguilement]" (38; ch. 9) or believe Miles to be "under some influence operating in his small intellectual life as a tremendous incitement" (39; ch. 9). In this context it is appropriate to note that Abraham and Torok propose that such "symptoms can occur when a shameful and therefore unspeakable experience must be barred from consciousness or 'kept secret' " (Rashkin 37).

When Flora plays with her bits of wood, her behavior is symbolic. The mistake made by critics has been to read this symbol as a hieroglyph standing for the structures of phallicism. But as Abraham understands it (Abraham's italics):

> *a first distinction must be made between, on the one hand, the symbol-thing considered as a hieroglyph or symbolic text — the symbol* dead as a symbol — *and, on the other hand, the symbol included within a process, that is, the* operating symbol, *animated by meaning and implying concrete subjects, all together considered as a functioning unit.* To interpret a symbol consists in converting the symbol-thing into an operating symbol. A thing *must never be taken as the symbol of another thing.* (Abraham, qtd. in Rashkin 47).

Flora's symbolic play constitutes this kind of functioning unit, representing her unsayable drama. Another example of the operation of "the phantom" in the effect of Flora's behavior on the governess is apparent in the toy boat episode: when the governess sees the apparition she notices that Flora's voluble chattering has abruptly ceased and she has turned her back to the water. This change convinces the governess that Flora "knows." But isn't it rather the case that Flora's spontaneous sounds would cease when she is compulsively reenacting a sexual experience with the two pieces of wood, producing a silence that the governess interprets as uncanny in relation to such an "innocent" activity as boatmaking, and this "causes" the ghost to appear? Flora didn't tell. The governess's comment, "Not a word — that's the horror. She kept it to herself! The child of eight, *that* child!" (30), is then true in another sense as well. Shoshana Felman registers the implication of Flora's action when she comments of the governess's exclamation "They *know* — it's too monstrous: they know, they know!" (30; ch. 7): that to know, indeed, is both 'to possess reliable information,' and 'to have sexual intercourse with' "; yet instead of following up the clear implication of this aperçue, Felman moves instead — like all other critics of the story — to the problem of the governess and, even in the section titled "A Child is Killed," manages to avoid the implication of her own perception (158; 161–177).

If the symptomatic behavior of the children and Mrs. Grose, circling around the "secret" of their having been sexually abused, creates an enigma that can only be resolved for the governess by her "filling in" the absent figures of Quint and Miss Jessel, the same can eventually be said of her own behavior towards the children, her own keeping of the "secret" that she does not "know." In Abraham and Torok's theory, the originator of the traumatic secret has to be simply "an identifiable member of a particular family whose secret, and whose reason for keeping a secret, are determined by a specific psychic constellation. By the same token, the effect on those to whom he [or, here, she] transmits the secret — as well as their identity (whether child, grandchild, nephew, niece, or non-relative) — cannot be predetermined or predicted'' (Rashkin 41).

The consequence of incomprehension in *The Turn of the Screw* is an increasing sense of interrelated suspicion and performance, on both sides, so that the governess works on her small charges as they work on her:

> the element of the unnamed and untouched became, between us, greater than any other, and . . . so much avoidance couldn't have been made successful without a great deal of tacit arrangement. It was as if, at moments, we were perpetually coming into sight of subjects before which we must stop short, turning suddenly out of alleys that we perceived to be blind, closing with a little bang that made us look at each other — for like all bangs, it was something louder than we had intended — the doors we had indiscretely opened. (50, 51; ch. 13)

The governess is in the role of mother to the orphaned children, handing on her unconsciousness to them through her unwillingness — indeed her inability — to articulate their situation (compare Rashkin 34). As she puts it, ''I flung myself about, but I always broke down in the monstrous utterance of names'' (53; ch. 13). What the governess thinks she means is the names of Quint and Jessel, but what she really fails to articulate — because she cannot think it — is the ''word'' that Mrs. Grose (similarly inarticulate, if better aware of the world) ''kept back.'' The subtle awareness of all four of what is not to be said undercuts the apparent harmony of their ''cloud of music and affection and success and private theatricals'' (39; ch. 9):

> What it was least possible to get rid of was the cruel idea that, whatever I had seen, Miles and Flora saw *more* — things terrible and unguessable and that sprang from dreadful passages of intercourse in the past. Such things left on the surface, for the time, a chill that we vociferously denied we felt (53; ch. 13)

In the end, this chill becomes so extreme as to cause Mile's death when he finally is forced to articulate the forbidden name: replying to the governess's interrogation ''Whom do you mean by 'he'?'' with ''Peter Quint — you devil!'' (88; ch. 24). Here a comment of Abraham and Torok's is particularly apposite. In *The Wolf Man's Magic Word* they claim:

> It is not a situation *including* words that becomes repressed; the words are not dragged into repression by a situation. Rather, *the words themselves, expressing desire, are deemed to be generators of a situation that must be avoided and voided retroactively*. . . . For this to occur, a catastrophic situation must have been created precisely by words. (20)

The words ''Quint'' and ''Jessel'' fulfill these criteria, when with catastrophic results Flora becomes suddenly aged, ''she was literally, she was hideously hard, she had turned common and almost ugly'' (73; ch. 20), by having to reencounter the traumatic word "Jessel"; and Miles is actually killed by the stress of articulating the name of "Peter Quint." A further argument of Abraham's in "Notes on the Phantom," may be brought into the discussion on this point of Miles's death on naming Quint:

> A surprising fact gradually emerges: the work of the phantom coincides in every respect with Freud's description of the death instinct. First of all, it has no energy of its own; it cannot be "abreacted," merely designated. Second, it pursues in silence its work of disarray. Let us add that the phantom is sustained by secreted words, invisible gnomes whose aim is to wreak havoc, from within the unconscious, in the coherence of logical progression. Finally, it gives rise to endless repetition and, more often than not, eludes rationalization. (291)

That the governess "always broke down in the monstrous utterance of names" (53; ch. 13) is an anticipation of the far more stressful effect of this naming on Flora and Miles. To name Quint, in the context of the governess's intervention, her insertion of Miles's unnamed experience into the frame of social opinion (or the symbolic order) is to strip away the child's defenses (his "innocence") in naming as disgusting or evil the activities he has been shaped by. This is what kills him: not simply his "fright" at the vehemence of her (or for that matter perhaps even his own) belief in the occult. In his article on the phantom, Abraham discusses the "special difficulty" in such analyses as the one that the Governess is in effect undertaking, which "lies in the patient's horror at violating a parent's or a family's guarded secrets, even though the secret's text and content are inscribed within the unconscious. The horror of transgressing, in the strict sense of the term, is compounded by the risk of undermining the fictitious yet necessary integrity of the parental figure in question" (290).

IV

> "the exposure indeed, the helpless plasticity of childhood that isn't dear or sacred to somebody!" Henry James, letter to Louis Waldstein, October 1898

WE ARE NOT SIMPLY in literature here (*pace* Felman); or if we choose to be so we are merely reenacting the systemic not-knowing of the culture which produces the text itself as symptom. In the period immediately preceding James's writing of *The Turn of the Screw* there *had* been an increase in public apprehension and concern about child sexual exploitation, but this attention was focused chiefly not on the abuse of small children by parents or other carers but on the scandal of under-age prostitution, into which such concern was rapidly diverted. In 1885 W. T. Stead's articles entitled "Maiden Tribute of Modern Babylon" in the July *Pall Mall Gazette* drew attention to the use of underage girl prostitutes. A brief alliance of Anglican bishops, free thinkers, and reformers then succeeded in a campaign to raise the age of consent from thirteen to sixteen years (Weeks 87).[8] On this issue of child prostitution, Deborah Gorham notes a division of attitudes to girl children who were conceived as either "the female child redeemer" or, on the other hand, "the little girl as evil incarnate." Illicit sexual intercourse was seen as producing permanent corruption, and "the earlier the 'corruption' took place, the more ingrained was the evil" (371). Stead's colorful version was that "the foul passion of the man seemed to enter into the helpless victim of his lust" *(Pall Mall Gazette* 8 July 1885, qtd. by Gorham 372). These attitudes are obviously relevant to *The Turn of the Screw's* dualisms, as is the direct connection of this crusade to the "germ" of the story, which lay in an anecdote by Archbishop Benson. It is, however, striking that studies of the history of sexuality in this period do not deal with child sexual abuse. Although documentary evidence from the period is often quite remarkably outspoken about homosexuality, masturbation, or "extreme" sexual practices, we find in the documentary evidence no more than innuendoes: "if only the parents are not completely demoralised and actually teach the children evil ways" (Bremner 2:592). G. J. Barker-Benfield's study of nineteenth-century American sexuality similarly does not acknowledge the existence of child abuse; his chapter on children is focused on the then-contemporary concerns about onanism.[9] Another and more famous example of the suppressions operating in society about this issue is of course the shift in Freud's reading of the meaning of his patients' accounts of sexual experience in childhood, away from their truth as testimony and towards instead the *symbolic* registration of infantile desire (Beigel 248–255).[10]

What this perspective on *The Turn of the Screw* produces is a reorientation of our position, a "change of gestalt and visible symmetries" so severe as to amount almost to a reversal. Instead of seeing the children as simply the occasion of adult interpretation and fantasy, we come to see implied pretextual but determining experiences as the cause of that whole problematic. Their actions and attitudes sketch for the inexperienced governess a history, a situation, that she cannot understand but equally cannot ignore, causing her to fill in the spaces of their communications with appropriate figures.[11]

No critic can resist another turn: there is in the governess herself an element that can perhaps be recognized as a species of sadism: for her own reasons she keeps the children incommunicado, retaining the letters they write to their uncle (54), and making them the *victims* — it is her own word — of her remorseless observation and lucidity: "My lucidity must have seemed awful, but the charming creatures who were the victims of it" (48; ch. 12) provides a typical example. Her imagination of them has a sinister note; she sees them as vulnerable in their beauty, as "blameless and foredoomed" (38; ch. 9), and muses on how the rough future would "handle them and might bruise them" (15; ch. 3). In this connection we may wish to put another gloss on the way that the governess finds herself repeating the actions of the ghosts: staring in at the window, sitting at the foot of the stairs or at the writing desk. At least potentially she too is drawn into a repetition of the servants' sadistic use of the children, their desire — when alive, and now in the children's memory — to get closer to them, to engage with them sexually.

And yet another turn: the governess thereby simply repeats the action of the text as a whole, a sadistic mechanism in which the children, and the young *ingenue* herself, are put on display, exposed to "the very worst action small victims so conditioned might be conceived as subject to," for the delectation, amusement, and even sexual frisson of those who, in James's words, are "not easily caught . . . the jaded, the disillusioned, the fastidious" (Preface; 176, 172). And here we must take some notice of the extraordinary way in which the children are constructed by the text, their uncanny beauty and charm. In his book *Child-Loving* James Kincaid has drawn attention to the stylized erotic presentation of children in Victorian literature in terms that virtually impose upon the reader a pedophilic voyeurism and potential sadism:

> This good child is, after all, so invitingly vacant that the goodness is utter blankness. Such blankness can suggest that the child's goodness, like that of Oliver Twist, is ordained, impervious to any wicked influence. Such a figuring may ironically open the good child up to sexual desire as no amount of imputed knowingness could. This blank child could be so loved, so made love to, that the goodness might rub off; if not, one can move forward with a clear conscience, the child being so very incorruptible. Doubtless this is one reason the Oliver image is so popular and why the child can be subject to such flagrant and unrestrained sadistic sexual mishandling. (223)

From this point of view, too, it is inevitable that a link be made between the sexualized child and death, both marking the end of innocence, substituting for the loss of the eroticized child-figure consequent on the process of growing up, and finally perhaps expressing the repression of the adult reader's inadmissable pleasures. That it should be Miles who dies, rather than the equally beautiful Flora, who simply turns hard and coarse (in effect, adult?) and is thereupon immediately shuffled off the scene, suggests that the focus here is mostly on homosexual attraction, in keeping with the period's dominant preoccupations: "What interested the Victorians in the way of perversion, at least in the last three decades of the century, seems primarily to have been not the size (or age) of the people involved, but the gender. The 'invert' or increasingly the 'homosexual' held public and medical attention" (191). The only textual evidence that we really have for Miles's presentation as an object of homosexual love is that Quint was "too free . . . with everybody" and that Miles spent long hours "going off with the fellow." That, and perhaps the stress on the school dismissal ("stupid sordid headmasters"), given that schools — even such elevated schools as Eton — were in the public eye for scandals involving homosexuality and notorious for the practice of beating their boys. For the rest, Miles is represented through the admiring intimacy of the governess's view of him — which enables, we might argue, guiltless proximities forbidden to a male onlooker.

That this representation of the eroticized child should also implicate James as well as those jaded and fastidious readers may give occasion for pause. But as Allon White remarks, "[t]he fascinating thing in James is the complex interpenetration of social and sexual censorship against a felt desire to 'know' things which he could not reveal without indicting himself by his own standards" (135). Most critics have displayed an astonishing reluctance to take any formal account of the pattern of (homosexual) desire displayed in James's life. As Eve Sedgwick remarks, perhaps they have been "motivated in this active incuriosity by a desire to protect James from homophobic misreadings in a perennially repressive sexual climate."[12] Similarly I would argue that the resistance to acknowledging that James, however unconsciously, may have based his charming ghost story on the sexual abuse of children has effectively energized the critical discussion into mutually opposing poles of interpretations based on *either* metaphysical evil *or* spinsterish heterosexual frustration.

James's disclaimer "Only make the reader's general vision of evil intense enough, I said to myself — and that is already a charming job — and his own experience, his own imagination, his own sympathy (with the children) and horror (of their false friends) will supply him quite sufficiently with the particulars. Make him *think* the evil, make him think it for himself, and you are released from weak specifications" (Preface 176), acknowledges the unsayable as nearly as possible. His success in making readers "think the evil" was apparent in contemporary reviews: "The feeling after perusal of the horrible story is that one has been assisting in an outrage upon the holiest and sweetest fountain of human innocence, and helping to debauch — at least by helplessly standing by — the pure and trusting nature of children. Human imagination can go no further into infamy, literary art could not be used with more refined subtlety of spiritual defilement" *(The Independent,* 5 January, 1899, qtd. in James, *Turn* 175). That he did not himself, however, consciously register the suggestion of reference to child abuse is suggested by his reaction to such reviews:

> How can I feel my calculation to have failed, my wrought suggestion not to have worked, that is, on my being assailed, as has befallen me, with the charge of a monstrous emphasis, the charge of all indecently expatiating? There is not only from beginning to end of the matter not an inch of expatiation, but my values are positively all blanks save so far as an excited horror, a promoted pity, a created expertness — on which punctual effects of strong causes no writer can ever fail to plume himself — proceed to read into them more or less fantastic figures. (Preface; 177)

That the story is constructed of "blanks" does not however preclude its having a strong current of suggestiveness as to their probable content. As John Carlos

Rowe says when discussing class issues in *The Turn of the Screw:* ''There is no 'proper' undecidability; it is always the effect or product of a certain forgetting of motives and drives that have awakened interest'' (145). To evade the censor in this manner is paradoxically to reinforce the sense of censorable (censurable) material. In a letter to Louis Waldstein in October 1898, on ''That Wanton Little Tale,'' James expressed in sentimental terms a hint of the complex that I have been here attempting to eludidate: ''My bogey-tale dealt with things so hideous that I felt to save it at all it needed some infusion of beauty or prettiness, and the beauty of the pathetic was the only attainable — was indeed inevitable. But ah, the exposure indeed, the helpless plasticity of childhood that isn't dear or sacred to *some*body! That *was* my little tragedy'' (qtd. in *Turn* 110). James's description of his intended readers as ''the jaded, disillusioned and fastidious,'' could however more harshly be seen as fin de siècle code for the knowing, or even corrupted, who relish the poignancy of the victims' exposure to the ''very worst,'' the worst, that is, that the culture contains but attempts not to admit into its discourse.

University of East Anglia, Norwich

NOTES

1. Here for example is the hallucination of Cranfill and Clark, seeing an invisible rowing boat:

> The explanation [of Mrs. Grose's reluctance to take the long way around the lake] is of course a simple one: there is no need to walk at all. Flora has of course *not* taken the boat. When the governess states that she has, Mrs. Grose stares ''at the vacant mooring place'' because it is *not* vacant. Before the very eyes of her confidante the governess, by failing to see what is there, betrays her derangement.

Cranfill and Clark then manage to *not* see the boat where it is; in the governess's words

> in the course of but few minutes more we reached a point from which we found the boat to be where I had supposed it. It had been intentionally left as much as possible out of sight and was tied to one of the stakes of a fence that came, just there, down to the brink and that had been an assistance to disembarking. I recognised, as I looked at the pair of short thick oars, quite safely drawn up, the prodigious character of the feat for a little girl.

To these critics, her version is ''stark, staring mad,'' and they continue:

> Miles and Flora devise, with devilish ingenuity, to frustrate their governess' eternal vigilance by Miles's piano playing so that Flora may slip away for her rendezvous with the ghost of Miss Jessel. The ghost and the child — though "at such times she's not a child: she's an old, old woman" — row the old flat-bottomed boat (each plying an oar?) across the lake, secrete it in a cove conveniently masked by trees and a projection of the bank, and thus secure for themselves a chance to carry on, clandestinely, afar, without fear of immediate interruption, their abominable communion. Oh, Laws, Laws, Laws! [as Mrs. Grose says]. (63–65)

2. See my article "The Occultism of the Text" on related points about the nature of the reading experience.
3. Warminski so argues in his study of "The Altar of the Dead," which ends (of course) in irony, the "negative echo" of the nameless woman's "Don't talk of it — don't think of it; forget it!" This is arguably just where we should begin.
4. The rhetorical figure of *preterition* is at work here, as conventionally, implying homosexuality, "the love that dare not speak its name." See Sedgwick 202.
5. I have referred extensively to Rashkin's useful summary of Abraham and Torok's thought.
6. Quoted by Sigmund Freud in "The 'Uncanny' " ("Unheimlich") 225.
7. See Rashkin 41.
8. James had the germ of his story told to him by an Anglican bishop, Edward White Benson, the Archbishop of Canterbury, with whose sons, A. C. and E. F. he closely associated (*Turn* 106).
9. But what little evidence we do find suggests that child sexual abuse must have been both endemic and under-reported. This was certainly the case during the twentieth century. A 1970 study of later-life effects of abuse, for example, found that on the evidence of respondents in a survey, sexual offences against children were rarely (in as little as 6% of cases) reported to the police (Shiloh 403). Curiously enough, for our purposes, that study also observed a disproportion in social class between middle-class victims and lower-class offenders, whom the authors tentatively identified as likely to be janitors or clerks in stores (415). In an earlier period we might wish to add "bad" servants to the list. This survey involved offences from considerably earlier than the date of the report, since it looked at lifetime effects of abuse. The social-class figures of course would be affected by issues of reporting, survey volunteers, etc. On the likelihood of large numbers of unreported cases in earlier generations, see Search 10.
10. In "A Child is Being Beaten" Freud shows how he relegated such abuse to the phantasy realm. See 188–89.
11. The problem of the Governess's accurate description of Quint has been variously addressed, perhaps most effectively by Renner, who discusses the stereotypical features of the apparition.
12. Sedgwick observes:

> It is possible that they fear that, because of the asymmetrically marked structure of heterosexist discourse, *any* discussion of homosexual desires or literary content will marginalize him (or them?) as, simply, *homosexual.* It is possible that they desire to protect him from what they imagine as anachronistically gay readings, based on a late twentieth-century vision of men's desire for men that is more stabilized and culturally compact than James's own. It is possible that they read James himself as, in

> his work, positively refusing or evaporating this element of his eros, translating lived homosexual desires, where he had them, into written heterosexual ones so thoroughly and so successfully that the difference *makes* no difference, the transmutation leaves no residue. Or it is possible that, believing — as I do — that James often, though not always, attempted such a disguise or transmutation, but reliably left a residue both of material that he did not attempt to transmute and of material that could be transmuted only rather violently and messily, some critics are reluctant to undertake the "attack" on James's candor or artistic unity that could be a next step of that argument. Any of these critical motives would be understandable, but their net effect is the usual repressive one of elision and subsumption of supposedly embarrassing material. In dealing with the multiple valences of sexuality, critics' choices should not be limited to crudities of disruption or silences of orthodox enforcement. (197)

I am not assuming here that James's putative homosexuality should be considered as directive of his choices in *The Turn of the Screw,* only that a similar collective critical act of denial and not-knowing seems to take place when confronting the issue.

WORKS

Abraham Nicholas and Maria Torok. *The Wolf Man's Magic Word: A Cryptonymy* 1976. Trans. Nicholas Rand. Minneapolis: U of Minnesota P, 1986.

Abraham Nicholas, "Notes on the Phantom: A Complement to Freud's Metapsychology." Trans. Nicholas Rand. *Critical Inquiry* 13.2 (Winter 1987): 287–92.

———. "The Phantom of Hamlet or the Sixth Act: Preceded by the Intermission of Truth." *Diacritics 18.4 (Winter 1988): 2–19.*

Barker-Benfield, G. J. *The Horrors of the Half-Known Life: Male Attitudes toward Women and Sexuality in Nineteenth-Century America.* New York: Harper Colophon, 1976.

Beigel, H.G. *Advances in Sex Research.* New York: Harper & Row, 1963

Bremner, Robert H. ed. *Children and Youth in America: A Documentary History.* Vol. 2. Cambridge, MA: Harvard U P, 1971.

Cranfill, Thomas Mabry, and Robert Lanier Clark, Jr., *An Anatomy of "The Turn of the Screw."* 1965. (New York: Gordian Press, 1971)

Felman, Shoshana. *"Turning the Screw of Interpretation."* in *Literature and Psychoanalysis: The Question of Reading: Otherwise.* Ed. Shoshana Felman. Baltimore: Johns Hopkins UP, 1982.

Freud, Sigmund. *"The 'Uncanny.'" Standard Edition of the Complete Psychological Works of Sigmund Freud* Ed. and trans. James Strachey. London: Hogarth, 1953. 17:215–52.

———. "A Child is Being Beaten." *Standard Edition. 179–204.*

Gorham, Deborah. The " 'Maiden Tribute of Modern Babylon' Re-examined: Child Prostitution and the Idea of Childhood in Late-Victorian England." *Victorian Studies* 21 3 (Spring 1978): 217–52.

———. "A Child is Being Beaten." *Standard Edition.* 17 179–204.

James, Henry. *The Art of the Novel: Critical Prefaces,* ed. R. P. Blackmur. New York: Scribners, 1962.

———. *The Turn of the Screw,* ed. Robert Kimbrough. New York: Norton Critical Editions, 1966.

Kincaid, James. *Child-Loving: The Erotic Child in Victorian Literature.* London: Routledge, 1992.
Lloyd Smith, Allan G. *Uncanny American Fiction.* London: Macmillan, 1989.
———. "The Occultism of the Text." *Poetics Today* 3 4 (Autumn 1982): 5–20.
Nardin, Jane. "The Turn of the Screw: The Victorian Background." *Mosaic* 12 1 (1978): 131–42.
Rand, Nicholas. "Towards a Cryptonomy of Literature." Translator's introduction to Abraham and Torok.
Rashkin, Esther. "Tools for a New Psychoanalytic Literary Criticism: The Work of Abraham and Torok." *Diacritics* 18.4 (Winter 1988): 31–52.
Renner, Stanley. "Sexual Hysteria, Physiognomical Bogeymen, and the 'Ghosts' in *The Turn of the Screw.*" *Nineteenth-Century Literature* 43 2 (1988): 175–94.
Rowe, John Carlos. *The Theoretical Dimensions of Henry James.* London: Methuen, 1985.
Search, G. *The Last Taboo: Sexual Abuse of Children.* London: Penguin, 1988.
Sedgwick, Eve Kosofsky. *Epistemology of the Closet.* London: Harvester Wheatsheaf, 1991
Shiloh, Ailon. *Studies in Human Sexual Behaviour: The American Scene.* Springfield, IL: Thomas, 1970.
Warminski, Andrzej. "Reading Over Endless Histories: Henry James's 'The Altar of the Dead' " *Yale French Studies* 74 (1988): 261–84.
Weeks, Jeffrey. *Sex, Politics, and Society. London: Longman, 1981.*
White, Allon. The Uses of Obscurity: The Fiction of Early Modernism. London: Routledge, 1981.

DISCOURSE AND SILENCE IN THE VICTORIAN FAMILY CELL: PROBLEMS OF SUBJECTIVITY IN *THE HISTORY OF SEXUALITY: VOL. I*

By Margot Gayle Backus

> "I think there's a pain somewhere in the room," said Mrs. Gradgrind, "but I couldn't positively say that I have got it."
>
> *Hard Times.*

I. Foucault's *Othered* Victorians

ALTHOUGH MICHEL FOUCAULT'S CENTRAL arguments in *The History of Sexuality, Volume I* turn on social changes occurring in eighteenth-century England and continental Europe, Victorian England constitutes the proving ground for most of the work's central assertions. Foucault's argument moves dialectically between eighteenth-century changes in the structure of the patriarchal family and late nineteenth-century social transformations through which the middle-class family cell discursively extended the pleasurable and quasi-erotic potentials inherent both in speech and in silence and, in the process, made itself increasingly available as a charged site for the extension of various institutional powers. Victorian society constituted an especially inviting site for an initial working out of Foucault's methodology because of this period's purportedly exemplary sexual repression, a mechanism the pre-eminence of which Foucault challenges.

Foucault disrupts prior notions of social power relations as predicated upon mechanisms of repression imposed from above by identifying discursive pleasure rather than bodily prohibition as the most compelling means through which power relations are constituted within the modern Anglo-European social order. In order to privilege the pleasurable incitement to discourse as a key factor in the production of societal power relations, Foucault contests prior models of Victorian society that posit legal, economic and social repression as that society's defining characteristic.[1] He critiques the popular construction of Victorian society as a monological social order governed exclusively by mechanisms of internal and external repression. He also dismisses contemporary dualistic models that complicated notions of a monologically repressed and sexless Victorian society by collapsing them, via Steven Marcus's *The Other Victorians,* into the model they formerly opposed.

In his introduction to *The History of Sexuality, Vol. I,* Foucault implicitly critiques Marcus's thesis by connecting it to the repressive hypothesis, the notion of Victorian repression he sets out to debunk:

> . . . those "other Victorians," as Steven Marcus would say — seem to have surreptitiously transferred the pleasures that are unspoken into the order of things that are counted. Word and gestures, quietly authorized, could be exchanged [in the brothel and the mental hospital] at the going rate. . . . Everywhere else, modern puritanism imposed its triple edict of taboo, nonexistence, and silence. (4–5)

Although Foucault does not go on to gainsay Marcus directly, in this opening move he weaves Marcus's construction of a dichotomous and self-eliding Victorian society into the conventional account of the "common sense" history of sexuality he opposes. This move suggests that Foucault, in order to reverse his readers' conditioned expectations concerning repression, first found it necessary somehow to dismiss the problems of sexual and economic exploitation and denial associated with the enormous Victorian trade in prostitutes. His discourse-centered, unitary account of modern subjectivity is, therefore, founded from the first on the occlusion of the experience of a vast number of women, men, and children whose lives and perspectives would have posed a formidable challenge to his own account of the implantation of eros into modern Anglo-European subjectivity through the installation of a pleasurable inducement to speak and self-interrogate.

In *The Other Victorians: A Study of Sexuality and Pornography in Mid-Nineteenth-Century England,* Steven Marcus challenged standard constructions of a sexually repressed Victorian era with his readings from a rich cross section of Victorian pornography and accounts of sexual practices, heterosexual and homosexual. From the standpoint of feminist literary criticism, Marcus's work was significant because it revived a long dormant awareness of the prevalence of prostitution and pornography within Victorian society and, moreover, explicated the impact of pornography and prostitution on "respectable" Victorian writing and vice versa. Despite his production of a series of fascinating readings foregrounding the interpenetration of pornographic, medical, and high literary discourses, however, Marcus ultimately salvaged earlier stereotypes of Victorian repression through a model that split Victorian society into isolated spheres, separate and opposed. The familiar repressive Victorian social order remained intact within Marcus's model, where it was incorporated as an autonomous sphere within a larger, binary social order. Outside the purview of Victorian repression, Marcus located a corresponding sphere of cultural alterity in which lust and carnality, elsewhere prohibited, were promoted as the sole motivating forces in human behavior.

Marcus's model was static and crudely hydraulic, but it did significantly and productively complicate critical perspectives on Victorian socio-cultural production. Moreover, the readings on which Marcus's model was based, but for which it could not, ironically, account, suggest that the pornographic discourse of the "Other Victorians" was constitutive of rather than alien to Victorian subjectivity *through* its very purported indecipherability. One example of the discursive power that is brought into being through the unacknowledged structuring presence of pornography as a "discipline" or way of knowing, for instance, occurs in Marcus's reading of a passage in William Acton's *The Functions and Disorders of the Reproductive Organs* (1857). In this passage, Acton elaborates an entire (implicit) "system of beliefs" through his discussion of the purported asexuality of "the 'majority of women.' " The characteristics of "the world which Acton creates," Marcus observes, are "nearly related" to "the world envisaged by pornography" (32). Marcus astutely deciphers the term "the majority of women" as a false generic through which the category of class is elided. Through a series of such elisions, working class women are, in Acton's work and elsewhere, reaffirmed as the legitimate targets of male sexual aggression, while the responsibility for domesticating male sexuality is "projected onto the role of [bourgeois] woman," who is thereby saddled with the responsibility of "sav[ing] man from himself" (32). Marcus explicates and critiques the irrational impact of pornographic "common sense" on the discourse of Victorian social theory, however, without actually accounting for the structuring relationship that clearly exists in this passage and elsewhere between Victorian sexual literature and praxis and Victorian "repression." He acknowledges that both "the world Acton creates" and the world of pornography feature a "split or divided consciousness" that is represented in the realm of pornography as "subversive and liberating" but in Acton's work as "grimly scientific and . . . tragic" (32). What Marcus fails to account for is the reality effect that pornographic conventions outside of pornographic literature achieve through covert appeals to "fantas[ies] [that] tend . . . to be larger [than those structuring the conventions of other discourses], [and a] submission of one's sense of reality to the fantasy [that is] more peremptory and absolute" (60). Such embedded pornographic conventions efface subjectivity by, for instance, dividing up sexual desire among women by class, with those within one group having none, and those in another group having it in such superfluity as to be in fact incapable of being raped or sexually exploited, since they "always already" incite sexual violation.

Marcus observes a similar effect at work in Henry Spencer Ashbee's *Index Librorum Prohibitorum: being Notes Bio-Biblio-Icono-graphical and Critical,* a privately printed 1877 volume purporting to explicate Victorian pornography and sexual praxis, in which women are said to "delight in administering the birch,'' observing that ''what began as investigation of a literature concludes as propaganda for a reality'' (60). He concedes that children were undoubtedly beaten as punishment, and that an enormous body of literature devoted to the subject testifies to the eroticization of flagellation in the imagination of some adult Victorians, but he points out that at a certain point ''a shift of levels of reality occurs, and the masculine sexual fantasy is projected onto women'' (61). A model capable of explaining the relationship between the two spheres of discourse — the socio-scientistic and the pornographic — as they coexist within the text would take into account the ways in which Ashbee creates a crisis of interpretation that emerges through the juxtaposition of differentially-empowered and authorized discourses. One of these, the medical, scientistic discourse, *must* be attended to; the other, the pornographic discourse of flagellation, *must* be discounted or, more accurately, relegated to a textual unconscious.

While Marcus's reading of the complex interaction between pornography and medical, sociological, and literary discourses implies an a priori, ongoing, and highly-structured interpenetration *between* the two spheres he identifies, Foucault's argument collapses the sphere of the ''Other Victorians'' into the more generalized world of the Victorian family, publishing, academy, and economy. The univocality that he ascribes to these various institutions reformulates the discourse of the ''Other Victorians'' as one among an array of sexualized discourses rather than as a specialized meta-discourse with a distinctive, constitutive relationship to its formally authorized and acknowledged institutional counterparts. In dismissing the dialectical potential of Marcus's model along with its static hydraulicism, Foucault in effect reinstates the undifferentiated Victorian subject that Marcus, and a generation of feminists who developed and refined similar but more sophisticated models, problematized.[2] The implied Foucauldian subject that emerges through this process, moreover, appears surprisingly bourgeois and masculine in its constitution. This implied subject, with its endless self-scrutiny, its interior dialogues, and its ongoing external vigilance, interpretation and self-expression, resembles the Cartesian individualist subject that Regenia Gagnier — whose exhaustive reading of Victorian autobiography qualifies her as an expert on Victorian subjectivity — identifies with male members of the Victorian bourgeoisie (148–49) more than it resembles Victorian workers or women of any class (95).

The emergence of bourgeois subjectivity in literature and culture has been increasingly recognized, through works such as Gagnier's *Subjectivities* and Firdous Azim's *The Colonial Rise of the Novel,* as having been enacted only at the expense of other perspectives, which bourgeois subjectivity eclipsed, or, as Azim would have it, serially obliterated (88). Azim illustrates her point concerning the violence that is routinely done to the perspectives of ''the Other subject, differentiated by class, race and gender'' (88) through the novel's consolidation of a unitary, bourgeois perspective by citing the words of Virginia Woolf, who disapproved of a number of troubling moments of duality in *Jane Eyre* in which more than one comforting, unitary perspective vied for ascendancy. Woolf complains of what she senses as Brontë's recurring "desire to plead some personal cause or to make a character the mouthpiece of some personal discontent or grievance" and observes that such special pleading "always has a distressing effect as if the spot at which the reader's attention if diverted were suddenly twofold instead of single" (Azim 105). Azim observes, in return, that: "the desired unity of reading that Woolf suggests can only result from a writing that ignores or remains unaware of social divisions and grievances" (105). In a set of "cautionary prescriptions" (Foucault 98) that I will take up at greater length in the next section, Foucault provides for precisely such a "desired unity of reading" by expressly banning consideration of "who has the power in the order of sexuality . . . and who is deprived of it" (99). In so doing, he renders subjectivity multiple and situational, but, ironically, he simultaneously relegates women, children, and workers throughout this now multiple and situational society to a realm of silence and shadow. Without the sense of uneven and asymmetrical social spheres that Marcus's analysis introduced, dynamic, oscillating discourses co-existing within and across Victorian social formations and fueled by interactions between differentially materially- and socially-empowered subjects are subsumed under a monolithic, unitary Victorian subject. Unlike the earlier, undifferentiatedly repressed Victorian subject, however, this subject is constituted not predominantly through social, legal, and intrapsychic forms of repression, but through social, legal, and intrapsychic inducements to discourse.[3]

Despite the gains this founding move enables, its elision of potentially differential relationships to speech and sexuality conditioned by class, gender, or, as I will argue, age, is a costly one. In this essay, I will assess the price of Foucault's dismissal of the work of Steven Marcus and a generation of feminist Victorianists as it is exacted in one specific area: his analysis of the Victorian family. My own counter-reading of Victorian subjectivity and the familial sex/gender system that gave rise to it conceives of these differential relationships as being, as *The Other Victorians* suggests, a central facet of the Victorian social order. In order to explore and critique the impact of Foucault's model on his analysis of Victorian culture, I will explicate several key passages in *The History of Sexuality, Vol. I* and the representational and theoretical rationales that underwrite them.

II. High Theory and the Problem of the Unitary Subject

In a well-known and influential essay, Abdul JanMohamed criticizes Homi Bhabha for countering Edward Said's "suggestion that colonial power and discourse is possessed entirely by the coloniser," by "assert[ing], without providing any explanation, the unity of the colonial subject (both coloniser and colonised)." JanMohamed concedes that he "do[es] not wish to rule out, *a priori*, the possibility that at some rarified theoretical level the varied material and discursive antagonisms between conquerors and natives can be reduced to the workings of a single 'subject' ''; but he argues that ''such a unity, let alone its value, must be demonstrated, not assumed'' (59–60) and argues for the reinstatement of Franz Fanon's ''definition of the conqueror/native relation as a 'Manichean' [or zero sum] struggle.'' This Manichean relationship, as Said famously observes (7), plays out representationally through a potentially-infinite series of morally-coded and power-imbued binary divisions (60).

It will be easy enough for most readers to see why such an intervention would be necessary in the field of Third World literature. In other areas of cultural analysis, however, the tendency of ''high theory'' to posit a unitary national or historical subject that is brought into being through the interactions of heterogenous players upon an implicitly even social terrain has stood more or less unchallenged.[4] Such unitary constructions, however, when uncomplicated by an accompanying attentiveness to socially- and economically-enforced power differentials, may obscure and thereby naturalize existing power inequities among first-world subjects. Foucault's revisionary reading of Victorian society and the Victorian family in *The History of Sexuality, Vol. 1* constitutes an at once disarmingly open and confoundingly slippery example of both the gains and the losses that accrue to such an approach.

Foucault's construction of the Victorian subject yields great analytical insight into power dynamics within Victorian society as a whole. The constitution of power in *The History of Sexuality, Vol. 1* as local, multiple, and consensual has unquestionably provided an enabling model for contemporary political praxis.[5] Paradoxically, however, in order to obtain its counter-intuitive emphasis on local effects and articulations, Foucault's model effaces the mass-scale material and representational power relations among heterogenous subjects through which these effects are brought into being.[6]

Foucault is able to make the basic assertion that Victorian discussion pertaining to sex, sexual activities, and sexuality was never silenced or repressed, that sex was always spoken, by everyone, all the time, or was withheld from speech or made secret only as a means by which Victorians intensified its importance and hence their pleasure, only by blotting out or making ineligible for our consideration the subjectivity of those whose bodies were the providers *of* the pleasure which he claims was the main enticement for (presumably) all Victorian subjects. He illustrates the ''singular imperialism that compels everyone to transform their sexuality into a perpetual discourse . . . [through] manifold mechanisms which, in the areas of economy, pedagogy, medicine, and justice, incite, extract, distribute, and institutionalize sexual discourse'' (33), through a story that, in its mode of narration, illustrates my point.

In 1867 a ''simple-minded'' farm hand who ''obtained a few caresses from a little girl'' was reported by the girl's parents to the mayor, by the mayor to the police, and by the police to psychiatrists, who measured his cranium, asked him innumerable questions, and, finally, institutionalized him for life (31–32).

The focus of this exemplary elaboration of sex into discourse is on discourse and not on the bodies (or not equally on all the bodies) these discourses render in Gagnier's apt term for the condition of Victorian women "ideologically somatic" (95). It undoubtedly may be that in 1867 an indigent farm hand was institutionalized for life for participating in the "inconsequential bucolic pleasures" that "a few [consensual] caresses" of his penis might arguably have represented. The coy reticence of Foucault's account, however, along with its notable recourse to a vocabulary conventional to the romantic, pastoral tradition that reconstitutes the rape of peasant women as an innocent, aristocratic idyll, cast more than a shadow of doubt on the absolute faithfulness of this rendition.[7] Moreover, the "innocent," "pastoral" events Foucault recounts derive much of their charm from the author's exclusion of the subjectivity of the little girl, which would, were it included, undoubtedly unsettle this otherwise beguiling account. This passage thus reenacts the same pattern that Marcus identified in the work of Acton and Ashbee: a silenced female body, positioned by the narrator within a system of sexualized power dynamics, eroticizes and thereby structures the reader's interpretation of a purportedly innocent and unbiased account. The reader is encouraged to identify with the male subject's sexual pleasure (here in order to solicit the reader's outrage at that subject's eventual reduction, via discourse, to the status of object), while questions concerning the impact of the sexual events the text records on the objectified female are suppressed. The reader's pleasure in the text, and his or her sympathetic identification with its male subject, are purchased only at the price of the dramatic relegation of an Other in the text to silence.

Throughout *The History of Sexuality, Vol. I* a textual focus on sexuality as discourse works as did the emphasis on the experiences of the farm hand in the above account. In both cases, a strict focus on the subject as being seduced, enjoined, or coerced into speech effaces the experiences of those whose lives are ruled by an edict of sexual silence or who are, like the little girl in the account, constituted as a specialized form of property that produces, among other things, accounts which may be, depending on the needs and wishes of their direct overseers, appropriated and circulated or suppressed. Prostitutes, rape victims, and sexually-abused children most saliently, but also Victorian women and children more generally, were silenced by dint of a sexuality that was "always already" attributed to them, as Foucault acknowledges when he observes that "a silence" among children grew in proportion to the proliferation of adult, institutional discourses on children's sexuality (27). The silences that enveloped those whose bodies provided the occasion for these discourses "[are] not one but many," as Foucault observes, "and they are an integral part of the strategies that underlie and permeate discourses" (27). If such silences are, however, an integral part of the discourses he interrogates, the nature of their role in the production of discourse is never elaborated on, and they are never mentioned again in the course of the volume.

The pointed absence from Foucault's analysis of a category in which to place sexual *dis*-pleasure, sexual victimization, or the sexual destruction of children and/or women is most evident in his discussion of the incest taboo in section 3 of "The Deployment of Sexuality." In this section, Foucault dances around the question of incest without ever unambiguously acknowledging that the "affective intensification of the family space" (109) he explores incites incest. He repeatedly hints that the post-industrial "family cell" symbolically forms itself around the incestuous exploitation of children by adults (at the emotional or physical level) regardless of whether the sexual violation of a specific child occurs or not, since the system prohibits not incest, but children talking openly about their own bodily and emotional experiences. Foucault's brief acknowledgement and dismissal of the question of silence earlier in the book, however, would lead readers to suppose that if repressively-enforced silence were integral to the family system he describes he would say so. His earlier denigration of direct prohibition within bourgeois western society as power's most "negative and emaciated form" (86) does not prepare us to find repression at the heart of the heterosexual patriarchal nuclear family, the social structure at the center of the social system Foucault redefines (38). The structures of the family that Foucault describes are, however, unquestionably Manichean; the family cell is ordered through a logic of binary power differentials that are, although he never says so, constituted through a converse relationship of discourse to silence, and self-expression to externally-imposed and internal repression.

The dynamics of Foucault's family cell are, in fact, productive in the manner that he describes precisely owing to the enormous power differentials that characterize relations with the patriarchal nuclear family. In order to outline the productive role of the family cell within society, however, Foucault found it necessary to set aside any consideration of the dynamic and immensely productive power differentials through which previous repressive, externally-imposed structures of power were incorporated into the patriarchal nuclear family.[8] He invokes four "cautionary prescriptions," including the "rules of continual variations," which specify that we must

> not look for who has the power in the order of sexuality (men, adults, parents, doctors) and who is deprived of it (women, adolescents, children, patients); nor for who has the right to know and who is forced to remain ignorant. We must seek rather the pattern of the modifications which the relationships of force imply by the very nature of their process. (99)

Through such exclusions, Foucault was enabled to bring forward, in its boldest outline, an extraordinary new way of looking at power. In an example given under the "rules of continual variations," for instance, Foucault points out that if we view the relationship between the parents, child, and psychiatrist as a matrix of transformation, rather than as a static exercise of ones *with* power over ones who lack power, we see that it is through the child-psychiatrist relationship that the sexuality of adults was called into question.

Obviously, we could usefully look at equivalent matrices of transformation that the growing volume of child sexual abuse charges brought against adults and juveniles in the United States may be enabling in the same way. In fact, Alexander Cockburn has been doing just this in a series of articles in *The Nation* documenting the opportunistic role that Attorney General Janet Reno appears to have played in several cases of alleged child abuse during her tenure as Dade County prosecutor. In one such case, a Cuban immigrant was sentenced to six life terms plus 165 years on the basis of testimony obtained from his wife, a seventeen-year-old undocumented Honduran worker. These events occurred after the couple's babysitting service became the target of allegations by the congregation of a local fundamentalist church. Testimony corroborating the allegations was obtained only after the seventeen-year-old woman was subjected to months of solitary confinement, including periods during which she was held naked, purportedly to prevent suicide attempts. During lengthy periods of isolation, she was subjected to repetitive and leading questioning by a spate of dubious "experts." At her trial, she stated "I am innocent of all those charges. . . . I am pleading guilty to get all of this over . . . for my own good" (297). Cockburn's analysis horrifyingly outlines the means by which a politically-ambitious public official exploited public paranoia to advance her own career, further attenuating legal protections for socially vulnerable persons in the process.

On the other hand, such a mode of analysis, directed as it is toward articulated power relations forged between children and law enforcement officials, perhaps necessarily effaces the differential power relations between these subjects that made such articulations possible in the first place. For instance, in the example that Foucault gives, in which a psychiatrist-child relationship forms a matrix of transformation through which parental sexuality is called into question, the child provides an anchor for the formation of a new social technology specifically because of children's powerlessness within modern society. Children's bodies and inner lives were, after all, specifically excluded from protections guaranteeing the bodies and psyches of (non-marginal) adults in the emergence of the liberal humanist dispensation. The individualist Cartesian subjectivity enabled and valorized under this dispensation was, in fact, constructed in opposition to and at the expense of children. As Ashis Nandy has observed, in seventeenth-century Europe children were re-constituted as both "blank slate[s] on which adults must write their moral code" and "inferior version[s] of maturity, less productive and ethical, and badly contaminated by the playful, irresponsible and spontaneous aspects of human nature" (14–15). The new Manichean opposition that resulted soon entered the rhetoric of international affairs, where it served to explain why natives cast as "children" in need of socializing were not yet prepared to enjoy the same fruits of liberty and democracy that were extended to literate, native-born adults within the colonizing powers.

Bearing the history of the subject position "child" and its relationship to the subject position "native" in mind, it becomes clear that Janet Reno was able to advance her own career through a series of attacks launched against purported child abusers largely because she chose her suspects wisely. Had Reno's career emerged in a locale that was not riven by the vast power differentials that traverse the Miami area, with its multiple and entrenched class, race, national, linguistic, and cultural cleavages, she could not so readily have broadly reconstituted fundamental civil liberties in a flamboyantly panicked response to unsubstantiated charges of child abuse.

Concerning the actual sexual exploitation of children, Foucault remains mute, although he makes a series of nervous, excited rushes at what appears to constitute his underlying subject throughout section three of "The Deployment of Sexuality." He repeatedly points to the incest taboo as constituting an obligatory ideological bulwark against the affective intensification that industrial capitalism's reconfiguration of the family precipitated. He strongly suggests that the supposed taboo against incest that social scientists of the nineteenth-century were so eager to discover within all societies has not been widely upheld in modern European society (109). Ultimately, however, Foucault fails to acknowledge the implications of a purported taboo that acts, insofar as it constitutes a blanket alibi unconditionally denying the possibility of certain acts or even desires, as a veritable incitement to sexualize children and thus as the guarantor of a sexual secret at the core of family life. Foucault does acknowledge the significance of the eroticization of parent-child bonds for the intense affective bonds out of which the modern patriarchal family was forged. His approach, however, in so far as it discounts physical and psychic repression as constitutive forces in modern society, minimizes the relevance of power differentials within the family for an understanding of the family's eroticization. Foucault's focus on discourse in the abstract, moreover, effaces the characteristic ways in which a familial erotics predicated on differential access to discourse shaped the subjective experiences of women and children within the patriarchal nuclear family.[9]

In order to demonstrate the significance of these erasures for a reader of Foucault, I will briefly turn to one especially interesting passage that exemplifies Foucault's caginess on the subject of abuse and the abject position of children within the family. Written over this passage in my own translation of Foucault is the single word "incest." I was interested to note when I checked out a copy in the original French from of my university's library to make sure that I was not misled in my reading by an ambiguity produced in translation that someone had written "incesto" in percil in the margin, exactly where I had written "incest." Both I and some anonymous Spanish-speaking colleague had felt it necessary to visibly mark this crux, to supply an absent signified that is present in the passage as a symbol but not as a potential act. Here is the passage in Robert Hurley's translation:

> But in a society such as ours, where the family is the most active site of sexuality, and where it is doubtless the exigencies of the latter which maintain and prolong its existence, incest — for different reasons altogether and in a completely different way [than in societies in which the mechanisms of alliance predominate] — occupies a central place; it is constantly being solicited and refused; it is an object of obsession and attraction, a dreadful secret and an indispensable pivot. (109)

In this passage, Foucault points to incest as ''occup[ying] a central place'' in the post-industrial Western family which, as he observes, ''constantly solicit[s] and refuse[s]'' it (109). Insofar as Foucault here suggests that the industrial capitalist society plays on and heightens (thereby soliciting) incestuous desire at the same time that it denies (and thereby refuses) the literal violation of children by older siblings, parents, uncles, aunts, grandparents, cousins, household employees, or visitors, he is perfectly correct. In effacing the subject from the above sentence, however, Foucault is tellingly able to have his analysis both ways: he makes his point about society's construction of a sexual dialectic that eroticizes the *telling* (of fantasies or experiences that can be treated as fantasies) and the *hiding* (of abuse) at the same time, while he evades the implications of this analysis for his larger argument. He describes incest as ''solicited and refused'' in a sentence which, if we trace carefully, makes society its subject: it is society which both solicits and then *refuses* incest — society solicits incestuous desires in the adult, whom it also provides with material and discursive opportunities within the locus of the now-affectively swollen family, and it then *refuses* the *telling* of incest through the discursive construction of women and children in general, and rape victims of all ages in particular, as both liars and traitors.

A different and more likely reading of Foucault's sentence, however, repeats the implicit assertion made by Freud when he instated the Oedipal complex as a way around the evidence supplied by his own analysands; in it, incest is ''solicited'' and then ''refused'' autonomously within the individual psyche of the child who initially desires the parent, who then represses or ''refuses'' the original desire, and who is later liable to *project* desire onto the (innocent) parent. Furthermore, a third possible reading of this sentence would have incest continually ''solicited'' by older family members but ''refused'' by children who are, in this reading, sufficiently empowered to fend off or ''refuse'' their elders sexual access to their bodies. So it is that Foucault is able to construct a sentence that provides three possible readings, although only one, if one hunts back several lines, is actually justifiable. A reader is unlikely to arrive at the one most justifiable meaning of this sentence, however. Foucault's emphasis on pleasurable sexualized discourse as the preeminent means through which powers are created and extended within bourgeois society and his eloquent silence concerning rape, trauma, or other forms of abuse greatly predispose a reader to arrive at either of the other readings, both of which deny incest as a literal possibility.

Foucault's own writerly strategy is, in fact, rhetorically locked into a peculiar but popular game, a game he himself describes throughout the book, in which power both reveals and denies its own workings, and in which the viewer of the game "enjoys" being simultaneously privy to and fooled by the inner workings of power because the continuation of the game forestalls an encounter with uncomfortable, damning, or even devastating truths.

Foucault's account of the family of alliance's eighteenth-century transformation into the family cell, to which affect and sexuality are central rather than peripheral phenomena, goes too far when it suggests that power deploys itself more richly and pervasively through pleasure than through prohibition and repression (86). This account distorts its subject matter insofar as it ignores important power differentials between subject positions (turning on who may speak and who may be believed) and in discourses (*what* may be said and be believed). Such an argument plays games with, and to a certain extent itself eroticizes or imbues with readerly desire, the construction of a unitary sexual subject for whom power is positively experienced exclusively as a pleasurable *participation mystique.* Such moves, when applied raw to Victorian culture, result in an alarming monologization of a society that is, for some purposes, better understood as consisting of mutually-dependent but mutually-excluding discourses. Applied to Victorian cultural production, Foucault's analysis cannot account for Manichean, or mutually-dependent but also mutually-excluding, Victorian discourses that, at times, conflicted with each other so violently that they gave rise to virtually indecipherable tropes in which the mutual incomprehensibility of split-off, contradictory discourses is unmistakably encoded.

At all levels of Victorian culture — as we can see when we retain an awareness of the mutually-excluding spheres that Steven Marcus documented while noting the ways in which the discourses proper to these supposedly discrete spheres are continually interpenetrating and defining each other — mutually excluding and dynamic discourses vie with and at the same time construct each other. These discourses and their deployment have their roots in the Manichean power arrangements instantiated in Victorian constructions of gender, familial arrangements, class organization, and international relations. A nostalgic appeal to essentially masochistic constructions of romantic love and the family and, on the other hand, sadistic depictions of brute domination of women and children by adult males represent contradictory, self-negating attempts at working out the wounds inflicted in Victorian Manichean technologies of subject formation within the family. Two split-off spheres of consciousness corresponding to these two objectively similar but subjectively binarized narratives seem to have saturated Victorian social space with antipathetic subject constructions that were mutually exclusive to the point of being mutually canceling. Within the world of Victorian pornography — the text, the photograph, the club, the brothel — the ''nice'' world ceased to exist except insofar as it functioned as a facade, a front for debauchery. Equally, within the world of nice literature, the world of pornography was denied and negated. A Victorian subject, moving easily from one register to the other as Thomas Carlyle was especially prone to do in his later writings such as *On Heroes, Hero-Worship, and the Heroic History,* could justify colonialist brutalities based on the a priori and sadistic assumption that natives are wayward children requiring punitive discipline and then move without a slip into a nostalgic appeal to England's supposed maternal and nurturing activities in the colonies. The connection between the mutually-occluding discursive spheres that make such oscillations possible and the power differentials that formed the basis for the Victorian family and subjectivity is acknowledged in Ashis Nandy's observation that European constructions of gender and of childhood were indispensable to the colonial enterprise.

Nandy himself, however, ignores the sense in which colonialist-era European constructions of gender and childhood were dependent upon mutually-contradicting sets of assumptions and awarenesses that must *both* be accepted as simultaneously, self-evidently, and non-paradoxically true. Power in Victorian society was, as this analysis is intended to show, brought into being and exercised through two modes, which must be considered in relationship to each other if power is to be accounted for fully. Both modes of power must be considered simultaneously, just as light must be simultaneously grasped as waves and as particles. Evidence for the simultaneous influence of both modes on Victorian culture and subjectivity may be found precisely in the moments at which the carefully nurtured exclusions and divisions of Victorian society cause Victorian representation to break down and become illegible to itself. The legacy of this divided and self-denying subjectivity remains in such self-alienated and culturally institutionalized breaches between language and materiality as the Clinton administration's ''compromise'' to a full lifting of the ban on lesbians and gay men in the military, the infamous ''don't ask, don't tell'' policy.

Foucault's own textual cruxes and ambiguities afford similar evidence for the existence of mutually contradictory systems that we ''Other Victorians'' still must strive to grasp simultaneously if our readings are to account for the interrelated workings of power. In order fully to account for power relations within modern society, we must commit ourselves to interrogating ''patterns of modification'' that ''relations of force imply by their very nature,'' but also to exploring how such relations of force may be established in the first place, through the Manichean power differentials that form the cogs of the larger machine Foucault so brilliantly described.

St. John Fisher College

NOTES

I am grateful to the following individuals for their assistance at various stages in this project's development: Ann Cvetkovich, Carol MacKay and Jane Marcus were especially generous in providing detailed and thoughtful responses to early versions of this essay; feedback from Allen Miller and other organizers and participants in the 1993 Texas Tech conference, ''Foucault's History of Sexuality'' enabled me to revise this essay substantially. Alice Batt, Jerome Bump, Jeffrey Carnes, Elizabeth Cullingford, Sandra Donaldson, Page du Bois, Janet Foster, Gordon Grant, Sean McMahon, Ed Madden, Susan Meigs, Adrienne Munich, and JoAnn Pavletich all provided invaluable help, feedback, encouragement, and inspiration along the way.

1. See especially Strachey's *Eminent Victorians* for an influential rendition of Victorians as repressed and the Victorian period as exceptionally repressive.
2. Two watershed examples of such feminist dualist models may be found in the work of Gilbert and Gubar and in Auerbach. Auerbach's model supplies an especially good example of the ways feminist extensions of early dualist models grew better able to account for the interpenetration and interdependence of binary but asymmetrically-authorized discourses that shaped Victorian cultural output. She begins a chapter entitled ''Angels and Demons: Woman's Marriage of Heaven and Hell,'' for instance, with the assertion:

> The towering woman who in so many guises possessed the Victorian imagination appears in art and literature as four central types: the angel, the demon, the old maid, and the fallen woman. The first two appear to be emanations of eternity; the latter two rise from within Victorian society. . . . In this chapter we shall see the ease with which the Victorian angel becomes demonic. . . . The old maid seems an innocent butt of comedy; the fallen woman is experienced and tragic; but in their exclusion from domesticity they amalgamate with each other at crucial moments. Discussing each type separately falsifies the fluid boundaries among them. (63)

Here we find a model that is capable, as Marcus's was not, of accounting for the overlap between differentially-empowered discourses within the work of individual authors and within individual texts.

3. Hints that scholars working in Victorian sexuality are beginning to find a purely Foucauldian mode of analysis restrictive can be found in the end notes of two recent articles by major gay/lesbian theorists Nunokawa and Cohen, both included in ''Victorian Sexualities,'' a special issue of *Victorian Studies* in 1993. For his brilliant and delightful analysis of the incest motif that underlies *Silas Marner,* Nunokowa cites a quote from Sedgwick's *Epistemology of the Closet,* then points out that this quote, unlike much of Sedgwick's work, does indeed reinstate the repressive hypothesis. Although he does not make clear what the implications of this move on Sedgwick's part, or of his own inclusion of Sedgwick's reinstatement of it, might be, it seems evident that the repressive hypothesis does, at times, explain phenomena that an emphasis on institutional discourses leaves out. Cohen, in his essay on ''ec-centric'' masculinities, is more explicit in observing that

> following Foucault, most of us working on "queer" topics in the Victorian period have focused our analyses at the level of what we might call "governmental" discourses. . . . As a consequence . . . we have [only a] rudimentary notion of how what I would call sexually "ec-centric" subjects lived out their dis-positions, let alone how they made sense of them. (354)

4. The work of Gagnier represents an important exception to this admittedly broad generalization. Gagnier explicitly calls attention to the analogous relationship that exists between First World/Third World economic relations as they are understood in light of Dependency theory and relationships between differential subjectivities within the industrialized nations. She observes that

> Jean Franco's summary of international Dependency theory can easily be translated into terms of class relations or the construction of subjecthood: "Dependency theory is based on the assumption that underdevelopment is structurally linked to development in the dominant nation. . . . Thus the theory cuts across the concepts of development and underdevelopment. . . . It is no longer possible to treat the two terms as if they were separable. . . ." . . . One must also say that bourgeois subjects were constituted within the same dialectic [as that which placed working-class writers in a problematic relationship to Cartesian individualist self-sufficiency]: they became individuated subjects because others did not. (148)

5. David Halperin has made an especially strong case for Foucault's influence on the current generation of gay/lesbian rights activists, especially on the highly localized and performative interventions of ACT UP.

6. This would be a prudent moment to observe that Foucault shows an awareness of most of the issues I raise. He does, for instance, acknowledge the role of local, differentially-empowered relations in the emergence of "a general line of force that traverses the local oppositions and links them together" producing "wide-ranging effects of cleavage" (94). His assertion that there is no a priori duality "extending from the top down" anchoring such effects, however, excludes from consideration the discursively-inscribed dualities that close the circuit between local oppositions and wide-ranging cleavages. While they do not "extend from the top down," representationally-produced binary oppositions certainly have the effect of naturalizing Manichean power relations between groups as efficiently as if these relations were legislated from on high. My arguments in this essay concern the effects of Foucault's emphasis on discourse over silence, his bracketing out of the universalizing *effects* of representation, and his elision of the subjectivity of those most commonly deprived of speech and self-representation *by* the discourses he interrogates. I do not mean to suggest that Foucault was oblivious to these problems; he in fact continually engages with them, arguing that such expedients are necessary for the promotion of a new analytics of power. However, just as the author of *My Secret Life*, as Foucault claims, unconsciously enacted social injunctions even as he sought to place himself outside of social controls (22), I feel warranted in pointing out ways in which Foucault reinscribes patterns of representation that support and naturalize Manichean power relations within our own society in spite of himself.

7. For a discussion of the structuring of peasant women relative to the courtly beloved as appropriate objects of sexual violation, see Ferrante.
8. For an exceptionally lucid account of the repressive and violent nature of law enforcement in early nineteenth-century England and its transformation from repressive to hegemonic forms of social control, see McGowen.
9. For an extraordinarily well-constructed and moving article in which the importance of the subjectivity of, to use Cohen's term, "ec-centric" individuals is affirmed, see Townsend.

WORKS CITED

Auerbach, Nina. *Woman and the Demon: The Life of a Victorian Myth.* Cambridge, MA: Harvard UP, 1982.

Azim, Firdous. *The Colonial Rise of the Novel.* New York: Routledge, 1993.

Carlyle, Thomas. *On Heroes, Hero-Worship and the Heroic in History*, 1841. Berkeley: U of California P, 1993.

Cockburn, Alexander, "Beat the Devil." *The Nation* 256.9 (8 March 1993): 296–97.

Cohen, Ed. "The Double Lives of Man: Narration and Identification in the Nineteenth-Century Representation of Ec-centric Masculinities." *Victorian Studies* 36. 3 (1993): 353–76.

Ferrante, Joan M. "Male Fantasy and Female Reality in Courtly Literature." *Women's Studies* 1. (1984): 67–97.

Foucault, Michel. *The History of Sexuality. Volume I: An Introduction.* Trans. Robert Hurley. New York: Vintage, 1978.

Gagnier, Regenia. *Subjectivities: A History of Self-Representation in Britain, 1832–1920.* New York: Oxford 1991

Gilbert, Sandra, and Susan Gubar. *The Madwoman in the Attic: The Woman Writer and the Nineteenth-Century Literary Imagination.* New Haven: Yale UP, 1979.

Halperin, David. *Saint Foucault: Towards a Gay Hagiography.* New York: Oxford UP, 1995.

JanMohamed, Abdul, "The Economy of Manichean Allegory: The Function of Racial Differences in Colonialist Literature." *Critical Inquiry* 12 (Autumn 1985) 59–87.

Mahood, Linda, and Barbara Littlewood. "The 'Vicious' Girl and the 'Street-Corner' Boy: Sexuality and the Gendered Delinquent in the Scottish Child-Saving Movement, 1850–1940." *Journal of the History of Sexuality* 4.4 (1994): 549–78.

Marcus, Steven. *The Other Victorians: A Study of Sexuality and Pornography in Mid-Nineteenth-Century England.* New York: Basic Books, 1966.

McGowan, Randall. "Punishing Violence, Sentencing Crime." *The Violence of Representation: Literature and the History of Violence. Ed. Nancy Armstrong and Leonard Tennenhouse. N32 York: Routledge, 1989. 140–56.*

Nandy, Ashis. *The Intimate Enemy: The Loss and Recovery of Self Under Colonialism.* Delhi: Oxford UP, 1983.

Nunokawa, Jeff. "The Miser's Two Bodies: *Silas Marner* and the Sexual Possibilities of the Commodity." *Victorian Studies* 36.3 (1993): 273–92.

Said, Edward. *Orientalism.* New York: Vintage, 1979.

Sedgwick, Eve Kosofsky. *Epistemology of the Closet.* Berkeley: U of California P, 1990.

Strachey, Lytton. *Eminent Victorians.* Garden City, NY: Garden City Publishing, 1918.

Townsend, Camilla. " 'I Am The Woman For Spirit': A Working Woman's Gender Transgression in Victorian London." *Victorian Studies* 36.3 (1993): 293–314.

READING THE SOCIAL TEXT: THE DISCIPLINARY RHETORICS OF SARAH ELLIS AND SAMUEL BEETON

By Margaret Shaw

> [In] order to perform my task with candor and faithfulness, I must renounce all idea of what is called fine writing; because the very nature of the duty I have undertaken, restricts me to the consideration of subjects . . . too familiar to produce upon the reader any startling effect — Sarah Ellis, *Women of England*

THE HISTORY OF THE RISE of conduct books and women's magazines, their set of positions, and some of their socio-political uses have been discussed extensively. Maurice Quinlan's 1941 *Victorian Prelude: A History of English Manners 1700–1830* is a good example of a long-respected form of social history — explaining circumstances responsible for changes in manners by referring to a history of ideas promoted by certain books, events, and individuals. The result of such a method is a chronological narrative of events which the writer typically does not see as problematical. And, while there is a wealth of information available about the literature of advice, none of it focuses on how the literature actually "worked" ideologically to produce gendered roles and practices.[1] The same is true for Cynthia White's *Women's Magazines 1693–1968* and Leonore Davidoff's *The Best Circles: Society, Etiquette and the Season*. White's book is indispensible as a descriptive source book for a wider number of women's magazines, but it does not claim to do extended political or cultural analysis. Davidoff's, on the other hand, explores the role of etiquette as a way of regulating daily life. Part of a larger study of domestic life and household management in Victorian and Edwardian Britain, Davidoff's more structuralist study tries to redefine social history by presenting a "picture" of the "total system" of social manners and some of its consequences for other institutions in society, that is, a picture of the "framework of constraints" within which people lived at the time (18). What the methodologies of such studies do not allow them to discuss is exactly how these social positions and constraints, designed to meet the often contradictory needs of heterogeneous groups of people, were constructed and then disseminated as a system of belief so pervasive that it was ultimately accepted as "common sense." Davidoff's concern to reconstruct a whole system of manners does not allow her to discuss how contradictions in the framework ultimately worked to construct or revise the sets of attitudes she says held the social fabric in place. A theory of representation could be applied to allow her to theorize the split she recognizes between the attitudes and behavior recommended in the advice literature and what she suspects were existing attitudes and behavior. Instead, she includes in her introduction a warning to the reader that much of the literature was "sheer fantasy" and that we need to balance these sources with personal memory (diaries, autobiographies, personal interviews). These alternative sources, however, are also implicated in representation and discourse.

Even when studies do discuss the significance of representation in such texts, few actually historicize its role:

> Despite recent interest in the history of representation *qua* representation, relatively few literary scholars and critics have explored the role of representation *in* history. While most of us pay lipservice to the power of literacy, we have not considered in a detailed and systematic way whether literature has played any part in political history. Indeed, it is the tendency of the disciplines in the United States and Britain to detach the writing we teach as literature from the other symbolic practices that compose history *per se.* Armstrong and Tennenhouse (21)

Consequently, most social historical approaches to conduct literature cannot describe the role it has played in the production of gender or theorize its relation to politics. Armstrong and Tennenhouse's collection (as well as Armstrong's *Desire and Domestic Fiction*) does discuss the means and political effects of such ideology. Rather than seeing writing as a reflection of other symbolic practices that compose history, the editors assume that writing can, in fact, create conditions for radical change or, conversely, the preservation of economic and political relations. Conduct books for women "strive to reproduce, if not always to revise, the culturally approved forms of desire," forms which "in fact constitute ideology in its most basic and powerful form, namely, one that culture designates as nature itself" (1–2). In their methodology, the essays break from previous work in their stated or implied argument that writing produced specific forms of desire which in turn created and maintained specific forms of political authority. Thus, *all* forms of literacy are relevant in the discussion of ideological production, including women's magazines and conduct books.

Analyzing the material of the everyday in this way means submitting it to different procedures, notably those that have come from feminist and poststructuralist theory. For example, Mary Poovey's 1988 book, *Uneven Developments: The Ideological Work of Gender in Mid-Victorian England,* focuses not on advice literature per se but on the ideological work of gender in general during the 1840s and 1850s. In its examination of the "uneven development" of this ideology, Poovey demonstrates how discourses not only conserved social beliefs about men and women but also, through their contradictions, opened up the possibility of oppositional voices in the culture. Poovey's methodology joins post-structuralist versions of formalism, Marxism, and psychoanalysis, which she applies to a variety of texts seen as signifying practices which always produce an excess of meanings. These meanings in excess of a text's actual form produce the multiple effects of ideology, including those which subvert that ideology.

How then do the material forms of the literature of advice for women promote certain reading practices which, in turn, contribute to the ideological reproduction and revision of gender? How were and are various forms of gendered literacy constructed through popular reading material? By bringing post-structuralist discourse analysis to bear on such texts, we can begin to see how non-literary discourses of advice worked to influence the way their readers "read" the social text and their roles within it.[2] Studying the construction and revision of positions for readers in the popular culture can also provide the basis for additional genealogical studies of the type suggested by Armstrong and Tennenhouse; the ideological work of certain representations and other discursive practices in history operates as well in today's women's magazines, self-help literature, and popular notions of women's literacy.

Applying Benjamin's analysis of the ideology of everyday life, Freud's notion of over-determination, and the concept of disciplinary function as used by the later Foucault and Pierre Bourdieu,[3] we can see that discourses of advice have power in the culture in part because of their ability to "discipline" their readers, that is, to produce, disseminate, and institutionalize overdetermined "ways of reading" and general habits of behavior through their rhetorics and pedagogic forms.

What were those "ways of reading"? By the 1850s, at the beginning of a genuine mass literacy in England, middle- and working-class women had available to them a large variety of reading material the primary ideological function of which was to socialize its readers into a newly-consolidated society.[4] In the first half of the century, novels generally shared this pedagogic function, constituting, along with advice manuals and women's periodicals, some of the dominant discourses for women (see Quinlan). While I cannot discuss all of them here, two of the more widely read dispensers of advice — one from early in the century and another from the middle — will suggest the method.

One of the most famous of the early advice-writers for women in the 1830s and 40s was Sarah Ellis. In addition to a number of novels, she also produced the *Women of England* series, three works published between 1838 and 1843, using the title of the first book as the series title. It became immensely popular in both England and America. As a Quaker-educated wife of a minister, most of Ellis's advice focused on re-establishing moral values at the center of women's education; she did more than probably any other writer at the time to directly promote the conscious adoption of self-abnegation as a social role for women, with its concomitant sphere of influence in the home. The role played by women's periodicals, on the other hand, is perhaps best illustrated by Samuel Beeton's *Englishwoman's Domestic Magazine,* first published in 1852 and credited with being one of the first magazines expressly published for middle-class women in England.[5] Covering fiction, advice, recipes, essays, and fashion, it was a huge success, claiming 25,000 sales a month in the first two years, 37,000 by 1856, and 50,000 by 1860 (White 46). The second, enlarged series, which began in 1861, claimed that year over 60,000 readers (Beeton, preface to April 1861 issue).[6]

One reason why advice literature had such influence in the culture was its sheer volume. In a five-year period, Ellis was able to produce three books of advice as well as her fiction and other non-fiction. Etiquette books were often published cheaply and in pocketbook size so that they could be carried about for handy reference. Likewise, the *Englishwoman's Domestic Magazine,* published monthly, could point to its cheap price (originally two-pence raised to a sixpenny series in the 1860s) as the reason why it was so readily accessible to middle-class and lower-middle class women. In addition to their omnipresence in the culture, these discourses were satisfying a real need and did so without violating existing notions of what was "proper" for women. Many of the early manuals, including those by Ellis, had a strong religious cast, and while they often simply carried on arguments already established by More and Trimmer earlier in the century, they offered women some element of power by establishing them as both the moral center and principal consumer in the family. But the real strength of these discourses comes from the practices they instituted, including a way of reading and writing.

Mrs. Ellis's Advice

SARAH ELLIS, LIKE MANY WRITERS of advice books, was nostalgic for a way of life that seemed to be passing in England. Therefore, the *Women of England* series was written to address what Ellis perceived as a problem. As she puts it, "One of the most striking features in the character of the young ladies of the present day is the absence of contentment" *(Women of England* 86). This problem, which she further characterizes as a deterioration of morals, was jointly caused by too much concern with self and ambition, an over-cultivation of the mental faculties at the expense of the moral, and a fascination with "false notions of refinement" which are "rendering [young women] less influential, less useful, and less happy than they were" (10). In her chapter on "Modern Education," Ellis describes the present schooling of young women in decidedly commercial terms, deploring the ambition it encourages:

> From the beginning to the end of school education, the improvement of *self*, so far as relates to intellectual attainments, is made the rule and the motive of all that is done. . . . To gain is the universal order of the establishment; and those who have heaped together the greatest sum of knowledge are usually regarded as the most meritorious. . . . [T]he whole system is one of pure selfishness, fed by accumulation, and rewarded by applause. To be at the head of the class, to gain the ticket or the prize, are the points of universal ambition. (62–63)

Clearly, young women were not to have "selves" — the product of a male-oriented and competitive economic system — but to gain satisfaction as a kind of repository of moral value, situated within a separate realm even while at school.

The result of attempts to move out of one's "sphere," according to Ellis, is an "unhealthy" woman, one of the large number of "languid, listless, and inert young ladies, who now recline upon our sofas, murmuring and repining at every claim upon their personal exertions" — a problem which demands "the attention of a benevolent and enlightened public, even more, perhaps, than some of those great national schemes in which the people and the government are alike interested" (80–81). Ellis's project, then, is "to penetrate into the familiar scenes of domestic life . . . to lay bare some of the causes which frequently lie hidden at the root of general conduct" (2–3). This was a problem demanding public attention as far as Ellis was concerned since she, as did many other advice writers, considered the "domestic character" of England to be an essential feature of the country's nationality; if England's women were losing their moral strength, then England itself was in danger of losing hers. Consequently, Ellis sets out, as she says, to "win back to the homes of England the boasted felicity for which they once were famed" (3).

But before Ellis promotes those practices or habits which she believes will develop moral character and happiness in a domestic sphere, she constructs an identity for her readers that will enable and motivate them to take up such practices. She does this by using what was to become a standard rhetorical move in the nineteenth century: she first recruits her readers under the categories of gender, class, and nation by appealing to their middle-class womanhood as the epitome of "Englishness"; then she equates this Englishness with morality; and, finally, she places them in opposition to a "foreign" upper class and a "faceless" and apparently de-sexed working class. This process begins in the preface to *The Women of England* where Ellis opens a space for her discourse among the "many valuable dissertations upon female character" by defining a new readership based on class:

> It is worthy of remark . . . that these writers [of previous advice manuals] have addressed their observations almost exclusively to *ladies,* or occasionally to those who hold a subordinate situation under the influence of ladies; while that estimable class of females who might be more specifically denominated *women,* and who

> yet enjoy the privilege of liberal education, with exemption from the pecuniary necessities of labor, are almost wholly overlooked. (2)

By asserting a difference and a unity, Ellis establishes her disparate readers as an educated, leisured class yet one whose situation is necessarily different from the "ladies" of the aristocracy. Once having designated the readers as "women," meaning a particular class of people, the next move is to universalize the label and make this class representative of all "English Women," in the aggregate. This is done by denying representativeness to other groups of women by means of a standard rhetorical process of classification and division:

> It is not therefore from the aristocracy of the land that the characteristics of English women should be taken, because the higher the rank, and the greater the facilities of communication with other countries, the more prevalent are foreign manners, and modes of thinking and acting common to that class of society in other countries. Neither is it entirely among the indigent and most laborious of the community, that we can with propriety look for those strong features of nationality, which stamp the moral character of different nations; because the urgency of mere physical wants, and the pressure of constant and necessary labor, naturally induce a certain degree of resemblance in social feelings and domestic habits, among people similarly circumstanced, to whatever country they may belong. (13–14)

Having denied "Englishness" to these groups, Ellis is left, by virtue of an arbitrary rhetorical construct, with a hierarchy and a ranking system of immense representational power: it immediately leads her to a metaphor of middle-class women as the "pillar" of a column with the base composed of the "laborious poor" and "its rich and highly ornamental capital" composed of the "ancient nobility of the land" (14). Thus, the poor become a necessary but faceless support for the middle-class while the rich, a decorative but useless ornament. The metaphor implies a rigidity of signification that denies class mobility and fixes Ellis's readers in a particular position, or more precisely, aspiring to it. This desire to fix social position once she has established the predominance of the middle class is repeated endlessly in the *Women of England* series. In *The Daughters of England,* she warns against marrying outside one's rank: "a sensible woman will easily see that the man of her choice must be as much as possible in her own sphere of life" (331). Marrying "down" is to be avoided at all costs and marrying "up" is all right only if the young woman "never *sought* her elevation" (332). Upward mobility is apparently unobjectionable as long as conscious efforts remain invisible, but for most women there is a proper sphere, not only in relation to other women, but to men and the public world as well:

> It is impossible that the teachers, or even the parents themselves, should always know the future destiny of the child; but there is an appropriate sphere for women to move in, from which those of the middle class in England seldom deviate very

> widely. This sphere has duties and occupations of its own, from which no woman can shrink without culpability and disgrace. *(Women of England* 70)

And, of course, the whole ideology of ''Women's Sphere'' soon follows.

Another important insight of Ellis's series is the recognition that concepts must be rooted in practice to be adequately disseminated. After constructing her readers as representatives of English moral life and therefore bound by social duty, she devotes the majority of her series to an argument for instilling habits of behavior which would gain their power from their sheer repetitive everydayness, a Foucauldean ''microphysics of power'' which, by training the body, goes beyond the power of representation to reproduce ideology.[7] Thus, while Ellis continually apologizes for her focus on the ''apparently insignificant detail of familiar and ordinary life'' *(Women of England* 2), she is also very much aware of the power of training and exercising women's behavior in exactly that sphere. In fact, her first objection to other discourses on women is that they are on too broad a scale; they offer ''no direct definition of those minor parts of domestic and social intercourse, which strengthen into habit, and consequently form the basis of moral character'' (2). In her chapter on education, Ellis admits that schools often promulgate a general ''system'' of morals in addition to their other subjects but that the system is not yet embedded in practice:

> [The] subject I would complain of is, that no means have yet been adopted for making the *practice* of this system the object of highest importance in our schools. No adequate means have been adopted for testing the generosity, the high-mindedness, the integrity of the children who pursue their education at school, until they leave it at the age of sixteen, when their moral faculties, either for good or for evil, must have attained considerable growth. (69)

Her solution is to introduce a set of instructional techniques that would teach the moral virtues of ''disinterested kindness'' and generosity, allowing young girls to practice the habits which would, in Bourdieu's terms, ''engrave'' ideology on their bodies.[8]

A similar emphasis is given to nursing the sick, visiting the poor, and doing housework. While Ellis describes her readers as leisured, she advocates domestic duties especially as a ''cure'' for their melancholy and dissatisfaction. For her, each domestic act carries within it the potential to exercise a moral principle:

> And thus it is with every act that falls within the sphere of female duty. The act itself may be trifling; but the motives by which it is sustained may be such as to do honor to the religion we profess. And we must ever bear in mind, that not only do we honor that religion by engaging in public services on behalf of our fellow-creatures, or for the good of our own souls; but by restraining evil tempers, and selfish dispositions, in the privacy of our own domestic sphere. (*Wives of England* 252–53)

By training the body to acts of selflessness, women would be enacting and reproducing an ideology of women's sphere rooted in religious principle in their daily lives. This activity would disseminate ideology as well since the servants "or other inferior members of a family" will learn from the habits of the mistress (254).

Ellis also argues for an "economy of time" which would keep a woman in constant employment and therefore free from "encroaching upon the rights of others" by "trifling" with time (*Wives of England* 257).[9] Her detailed discussion of this economy relies heavily on the metaphor of the machine, extending it to a description of the motion a body assumes when working correctly:

> Habitually idle persons are apt to judge of the difficulty of being industrious, by what it costs them to do any thing they may happen to undertake; the movements of a naturally indolent person being composed of a series of painful exertions, while the activity of an industrious person resembles the motion of a well-regulated machine, which having been once set at work, requires comparatively little force to keep it going. (259)

The mechanical metaphor suggests Ellis's ideal: the woman who adopts habits or the practice of moral virtue will function almost without thought, mechanically and efficiently:

> It is subsequently by making industry a habit, and by no other means, that it can be thoroughly enjoyed; for if between one occupation and another, time is allowed for sensations of weariness to be indulged, or for doubts to be entertained as to what shall be done next, with those who have much to do all such endeavors to be industrious must necessarily be irksome, if not absolutely laborious. (259)

The machine metaphor for production applies as well to the instrumentalist writing practice Ellis's text itself promotes. Soon after publishing *The Women of England* and allowing no time for "doubts to be entertained as to what shall be done next," Ellis proceeded to write two more books in the series. Her method of production is guided by the principle of classification and division as well as the movement into ever greater detail about women's lives, insuring a treatise that could go on forever. In the preface to *The Daughters of England,* Ellis expresses her gratitude that thousands of readers have begun entertaining her views and that she has been induced to continue writing:

> The more minute the details of individual, domestic, and social duty, to which allusion is made, the more necessary it becomes to make a distinct classification of the different eras in woman's personal experience; the Author, therefore, proposes dividing the subject into three parts, in which will be separately considered, the character and situation of the Daughters, Wives, and Mothers of England.

By classifying women's lives into "eras," she has a ready-made series of books, each carrying with it the ideological weight of classifying by marital status — a perfect writing machine.

The texts, their predecessors, and their imitators are an excellent example of intertextuality at work; familiar phrases, situations, and concepts are produced and reproduced, echoing the advice of a Hannah More or being itself echoed in a treatise on women by Maria Grey ten years later.[10] The value of this prosaicism seems to underlie Ellis's own rejection of "fine writing," preferring the weight of "homely detail" to a writing that would call attention to itself as "produced" by an individual mind:

> [In] order to perform my task with candor and faithfulness, I must renounce all idea of what is called fine writing; because the very nature of the duty I have undertaken, restricts me to the consideration of subjects, too minute in themselves, to admit of their being expatiated upon with eloquence by the writer — too familiar to produce upon the reader any startling effect. Had I even felt within myself a capability for treating any subject in this manner, I should have been willing in this instance to resign all opportunity of such display, if, by so doing, I could more clearly point out to my countrywomen, by what means they may best meet that pressing exigency of the times, which so urgently demands a fresh exercise of moral power on their part. (*Women of England* 3)

Prosaicism actually takes on an ideological function. Its sheer reproducibility normalizes not only certain attitudes but, more importantly, its own way of speaking, writing, and reading by displacing other possible styles, other ways of representing. Thus, "fine writing" is excluded, given a pejorative value because it cannot perceive the "homely detail." The "insignificant detail" now becomes the focal point of discussion, defining for women a particular "quality" to their lives.

This process is even more significant once we begin to see this way of writing and reading as reproducing an epistemology as well, a way of knowing which will determine to a large extent what certain readers will perceive in their culture. The constant repetition of ever more familiar phrases produces equally familiar observations about women's lives which, through accumulation and eventual anonymity, lose their identity as the property of an author and become, instead, part of the public domain, part of the received truths of the culture. Politically, such stylistic attention to the domestic detail works to validate a woman's sphere as much as any overt argument might; the irony is that it validated certain perceptions linked to women which both increased women's stature and delimited it at the same time.

Works like Ellis's make the world immediately self-evident and without contradictions. They were written by popularizers of bourgeois thought, only reduced to a kind of public philosophy. The reading habits such texts encourage are equally reductive. The reader consumes each seamless book effortlessly with no gaps in the text to allow for doubts or questions. She is kept busy and at the same time involved enough not to critique what she reads. Consequently, the reader enacts, in the process of reading, those habits encouraged by the text: constructed as free to will an unwillful relation to the rest of the world, she practices that relation with the daily exercise of reading Ellis's advice. In this way, the practice of reading and not so much the representing of advice is the key to the ideological mechanism.

Beeton's New Magazine

MAGAZINES FOR WOMEN developed different strategies and for different purposes. Samuel Beeton and his wife Isabella claimed the purpose of the new magazine for middle-class women was to be educational and, true to their word, the monthly periodical which began in 1852 produced everything from domestic fiction to essays on English history and botany. Setting his notion of education against the upper-class version of "showy accomplishments," Beeton encouraged female achievement even further by sponsoring writing contests and printing winning essays. It was a time of heated debates on the woman question; the labor market was overcrowded and thousands of cultured but untrained gentlewomen had little work of significance to do. Beeton's magazine gave them a vehicle for expressing their concerns as well as a way to pass the time in a way that appeased the conscience. But more than anything else, the magazine, like most of the women's periodicals that followed, was designed to make money, schooling women in consumption as well as bourgeois habits of domestic industry and usefulness. While Beeton himself announced the magazine as providing a "Receipt for succeeding in the world," namely, "to work much and spend little" and to practice "wholesome thrift as will disinduce us to spend our time or money without an adequate return in gain or enjoyment" (qtd. in White 44), he also proudly published his monthly sales and made sure women were aware of the latest fashions and newest books.

The juxtaposition of articles by Isabella Beeton on the latest fashions in Paris with the innovative inclusion of sewing patterns suggests that the Beetons knew their audience well: while the ideology of women's magazines implied a life of leisure and means, many women who read them were not "daughters-at-home" or married women, but women pressured to contribute to their own financial support (Gorham 27). The possibilities open to such women in the first part of the century were discouraging, and articles of concern did appear in the periodical press (28). But the great success of magazines such as Beeton's suggest the psychological structures of desire were more easily manipulated than were the political, economic, and social realities of the 1840s and '50s. The magazines diverted such women's concerns away from economic problems by promising them a chance to transform their lives through consumerism; even if they had to support themselves, they had some consolation in the prospect of at least being able to acquire some of the outward signs of a leisured life.

This construction of the middle-class woman had clearly changed somewhat from that of Mrs. Ellis's "women of England." Beeton's use of an advice column on courtship, "Cupid's Letter Bag," and, later, a more general column of chatty advice on general topics, "The Englishwomen's Conversazione," suggests that women were seeking advice outside the home more publicly than ever and on more intimate topics. It also suggests that social changes had made it possible for women to meet men socially without a chaperone, making a resource such as the *Englishwoman's Domestic Magazine* particularly important. However, while the columns did give women a voice in the culture and therefore made their social concerns more visible, in general the concerns that got voiced, considering Beeton's advice, conspicuously avoided the whole subject of women's rights. For example, typical "Conversazione" columns from the new 1860s series include advice about a cold-hearted governess, the definition of a "flirt," advice about poor servants, about how to get letters read by a publisher, what to do about "love at first sight," and other bits of general information (1862, 48, 96, 144, 182, 240, and 288). The general tone of each column is light and humorous, in line with its claim to provide "conversation" for young women. It was a magazine written for young women who wanted to know how to manage the daily events of their lives, not the political and economic realities of women's general condition.

The essays published by the magazine were equally light in tone, even though they were written on more serious subjects. The essays from several issues from the same period, for example, included a semi-serious complaint about "The Popular Man," the life-of-the-party who leaves his loved one at home worrying about him (73), and "Palace Gardens" (121), a heavy-handed satire on other satires of social fashion, jabbing at the middle-class desire to ape the manners of the aristocracy. The only serious note the latter strikes is when it praises the working class for "being above" the vanity fair, a remark that reveals its political bias in the immediate disclaimer that reformers were not to be included in this group. Finally, the essay entitled "Dismay" is another light satire, this time on perambulators and crinolines. Avoidance of the woman question was typical of the leading periodicals for women, except for an occasional derogatory or joking comment. While a large number of new magazines for women has entered the field during this period, no magazine which took up the cause for women's rights lasted for more than one or two years (White 47). The resulting image we get of middle-class women's conversation based on these magazines is that it was chatty, clever, but essentially apolitical and limited to questions of morality or manners.

The commercialism of the magazine is probably most apparent in the reading practice it constructs. Unlike the seamlessness of Ellis's prose, the magazine is marked by the juxtaposition and interpenetration of various types of discourse. While the index of each magazine groups types of discourse together, the actual organization of the magazine mixes essays with a chapter or two of a short story with cooking recipes. One issue begins, for instance, with several chapters of "Constance Chorley," followed by a poem and an article on "historical female biographies," followed by chapters from another short story, an essay on "The Church Militant," the beginning chapter of a third story, a Book of the Month review, an article on Paris fashions, advice to correspondents on domestic matters, more chapters of "Constance Chorley," and an article on the nature of color. Ads for other publications by Samuel and Isabella Beeton are occasionally thrown in as well. The underlying principle of such an organization is the commodity form — the reification of bits of knowledge, all levelled in significance by their juxtaposition.[11] Thus, an article on English history is given as much weight as a recipe for stew, while colored fashion plates mount drawings of stiffly-posed women like cut-outs against an all-white background: all items are detached, without context or frame, juxtaposed or interpenetrated by each other in ways which soon numb any awareness of incongruity or contradiction. Like the newspapers which dominated male culture at the time, magazines like the *Englishwoman's Domestic Magazine* amounted to a routine, monthly recurrence of the same: a prosaic, commercial, commodification of women's lives, even in its enlightened attempt to educate women to more than just the fashions of the day.

Such exposure helped women to develop habits of consciousness and of socio-economic practice which encouraged consumerism. The language of "turn over" with its implications of "wearing out" dominates the seasonal metaphors found in "The Book of the Month" column or the references to "the clothes of the season" in Mrs. Beeton's fashion column, stressing qualities of impermanence that may not necessarily inhere in the product itself. The constant repetition of references to which product "has taken the place of" another mediates the meaning of fashion and encourages women in habits of consumption. The selection and classification of types of dress (appropriate for the seaside or for town, for instance), shape readers into a particular class and close out those who can not diversify their wardrobes in these ways. In addition, the habit of passively "looking at" fashions and disembodied articles in this way encourages a passive perception in general, a reading-as-browsing that reduces the adversarial nature of both reading and shopping, saturating them in consumerism. The result is a highly efficient transmission of a particular ideology and construction of women who can act within it, albeit as consumers.

1. EDM fashion plate. Courtesy of the Kent State University Library

The Contradictions

WHILE ELLIS AND BEETON developed their own particular strategies for reproducing gender- and class-based ideologies and did so for different purposes, we can see, now, that they also produced "transdiscursive" devices, overdetermined rhetorical practices which disciplined generally willing readers into particular habits of mind and body. Both discourses of advice focus on how to approach, read, and enter the social world; both offer representations and practices which transmit ideological belief; and both construct, through the discursive work of each text, a subject (or reader) who could function as the site for the integration of those representations and practices. They use rhetorical devices such as the "objective" structures of classification and division as a way of normalizing politically-charged hierarchies or defining an undesirable Other against which the readers might consolidate their identities as a coherent whole: the group of middle-class English women of London as opposed to the upper-or lower-class woman, the foreign woman, or the Northerner. And, since both pedagogic forms purport to give advice, they share a common trope, a master/pupil relationship between reader and writer which became a powerful social conjuncture in the nineteenth century, especially for women. The initiator in such a relationship is in a position of immense power since she or he has the potential to determine meaning for the novice and to pass on the representations by which the novice can act in society. But, while the initiator is clearly set in a position of mastery, the promise is that the novice will someday acquire that position as well, as surveyor and consumer of the social text. She too will learn to read and acquire the marks of distinction and, by practicing ideology directly, eventually function within a privileged social group.

Of course, such devices and tropes could not, by themselves, control and homogenize reader response. But as part of a larger cultural network — one whose articulations I can only suggest here — they did come to exert a great deal of influence. Because the rather limited subject positions they offered readers were so overdetermined, both within the discourses and within the cultural as a whole (in the home, in schools, in the church, and in marriage), the women who read such material soon found their diverse needs and desires channelled into a relatively few number of roles they might play. But even more importantly, these limited subject positions were able to determine, to a large extent, the horizon of intelligibility for many women's understanding of their own predicament — a perception which, in conjunction with an attractive promise of mastery and status, must have made resistance seem not only difficult, but also simply unnecessary.

In spite of this, a paradox remains, a paradox produced by the fact that advice literature operates in the register of two contradictory discourses: the first argues that a woman's identity is free from cultural determination and therefore she is able to claim she is the origin of her acts and outside the grid of social power. The second argues that a woman's identity is, in fact, produced by taking on a system of marks or linguistic representations which pre-exist her. This paradox is apparent in Ellis's texts in a number of places, but it is probably most obvious in her insistence that women ought to learn what she also wants to claim is natural to their sex: a disinterested selflessness and dedication to others. In addition, the woman must be able to actively choose this, that is, actively will the abnegation of the will, a contradiction middle-class advice literature tries to suppress for obvious reasons. Therefore, the reader of advice literature must finally be represented as "self-sufficient," free from the network of social power relations. The reader becomes the privileged site of human agency and mastery, capable of self-denial only because of supreme self-control, a Judeo-Christian middle-class value which effectively silences other values and other practices.

The same contradiction exists in any discourse of advice when one class of people are privileged as the natural origins of certain marks of distinction and others are not; in order to maintain their superiority, this class must deny the constructed nature of their behavior and yet, as educators, they must insist on it. Because of these contradictions in the texts, the reading practices they promote are crucial. Whether through a persistent, easily reproducible prosaicism and intertextuality or through habits of consumption which reach beyond the marketplace into the printed text, such discourses exercised power because they separately and inadvertently conjoined to produce and naturalize ways of reading with remarkably similar effects. The resulting grid of intelligibility that was offered large number of readers in the period suggests how it is possible that writers who sought to subvert the representations of such discourses of advice often found their own texts, wittingly or not, implicated in a paradoxical repetition of ideology, even when the ostensible ''content'' of those texts seems subversive.

This latter realization shows us how important it was to preserve the possibility of ''resistant readings'' by opening up the gaps produced, in Poovey's words, by the ''uneven development'' of such discourses. It is no less important today. While Sarah Ellis and Samuel Beeton are no longer household names, the ideology and practices their discourses constituted or reproduced are with us still. What a post-structuralist examination of advice literature shows us is how pervasive an ideology can be in its construction of readers of diverse needs — a power other critical perspectives have seen, but not seen through. But that same critical practice also allows us to expose the limits of the discourse and make visible those contradictions in its practice which continue to open up possibilities for change — not only a broadened practice, but a political one as well.

Kent State University

NOTES

1. Ryan in 1983 calls for a new ''cultural science'' to broaden and politicize traditional studies in the humanities and social sciences (105); his article speaks to the need to investigate non-canonical documents and to cross disciplinary lines.
2. While there was no shortage of advice in women's conduct books and magazines on how and what to read, I am more interested in the ways discourses of advice actually worked to *produce* certain habits of mind and body through their rhetorical and pedagogic forms, whether or not they mentioned reading directly. So a ''reading practice'' has more to do with taking on a perceptual frame than it does a specific set of rules about how to read.

3. These terms and practices are developed especially in Benjamin, *Illuminations;* Freud, *The Interpretation of Dreams;* Foucault, *Discipline and Punish: The Birth of the Prison;* and Bourdieu, *Outline of a Theory of Practice.*
4. Altick's *The English Common Reader* continues to be the most respected and useful of traditional social histories on the subject. For the purposes of this study, I limit myself to materials produced for white, middle- or lower-middle class women of different ages; by the middle of the century, working class women had a number of popular forms directed at them as well. A useful study might compare the rhetorical practices of the *London Journal* or the *Family Herald,* for instance, with those addressed here.
5. Of course, *The Ladies' Magazine* had been in existence since 1749, and was directed exclusively toward the middle class and women's perceived interests by around 1770. The period of its last influence was the 1820s, some thirty years before the period I am discussing here (Quinlan 64).
6. Previous work on Ellis and Samuel Beeton has been sparse and largely descriptive in nature. While a new biography on Ellis is apparently underway, major critical work exclusively on these figures has yet to be published. Gorham's work discusses Ellis's *Daughters of England* in her chapter on Victorian advice to adolescent girls, but not its rhetorical strategies or ideological content. Ellis's book is seen as providing advice about the "intellectual, practical, and emotional content" of the young girl's transformation from child to woman, including the admonition that she accept her "inferiority" to men. White provides factual information about Beeton's magazine and about his wife Isabella, emphasizing the magazine's innovative targeting of middle-class women. She places the magazine in the context of larger trends in women's publications over two centuries. Excellent descriptive material on Beeton's magazines and their place among a large variety of women's magazines of the period, including radical journals, appears in Doughan. Finally, Branca's *Silent Sisterhood* discusses the Beetons and Ellis as important sources of information about the material culture of middle-class women, especially when letters from the women themselves were published. However, she reminds us that the Beetons' advice still reflected upper-class life in its emphasis on leisure time and that Ellis's series was too nostalgic of older social forms to always represent current desire. Branca's book thus offers a corrective to the stereotyped versions of middle-class women's lives often based on popular literature and biographies of eminent women only.
7. The definitive example of such a "microphysics of power" is, of course, Michel Foucault's *Discipline and Punish: The Birth of the Prison.*
8. This notion of "engraving" ideology on the body is particularly useful for explaining some of the socio-political effects of etiquette as well. Compare to Bourdieu's discussion below:

   If all societies . . . that seek to produce a new man through a process of "deculturation" and "reculturation" set such store on the seemingly most insignificant details of *dress, bearing,* physical and verbal *manners,* the reason is that, treating the body as a memory, they entrust to it in abbreviated and practical, i.e. mnemonic, form the fundamental principles of the arbitrary content of the culture. The principles embodied in this way are placed beyond the grasp of consciousness, and hence cannot be touched by voluntary, deliberate transformation, cannot even be made explicit; nothing seems more ineffable, more incommunicable, more inimitable, and, therefore, more precious, than the values given body, *made* body by the transubstantiation achieved by the hidden persuasion of an implicit pedagogy, capable of instilling a whole cosmology, an ethic, a metaphysic, a political philosophy, through injunctions as insignificant as "stand up straight" or "don't hold your knife in your left hand." (94)

9. Compare to Foucault's comments on this notion of "disciplinary time" which, he argues, was gradually imposed on bodies to train them more efficiently:

[It was] an important phenomenon: the development, in the classical period, of a new technique for taking charge of the time of individual existences; for regulating the relations of time, bodies and forces; for assuring an accumulation of duration; and for turning to ever-increasing profit or use the movement of passing time. How can one capitalize the time of individuals, accumulate it in each of them, in their bodies, in their forces or in their abilities, in a way that is susceptible of use and control? How can one organize profitable durations? The disciplines, which analyse space, break up and rearrange activities, must also be understood as machinery for adding up and capitalizing time. (157)

10. While Grey and Sherriff's *Thoughts on Self-Culture,* published in 1854, and More's *Strictures on the Modern System of Female Education,* published in 1799, were both primarily reactions to feminist arguments for equality, each makes her case in many of the same terms as Ellis, advocating a "proper sphere" of moral influence for women, paying careful attention to habits and details of domestic economy, and repeating phrases still familiar today as conservative ideology. Like Ellis, Grey argues for the "power and influence of habit," the value of time, and the role of duty; and More produces similar arguments on self-regulation in her discussion of women's education: "[A lady] is to read the best books, not so much to enable her to talk of them, as to bring the improvement which they furnish, to the rectification of her principles and the formation of her habits. The great uses of study to a woman are to enable her to regulate her own mind, and to be instrumental to the good of others" (2:2).
11. See Benjamin, "The Work of Art in the Age of Mechanical Reproduction" (217–51).

WORKS CITED

Altick, Richard. *The English Common Reader: A Social History of the Mass Reading Public 1800–1900.* Chicago: U of Chicago P, 1957.

Armstrong, Nancy. *Desire and Domestic Fiction: A Political History of the Novel.* New York: Oxford UP, 1987.

Armstrong, Nancy, and Leonard Tennenhouse, eds. *The Ideology of Conduct: Essays in Literature and the History of Sexuality.* New York: Methuen, 1987.

Beeton, Samuel. *Englishwoman's Domestic Magazine.* London: S. B. Beeton, 1852–1879.

Benjamin, Walter. *Illuminations.* Trans. Harry Zohn. Ed. Hannah Arendt. New York: Schocken Books, 1969.

Bourdieu, Pierre. *Outline of a Theory of Practice.* Trans. Richard Nice. Cambridge Studies in Social Anthropology. Cambridge: Cambridge UP, 1977.

Branca, Patricia. *Silent Sisterhood: Middle Class Women in the Victorian Home.* Pittsburgh: Carnegie Mellon UP, 1975.

Davidoff, Leonore. *The Best Circles: Society, Etiquette and the Season.* London: Croom Helm, 1973.

Doughan, David T. J. "Periodicals by, for, and about Women in Britain." *Women's Studies International Forum* 10.3 (1987): 261–73.

Ellis, Mrs. *The Daughters of England, Their Position in Society, Character and Responsibilities.* London: Fisher [1842].

———. *The Wives of England, Their Relative Duties, Domestic Influence, & Social Obligations.* London: Fisher, n.d.

———. *The Women of England, Their Social Duties and Domestic Habits.* London: Fisher, 1838.

Foucault, Michel. *Discipline and Punish: The Birth of the Prison.* Trans. Alan Sheridan. New York: Vintage, 1979.

Freud, Sigmund. *The Interpretation of Dreams.* Trans. and ed. by James Strachey. New York: Avon, 1965.

Gorham, Deborah. *The Victorian Girl and the Feminine Ideal.* Bloomington: Indiana UP, 1970.

Grey, Maria, and Emily Shirreff. *Thoughts on Self-Culture.* N.p.: 1854.

More, Hannah. "Strictures on the Modern System of Female Education" (1799). *The Works of Hannah More.* 2 vols. New York, 1844. 1: 311–415.

Poovey, Mary. *Uneven Developments: The Ideological Work of Gender in Mid-Victorian England.* Chicago: U of Chicago P, 1988.

Quinlan, Maurice J. *Victorian Prelude: A History of English Manners 1700–1830.* New York: Columbia UP, 1941.

Ryan, Michael. "Literary Criticism and Cultural Science: Transformations in the Dominant Paradigm of Literary Study." *North Dakota Quarterly* 51.1 (Winter 1983): 100–12.

White, Cynthia L. *Women's Magazines 1693–1968.* London: Michael Joseph, 1970.

HISTORY, HYSTERIA, HISTRIONICS: THE BIOGRAPHICAL REPRESENTATION OF CHRISTINA ROSSETTI

By Alison Chapman

> If only my figure would shrink somewhat! For a fat poetess is incongruous, especially when seated by [t]he grave of buried hope!
> ———Christina Rossetti to Dante Gabriel Rossetti, *Family Letters*

> Wrapt in fire, indeed, was that pure and perfect spirit, that disembodied soul of song.
> ———William Sharp on Christina Rossetti, *Atlantic Monthly*

WHO WAS CHRISTINA ROSSETTI? The biographies — all dependent upon William Michael Rossetti's management of his sister's posthumous affairs — and reminiscences present us with a character at once enigmatic and prosaic but always inherently contradictory. Dichotomies ascribed to Rossetti — passion/repression, aestheticism/asceticism — define for Georgina Battiscombe, and for most of Rossetti's biographers, what is distinctive in her life: "outwardly, Christina Rossetti's life was an uneventful one; inwardly, it was a continual conflict" (13). The mythically constructed split character of Christina Rossetti allows the biographer to move the normal goalposts of the genre. Instead of presenting a factual account of the life of an historical personage, the subject for the biographer becomes a wholly interior life, an emotional drama. With this shift of arena, the biographical subject is still presented as an historical personage, but this has become an ambiguous position, for with the shift comes an insistence that the personage is also ahistorical, that she is removed from history by virtue of living an essentially emotional life and acquiring a status as a feminine ideal, a saintly poetess. It is this doubleness — the insistence upon an historical subject and the concurrent insistence that the subject is ahistorical — that I wish to investigate.

Conventionally depicted as a devout spinster whose lyrical poetry directly transcribes her unrequited love, the biographical representation of Rossetti subscribes to the aesthetic construction of femininity while attempting to place such an operation under erasure. Contemporary criticism continues to be infected with the image of Rossetti as one that inhabits her poetic discourse without an interrogation of the nature of this representation. Writing about the surge of biographical interest at Rossetti's centenary (5 December 1930), Virginia Woolf begins to explore the problems of biography as a genre:

> As everybody knows, the fascination of reading biographies is irresistible. . . . Here is the past and all its inhabitants miraculously sealed as in a magic tank; all we have to do is to look and to listen and to listen and to look and soon the little figures — for they are rather under life size — will begin to move and to speak, and as they move we shall arrange them in all sorts of patterns of which they were ignorant, for they thought when they were alive that they could go where they liked. (237)

Woolf expresses dissatisfaction with the biographical mode that positions and frames people and events in artificial patterns, while she also relishes the various Rossetti anecdotes. An apocryphal anecdote is recounted of a tea party at which, possibly in response to some remark about poetry, "suddenly there uprose from a chair and paced forward into the centre of the room a little woman dressed in black, who announced solemnly, 'I am Christina Rossetti!' and having so said, returned to her chair" (240). The anecdote might well have the same source as that offered by Ellen Proctor in her *Brief Memoir of Christina G. Rossetti.* During a tea party, Proctor spoke at length to a lady whom she was later surprised to learn was Christina Rossetti:

> I turned to my late companion, and said, "Are you Miss Rossetti?" "Yes," she said cheerily, "I am." "Miss Christina Rossetti?" I continued. "Christina Rossetti at your service!" was the reply. She was smiling now, and her face seemed to say, "What a wonder you make of me!" (45-46)

For Woolf, Christina Rossetti's name denotes something more than a name: it signifies a poetess trapped and framed by the biographies but nevertheless removed from cultural, social, and historical shapings: "Years and the traffic of the mind with men and books did not affect you in the least" (242). Proctor, however, tells of how Rossetti's use of her own name undermines the value Proctor herself has put on it. By inscribing into her account the supposed puncturing by Rossetti of the significance of her own name, Proctor insists upon the actual historical existence of Rossetti, rendered as her prosaic ordinariness, while also constructing her name as a signifier for something more than a name. Once again, the signification process whereby the name exceeds its own designation as a name bears within it the attempted erasure of this process, the mask of its operation. The presentation in the biographies of a complete and unified historical personage emerges plainly as a fallacy, an illusory by-product of the text. To read into this fallacy, furthermore, is to see that "Christina Rossetti" as understood in the biographies is a trope.

For a woman who lived to be sixty-four and was associated with a literary and artistic coterie, there are surprisingly few anecdotes about her in circulation. The source of much information is the first full-length biographical and critical study, by Mackenzie Bell, which utilizes explicitly the information given him by William Michael Rossetti and from which subsequent biographers have culled much detail. Across the biographies the material is retold in a similar pattern and the same incidents are repeated with an almost tedious regularity.[1] We are told of Rossetti's impressive vocabulary as a child, illustrated on the occasion when, less than six years old, she remarked to a visitor that "the cat looks very sedate"; the young poet's first verse: "Cecilia never went to school / Without her gladiator"; her canary dream, told to Dante Gabriel Rossetti (who planned to paint it) and passed down by William Sharp, in which Christina Rossetti saw a yellow cloud of escaped canaries converging over London rooftops and later returning to their cages (W. M. Rossetti, *PW* xlix–l; Bell 11). There are other, more apocryphal anecdotes: her unwillingness to step on a scrap of paper on the street in case it had written upon it the Holy Name (Hinkson 187); her habit of carrying her cat, Muff, on her shoulders around the house in Torrington Square (Jones 224); finally, her method of dealing with a young poet who wished to discuss his work with her: upon seeing the manuscript in his pocket, Rossetti denounced modern poetry so vehemently that he was terrorized from producing it (Jones 206).

Following Elizabeth Cowie's influential article "Woman as Sign," Deborah Cherry and Griselda Pollock analyzed the representation of Elizabeth Siddall in Pre-Raphaelite literature and the extent to which she functions as a sign for masculine creativity. Cherry and Pollock distinguish between her historical and semiotic construction, and they postulate restoring Siddall as an artist and as an historical personage. Both procedures fail, the first because "attempting to restore Elizabeth Siddall in this empirical and monographic manner cannot effect the necessary alteration of the gendered discourses of art history" ("Woman as Sign" 210), particularly in view of the fact that Siddall's work has been predominantly placed relative to Dante Gabriel Rossetti's. The second strategy breaks down due to a lack of information and because, as Cherry and Pollock emphasize, archives are themselves historically shaped and cannot be employed "as a transparent window to the past" (211). Instead, they explore the textual construction of Elizabeth Siddall.

Cherry and Pollock's work has implications for the study of representations of Christina Rossetti. Although not on the same scale as in the case of Siddall, there is only a limited historical record of Rossetti: the Rossetti family's habit of destroying material made possible their control of information in the tropic construction of Rossetti.[2] Although, like Elizabeth Siddall, Rossetti is represented as a trope, she is also, due to her status as a poetess, more historically (or, rather, factually) recoverable. In effect, whereas Siddall's artistic output was never perceived to be more than an extension of Dante Gabriel Rossetti's oeuvre, Christina Rossetti is a producer of meanings. Because she is a relatively independent figure, the value of the fallacy of historicism increases in importance. Historical accuracy is masked as pleonasm, in excessively prosaic and excessively repetitious anecdotal material across the biographies. Mackenzie Bell was criticized by contemporaries for his attention to commonplace detail, and he is reported as defending himself to Godfrey Bilchett thus:

> Bell told me . . . that he gave so much prosaic matter of Christina Rossetti's because he wished to bring out her . . . absolutely practical everyday mind combined with the gift of the visionary, artist & poet; & Bell said his father had found the same combination in the Italians in the Argentine. (Kohl 424)

As Bell seems to have suggested, anecdotal information is inserted as part of a wider tropic concern: here, Rossetti is portrayed as an Englishwoman who is quintessentially Italian, a duality widely presented as a facet of her characteristic ambivalence. The inclusion of so much detail is equivalent to what Elisabeth Bronfen terms an attempt to parenthesize subjectivity: the biographical subject as an "accurate" historical personage is present but as an empty shell, bracketed or displaced to "make room for the concept it is used to signify." Consequently, "the body is deprived of history [and] changed into a gesture" (228). This presence-in-absence is fundamental to the mythological construction of the Christina Rossetti personage. The trace of displaced subjectivity, the notional inclusion of an emptied trope (Rossetti as an historical personage), is rendered biographically as her "divided life," a duality of "inner" and "outer" lives, between "natural" passion and imposed repression, between asceticism and aesthetics. Her "outer" life, or historical existence, is seen as a cover for her "inner" turmoil. As Cherry and Pollock conclude in relation to Elizabeth Siddall, ultimately only a textual analysis of the biographical subject can expose the construction given as "Christina Rossetti."

As a fragmentary narrative which must have, in order to work, an epiphanic moment, the biographical anecdote discloses the cultural constructions of femininity behind its operation in a biographical text. The disclosures are most fruitful when the very point of the anecdote — its epiphanic moment — is explicitly in question. This example signposts an elision of data that agitates the binary construction (inner/outer, passion/repression) of the subject's supposed identity, when an ambivalent textual silence seems to expose the gap between sign (the person labelled "Christina Rossetti") and signified (Rossetti as trope). Mackenzie Bell's biography and William Michael Rossetti's memoir cautiously describe Rossetti's adolescent crisis and last illness. In 1845, when she was fifteen, Rossetti's health became delicate. Bell briefly mentions that at this time she was attended by Dr. Hare, whose opinion of Rossetti's beauty and filial love is recounted, but not his diagnosis (Bell 20-21). No further details are offered as to the cause of her illness, which later biographers tend to interpret as a form of breakdown which transformed her from a vivacious child into a solemn and sickly adult. In his memoir, William Michael Rossetti is also vague in his description of his sister at this period:

> Christina was, I think, a tolerably healthy girl in mere childhood; but this state of things soon came to an end. She was not fully fifteen when her constitution became obviously delicate. . . . There was angina pectoris (actual or supposed), of which, after some long while, she seemed cured; then cough, with symptoms which were accounted ominous of decline or consumption, lasting on towards 1867; then exophthalmic bronchocele (or Dr. Graves's Disease), which began in 1871, and was truly most formidable and prostrating. . . . All these maladies were apart from her last and mortal illness, of which I must say a few words in its place. I have naturally much more reluctance than inclination to dwell upon any of these physical ills; but any one who did not understand that Christina was an almost constant and often a sadly-smitten invalid, seeing at times the countenance of Death very close to her own, would form an extremely incorrect notion of her corporal, and thus in some sense of her spiritual, condition. (W. M. Rossetti, *PWl*)

William Michael Rossetti does not name the illness that began in 1845, but Bell's friend, Godfrey Bilchet, transcribed the following note in the back of his copy of Bell's book:

> the doctor who attended on Christina Rossetti when she was about 16-18 said she was then more or less out of her mind (suffering, in fact, from a form of insanity, I believe, a kind of religious mania). (Kohl 423)

Around 1845 the family were in great financial difficulty owing to the ill health of the father Gabriele, and preparations were made for Christina Rossetti to take up a post as a governess. It is also known, from her manuscript notebooks, that she was continuing to write poetry at this time. It seems likely that the contemporary diagnosis of the mysterious illness, which William Michael Rossetti and Bell would be naturally reluctant to mention, was hysteria.

It is necessary to distinguish between definitions of hysteria. As Elaine Showalter argues in *The Female Malady,* the symptoms and cultural meaning of hysteria changed from era to era. For the Victorians, hysteria was a disorder of the womb and a sign of dysfunctional femininity for which the prescribed cure was rest, marriage, or motherhood.[3] The Victorians, in a much documented ambivalence, also construed women's illness as an affirmative sign of femininity; hysteria then becomes a sign of excess which challenges this cultural code, a sign for extremes of emotion and of physical symptoms. The significance of hysteria has subsequently evolved through the work of Freud and Breuer, and feminist readings of their *Studies on Hysteria* and Freud's *Fragment of an Analysis of a Case of Hysteria* develop its designation as a neurotic illness into a gender ambivalence that emerges in the hysteric's discourse. Thus, hysteria as the excessive sign for what the Victorians understood as "feminine" becomes in hysterical discourse a vacillation between masculine and feminine, both an acceptance and refusal of the feminine position as dictated by society. The biographical representation of Christina Rossetti emerges as an illusory historical personage presented as both historically accurate and removed from the workings of history: the suggestion and biographical suppression of her hysteria helps unravel this paradox.

As Kathleen Jones notes in her recent biography of Rossetti, hysteria would almost certainly have been mentioned as a cause of her illness: she was seen by a gynecologist, and one symptom was described as a suffocating sensation, typical of psychosomatic illness (19–20). William Michael Rossetti's comment that to understand that his sister was an invalid is to understand her "corporal, and thus in some sense her spiritual, condition" (see above) suggests that illness is both the sign of a suffering saint and the outward sign of a psychical or spiritual malaise, two different notions attesting to the Victorian ambivalence towards illness and femininity. At a time when she had extreme reluctance for governessing[4] and an increasing poetic output, we witness in the seminal biographies intimations of hysteria when her behavior could not be presented in line with nineteenth-century concepts of femininity. The suggestion of hysteria is even more pertinent when one considers the contemporary interrelationship of writing, motherhood, and disease, for both literary output and nervous illness were thought to originate in the womb.

Another highly significant passage occurs in Bell in an uncharacteristically explicit description of Rossetti's last illness, breast cancer, which caused her much pain and distress:

> Her brother has said to me, and wishes me to mention, that about a "couple of years" before her death Dr. Stewart told him "she was very liable to some form of hysteria." For a while in her final illness, though appreciably less in her last fortnight of life, such symptoms were apparent, particularly during semi-consciousness, chiefly manifesting themselves in cries, not so much, as far as could be observed, "thro' absolute pain" as "thro' some sort of hysterical stimulation." (170)

Bell's tentative reference to hysteria, which William Michael Rossetti refuted (Packer 397–98, Jones 223), is further amplified by a previously unpublished letter quoted in Packer's biography, in which a neighbor complains of Rossetti's "distressing screams that sound clear from her Drawing-room to mine" (399). To label her understandable distress during the closing stages of her illness hysteria *and* to suppress this diagnosis indicate another incident when her behavior could not be accounted equivalent to the assigned "character" of Christina Rossetti.

Furthermore, it is possible to apply contemporary theories of hysteria to the biographical texts themselves. By both fetishistically stating and refuting the diagnosis that Rossetti was an hysteric, these texts appropriate the other they wish to deny — the trope "Christina Rossetti" as historically constructed. To include and withdraw the designation of Rossetti as an hysteric (in the sense understood by the Victorians) is to intimate an ambiguity and vacillation of sexual identity — particularly in the insistence that a saintly asexuality and a perpetual sickness is concurrent with her femininity. The texts thus refuse the "ordering" of a sexuality construed as normal: the classic symptom, the classic failed repression, of the twentieth-century's definition of hysteria. The ensuing uncanny duplicity is both a denial and an affirmation not only of the diagnosis of hysteria but also of the biographical subject as a feminine subject. As Bronfen succinctly asserts, the hysterical textual voice is a function of the cultural equivalence of femininity and death:

> The hysteric's is a superlatively uncanny position, and as such another aspect of death's figure in life. Precisely because of the hysteric's doubleness between self and image and her oscillation between sexual signifiers, she uses her body to collapse the difference between opposite terms like masculinity/femininity, object/agent of spectatorship, confirmation/disclosure of cultural values, only to pose undecidable questions. (282)

The biographical *representation* of an alleged clinical hysteric subscribes to the same operation; the textual appropriation of the included and refuted hysterical feminine subject positions the text within an hysterical discourse.

In a discussion of Levi-Strauss's analysis of woman as a commodity for exchange within culture (which also concerns Elizabeth Cowie), Bronfen notes that "Woman-as-sign," "also marks a self-reflexive moment within the process of signification to become a signifier for exchange itself." She is both body and trope, and her historical existence and subjectivity are different from the way she is spoken of "in figure" (226). Thus, "Woman" comes to represent in herself the meaning process she is part of. This semiotic function is inherently associated with the feminine subject represented within a discourse that positions the subject as hysterical, for by definition the hysterical symptom is histrionically somaticized and dramaticized by the subject in an enactment of the self-doubling that comes with the resistance to gender identity and the disjunction inscribed into the textual position. The explicitly unknown and unknowable trope of Christina Rossetti in the biographical texts emerges as both a figure of represented "Woman" and a figure for the actual process of representation, for the self-enacting and histrionic nature of the trope.

That Christina Rossetti is a sign for representation is suggested most forcefully in a recurrent biographical anecdote of her stay at Penkill Castle, the home of Alice Boyd in Ayrshire, in the summer of 1866. Quotation from five of the principal biographies will suggest not only a tendency of the authors to repeat similar material and even similar phrases but also a tendency literally and figuratively to frame Rossetti as object and as trope.

Mr. Arthur Hughes, in the course of conversation, has described to me in a very vivid manner the little four-cornered window of Christina Rossetti's bedroom at Penkill, which commanded a view over an old-fashioned garden, and in which, according to Miss Boyd, as quoted by my informant, she used to stand, leaning forward, "her elbows on the sill, her hands supporting her face" — the attitude in which she is represented in Dante Gabriel's drawing of 1866, just alluded to. "The little window exactly framed her," added Mr. Hughes, "and from the garden she could be seen for hours meditating and composing." (Bell 51)

At Penkill the room assigned to the shy, dark-haired lady from London looked out upon an old garden and has a little four-cornered window at which that lady used to stand for hours together, "her elbows on the sill, her hands supporting her face," lost in meditation. How she must have looked standing there we may guess from Dante Gabriel's chalk drawing made about this time and used by Mr. Mackenzie Bell as the frontispiece to his monograph. . . . The wistful look of the earlier Christina has given place to an aspect at once passionate and austere. Here is the image of the woman who wrote:

My heart goes singing after swallows flown
On sometime summer's unreturning track.

(Stuart 79-80)

From the old-fashioned garden below, Christina was often seen standing in front of the little four-cornered window which, Arthur Hughes tells us, "exactly framed her." Her habitual position was to lean forward, "elbows on the sill, hands supporting her face," and she could be seen for hours "meditating and composing."

But she could see as well as be seen. Her room commanded a view of the garden with its sundial, moss-covered stone benches, and lattice arbors overarched by roses, of the dark leafy depths of the glen, of Girvan stretching out into the distance, and further, beyond the town, the sea and Ailsa Craig. (Packer 222)

In spite of these occupations, however, much of her time was spent alone in her room, the topmost one in the tower, and originally known as "the ladies' bower." From its windows she could see the distant sea and the rocks of Ailsa Craig. She would stand for hours on end, her elbows on the window-sill, her chin cupped in her hands, looking out over the garden and the more distant landscape, "meditating and composing" (Battiscombe 126).

Alice told Arthur Hughes that it [Rossetti's room at Penkill] had a "little four-cornered window . . . which commanded a view over an old fashioned garden . . ." where Christina stood leaning on the sill for hours at a time "meditating and composing." Or so Alice Boyd thought. It was more than likely that Cayley was the object of her thoughts. At Penkill she wrote another haunting, allusive lyric. (Jones 139)

The repetition of a "little four-cornered window" at which Rossetti was to be seen is highly suggestive of the frame of a portrait, as if Rossetti was herself a living "framed" picture,[5] for she both looks out and is seen. The tropic construction that yokes representation *of* "Woman" and the sign for representation *as* "Woman" becomes also in these descriptions part of the contemporary discourse of the creative female as both object and subject, as both surveyed and spectated. Both Bell and Stuart follow their description of Rossetti at the turret window with a reference to Dante Gabriel's 1866 drawing of his sister to provide an index to how she actually appeared at the window. As Cherry and Pollock have shown with reference to Elizabeth Siddall, representations of Pre-Raphaelite women cannot be taken as simple reflections of their appearance. Such a myth of the accuracy of Pre-Raphaelite representation does, however, prevail in the biographies and was instigated principally by William Michael Rossetti's memoir in the posthumous edition of his sister's *Poetical Works* where he explains the extent of the likeness of each portrait of Rossetti to the model. Significantly William Michael Rossetti declares the 1866 colored-chalk drawing (which Bell and Stuart refer to) to be the best of all the portraits:

> This is a beautiful drawing, showing a face very chaste in outline, and distinguished in expression; it would be hard for any likeness to be more exact. I have seen it stated somewhere (and I believe it apropos of this very drawing) that one cannot trust Rossetti's likenesses, as he always idealized. Few statements could be more untruthful. Certainly he aimed — and he succeeded — at bringing out the beauty and the fine expression of a face, rather than its more commonplace and superficial aspect; but his likenesses are, with casual exceptions, very strict transcriptions of the fact. (lxiv)

To confuse actual appearance and representation, sign and signified, at the very site where Christina Rossetti watches and is herself watched suggests the process by which the iconic image of Rossetti is mistaken for that which it represents. To present Rossetti at a window in an act of composition and contemplation is also to involve her poetics in the trope of representation, for poetry here becomes an act of perceptual cognition, a reflex of sight. The biographies compound this trope by giving a description of the view that Rossetti would have seen.

Interestingly, contemporary commentators claim that her poetry describes an identifiable locale.[6] Edmund Gosse writes:

> Unless I make a great mistake, she has scarcely visited Italy, and in her poetry the landscape and the observation of Nature are not only English, they are so thoroughly local that I doubt whether there is one touch in them all which proves her to have strayed more than fifty miles from London in any direction. (139)

Arthur Symons declares that her style is "sincerity as the servant of a finely touched and exceptionally *seeing* vision" (Bell 331). Bell also quotes William

Michael Rossetti's analysis of his sister's poetics: "there is no poet with a more marked instinct for fusing the thought into the image, and the image into the thought: the fact is always to her emotional, not merely positive, and the emotion clothed in a sensible shape, not merely abstract" (328). We are presented with a poetess whose work is given to constitute a direct collapsing of thought into image, perception into poetry. What Lynne Pearce terms the Victorian anxiety over the "slipperiness" of signification (36), or the difficulty of fixing sign to signified, manifests itself as a sequence of mirrorings of life into art and of sight into poetry.

The object of the gaze is also the subject of his/her own gaze upon others, and, as such, that which is objectified by the gaze bears within itself the potentialities for subjectivity. The doubleness in the representation of Christina Rossetti at the window is thus apparent not only in the fact that the gazer seeing through the window may also view herself reflected in the pane, but also in the very status of the gazer who both sees and may be seen. Lacan defines the gaze as an excess of seeing, as desire, and not just a perceptual mode. To the subject (defined as that which is capable of being seen and shown), the possibility of being seen has primacy over the recognition that a reciprocal gaze is possible. Thus, the potential for subjectivity emerges as only a trace: this is apparent in the suggestion that Rossetti's gaze (delimited already within the aesthetics of feminine representation) is secondary to and predicated on the spectacle of viewing her.[7]

Over an analysis of the Victorian construction of the feminine subject always falls the shadow of the Lady of Shalott, reformed by the Pre-Raphaelites into their own parable for feminine transgression: an attempt to reinstate displaced subjectivity into the signification process is an attempt that ends in death.[8] Rather than being a critical dead-end, however, this topos of death is highly pertinent to an interrogation of the representations of Christina Rossetti: death as both a literal threat (Rossetti as an almost constant invalid from her adolescence, rendering her position literally in-valid) and figural (death as non-existence, a no-place from which the subject of Rossetti's poetry is predominantly positioned).

The highly ambivalent subject position of the trope Christina Rossetti emerges from the concept of "Rossetti" as both a sign of the representation of "Woman" and a sign for that signification process itself. This self-reflexive doubleness blurs the distinction between the socio-economic and semiotic functions of the trope, and the resultant indeterminacy becomes one of the signifieds of the sign. "Woman" may thus turn into the subject and producer of this operation, thereby blurring the difference between active and passive.[9] The dualism of Rossetti as an historical personage and as a sign for representation emerges in the depiction of Rossetti as a living saint, as dead before her death; thus the subject is always already posthumous and conceptually disembodied. The dichotomy is apparent in the descriptions of her appearance, which posit her as both "real"/historical and outmoded (or always outmoded and thus ahistorical). There is a widespread biographical interest in her unfashionable appearance (and thus non-contemporary, not of her time and therefore situated outside of her historical context), and in her illnesses which are inscribed in the text to re-figure Rossetti as trope, to present her as literally equivalent to the subject position of death that the trope occupies. Emphasis is placed upon her manner of dressing, particularly in her later years when she was heralded as a virginal suffering saint. Max Beerbohm's cartoon wittily presents the ambivalence of Rossetti as a Pre-Raphaelite heroine and as an old-fashioned plain dresser (reproduced in Battiscombe, facing p. 18). Rossetti, dressed in black, is remonstrated with by Dante Gabriel Rossetti for her dowdiness, and he offers other, more fashionable material, declaring: "What *is* the use, Christina, of having a heart like a singing bird and a water-shoot and all the rest of it, if you insist on getting yourself up like a pew opener." She is distinctive by virtue of her inappropriate dress (her face could be that of any female, whereas Dante Gabriel Rossetti is clearly identifiable) — if she was to wear the cloth he offers, she would no longer be identifiable as Christina Rossetti. Katherine Tynan Hinkson tells how she was initially disappointed with Rossetti's appearance:

> I remember that it was something of a shock to me to receive at my first sight of Christina an impression of short-petticoated sturdiness. . . . Doubtless it was a mortification of the flesh or the spirit to wear, as she did, thick boots and short rough grey skirts. As far as they could they made her almost ugly, for the spiritual face, with the heavy-lidded eyes, had nothing to do with those garments fit for a ten-mile walk over ploughed fields. . . . Something of a death-in-life it seemed to the girl coming in from outside, to be shut up in an ill-lit house in Torrington Square, with two or three old ladies getting up their centuries. (186)

William Sharp recounts the story of his first encounter with Rossetti during his visit to the home of friends. As he sat in the twilight he was conscious of a laughing, musical voice which attested to the right to prefer London to the countryside. A servant entered announcing the arrival of a guest and bearing a light, and the woman who had just spoken swiftly and mysteriously covered her face with a veil and left (736-38). The reclusiveness and preference for the anonymity of twilight is explained in Rossetti's correspondence as the result of Graves' disease, which dramatically altered her appearance. Most noticeable was a darkening of the skin and protruding eyes, along with other distressing non-visual symptoms (Bell 52–53, Jones 154). Rather than representing her as disfigured, however, the change in appearance is taken by biographers and commentators to signify spiritual beauty in suffering. Sensitivity to the symptoms would doubtless explain the use of the veil, but it also becomes part of the enigma of Rossetti as an idealized feminine figure in a play between what is seen and what is elusively covered up. Rossetti belongs comfortably to the twilight and must veil the visual signs of her illness. In physical suffering she is represented as supremely non-physical. The descriptions of her debilitating illness, and her own documented acute awareness of and attempts to conceal it, enact the nineteenth-century aporia of illness as the superlative sign of the feminine and illness as a sign of spiritual malaise.

Other references to Rossetti's appearance emphasize her unfashionable plain dress (which William Michael Rossetti comments was a family tradition, *PW* xlvii), the link between her clothes and separation from the outside world (which Hinkson aptly terms "death-in-life"), the correlation of her dress with domestic and pious passivity. All serve to construct Rossetti as a saint — dehistoricized, decontextualized — and, as a saint that is alive yet also posthumous, to posit her intrinsic identification with death. Roland Barthes, in "The Iconography of the Abbé Pierre," declares "the saint is first and foremost a being without formal context; the idea of fashion is antipathetic to the idea of sainthood." He comments upon the ambivalent haircut of the Abbé Pierre, which seems to be neutral, unfashionable, "a sort of zero degree of haircut," but he concludes that "neutrality ends up by functioning as the *sign* of neutrality, and if you really wished to go unnoticed, you would be back where you started" (53). An attempt to exempt oneself from fashion becomes a statement about fashion. For representations of Christina Rossetti, her unfashionable clothes do not simply decontextualize her but also place her relative to her context and become a statement about her difference, her spirituality, her asexuality and saintliness; her dress becomes an excessive sign, one that theatricizes her, renders her histrionic. This ambiguous attempt to decontextualize is also apparent in the depictions of Rossetti as an invalid, which seem to be a figure for the process whereby she is immobilized, fixed semantically and socio-historically as an identity: reclusive poetess, devoted daughter, pious spinster. The essence of feminine purity is couched ahistorically, beyond outside influences, and the feminine identity of Rossetti is constructed in terms of the fallacy that it transcends history.[10]

The body as physical entity and as presence is thus represented as a literal or actual portrayal in order to conceptually disembody Rossetti. Emphasis upon her literalness is ironic, for the inclusion of details supposedly attesting to her historical identity only serves to dehistoricize. It is significant that the literal serves a special purpose. Comments upon Rossetti's thought processes — her analysis of the Scriptures, her non-intellectual faith, her spontaneous and "natural" poetry — all serve to construct her thought as literal, feminine, and non-participatory in masculine literary tradition and masculine symbolism. In contrast, Elizabeth Barrett Browning's public and political poetry was interpreted by contemporaries as a transgression of the scope of women's poetry, and she was denounced by some as a hysteric and as masculine.[11] The biographies widely claim Rossetti's literalness in her interpretation of the Scriptures[12] and circulate the anecdote of how she disapproved of cremation because of her literal notion of the Resurrection (Bell 155). They also recount the anecdote given in Rossetti's *Time Flies* of how her sister Maria would not visit the Mummy Room at the British Museum because "it would be very unseemly if the corpses had to put on immortality under the gaze of mere sightseers" (retold in Bell 62, Woolf 238).

The significance of assigning the literal as inherent to femininity is explored by Lacan. The mother is connected, in Lacanian semiotics, to the literal and the absent referent: both the feminine and the literal in language are always located elsewhere. Thus to conceptualize literality as inherent to femininity becomes part of the tropic construction of "Woman" as the sign for representation itself, as the Lacanian subject is displaced into a position which is constantly fading.[13] To construct Christina Rossetti's mode of thought and poetry as non-participants in a dominant masculine signification process and her physical entity as actual and literal is to reposition her as already posthumous: a fading and elusive presence-in-absence. There is, of course, an irony: biographies are conventionally written after the subject's death, but Christina Rossetti's death is the crescendo of her representations.

The complex and paradoxical nature of such representations is suggested by Mackenzie Bell's account of Rossetti's deathbed, in which the literal and the abstract become confused. Bell narrates how he arrived one afternoon at 30 Torrington Square to find that Rossetti had died earlier that day. He is told of the events of her last hours and is shown upstairs to see the body:

> As I entered what had formerly been Christina's drawing-room I thought how unchanged yet how changed was the room. All the pictures, and well-nigh all the pieces of furniture, even to the miscellaneous articles which stood usually on the large drawing-room table, were in the same places as I had been in the habit of observing them. This, paradoxical as it may seem at first sight to say so, added vastly to the sense of impressiveness, just as the contrast between the commonplace — almost the prosaic — details and the supernatural element indissolubly linked with the poem, adds to the impressiveness of that lyric by Christina which her brother Gabriel named for her "At Home." (174–75)

Bell continues to describe the room and comments that, "With the sharpening of the perceptive faculties that comes to us sometimes, at moments like these, I thought I had never before seen Dante Gabriel's large chalk drawing of his sister — that drawn in 1866 — appear so lovely" (175). He then describes the face:

> I saw that, though slightly emaciated, it was not greatly changed since the last time I had beheld it in life. Perhaps I was hardly so much struck with the breadth of her brow — I mean in regard to its indication of intellectual qualities — as I had often been when conversing with her, but on the other hand I was struck more than ever before both by the clear manifestation of the more womanly qualities and by the strength of purpose shown in the lips. . . . My spirit was moved by the

> contrast I felt between the holy — almost the saintly atmosphere of the house and its commonplace surroundings. (175)

The juxtaposition of spiritual and prosaic, the collapsing of poetry into life (indicated in Bell's mention of "At Home"), and the heightened appreciation of the 1866 portrait suggest that death itself signifies all that is essentially feminine.

Rossetti's face in death, in fact, becomes the true representation and a figure for feminine purity. As the epitome of absence, the corpse of Rossetti is the ultimate trope for displaced subjectivity and for a disembodied historical personage. Under the guise of an authoritative chronicle, Bell's account, repeated through the genealogy of Rossetti biographies, subscribes to cultural notions of femininity which insist upon the absence of subjectivity and historical identity, but it nevertheless purports to give Rossetti within the framework of historical reference. In Bell's description of the deathbed scene, the attempted repression of historical identity is epitomized by the inert figure of Rossetti. The biographical subject, only precariously inhabiting the world in which it is a female paragon, now comes fully to be that which it has represented — disembodied, denatured, and ideally feminine.

The University of Dundee

NOTES

I am immensely grateful to Richard Cronin who assisted with the evolution of this article.

1. Groundbreaking work on the representation of Pre-Raphaelite artists in literary biography has been undertaken by Cherry and Pollock. In "Patriarchal Power and the Pre-Raphaelites" they expose the reminiscences of the Brotherhood as historically and culturally determined and not simply a window to the past. Similarly, in "Woman as Sign in Pre-Raphaelite Literature," to which this article is indebted, representations of "Elizabeth Siddal" are separated from the historical personage Elizabeth Siddall (see below for a fuller discussion of this essay). Both articles also point to the circulation of similar material in biographical texts.
2. The Pre-Raphaelite circle displayed a general tendency to destroy or control personal material. Christina Rossetti had a habit of destroying letters addressed to her upon receipt. She also requested that her letters to her long-term intimate friend Charles Cayley be destroyed at his death (Packer 362). At Dante Gabriel's death, she helped William Michael select letters that were suitable for publication (Packer 354–56). All the Rossettis, but Christina perhaps more than any, were acutely aware of their literary persona; certainly the dearth of historical information about her life is a result of the deliberate construction of her mythical and idealized image. "Christina Rossetti complicates but never disentangles herself from attendant men's angelic dream of her" (Auerbach 115–16).
3. Chapter 6 of *The Female Malady* is relevant here; also, for an overview of the history of hysteria, see the introduction to *In Dora's Case,* Bernheimer and Kahane.
4. She later so confessed in letters to Swinburne and William Michael Rossetti (Packer 21).

5. The actual window of her bedroom at Penkill Castle does indeed resemble a picture frame. On the cover of the Penkill Foundation newsletter, *The Order of the Owl,* is a photograph of a woman dressed as Rossetti sitting at the window. The frame of the window has a triple stone border, the middle section resembling lattice work; it uncannily suggests a painted portrait of Rossetti (the photograph itself makes this point by "picturing" a Rossetti double looking out of the window). For a general survey of representations of women at windows, see Shefer.
6. Compare my forthcoming article in *Victorian Poetry,* in which I demonstrate how Dante Rossetti's revisions to his sister's poetry replace the feminine subject with a locale and prioritize the experiential over the imagination.
7. See Wright 448–49, in which Lacan's stress on the primacy of the subject's possibility of being seen is distinguished from Sartre's notion of the reciprocal gaze. See also Lacan 182–83.
8. Belsey and Belsey 45. Saville makes an important clarification about the realm of Camelot which the Lady of Shalott yearns to enter, and enters to die: it is the hub of chivalric fiction which the Lady, and many readers, mistake for "real life." Thus Camelot is by definition a site for a dominantly masculine discourse, the chivalric tradition (77–78).
9. See Bronfen, 225–28.
10. Many feminist critiques are concerned with the dominant Victorian representational system's denotation of the feminine as private, in opposition to the masculine as public. Most pertinent here is an excellent article by Psomiades, "Body's Beauty," and see also her "Feminine and Poetic Privacy." At issue here is the removal of the feminine from capitalist production; in representations of "Rossetti" as a biographical subject this removal extends to an effacement of social and historical contexts that produced such representations. Kaplan argues that Rossetti's lyrics witness to a female psyche deliberately defiant of the social in order to forefront the psychological (ch. 5). I would argue that, rather than an *intentional* attempt to erase contexts, the poetry is largely predicated by the aesthetic which equated female poetry with the feminine subject position constituted within the realm of privacy, domesticity, and the a-contextual. Until quite recently, criticism of Rossetti continued to be affected by this representational discursive practice and insisted on divorcing the poet from her various social contexts. With Jerome McGann's reassessment, and the developing trend in New Historicism, Rossetti's social, literary, and economic contexts are now being reclaimed.
11. Dante Gabriel Rossetti refers to Barrett Browning derogatively with masculine imagery: "modern vicious style," "falsetto muscularity" (W. M. Rossetti, *PW* 460).
12. For example, see W. M. Rossetti, *PW,* p. lxvii.
13. Homans, ch. 1.

WORKS CITED

Auerbach, Nina. *Woman and the Demon: The Life of a Victorian Myth.* Cambridge, MA: Harvard UP, 1982.

Barthes, Roland. "The Iconography of the Abbé Pierre." *Mythologies.* London: Paladin, 1973; repr. 1989. 53–55.

Battiscombe, Georgina. *Christina Rossetti.* London: Constable, 1981.

Bell, Mackenzie. *Christina Rossetti: A Biographical and Critical Study.* London: Hurst and Blackett, 1898.

Belsey, Andrew and Catherine Belsey. "Christina Rossetti: sister to the Brotherhood." *Textual Practice* 2.1 (1988): 30–50.

Bernheimer, Charles, and Claire Kahane, eds. *In Dora's Case: Freud-Hysteria-Feminism.* London: Virago, 1985.

Bronfen, Elisabeth. *Over Her Dead Body: Death, Femininity, and the Aesthetic.* Manchester: Manchester UP, 1992.

Chapman, Alison. "Defining the Feminine Subject: Dante Gabriel Rossetti's Manuscript Revisions to Christina Rossetti's Poetry." *Victorian Poetry,* forthcoming.

Cherry, Deborah, and Griselda Pollock. "Patriarchal Power and the Pre-Raphaelites." *Art History* 7.4 (December 1984): 480–95.

———. "Woman as Sign in Pre-Raphaelite Literature: A Study of the Representation of Elizabeth Siddall." *Art History* 7.1 (March 1984): 206–27.

Cowie, Elizabeth. "Woman as Sign." *m/f* 1.1 (1978): 49–63.

Freud, Sigmund. *Standard Edition of the Complete Psychological Works of Sigmund Freud.* Ed. and trans. James Strachey. 24 vols. London: Hogarth Press, 1955.

Gosse, Edmund. "Christina Rossetti." *Critical Kit-Kats.* London: Heinemann, 1896.

Hinkson, Katherine Tynan. "Santa Christina." *The Bookman* (London) 41 (Jan. 1912): 185–90.

Homans, Margaret. *Bearing the Word: Language and Female Experience in Nineteenth-Century Women's Writing.* Chicago: U of Chicago P, 1986.

Jones, Kathleen. *Learning Not to be First: The Life of Christina Rossetti.* Oxford: Oxford UP, 1992.

Kaplan, Cora. *Sea Changes: Essays on Culture and Feminism.* London: Verso, 1986.

Kohl, James A. "A Medical Comment on Christina Rossetti." *Notes and Queries* 213 (Nov. 1968): 423–24.

Lacan, Jacques. *The Four Fundamental Concepts of Psycho-analysis.* Trans. Alan Sheridan. London: Hogarth Press, 1977.

McGann, Jerome J. "Problems of Canon and Periodization: The Case of Christina Rossetti." *The Beauty of Inflections: Literary Investigations in Historical Method and Theory.* Oxford: Clarendon, 1985.

Packer, Lona Mosk. *Christina Rossetti.* Berkeley and Los Angeles: U of California P, 1963.

Pearce, Lynne. *Woman/Image/Text: Readings in Pre-Raphaelite Art and Literature.* London: Harvester, 1991.

The Penkill Foundation. *The Order of the Owl* 3.1 (1987).

Proctor, Ellen A. *A Brief Memoir of Christina G. Rossetti.* 1895. N.p.: Norwood, 1978.

Psomiades, Kathy Alexis. "Beauty's Body: Gender Ideology and British Aestheticism." *Victorian Studies* 36.1 (Fall 1992): 31–52.

———. "Feminine and Poetic Privacy in Christina Rossetti's 'Autumn' and 'A Royal Princess'." *Victorian Poetry* 31.2 (Summer 1993): 187–202.

Rossetti, Christina. *Time Flies: A Reading Diary* London: S.P.C.K., 1885.

Rossetti, William Michael, ed. *The Family Letters of Christina Georgina Rossetti.* London: Brown and Langham, 1908.

———. "Memoir" and Notes. *The Poetical Works of Christina Georgina Rossetti.* London: Macmillan, 1904; repr. 1906.

Saville, Julia. " 'The Lady of Shalott': A Lacanian Romance." *Word & Image* 8.1 (Jan.–March 1992): 71–87.

Seymour, Miranda. Review of Frances Thomas's *Christina Rossetti. The Sunday Times* 24 May 1992: 6.8

Sharp, William. ''Some Reminiscences of Christina Rossetti.'' *Atlantic Monthly* 75 (June 1895): 736–49.

Shefer, Elaine. ''The Woman at the Window in Victorian Art and Christina Rossetti as the Subject of Millais's *Mariana.*'' *Journal of Pre-Raphaelite Studies* 4.1 (1983): 14–25.

Showalter, Elaine. *The Female Malady: Women, Madness, and English Culture, 1830–1980.* London: Virago, 1987.

Stuart, Dorothy Margaret. *Christina Rossetti.* London: Macmillan, 1930.

Woolf, Virginia. *The Common Reader: Second Series.* London: Hogarth, 1932.

Wright, Elizabeth, ed. *Feminism and Psychoanalysis: A Critical Dictionary.* Oxford: Blackwell, 1992.

THE BODY POLITIC AND THE BODY FLUID: SOCIAL EXPECTORATIONS AND DICKENS'S *AMERICAN NOTES*

By Laura C. Berry

> But however much I like the ingredients of this great dish, I cannot but come back to the point from which I started, and say that the dish itself goes against the grain with me, and that I don't like it.
>
> Charles Dickens on America, in a letter of 22 March 1843

ALL OF THE PRODUCTS OF THE BODY convey a double message, since we revile them even as we recognize their positive necessity, but this is especially so of saliva. Our usual associations connect spit to a paradoxical sense of both sustenance and breakdown, if only digestive. Then, too, spit is neither consistently out of our control nor necessarily willful. It certainly does not enjoy the dramatically involuntary status of blood or tears, but neither is it as notoriously subject to the will as some other body products. To our common imagination — certainly not to Science! — it sometimes appears that saliva is useless in comparison with more noteworthy body fluids. Blood and semen, for example, vividly invoke the living body, and even sweat, in its association with a release of toxins or cooling properties, bespeaks a folksy justification for its existence. Saliva is set apart by the way that it insists upon working *on* or *with* something else. It is not a strictly internal, one might even say private, flow that governs the movement of saliva, as is the case with blood; nor is this circulation directed outward and away from the body, as in matters of waste. Instead, saliva's utility is defined by its unique action of mingling and then returning to the body's interior. Our tendency to connect spit with figures of helplessness — consider the infant's and the madman's drool — suggests that we fear a loss of control over its flow. And indeed, the problem with spit is that we must employ it while we wish to have no more than what we need of it. Spit is only visible — and visibly worrisome — when it appears outside its purely utilitarian role. We are alarmed when there is extra, and the more we have of it the less we care for it. A literal-minded physiology might argue that saliva is vital, but common sense rightly insists there can be too much of it.

That very excess is emphatically registered by Charles Dickens during his first American travels, when he is suddenly "attracted to a remarkable appearance" in a railroad car. At first he believes he is seeing

> a number of industrious persons inside, ripping open feather-beds, and giving the feathers to the wind. At length it occurred to me that they were only spitting . . . though how any number of passengers which it was possible for that car to contain, could have maintained such a playful and incessant shower of expectoration, I am still at a loss to understand: notwithstanding the experience in all salivatory phenomena which I afterwards acquired. (*Notes* 144)

American Notes indulges, not to say bathes itself, in that "phenomena," taking seriously a housekeeper's mission to find filth everywhere. An obsessive attention to hygiene, particularly the hawking and spitting of tobacco juice, is one reason that the book is seldom discussed. Another is the unspoken, but nevertheless present, issue of copyright. In the absence of a binding law, Dickens's books circulated too freely, and without economic return. Perhaps it was this subtextual rumbling that Samuel Warren recognized when he criticized the book shortly after its publication. "[T]here is . . . too much about the personal *trivia* of his journeys," Warren remarked in *Blackwood's*, and then ended the sentence definitively, "too much about spitting" (Collins 120). If Dickens came to America prepared to laud it, he left eager to condemn, and the non-fiction account he produced of his journey has largely been dismissed. But *American Notes* demands a sustained reading because in this text a focus on unsavory manners can be read as something more than mere neurotic symptom. *American Notes* takes America as its nominal subject, but it is produced in a British context, both for Dickens and for England generally, heavily marked by social tensions. The 1840s have in fact been seen as "the decisive period in which the consciousness of a new phase of civilization was being formed and expressed."[1]

In particular, *American Notes* brings shifting class relations into focus, registering a concern that increased social circulation might be a necessary result of industrialism and its effects. The greatest threat that social levelling presents, in *American Notes*, is to individual identity. *American Notes* confronts the potential for a too-fluid social circulation by way of its attention to the contaminating circulation of bodily fluids, and thus confines pollution to a foreign, almost entirely masculine realm. But in the novels that follow this travel book, Dickens's narratives engage, rather than flee from, social transgressions. The novels move decisively toward social fluidity and a more instrumental use of the poor. However monotonous *American Notes* might be as a travelogue, it ultimately produces a more mobile subjectivity than had been possible in Dickens's earlier work. That is, greater fluidity in the later novels enables the construction of a flexible subjectivity than can withstand, perhaps even capitalize on, social change. Moreover, that fluidity encourages the prolific production of narrative. *American Notes* itself remains, however, a stalled narrative vehicle that only reveals the horrific dangers — no less than loss of self — contingent upon social mobility and the levelling of class differences.

Both in the jarring effect it seems to have had on his personal life, and in its sheer physical ruggedness, Dickens 1842 journey to American was by all accounts a rocky one. The enthusiastic author left England a democratic champion, ready in the belief that "European misery had its root in social, political, and economic exploitation embedded in the class structure . . . " (Kaplan 125).[2] He felt certain that "[n]o visitor can ever have set foot on those shores, with a stronger faith in the Republic than I had, when I landed in America."[3] But his trip was punctuated by his famously disaffected cry, "I *am* disappointed. This is not the Republic I came to see. This is not the Republic of my imagination. I infinitely prefer a liberal Monarchy . . . to such a Government as this" (*Letters* 3: 156). And when he returned to England, Dickens admitted that it was "with a corrected and sobered judgment," and that he "went [to America] expecting greater things than I found."[4]

American Notes is propelled forward by a chronological roll call of stops on an itinerary or descriptions of the means by which each destination is reached. For instance, the title of chapter nine, a catalog of conveyances and destinations, fairly reflects the preoccupations of the book: "A Night Steamer on the Potomac River. A Virginia Road, and a Black Driver. Richmond. Baltimore. The Harrisburg Mail, and a Glimpse of the City. A Canal Boat." Vast rural expanses are not the sole objects of this attention to locomotive detail; the city produces its own mobile notorieties: "No stint of omnibuses here!" Dickens enthuses, " . . . [p]lenty of hackney cabs and coaches too; gigs, phaetons, large-wheeled tilburies, and private carriages . . . " (128). The "plot" of *American Notes*, and perhaps this must be accepted as simply endemic to travel accounts, is as rigid as a set of railroad tracks, and just about as tiring.

That plot may result in a kind of progress, in which we are always arriving somewhere new, but it also describes a tedious circularity, as we move in a rough circle that will eventually return us almost to our starting point. Physically, we end in New York, having begun in Boston, but narrative barely advances. The "story," as it is usually read by critics, is in the dashing of Dickens's youthful political idealism. But if this is what happens, it takes place only in the margins. *American Notes* itself does not record a change of heart; it barely records, in any depth, a change of scenery.

The book was largely considered a failure or dismissed as mere insult when it was published, and it seldom is treated at length. Even critics who take the American trip as central to a biographical or semi-biographical reading of Dickens's novels avoid any extended discussion of the text itself.[5] The superficiality of Dickens's reading of America has defied any truly good reading of *American Notes*.[6] And it certainly is not a diverting ride. By the time we have reached the

Looking Glass Prairie, we have, like Dickens's party, grown exhausted. *American Notes* resembles nothing so much as the long car trips of youth. At last one feels "[a]s the time draws nearer . . . FEVERED with anxiety for home . . . oh home-home-home-home-home-home-HOME!!!!!!!!!!!" (*Letters* 3: 248).

Dickens's longing was no doubt influenced by the formidable pressures of his public appearances. Dickens in America was as much tourist attraction as he was tourist.[7] It is the literal circulation of Dickens's body across the landscape that locomotes *American Notes*, yet these travels are fraught from the start by the confusion engendered by the embodiment of Dickens's literary self. That is, a confusion develops between Dickens, a tourist seated in a carriage and examining the sights, and the Author who created Little Nell. At times this produces the most disjunctive interchanges, as when a gentleman speaks in the author's "very ear, and could not have communicated more directly with me, if he had leaned upon my shoulder, and whispered. . . . " Yet the secret so provocatively imparted could hardly be news to the listener, for the man speaks to Dickens about, of all things, Dickens, saying, "Boz keeps himself very close." The difficulty of reconciling spectator and spectacle gathers around the difficulty of mingling Dickens's public and private selves, as when the peculiar gentleman "broke out again, with 'I suppose that Boz will be writing a book by-an-by, and putting all our names in it' " (242). The distance between those selves is at times very painfully diminished, as when a rail passenger becomes "exceedingly anxious to expound at great length . . . the true principles on which books of travel in America should be written by Englishmen" (119). Or, worse, on the occasion when Dickens's carriage is rushed by men and boys who "let down all the windows; thrust in their heads and shoulders; hooked themselves on conveniently, by their elbows; and fell to comparing notes on the subject of my personal appearance, with as much indifference as if I were a stuffed figure" (161). The visit is thus, biographically speaking anyway, marked by an uncomfortable intimacy that, in acknowledging Dickens as a literary lion — and therefore curiosity — effectively erases him in his capacity as an individual subject. He becomes, in this strange mixing and mingling, a "stuffed figure," while the mass of onlookers are paradoxically able to maintain a corporeal selfhood in spite of their being one of a crowd. Those individual selves are registered in the insistent specificity of their "shoulders," and "elbows," and "heads" and in their usurpation of the author's prerogative as they fall to "comparing notes."

More troubling with regard to Dickens's progress is that *American Notes* begins — or rather, does not quite begin — with an angry jibe at the financial problems of circulation: the circulation of his books. That the issue of the copyright agreement stands very much behind the text is signalled in the title: these are, after all, notes "for General Circulation." And in fact the title is a bitter joke, referring to the profitless circulation the *Notes* would enjoy across the Atlantic. At the last minute Dickens omitted an epigraph, taken from the *Old*

Bailey Report, that would have underscored the point: "In reply to a question from the Bench, the Solicitor for the Bank observed, that this kind of notes circulated the most extensively, in those parts of the world where they were stolen."[8] The quotation also, of course, figures Dickens's own books as currency made counterfeit in America.

Dickens's novels were fantastically popular in the States, but in the absence of a copyright agreement between England and America, that healthy circulation was profitless for Dickens. The lack of an agreement was at issue at every juncture, both public and private, during the trip. Dickens created an "enormous furore" (Johnson 376) in using the American journey to press his case for copyright law, even though the public "outcry" included "[a]nonymous letters; verbal dissuasions; newspaper attacks . . . assertions that I was no gentleman, but a mere mercenary scoundrel; coupled with the most monstrous mis-representations relative to my design and purpose in visiting the United States" (*Letters* 3: 83). But on the subject of this enormous furor, *American Notes* is curiously silent. Although Dickens made countless speeches, prepared a petition, wrote angry letters home, and even lobbied Congress on behalf of his cause, there is no direct mention in his published account of the trip. The silence maintained about copyright everywhere but in the title, and the noisy engagement of the topic outside the *Notes*, must call attention to itself.

American Notes, in its rare and oblique references to the copyright issue, constructs the problem as precisely one of cleanliness and virtue. The newspapers, for example, which serialized Dickens's novels (making them available for pennies, and cheating him of his profits) and participated in the gossipy, often quite mean, reports of his visits (including his agitations on behalf of copyright), become in *American Notes* a species of hysterical pornography,

> pimping and pandering for all degrees of vicious taste, and gorging with coined lies the most voracious maw; imputing to every man in public life the coarsest and the vilest motives; scaring away from the stabbed and prostrate body-politic, every Samaritan of clear conscience and good deeds; and setting on, with yell and whistle and the clapping of foul hands, the vilest vermin and worst birds of prey. (136)

This metamorphosis translates an allegation of slander into a question of hygiene; like the trouble associated with the movement of Dickens's body through America, the copyright dilemma puts forward a problem: how to make progress while maintaining a profitable and authentic self. On the one hand, a dangerous transgressing of social bounds potentially erases Dickens's individual selfhood. And on the other hand, an equally dangerous freedom of movement threatens to erase the author's profits. What is evidently required is greater control over movement. Things, it would seem, must be brought to rest, and in their proper places.

American Notes exchanges these dilemmas of self and wealth for a single-minded obsession with ill-health. Dickens's penultimate paragraph in *American*

Notes peculiarly sums up his book by begging for "a few common precautions" to promote an acceptable standard of hygiene:

> Greater means of personal cleanliness, are indispensable to this end; the custom of hastily swallowing large quantities of animal food, three times a-day, and rushing back to sedentary pursuits after each meal, must be changed. . . . Above all, in public institutions, and throughout the whole of every town and city, the system of ventilation, and drainage, and removal of impurities requires to be thoroughly revised. (292)

This weird conclusion is nevertheless amply prepared for by a text which collapses the journey, after some commentary on American institutions, into little more than an index to dirt and decay. In America, we find, "[e]ach pool of stagnant water has its crust of vegetable rottenness," found "in every possible stage of decay, decomposition, and neglect" (113), while a river is a "dismal swamp" that is "a breeding-place of fever, ague, and death" and "teeming . . . with rank unwholesome vegetation" (215). The city fares no better, where a visitor encounters "these narrow ways . . . reeking everywhere with dirt and filth" (136). In short, "all that is loathsome, drooping and decayed" presides in the States; there is a never-ending "air of ruin and decay abroad" (180).

Movement in this book tends to unearth a filthy subtext. Indeed, travel itself is dirty.[9] On a steamer boat, the "atmosphere of the cabin is vile in the last degree"; and worse, "everybody" uses the single available comb and brush (176). Traveling in general results in a most distasteful grime, for,

> [i]n all modes of travelling, the American customs, with reference to the means of personal cleanliness and wholesome ablution, are extremely negligent and filthy; I strongly incline to the belief that a considerable amount of illness is referable to this cause. (203)

This concern for American hygiene soon reveals itself as an anxiety about social boundaries. For example, there is the first significant rail trip. We learn immediately that "[t]here are no first and second class carriages as with us," and that the cars are "shabby omnibuses." Genteel behavior is lacking, since "[t]he conductors or checktaker, or guard, or whatever he may be" — Dickens will not deign to know or guess — "wears no uniform." In fact, he walks about "as his fancy dictates" and even "stares at you." The most appalling indignity seems to be that "[e]verybody talks to you, or to anybody else who hits his fancy" (111–12).[10]

The result is an unbearable social proximity. A steamer that traverses the Potomac, to Dickens's "horror and amazement," is "full of sleepers in every stage, shape, attitude and variety of slumber" (176). In coaches passengers are squeezed mercilessly (177), and the coachmen are as filthy as the coaches (187). On a canal boat the closeness at night is sickening, and Dickens is lucky enough to get a place "in some degree removed from the great body of sleepers" (193). This turns out to be particularly fortunate, since we are soon warned against "that class of society who travel in these boats" (194). A steamboat affords a much-needed separation, for it "was unspeakable relief to have any place, no matter how confined, where one could be alone" (201).

Most objectionable, and most memorable, is the saliva that is relentlessly associated with a contaminating closeness that will not admit separation; it equalizes as it flows. In *American Notes* spit wells up everywhere. It is what is on everyone's lips, and what defines the social context. For the fascinated reader, as apparently for the writer, spit substitutes for a lively description of the sights. But as the trip progresses, "those two odious practices of chewing and expectorating began . . . to be anything but agreeable, and soon became most offensive and sickening" (160).[11]

Spit is at the heart of the American democracy Dickens was at first so eager to approve. "Washington may be called the head-quarters of tobacco-tinctured saliva" (160), he says. The House and Senate display hideously discolored carpets, caused by "universal disregard of the spittoon" (169). The President's "mansion" is "like an English club-house" (170) but that it is defiled by the same cause, as the men "bestowed their favors so abundantly upon the carpet, that I take it for granted the Presidential housemaids have high wages . . . " (172).

But the most peculiar thing about spit in *American Notes*, having once accepted its so-tangible presence in the book at all, is the fact that it is simultaneously the most disgusting thing Dickens finds in America and the very thing that keeps things going. The practice of spitting is implicated in the very functioning of commerce and community. Situated at the heart of every crucial segment of the social body, spit comes to seem the circulatory fluid that makes life possible. The "dignified and decorous" body of the Senate is interrupted by the "universal disregard of the spittoon with which every honourable member is accommodated" (169). As this lengthy passage goes on to describe the workings of Congress, nothing comes across so much as the regularity of their chewing, the inextricable connection between spit and the political business of the day.

To chew and to spit is part of every aspect of civil life in America. Dickens lists the sites for this dirty practice, omitting no social body of significance. His specificity emphasizes how pervasive the practice is; indeed, he wants to insist on the institutionalization of expectoration:

> In all the public places of America, this filthy custom is recognized. In the courts of law, the judge has his spittoon, the crier his, the witness his, and the prisoner his; while the jurymen and spectators are provided for, as so many men who in the course of nature must desire to spit incessantly. . . . (160)

It is not only an institutionalization, but a kind of equalization, this passage implies. Spitting brings people together, even prisoner and prosecutor; it is at the heart of the justice system; when people are together at business it is "in the course of nature" that they will "spit incessantly."

> In the hospitals, the students of medicine are requested . . . to eject their tobacco juice into the boxes provided. . . . In public buildings, visitors are implored . . . to squirt the essence of their quids . . . into the national spittoons, and not about the bases of the marble columns. (160)

But above all, spit is the fluid that greases the wheels of social intercourse. The passage ends in decrying the fact that "in some parts, this custom is inseparably mixed up with every meal and morning call, and with all the transactions of social life" (160). In America, "[t]here is no conversation, no laughter, no cheerfulness, no sociality, except in spitting" (203).[12]

Spitting, implicated as it is in Dickens's conception of things with the very commerce and forward motion of life in America, is as necessary as it is deplorably unsanitary. Although certainly chewing tobacco and spitting was not crucial to American democracy or social life, and although surely Dickens was aware of this, in portraying America as awash in tobacco-colored spittle, Dickens finds it possible to condemn the entire country. The recurring motif of the vulgar, expectorating American becomes a textual touchstone, a reference point from which a rejection of the democratic experiment begins to seem natural. One reason for this is that, as we have seen, the failure of hygiene in America is imagined partly as a failure of social separation. A breakdown in civility is equated with a breakdown in class barriers. Prisoner and judge are brought nearer in their common dependance on the "national spittoons." The closeness is horrific, and the horror is defined by the impossibility of locating a space "no matter how confined, where one could be alone."

To be alone: as Dickens's text progresses, or fails to, social proximity takes shape around a specific fear — that striking down class barriers will produce a hopelessly homogeneous populace. During a meal on board "The Messenger," Dickens designates this commuter steamer a floating container for mediocity:

> The people are all alike, too. There is no diversity of character. They travel about on the same errands, say and do the same things in exactly the same manner, and follow in the same dull cheerless round. All down the long table, there is scarcely a man who is in anything different from his neighbor. (204)

It is "the usual dreary crowd of passengers" from whom Dickens strives, with only limited success, to maintain adequate distance. They are "the depressing influence of the general body. There was a magnetism of dulness in them which would have beaten down the most facetious companion. . . . Such deadly leaden people; such systematic plodding weary insupportable heaviness" (215). Proximity between classes threatens English middle-class subjectivity. That is, lapses in social boundaries can mean a virtual loss of self.[13]

Dickens's disgust at American hygiene and travel conditions and his concerns about individual identity are openly manifest as he heads home. No sooner is he afloat on the Atlantic than he finds it possible to adopt the role of social reformer — but only now that he is safely sequestered. Of the crowds in steerage, he remarks, the "whole system of shipping and conveying these unfortunate persons . . . stands in need of thorough revision" (265). The massing of the lower classes below decks actually produces personal identity, unlike the featureless crush experienced on American vehicles:

> We carried in the steerage nearly a hundred passengers: a little world of poverty: and as we came to know individuals among them by sight, from looking down upon the deck where they took the air in the daytime, and cooked their food, and very often ate it too, we became curious to know their histories. (264)

The safe distance and the nearness of home enables Dickens to once again discover in the poor suitable subjects for history-taking, presumably with a thought to turn those individuals into fictional characters. This attitude, a reformed liberalism that is authorized only by Dickens's safe status above decks, is the one Dickens characteristically displays toward American slaves. He is at ease taking up their cause and chastising backward America, and he devotes an entire chapter to this effort; this is possible to do because the slaves, whether free or not, are in no danger of coming closer to *him*.

Similarly, in his observation of state institutions in Massachusetts, Dickens opines that government in England has singularly failed to "display any extraordinary regard for the great mass of people or to recognize their existence as improvable creatures" (78). That is to say, in offering nothing beyond "the workhouse and the jail," which have come "to be looked on by the poor rather as a stern master, quick to correct and punish, than a kind protector, merciful and vigilant in their hour of need" (78), his countrymen have not sufficiently differentiated the poor. To be merciful — and vigilant — defines Dickens's reformist stance; what he applauds above all is an organized system that can both maintain order and resist creating featureless crowds: the indigent, blind, and imbecile must maintain the (distant) individuality that will authorize Dickens's authorial interventions. Thus, at The Perkins Institution and Massachusetts Asylum for the Blind, the lack of a uniform — uniforms were of course standard in England — is what stands out in Dickens's mind:

> the absence of these things presents each child to the visitor in his or her own proper character, with its individuality unimpaired; not lost in a dull, ugly, monotonous repetition of the same unmeaning garb. (80)

That this tableau is understood to be important primarily from the visual perspective of Dickens and his reader is of course indicated in the phrase "to the visitor": what matters is the effect on the bourgeois observer.

The State Hospital for the Insane gains approval because a necessary order is not imposed at the cost of the illusion of individuality, marked by the endurance of manners. Patients, however mad, are encouraged to "exchange[ ] . . . the most dignified salutations with a profound gravity and respect" (96), and the selfhood of the inhabitants is assured by an insistence on civility. Civility, indeed, imparts subject status even as, absurdly enough, it prevents homicide attempts:

> Every patient in this asylum sits down to dinner every day with a knife and fork . . . At every meal, moral influence alone restrains the more violent among them from cutting the throats of the rest. (96)

Restraint is equated with cure, and moral influence is "a hundred times more efficacious than all the strait-waistcoats, fetters, and handcuffs" ever produced (96).[14] At the House of Industry it is a "mild appeal" (97) that greets paupers, and "[i]nstead of being parcelled out in great, long, rambling wards, where a certain amount of weazen life may mope, and pine, and shiver, all day long, the building is divided into separate rooms, each with its share of light and air" (98). In summarizing his view, Dickens enthuses:

> Such are the Institutions at South Boston! In all of them, the unfortunate or degenerate citizens of the State are carefully instructed in their duties both to God and man . . . are appealed to, as members of the great human family . . . are ruled by the strong Heart, and not by the strong (but immeasurably weaker) Hand. (103)

For Dickens, only in a divided society is the "individual" a possibility. And only in positioning himself as a social reformer — advocate of the heart and not the hand — is that division fully comfortable. The individual middle-class subject is portrayed "looking down upon the deck," pondering the "need of thorough revision." And in the modern institutions of Boston, Dickens encounters the sort of revision he will employ in rewriting his own narratives of the poor.

It is the preservation of identity that consumes Dickens as he travels; it is the continual threat of class boundaries that incites his fears. The democratic experiment must be, for Dickens, a failure. *American Notes* records Dickens's disillusionment, but it also holds a clue to the solution that the author will offer in his later novels: the saving enclosure of domestic life. While Dickens's obsession with saliva allows him to partition himself from the filth he perceived all around him, it also requires that he virtually erase women from his text. It is this erasure which contributes most to the stalemate of this narrative.

For spitting is manifestly part of an all-male universe. One of the problems *American Notes* encounters is an inability to fully imagine a female subject, a project crucial to Dickens's novels, if not to Victorian fiction more generally. If it is gender, as I will suggest, that assists in resolving social anxieties in Dickens's later novels, it is no wonder that *American Notes* has such trouble sentimentalizing the currents of social circumfluency. Women labor only at the margins of the text. There are, for one small example, the White House maids, charged with cleaning the spittoons. Boston women are briefly mentioned: "The ladies are unquestionably very beautiful — in face; but there I am compelled to stop" (106). Two fuller accounts (discussed below) of women in *American Notes* emphasize once again the importance to Dickens of making individuals of the poor, but neither example provides the text with that fixture of the English novel, the idealized domestic woman.

The Lowell factory girls are not "women," but rather working-class objects of a kind of charity. They exemplify how poor girls who work, rather than simply allow themselves to remain indigent, can be made manageable. The girls are models of "extreme cleanliness," and "[t]he rooms in which they worked, were as well ordered as themselves" (115). What Dickens delights most to report, although it may "startle a large class [English] readers" (116), is that the factory girls display traditional English markers of a higher status; their boarding houses typically have a piano, they subscribe to circulating libraries, and they produce a periodical magazine. Dickens rhapsodizes:

> Are we quite sure that we in England have not formed our ideas of the "station" of working people, from accustoming ourselves to the contemplation of that class as they are, and not as they might be? (117)

Dickens's fascinated re-telling of the story of Laura Bridgman at the Perkins Institution typifies the desire to link institutionalized and regulated charity with individuality. Bridgman can neither see nor hear nor speak. She is an absolutely inarticulate subject with whom it is impossible to communicate, perpetually and perfectly the faceless object of charity. Dickens lovingly narrates the elaborate process of communication developed at the Institute, a miraculous story that reaches its apothesis when "self-consciousness" and "identity" coincide in the recognition of a mother. Laura's entry into the world is effected when she finds her mother; the visit instates Laura as an articulated and articulate subject:

> at this moment of painful uncertainty, the mother drew her [daughter] close to her side, and kissed her fondly, when at once the truth flashed upon the child, and all mistrust and anxiety disappeared from her face . . . she eagerly nestled to the bosom of her parent, and yielded herself to her fond embraces. (88)

This mother, however, is rapidly banished from the pages of *American Notes*. Laura Bridgman must remain an inmate of the Institution, her story serving to hint at what Dickens needs to remodel his own fictions.

Later, on the prairie, the furthest Dickens gets from London and its comforting divisions, we encounter a final nurturing figure who, like Laura Bridgman's mother, cannot provide the sustaining story of self for long and quickly disappears from the text:

> The track of to-day had the same features as the track of yesterday. There was the swamp, the bush, [and] the perpetual chorus of frogs, the rank unseemly growth, the unwholesome steaming earth. Here and there, and frequently too, we encountered a solitary broken-down waggon, full of some new settler's goods. It was a pitiful sight to see one of these vehicles deep in the mire; the axle-tree broken; a wheel lying idly by its side; the man gone miles away, to look for assistance; the woman seated among their wandering household gods with a baby at her breast, a picture of forlorn, dejected patience; the team of oxen crouching down mournfully in the mud, and breathing forth such clouds of vapour from their mouths and nostrils, that all the damp mist and fog around seemed to have come direct from them. (227)

It is a portrait of the stalemate that aimless movement can produce and of the stalemate of narrative itself. Nature displays the sameness and mediocrity that is the result of a too-free locomotion. The American settlers, allowed to roam the frontier at will, have met with disaster; families are broken apart, identity lost. The nursing mother, "picture of forlorn, dejected patience," stands as the one fixed human point in a drama of unwise circulation. She represents the safe haven of family, a welcome infusion of feminine "patience" in a dirty male world of contagious proximity. In *American Notes*, mediocrity and sameness are not even relieved by human companionship. Here, there is neither social proximity nor personal identity. There is simply a solitary unwholesomeness. All that remains is a woman nursing her child.

In the novels that follow *American Notes*, the soothing flow of the milk of human kindness replaces an aggressive spurting of the "essence of [tobacco] quids," an exchange not only of fluids but of gender. The apparent political and professional reassessment in which Dickens engaged during and after 1842 has led some critics to think of it as a turning point in his career. The novel that immediately followed the trip abroad, and to some extent makes fiction of it, *Martin Chuzzlewit*, is less frequently discussed, but with the publication of *Dombey and Son* beginning in 1846, Dickens is almost universally said to have laid the foundation for the later novels. Kathleen Tillotson claims that "*Dombey and Son* stands out from among Dickens's novels as the earliest example of responsible and successful planning; it has unity not only of action, but of design and feeling. It is also the first in which a pervasive uneasiness about contemporary society takes the place of an intermittent concern with specific social wrongs" (157). Steven Marcus accords *Dombey and Son* a special place in his account of the author's literary progress: "This is the first of Dickens's novels whose movement seems to obey the heavy, measured pull of some tidal power. And it is not just a massive novel, but a monolithic one as well: all its parts seem to move together when they move at all. It begins slowly and ponderously, and only gradually, like a departing train or an ocean wave, picks up speed; but its motion then is irresistible" (296). Or, yet again, J. Hillis Miller says that "[t]he novel is really not so much a continuous course as a series of short, nearly straight lines, each of which advances the action a little way. Seen from a distance as we view the totality of the novel these lines organize themselves into a single curve'' (143).[15]

These comments find their common source in John Forster who, in his eagerness to dispute complaints that Dickens killed off little Paul Dombey in chapter 16 purely to boost sales of the earlier numbers, initiated the dominant theme in discussions of Dickens's literary transformation: an intentional, carefully worked out *plan.* In his biography of Dickens, Forster is quick to insist that ''the design affecting Paul and his father had been planned from the opening, and was carried without real alteration to the close'' (2: 20). Tillotson, Marcus, and Miller value ''responsible and successful planning''; the writer makes narrative ''obey.'' Dickens's ability to ''organize'' into a whole, to keep all of the parts in motion together, to *design* narrative is stressed. But what Tillotson and others perceive as ''design'' and as a grander social scale in the ''mature'' novels might also be understood as a more disciplined allegiance to a revised ''social vision'' that critics find easy to swallow. A seminal aim of that vision is to mediate the conflicts between social class and identity that *American Notes* demonstrates; one of the achievements of Dickens's novels after the *Notes* is that they at once rescue and reject the poor. The sense of purpose and design so often remarked upon as originating in *Dombey and Son* says less about *Dombey* itself than it does about the comfort critics feel in accepting the form of the social ''critique'' of the later works.

In *Dombey,* Dickens insists upon creating an equalizing flow between social strata. A more fluid relationship between classes is made to seem necessary, even instrumental, and dangerous pollutants are transformed from their negative flow to a positive charge. Dickens uses the figure of wet-nurse Polly Toodles, as well as her husband, the railway worker, to amend the nature of the circulation of body fluids found so threatening in *American Notes.* Polly's milk maintains little Paul Dombey's life, and it is largely the loss of that vital fluid, flowing from the poor woman's body to nourish her upper class charge, that means the certain doom of the child. By allowing a controlled transgression between classes, Dickens organizes a change that allows for more fluid narrative. In *Dombey and Son,* Polly's breast milk flows into Paul's body, where it is associated with that other maternal presence, Florence Dombey. Working-class contamination is imaginatively transformed, reorganized under the class-effacing sign of feminine ''influence.'' Meanwhile, ''influence'' comes crucially to be associated with the devouring plots of Carker, whose middle-class manipulations stand in for, and therefore diminish, the power of working-class men, represented and simultaneously rendered benign in the novel through the presence of Polly's bumbling husband. In *Dombey and Son,* gender becomes a means for coping with class.[16] In examining *American Notes* in detail, it is possible to see the need for this transformation from ''contamination'' to ''influence'' as it emerges in the course of the journey. In one important sense, *American Notes* finally cries out for the (ideologically) comforting presence of a woman.

After *Dombey*, Dickens makes narrative obey by letting go, increasingly by way of a more thoroughgoing use of images of circulation — the river, the fog, the Circumlocution Office, Pip's expectations — that work to complicate and to ease tension about class issues. What defines these tropes is their singular fluidity, and the intensity with which they flow *throughout* society.[17] Even as social forms and separations are reaffirmed, the novels enlist organizing metaphors that imply a circumfluency. Thus, in the world of *Bleak House* there is "fog everywhere" (5), murkily misguiding everyone in the novel, from the filthy inhabitants of Tom All Alone's (subject to the literal contagion of disease that can infect not only the poor, but migrate into the body of Esther Summerson as well), to much loftier heights where what has passed around circulates via the equally poisonous "fashionable intelligence." The river runs through *Our Mutual Friend* without regard to rank; it drags into itself or disgorges according to need or merit rather than status. Similarly Pip's expectations appear to float — in Pip's and in the reader's mind — from the dubious but sanitary grasp of Miss Havisham to the grasping and unclean hands of Magwitch. And of course, in *Little Dorrit*, Dickens offers a most ambitious representation of a pervasive fluidity that ruins — or simply runs down — all those in its path, which of course comprises everyone and everything. The Circumlocution Office "went on mechanically," and it is

> this spirit of national efficiency in the Circumlocution Office that had gradually led to its having something to do with everything. Mechanicians, natural philosophers, soldiers, sailors, petitioners, memorialists, people with grievances, . . . jobbing people, jobbed people, people who couldn't get rewarded for merit, and people who couldn't get punished for demerit, were all indiscriminately tucked up under the foolscap paper of the Circumlocution Office. (146)

Indeed, *Little Dorrit* represents the very flow of currency as an epidemic that infects every social sector, from Bleeding Heart Yard to its high source in Merdle. The name of Merdle spreads like a plague:

> That it is at least as difficult to stay a moral infection as a physical one; that such a disease will spread with the malignity and rapidity of the Plague; that the contagion, when it has once made head, will spare no pursuit or condition, but will lay hold on people in the soundest health, and become developed in the most unlikely constitutions; is a fact as firmly established by experience as that we human creatures breathe an atmosphere. A blessing beyond appreciation would be conferred upon mankind, if the tainted, in whose weakness or wickedness these virulent disorders are bred, could be instantly seized and placed in close confinement (not to say summarily smothered) before the poison is communicable. (627)

Merdle's poisonous economics "spare no pursuit or condition." Dirty currency infects wherever it flows, and it flows everywhere.

American Notes thus prepares for, even as it necessitates, the ''circulatory'' novels that follow in that the *Notes* present an unhealthy circulation that cannot be sanitized and therefore must be confronted. The vacillation between need and disgust that characterizes our view of saliva also defines the Dickensian picture of the undifferentiated poor. The threat of loss of control, the dread mixing and mingling — these things make spit abhorrent, and they describe with specificity the anxieties about class represented in *American Notes*. But if, at the end of the journey, we long to return ''home-home-home-home-home-home-HOME!!!!!!!!!!!,'' we have also been tutored to yearn for, and in the later novels will be invited to take our comfort in, the bosom of the family.

University of Arizona

NOTES

1. Williams makes this comment in his introduction to the Penguin *Dombey and Son* (11). For discussion of the unique tensions of the 1840s, see Perkin, Thompson, and Jones, to name just some major sources.
2. This is biographer Kaplan's assessment, but it also accords with the sense of Dickens's letters on the subject. See also Magnet who, pursuing a thesis linking *Nicholas Nickleby, Barnaby Rudge, American Notes,* and *Martin Chuzzlewit,* calls the 1842 trip one ''with a primarily political interest'' (175). Magnet goes on to argue that Dickens saw in America (or imposed upon it) a realization of the political theory he had formulated during the writing of *Barnaby Rudge.* Magnet describes this political stance as fundamentally more conservative than the familiar Dickensian liberal reform and uses his readings to detail an early ''*other* Dickens'' (1).
3. See the ''preface to the Cheap Edition,'' added in 1850 and included in the Penguin edition of *American Notes* (47).
4. This is taken from Dickens's discarded introduction to the first edition of *American Notes*. On John Forster's advice Dickens decided against publishing the introduction, but it is contained in the Penguin edition of *American Notes* cited above (300).
5. See Magnet, and especially Welsh. There are four book-length treatments of *American Notes* of which I am aware. Slater, in *Dickens on America and the Americans*, offers an excellent introduction, but his text is largely a collection of pictorial representations of the trip or the territory in 1842, together with excerpts from the *Notes* and from *Chuzzlewit.* Moss's *Charles Dickens' Quarrel with America* gives a volume of facts, clears up a number of controversies that arose during the trip, but does not address the issue of the literary quality of the book. Meckier has written a more recent book that extends the arguments of his 1984 journal article. Wilkins has also written a book. Parker has written an article in which he argues that Dickens responded with such hostility to matters of manners, and to America more generally, for psychological reasons: namely, that it called up ''unresolved conflicts'' and offered parodies of his own behavior and attitudes (58).
6. Ford remarks: ''It was reviewed extensively on both sides of the Atlantic, and [for the most part] its reception in England was predominantly hostile. . . . It was provoked because Dickens had ventured to talk authoritatively about something of which he was plainly ignorant.'' It was a ''superficial tourist's picture of American life'' (46).

7. Meckier ascribes Dickens's disaffection with the States to this "persecution," in "Dickens Discovers America."
8. On the matter of the omitted epigraph, see Forster (262). Dickens apparently took the quotation from a recent trial, but he does not identify the specific case, nor have I been able to locate it.
9. This is an appropriate moment at which to acknowledge a compelling recent essay, one which I located only in the last stages of my own revisions — that of Edgecombe, who places *Martin Chuzzlewit* in the context of colonial discourse. He notes that Dickens uses the American landscape "as a vehicle for social judgement" (37). This is to greatly oversimplify his argument, however. Edgecombe turns to *American Notes* to record the evolution of Dickens's "topographic disaffection." While the argument obviously takes a different route than my own, concerned as it is with the tropes and strategies of colonialism and with the land itself, Edgecombe nevertheless pursues some similar themes — disgust and infection for example — as part of a fascinating discussion of Dickens's development.
10. Dickens's concerns about rail travel in the United States were exacerbated by the fact that, in 1842, American railway cars were modelled on canal boats. The seats faced one another in long rows, there were no class divisions, and there was little sense of privacy. English coaches were, as Dickens points out, class divided and lavishly appointed. English rail coaches found their model in upper-class carriages with which travelers were familiar, and which positioned the first class passenger in a small private box that preserved, even fostered, the idea of the individual subject.
11. Although he is, for the most part, speaking of chewing-tobacco spit, Dickens seldom distinguishes among "types" of expectoration. Spit, as far as he is concerned, is spit. But apologists for American manners may wish to point out that the ill-mannered Yankees had, at least, reason to expectorate.
12. Dickens's very elaborate descriptions of expectoration understandably ask that we read them at least partly as exaggerations — in the spirit of the exaggerated personal peccadilloes found everywhere in his fiction. But for an argument that Americans really were as disgusting as Dickens implies, see Hughes. Hughes concludes that few American gentlemen would spit so profusely, and that Dickens's observations were probably of imposter-gentlemen, for "[t]he fact is, every man who could get together enough cash to purchase a frock coat and a top hat, called himself a gentleman" (74).
13. Magnet also sees Dickens concerned with the issue of individuality: "Like some vast Solitary Prison, America denies men participation in a fertile communal life, and as a result it characteristically produces stunted, undeveloped selves, whose individuality never blooms" (187).
14. The use of moral suasion over the insane is not unique to South Boston but represents a generally accepted theory employed in many institutions of the day.
15. The idea is hardly restricted to these three critics, but they are among the most influential of Dickens's earlier twentieth-century critics and represent three relatively different positions in relation to Dickens yet arrive as similar conclusions.
16. I develop this argument at length in an essay, "In the Bosom of the Family: The Wet-Nurse, the Railroad and *Dombey and Son*."
17. It is this "transgressive" flow, I would argue, that distinguishes the tropes of circulation in the novels written after 1846 from those of the earlier novels. While travel and other versions of circulatory movement are obviously present in works such as *Pickwick Papers* and *The Old Curiosity Shop*, there is not the same managed and

manageable movement across the entire social field that is dominant in Dickens's later fiction.

WORKS CITED

Berry, Laura C. "In the Bosom of the Family: The Wet-Nurse, the Railroad and *Dombey and Son.*" *Dickens Studies Annual*, forthcoming.

Collins, Philip, ed. *Dickens: The Critical Heritage.* New York: Barnes and Noble, 1971.

Dickens, Charles. *American Notes for General Circulation.* London: Penguin, 1972.

———. *Bleak House.* ed. George Ford and Sylvère Monod. Norton: New York, 1977.

———. *Dombey and Son.* London: Penguin, 1988.

———. *The Letters of Charles Dickens* Vol. 3. Ed. Madeline House, Graham Storey, and Kathleen Tillotson. 6 vols. Oxford: Clarendon, 1974.

———. *Little Dorrit.* London: Penguin, 1983.

Edgecombe, Rodney Stenning. "Topographic Disaffection in Dickens's *American Notes* and *Martin Chuzzlewit.*" *Journal of English and Germanic Philology* 93.1 (January 1994): 35–54.

Ford, George H. *Dickens and his Readers.* Princeton, NJ: Princeton UP, 1955.

Forster, John. *The Life of Charles Dickens.* 2 vols. London & Toronto: J.M. Dent, 1927.

Hughes, Dean. "Great Expectorations: Dickens on America." *The Dickensian* 79: 2, no. 400 (Summer 1983): 67–76.

Johnson, Edgar. *Charles Dickens: His Tragedy and Triumph.* 2 vols. New York: Simon & Schuster, 1952.

Jones, Gareth Stedman. *Outcast London: A Study in the Relationship Between Classes in Victorian Society.* New York: Pantheon, 1984.

Kaplan, Fred. *Dickens, A Biography.* New York: William Morrow, 1988.

Magnet, Myron. *Dickens and the Social Order.* Philadelphia: U of Pennsylvania P, 1985.

Marcus, Steven. *Dickens: From Pickwick to Dombey.* London: Chatto & Windus, 1965.

Meckier, Jerome. "Dickens Discovers America, Discovers Dickens: The First Visit Reconsidered." *Modern Language Review* 79.2 (1984): 266–77.

———. *Innocent Abroad: Charles Dickens's American Engagements.* Lexington: U of Kentucky P, 1990.

Miller, J. Hillis. *Charles Dickens: The World of His Novels.* Cambridge, MA: Harvard UP, 1958.

Moss, Sidney P. *Charles Dickens' Quarrel with America.* Troy, NY: Whitston, 1984.

Parker, David. "Dickens and America: The Unflatttering Glass." *Dickens Studies Annual* 15 (1986): 55–63.

Perkin, Harold. *The Origins of Modern English Society 1780–1880.* London: Routledge, 1969.

Slater, Michael. *Dickens on America and the Americans.* Brighton: Harvester P, 1979.

Thompson, E. P. *The Making of the English Working Class.* New York: Vintage, 1966.

Tillotson, Kathleen. *Novels of the Eighteen-Forties.* Oxford: Clarendon, 1954.

Welsh, Alexander. *From Copyright to Copperfield: The Identity of Dickens.* Cambridge, MA: Harvard UP, 1987.

Wilkins, William Glyde. *Charles Dickens in America.* New York: Haskell House, 1970.

Williams, Raymond. "Introduction." *Dombey and Son.* London: Penguin, 1972.

PROFESSIONALISM, AUTHORITY, AND THE LATE-VICTORIAN MAN OF LETTERS: A VIEW FROM THE MACMILLAN ARCHIVE

By John L. Kijinski

THE LATE-VICTORIAN MAN of letters has received a good deal of attention recently. Scholars of Victorian literature, historians interested in the rise of professionalism in Britain, people in cultural studies hoping to map out the relationship of literature to politics, and investigators of the rise of English studies have all looked to the man of letters as a figure crucial to our understanding of late-Victorian culture.[1] Neither a "Victorian sage," nor a specialist speaking to other specialists, nor even primarily a journalist, the man of letters was a professional writer who attempted to earn a living by selling "serious" writing to what he still considered a general, middle-class readership. On this we can agree. What continues to be debated, however, is the exact cultural role these writers played: how exactly they defined their relationship to the general culture; on what grounds of authority they rested their pronouncements to this general culture; and how exactly these professionals were involved in the rise of professionalism and specialization, particularly within the emergent discipline of English studies.

A vast repository of information on the day-to-day activities of the "serious" late-Victorian professional writer is the 1,250-volume Macmillan Archive, housed in the British Library. In this collection we have access to the outgoing and incoming letters of the firm that published more serious work by more important professional men of letters (e.g., Matthew Arnold, Leslie Stephen, John Morley, Walter Pater, Edmund Gosse, J. A. Froude, Thomas Huxley — the list goes on) than any other British house of the time. The people who made up this group of writers are a distinguished and representative set of end-of-the-century professionals who directly spoke to the general culture about the role that the national literature and figures of the nation's literary past should play within that culture. What I offer here is a picture of the late-Victorian professional writer that emerges from the letters of these writers to their publisher as well as the letters that the Macmillans — Alexander, Frederick, and George — wrote in response. Obviously, when dealing with an archive as large as this one, a limiting principle is required, and I have focused my investigation on the correspondence with Macmillan's of John Morley and the important writers who contributed to his "English Men of Letters" series (1878–92).[2]

Certainly one of the most influential figures in literary London during the 1870s and 1880s, Morley was, at various times, editor of the *Fortnightly Review, The Pall Mall Gazette,* and *Macmillan's Magazine.* His influence as a reader and editor at Macmillan's was enormous, and his importance to the Macmillans is indicated in that firm's Letterbooks of the 1870s and 1880s: during any given year, more letters are addressed to Morley than to any other individual. On top of all this, Morley had by 1883 already begun his political career (for which he would be primarily remembered) by taking a seat in the House of Commons.

The picture of the late-Victorian man of letters that emerges from the correspondence of this group — of his perceived grounds of authority for making pronouncements about literature, of his relationship to the general culture, of his hopes for influencing the general culture — are particularly important when considered in light of Ian Small's recent investigation of late-Victorian writing about literature, *Conditions for Criticism.* Briefly, Small argues that the relationship between authority and knowledge in many fields (e.g., history and political science) underwent a fundamental change toward the end of last century. This change, in fact, amounted to an epistemological crisis, and the response was the creation of professional disciplines within the universities. These disciplines claimed communal, institutionally-sanctioned, and precisely-defined authority over specialist bodies of knowledge. This new and methodologically precise claim to authority undermined the position of the lone individual making pronouncements about culturally complex matters, one of the reasons that the concept "Victorian sage" seemed so antiquated by end of the century. Although he bases his argument on a wide knowledge of the creation of a number of disciplines, Small is, of course, most interested in the impact this epistemological crisis had on the possibility of making authoritative statements about literature and how this change is related to the specializations that would be included in the discipline of English studies. He persuasively explains the work of Pater and Wilde as resounding rejections of specialization, as reaffirmations on new and radical ground of the authority of the individual. Small, then, deals with the specialist response to this perceived epistemological crisis and with two great writers who oppose the move toward specialization and point toward a modernist relationship between literature, culture, and the authority of the individual. What the letters of the Macmillan Archive add to this picture is a third element, the view of mostly traditional, non-specialist, and (much more than Pater or Wilde) representative professionals writing for a most respectable publisher.

The importance of Macmillan's — and other well-established publishers — as a cultural institution and underwriter of professional literary-critical activity needs to be taken into account as we sharpen our view of how authority to speak about literature could be gained toward the end of last century. As N. N. Feltes has demonstrated, it was during the late-Victorian period that publishers began to see their books as "branded goods" that offered customers a known "reputation value" (*Modes of Production* 84). Furthermore, Feltes shows that at this time publishers began to split into two groups: "entrepreneurial" houses put forth a book in hopes of making a large and quick profit on it; "list" houses were more interested in publishing works that would last, in building a "list" of works that would be seen by the book-buying public as having more than topical interest. As Feltes explains, the list became a tradition of the publishing house, and thus a valuable commodity in itself (*Literary Capital* 27). Macmillan's was, of course, among the most respectable of the list publishers; readers could be assured that the Macmillan name on a book was, in itself, an indicator that what was offered within the book was authoritative. What emerges from an examination of the correspondence of Morley and the writers who worked under his editorship is a vivid picture of how these late-Victorian arbiters of culture viewed their relationship to literature and the general culture to which they address their professional comments on this body of knowledge: these writers seldom endorse the stance of the specialist; although many of them were affiliated with university education, there is a sense conveyed that their authority comes not from the underwriting apparatus of an organized discipline, but rather from their individual talent and their standing as *public* figures within a sphere wider than that of a given discipline; finally, they convey a continuing belief that their work can have a direct and salutary impact on a general culture that they thought could still be reached and improved by their serious writing on the important figures of the nation's literary past.

The Choice of Contributors

WHAT IMMEDIATELY STRIKES the twentieth-century reader of the letters that Morley and the Macmillans wrote about the establishment of the "English Men of Letters" series is the role that respectability played in their estimation of fit contributors to the series. The series would be comprised of short (160 to 200 page) biographical/critical studies of the great writers of England's past. Morley and Alexander Macmillan hoped that this would be an important and lasting series, and of course they hoped to employ only the best writers they could find to author the individual volumes. What is surprising, however, is just how important they thought it was to attract respectable writers to their series. A revealing example is Morley and Alexander Macmillan's attempt to engage Richard W. Church, Dean of St. Paul's, to do a volume for the series. In a letter of 6 August 1877, Morley presents Macmillan with a list of writers he would like to see treated early in the series — Swift, Milton, Wordsworth, Gibbon, Scott, Shakespeare, and Johnson — and then comments, "The list would do for a launch, provided we can only get *one* recognized divine, Cain, or Dean Church. We need that for respectability's sake." Writing several days later, 22 September 1877, Morley had met with Church, had been delighted with the meeting, and notes to Macmillan, "If we can secure him we are all right." He reiterates the importance of Church a few days later: "Of course we cannot launch our list until he comes in." Yet at this point, Morley and Macmillan are not even sure of which volume for the series Church would do; the Dean would be allowed to select between Spenser, Taylor, and Dryden (letter to Alexander Macmillan, 30 September 1877). Similarly, Morley speculates on the appropriateness of asking Church's friend, the eminently respectable Lord Coleridge (who never did finally contribute to the series) to do the volume on Swift, even though he is not confident that he would be the most appropriate person to treat the subject: "I do not suppose Lo. Coleridge will make much of Swift, but his name would help the Series very much. So let us ask him" (letter to Alexander Macmillan, 3 October 1877).

This is not to suggest that Morley and Macmillan overlooked the quality of the writers for this series; it is just to note how large a function respectability played in the establishment of authority. Ideally, what they sought was a combination of respectability and the highest professional qualifications. As Morley notes to Macmillan on 5 October 1877: "The highest respectability — and the highest capacity — an impossible union, O my Macmillan. But I accept your command all the same." This emphasis would have a strong influence on how the "less respectable" writers (e.g., Burns, Byron, Defoe) who would become part of the twentieth-century canon of English studies would be viewed. Macmillan books spoke to a solid, middle-class readership. Such readers could be edified by studies of the lives and works of "non-respectable" literary figures only if they were written by the most respectable professional writers. Here, for example, are the grounds on which Macmillan is pleased about Dean Church's interest in doing the volume on Dryden: "I see that he [Church] leans to Dryden, and as he is a rather ticklish subject I am much inclined to entrust him to such refined hands" (letter to Morley, 2 October 1877). The phrases "ticklish subject" and "refined hands" speak volumes: only when passed through the refined hands of a public cleric who was also a public man of letters could the suspicious Dryden become an appropriate representative of the national tradition to the respectable reader. This is true of figures other than Dryden, as Macmillan comments to Morley in a letter from a few days later: "Three of our subjects, Swift, Dryden, and Burns should be given to people who have as much respectability as is compatible with capacity, a nice problem" (4 October 1877).

Although respectability was an important qualification for a writer who hoped to become part of the Macmillan list, the letters also offer evidence that respectability without the right kind of capacity could disqualify a writer. For example, Alexander Macmillan writes to Morley on 18 March 1878, "Please put a word into my mouth that I may speak to Sir Edward Strachey. I doubt whether we ought to give Coleridge yet, at all, and if we do give him it certainly should be as a man of letters mainly & not as a philosopher which probably would be Sir Edward's view of him." The respectability Strachey's name would add to the series is outweighed by the fear that he might treat Coleridge as a philosopher rather than as a man of letters — and thus make the volume inappropriate for the general readership at which it would necessarily be aimed. This dilemma demonstrates clearly that Macmillan saw the man of letters — both of the past and of the present — as a non-specialist who could speak to the general reader about matters of wide cultural — rather than narrowly disciplinary — interest.

Beyond comments on respectability, it is surprising how infrequently Morley discusses his grounds for selecting writers for his series with Macmillan. Macmillan and Morley both thought that they were finding "illustrious workers for the Series" (letter to Morley from Alexander Macmillan, 19 July 1877), and certainly, as I have pointed out, the list of people who ended up writing for the series reads like a who's who of professional London literary life during the 70s and 80s. Yet how Morley went about selecting them and on what grounds he saw them as *the* authorities to write the volumes they did is seldom discussed in the letters. Obviously, in his capacity as an editor of the *Fortnightly* and reader at Macmillan's, he had a working relationship with most of the important writers of London, as well as those at Oxford, Cambridge, and other universities of the time. Furthermore, it is clear that he was known and valued — socially as well as professionally — by members of the literary world. As Arnold testifies to Alexander Macmillan: "All you say in Morley's praise is true. He is indeed a delightful companion . . . " (27 August 1878).

Some of their discussions of selection and authority focus on the attempts that Morley and Macmillan made to enlist those seen as the literary stars of the time. For example, both George Eliot and Arnold were approached to do Shakespeare, and both refused. Morley speculates on what Eliot's name could do for the series: "Of course we could not press Mrs. Lewes for time, but it would be worth much silver and gold to us if she could start the Series — say in April" (letter to Alexander Macmillan, 9 November 1877). Macmillan was enthusiastic enough about the possibility of Eliot writing for them that he authorized Morley to pay her three to five times the normal one hundred pounds for the volume (letter to Morley, 9 November 1877).

However, apart from these discussion of how to win the help of the *most* respectable and the *most* famous writers, what we often find is a rather informal system of recommendation and a "common sense" of who the right people would be to do these volumes. For example, there was an unexplained agreement that John Seeley should do the volume on Shakespeare (he was offered this volume before it was offered either to Arnold or to Eliot). Morley writes to Macmillan on 16 December 1878, "Of course Seeley is the man for Shakespeare; I always said it" — an assumption that seems strange today as Seeley was known primarily for the work he did as Professor of Modern History at Cambridge. In other instances we find informal recommendations. Morley, for example, explains to George Craik (an important administrative assistant to Alexander within the Macmillan firm) that Charles Eliot Norton had recommended W. D. Howells for the volume (never actually to be completed) on Washington Irving (15 January 1878). Or we find Dean Church suggesting Arthur Stanley and John Campbell Shairp (who did, eventually, write the volume on Burns) as likely candidates for the series (Alexander Macmillan to Morley, 20 September 1877). Or Frederick Macmillan, suggesting to Morley, that — because they cannot get James Russell Lowell to do it — the Hawthorne volume should be offered to Henry James: "What do you think of Henry James for Hawthorne? There seems to be no chance of getting Lowell. James writes well and I am sure would put his best work into it" (5 October 1878). Or we have Frederick Macmillan mentioning Alfred Ainger to Morley (first reminding Morley that he had met Ainger and would surely remember him) and noting, "Ainger is a man of a fine and delicate humour and knows his Lamb thoroughly" (29 October 1880). The grounds on which this recommendation is made are, indeed, interesting and revealing. What is just as important as a knowledge of Lamb is the writer's connectedness to the professional literary establishment of which Macmillan's is such an important part — Morley already *knows* him and will remember him — as well as his *refinement*, his "fine and delicate humour."

This selection process — so different from what would now be employed by a major publisher for a definitive critical/biographical series on great literary figures of the past — did, as we have seen, yield a distinguished group of writers. What is equally noteworthy is these writers were willing to publish in the series at a payment rate that must have looked like "minimum wage" to many of them. This agreement is actually a part of what we may call the professional stance of the time. Harold Perkin, in his study of the rise of professionalism in Britain, notes that the professional must always find a way to press "his own social ideal, his own vision of society and how it should be organized, upon other classes" (8). The professional, of course, needs to convince society that his views are based on purely logical grounds and that their adoption will be in the best interest of all classes. Robert L. Patten has argued that one of the ways this impression was created by the late-Victorian professional writers was through "the mantle of *secular sanctity*" (27) in which they wrapped their pronouncements. Certainly the Macmillans and those who wrote for them were interested in profits and sales, but there is a kind of "secular sanctity" that is reflected in their ideas about presenting the general reader with access to the great literature of Britain's past, and it manifests itself in part in the willingness of writers to contribute their work to this series for the rather small wage of one hundred pounds per volume.

Many of the contributors could have earned by their pens much more on less difficult work. The case of William Black, author of the volume on Goldsmith, is revealing. Although he is almost forgotten today, he was famous as a journalist turned novelist. His novels *A Daughter of Heth* (1871) and *A Princess of Thule* (1874), for example, were both best sellers. His importance is attested in the *Dictionary of National Biography* entry on him that Richard Garnett wrote: "Few men of letters were more widely known in literary circles, and none more generally esteemed and beloved." Evidence of his high earning power can be found in a contract, preserved in the Macmillan Archive, which he signed on 29 March 1878 for the novel *Macleod of Dare*. The contract gave him one thousand pounds in advance as well as one-sixth of the selling price of every copy as a royalty. Compare this to the one hundred pounds — with no royalties — he was paid in the same year for *Goldsmith*. It is no wonder that in a letter of 13 April 1878 he protests to George Craik that he could easily get five times as much writing serialized fiction, which he claims is much less demanding work than he is putting into his study of Goldsmith. Yet, he says he will presevere in his critical/biographical task. And it is telling that when his volume was completed, Black asked Craik to send a complimentary copy to Carlyle, a writer whose spirit informs the publishing ventures of Macmillan's (3 February 1879); Black must have felt that, unlike his novels, *Goldsmith* represented the sort of earnest work of which Carlyle could approve. I think it is also significant that the Macmillans instructed Morley to be sure that every contributor to this series was given a copy of each volume as it was completed (letter to Morley, 24 June 1878). Thus the writers were encouraged to see themselves as a part of a large project of public significance which would provide readers with a unified set of works on the great figures of the nation's literary past.

Of all the people who wrote for this series, I can find evidence that only Huxley was given extra money: in a letter of 27 March 1878, Craik tells Morley that he may give 150 pounds to Huxley for his volume on Hume. Thus all the rest of the distinguished contributors — Anthony Trollope, Henry James, Leslie Stephen, Sidney Colvin, J. A. Froude — produced works of from 170 to 200 pages in length for one hundred pounds. The payment is slight even when the comparison category is other critical work for Macmillan. For example, Gosse's contract for doing an edition of the poetry of Gray shows that he earned 250 pounds for that (April 1884), and Arnold received fifty pounds for his Preface to Ward's *English Poets* (this rather brief essay would be republished as "On the Study of Poetry") (contract, 25 December 1879).[3] Apparently, more important than money was having one's name as a contemporary man of letters associated with this series that would bring to the general public guidance in the national literary tradition.

The Publisher's Commitment

THE LETTERS THE MACMILLANS wrote to this distinguished set of contributors help to clarify exactly what they thought the work of serious writers could accomplish for the general culture. They were convinced that good writing, addressed to the general reader, about great writers of the past could have a positive influence on the culture and that they, as publishers, had a commitment to promoting this task. Particularly striking is the working relationship the Macmillans established with the writers. Alexander Macmillan — probably the most influential publisher in Britain — never saw himself as a mere businessman, a mere provider of commodities for a profit. He shows, of course, an interest in sales, but he sees a kind of symbiotic relationship between his firm's turning a fair profit and the general health of the culture. In his letters, we find him consistently dealing directly with writers, commenting even on such concerns as possible errors in a given manuscript or the effectiveness of the general treatment of a given subject. When Alexander did not personally deal with these important writers, the task was assigned to his nephew Frederick or his son George (Craik, however, handled most correspondence that dealt with money details). The firm seemed to run much more like a family enterprise than along the lines of a fully capitalist publishing house.[4] Writers were treated as collaborators with the publishers in a public enterprise that would serve the culture.

Alexander Macmillan saw his firm as carrying on the Victorian tradition of the literature of cultural improvement, and it is not suprising that he saw the "English Men of Letters" series as descending from the work of Carlyle. Here in an letter to Richard Church, Macmillan tellingly links his expectation of a large audience for the series with the legacy of Carlyle: "I enclose a prospectus of a Series of Books to be sold at 2/6 or so; we would hope for a sale on Railway Stalls and the like. The length should be double that of an Edinburgh or Quarterly article. Carlyle's Burns in his critical Essays, with a little more biography would be the sort of mode of treatment aimed at" (19 September 1877). He also tells Morley that he likes the title of "men of letters" for the series because of the echo that it carries of Carlyle's essay on the man of letters as hero in *Heroes and Hero-Worship* (10 November 1877). Thus the legacy of Carlyle — the antithesis of the specialist, or academic, writer on literature — is still very much alive at the end of the 1870s in the mind of the most influential publisher of books on literature and culture in Britain. In spite of questions about authority and knowledge that were being taken up in academic circles, this publisher still saw his firm as a site of considerable authority at that crucial ideological point where judgments on the national literature are made for a wide public.

In their letters, the Macmillans, Morley, and writers publishing under the Macmillan imprint reveal that they felt no need to derive authority for their critical pronouncements from a formal community of scholars with specialist training. Instead, the primary site of authority, as they saw it, was the individual professional, writing as a public man of letters, in direct, essential contact with a public man of letters of the nation's past. In effect, the ideal was to have the contemporary man of letters working to treat the great man of letters of the past about whom he was writing as a kindred spirit rather than primarily as an object of specialist research. This standard of authoritative treatment is revealed, in part, in those comments that Morley and the Macmillans make on writers who fall short of this ideal. Morley, for example, complains of J. C. Shairp's manuscript on Burns, stating that although it is about such a colorful figure, it is itself "colourless" as "there is nothing of the writer [Burns, that is] himself in it." He will finally accept the MS as "suitable & readable," but he clearly thinks more could have been done to treat the subject appropriately and authoritatively (letter to Alexander Macmillan, 27 March 1878). In a similar vein, he complains to Craik about Richard Holt Hutton's *Scott*: "It is just, but, entre nous, it rather wants *character*, and that is just what Scott ought to have had — the faithful admirable man" (6 June 1878). Or note this particularly telling criticism that Alexander Macmillan makes of Goldwin Smith's *Cowper* in a letter to Morley: "As it stands, I don't think it would at all do. Of course with his really fine power of thought & utterance there is much that has merit, but the *whole man* Cowper has not impressed itself on the retina of mind's eye, or if it has he has not *said it again* as an artist should" (4 July 1879). These are not the sort of complaints one makes about biographical/critical accounts of great writers of the past if one is judging primarily by scholarly or specialist standards. Morley and the Macmillans want their writers to treat great writers of the past so that the living writer captures — in a complementary fashion — the *essence* of the writer of the past. The ultimately authoritative act of criticism is the passing on of this captured essence to the general reader, who can then rely on the "essential author" as the site of authority for the reading and interpretation of the literary works of that author.

We can see this standard being invoked as a grounds for praise when Alexander Macmillan finds a volume particularly successful. Morley, it is true, sometimes seems to be satisfied if a volume is simply "readable and workmanlike" (letter to Alexander Macmillan, 5 February 1878). However, if praise was given, it was generally based on a more exalted idea of what the critic writing about a great writer of the past could do. Note here the grounds on which Alexander Macmillan praises Church's *Spenser*: "It is an excellent work, with fineness, health, discrimination, charity, moral and intellectual" (letter to Morley, 16 March 1879). For Macmillan, Church had captured those special features that mark the essential Spenser. Furthermore, the idea of the *health* of the work is important and comes up frequently in other Macmillan writers about literature. Good literature is created by great writers who are morally healthy, and good criticism captures this quality and allows the general reader to share in it.

Shelley, of course, provided a particular challenge to the idea of respectability as a poetic quality, so it is significant when Macmillan congratulates J. A. Symonds on his treatment of this subject. Here, Macmillan gives us a clear picture of what a very good critic could do for his subject, how he could capture the essence of a great writer of the past — the "whole man," purged of the non-essential — and offer it to the general public for their edification:

> I like your book very much, and think it must be the clearest & simplest complete presentation of the man we have. . . . [He refers to Shelley as "The Divine Poet."] Shelley was a unique man in himself & in spite of deflections of a very pure high nature. As an utterer of noble thought in noblest word, he is unsurpassed. My admiration for him is of more than forty years['] standing, and is as strong now as it ever was. But as St Paul exhorted people to pray with the understanding, so I think we ought to admire with the understanding. People have both admired & abused him with much too little of this valuable gift. I cannot help being gratified that we have had the honour of publishing what is on the whole the best, completest, and most rational account of so noble and beautiful, if also erratic & perplexing a character. (22 November 1878)

Certainly one could do worse than to point to this passage from Macmillan to demonstrate what Victorian publishing at its most respectable was about. Here we have the most powerful publisher in England expressing his solidarity with the biographer/critic, joining with him in his effort to present the public with an authoritative guide to how an important but problematic part of the English tradition is to be viewed.

Completely compatible with this high view of serious works about literature, we find a confidence that such works could reach a significant reading public. Macmillan assumed that these volumes spoke to the general adult reader — neither a student nor a specialist — so that something like the existence of an influential "public sphere" that is interested in literature is still taken for granted. Macmillan distinguishes Morley's series from less ambitious attempts — also published by Macmillan — to reach a *student* audience. Macmillan reminds Morley that his series is to be quite different from J. R. Green's literary primers (letter to Morley, 1 February 1879). This difference, and the greater care and importance placed on choices for a general adult readership, is illustrated by the fact that Morley and Macmillan never considered Edward Dowden — who did the volume on Shakespeare for Green — as a possible candidate for the more important volume on the author in Morley's series. In a letter to Goldwin Smith, Alexander Macmillan explains exactly what serious books on literary figures of the past could do for the general adult reader:

> The essence of such a series as we are attempting is that the Reader [sic] should carry away with him an impression of the man & his work, that would be living and real whether the reader knew the subject before or did not. In the first case it ought to recal [sic] and vivify previous knowledge, in the second place to whet the appetite for more complete knowledge, and even be fairly satisfactory if a man had not time to go further. (4 July 1879)

Note here that once again we have the insistence that the basis of authority of such work lies in the fact that a contemporary writer captures a great writer from the past as a living reality for the general reader.

Alfred Ainger, a Macmillan writer who, as I have noted, wrote a volume on Lamb, expressed a clear sense of what he thought the professional writer could do for the general reader. In a letter of 1882, he explains that he would like to write a volume on Shakespeare, in spite of the fact that so much had been written about him, because, in the past, he had been treated too often "for *school boys* and the *experts*. What he [Shakespeare] wants doing for — is to be written about for the average Englishman — & I *should* like to do it"(letter to Craik, 25 April 1882). He further explains, in a letter to Frederick Macmillan, that if he were allowed to write the volume his goal would be to tell the "middle class what Shakespeare did, was, and ought to be to us" (5 June 1882). This comment could be used as a summing up of what so much of the serious professional writing of the time on literature attempted to do: tell the middle class what their own national literary tradition did, was, and ought to be to them.

Macmillan and Morley were both confident that there were enough of these "average," middle-class readers to buy serious literary books to make their publication profitable. They estimated that serious treatments of great writers of the past, done by respectable writers of the present, would be well received and would continue to sell for a long time. Even before the series was begun, Macmillan remarks, "My own feeling is that the books will do well, very well, and last" (letter to Morley, 30 November 1877). As was appropriate for a "list" publisher, Macmillan hoped that a fit audience for such books could be found that would buy them year after year. Just how well founded his hopes were can been seen by glancing through *A Bibliographic Catalogue of Macmillan and Co.'s Publications from 1843–1889* (published by the firm in 1891), which shows how often so many of the volumes of the "English Men of Letters" series went into numerous editions. Evidence that there was a public out there to purchase such volumes is also found in the comments that George Macmillan makes to Morley on how to make the most of this market:

> Our country traveler, a very shrewd person, & of much experience, has been in today, and is very strong of opinion [sic] that we ought not to publish another volume till about the 25th so as to give the first time to make its mark, or "get a good swing" as he expresses it. . . . It is after all probably better for the Series not to cram too many books down the public throat at the same time. (2 June 1878)

The letters are also sprinkled with comments on how well the volumes of this series sold. About three months after the first book in the series (Stephen's *Johnson*) was published, Macmillan writes to Morley: "We are over 2000 copies and every day the sale goes on. We will want to reprint very soon" (24 June 1878). Again, shortly after the publication of Shairp's *Burns*, Macmillan tells the author, "We have sold about 4500 copies of your Burns, and the sale goes on steadily" (5 August 1879). George Macmillan also notes to Morley that, upon the very first printing of Symonds' *Shelley*, there is an immediate order "of considerably over 2000 straight off — which is certainly encouraging" (18 October 1878). Perhaps the most important statement on sales figures, and how these reflect the cultural mission of the writers employed by Macmillan's, is found in a letter of 27 January 1881 written by Alexander Macmillan to F. W. Myers, author of *Wordsworth*. Macmillan notes that two months after its publication, the volume has already sold about 4,500 copies. He compares this with the sales figures for two months with some of the other books in the series: *Hume* sold 6,000; *Byron* about 4,700; *Locke* 3,700. These, he remarks, are about average for how all of the volumes so far published had sold during their first two months of publication. He then goes on to say, "Of course the subject tells a good deal. But it is comforting that Wordsworth is so near Byron [in sales]. People are constantly telling me that Wordsworth is little read now, and yet we have sold over 4000 of Matthew Arnold's Selections & your book too." Macmillan is, of course, encouraged by profitable sales, but he is also pleased that the series is serving the cultural mission of promoting the popularity of Wordsworth.

To gauge the confidence in this cultural mission that was felt by those associated with Macmillan's, it is useful to turn to Morley's brief monograph on literature for the general reader, *On the Study of Literature*, originally given as an address to the students of the London Society for the Extension of University Teaching in 1887 and published by Macmillan in the same year. Late in the '80s, Morley expresses an undiminished confidence that serious reading will reward the general reader with intellectual capital. Systematic reading, even if done for only thirty minutes per day, will pay off. He offers this calculation to those willing to put in the needed thirty minutes: "Then multiply that half hour by 365, and consider what treasures you might have laid by at the end of the year; and what happiness, fortitude, and wisdom they would have given you for a lifetime" (*Study* 26-27). This analogy of intellectual capital with real capital — found frequently in the critical works of Macmillan writers of the time — underlines the value the professional man of letters could still claim for serious reading. Morley, then, speaking at the end of the '80s, shows no evidence that he felt an epistemological crisis had undermined the authority of the individual to speak about literature to a wide public.

Just as significantly, Morley never suggests that the authority of serious writing about literature need be underwritten by specialized knowledge backed by a formal discipline. For Morley, it was more important that the man of letters have a wide and active awareness of many phases of the culture. In what relationship should such an independent professional stand to the new discipline of English then developing at the universities? Although Morley was a supporter of English studies at the universities, he also claimed authority for the man of letters that went beyond the confines of any narrow notion of disciplinarity or specialization. In *On the Study of Literature*, for example, he notes that the serious writer on cultural issues can also take an active role in the important political and social concerns of the culture. In fact, he implies that such writers amplify their authority by taking on the character of the "public man." Morley is eager to dispel any notion that men of letters are fit to engage only in retiring work; he insists that they may also succeed in activities that are clearly gender-marked as "manly": "I venture to say that in the present Government, from the Prime Minister downwards, there are three men at least who are perfectly capable of earning their bread as men of letters" (*Study* 8). Note the emphasis here on earning power and on seeing the man of letters as a public character. He also claims that "some of the best men of business in the country are men who have had the best collegian's equipment, and are the most accomplished bookmen" (*Study* 8).

If the ideal man of letters for Morley and the Macmillans was something more than a university specialist, this does not mean that they were opposed to drawing on the labors of university professors. The House of Macmillan had throughout its history been connected with the universities: Macmillan had begun his career as a bookseller in Cambridge, and he was publisher to Oxford University from 1863 until 1880. Morley believed that one of his strengths as an editor and reader was his ability to draw on talented young people coming out of the universities. In fact, one of the reasons he took only an advisory position for the second "English Men of Letters" series (published by Macmillan beginning in 1902) was that he felt he was no longer adequately acquainted with people at Oxford and Cambridge. Many of the professional writers published by Macmillan also held university appointments; some of them held chairs in English. For example, Edward Dowden held the chair of English literature at Trinity College, Dublin. John Nichol was chair of English Language and Literature at the University of Glasgow. David Masson was professor of English first at University College, London, and then at Edinburgh University, where he was succeeded by George Saintsbury. And Goldwin Smith was the first professor of English at Cornell University in the United States.

The letters, however, never convey the sense that these people were called upon primarily as specialists, that their work somehow had more value and authority because the writer spoke from a position at a university. Quite to the contrary, the Macmillans made decisions about publishing, about who would become part of their firm's list and tradition, on authoritative grounds that went beyond university or disciplinary bounds. The relationship of what the Macmillans saw as their own authority to the authority of the universities can be epitomized in a series of judgments that Morley was asked to give for the firm. Morley was regularly called upon to judge the worth of manuscripts that had already received the imprimatur of either Cambridge or Oxford. I cite three of many such examples: On 6 April 1883 Alexander Macmillan sends Morley a manuscript that had been designated a Cambridge Prize Essay. Macmillan thinks it "too slight for publication but we should be glad to know whether you think the writer shows promise. If so we might encourage him to send us something more substantial at a future date." A similar instance occurs when George Macmillan asks Morley the following question: "I send you the work of a young economist; it got the Cobden Prize at Oxford lately. Question, is it worth publishing?" (19 December 1878). Or again, George Macmillan seeks Morley's advice: "We are asked to publish the Essay on Roman Provincial Administration which has just gained the Arnold Prize at Oxford." He wants Morley to advise him if it has "literary quality & promise" (22 March 1879). Clearly the opinion of the reader for Macmillan's carried more weight than the distinction of prizes at the nation's premier universities — even when the prize-winning manuscript was on a subject in which the reader could not claim any specialist's knowledge.

The range of subjects that the Macmillans and Morley felt competent to comment on is astonishing. Letter after letter to Morley asks for his opinion on manuscripts that deal with any number of topics treated from any number of different perspectives: treatises on logic and rhetoric; accounts of South African affairs; translations of German classics; classical history and theory; the history of India; the state of contemporary socialism; archaeology — and along with all of this, Morley was also commenting on numerous manuscripts of novels as well as on volumes of poetry. The Macmillans would sometimes send him an extra novel and suggest that he might read and evaluate it in his spare time on a given Sunday. Morley was not exaggerating when he told a London audience, "It has been my lot, I suppose, to read more unpublished work than any one else in this room, and, I hope, in this city" (*Study* 44).

A particularly interesting request for advice about publication comes to Morley from George Macmillan about a "popular book on Greek Art, delivered as lectures at the British Museum by a lady [Jane Harrison, who would become a distinguished classicist and publish under the Macmillan imprint] whom I know to be a sound archaeologist." In view of the special role that Greek art and culture played within the exclusively male, homosocial, university tradition of the time, it is interesting to see Macmillan react to the presence of a woman within this domain. He comments, "I have read it myself and think it good except for traces of feminine gush which could be pruned away" (18 December 1883). A strange comment to make on the work of someone he knows to be a sound archaeologist. But more significantly, he goes on to ask Morley if the book is worthy of publication.

The Macmillans' and Morley's assumption that the wide cultural range of the professional man of letters overrides specialist knowledge is also reflected in the way many of the Macmillan writers approached their tasks as critics, biographers, or editors of great writers of the past. We find, for example, William Black commenting in January of 1878 that he plans soon to begin work on his book on Goldsmith, the completed manuscript of which is due at the publishers in May or June (letter to Craik, 9 January 1878). In April he notes that he is just getting started on the book (letter to Craik, 8 April 1878). Furthermore, as he approached this formidable task, he requested from Macmillan a complete edition of Goldsmith so that he could work up his subject (10 January 1878). This practice must not have been all that unusual, as we also find Alexander Macmillan instructing Morley to send any books to James Russell Lowell that might aid him in working up what they had hoped would be his volume on Hawthorne (20 November 1877). Such an approach to doing definitive critical/biographical studies of great writers reveals assumptions about critical authority that run counter to specialism and disciplinarity.

Nor is it unusual to find independent writers — without the aid of university resources or specialist training in textual studies — proposing to do editions of major English writers. For example, Austin Dobson — certainly an authority on eighteenth-century literature but not a textual specialist — offered to do an edition of Fielding (a project Macmillan decided not to underwrite) (Frederick Macmillan to Austin Dobson, 22 May 1883). William Benham was commissioned to do an edition of the letters of Cowper (Frederick Macmillan to Austin Dobson, 8 June 1883). Sidney Colvin and Edmund Gosse both asked to do editions of Landor and Gray respectively, as a sort of follow-up to the volumes they did on the lives and works of the two writers (Gosse to Macmillan, 10 October 1882). Alfred Ainger, in light of his book on Lamb, also urged Macmillan to allow him to do an edition of Lamb's prose and verse. He argues, "What I feel is that *time* is everything — if *you* don't announce such a thing, Paul (or Peter) or somebody will cut in — & cut us out" (27 January 1882). In each of these cases, the independent professional feels competent to take on a task (and proposes to complete it quickly) that would now take years to be completed by a textual expert working in conjunction with a university publishing project.

One significant note of reluctance about what a non-specialist writer might take on with authority comes, interestingly enough, from Walter Pater. Pater was asked to do a volume on Coleridge, but George Macmillan informs Morley, "He shrinks from the vastness of the subject" (28 April 1879). Strangely, the same man who was willing to write books on subjects as big as Plato and the Renaissance from the non-specialist perspective says he was put off by the notion of writing on Coleridge.

In general, however, the letters indicate that the professional writer of wide cultural experience needed no specialist certification from a community of scholars. Quite to the contrary, people at the universities could learn from them. This attitude is expressed by George Macmillan in a letter to Sidney Colvin (who was, at the time, employed at the British Museum). He notes that Colvin's book on Landor would soon be reprinted, and he explains why: "It is a large demand in India that has quickened the sale. They have an admirable habit of setting such books now & then for University Examinations there. Why do not our Universities follow so good an example?" (22 April 1885). Such a comment indicates confidence — rather than a sense of epistemological crisis — in the professional man of letters published by one of Britain's most respectable publishers during the 1880s.

Thus the view one gets from the letters of the Macmillan Archive on the state of professionalism among literary men during the 1870s and '80s indicates that, although there was a sense of a declining shared culture, there was still a confidence that the general public could be profitably addressed, that there was still a readership for serious works by serious writers about the great figures of England's literary past, and that these works could do something to improve the general culture. And all of this could be accomplished through a system of authorization based on the talent of the man of letters — particularly a highly respectable and public man — capturing and then recreating for the reader the essence of another great public figure of the past. Dowden presents this view as a matter of simple logic and common sense when, in 1885, he explains how he would go about writing a proposed history of English literature after 1780:

> My notion is that, what I may call the *unit of criticism*, when it is possible, to be an *author* not a *book*. . . . My notion is that the works ought to group around the author, & minor authors around the masters, while the leading ideas of the time ought to glance in & out everywhere, forming an underlying web binding the whole together but not obtruded in a doctrinaire fashion — (5 June 1885)

What clearer statement could we have that the cultural arbiters of the time — speaking from the established position of Macmillan writers — continued to see their professionalism as a matter of individual talent rather than specialization, a matter of one man coming to terms with the lives of other (like) men of the past? Nor can we find a clearer statement of the notion of the unitary self of the author as the true site of authority for the reading and organization of literary texts and historical accounts of these texts. The professionals writing for Macmillan's saw their authority as coming not from specialization but rather from a kind of personal interaction between the past and present, an interaction between kindred spirits committed to literature and the impact it could have on the culture. The view from the Macmillan Archive does, of course, offer elements of alarm about the state of the culture and the reading public, but it is dominated by confidence that the public literary man still can make a salutary impact on a general public.

Idaho State University

NOTES

I thank Macmillan Publishers Ltd. for kindly granting me permission to quote material from the Macmillan Archive in the British Library. I also thank Idaho State University for a Faculty Research Grant which enabled me to do work at the British Library.

1. Eagleton has explored how the late-Victorian professional writer functions within a culture whose "public sphere" (using Habermas's term) has been severely eroded. Christ has argued that the creation of the late-Victorian professional man of letters played an important role in gender-marking serious nonfiction prose as masculine by the turn of the century. Clarke has explored the vexed relationship between the concept of masculinity and the idea of "letters" as a manly profession. Court has recently provided the first fully-documented study of the development of English studies in England, including the role that men of letters played in the process. Throughout this article, I refer to the late-Victorian professional writer as "he"; of course, a number of women published under the Macmillan imprint, but the formation of the concept "man of letters" in the material I am working with deals almost exclusively with male writers.
2. For an overview of the cultural significance of the "English Men of Letters" series, see Kijinski.
3. Morley himself did much better as the editor of the series. He was given 250 pounds for his first year's work on the series — no matter how many volumes were sold — a guarantee of at least another 250 for the second year (or 5% of all English sales, whichever was higher), and thereafter 5% royalty on all copies sold in England as long as the series was published (contract, November 1877).
4. Ironically, it was Frederick Macmillan who worked successfully to bring about the Net Book Agreement of 1899 which made possible in Britain a fully capitalist, mass-market publishing industry (Feltes, *Modes of Production* 78–81).

WORKS CITED

Ainger, Alfred. Letter to George Craik. 25 April 1882. British Library ADD MSS 55097.

———. Letter to Alexander Macmillan. 5 June 1882. British Library ADD MSS 55097.

———. Letter to Alexander Macmillan. 27 January 1882. British Library ADD MSS 55097.

Arnold, Matthew. Letter to Alexander Macmillan. 27 August 1879. British Library ADD MSS 54978.

———. Contract for Preface to Ward's *English Poets*. 25 December 1879. British Library ADD MSS 54978.

Black, William. Letter to George Craik. 9 January 1878. British Library ADD MSS 54929.

———. Letter to George Craik. 10 January 1878. British Library ADD MSS 54929.

———. Contract with Macmillan's for *Macleod of Dare*. 29 March 1878. British Library ADD MSS 54929.

———. Letter to George Craik. 8 April 1878. British Library ADD MSS 54929.
———. Letter to George Craik. 13 April 1878. British Library ADD MSS 54929.
———. Letter to George Craik. 3 February 1879. British Library ADD MSS 54929.
Christ, Carol T. " 'The Hero as Man of Letters': Masculinity and Victorian Nonfiction Prose." In *Victorian Sages and Cultural Discourse: Negotiating Gender and Power*. Ed. Thais Morgan. New Brunswick: Rutgers UP, 1990. 19–31.
Clarke, Norma. "Strenuous Idleness: Thomas Carlyle and the Man of Letters as Hero." In *Manful Assertions: Masculinities in Britain since 1800*. Ed. Michael Roper and John Tosh. London: Routledge, 1991. 25–43.
Court, Franklin E. *Institutionalizing English Literature: The Culture and Politics of Literary Study, 1750–1900*. Stanford: Stanford UP, 1992.
Craik, George. Letter to John Morley. 27 March 1878. British Library ADD MSS 55405.
Dowden, Edward. Letter to Alexander Macmillan. 5 June 1885. British Library ADD MSS 55019.
Eagleton, Terry. *The Function of Criticism: From "The Spectator" to Post-Structuralism*. London: Verso, 1984.
Feltes, N. N. *Literary Capital and the Late Victorian Novel*. Madison: U of Wisconsin P, 1993.
———. *Modes of Production of Victorian Novels*. Chicago: U of Chicago P, 1986.
Gosse, Edmund. Letter to Alexander Macmillan. 10 October 1882. British Library ADD MSS 55012.
Kijinski, John L. "John Morley's 'English Men of Letters' Series and the Politics of Reading." *Victorian Studies* 34.2 (Winter 1991): 205–25.
Macmillan, Alexander. Letter to John Morley. 19 July 1877. British Library ADD MSS 55403.
———. Letter to Richard Church. 19 September 1877. British Library ADD MSS 55403.
———. Letter to John Morley. 20 September 1877. British Library ADD MSS 55403.
———. Letter to John Morley. 2 October 1877. British Library ADD MSS 55403.
———. Letter to John Morley. 4 October 1877. British Library ADD MSS 55403.
———. Letter to John Morley. 9 November 1877. British Library ADD MSS 55404.
———. Letter to John Morley. 10 November 1877. British Library ADD MSS 55404.
———. Letter to John Morley. 20 November 1877. British Library ADD MSS 55404.
———. Letter to John Morley. 18 March 1878. British Library ADD MSS 55405.
———. Letter to John Morley. 24 June 1878. British Library ADD MSS 55406.
———. Letter to John Morley. 18 October 1878. British Library ADD MSS 55407.
———. Letter to J. A. Symonds. 22 November 1878. British Library ADD MSS 55407.
———. Letter to John Morley. 1 February 1879. British Library ADD MSS 55408.
———. Letter to John Morley. 16 March 1879. British Library ADD MSS 55408.
———. Letter to John Morley. 4 July 1879. British Library ADD MSS 55409.
———. Letter to Goldwin Smith. 4 July 1879. British Library ADD MSS 55409.
———. Letter to J. C. Shairp. 5 August 1897. British Library ADD MSS 55409.
———. Letter to F. W. Myers. 27 January 1881. British Library ADD MSS 55411.
———. Letter to John Morley. 6 April 1883. British Library ADD MSS 55415.
Macmillan, Frederick. Letter to John Morley. 5 October 1878. British Library ADD MSS 55407.
———. Letter to John Morley. 29 October 1880. British Library ADD MSS 55411.
———. Letter to Austin Dobson. 22 May 1883. British Library ADD MSS 55414.
———. Letter to Austin Dobson. 8 June 1883. British Library ADD MSS 55415.
Macmillan, George. Letter to John Morley. 2 June 1878. British Library ADD MSS 55406.

———. Letter to John Morley. 24 June 1878. British Library ADD MSS 55406.
———. Letter to John Morley. 19 December 1878. British Library ADD MSS 55407.
———. Letter to John Morley. 16 March 1879. British Library ADD MSS 55498.
———. Letter to John Morley. 28 April 1879. British Library ADD MSS 55408.
———. Letter to John Morley. 18 December 1883. British Library ADD MSS 55416.
———. Letter to Sidney Colvin. 22 April 1885. British Library ADD MSS 55419.
A Bibliographical Catalogue of Macmillan and Co.'s Publications from 1843–1889. London: Macmillan, 1891.
Morley, John. Letter to Alexander Macmillan. 6 August 1877. British Library ADD MSS 55055.
———. Letter to Alexander Macmillan. 22 September 1877. British Library ADD MSS 55055.
———. Letter to Alexander Macmillan. 30 September 1877. British Library ADD MSS 55055.
———. Letter to Alexander Macmillan. 3 October 1877. British Library ADD MSS 55055.
———. Letter to Alexander Macmillan. 5 October 1877. British Library ADD MSS 55055.
———. Contract for "English Men of Letters" series, November 1877. British Library ADD MSS 55055.
———. Letter to Alexander Macmillan. 9 November 1877. British Library ADD MSS 55055.
———. Letter to George Craik. 15 January 1878. British Library ADD MSS 55055.
———. Letter to Alexander Macmillan. 5 February 1878. British Library ADD MSS 55055.
———. Letter to Alexander Macmillan. 27 March 1878. British Library ADD MSS 55055.
———. Letter to George Craik. 6 June 1878. British Library ADD MSS 55055.
———. Letter to Alexander Macmillan. 16 December 1878. British Library ADD MSS 55055.
———. *On the Study of Literature.* London: Macmillan, 1887.
Patten, Robert L. " 'The people have set Literature free': The Professionalization of Letters in Nineteenth-Century England." *Review* 9 (1987): 1–34.
Perkin, Harold. *The Rise of Professional Society: England Since 1880.* London: Routledge, 1989.
Small, Ian. *Conditions for Criticism: Authority, Knowledge, and Literature in the Late Nineteenth Century.* Oxford: Clarendon, 1991.

SPECIAL EFFECTS

NOFRIANI UNBOUND: THE FIRST VERSION OF FLORENCE NIGHTINGALE'S "CASSANDRA"

By Katherine V. Snyder

Introduction

THERE IS NO CASSANDRA in the essay by Florence Nightingale entitled "Cassandra," at least not in the version that appears as part of the three-volume theological meditation, *Suggestions for Thought to Searchers after Religious Truth*, that Nightingale had privately printed around 1860. But the earliest version of "Cassandra," which Nightingale wrote sometime between 1850 and 1852, does feature a Cassandra, or at least a character who rhetorically names herself after the cursed prophetess of ancient myth:

> "Oh! call me no more Nofriani, call me Cassandra. for I have preached + prophesied in vain. I have gone about crying all these many years, Wo to the people! And no one has listened or believed. And now I cry, Wo to myself! For upon me the destruction has come."

Nightingale removed both Nofriani and Cassandra in the course of revising the manuscript of *Suggestions* prior to the printing of the private edition; all that remains of the "Cassandra" section are the disembodied words of Nofriani with perfunctory changes in pronouns and verb tenses used to disguise her tragic life story as the story of the suffering of all women in society. Nightingale's revisions transformed what was originally a fictionalized dialogue, or autobiographical novel in the first-person, into a choppy and generalized third-person essay. This landmark feminist document, which has been called "the missing link in English feminism," has been available to twentieth-century readers since it was first reprinted as an appendix to Ray Strachey's *The Cause* (1928), and later in editions from the Feminist Press (1979) and New York University Press (1992), but until now it has been available only in the expurgated form in which Nightingale abandoned it.[1]

Nightingale wrote ''Cassandra,'' and indeed all of *Suggestions*, in a state of profound, even suicidal, depression; this rage-turned-inward was her response to her family's seemingly insurmountable resistance to her desire for active public work.[2] In 1853, however, Nightingale received from her father an independence of £500 per year and several months later she accepted a post as the Superintendent of the Institution for the Care of Sick Gentlewomen in Distressed Circumstances at 1 Upper Harley Street in London. In 1854, she left for the Crimean War and the nursing work that was to make her an international legend.

In 1858, two years after Nightingale returned from the Crimea, she set about revising the manuscript of *Suggestions*, including the section called ''Cassandra'' which appears at the end of the second volume, subheaded ''Practical Deductions'' (see the ''Note on the Text'' following this introduction for a more detailed description of the manuscript). She went on, in late 1859 and 1860, to have the extensively revised manuscript privately printed in a three-volume review edition, with wide margins for annotations. The six copies in this private edition were sent to men whom she knew personally or on account of their intellectual stature: her father, her uncle Samuel Smith, Richard Monckton Milnes, Sir John McNeill, Benjamin Jowett, and John Stuart Mill.[3] Nightingale undertook no further revisions of ''The Stuff,'' as she customarily called it.[4]

Nightingale revised her text with this audience of selected readers in mind; she put it aside after she had gotten their actual responses to her work. But when she first wrote *Suggestions*, she was writing for herself, writing as a symptom of her emotional and intellectual suffering and as a cure for it. In ''Cassandra,'' she was also writing *about* herself, with the fictional heroine, Nofriani, and her tragic life story standing in for Nightingale and her own plight, the enforced idleness and domestic confinement of this upper-class Victorian woman. Nightingale develops her theme through the device of a dialogue between Nofriani and her brother, Fariseo, as reported by Fariseo after Nofriani's death (the manuscript begins by using an omniscient third-person narrator to report their conversation, then oscillates between third- and first-person, and eventually settles on Fariseo as first-person narrator; see my article for more on the significance of this narrative shift). This dramatized discussion apparently takes place over an extended period of time, since the second chapter takes place on a fiercely hot day with the two characters lounging beside a cooling fountain, and the third chapter describes them looking out upon a snow-laden landscape. The piece ends with Nofriani on her deathbed at the age of thirty, with Fariseo among the mourners recounting her last requests and her final words: ''Free, free, oh! divine Freedom, art thou come at last? Welcome, beautiful Death!''

These final words are virtually the only ones retained as direct discourse (that is, as words given in quotation marks to indicate that they have been spoken by a character) in the essayistic version; in that later version, however, they are attributed to some unspecified "dying woman to her mourners." Elsewhere in the essay, Nightingale removed Nofriani's speeches from their quotation marks, and changed the "I" of her first-person singular narration to the first-person plural — women as "we" — or to the more generalized third-person plural — women as "they." With these changes in the personal pronoun comes a shift in tense — the historical past of one woman's life is transposed to the present condition of women in general. For example, one paragraph that originally read:

> "Thus I lived for other [sic] seven years dreaming always, never accomplishing, — too much ashamed of my dreams, which I thought were 'romantic,' to tell them where I knew that they would be laughed at, if not considered wrong. So I lived, till my heart was broken. I am now an old woman at 30."

Nightingale revised to read:

> Dreaming always, never accomplishing, thus women live — too much ashamed of their dreams, which they think "romantic," to tell them to be laughed at, if not considered wrong.[5]

In this example, the shift in person and tense coincides with certain other alterations. These alterations, which characterize the revision of the manuscript as a whole, can be grouped into two categories. First, she cut or disguised autobiographical details, such as "at 30," Cassandra's age at death and Nightingale's age when she first wrote "Cassandra." At the same time, she excised stylistic details that may have seemed overly fanciful, or "romantic," such as "till my heart was broken." In fact, the two categories of revised or excised material tend to overlap because Nightingale fictionalized many details of her life by framing them in fanciful or sometimes highly spiritualized language and settings. Thus, Nightingale's revisions resemble the self-censorship described in the passage quoted above; that is, women's concealment of their "romantic" dreams suggests a paradigm for Nightingale's censorship of "romantic" or "dreamy" passages from her own manuscript. By eliminating the exotic settings and atmospheric effects of the original version, as well as foreshortening accounts of women's compensatory fantasy that were themselves particularly fanciful, the essay actually enacts the censorship that the novel vividly describes.

Nightingale's revisions transformed *Suggestions* from private writing — her imaginative, concealed response to the emotional and intellectual privations of enforced domesticity — to public writing in a seemingly more "objective," non-narrative mode, intended for an audience wider than one. And while the feedback from Nightingale's selected readers did not influence her accomplished revisions since their responses came only *after* the printing of the review copies, their commentary may well have dissuaded her from continuing to revise. The quantity as well as the nature of their suggested revisions were daunting —

only Mill suggested minor changes, whereas both Jowett and McNeill advised substantive changes that would actually undo the revisions she had already made. Jowett, a professor of Greek at Oxford to whom Nightingale sent installments of *Suggestions*, thereby launching their life-long friendship and correspondence, explicitly advocated back-tracking — "[S]uppose you were to publish the novel & imaginary conversations as they stood originally" — as well as numerous other changes. Despite his agreement with Nightingale that the "value" of her papers depends on "their being a record of your own experience," Jowett repeatedly objected to just this feature of her writing:

> it would add to the effect of what is said . . . if the reflections on the family took less the form of individual experience; this appears to me to lessen the weight of what is said & may, perhaps, lead to painful remarks.
>
> The difficulty I should find would be to separate the part which expresses your own feelings & thoughts from those which belong to other characters. (Quinn and Prest 4, 9)

Even in its revised essayistic form, "Cassandra" was still too emotional and too personal for Jowett's sense of decorum. Apparently, it seemed even more personal and emotional than a fully novelized version might have because no characters were there to interpose between writer and reader; as nonfiction, it displays undisguised the feelings and experience of the author. To Jowett, the nonfiction essay left the woman writer indecently exposed, whereas the trappings of fiction would have provided fittingly modest attire for "Cassandra" and for Nightingale's life.

Whereas Nightingale's male readers tended to see the essayistic version of "Cassandra" as too revealing, I would argue that version was more of a cover-up. The gutted manuscript (see the photographic facsimile of the first page) suggests that the essay was a form of protective self-concealment for Nightingale, compared with the impassioned and vivid testimony offered by her alter-ego Nofriani. The gaps and the awkward, sometimes incoherent, passages that characterize the essay testify to the predicament Nightingale faced when she aligned herself with the masculine authority that was the subject of her feminist critique. Speaking with the voice of a definitively masculine social authority required Nightingale to dissociate herself from the sufferings of her fictionalized heroine and the other Victorian women who shared her plight. While her revisions reflect a new control over her fantasy life, and may even have helped her to gain self-control, this control came at a heavy price, both for Nightingale and for the voice of her "Cassandra."[6]

Most critics and historians agree that Nightingale was no feminist. "I am brutally indifferent to the rights and wrongs of my sex,"[7] Nightingale unabashedly proclaimed in a letter to Harriet Martineau, one of the few women in whom she showed any interest. Surprisingly, in light of the incisive and compassionate analysis offered in ''Cassandra,'' Nightingale's private letters and published writings repeatedly express her impatience with, and even contempt for, the women who suffered from the enforced passivity she herself had endured earlier in her life. Her refusal to work actively for, or even wholeheartedly to endorse, the chief causes of the women's rights movement of her time — suffrage and equal education for women — can be attributed at least in part to her belief that economic rights, particularly for married women, were more vital. But Nightingale ultimately identified herself with men and their work, referring to herself in her private correspondence as a ''man of action'' and a ''man of business.'' While she capitalized on the popular feminine image of ''the lady with the lamp,'' she worked with men on what was conventionally considered man's work — army sanitation and medical affairs — albeit from the socially irreproachable distance of the ''little War Office,'' the back-bedroom of her own apartment. And while she helped to develop respectable, well-paid professions for women, she never questioned the gendered hierarchy that made nurses and midwives answerable to doctors.

For Nightingale, the ''moral activity'' of work and its immediate, concrete results took precedence over the struggle for women's rights. Although Nofriani wondered ''whether Christ was called a complainer against the world,'' and recognized that ''[t]he great reformers of the world turn into the great misanthropists, — if circumstances or organization do not permit them to act,'' her creator would later rail against this ''enormous jaw, the infinite female ink'' spilled in pursuit of educational equality. The author of ''Cassandra'' came to see women's rights as an abstraction, and the struggle for them as mere complaining.

Thus, just as much as this reconstructed edition of ''Cassandra'' presents the unalloyed feminist complaint of an eminent Victorian woman, its hidden status represents her eventual turning away from her own anguished outcry. Once the celebrity of her Crimean work had attained leverage for her within her family and with the representatives of the War Office, Nightingale disowned her earlier suffering and the cause of female sufferers in Victorian society. In her life and her work, Nightingale found a solution to the restrictions imposed upon Victorian women of her class, but the silenced voice of ''Cassandra'' reveals what was at stake in her choice. This edition does not pretend to restore ''Cassandra'' to the condition that Nightingale ''would have wanted''; it is more than likely that Nightingale would have been appalled to see this hidden record unearthed and publicly displayed. But the private and literary history that this textual excavation undertakes is vital to the continuing project of recovering, and rereading, what has been censored in Victorian women's writing and their lives.[8]

University of California, Berkeley

NOTES

1. Elaine Showalter thus assessed the significance of "Cassandra" in a 1989 MLA special session, "Illuminating the Lady with the Lamp: Writings by and about Florence Nightingale."
2. For accounts of Nightingale's emotional and intellectual outlook during this period and after her return from the Crimea, see the standard biographies by Cook and Woodham-Smith. See also Showalter, 1981.
3. This list of recipients is from Quinn and Prest, xii. Neither Woodham-Smith nor Showalter mentions Nightingale's father or uncle, although Showalter [1981, 407] includes historian J. A. Froude among Nightingale's selected readers of *Suggestions*.
4. An unknown number of copies, probably very few, were printed in 1860; these books were identical to the review copies but without the wide margins. Copies of the narrow-margin book are in the British Library and in the Florence Nightingale Museum in London.
5. The printed edition varies slightly from the revised manuscript here — it reads "to tell them where they will be laughed at, even if not considered wrong" [Stark 39] — and elsewhere in "Cassandra." These differences indicate that Nightingale made further revisions in proofs which are no longer extant. Most of these late revisions are minor, although several changes are more substantive, including two discursive footnotes added in the proof stage which can be read in Stark 50 and 53. Another substantive revision in proof tones down a scathing analogy likening marriage to prostitution. The passage originally read:

   And now they are married. . . . The woman is as often a prostitute as a wife. She prostitutes herself, if she has sold her person for an establishment, as much as if she had sold it in the streets. She prostitutes herself, if, knowing so little of her husband as she does, she begins immediately, without further acquaintance, to allow him the rights of a husband over her person. She prostitutes herself later, if, against her own desire, she allows herself to be made the blind instrument of producing involuntary children. It will be said, + truly, that, when she marries, her husband understands all these privileges as granted, + that she would drive him mad + deceive his understood expectation, if she did not grant them. But how is she to ascertain her husband's opinion on these points before marriage? [ms 277]

   Only the sentence about allowing "the rights of a husband over her person" was initially marked-out in the manuscript, but the entire passage was later abbreviated, presumably in proofs, to read: "And now they are married. . . . The woman who has sold herself for an establishment, in what is she superior to those we may not name?" [Stark 48]. See the Note on the Text for a discussion of the manuscript's multiple stages of revision.

6. My article in *The Politics of the Essay* discusses at greater length the implications for gender and genre of Nightingale's revisions.
7. Cook 1: 385.
8. Many people have helped me with this project; I would like to express my particular thanks to Nancy Armstrong, Catherine Gallagher, Janet Larson, Linda Peterson, Mary Poovey, Catharine Stimpson, and Herbert Sussman. I am grateful to Freya Johnson for her proofreading and suggestions.

WORKS CITED

Cook, Edward T. *The Life of Florence Nightingale*. 2 vols. London: Macmillan, 1913.

Nightingale, Florence. "Cassandra." Additional Manuscript 45839. Nightingale Papers. British Library.

———. *Cassandra and Other Selections from Suggestions for Thought*. Ed. Mary Poovey. New York: New York UP, 1992.

———. *Cassandra: an Essay*. Ed. Myra Stark. Old Westbury, N.Y.: Feminist Press, 1979.

———. *Suggestions for Thought to Searchers after Religious Truth*. 3 vols. Privately printed. London: Eyre & Spottiswoode, 1860.

Quinn, Vincent, and John Prest, eds. *Dear Miss Nightingale: A Selection of Benjamin Jowett's Letters to Florence Nightingale, 1860–1893*. Oxford: Clarendon Press, 1987.

Showalter, Elaine. "Florence Nightingale's Feminist Complaint: Women, Religion, and *Suggestions for Thought*." *Signs: Journal of Women in Culture and Society* (6) 1981: 395–412.

Snyder, Katherine v. "From Novel to Essay: Gender and Revision in Florence Nightingale's 'Cassandra'." *The Politics of the Essay: Feminist Perspectives*. Ed. Ruth-Ellen Boetcher Joeres and Elizabeth Mittman. Bloomington: Indiana UP, 1993.

Strachey, Ray. *"The Cause": A Short History of the Women's Movement in Great Britain*. London: Virago, 1978.

Woodham-Smith, Cecil. *Florence Nightingale 1820–1910*. New York: McGraw-Hill, 1951.

Note on the Text

"Cassandra" appears roughly at the midpoint of the manuscript for *Suggestions for Thought to the Searchers after Truth*, now located in the Nightingale Papers at the British Library (Add. Mss. 45837, 45838, and 45839). This 51–page section is separated from the preceding text by a title page (ms. 236) with the heading, "Cassandra," which has been crossed out. The entire manuscript of *Suggestions* is in Nightingale's own hand on standard-size, loose, white sheets in brownish ink, with writing on only one side of each sheet, except for page 12 (ms. 248), on the reverse of which appear four paragraphs and which is numbered "12a"; page numbering 1 through 51 appears in the top-right corner of the manuscript pages. Revisions and corrections occur throughout the manuscript, which seems to be complete, although one page in the "Cassandra" section (ms. 253) has been ripped in half with the added notation, "Go on to III. P. 21," indicating that the largely unmarked four-page *paysage moralisé* that follows (Nofriani's description of the fountain and its striving "spirits" to Fariseo) is not meant to appear in the printed edition. Before revision, section "III" had begun on page 20 (or ms. 257), but a new "III" is inserted on page 21 (ms. 258), with a carat and a circle drawn around it.

Some words and sentences in the manuscript have single or multiple lines drawn through them indicating that they were to be excised; these passages range from one word to 11 lines. Some sections, ranging from 5 to 23 lines, are marked through with repeated diagonal lines or, more typically, with a large "X," the corners of which are connected to form a box. There are also some individually crossed-out words and lines within these "X"-boxes, and sometimes marked-through single lines immediately precede or follow the "X," indicating that revision probably occurred in multiple stages. Some words and sentences are simply excised while others are replaced with words and sentences written in above them, sometimes with carats to mark the point of insertion. These variations, as well as minor variations in the shade and line-width of the ink and in the quality of Nightingale's handwriting, also indicate more than one stage of revision. (There are also several discrepancies between the revised manuscript and the printed edition, indicating that Nightingale made further revisions at the proof stage; see note #5). In all, more than one third of the earliest version of the text has been excised, and an even larger percentage of that early text has been altered, if we include words and passages that have been added or otherwise revised.

The manuscript of "Cassandra" thus reveals multiple stages of writing and rewriting, but it is not clear from biographical information on Nightingale nor from the manuscript itself precisely when most of these changes took place, whether in composition or revision. The biographical background seems to suggest that the major textual shift from first-person fictional narrative to third-person nonfiction essay took place after Nightingale returned from the Crimea, but this is not certain. It is equally uncertain whether the more minor revisions, such as the superscription of synonymous words, or the insertion of qualifying phrases, took place in the pre-Crimean composition of the text or in the post-Crimean revision of the text.

Although the timing of the revisions remains open to question, the sequence of these revisions is fairly clear. For this reason, I have chosen to use the earliest variant that I can make out, even when it means omitting alternate phrasings or insertions that do not appear in the printed edition (such as much of the intermediate phase in which the narrative voice oscillates between referring to Fariseo in the first-person and in the third-person). In other words, this editorial strategy risks losing some details that may have been part of Nightingale's early writing, even possibly her original composition, in the interest of reconstructing the earliest version of the text. I have, however, found that a system of graphical notation showing all the variants within the revised manuscript tends to make the text virtually unreadable, so I have chosen to use this less subtle, but more accessible, method. I have included in footnotes some, though not all, alternate phrasings that this strategy occludes.

I have also used boldface type to indicate the larger sections of text that Nightingale excised from her manuscript. While this editorial device effectively indicates Nightingale's grosser expurgations, it has several shortcomings about which I would caution the reader. For one thing, it fails to mark the alterations in person and tense throughout the text, but since these are fairly consistent, and since they are stressed in my introduction, I hope that readers will be able to make these transpositions mentally. More problematically, this use of boldface fails to highlight those smaller and more subtle, yet still significant, changes in the text, such as Nightingale's toning down of "To be absent from dinner is equivalent to being at the point of death" in the original, to "To be absent from dinner is equivalent to being ill" in the revised version, or her changing of "your sister-in-law" in the original, to "Mrs. A" in the revised version, to name just two of many examples. Thus, the boldface may mislead readers into thinking that the excision of these larger "chunks" of text was the only or the most important part of Nightingale's revisions, when in fact it is merely the most easily representable of the different kinds of changes that she made. I would, however, encourage readers to read this reconstruction of the early "Cassandra" with one of the published editions of "Cassandra" close to hand, in order fully to grasp the differences, both subtle and profound, between the early "Cassandra" and the revised version (if only in those parts of the text that remain in the printed edition.

Finally, to preserve Nightingale's voice, I have left her distinctive orthography — her ampersands and dashes — intact.

Cassandra

I

> "The voice of one crying in the" *crowd*, "Prepare ye the way of the Lord."

The night was mild + dark + cloudy. Nofriani was walking to + fro before the beautiful facade of a Palladian palace. All was still. Not one light through the window betrayed the existence of any life stirring within. "I, I alone, am wandering in the bitterness of life without,**" she said. She went down where on the glassy dark pond the long shadows of the girdle of pines the tops of which seemed to touch heaven, were lying. The swans were sleeping on their little island. Even the Muscovy ducks were not yet awake. But she had suffered so much that she had outlived even the desire to die. "***All* must be gone through,**" she said,** "Why not this side the grave as well as the other? Perhaps, if prematurely we dismiss ourselves from this world, all may even have to be suffered through again. The premature birth may not contribute to the production of another being, which must be begun again from the beginning."

She resumed her walk on the terrace, by the struggling light of the moon, which at this moment shone out from between the clouds. The sharp cornice of the Venetian palace building stood out clear against it in the clear pale blue of the morning dawn.

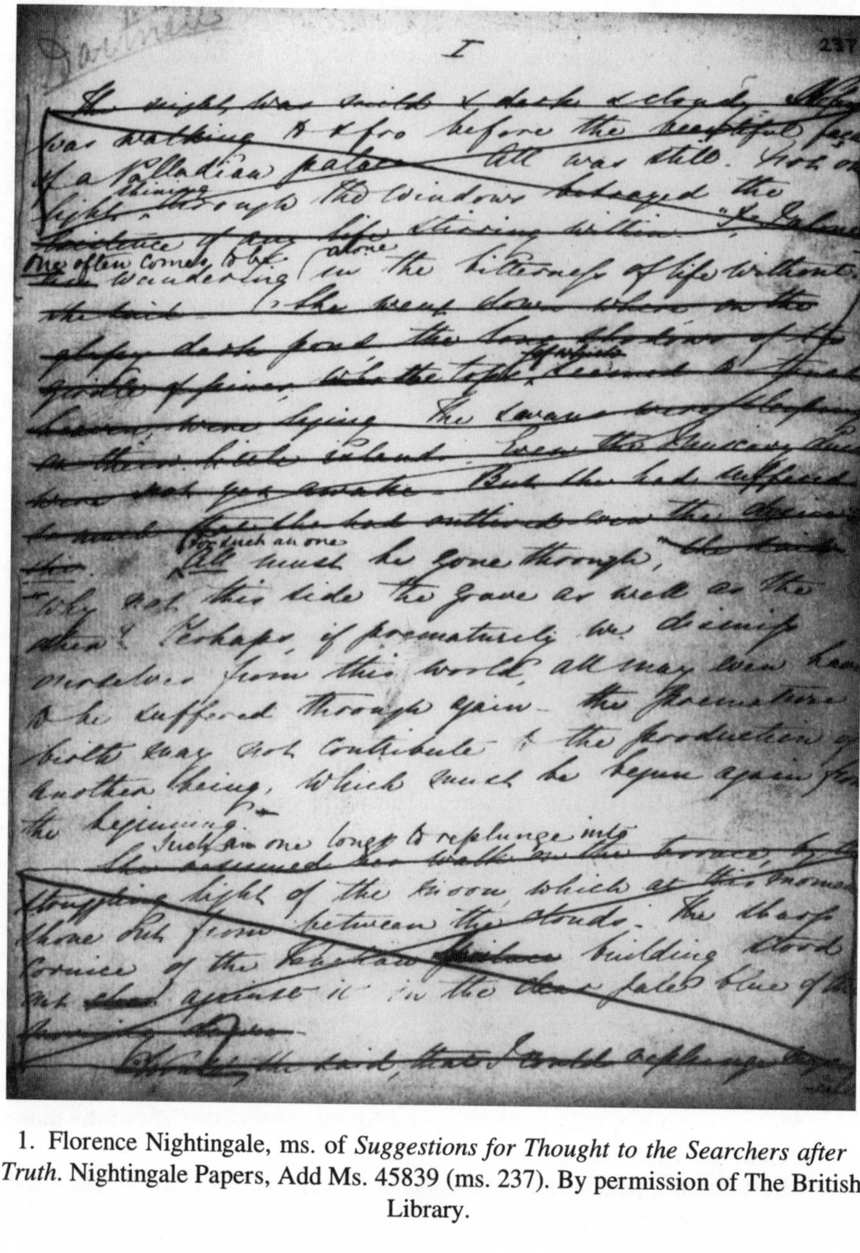

1. Florence Nightingale, ms. of *Suggestions for Thought to the Searchers after Truth*. Nightingale Papers, Add Ms. 45839 (ms. 237). By permission of The British Library.

"Would," she said, "that I could replunge myself into the happy unconscious sleep of all my race! They slumber in one another's arms. They are not yet awake. To them evil + suffering are not, for they are not conscious of evil. While I, alone, awake + prematurely alive to it, must wander out in silence + solitude. I have risen up too soon, I have awakened too early. I have rejected the companionship of my race. I am unmarried to any human being. I see the evil they do not see yet I have no power to discover the remedy for it. Would that I were back again warm + innocent in sleeping ignorance, but not alone!

She re-entered the palace, + reached her balcony, where, throwing herself down on its cold pavement, + resting her arm upon the stone balustrade, her long hair, of the golden tint which the Venetian painter delighted to honour, bound with radiant gems which sparkled in the moonlight, fell upon her bare arm. But hardly for a moment could her energetic nature requiesce in this humiliated despairing posture. She started up, like the dying lioness who fronts her hunters, + standing at bay, as it were, she bared her forehead to the night breeze, + stretching out her arms, she cried,

"God, to thee alone can I say all. God, hear me. Why didst Thou create us with passions, intellect, moral activity — these three — + place us in a state of society where no one of the three can be exercised? God, to none else can I make my complaint, without being rebuked for complaining, scourged for suffering! There are those who say that Thou too dost punish us for complaining. I do not believe it. Men are angry with misery. They are irritated with us for not being happy. They take it as a personal offence. To thee, to thee alone may we complain, without insulting thee. Oh Eternal Patience of God! Him! God, how passionate hast thou created us! And the women, who are afraid to own that God's work is good + wish to say, Thy will be *not* done, (declaring another order of society from that which Thou hast made,) go about maulding to each other + teaching to their daughters that "women have no passions." In the conventional society, which men have made for women, + women have accepted, they *must* have none, they *must* act the farce of hypocrisy, the lie that they are without Passion — + therefore what else can they say to their daughters, without giving the lie to themselves?

"Oh! miserable suffering female "humanity"! + what are these feelings which you are taught to consider as disgraceful, to deny to yourselves. Let us see what form do the Chinese feet assume when denied their proper development? Speak, young maidens of the "higher toned classes," ye who never commit a false step, whose justly earned reputations were never sullied even by the stain which the fruit of the mere "knowledge of good + evil" leaves behind. Speak Ye, what are your thoughts employed upon, your *thoughts*, which alone are free."

And, moved by the spell of the enchantress, there appeared the phantasms, the larvae of the most beautiful race of the world, the maidens of the

ranks, whose white hands have never been made hard by toil — Graceful + lovely, pure + etherial they floated by — + their thoughts and fancies took shape + form at the word of the Magician. With each maiden there was a Phantom one! there were two, three, twenties, hundreds, ever varying, ever changing, but *never* was she *alone.* With the Phantom companion of her fancy, she talked (not love, she was too innocent, too pure, too full of genius and imagination + high toned feeling for that, but she talked, in fancy, of that which interested them most. They sought a companion for every thought, the companion she found not in reality she sought in fancy, or if not that, if not absorbed in endless conversations, she saw herself engaged with him in stirring events, circumstances which called out the interest wanting to them. Yes, fathers, mothers, you who see your daughters proudly rejecting all semblance of flirtation, primly engaged in the duties of the breakfast table, you little think how her fancy compensates itself by endless interviews + sympathies (sympathies either for ideas or events) with the fancy's companion of the hour! And you say, "she is not susceptible, women have no passion." Ah! Mothers, who cradle yourselves in visions about the domestic hearth, how many of your sons + daughters are *there*, do you think, while sitting round under your maternal complacent eyes? Were you there yourself during your own (now forgotten) girlhood?

Tell your thoughts for once, maidens, while one is singing that divine music, another is reading the Review, + a third is doing crochet, where are your thoughts? Is not one fancying herself nurse of some new friend in sickness, another engaging in romantic dangers with him, such as call out the character + afford more food for sympathy than the monotonous events of domestic society, another undergoing unheard of trials under the observation of someone whom she has chosen as the companion of her dream?

And is not all this most natural, inevitable? Are they, who are too much ashamed of it to confess it even to themselves, to be blamed for that which cannot be otherwise, the causes of which stare one in the face? *if one's eyes were not closed*

"Alas! Oh!" cried poor Nofriani, "how I have struggled against this! **How I have martyrized myself, put myself to the torture!** No Trappist ascetic has done so more in the body than I have done in the soul! Oh! how well I can understand the discipline of the Thebaid, the life-long agonies which those strong moral Mohicans put themselves through! How cordially I could do the same if I believed in their effect in order to escape the worse torture of sin! But I know that the laws of God for moral well-being are not to be obeyed thus. How I have fasted mentally, scourged myself morally, used the intellectual hairshirt, in order to subdue that perpetual day-dreaming, which I know was so dangerous! I have resolved "this day month I will be free from it! twice a day with prayer + written record of the times which I have indulged in it, I have endeavoured to combat it, never, never with the slightest success. **Then I thought, "through**

Vanity it comes, through vanity it must be conquered." And I selected a person to whom to make my confession, the confession of my whole life of dreaming, I remember the day. It was like a day of Crucifixion to me. It was like death. As each confession came out, I feared I should not have strength to make the next confession to drive the next nail. But I did. I went through the whole. And when it came to piercing the side, I did it too. For a fortnight it delivered me. Then all was as bad as ever. By mortifying vanity, I had done myself no good. I did not see that it was the want of interest in my life which produced it, that, by filling up that want of interest in my life, I could alone remedy it. And, had I even seen this, how could I make the difference? How could I obtain the interest which Society declared *she* did not want, + *I* could not want?

But now it seems to me that no one cares about sin, no one feels it, no one thinks it a matter of much importance.

What are novels? What is the secret of the charm of every romance that ever was written? The first thing that you observe in a novel is that persons are placed together in circumstances which naturally call out the high feelings + thoughts of the character, which afford food for sympathy between them on these points — "romantic events" they are called. The second is that the heroine has *generally* no family ties, (almost *invariably* no mother). Or, if she has, these do not interfere with her entire independence.

These two things constitute the main charm of reading novels. Now, in as far as these are good + not spurious interests, let us see what we have to correspond with them in real life. Can the high sympathies be fed upon the Opera, the Exhibitions, the debate in the House of Commons + the caricature in Punch? If, together, man + woman approach any of the high questions of social, political, or religious life, they are said + justly to be going "too far"! God, that such things can be?"

And again she threw herself down in the extremity of her suffering. It seemed a little thing to awaken such anguish. It was the ferment of a life of inaction and solitude. Again she raised herself up and looked abroad. The moon was shining brightly. A heavy shower of rain, which had just fallen (upon her all unconscious head) had moistened the pavement of the noble terrace. The moon was reflected from the moisture below, doubling the light. Above her head + beneath her feet there was a flood of radiance. The swollen rivers at the bottom of the valley rushed + roared from afar. The distant circle of mountains gave liberty to the thought which is fettered by a circumscribed horizon. She fixed her eyes upon the splendid [illeg] expanse beneath her, when suddenly there came that darkening of the world, which we have all observed on a night when fleecy clouds veil unexpectedly the face of the moon, + which is like the wings of the Almighty overshadowing suddenly the world, as in that inspired representation of Him in Michael

Angelo's Sistine Chapel. She felt the overshadowing wings above her, which had darkened *her* lowered world. She said, "Is it Thou, Lord?" And He said, "It is I." + her heart was still.

II

"Yet I would spare no pang,
Would wish no torture less,
The more that anguish racks
The earlier it will bless."[1]

Nofriani + Fariseo were sitting together under a tree by the side of a fountain which shot up its single solitary spire towards Heaven. The heat was intense, they had agreed to spend there together the hours when every man is idle. Little fountains played all around them in the beautiful Italian garden. The white blossoms and shining green of the orange trees glistened among the cypresses.

"But why, my sister," said Fariseo, "have you quarrelled with the world? Enjoy it as I do, + do not complain of it."

Nofriani was speechless. What could she say? A crowd of thoughts rushed into her mind at the moment. "Oh! give me, give me back my suffering," she cried to Heaven in her heart. "Suffering rather than Indifferentism! For out of nothing comes nothing. But out of suffering may come the cure. Better Pain than Paralysis! A hundred struggle + drown in the breakers. One discovers the New World. But rather, ten times rather die in the surf, heralding the way to that new world, than stand idly on the other shore!"

Fariseo scarcely remarked her silence. "You have everything to make a woman happy," he said, "Why are you so cast down?"

"I cannot answer the question, it is too long an one. Passion, Intellect, Moral Activity — these three have never been satisfied in me. In this cold + oppressive conventional atmosphere, they cannot be. To go farther would be to enter into the whole history of society, of the present state of civilization."

"But let us do so. We have nothing else but this hot noon," said Fariseo, "only be as short as you can."

This morning Nofriani was so discouraged she did not wish even for the power of expression. "Look, **brother," she said, "**at that lizard. 'It is not hot,' he says, 'I like it. The atmosphere which enervates you is life to me.' The state of society which I complain of makes you happy. Why should I complain to you? You do not suffer. You would not understand it, any more than that lizard would comprehend the sufferings of a Shetland sheep."

"Never mind," said Fariseo, "try, + I will do my best."

---

1. Excerpted from Emily Brontë, "The Prisoner" (1845).

It was not pride — unless pride is the fear of not finding sympathy. It was the reluctance of wounded feeling which kept Nofriani silent.

"Speak," said Fariseo, "I am ready. With all the gifts which Heaven has bestowed on your ingratitude, I cannot understand your suffering + I want to understand it."

"Must I enter into all the history of my life," said Nofriani, "*Cui bono*? I do not quarrel with you, as you often accuse me of doing. The progressive world is necessarily divided into two classes. Those who take the best of what there is + enjoy it — those who wish for something better + try to create it. Without both these two classes, both the one and the other, the world would be badly off. They are the very conditions of progress. Were there none who were discontented with what they have, the world would never reach anything better. And through the other class, which is constantly taking the best of what the first is creating for them, a balance is secured, + that which is conquered is held fast. But with neither class must we quarrel for not possessing the privileges of the other. The laws of the nature of each make it impossible."

"Then you do esteem, discontent a privilege?" **said Fariseo, with a smile which chilled poor Nofriani's blood.**

"Yes, it is a privilege to suffer for your race, a privilege not reserved alone to the Redeemer + the Martyrs, but one enjoyable by numbers in every age. **But if you *will* hear what I have been doing, listen. It is a** vulgar common-place life enough — And in that is its only interest, it's [sic] only merit as a history. It is the type of vulgar sufferings — the story of one who has not the courage to resist nor to submit to the civilization of her time — is this.

Poetry and imagination began life in me, as they do in most. I remember, when I was a child falling on my knees on the ground at the sight of a pink hawthorne in full flower, + one day when I was by myself, to praise God for it.

Then came Intellect. I wished to satisfy the wants which my Intellect created for me. But there is a physical, not moral, impossibility of supplying the wants of the Intellect in the state of civilization at which we have arrived. The stimulus, the training, the time are, all three, wanting to us — or, in other words, the means of inducements are not there.

Look at the poor lives we lead. It is a wonder to me that we are so good as we are, not that we are so bad. In looking round me, I am struck with the power of the organizations about me, not with their want of it. Now + then, it is true, I am conscious that I am in *the* presence of an inferior organization. But, in general, just the contrary. Your sister-in-law has the imagination, the poetry of a Murillo, + a sufficient power of execution to shew that she might have had a great deal more. Why is she not a Murillo? — From a physical difficulty, not a mental one. If she has a knife and fork in her hands during three hours of the day, she cannot have a pencil or brush. Dinner is the great sacred Ceremony of this day, the great Sacrament. To be absent from dinner is equivalent to being at the point of death. Nothing else will excuse us from it. Bodily incapacity is the only apology valid. If she has a pen + ink in her hands during other three hours, writing answers for the Penny Post, — again she cannot have her pencil, + so *ad infinitum* through life. People have no type before them in their lives, neither fathers + mothers, nor the children themselves. They look at things in detail. They say, ''It is very desirable that A, my daughter, should go to such a party, should know such a lady, should sit by such a person'' — It is true. But what standard have they before them? — of the nature and destination of man? The very words are rejected or pedantic. But might they not, at least, have a type in their minds that such an one might be a discoverer through her intellect, such another through her art, such a third through her moral power?

I tried one branch of Intellect after another in my youth. I tried Mathematics. But that, least of all, is compatible with the life of our society. It is impossible to follow up any thing systematically. **I thought seriously at one time of running away — + (putting on men's clothes) + entering myself at College, where I** should have found direction, — competition, (or rather the opportunity of measuring the intellect with others, — +, above all, time.

In those wise Institutions, — mixed as they are with many follies which will last as long as the human race lasts, because they are adapted to the wants of the human race. Those Institutions which we call monasteries + which, embracing much that is contrary to the laws of nature, are yet better adapted to the union of the life of action + that of thought than any other mode of life with which we are acquainted — in such, 4 1/2 hours, at least, are daily set aside for thought, rules are given for thought, training and opportunity afforded. Among us, there is *no* time appointed for this purpose, + the difficulty is that, in our Social Life, we must be always doubtful whether we ought not to be with somebody else or be doing something else.

''But do you fancy,'' I said,[2] **''that** men are so much better off than women?''

''It happened to me, calling twice upon a friend in London, to see both times her son in the drawing room, it struck me as odd to find a young man sitting idling in his mother's drawing-room in the morning. For men, who are seen much in those haunts, there is no end of the epithets we have[:] ''knights of the carpet,'' ''drawing room heroes,'' ''ladies men,'' to mark our contempt. But suppose we were to see a number of men in the morning sitting round a table in the drawing room, looking at prints, doing worsted work + reading little books, how we should laugh! **I knew a man once,** an Hon. member of the House of Commons, who did a great deal of worsted work. Of another man a friend said to me once, ''his only fault is that he is too good. He drives out with his mother every day in the carriage + if he is asked anywhere, he answers that

2. At an intermediate stage of revision, ''I said'' was altered to read ''said Fariseo.''

he must dine with his mother, but, if she can spare him, he will come in to tea, + he does not come.''

Now why is it more ridiculous for a man than for a woman to do worsted work + drive out every day with his wife? Why should we laugh, if we were to see a parcel of men sitting round a drawing-room table in the morning, + think it all right if they were women?

Have women confessedly nothing to do? Is man's time essentially more valuable than woman's?

Women are never supposed to have any occupation of sufficient importance *not* to be interrupted, except ''suckling their fools'' + the most curious part of it is that women themselves have accepted this, have written books to support it, + have trained themselves to consider nothing that they do as of sufficient value to the world or to others, but to throw it up at the first ''claim of social life.'' They have accustomed themselves to consider intellectual occupation as a merely selfish amusement, which it is their ''duty'' to give up for every trifler more selfish than themselves.

A young man, (who was afterwards useful + known in his day + generation), when busy reading, + sent for by his proud mother + sisters to shine in some social reunion, came; but, after it was over, he said, ''now remember, this is not to happen again, I came that you might not think me sulky, but I shall not come again.'' But for a young woman to send such a message to her mother + sisters, would be considered impertinent + impossible! A woman of great power told me once that she never undertook anything which ''she could not throw by at once, if necessary.''

''But how do you explain,'' **said I (I am Fariseo),** ''the innumerable cases of women who have distinguished themselves in Classics, Mathematics, even in Politics?''

''Widowhood, ill-health, or want of bread, these three explanations or excuses are supposed to justify a woman in taking up an occupation. In some cases, no doubt, an indomitable force of character will suffice without any of these three, but such are rare. But see how society fritters away the intellects of those committed to her change! It is said that society is necessary to sharpen the Intellect. But what do we seek society for? It does sharpen the intellect because it is a kind of *tour-de-force* to say something at a pinch — unprepared + uninterested with any subject to improvise something under difficulties. But what ''go we out for to seek''? To take the chance of someone having something to say which we want to hear? Or of our own finding something to say which *they* want to hear? You have a little to say, but not much. You often make a stipulation with some one else, Come in ten minutes, for I am sure I shall not be able to find enough to spin out longer than that. You are not to talk of anything very interesting, for the essence of society is to prevent any long conversations + all *tete-a-tetes.* ''Glissez, n'appuyez pas'' is its very motto. The praise of a maitresse de salon is that she allows no one to be too much absorbed in, or too long about, a conversation. She always recalls them to their "duty." People do not go into the company[3] of their fellow creatures for what would seem a very sufficient reason, namely, that they have something to say to them, or something that they want to hear from them, but in the vague hope that they may find something to say.

Now for our solitary opportunities. I never had half an hour in all my life (excepting before anybody was up in the house) that I could call my own, without fear of offending or of hurting some one. Why do people sit up so late, or, more rarely, get up so early? Not because the day is not long enough, but because they have "No time in the day to themselves."

"But can't you do anything when anybody else is in the room?" I said. "If not, the best advice I can give you is to learn as soon as possible. School boys do."

"And, if we do attempt to do anything in social company, what is the system of literary exercise we pursue? Every body reads aloud out of their own book, or, every five minutes, something is said. And what is it to be "read aloud to"? The most miserable exercise of the human intellect. Or rather, is it any exercise at all? To me it is like lying on my back, with my hands tied + having food poured down my throat. Worse than that, because suffocation would immediately ensue + prevent that operation. But no suffocation would stop the other.

So much for the satisfaction of the Intellect. Yet for a married woman in society — it is even worse. I once heard a married woman wish that she could break a limb that she might have a little time to herself. **I am sure I have often wished the same.**

It is a thing *so* set down among women that they have nothing to do that a woman has not the least scruple of saying, "I will come + spend the morning with you." And you would be thought quite surly and absurd, if you were to refuse it. Nay, it is thought a mark of amiability + affection, if you are "on such terms" that you can "come in" "any morning you please." The last time I was in the country, in the neat country house, there was a large party of young people. "You will spend the morning with us," they said, "we will drive together in the afternoons," "we will walk together," "tomorrow we will make an expedition," "+ we will spend the evening together." And this was thought friendly + pretty. And they went away, at the end of some weeks, without the smallest idea that they had not been perfectly acceptable, + thinking that their time had been spent in a very pleasant manner, + that "we had seen each other every day." So women play through life. Yet time is, I suppose, the most valuable of all things. If they had come every morning + afternoon + robbed

3. "the company . . . " is preceded by the incomplete phrase "society becau," which has been crossed out.

me of half-a-crown, I should have had redress from the Police. But it is laid down, among us, that our time is of no value. If you offer a morning visit to a professional man, + say, "I will just stay an hour with you, if you will allow me, till So + so comes back to fetch me," it costs him a guinea, + therefore he has a right to complain. But women have no right."

"Well, but do you mean to say that you can't resist?" said Fariseo.

"Women have no means given them, whereby they *can* resist the "claims of social life," **as they are called," she answered.** "They are taught from their infancy upwards that it is wrong, ill-tempered, + a misunderstanding of 'woman's mission,' (with a great M), if they do not allow themselves, *willingly* to be interrupted at all hours. If a woman has once justified a claim to be treated as a man by some work of Science or Art or Literature, which she can *shew* as the "fruit of her leisure," then she will be considered justified in *having* leisure, (hardly perhaps then). But if not, not. If she has nothing to show, she must resign herself to her fate."

Nofriani was silent + so was I, for I did not know what to say.[4] I sate looking at the fountain + the beautiful solitary spire of water. At last she said in a low voice,

"See, how it strives + strives + strives to heaven. It cannot reach it. It is shedding tears of grief + of disappointment. And now it makes another + another spring. Alas! It has chains about its wings + about its feet. And it falls, falls, falls heavily to the ground, + is lost upon the earth. And that which escapes is scattered among the clouds + before the wind + never finds its way again.

See, it struggles up towards heaven again. And this time it will succeed. Behold, it scales Infinity. It is rising higher and higher. That mighty heart will climb to heaven. Now it has conquered Earth. It is out of the sphere of its attraction. Oh! it is rising now! It has ascended up on high. It is leading Gravitation captive. The earth cannot reach it to pull it down again. Shoot up, brave spirit, brave spirit, soar higher! Thou hast mastered matter. Be of good cheer, thou hast overcome the world!

Alas! the wind has carried away large fragments of its column. It has made wide gaps in its shaft. Will it fall? Will it fall? It has no support, + it has but a cloud to cling to.

No, it does not fall, brave spirit. It soars higher + higher. Oh! living soul, oh unconquerable heart! though it has lost its foundation, by its own impulse it has struggled on.

Alas! Where is it now? its impulse is exhausted; its strength is at an end; its life is blasted; its struggles done; its hope destroyed. And it falls lifeless on the grass — it, which had so lately been striving to heaven. For it is dead.

---

4. At an intermediate stage of revision, "I, for I did not know what to say" was crossed out and replaced with "her brother, for, in truth, he knew not what to say."

And is there no comfort? Were all its struggles vain? did that noble heart seek heaven in vain?

The ungrateful ground had been fertilized by it. It struggled to the skies — + it watered a weed. It thought to scale Infinity — + it made verdant a blade of grass."

And Nofriani positively shed tears — I had never seen her cry for herself.[5] And how she was actually in tears for the fountain. I did not know how to amuse her. So I attracted[6] her attention to the other little sparkling fountains which were playing in the sun, + though I am nothing of a Mysticist myself I made shifts to improvise a "Ballata" for her benefit, to shew her that her sick fancies were not those of all the world.[7]

"See, how the infant founts spring + gambol + dance in the sun-beams! There is one! He is shooting with his tiny arrow at the sun. He stands, the mimic Apollo, erect + fearless, + laughing sends the missile at the mark. And when the harmless arrow falls playful at his foot, he runs, with joyous laughter, back, + hides his merry face in his mother-fountain, while he tells her how the sun held out his noble hand to catch the infant spear, + could not.

See, there is a brother plashing in the bright waters below. He spreads out his little arms + feet in exciting sport. He thinks he is swimming. And another stands by the edge already reached + cries, Thou canst not come so far.

And here are young spirits in merry multitude, playing shuttlecock with drops of water. Two, tired with the long summer's holiday, have laid their dimpled cheeks on one another + are dreaming of the rich marvels in the upper air. What flushes his cheek like a bright rose-leaf in sleep? He sees a snowy cloud tinged with pomegranate, + thinks how wonderful it must all be up there. Shall he not fly thither + see those dazzling white + purple walls? He climbs with his tiny foot upon his companion to help him a step higher, + his rosy wings quiver like a butterfly's about to fly. But those playful pinions are all too small to carry up the aspiring fount — till a bright sun-beam leaves his etherial home + shoots down with out-stretched helping hand — and he catches the kindly ray, + reaches the top-most spring by that sweet brother's arm. There, pouring his joyous soul in song, he waves his little lance on high. Glad morning vision of *light* and merry *life* as brothers! Not long does he remain there, but eager to rejoin his

---

5. At an intermediate stage of revision, "I had never seen her cry" was made to read "her companion had never seen her weep."

6. At an intermediate stage, "I did not know how to amuse her. So I attracted" was made to read "Seeking how to amuse + calm her, he drew"

7. "I am" was changed to "he was"; "myself I" was changed to "himself he."

Mother Earth, down he springs — + his sister fount welcomes him back with her glad eyes. In loving triumph, she holds up her watery mirror, while he, the daring little soarer, successful Icarus, admires his scatheless wings.

And now they all unite in merry ring, to gather the sunny drops which fall from on high — one, more eager than the rest, darts from the circle to collect a heap in his infant lap. But see, tis but to throw again the sparkling fruits among his brothers! And here, a fairy sister spirit riding in a little boat, while a stout young fount pushes behind with exulting voice, + two brother springs harness themselves in front with wreaths of Childhood's own heavenly colour, blue chains of forget-me-not.

And lo! one solemnly teaching a fraternal fount the principles of the circle on the watery surface, + while his circle spreads + spreads + escapes beyond his little compasses + vanishes out of the reach of his eyes, the other laughs with joyous glee, + trying to stop the run-away, tumbles headlong into the circle's midst, scattering all the glittering fragments into water. And see (oh wonder of wonders!) the little Archimedes stands amazed! The solid walls of his marble house are broken into a thousand glistening jewels, wavy lines, sparkling gems of light, while the commotion lasts which the little Diver has made in the reflecting mirror. And fresh sport succeeds as they dance round their King — their smiles light up the very sky. Blest spirits! glad, sunny fairies every one! But their king, the boldest, loveliest of them all! Joy to thee, glorious Child — for lo! the bird of love, the noble Eagle, floating, descending, not swooping from the skies, paternal in his might, fondly raises the little Ganymede clinging round his neck + looking confidingly in his face + bears him to the feet of love, where Innocence + Power have kissed one another, + are for ever hand in hand."

III

Nofriani sate alone, in her pale cold arid life. She sate, looking at the falling snow, which came down silently, silently, ever slowly + silently falling, till it had covered up all her spring flowers, all her evergreens. And there was nothing but one dreary expanse of untrodden white. The air was full of snow + fog, so that, a few yards off even that white sheet was lost in a wall of dirty mist. She thought of the consolations which she had so lately received, the advice to "come to a compromise with Society," to "let Society have its share + take the other herself," not "to quarrel with the world," "to take things as they were" + e [sic]. And she felt that it was like telling the bush "not to quarrel" with the heavy load which over-powered it + crushed it down, that it was like telling the snow-drops to "make a compromise" with the superincumbent weight.

"My life is like that snow-oppressed land-scape," she said. "There is nothing to be seen but snow + mist on all sides. They say God intended it.

Did God intend that waste of snow to press down all life + green spring beneath it? Yes, I suppose He did — But only for a time. "You must look at life cheerfully," they say. Say to a wretch writhing on her bed in horrible spasm, "God intended it you must take life cheerfully."

"Well, but you are at ease now," they say, "such + such a grievance is not here. *I* like riding about this beautiful place, why don't you? I like walking about the garden, why don't you?"

As if I were a child, whose spirits rise during a fortnight's holiday, who thinks that they will last for ever, + who looks neither backwards nor forwards.

"Oh! pale + cold existence of a broken heart!" I heard her saying.

"And why art thou broken," I asked, "thou that hast everything that Earth can give?"

"I everything!" she said, "I who have now nothing I can desire + nothing I can rejoice in on this Earth."

"How can that be?" I said.

"Do you wish to know? Listen + you will see. Society has triumphed over me. I wished to regenerate the world with my Institutions, with my Moral Philosophy, with my Love. Now I am satisfied to live from breakfast till dinner, from dinner till tea, with a little worsted work, + to look forward to nothing but my bed.

Oh! When shall we see a life full of steady enthusiasm, walking straight to its aim, flying home, as that bird is now, against the wind with the calmness + the confidence of one who knows the laws of God + can apply them? When shall I see it?

And what *do* I see? I see great + fine organizations deteriorating. I see girls + boys of 17, before whose noble ambitions, heroic dreams, + rich endowments I bow my head, as before *God incarnate in the flesh*. But before they are 30, they are withered, paralyzed, anchylosed. "Oh! I have forgotten all my visions," they say themselves.

The "dreams of youth" have become a proverb. That organizations, early rich, fall far short of their promise has been repented to satiety. But is it extraordinary that it should be so? For do we ever *utilize* this heroism? Look how it lives upon itself + perishes for lack of food. We do not know what to do with it. We had rather that it should not be there. Often we laugh at it. Look at the poorness of our life! Can we expect anything else but poor creatures to come out of it? Did Michael Angelo's genius fail, did Pascal's die in its bud, did Sir Isaac Newton become a commonplace sort of man? Yes, in two of these cases the knife wore out the sheath. But the knife itself did not become rusty, till the body was dead or infirm.

Why cannot we *make use* of these noble rising heroisms instead of leaving them to rust.

They have nothing to do.

Are they to be employed in sitting in the Drawing-Room, saying words which may as well not be said, which they could say as well if *they* were not there?

Oh love! Oh Intellect! Oh Activity! ye sun, moon, + stars of human existence! Are ye all set? Departed from my sky?

For seven years I lived in the light of the moon. She was pale, it is true. The clear, brilliant, sharp radiance of Intellect's moonlight rising upon the expanse of snow was dreary. But I loved its solemn desolation, its silence, its solitude — if I had been *allowed* to live in it, if I had not perpetually been baulked, + disappointed. But a woman cannot live in the light of Intellect, Society forbids it. Those conventional frivolities, which are called her ''duties,'' forbid it. Her ''domestic duties,'' high-sounding words, which for the most part, are but bad habits, (which she has not the courage to enfranchise herself from, the strength to break through), forbid it. What are these duties? (or bad habits?) — answering a multitude of letters, which lead to nothing, from her so-called friends, keeping herself up to the level of the world that she may furnish her quota of amusement at the breakfast-table, driving out her company in the carriage. And all these things are exacted from her by her family which, if she is good + affectionate, will have more influence with her than the world.

What wonder if, wearied out, sick at heart with hope deferred, the springs of will broken, not seeing clearly *where* her duty lies, she abandons Intellect as a vocation + takes it only, as we use the moon, by glimpses through her tight-closed window-shutters.

The family? It is too narrow a field for the development of an immortal Spirit, be that spirit male or female. The chances are a million to one that, in that minute sphere, the task, for which that immortal spirit is destined by the qualities + the gifts which its Creator has placed within it, should be found.

The family uses people, *not* for what they are, not for what they are intended to be, but for what it wants them for — for its own uses. It thinks of them not as what God has made them, but as the something which *it* has arranged that they shall be. If it wants some one to sit in the Drawing Room, *that* someone is to be supplied by a member of the family, though that member may be destined for Science or for Education or for active Superintendence by God, i.e. by the gifts within.

This system dooms some minds to incurable infancy, others to silent misery. And family boasts that it has performed its mission well, in as far as it has enabled the individual to say, ''I have *no* peculiar work, nothing but what the moment brings me, nothing that I cannot throw up at once at any body's claim''; in as far, that is, as it has *destroyed* the individual life. And the individual thinks that a great victory has been accomplished when, at last, she is able to say that she has ''no personal desires or plans.'' What is this but throwing the gifts of God aside as worthless, + substituting for them those of the world?

Marriage is the only chance offered to women for escape from this death — + oh how eagerly + how ignorantly it is embraced!

At present, we live to impede each other's satisfactions. Competition, Domestic Life, Society, what is it all but that? We go somewhere when we are not wanted + where we don't want to go. What else is Conventional Life? *Passivity* when we want to be active. So many hours spent every day in passivity doing what Conventional Life tells us, when we would so gladly be at work. And is it a wonder that all individual life is extinguished?

I lived seven years by the wax-lights of conventional Society, striving to see the moonlight of Intellect. She does not warm, she is cold + dreary, with sharp harsh lights + blackest shadows. but oh! she is fair + brilliant, compared with the glare of the candles.

At the end of that time, I gave up the point, or rather, the point gave up me. And I began to dream of other lights. I dreamed of a great sphere of steady, not sketchy benevolence, of Moral Activity for which I should be trained and fitted, instead of working in the dark. Not knowing + not registering whither my steps led me, whether farther from or nearer to my aim.

For how do people exercise their moral activity now? We visit, we teach, we talk, among "the poor," we are told, "don't look for the fruits, cast thy bread upon the water: for thou shalt find it after many days." I say, too, "don't look," for you won't see. You will *not* find it, + then you would strike work.

Oh! How different would be the heart for the work, and how different would be the success! If we learnt our work as a serious study + followed it out steadily as a Profession.

Were the Physician to set to work at *his* trade as the Philanthropist at his does, how many bodies would he not spoil before he cured one!

Ah! true, I had forgotten. We set the treatment of bodies so high above the treatment of souls that the Physician occupies a higher place in society than the schoolmaster. The governess is to have every one of God's gifts, she is to do that which the mother herself is incapable of doing, but our son must not degrade himself by marrying the governess, nor our daughter the tutor, though she might marry the Medical Man.

But my medical man does do something for me, you say, my tutor has done nothing.

This is true, that is the real reason. And what a condemnation of the state of mental science is here! Low as is Physical Science, that of the Mind is still lower.

Well, I dreamed an education **(it was but a dream)** to teach me *to teach*, to teach me the laws of the human mind + how to apply them, + knowing how imperfect, in the present state of the world such an education must be. I dreamed of experience, not patch-work experience, but experience followed up + systematized to enable me to know what I was about + *where* I was "casting my bread" + whether it was "*bread*" that I was casting or a stone.

But vain, vain were all my dreams, killing my disappointments, heart-sickening my struggles.

How should you learn a language, if you give to it an hour a week? A fortnight's steady application would make more way in it than a year of such work. So was it with all my plans. A ''lady'' can hardly go to ''her school'' two days running. She cannot leave the breakfast-table or she must be fulfilling some little frivolous ''duty,'' which others ought not to exact, or which might just as well be done some other time.

Thus I lived for other [sic] seven years dreaming always, never accomplishing, — too much ashamed of my dreams, which I thought were ''romantic,'' to tell them where I knew that they would be laughed at, if not considered wrong. **So I lived, till my heart was broken. I am now an old woman at 30.**

I do not say that, with greater strength of purpose, I could not have accomplished something. If I had been a hero, I should not need to tell my story for then all the world would have read it in the mission I should have fulfilled. It is because I am a common-place, every-day character that I tell my tale, because it is the sample of hundreds of lives (or rather deaths) who cannot fight with Society, or who, unsupported by the sympathies about them, give up their own destiny as not worth the fierce + continued struggle necessary to accomplish it. *One* struggle they *could* make + be free, (+, in the Church of Rome, many, many, unallured by any other motive, make this one struggle to enter a Convent). But the perpetual series of petty spars, — with doubts + discouragements between whether you are right, — wears out the very life necessary to make them.

So I lived, then, for 7 years. And, at the end of that time, I was dead. My pole star was still in the sky, — for it could not set. But my eyes were too dim to see it. I lost my way + perished.

If a man were to follow up his Profession or Occupation at odd times, how would he do it? Would he become skilful in that Profession? It is acknowledged by women themselves that they are inferior in every occupation to men. Is it wonderful? *They* do everything at odd times.

And, if a woman's music and drawing are only used by her as an amusement, (a *pass-time*, as it is called), is it wonderful that she tires of them, that she becomes disgusted with them?

During all these fourteen years, I had been waiting for my sun to rise, the sun of a perfect human sympathy, the sun of Passion, as it is called, not consciously looking out for. Our pride + our ignorance are alike too great for that, but unconsciously shadowing it in idea. In every dream of the life of intelligence or that of activity, I was accompanied by a phantom, a sympathy, say, warming me, guiding me, lighting me. **It was only in idea — it never reached, even in my own mind, reality.**

I sacrificed marriage — because I must have sacrificed all other life, had I accepted that. That man + woman have an equality of rights even is accepted by woman even less than by man. Behind *his* destiny woman must annihilate herself. I felt that, I knew that I must be only his complement. A woman dedicates herself to the vocation of her husband. She fills up + performs the subordinate parts in it. But, if she has any destiny, any vocation of her own, she must renounce it, in nine cases out of ten. Some few, like Mrs. Somerville, Mrs. Chisholm, Mrs. Fry, have not done so. But these are exceptions. The fact is that woman has so seldom any vocation of her own that it does not signify. She has none to renounce. A man gains everything by marriage. He gains a "help-mate." But a woman does not.

I felt that I must choose, either to hold myself ready to sacrifice, *if* called upon, feelings, religious, social, political (but when these were all gone, there was not [illeg] |———| of me left),[8] or I must sacrifice love + marriage. I preferred the latter. And now I have lost all, the prize + the penalty, the crown I dream for + the way-side happiness I despised. And I am dead.

I dared presumptuously to measure my strength. And it has been found wanting.

I have fallen so low that I now regret even the conventional importance of marriage.

The glory has departed. The life is gone out of me.

I now only recognize my existence but by suffering. Otherwise I should believe that I was dead. I cannot even remember the motives which caused me to overstep the easy landing-place of marriage. I have lost even the memory of my former self.

Once only did I recover the sentiment of my vocation, the recollection of former springs of action.

Those dreams of a human sympathy had pursued me day + night, tortured + driven me to within a hair's breadth of losing all consciousness of actual existence. I now think that I should have done better to satisfy them at any price. But it was now too late.

When all was lost, I was called for three months (it was the only romantic incident of my life) to see + nurse sickness + crime + poverty in masses. The practical reality of life revived me. I was exhausted, like a man who has lived on Opium or on novels all his life, exhausted with feelings which led to no action. Here I came in contact with a continuous line of action, with a full + interesting life, [illeg — word fragment?] with training constantly kept up to the occupation, occupation constantly testing the training. It was the beau-ideal of practical, not theoretical education — I was re-tempered. My destiny accomplished, my life filled, my intellect — + activity satisfied. I had found my work + the means to do it.

8. Intermediate revisions alter this sentence to read, "(but when these were all gone, there would not be thus much |———| of me left)."

I remember, when I was young, I used to think that an actress's life might be a very happy one. Not for the sake of the admiration, not for the sake of the fame. I did not think of that. But, because in the morning she studied, — in the evening she embodied those studies. She had the means of testing them by practice, of correcting them by incarnation, + of resuming her studies in the mornings to improve the weak parts, remedy the failures, and in the evening try the corrections again. In this way, I thought there was no end to the progress which might be made."

"But why, why," said I at last, "can't you be satisfied with this life, which so many love + enjoy? I never wanted five minutes' solitude, I never wanted a profession, why do you?"

"And I, to stop this little breath + with it all this load of misery, how often have I been tempted to do it?"

"And why don't you? What has held you back?"

"**Only** because it is more than anything else saying to God: 'I won't, I won't do as Thou would have me.' + because it is 'no use.' "

"Well, but tell me, tell me the cause of this misery, I can't understand it. You have told me a great deal, + I can only say, 'Is that all?' "

"To have no food for my head, no food for my heart, no food for my activity — and you call that not enough? Oh! if we have no food for the body, how we do cry out, how all the world hears of it, how all the newspapers talk of it with a paragraph headed in great capital letters, *Death from Starvation*! Suppose I were to put a paragraph in the "Times," Death of the Head from Starvation or Death of Moral Activity from Starvation, how people would stare, how they would laugh + wonder! One would think we had no heads nor hearts, by the total indifference of the public towards them. Our bodies are the only things of the least consequence."

"Well, but just tell me what you complain of," said I. "I am sure I don't know."

"I have nothing to do which raises me. No food which agrees with me. I can never pursue any object for a single two hours. For we can never command any regular leisure or solitude."

"But cannot you do anything with anybody in the room? If not, the best advice I can give you is to learn as soon as possible. School-boys do."

"But in Social + Domestic Life, every body reads aloud out of their own book or newspaper, + one is bound, under pain of being thought sulky, to make a remark or to speak every two minutes."

"Yes, to be sure, one might as well be alone, if one is to sit mute."

"You see, you are on the side of Society. You blow hot + cold. You say, 'why can't you employ yourself in Society?' and then 'why don't you talk in Society?' I can pursue a connected conversation, or I can be silent, but to drop a remark, as it is called, every two minutes, how wearisome it is! It is impossible to pursue the current of one's own thoughts because one must keep oneself ever on the alert "to say something," + it is impossible to say what one is thinking, because the essence of a remark is not to be a thought, but an impression. With what labour I have labored to break down all individual and independent life in order to fit myself for this social + domestic existence, thinking it right. And now that I have killed myself to do it, I have awakened (too late) to [illeg] [is?] [illeg].[9]

For now I could not make use of Leisure + Solitude, if I had it! Like the Chinese woman, who could not make use of her feet, if she were brought into European life.

I was born with an attention like a battering-ram, which, slowly brought to bear, could work upon a subject for any length of time. I could work ten hours just as well as two upon the same thing. But this age is like the musket which you can load so fast that nothing but its taking fire puts any limit to the number + frequency of times of firing, + at as many different objects as you please.

Now I cannot use my battering-ram. My attention, like Society's goes off in a thousand different directions. I am an hour before I can fix it, + by the time it is fixed, the leisure is gone. I am become incapable of consecutive or strenuous work.

What I have suffered from the want of such work no one can tell. Even physically. The accumulation of nervous energy, which had had nothing to do during the day, made me feel every night, when I went to bed, as if I were going mad. And I was obliged to lie long in bed in the morning to let it evaporate + keep it down.

Now I am suffering at once from disgust of the one + incapacity for the other, from loathing of conventional idleness + powerlessness to do work when I have got it. "Now go, you have several hours," say people, "you have all the afternoon to yourself." Yes, when I am all frittered away, I am to begin to work. When I am broken up into little bits, I am to hew away.

Oh! call me no more Nofriani, call me Cassandra. for I have preached + prophesied in vain. I have gone about crying all these many years, Wo to the people! And no one has listened or believed. And now I cry, Wo to myself! For upon me the destruction has come."

IV

"Oh world! oh life! oh time!
On whose last steps I climb,
Trembling at that where I had stood before,
When will return the glory of your prime?
No more — oh never more!"[10]

---

9. The illegible words at the end of this sentence are written over with the words "think it wrong."

10. From Percy Bysshe Shelley, "A Lament" (1821, published 1824 in *Posthumous Poems*).

"Yes," she said to me one day, "I feel that my youth is gone. I used to laugh at the poets' sunny description of the May-time of youth, + say that *I* had never felt anything like that. But now I see the great difference between Youth + Middle Age. Before, I suffered, but I always thought that I *should* carry out my schemes. I lived but for that. I lived upon desire, upon the dream of my hopes fulfilled. Now I see that I never shall fulfill them. I have lost the vigour to hope, the zest to desire, the sap to dream. I have come even to regret the enjoyments which I thought unworthy of me, to pick up as I went by.

Moral Activity? Why, there is not such a thing possible! Every thing is sketchy. The world does nothing but sketch. One Lady Bountiful sketches a school, but it never comes to a finished study, she can hardly work at it two weeks consecutively. Here + there a solitary individual, it is true, makes a study, as Mrs. Chisholm of Emigration, or Mrs. Dowes of a school Education, as Mrs. Fry of Prison Discipline. But, in general, a "lady" has too many sketches on hand. She has a sketch of Society, a sketch of her children's education, sketches of her "charities," sketches of her reading. She is like a painter who should have five pictures in his [illeg][11] at once, + giving now a stroke to one, + then a stroke to another, till he has made the whole round — How would he paint, do you think?

Alas! all life is sketchy — the Poet's verse (compare Tennyson, Milnes, + Mrs. Browning with Milton or even Byron — it is not the difference of genius which strikes you so much as the unfinished state of these modern sketches, compared with the studies of the Old Masters). The artist's picture, the author's composition, all are rough, imperfect, incomplete, even as works of art.

And how can it be otherwise? A "leader" in a newspaper, an article out of a Review, five books read aloud in the course of an evening, such is our literature. What mind can stand three leading articles every morning as its food?

Alas! for Moral Activity! When shall we see a woman making a *study* of what she does? Married women cannot, for a man would think, if his woman undertook any great work with the intention of carrying it out, — of making anything but a sham of it, — that she would "suckle his fools" + "chronicle his small beer" less well for it, that he would not have so good a dinner, but that she would destroy, as it is called, his domestic life.

And I, who dreamed of Institutions to shew women their work + to train them how to do it, to give them an object + to incline their wills to follow it. I, in whom thoughts of this kind put aside the thought of marriage, who sacrificed my individual future for great hopes, glimpsed a great general future, I have fallen so low that I can look back with a sigh after the conventional dignity of a married woman, the vulgar incident of the pomp

[11]. "Studio" has been written over another word that is now illegible.

+ circumstance of marriage + say with a sigh, "Such might have been mine, if I had chosen!"

Yes, I thought that I could despise Passion. I thought, the intercourse of man + woman, how frivolous, how unworthy it is! Can you call *that* the true vocation of woman, her high career? I looked round at the marriages which I knew + I said, "The true marriage, that noble union, by which man + woman become together the one perfect being, probably does not exist at present upon this earth."

I am not surprised that husbands + wives seem so little part of one another, I am surprised that there is so much love as there is. For I see no food for it. I don't know what it lives upon, what nourishes it? Husbands + wives never seem to have anything to say to one another. What do they talk about? Not about any of the great religious, social, political questions + feelings. They talk about who shall come to dinner, who is to live in this lodge + who in that, about the improvements of the place, or when they shall go to London. If there are children, they form a common subject of some nourishment. But, even then, the case is oftenest thus — the husband is to think of how they are to get on in life, the wife of bringing them up at home.

But any real communion between husband + wife, any descending into the depths of their being + drawing out thence what they find there + comparing it, do we ever dream of such a thing? Yes, we may dream of it during the season of "passion," but we shall not find it afterwards. We even *expect* it to go off, + lay our account that it will. If the husband has, by chance, gone into the depths of *his* being + found anything there unorthodox, he, oftenest, conceals it carefully from his wife, he is afraid of "unsettling her opinions," of "shocking her feelings."

What is Passion[?] Blind passion, as it has most truly been called, seems to come on, in man, without his exactly knowing why, without his *at all* knowing why for *this* person rather than for *that*, and (whether it has been satisfied or unsatisfied) to go off again after a while, as it came, also without his knowing why.

The woman's passion is generally more lasting.

It is possible that this difference may be because there is really more in man than in woman. There is nothing in her for him to have this intimate communion *with.* He cannot impart to her his religious beliefs, if he have any, because she would be "shocked." Religious men are + must be heretics now, for we must not pray, except in a "form" of words, made beforehand, or think of God but in a pre-arranged idea.

With [illeg][12] political ideas, if they extend beyond the merest Party Politics, she has no sympathy.

12. Illegible word written over "the man's."

His social ideas, if they are "advanced," she will probably denounce without knowing why, as savouring of "Socialism" (a convenient word, which covers a multitude of new ideas + offences) + fears that they will lead to a "community of women."

Woman has nothing but her affections, + these make her at once more loving + less loved.

But is it surprising that there should be so little real marriage, when we think what the process is which leads to marriage?

Under the eyes of an always present mother + sisters, whom even the most refined + intellectual cannot abstain from a jest upon the subject, + of whom the mother, at least, thinks it the *duty* to be anxious, to watch every germ + bud of it, the acquaintance begins. It is fed — upon What? — the gossip of Art, musical + pictorial — the party politics of the day — the chit-chat of Society — + people marry — or sometimes they don't marry, discouraged with the impossibility of knowing any more of one another than this will furnish.

They prefer to marry in *thought*, to hold imaginary conversations with one another in idea, rather than, on such a flimsy pretext of communion, to take the chance (*certainty* it cannot be) of having more to say to one another in marriage.

Men + women meet now *to be idle* — is it extraordinary that they do not know each other, + in their mutual ignorance, form no surer friendships? Did they meet to *do* something together, then indeed they might form some real tie.

But, as it is, *they* are not there, it is only a mask which is there, **a talker** of ready-made sentences about the "topics of the day" which you see. And then people rail against them for choosing a woman "for her face" — why what else to they see? It is very well to say "be prudent, be careful, try to know each other" — But how are you to know each other? Unless a woman has lost all pride, unless she has the impudence of that which we must not name, how is it possible for her, under the eyes of all her family, to indulge in long exclusive conversations with a man? Such a thing must not take place till after her "engagement." And how is she to make an engagement, if such a thing has not taken place?

Besides, young women at home have so little to occupy + to interest them — they have so little reason for *not* quitting their home that a young + independent man cannot look at a girl, without giving rise to "expectations" — if not on her part, on that of her people. Happy he, if he is not said to have been "trifling with her feelings," or "disappointing her hopes"! Under these circumstances, how can a man, who has any pride or principle, become acquainted with a woman in such a manner as to *justify* them in marrying?"

"Yet people do marry," said I.[13]

13. This sentence is crossed out with a double line, and followed by another version of the sentence — "Yet people have married," said I, "+ we do see them marrying even now" — that is crossed out with a single line.

— There are four ways in which people marry. First, accident or relationship has thrown them together in their childhood — + acquaintance has grown up naturally + unconsciously. Accordingly, in Novels, it is generally cousins who marry. And I confess that it seems to me the only natural thing, the only possible way of making an intimacy. And yet, we know that intermarriage between relations is in direct contravention of the laws of Nature for the well-being of the race — vide the Quakers, the Spanish grandees, the royal races, the secluded vallies of mountainous countries, where madness, degeneration of race, defective organization + Cretinism flourish + multiply. **The laws of nature have said, 'marry your cousin, be happy, + cause the race to degenerate.' "**

"And have they said, Marry a foreigner + be miserable + improve the race?" said I.

"I believe so, or pretty nearly so. The second way, + by far the most general, in which people marry, is this. A woman, thoroughly uninterested at home, + having formed a slight acquaintance with some accidental person, accepts him, if he "falls in love" with her, as it is technically called, + takes the chance. Hence the vulgar expression of Marriage being a lottery, which it most truly is — for, that the *right* two should come together has as many chances against it as there are blanks in any Lottery.

The third way is that some person is found sufficiently independent, sufficiently careless of the opinions of others, or sufficiently without modesty to speculate thus, "It is worthwhile that I should become acquainted with so + so. I do not care what his or her opinion of me is, if, *after* having become acquainted, to do which can bear no other construction in people's eyes than a desire of marriage, I retreat! I do not care what others think of me. It is worth while." But there is this to be said that it is doubtful whether, under this unnatural tension which, to all susceptible characters, such a disregard of the opinions which they care for, must be, a healthy or a natural feeling can grow up.

And now they are married, that is to say, two people have received the license of a man in a white surplice. But they are no more man + wife for that then Louis XIV + the Infanta of Spain, married by proxy, were man + wife. The woman is as often a prostitute as a wife. She prostitutes herself, if she has sold her person for an establishment, as much as if she had sold it in the streets. **She prostitutes herself, if, knowing so little of her husband as she does, she begins immediately, without further acquaintance, to allow him the rights of a husband over her person.** She prostitutes herself later, if, against her own desire, she allows herself to be made the blind instrument of producing involuntary children. It will be said, + truly, that, when she marries, her husband understands all these privileges as granted, + that she would drive him mad + deceive his understood expectation, if she did not grant them. But how is she to ascertain her husband's opinion on these points before marriage?

Lastly, in a few rare, very rare cases, such as circumstances, always provided in novels, but seldom to be met with in real life, or the accident of parents' neglect, or of parents' unusual skill + wisdom, or of having no parents at all, which is again generally the case in Novels, or marrying out of the person's rank of life, by which the usual restraints are removed, + there is room + play left for attraction, or extraordinary events, isolation, misfortunes, which I am sure that many wish for, even though their imaginations be not tainted by romance-reading, such alternatives as these give food + space for the development of character + mutual sympathies. But a girl, if she has any pride, is so ashamed of having something she wishes to say out of the hearing of her own family, she thinks it must be something so very wrong that it is ten to one, if she have the opportunity of saying it, that she will not.

And yet she spends her life, perhaps, in dreaming of accidental means of unrestrained communion.

And then it is thought chastely pretty to say that ''women have no passion.'' If passion is excitement in the intercourse with men, I am sure that women think about marriage much more than men do — it is the only event of their lives. It ought to be a sacred event, but surely not the only event of woman's life, as it is now, when many women spend their lives in asking men to marry them, in a refined way. Yet it is true, I believe, that women are seldom in love. How can they be? Oh! how cruel are the revulsions which women suffer! **I remember, on the ruins of Palmyra, amid the wrecks of worlds + palaces + temples, thinking of** one I had loved, in connection with great deeds, noble thoughts, devoted feelings. I saw him again. It was at one of those crowded parties of Civilization which we call Society. His words were, ''the buzz tonight is like a manufactory.'' Yet that man loved me still.

And now, I have soon done with this world — The life of it has departed from me.''

V

> ''L'enthousiasme + la faiblesse
> d'un temps ou l'intelligence
> monte tres haut, entrainee
> par l'imagination, + tombe
> tres bas, ecrasee par une
> realite, sans poesie + sans grandeur.''

And now I have no longer the strength to dream those dreams, against which I did so struggle, so honestly, vigorously + conscientiously + so in vain, which I did so curse in their time, + which I now know were my life, without which I could not have lived. Those dreams are gone, all my plans + visions seem vanished + I know not where — gone + I cannot recall them. I do not even remember them. And I am left without the food either of reality or of hope.

I neither desire nor dream now, neither of activity, nor of love, nor of intellect. Yes, the last has survived the longest. I should like, if my experiences would benefit anybody, to give them to some one. But I never find an hour free in which to collect my thoughts, + so discouragement becomes even deeper + deeper, + I less + less capable of undertaking anything.

Oh! miserable fate of the woman! It seems **to me when I hear that eternal wind sighing + lamenting I know not where** as if it were the female spirit of the world mourning everlastingly over blessings — *not* lost, but which she has never had, — which, in her discouragement, she feels that she never will have, they are so far off.''

"But why do not other women feel this?"

''The more complete her organization, the more she will feel it, till at last there will come a woman, who will resume, in her own person, all the sufferings of her race, + that woman will be the Saviour of her race.

Jesus Christ raised us above the condition of mere slaves, mere ministers to the passions of the man, by His sympathy, to be ministers of God. He gave us Moral Activity. But the Age, — the World, — Humanity must give us the means to exercise this moral activity, must give us intellectual cultivation, spheres of action.

There is perhaps no century where the woman shows so meanly as in this. Because her education seems entirely to have parted company with her vocation. I mean that she as inwardly developed, + she as outwardly manifested no longer run parallel.

In the last century, it was not so. In the succeeding one, let us hope that it will no longer be so.

But now she is like the Archangel Michael as he stands upon Sant' Angelo at Rome. She has an immense provision of wings, which seem as if they would bear her over earth + heaven — but when she tries to use them, lo' she is petrified into stone, her feet are grown into the earth, chained to the bronze pedestal.

Nothing can well be imagined more painful than the present position of woman — unless, on the one hand, she renounces all outward activity + keeps herself within the magic[14] sphere, the bubble of her dreams — or, on the other, surrendering all aspiration, she gives herself to her real life — soul, + body. For those to whom it is possible, I recommend the latter — for out of activity may come thought — out of mere aspiration can come nothing.

But now, — when the young imagination is so high + so developed — + reality is so narrow + conventional, — there is no more parallelism between life in thought + life in the actual than between the corpse, which lies motionless

14. ''Magic'' is preceded by a crossed-out word, ''ephe,'' which was probably to have been ''ephemeral.''

in its narrow bed, + the spirit, which, in our imagination, is at large among the stars.

The ideal life is passed in noble schemes of good consecutively followed up, — of devotion to a great object — of sympathy given + received for high ideas + generous feelings. The actual life is passed in sympathy given + received for a dinner, a party, a piece of furniture, a house built or a garden laid out well — in devotion to your guests, — (a too real devotion, for it implies the sacrifice of all your time) — in schemes of schooling for the poor, which you follow up perhaps in an odd quarter of an hour, between luncheon + driving out in the carriage, broth + dripping are included in the plan, + the rest of your time goes in ordering the dinner, hunting for a governess for your children, + sending pheasants + apples to your poorer relations. Is there anything in *this* life which can be called an incarnation of the ideal life within? Is it a wonder that the unfortunate woman should prefer to keep them entirely separate? not to take the bloom off her Ideal by mixing it up with her Actual — not to make her Actual still more unpalateable by trying to *inform* it with her Ideal? And then she is blamed, + her own sex unites against her, for not being content with the "day of small things" — she is told that "trifles make the sum of human things" — they do indeed — she is contemptuously asked, "would she abolish domestic life?" Men are afraid that their dinners will not be so comfortable, that their wives will make themselves so good, women that they will make themselves distasteful to men — they write books (+ very wisely) to teach themselves to dramatize "little things," to persuade themselves that "domestic life is their sphere" + to idealize the "sacred hearth." Sacred it is indeed — virgin from the touch of their sons almost as soon as they are out of childhood — (from its dulness + its tyrannous trifling *these* recoil —) virgin from the grasp of their daughters' affections, upon which it has so light a hold that they seize the first opportunity of marriage — *their* only chance of emancipation — the "sacred hearth," sacred to their husbands' sleep, their sons' absence in the body + their daughters' in mind.

Oh! mothers, who talk about this hearth, how much do you know of your sons' real life — how much of your daughters' imaginary one? Awake, ye women, all ye that sleep, awake — if this domestic life were so very good, would your young men wander away from it, your maidens think of something else?

The time is come when women must do some thing more than the "domestic hearth," which means nursing the infants, keeping a pretty house, having a good dinner + an entertaining party.

You say, "it is true, our young men see visions + our maidens dream dreams, but what of? Does not the woman intend to marry + have over again what she has at home? + the man ultimately too?" Yes, but not the same. She *will* have the same, that is, if circumstances are not altered to prevent it, but her *ideal* is very different — though that ideal will never come.[15]

VI

"Well," said I, "we are now going into the world, + if you would cease quarrelling with it, + would open your eyes to its joys, which you don't seem inclined to do, I think you might make yourself very tolerably happy."

This was a cruel speech, I admit, to such deep discouragement, such old griefs as hers. But it was a true one.[16] She answered me never a word, but, in the course of the evening, she said,

"I wonder whether Christ was called a complainer against the world? Yet all these great teachers + preachers must have had a most deep + ingrained sense, a continual gnawing feeling of the miseries + wrongs of the world. Otherwise they would not have been impelled to devote life + death to redress them. Christ, Socrates, Howard,[17] they must have had no ear for the joys, compared to that they had for the sorrows of the world."

"Ah! but," I said, "they acted + we complain."

"Yes," she said, "I suppose that is the difference. The great reformers of the world turn into the great misanthropists, — if circumstances or organization do not permit them to act. Christ, if He had been a woman, might have been nothing but a great complainer. Peace be with the misanthropists! They have made a step in progress. The next will make them great philanthropists. They are divided but by a line.

"The next Christ will be a female Christ, I believe. But I do not see one woman who looks like a female Christ. **I don't see any one who looks, in the least, like her Precursor even.** If I could see one, I would be "the messenger before" her "face," to go before her + prepare the hearts + minds for her.

"Now I don't wonder," said I, "at your being unhappy. If you have that insane ambition to be a Christ or a John the Baptist! Do you know that half the inmates of Bedlam began in that way, by fancying that they were "the Christ"?

"Yes," she said, "that is just like you all. You talk about imitating Christ + you imitate Him in the little trifling formal things, such as washing the feet, saying his prayer + so on. But if anyone attempts the real imitation of Him, there are no bounds to the outcry with which the presumption of that person is condemned."

15. "will never come" is crossed out, and the sentence reads "though that ideal and the reality will never come together to mould each other."

16. "My true one" is written over and the sentence revised to read "but it was my true impression, and good advice too."

17. John Howard (1726?–90), philanthropist.

''Presumption indeed! It is mad pride, downright insanity!''

''For instance, Christ was saying something to the people one day, which interested Him very much + interested them very much. And Mary + his brothers came in the middle of it, + wanted to interrupt him, to take him home to dinner very likely (how natural that story is! I want no 'historic Evidences' of the Gospel) + he, instead of being angry with their interruption of Him in such an important work for some trifling thing, answers ''Who is my mother? + who are my brethren? Whosoever shall do the will of my Father which is in heaven, the same is my brother + sister + mother.'' But if *we* were to say that, we should be accused of ''destroying the family tie'' — of diminishing the obligation of the ''home duties.''

He might well say ''Heaven + earth shall pass away, but my words shall not pass away.'' His words will never pass away. Only think if he had said, ''Tell them that I am engaged at this moment in something very important — that the instruction of the multitude ought to go before any personal ties — that I will remember to come when I have done,'' no one would have been impressed by his words — But how striking is that, 'Behold my mother + my brethren!' ''

VII

Before I go on, I had better tell who ''I'' am. My name is Fariseo. I am one of those, who are called the Cynics of the age, who openly confess their own selfishness, admit the wants of the times, + preach that we should bear with them, making this confession, not with sorrow of heart, nor well-trained resignation, but without shame + without difficulty, as, on the whole, the best state of mind. I am the brother of poor Nofriani, + I tell her story as she told it me, one day when I blamed her for not finding her happiness in life as I + her contemporaries have done, + she answered that I did not know whether her life had been such that she could either find happiness in it or alter it. I made some few notes of our conversation, for it occurred a short time only before her death — My poor sister! She died at 30, wearied of life, in which she could do nothing + having ceased to live the intellectual life long before she was deserted by the physical life. I saw her on her death-bed, + giving way to the tears + exclamations natural on such occasions, was answered by her,

''Oh! if you knew how gladly I leave this life, how much more courage I feel to take the chance of another than of anything I see before me in this, you would put on your wedding- clothes instead of mourning for me!''

''But,'' I said, ''so much talent! So many gifts! Such good which you might have done!''

''The world will be put back some little time by my death,'' she said, ''you see I estimate my powers at least as highly as you can, but it is by the death which has taken place some years ago in me, not by the death which is about to take place now. So is the world put back by the death of every one who has to sacrifice the development of his or her own peculiar gifts to conventionality which were meant, not for selfish gratification, but for the improvement of that world.

My people were children playing on the shore of the 18th century. I was their hobby-horse, their plaything. And they drove me to + fro, dear souls! Never weary of the play themselves, till I, who had grown to woman's estate + to the ideas of the 19th century, lay down exhausted, my mind closed to hope, my heart to strength, + all was still + dark + dreary.''

She lay some time silent. Then starting up + standing upright for the first time for many months, she stretched out her arms + cried, ''Free, free, oh! divine Freedom, art thou come at last? Welcome, beautiful Death!'' She fell forward on her face. She was dead.

One of her last requests had been that neither name nor date should be placed on her grave. Still less the expression of regret or of admiration, but simply the words, ''I believe in God.''

WORKS IN PROGRESS

Carolyn Dever's essay, "Calling Dr. Darwin: Phylogeny, Parthenogenesis, and the Phantasy of the Dead Mother," is from a forthcoming Cambridge book considering representations of dead and missing mothers in mid-nineteenth century fiction.

John Woolford's essay, "The Protean Precursor: Browning and Edward FitzGerald," will form part of a book on literary networking in the nineteenth century.

CALLING DR. DARWIN: PHYLOGENY, PARTHENOGENESIS, AND THE PHANTASY OF THE DEAD MOTHER

By Carolyn Dever

TOWARD THE END of his *Autobiography* (1887), assessing the process of his intellectual development, Charles Darwin writes: "My mind seems to have become a kind of machine for grinding general laws out of large collections of facts. . . . I think I am superior to the common run of men in noticing things which easily escape attention, and in observing them carefully."[1] In his articulation of the link between general laws and "large collections of facts," Darwin draws attention to the relationship of evidence to conclusion, of part to whole, of individual to species. Making explicit the uniquely synecdochal logic of his scientific texts, Darwin casts himself as the Sherlock Holmes of Victorian natural philosophy, capable of understanding what others cannot even see, and of developing "general laws" for scientific and behavioral theories alike.

This logic prevails throughout his autobiography; like *The Origin of Species,* Darwin's autobiographical text is a narrative of origins which recasts the larger questions of his intellectual life onto a smaller, personal framework. However, the translation of the phylogenetic, or group, narrative of origins, to the ontogenetic, or personal narrative, exposes a set of anxious displacements behind and within Darwin's self-construction. When Darwin represents *himself* as the evolutionary subject, the generic and practical conventions of autobiography require the explication of a family structure, and specifically, of a parent-child structure. Darwin's descriptions of his parents demonstrate anxieties regarding questions of gender and power, desire and knowledge. He represents himself as a subject engaged at once in a relationship of vexed desire for a mother who is dead, and of intense rivalry with a father who is all too present. The patterns of displacement and aggression produced through these relationships are the patterns that implicitly subtend Darwin's theories of origins, on the phylogenetic and the ontogenetic levels.

In his construction of an autobiographical persona in an evolutionary framework, Darwin directly anticipates the efforts that will be made in the next decade by Freud: both men utilize the discourse of science to comprehend the puzzle of human development, and both present their conclusions in narratives noteworthy for their literary qualities.[2] As a writer, Darwin, like Freud, consistently anticipates his critics through the meticulous analysis of physical evidence and the constant, self-conscious reformulation of his argument. On a more subtle level, however, Darwin, like Freud, *acts out* anxieties — particularly when they are related to questions of gender and power — through rhetorical structures which are symptomatic in their display of ambivalence and aggression.[3] In this essay, I will analyze the ways in which Darwin acts out representational anxieties on the level of rhetorical presentation; thus the rhetorical becomes a lens through which to understand the ideologies of domesticity and desire displaced from home in particular to culture at large in Darwin's larger scientific project.

I. *Figuring the Mother*

IN A DISCUSSION of his boyhood creative impulses, Darwin makes an explicit connection between creativity and creation. He writes, "I told another little boy (I believe it was Leighton, who afterwards became a well-known Lichenologist and botanist) that I could produce variously coloured Polyanthuses and Primroses by watering them with certain coloured fluids, which was of course a monstrous fable, and had never been tried by me. I may here also confess that as a little boy I was much given to inventing deliberate falsehoods, and this was always done for the sake of causing excitement" (23). Darwin's "deliberate falsehood" causes excitement focused on his own generative powers; this "fable" represents an early desire for agency within the world of nature. Notably, however, such a production of agency is linked explicitly with the production of narrative; telling tales about nature generates excitement and attention for the child as for the man.

In a 1921 reading of this anecdote, Edward J. Kempf locates the source of "agency" in Darwin's body; the anecdote, he argues, "was told at the age when children are inclined to wonder seriously about the possible genetic qualities of their excreta."[4] For Kempf, an early practitioner of Freudian psychoanalysis in the project of literary theory, Darwin himself, rather than Darwin's text, is the object of analytic scrutiny. In Kempf's view, Darwin's various blindnesses to and manipulations of childhood memories lead to personal psychodramatic issues, rather than to Darwin's engagement with larger cultural dynamics reflected in his various modes of self-presentation. Thus for Kempf, Darwin's story "had the value of being a fertilization curiosity," in which Darwin, by urinating, was capable of producing "variously coloured Polyanthuses and Primroses." The boy has constructed himself as a paternal figure both in relation to the flowers he generates and the stories he generates. Darwin's story describes a myth of parthenogenetic fertility, in which generation occurs paternally, and in which the maternal is elided altogether: the source of flowers, or ordinary narratives, is Charles Darwin alone.

A footnote added to the *Autobiography* after its initial publication suggests that Darwin's ''monstrous fable' is linked by complex means to the ''generation'' of Darwin himself. Darwin's son Francis adds the following explanatory account to his father's tale: ''Rev. W. A. Leighton, who was a schoolfellow of my father's at Mr. Case's school, remembers [Charles Darwin] bringing in a flower to school and saying that his mother had taught him how by looking at the inside of the blossom the name of the plant could be discovered. Mr. Leighton goes on, 'This greatly roused my attention and curiosity, and I inquired of him repeatedly how this could be done?' — but his lesson was naturally enough not transmissible'' (23, n1). Leighton's story is noteworthy in its differences from Darwin's: rather than generating flowers himself, Darwin is shown, in Kempf's narrative, describing their proper names by ''looking at the inside of the blossom.'' While Darwin's memory of the episode presents its events as a generative phantasy, Leighton's anecdote tells a tale of reading, of peeking inside a blossom and learning its secrets. The erotic symbolism of the two memories is quite notably different; Leighton's recollection seems to focus on the interaction of boy and blossom, a relationship mediated by the instructive presence of the mother. In Darwin's story, on the other hand, the mother-figure is elided altogether, in favor of a focus on one small but powerful boy. Darwin's version of this story is both more aggressive and more paternalistic, although its potency is twice undercut by qualification as ''deliberate falsehood'' and as ''fable''; the apocryphal nature of the anecdote within the autobiography, in combination with Leighton's corrective version, signals its symptomatic complexity.

Kempf speculates on the significant differences between Darwin's and Leighton's stories:

> Whether or not Darwin's mother actually propounded her enchanting riddle to her boy is not quite so important as the fact that he said she did, showing how keenly his wishes relished the fancy that she had revealed to him the one secret of life that fascinated her — the secret, which, if read, would reveal the origin and creation of life and — himself. Children from seven to ten are usually passionately fond of riddles. It is the trial and error method of finding the answer to the omnipresent riddle as to their origin. Soon after this innocent exchange of confidences with her boy, the beautiful mother died — went on a long journey into the night. . . . At ten, this boy was still collecting minerals with much zeal, still searching for the answer to his mother's riddle and her wish that he could know.[5]

Kempf sees a direct relationship between Darwin's scientific work and the death of his mother in his youth, a relationship articulated, he argues, in both Leighton's anecdote and in the version Darwin presents in the *Autobiography.* ''Looking at the inside of the blossom,'' exploring the secrets of the scientific universe, signifies for Darwin as the means of connection with his missing mother. Kempf argues that Darwin's fascination with ''naming,'' with empiricism, and with origins, is immediately traceable to his desire to please, to imitate, and ultimately, to recover, his mother, as well as his desire to understand the means by which his own life was created. To act after her example is not only to indulge his curiosity about flowers, but also to explore the acts and means of physical generation, of sexuality. Empirical investigation, the observation of events and the generation of "general laws," functions for Darwin as a complex means of articulating his powerful desire for a lost mother, while compensating for that loss through the assertion of a male generative phantasy.

Darwin mentions only briefly, and even then obliquely, his mother's death, the most significant loss of his youth: "My mother died in July 1817, when I was a little over eight years old, and it is odd that I can remember hardly anything about her except her death-bed, her black velvet gown, and her curiously constructed work-table" (22). Darwin repeats his mother's loss on the level of his narrative: she is lost to him in memory, represented only by a few scattered objects, and thus remains coextensive with those objects throughout the text. One of Darwin's early biographers, in a book titled, appropriately enough, *Charles Darwin: The Fragmentary Man,* responds to the simultaneous centrality and obliquity of this passage: "Even [his mother's] death made far less impression upon him than the local burial of a dragoon which he witnessed about the same time, and certain details of which . . . remained vivid after sixty years, though of the other, and one would have supposed much more moving, event he could recall no more than being sent for, going into his dying or dead mother's room and finding his father there (again the memory was of anything *but* his mother)."[6]

In an "Autobiographical Fragment" that Darwin composed much earlier, in 1838, his memory of his mother's death is at once equally elliptical and far less dramatically embellished. He writes:

> When my mother died I was 8 1/2 years old, and [Catherine] one year less, yet she remembers all particulars and events of each day whilst I scarcely recollect anything (and so with very many other cases) except being sent for, the memory of going into her room, my father meeting me — crying afterwards. I recollect my mother's gown and scarcely anything of her appearance, except one or two walks with her. I have no distinct remembrance of any conversation, and those only of a very trivial nature. I remember her saying 'if she did ask me to do something,' which I said she had, 'it was solely for my good.'[7]

Memory functions as an impediment for Darwin, blocking access both to his mother and to the scene of her death. His limited memory of her, however, is as the quintessential "good object"; she claims to act "solely for [his] good," and he recalls mourning her loss. Although he recollects her gown, this version of the maternal death-scene has not yet generated the series of objects through which she is later personated. In this much earlier version of his autobiographical record, the death of Darwin's mother is recorded in — and as — a rhetorical construction: her death is reported in the hyphen which divides his encounter with his father from his emotional response after the fact of the death. Represented variously by a series of objects or a series of dashes, Susannah Wedgwood Darwin is always already demarcated as absent.

Present in this text only by means of ellipsis and substitution, Darwin's mother figures the centrality of loss and repression in the *Autobiography* and in the developmental narrative that it describes. As a mother and as a woman, her status as an embodied presence is displaced by a series of objects which only ever remain, unanalyzed, a series of objects. Darwin constructs her person in terms of proximity through the vehicle of metonymy; the collection of things that surround her body literally efface her physical presence. But at the same time, the convocation of bed, gown, and work-table remains provocatively suggestive, seductive even, for these objects delineate the spatial parameters of a body even as they attempt to describe a gesture of displacement. The combination of seduction and aversion locates the mother as a problematic but powerful figure within this passage and for the text as a whole.

As a rhetorical mode, metonymy is an extremely effective way to describe Darwin's evolutionary paradigm, which relies on a logic of non-teleology, but also of consistent renewal: in the evolutionary model, generations are contiguously related to but different from one another, configured as a chain of progression but, theoretically, not of telos. Similarly, in Melanie Klein's description of infantile development, the chain of substitutions invoked against the threat of maternal loss bears a metonymic relationship to the maternal referent. Klein writes:

> The process by which we displace love from the first people we cherish to other people is extended from earliest childhood onwards to things. In this way we develop interests and activities into which we put some of the love that originally belonged to people. In the baby's mind, one part of the body can stand for another part, and an object for parts of the body or for people. In this symbolical way, any round object may, in the child's unconscious mind, come to stand for his mother's breast. By a gradual process, anything that is felt to give out goodness and beauty, and that calls forth pleasure and satisfaction, in the physical or in the wider sense, can in the unconscious mind take the place of this ever-bountiful breast, and of the whole mother.[8]

In the terms of Klein's argument, all structures of substitution refer back to the mother, and especially to the maternal body. The subject's grid of positive associations is formulated initially with reference to the "ever-bountiful breast"; conversely, however, the subject's earliest aggressive impulses also occur within this referential structure, in the desire to destroy the breast, the body, the mother, which has the power to withhold that bounty. The significance of metonymic substitution, then, refers to a structure of ambivalence directed toward the maternal object. The gesture of substitution or displacement functions as the attenuation of the conflicted emotional responses surrounding the division from — and, indeed, the connection to — the powerful mother. In Klein's terminology, the child's construction of its own subjectivity, authority, and agency depends on its ability to negotiate this particular conflict; thus the "epistemophilic impulse," the drive to and construction of knowledge, is predicated on an aggressive response to the danger of maternal loss.[9] That Darwin should use the vehicle of metonymy as a way of describing his mother's death represents, in this formulation, the perfect coincidence of vehicle and message: Darwin's displacement, as Klein suggests, is at once protective and suggestive, seductive and aggressive. As a means of expressing, rather than of occluding, his experience of his mother's death, Darwin introduces his own impeded memory and the vehicle of metonymy as critical signifiers within the *Autobiography*. In his representation of the mother-figure, Darwin's deployment of metonymy suggests a specificity of relationship between the mother and the rhetorical logic of the text.

In "The Agency of the letter in the unconscious," Lacan's reading of the metonymic structure extends the implications of the Kleinian paradigm. For Lacan, metonymy not only describes a reference back to maternal loss; it also describes the interaction of drive and substitution that constructs sexual desire. Lacan suggests that metonymy is the figure for infinite desire precisely because it presupposes a dynamic of perpetuation, of endlessness; he describes it as "being caught in the rails — eternally stretching forth towards the *desire for something else.*"[10] Darwin's dead mother, receding from view in her only appearance in her son's autobiography, figures the infinite desirability of an object that can be neither appropriated nor demystified. For Darwin, the desirability of the maternal represents a desire for the originary, just as his impulse toward the originary is implicated in an impulse toward the maternal: in Darwinian evolutionary theory as in Freudian psychoanalytic theory, the "originary," the mother of all mothers, is located just over the horizon. Darwin's rhetorical figuration of the exchange of maternal loss for sexual desire is central to the terms by which he constructs his appropriation of the epistemophilic impulse, and therefore his appropriation of narrative and scientific authority, within the *Autobiography.*

Nancy Vickers suggests that the poetic strategy of description that presents a woman in terms of a series of scattered objects works to construct an inaccessible ideal, as well as to contain the actuality, the subjectivity of that woman: "bodies fetishized by a poetic voice logically do not have a voice of their own; the world of making words, of making texts, is not theirs." In other words, to describe a woman through the vehicle of the blazon, in terms of fragmented, scattered body parts, is effectively to fragment and scatter the whole woman. The chivalric construction of an ideal thus divides the narrative representation of the woman, and of female desirability, from the agency of narrative production; the woman represented through the vehicle of the blazon is deprived of the opportunity to speak. Vickers, arguing that Petrarchism represents a powerful force in the textual construction of "woman," reads Petrarch's representation of the Actaeon-Diana myth as a struggle toward the rhetorical containment of a woman's power: "A modern Actaeon affirming himself as poet cannot permit Ovid's angry goddess to speak her displeasure and deny his voice; his speech requires her silence. Similarly, he cannot allow her to dismember his body; instead he repeatedly, although reverently, scatters hers throughout his scattered rhymes."[11]

The implications of Vicker's argument for a reading of Darwin's *Autobiography* suggests the issues at stake for Darwin in the representation of his dead mother as a figure dispersed among several inanimate objects. In Kempf's terms, the "mother's riddle" is, for Darwin, the secret of human origins. In order for Darwin to pursue that riddle, it is necessary for him to circumscribe the sphere of maternal influence, particularly in the emotionally-charged aftermath of her death. The gesture of dispersal and objectification signifies the circumscription of that power. Throughout the rest of the *Autobiography,* therefore, the "mother" is represented obliquely and doubly: through Darwin's persistent claims to poor memory; and through his elision, containment, and displacement of other women, particularly of the objects of his desire.

For throughout the *Autobiography,* the "Woman Question" is addressed only by means of rhetorical misdirection and the "scattering" of individual women as active agents in Darwin's life. An entire section of the *Autobiography* is dedicated to a detailed, stream-of-consciousness account of the men whose company Darwin has found most influential, including Lyell, Buckland, Murchison, Brown, Owen, Falconer, Hooker, Huxley, Herschel, Babbage, Spencer, Buckle, Smith, Macaulay, Stanhope, and Carlyle. In contrast to his detailed accounting of professional contacts, however, the same chapter opens with the following description of his wife:

> You all know well your Mother, and what a good Mother she has ever been to all of you. She has been my greatest blessing, and I can declare that in my whole life I have never heard her utter one word which I had rather have been unsaid. She has never failed in the kindest sympathy towards me, and has borne with the utmost patience my frequent complaints from ill-health and discomfort. I do not believe she has ever missed an opportunity of doing a kind action to anyone near her. I marvel at my good fortune that she, so infinitely my superior in every single moral quality, consented to be my wife. She has been my wise adviser and cheerful comforter throughout life, which without her would have been during a very long period of a miserable one from ill-health. She has earned the love and admiration of every soul near her. (96–97)

The function of this paragraph as a standard set-piece of domestic narrative is underscored by the fact that this is the only moment in the text in which Darwin uses the form of direct address. Earlier he has declared that this autobiography is intended to amuse him, "and might possibly interest my children or their children" (21), but it is only at this point that Darwin shifts from public to private discourse. The effect of this rhetorical shift is to place his wife in the structural position of mother, and Darwin in the dual positions simultaneously of husband and son; in fact, Emma Wedgwood Darwin, his wife, was niece to his mother, Susannah Wedgwood Darwin. The contrast of this description with Darwin's detailed account of his professional relationships structures a distinction between private life and public life, in which women remain, undescribed, in the sphere of the private. The rhetorical invocation of privacy in this description implies that information about Emma Darwin is only available to those who know her already, and even they are presupposed to share Darwin's perceptions and conclusions. Despite its claims of Emma Darwin's centrality, however, the effect of this passage is to preserve her by means of rhetorical effacement in complete anonymity, the generic Victorian wife. Darwin's construction of this description demonstrates ambivalence through misdirection: that he has "never heard her utter one word which I had rather have been unsaid," that she has "never failed in the kindest sympathy," that he does "not believe she has ever missed an opportunity of doing a kind action" signifies ambivalence through the very accumulation of negative statements. Yet Emma Darwin's insignificant appearance here is apparently unreflective of her powerfully influential position over Darwin's personal and professional identities; her editorial influence shaped the posthumous production of Darwin's *Autobiography,* and her own letters, which fill two volumes, were published posthumously in 1915.[12] Around the time of his marriage in 1839, Darwin mysteriously lost the vigorous health that had enabled him to spend five years exploring with the *Beagle*, a fact that has been variously attributed to any number of physical and nervous diseases. The only fact that is certain is that Emma Darwin alone guarded and protected her husband; Kempf writes that Darwin obviously married a "mother image": "For over forty years she was his wife-mother-nurse."[13]

Emma Darwin, like Susannah, is meticulously represented as Other to the world of scientific and theoretical discourse presented in her husband's autobiography. But Melanie Klein suggests, like Kempf, that these two women bear a more direct relationship to Darwin's scientific pursuits than is first apparent. In *Love, Hate and Reparation,* Klein suggests that scientific exploration occurs as an attempt to regain access to, to reconstruct, the lost "good object" of infancy, the mother: "The drive to explore need not be expressed in an actual physical exploration of the world, but may extend to other fields, for instance, to any kind of scientific discovery. Early phantasies and desires to explore his mother's body enter into the satisfaction which the astronomer, for example, derives from his work."[14] Within the terms of Klein's argument, scientific exploration occurs in the service of two impulses, aggressive and reparative; these impulses describe the "depressive position," in which the infant desires the simultaneous presence and destruction of the mother-object.[15] Klein suggests that the activity of collecting, along with scientific exploration, contributes later to the adult's attempt to resolve tensions left over from turbulent infancy. She writes:

> In the explorer's unconscious mind, a new territory stands for a new mother, one that will replace the loss of the real mother. He is seeking the 'promised land' — the 'land flowing with milk and honey.' We have already seen that fear of the death of the most loved person leads to the child's turning away from her to some extent; but at the same time it also drives him to re-create her and to find her again in whatever he undertakes. Here both the escape from her and the original attachment to her find full expression.[16]

For Charles Darwin, who sailed around the world for five years on the *Beagle,* the activity of exploration is the act of reclaiming the lost mother, of exonerating himself from guilt in her disappearance, of supplementing his faulty memory at her loss. Simultaneously, however, he is now able to reclaim her on his own terms, as an adult, and through its strategic representation, to act as master of the scene.

Notably, then, Darwin's loss of mother — as well as his loss of memory regarding that mother — is inversely proportional to his investment in collecting, which he consistently describes as his "greatest passion"; at one point he writes, "It seems therefore that a taste for collecting beetles is some indication of future success in life!" (63). In contrast to his obscured memory of his mother, Darwin writes, "I am surprised what an indelible impression many of the beetles which I caught at Cambridge have left on my mind" (63); in support of his passion for beetles, he offers the following anecdote:

> I will give proof of my zeal: one day, on tearing off some old bark, I saw two rare beetles and seized one in each hand; then I saw a third and new kind, which I could not bear to lose, so that I popped the one which I held in my right hand into my mouth. Alas it ejected some intensely acrid fluid, which burnt my tongue so that I was forced to spit the beetle out, which was lost, as well as the third one. (62)

As a cautionary tale, this narrative suggests the potential dangers of a "zeal" for collecting. And as always within Darwin's *Autobiography,* the narrative's symbolic content participates in a larger set of theoretical issues: Darwin's overwhelming desire to possess all three beetles creates a situation first of pain, then of loss. That the pain is located in his mouth links this story symbolically with his attempts to narrate other painful stories in the text, most specifically, of course, with the story of desire, pain, and loss surrounding his mother's death. Both mother and beetle do injury — the first symbolic, the second literal — to Darwin's tongue, to his ability to tell the story of his life and his discoveries. These injuries produce rhetorical symptoms, made manifest in the representational anxieties surrounding these three central issues, desire, pain, and loss.[17]

Thus there is a tension in Darwin's *Autobiography* between his inability to recollect and his drive to collect. Melanie Klein makes an explicit connection between an infant's primal love for the mother and its later love for objects or abstract concepts. The attempt to collect or codify these objects, to generate theories based on abstractions, signals a desire to reconstruct the primary, mother-child relationship; the relationship between mother and objects is not one of displacement but of symbolic equation. Darwin's passion for collecting recalls the only set of objects he collects, but which he actively chooses *not* to codify and analyze: the bed, gown, and curiously constructed work-table that belong to and signify as his mother. The epistemophilic impulse only breaks down at the scene of *actual* maternal loss, at the destruction of the truly good object. The mother functions as the missing link in both the evolutionary chain and the chain of signification.

As a narrative representation of a "family," the *Bildungsroman* of *The Origin of Species* is profoundly patriarchal and paternalistic, and is especially symptomatic of the narrative anxieties that persistently produce the "mother" as the text's most noteworthy absence. For with one or two exceptions, the question of gender difference in Darwin's major works, *The Origin of Species* (1859) and *The Descent of Man* (1871), is completely elided in favor of a universal paradigm that describes the genetic and reproductive capacities of men alone. Although Gillian Beer points out that Darwin "retains the idea of *natura naturans,* or the Great Mother, in [his] figuring of Nature," that mother remains simply a metaphor for the natural world, the untamed context in which the paternalistic line of evolution occurs.[18] In *The Origin of Species* Darwin describes the evolution of a species gendered male against the backdrop of "nature," rhetorically figured as female:

> Man can act only on external and visible characters: Nature, if I may be allowed to personify the natural preservation or survival of the fittest, cares nothing for appearances, except in so far as they are useful to any being. She can act on every internal organ, on every shade of constitutional difference, on the whole machinery of life. Man selects only for his good: Nature only for that of the being which she tends. Every selected character is fully exercised by her, as is implied by the fact of their selection . . . How fleeting are the wishes and efforts of man! how short his time! and consequently how poor will be his results, compared with those accumulated by Nature during whole geological periods! Can we wonder, then, that Nature's productions should be far 'truer' in character than man's productions; that they should be infinitely better adapted to the most complex conditions of life, and should plainly bear the stamp of far higher workmanship?[19]

"Nature" appears here in the guise of Darwin's mother, as well as his wife: if Nature selects only for the good "of the being which she tends," she is like Darwin's mother, who, he recalls, said she asked him to do something " 'solely for [his] good.' " In contrast to capitalistic, solipsistic "Man," Darwin's "Nature" is selfless, timeless, nurturing, and primarily invested in the well-being of her dependents, identical in form to Darwin's brief sketch of Emma Darwin in the *Autobiography.* By gendering these abstractions, Darwin maintains the division between ideality and reality, between private and public spheres, that characterizes his description of his wife. When Darwin personifies "Nature" as woman and as mother, he appropriates the terminology of the chivalric ideal, gendering an abstraction in order to maintain the circumscription of female subjectivity.

II. *Figuring the Father*

DARWIN'S AUTOBIOGRAPHICAL REPRESENTATION of his mother's death betrays ambivalence about her, both in terms of her authority during life, and in terms of her premature "abandonment" of her son. His representation of his father's death is similarly vexed, but I want to argue that it involves a different set of representational and narrative issues. Darwin introduces the fact of his father's death in the context of a discussion of his own hypochondria:

> Although I was employed during eight years on this work [a study of barnacles], yet I record in my diary that about two years out of this time was lost by illness. On this account I went in 1848 for some months to Malvern for hydropathic treatment, which did me much good, so that on my return home I was able to resume work. So much was I out of health that when my dear father died on November 13th, 1847, I was unable to attend his funeral or to act as one of his executors. (117)

Despite his precision throughout this passage, despite the citation of his diary and his awareness that his voyage to Malvern occurred in 1848, Darwin shows a significant lapse of precision with respect to his "dear father's" death. The autobiography's editor, Nora Barlow, adds the following footnote to the passage: "The date of Dr. Robert's death is given as 1848 in *Life and Letters.* In the MS. the date is clearly written 1847 — a curious error" (117, n3). The death of Dr. Robert Darwin did, in fact, occur in 1848; Charles Darwin's parapraxis is a complex signifier of aggression and ambivalence.

When Charles Darwin places his father's death in 1847 rather than 1848, he implies a causal relationship between that death and the prolonged disability which left Charles "unable to attend his funeral or to act as one of his executors." It is ironic, perhaps, that Dr. Robert Darwin was his son's physician. Rather than the loss of his doctor/father, however, it is the figure of his doctor/father that "caused" his illness. For Darwin's persistent illness is extremely useful to him, functioning as one of the central signifiers by which he challenges his father's authority, both as a medical man and as a socially important figure. Primarily, Darwin's illness enables him to reconstruct his lost maternal relationship with the wife who is dedicated to his care and recuperation, thus reclaiming the missing mother of his youth. And secondarily, it literalizes the disadvantage that the younger Darwin faces in his assertion of authority: Darwin succeeds in the world *despite* his illness, and despite the father who "strongly objected" (71) to the voyage of the *Beagle* and disapproved of his son's line of work. Charles Darwin reports his illnesses and his inadequacies as a direct challenge to his father, who is figured throughout the *Autobiography* as the center of both authority and vitality. By means of these challenges, Darwin is able to claim that position as his own.

Much contemporary backlash against Darwin's work came from natural theologists, who resisted a theory of evolution that was simultaneously organic and agnostic. Basil Willey writes that Darwin was thought "to have banished from the world the idea of God as Creator and Designer, and to have substituted the notion of 'blind chance,' thus undermining the basis of religious belief."[20] The question at the time was one about the sources and symptoms of power. But ironically, while natural theologists would have argued that there is no Father in the work of Darwin, the figure of the Father is not only present in his *Autobiography,* but provides a powerful standard of identification for his son.[21] In Darwin's presentation and appropriation of the figure of the "Father" in his *Autobiography,* he attempts to appropriate the status of the "originary figure" for his own. But like the Holy Trinity of the original model, the Oedipal triangle presented in Darwin's *Autobiography* offers as its third term a Ghost: what is suppressed most literally in this text is the figure of the mother. Articulated over the circumscribed space of the woman, the mother, the Ghost, is the sense of powerful continuity from father to son, as well as the powerful rivalry of two competing intellects.

In order for Darwin to articulate the terms of his power, he must pay homage to an authoritative patriarchal structure while simultaneously appropriating it to his own ends. Significantly, then, the Father-figure in Darwin's *Autobiography* is consistently God-like. In the sense that Darwinian evolution was culturally perceived as a direct challenge to the genetic powers of God, Darwin is multiply implicated in the act of father-slaying. For example, he describes the following anecdote of his childhood pranks:

> I once gathered much valuable fruit from my Father's trees and hid them in the shrubbery, and then ran in breathless haste to spread the news that I had discovered a hoard of stolen fruit. . . . About this time, or as I hope at a somewhat earlier age, I sometimes stole fruit for the sake of eating it; and one of my schemes was ingenious. The kitchen garden was kept locked in the evening, and was surrounded by a high wall, but by the aid of neighbouring trees I could easily get on the coping. I then fixed a long stick into the hole at the bottom of a rather large flower-pot, and by dragging this upwards pulled off peaches and plums, which fell into the pot and the prizes were thus secured. When a very little boy I remember stealing apples from the orchard, for the sake of giving them away to some boys and young men who lived in a cottage not far off, but before I gave them the fruit I showed off how quickly I could run and it is wonderful that I did not perceive

> that the surprise and admiration which they expressed at my powers of running, was given for the sake of the apples. (23–24)

In a single paragraph, Darwin documents three separate fruit-stealing schemes. Two of these, the first and the last, were accomplished for the fact of self-aggrandizement: he stages these scenes in order to make himself a young celebrity, in the minds of his family, grateful for his discovery of a theft, and in the minds of the young men who admire his running. The second anecdote, which reports on the intricate scheme the boy developed for stealing from his father's *hortus conclusus,* positions the child as a young Satan-figure in his desire to infiltrate the garden. The "staging" and the narration of each of these scenes is implicated in a highly subversive goal: Darwin utilizes them to articulate a direct challenge to the Law of the Father. The theft of forbidden fruit, not once but three times, signifies an appropriation of the terms of "truth" and "knowledge."

As a challenge to conventional structures of authority, these three scenes incorporate and attempt to subvert both Biblical and Miltonic precedent.[22] Notably, the second anecdote in particular contextualizes Darwin's autobiography in a generic and epistemological tradition which includes Rousseau. In the *Confessions,* another autobiographical text preoccupied with the problematic of maternal death, Rousseau describes a strikingly similar scene in which he steals an apple. Rousseau writes,

> One memory of an apple-hunt that cost me dear still makes me shudder and laugh at the same time. These apples were at the bottom of a cupboard which was lit from the kitchen through a high lattice. One day when I was alone in the house I climbed on the kneading through to peer into this garden of the Hesperides at those precious fruits I could not touch. Then I went to fetch the spit to see if it would reach; it was too short. So I lengthened it with one which was used for game — my master being very fond of hunting. I proved several times in vain, but at last I felt with delight that I was bringing up an apple. I raised it very gently, and was just on the point of grasping it. What was my grief to find that it was too big to pass the lattice! I resorted to the most ingenious devices to get it through. I had to find supports to keep the spit in position, a knife long enough to cut the apple in two, and a lath to hold it up. With time and perseverance I managed to divide it, and was in hopes of then bringing the pieces through one after the other. But the moment they were apart they both fell back into the cupboard. Kind reader, sympathize with me in my grief! . . . Next day, when the opportunity offered, I made a fresh attempt. I climbed on my perch, fastened the two spits together, straightened them, and was just going to probe. . . . But unfortunately the dragon was not asleep; the larder door suddenly opened; my master came out, folded his arms, looked at me, and said "Bravo!" The pen falls from my hand.[23]

Rousseau's apple-appropriation scene is at once more elaborate, more vexed, and more immediately dramatic than Darwin's is. The appearance of the "master" clearly halts the boy's attempts at apple-stealing, at father-slaying, and at narrative. Rousseau therefore makes explicit the implications of the act of theft: the boy's intricate machinations are thwarted simply by the master's appearance. While the tension between the object of desire and the forbidding father-figure remains unresolved in Rousseau's text, Darwin's successful appropriation of the paternal fruit demonstrates his success in the project of subversion. The redoubled nature of Darwin's gesture, as an allusion to Rousseau and a challenge to paternalistic authority, locates the *Autobiography* within a powerful intellectual tradition at the same time as it represents the direct subversion of theodicy.

Darwin's representation of his father demonstrates ambivalence through its rhetorical equivocations and often-strained emotional justifications. The means by which he describes the father-son relationship are just as critical as the events he describes. The following is a typical example:

> When I left the school I was for my age neither high nor low in it; and I believe that I was considered by all my masters and by my Father as a very ordinary boy, rather below the common standard in intellect. To my deep mortification my father once said to me, "You care for nothing but shooting, dogs, and rat-catching, and you will be a disgrace to yourself and all your family." But my father, who was the kindest man I ever knew, and whose memory I love with all my heart, must have been angry and somewhat unjust when he used such words. . . . I may here add a few pages about my Father, who was in many ways a remarkable man. (28)

This statement is a model of ambivalence. Darwin's inconsistent capitalizations of the word "father" — Father, father, father, Father — persist throughout the *Autobiography* in no discernible pattern. If the keynote of the passage is Darwin's status at school, "neither high nor low," then that pattern of neither/nor is reflected throughout in the way he describes his father's response to his supposed "ordinariness." Robert Darwin and the boy's schoolmasters obviously misjudged the intelligence of their pupil; the prominence of Charles Darwin within Victorian intellectual circles is evidence enough of that fact. Within this context, though, Darwin's justification of his father's aggressive misjudgment rings hollow: if Robert Darwin had truly been "in many ways a remarkable man," he would not have made such a signal mistake about his own child. But Charles Darwin has competing desires regarding his father, the desire to exact revenge for this underestimation, as well as to preserve his father's "remarkable" qualities intact for posterity. The ambivalence of the *Autobiography* therefore demonstrates Darwin's attempt to preserve and to slay Robert Darwin at once; the authority of Charles Darwin is dependent on his ability to accomplish that task.

Thus Robert Darwin offers his son a model of authority to emasculate, even as he offers him a model to emulate. If Dr. Darwin was consistently God-like, he was also Freud-like, and in this regard, offered his son a powerful precedent for scientific authority. Dr. Darwin, Charles explains, found great success in treating his female patients' emotional ailments, as well as their physical ones, simply by listening and by advising them on the volatility of male-female relationships. "Owing to my father's skill in winning confidence he received many strange confessions of misery and guilt. He often remarked how many miserable wives he had known" (32). But as his son inadvertently reveals, Dr. Darwin turns confidence into a confidence-game. This is one of a number of examples that Charles Darwin cites in the autobiography:

> As a boy, I went to stay at the house of Major B — , whose wife was insane; and the poor creature, as soon as she saw me, was in the most abject state of terror that I ever saw, weeping bitterly and asking me over and over again, "Is your father coming?" but was soon pacified. On my return home, I asked my father why she was so frightened, and he answered he [was] very glad to hear it, as he had frightened her on purpose, feeling sure that she could be kept in safety and much happier without any restraint, if her husband could influence her, whenever she became at all violent, by proposing to send for Dr. Darwin; and these words succeeded perfectly during the rest of her long life. (40)

As an illustration of the means by which women were "contained" or "kept in safety," this anecdote reveals the extreme of the logic Darwin appropriates in his "containment" of mother and wife through rhetorical, rather than physical, means. The powerful figure of "Dr. Darwin" is installed for Mrs. Major B— , as for his son, as the superego, as the terrifying, punitive source of law and order. That the mere invocation of Dr. Darwin's name is enough to silence this woman signifies the extent to which the Law of the Father prevails within Charles Darwin's universe.

Charles Darwin himself appropriates this model of authority to his own ends, but not without ambivalence. Early in the *Autobiography,* he writes, "I can say in my own favour that I was a boy humane, but I owed this entirely to the instruction and example of my sisters. I doubt indeed whether humanity is a natural or innate quality" (26). Darwin represents his "humanity" in terms of his ability to restrain himself: "I never took more than a single egg out of a bird's nest" (26–7); "I never spitted a living worm" (17). But his representation of his personal "power" vacillates wildly between extremes of humanitarianism and outright cruelty:

> Once as a very little boy, whilst at the day-school, or before that time, I acted cruelly, for I beat a puppy I believe, simply from enjoying the sense of power; but the beating could not have been severe, for the puppy did not howl, of which I feel sure as the spot was near to the house. This act lay heavily on my conscience, as is shown by my remembering the exact spot where the crime was committed. It probably lay all the heavier from my love of dogs being then, and for a long time afterwards, a passion. Dogs seemed to know this, for I was an adept in robbing their love from their masters. (27)

Darwin is aware that beating the puppy reveals an investment in the manifestation of power over a smaller creature; like the anecdote of his father and Mrs.

Major B — , there is something sadistically, personally gratifying about his ability to demonstrate potency. His compensatory "passion" for dogs, however, conforms to what Melanie Klein describes as the depressive position: his guilt at damaging that puppy causes a disproportionate desire to adore all puppies, as an infant's desire to aggress against the mother is mediated by a need for that mother, and therefore the compensatory reassertion of the love-relationship. Darwin's "need" is demonstrated here in his ability to steal love, a rhetoric of theft that continues from his fruit-stealing adventures, a rhetoric which occurs consistently with references to his father. "[R]obbing their love from their masters" is a means of stealing love, of appropriating the admiration of a dog for its master, or of a community for a Darwin. The rhetoric of theft represents Darwin's conversion-phantasy, in which all the admiration Darwin describes as directed toward his father is made available to him. The pattern that Darwin describes here, in which his aggressive impulses are ultimately rewarded with slavelike adoration and the acknowledgment of his absolute mastery, is an appropriation of the epistemophilic impulse, in which knowledge is equated with sadism, with the expulsion of a mother, and with the appropriation of paternalistic mastery. The connection between this disturbing incident and Darwin's more subtle means of containing women becomes explicit in an appendix to the *Autobiography,* which reproduces notes scribbled on scraps of paper in 1837 or 1838, in which Darwin debated the question of whether or not to marry. Under the heading "Marry," he lists the following reasons: "Children — (if it please God) — constant companion, (friend in old age) who will feel interested in one, object to be beloved and played with — better than a dog anyhow."[24]

Within the tension of the father-son relationship, the question of "memory" is a central signifier. "Memory" denotes not only Charles Darwin's ability or inability to recall the events of his youth. His reputation, the way in which he and his father will be remembered after death, is also implicated in his desire to construct his memories accurately, authoritatively, in his autobiography. Darwin writes, "I have heard my Father say he believed that persons with powerful minds generally had memories extending far back to a very early period of life. This is not my case for my earliest recollection goes back only to when I was a few months over four years old, when we went to near Abergele for sea-bathing, and I recollect some events and places there with some little distinctness" (21–22). From the beginning, then, the fallibility of Darwin's memory, the limitations of his particular subject position, present him with a distinct methodological challenge. Throughout the autobiography, as in his theoretical works, he praises the scientific mind as one which consistently attempts to universalize, taking the part, even the minute example, as evidence of a grander, invisible whole. But Darwin's desire to collect all the facts, to construct empirical chains of evidence leading to universal conclusions, is frustrated by the formal constraints of his project. For in the genre of autobiography, memory is a primary form of authoritative citation. Darwin's memory, unlike his father's, is faulty.[25] He writes of Robert Darwin:

> My father possessed an extraordinary memory, especially for dates, so that he knew, when he was very old the day of the birth, marriage, and death of a multitude of persons in Shropshire; and he once told me that this power annoyed him; for if he once heard a date he could not forget it; and thus the deaths of many friends were often recalled to his mind. Owing to his strong memory he knew an extraordinary number of curious stories, which he liked to tell, as he was a great talker. He was generally in high spirits, and laughed and joked with every one — often with his servants — with the utmost freedom; yet he had the art of making every one obey him to the letter. Many persons were much afraid of him. (39)

Memory is what Darwin lacks and his father has. Memory is also the source of his father's good reputation, as well as his power as an authority-figure; that "many persons were much afraid of him" underscores Robert Darwin's representation as a god, powerful and potentially angry, in this text. In contrast, throughout the *Autobiography,* Darwin qualifies his own ability to remember events adequately, and contrasts his poor memory with his father's perfect memory, his embattled position within contemporary scientific circles with his father's ease and authority as a community leader. As an index of comparison, the ability to remember constitutes the power differential between father and son; the rhetoric of memory becomes for Darwin the vocabulary of a struggle to prevail against the high standards of the father-figure.

Thus memory functions within this text and within the father-son relationship as the signifier of rivalry and competition — a competition which the son always fails. Clearly the most problematic instance of Charles's memory-failure occurs with reference to the death of his mother, yet memory is what gives Robert Darwin access to this dead woman, while it impedes Charles from that very connection. As represented through the figure of Robert Darwin, the ability to remember represents the ability to have, to possess, to master. Notably, then, Charles Darwin uses writing to supplement his inadequate memory: research allows him to accumulate data and to "master" a body of knowledge. And as Kempf suggests and Klein implies, such a gesture of intellectual mastery is linked with the desire to recuperate, to dominate, the "mother's riddle": the question of origins is always already a question of gender, power, and representation.

If collection and scientific exploration supplement the loss of the mother, then these activities supplement Darwin's loss of memory, as well. Darwin comments that he needs a written text in order to prompt his memory: "I had, also, during many years, followed a golden rule, namely, that whenever a published fact, a new observation or thought came across me, which was opposed to my general results, to make a memorandum of it without fail and at once; for I had found by experience that such facts and thoughts are far more apt to escape from the memory than favourable ones. Owing to this habit, very few objections were raised against my views which I had not at least noticed and attempted to answer'' (123). Here Darwin articulates his resistance to challenge in the course of describing the measures he takes to disarm surprising ''objections.'' The written text is central not only to Darwin's description of his work habits, however, but also to the psychological drama he describes in the *Autobiography.* When Darwin writes about his scientific writings, he speaks of them as his offspring. For example, in the chapter entitled ''My Several Publications,'' he describes the popular response to his first independent publication, *Journal of Researches,* published in 1845: ''The success of this my first literary child always tickles my vanity more than that of any of my other books. Even to this day it sells steadily in England and the United States, and has been translated for the second time into German, and into French and other languages'' (116). Darwin's delight at his ''child's'' success stands in marked contrast to his father's skepticism regarding his son's abilities. Darwin consistently constructs himself as the good father, and, for that matter, the good mother, as well. The production of the texts describing his activities in research, exploration, and collection provides him with a supplementary parental structure, in which he is father and mother alike, and in which the ''literary child'' reflects positively on its progenitor. Thus Darwin constructs a positive model for his own paternity, as well as a positive phantasy for his relationship with his own father.

Darwin's *actual* first child doesn't appear in the text for another fifteen pages, and even then young Francis Darwin acquires significance only by providing evidence for Charles Darwin's attempts to study the evolution of infantile expression: ''My first child was born on December 27th, 1839, and I at once commenced to make notes on the first dawn of the various expressions which he exhibited, for I felt convinced, even at this early period, that the most complex and fine shades of expression must all have had a gradual and natural origin'' (131–132). The ''origin of species'' is grounded explicitly in a Romantic notion of individual origins. When Wordsworth describes the sense of continual progression from father to son in the line ''The Child is father of the Man,'' he posits a model of evolution within one individual as between two, collapsing the phylogenetic paradigm into the framework of ontogenesis. It is this redoubled sense of continuous, unbroken progression that Darwin struggles to ''remember'' in the *Autobiography,* despite the fact that his memories, when they exist, usually illustrate only fragmentation, ambivalence, and loss. At stake in Darwin's overdetermined descriptions of paternal continuity is a position of authority, within the autobiographical text, as well as within the scientific and cultural discourses which the autobiography attempts to construct as continuous.

In his *Autobiography,* Darwin demonstrates a direct relationship between the origin of an individual and the origin of species, between ontogeny and phylogeny. The translation of the evolutionary model to the autobiographical mode makes clear the tensions regarding gender, gender roles, and questions of power that underpin, and often undercut, Darwin's representation of the "originary." Through the rhetorical presentation of his mother as effectively "missing," and through the accompanying representation of his father as a notably overdetermined figure of potency, Darwin aligns himself — not unproblematically — with the powerful father. Thus Darwin's articulation of narrative authority occurs in the sacrifice of that mother to the all-powerful, all-knowing father. This parthenogenetic phantasy, the phantasy of continuity from "Father" to son, produces the "origin of species," and arguably, *The Origin of Species.*

New York University

NOTES

1. Charles Darwin, *The Autobiography of Charles Darwin, 1809–1882,* ed. Nora Barlow (New York: Norton, 1958) 139, 140–41. All quotes refer to this edition and will be cited parenthetically in the text.
2. For an analysis of the literary qualities of Freud's prose, particularly in his case study of Dora, see Steven Marcus, "Freud and Dora: Story, History, Case History," *In Dora's Case: Freud — Hysteria — Feminism,* ed. Charles Bernheimer and Claire Kahane (New York: Columbia UP, 1985) 56–91.
3. For Freud's elaboration of the concept of "acting out," see "Remembering, Repeating, and Working-Through" (1914). *The Standard Edition of the Complete Psychological Works of Sigmund Freud,* ed. and trans. James Strachey (London: Hogarth P and Institute of Psycho-Analysis, 1986).
4. Edward J. Kempf, *Psychopathology* (St. Louis: Mosby, 1921) 214.
5. Kempf 214. Kempf argues that Susannah Wedgwood Darwin's fascination with her father-in-law, Erasmus Darwin's work, especially his *Zoonomia,* was the source of *her* engagement with the riddle of origins (212–13).
6. Geoffrey West, *Charles Darwin: The Fragmentary Man* (London: George Routledge, 1937) 45.
7. Charles Darwin, "An Autobiographical Fragment Written in 1838," in Charles Darwin and Thomas Henry Huxley, *Autobiographies,* ed. Gavin de Beer (New York: Oxford UP, 1983).
8. Melanie Klein, "Love, Guilt and Reparation," in Melanie Klein and Joan Riviere, *Love, Hate and Reparation* (New York: Norton, 1964) 102–03.
9. Melanie Klein describes the "epistemophilic impulse" as a sadistic impulse consisting of the phantastic construction and prompt destruction of an "object." As a little cannibal, oriented to and dependent on the mother's breast for survival, the infant's desire to incorporate the maternal body represents a drive to "epistemology" predicated on the assimilation of a multiply symbolic object and the assumption of a position as controller and interpreter of all of these symbols. The child's relative success at the "epistemophilic impulse" determines "the subject's relation to the outside world and to reality in general." At the heart of ego-formation, then,

is the production and destruction of a symbolic object personated by the child as "mother." See Melanie Klein, "The Importance of Symbol-Formation in the Development of the Ego," *The Selected Melanie Klein,* ed. Juliet Mitchell (New York: Free Press, 1986) 96–98.

10. Jacques Lacan, "The Agency of the letter in the unconscious," *Écrits: A Selection,* trans. and ed. Alan Sheridan (New York: Norton, 1977) 167.
11. Nancy Vickers, "Diana Described: Scattered Woman and Scattered Rhyme," *Writing and Sexual Difference,* ed. Elizabeth Abel (Chicago: U of Chicago P, 1982) 107, 109.
12. See Mrs. Henrietta Emma Darwin Litchfield, *Emma Darwin: A Century of Family Letters,* ed. Henrietta Litchfield (London: Murray, 1915).
13. Kempf, 244. Kempf attributes Darwin's illness to an anxiety neurosis, while Douglas Hubble, in an article titled "The Evolution of Charles Darwin," suggests that "Charles suffered not from an organic disease but from an autonomic disorder," from an illness deriving from emotion and conscious thought *(Horizon* 80, 1946, 83). In a note following the text of Darwin's *Autobiography,* editor Nora Barlow writes,

    The nausea, giddiness, insomnia and debility from which he suffered, follow the now familiar pattern of the ills of other eminent Victorians, with the Victorian Hydropathic establishment, the sofa and the shawl as characteristic hall-marks. Charles Darwin's forty years of invalid existence, moreover, were an unexpected sequel to his youthful vigour, for his strength and endurance were well above the average, as Captain Fitz-Roy has recorded in his accounts of various incidents during the Beagle Voyage. . . . Yet health anxieties did trouble Charles Darwin even in the early days before the voyage, so that his marriage to a deeply sympathetic wife can hardly have done more than increase a deep-seated tendency. Her over-solicitude helped to cast that faint aura of glory on the Symptom, an attitude that was carried on into adult life by several of their children. (240–1)

    For a discussion of Darwin's illness, as well as an annotated bibliography suggesting various diagnoses, see Barlow's note, "On Charles Darwin's Ill-Health," *The Autobiography of Charles Darwin* (240–43).
14. Klein, "Love, Guilt, and Reparation" 105.
15. Klein, 104.
16. Klein, 102–03.
17. Interestingly, in *The Interpretation of Dreams,* Freud analyzes at some length the "May-Beetle Dream," in which one of his patients, "an elderly lady," has symbolized anxieties about her daughter, her husband, and questions of sexuality in a dream about two beetles escaping from a box. See *The Interpretation of Dreams, Standard Edition* 4: 289–92.
18. Gillian Beer, *Darwin's Plots: Evolutionary Narrative in Darwin, George Eliot and Nineteenth-Century Fiction* (Boston: Routledge & Kegan Paul, 1983) 9.
19. Darwin, *The Origin of Species,* 90. The gender construct that Darwin invokes is a variation on the ancient division between (female) receptacle and (male) logos; in the *Timaeus,* still another originary narrative, Plato describes the receptacle: "Therefore we must not call the mother and receptacle of visible and sensible things either earth or air or fire or water, nor yet any of their compounds or components; but we shall not be wrong if we describe it as invisible and formless, all-embracing, possessed in a most puzzling way of intelligibility, yet very hard to grasp." Plato, *Timaeus,* trans. Desmond Lee (New York: Penguin, 1977).

20. Basil Willey, "Darwin and Clerical Orthodoxy," *1859: Entering an Age of Crisis,* 52, quoted in Monica Correa Fryckstedt, "Defining the Domestic Genre: English Women Novelists of the 1850's," *Tulsa Studies in Women's Literature* 6: 1 (Spring 1987) 22.
21. For an uncannily similar description of father-son ambivalence, as well as for a contemporary discussion of evolutionary theory, see the autobiography of Edmund Gosse, *Father and Son* (1907).
22. Milton plays a multiply significant role in Darwin's *Autobiography.* Darwin announces at one point that *Paradise Lost* was the only book he brought with him on the voyage of the *Beagle,* the trip which provided him with the raw material to construct *The Origin of Species.* Gillian Beer makes much of this connection:

    Darwin was to rejoice in the overturning of the anthropocentric view of the universe which Milton emphasizes, yet his language made manifest to Darwin, in its concurrence with his own sense of profusion, destiny, and articulation of the particular, how much could survive, how much could be held in common and in continuity from the past. Milton gave Darwin profound imaginative pleasure — which to Darwin was the means of understanding. (36)

23. Jean-Jacques Rousseau, *The Confessions,* trans. J. M. Cohen (New York: Penguin, 1984) 42. For an analysis of the implications of Rousseau's own originary crisis, the death of his mother at his birth, see Jacques Derrida, *Of Grammatology,* trans. Gayatri Chakravorty Spivak (Baltimore: Johns Hopkins UP, 1976) 144–52.
24. Charles Darwin, "The pencil notes of 1837–38: 'This is the Question,' " Note three to Darwin's *Autobiography,* 232–33.
25. Darwin refers continually to his poor memory throughout the *Autobiography,* and indeed, a slip of the memory was responsible for the central crisis of his later career. Samuel Butler accused Darwin in print of harboring a grudge against him, a misunderstanding perpetuated by the fact that Darwin forgot to mention that a certain article had previously been published elsewhere, and therefore could not possibly be an attack on Butler. For an overview of the Samuel Butler controversy, see the second appendix to Darwin's *Autobiography,* 167–219, which reproduces the articles and correspondence in question.

THE PROTEAN PRECURSOR: BROWNING AND EDWARD FITZGERALD

By John Woolford

1. Ezra on Omar

In 1864 Browning published "Rabbi ben Ezra," an early expression of what DeVane describes as "the peculiar quality of robust hope and cheerfulness which is [his] contribution to the spirit of English literature" (294–95). In 1909 F. L. Sargent pointed out that certain passages in this poem appear to respond to Edward FitzGerald's *The Rubáiyát of Omar Khayyám,* and until quite recently there was a consensus that, as DeVane concludes, "the spark which caused Browning to write the poem was unconsciously supplied by Edward FitzGerald . . . Browning's philosophy of life, which he puts into the mouth of the Rabbi, meets squarely the way of life which is laid down by the Persian tent-maker" (293). The best internal evidence for this reading is provided by a passage in which Ezra's "philosophy of life" is cast in the teeth of an unnamed antagonist:

> Thou, to whom fools propound,
> When the wine makes its round,
> "Since life fleets, all is change; the Past gone, seize today!"
>
> Fool! All that is, at all,
> Lasts ever, past recall;
> Earth changes, but thy soul and God stand sure:
> What entered into thee,
> That was, is, and shall be:
> Time's wheel runs back or stops: Potter and clay endure. (151–162)[1]

This certainly appears to rebut stanzas 36–37 of FitzGerald's poem[2]:

> For in the Market-place, one Dusk of Day,
> I watch'd the Potter thumping his wet Clay:

And with its all obliterated Tongue
It murmur'd — "Gently, Brother, gently, pray!"

Ah, fill the Cup: — what boots it to repeat
How Time is slipping underneath our Feet:
Unborn To-morrow and dead Yesterday,
Why fret about them if To-day be sweet! (141–48)

In both passages the relation of a potter to a pot becomes a figure for the meaning of existence. To Omar Khayyám (in FitzGerald's portrayal), life is meaningless because time "is slipping underneath our Feet," and the potter (God) is therefore imagined as cruel to the pot, his (human) victim. In the "Kúza-Náma" section of *The Rubáiyát,* this argument expands into a critique of divine predestination articulated with the aid of the same image:

Another said — "Why, ne'er a peevish Boy,
"Would break the Bowl from which he drank in Joy;
"Shall He that made the Vessel in pure Love
"And Fansy, in an after Rage destroy!"

None answer'd this; but after Silence spake
A Vessel of a more ungainly Make:
"They sneer at me for leaning all awry;
"What! did the Hand then of the Potter shake?" (245–52)

FitzGerald equates the making of the pot with God's production of the human individual in a certain distinctive and unalterable shape (humans cannot rectify the defects conferred on them by God). The breaking of the pot signifies death and/or divine punishment. Life, then, is at once divinely pre-determined and threatened with divine retribution, as Khayyám satirically laments: "Thou wilt not with Predestination round / Enmesh me, and impute my Fall to Sin?" (227–28). In the face of this "Impertinence," (120) which deprives life-in-time of development and therefore of any real meaning, only the present moment — "To-day" — counts for anything, and only wine and, to a lesser extent, sexual love can make it endurable.

By contrast, Browning's Ezra argues that time is an illusion generated to provide a medium within which the human soul can develop:

He fixed thee mid this dance
Of plastic circumstance,
This Present, thou, forsooth, wouldst fain arrest:
Machinery just meant
To give thy soul its bent,
Try thee and turn thee forth, sufficiently impressed. (163–68)

Human beings are clay on the wheel which God the potter progressively shapes into the ''consummate cup'' from which, after their physical death, he drinks a toast:

> Look not thou down but up!
> To uses of a cup,
> The festal board, lamp's flash and trumpet's peal,
> The new wine's foaming flow,
> The Master's lips a-glow!
> Thou, heaven's consummate cup, what needst thou with earth's wheel? (75–80)

FitzGerald's ''pot'' is transfigured into ''heaven's consummate cup'' and his ''wine'' into the ''new wine'' of immortality, itself a condition rejected or questioned throughout *The Rubáiyát.*

2. Influence and Evidence

But this analysis is thrown into doubt by the absence of any proof that when Browning wrote ''Ezra'' he had read *The Rubáiyát.* FitzGerald's translation was published four years before ''Ezra,'' in 1859, but anonymously and in pamphlet form, not becoming widely known until long after the publication of the second edition in 1868. There is no mention of it in Browning's correspondence until 1889. Following a shadowy tradition, DeVane posits an intermediary in the shape of Dante Gabriel Rossetti, who, he speculates, ''picked up a dozen copies of the *Omar* . . . and probably . . . made Browning acquainted with FitzGerald's translation'' (293), but the uncertainty of this kind of argument,[3] coupled with Browning's 1889 denial of any knowledge of FitzGerald until ''a few years ago,'' has caused some recent scholars, quite reasonably, to doubt the whole tradition.[4]

So the evidence for FitzGerald's influence on Browning actually rests upon ''the figure of the potter's wheel'' in which, according to DeVane, ''Ezra'' ''definitely . . . meets FitzGerald's wonderful but perversive [sic] poem.'' But as DeVane also notes, man-as-pot to God-as-potter are frequent figures in both the Old and the New Testaments, and both poets allude to these sources. In the last-quoted passage from *The Rubáiyát* FitzGerald refers to Jeremiah's comparison of God's punishment of the Israelites to the shattering of a badly-made pot:

> Then I went down to the potter's house, and, behold, he wrought a work on the wheels.
> And the vessel that he made of clay was marred in the hand of the potter: so he made it again another vessel, as seemed good to the potter to make it.
> Then the word of the LORD came to me, saying,
> O house of Israel, cannot I do with you as this potter? saith the LORD.
> Behold, as the clay is in the potter's hand, so are ye in mine hand, O house of Israel. (Jer. 18.3–6)

Later, Jeremiah reifies this trope by smashing an actual ''potter's earthen bottle,'' to illustrate how ''the LORD of hosts . . . will . . . break this people and this city, as one breaketh a potter's vessel, that cannot be made whole again'' (19.11). FitzGerald develops this imagery to express incredulity that God, having made humanity ''awry,'' as the potter's vessel ''was marred in the hands of the potter,'' could then reasonably punish it for being defective. He may also have in mind St. Paul's development of the image in the interests of an argument for divine election,[5] ''Hath not the potter power over the clay, of the same lump to make one vessel unto honour, and another unto dishonour?'' (Rom. 9.21). For FitzGerald the combination of divine predestination with divine judgment is a moral absurdity; he therefore ''reads'' the Biblical use of the pot-image as an inherent exposure of that absurdity.

Browning alludes to passages from Isaiah rather than Jeremiah. In Isaiah, Israel's devastation is commonly associated with the witholding of wine:

> The earth also is defiled under the inhabitants thereof; because they have transgressed the laws . . .
> Therefore hath the curse devoured the earth, and they that dwell therein are desolate . . .
> The new wine mourneth, the vine languisheth . . .
> They shall not drink wine with a song; strong drink shall be bitter to them that drink it . . .
> There is a crying for wine in the streets; all joy is darkened, the mirth of the land is gone. (Isa. 24.5–11)

Earlier, the human-as-pot trope had been used:

> Woe unto them that seek deep to hide their council from the LORD, and their works are in the dark, and they say, Who seeth us? and who knoweth us?
> Surely your turnings of things upside down shall be esteemed as the potter's clay: for shall the work say of him that made it, He made me not? or shall the thing framed say of him that framed it, He had no understanding? (19.15–16)

In contrast to *The Rubáiyát's* use of the image, following Jeremiah, to represent the vengefulness or arbitrariness of God, these passages emphasize humanity's inevitable creatureship, our emergence from and dependence on God's hand. Hence the force of the final, climactic occurrence; ''But now, O LORD, thou art our father; we are the clay, and thou our potter; and we are all the work of thy hand'' (64.8). It is this passage which Browning had most in mind in ''Ezra.'' The image of God's ''hand'' runs through the poem (''Our times are in his hand''; ''My times be in Thy hand!''); God should ''take and use Thy work''; ''Potter and clay endure'' (lines 4, 190, 187, 162). And God's response to this plea in the following chapter of Isaiah begins, ''Thus saith the LORD, As the new wine is found in the cluster, and one saith, Destroy it not; for a blessing is in it: so I will do for my servants' sakes, that I may not destroy them all'' (65.8). Browning has fused these two images by imagining that humanity, the ''cup'' manufactured on the potter's wheel, can both become and contain the ''new wine'' which God elects to conserve; he formulates this exegesis through the bold trope of a celestial feast at which that wine, borne by and in the believer, is to be drunk by God.

So if the Bible provides sources for both FitzGerald's and Browning's applications of their mutual figure, how are we to argue that the one stimulated the other? This is a general problem for influence-study. My own experience as an editor has constantly warned me that what looks like a straightforward textual genealogy can turn out to reflect separate borrowings from the inherited stock of stories, structures, and tropes in which cultural self-narration is conducted. In order to distinguish this kind of common inheritance from specific poet-to-poet influence, I suggest that the grounds of enquiry need to be shifted from comparison of specific figures to examination of their figural collocation. Any given figure taken separately might derive from a cultural source common to both the writers in question. But if a poet rearranges a set of figures from the common cultural source, and if a second poet then echoes not only those figures but the first poet's collocation of them, it seems reasonable to conclude that the first poet has intervened as an influence between the second poet and their common source. This is not of course to deny that the second poet also refers to the common cultural source, but such reference will be motivated, whether positively or negatively, by the first poet's collocation.

I have noted that Ezra represents God as a potter and the believer both as a cup and as the wine within that cup. There is no precedent for this combination of figures in Isaiah,[6] or in Browning's earlier work. Occurrences of ''cup'' normally denote either a wine-cup (11 instances) or flower-cup (10). More metaphorically it can mean ''the cup of life'' (7), but is then synonymous with ''secular bliss'' rather than ''personal essence.'' Likewise, ''wine'' is used to mean, literally, an intoxicant, metaphorically the consolations of secular life: it is never made to stand for personal essence, or drunk by God. The word ''potter'' appears only once before ''Ezra,'' in ''In a Balcony'': ''The grappling of a potter with his clay'' (707), referring to a politician's control over the populace.[7] The concatenation by which the believer becomes both the cup moulded by God-the-potter and the wine contained in the cup he has made is foreshadowed not in Browning's earlier poetry but both in stanza 61 (above) and in stanza 22 of *The Rubáiyát:*

> Lo! some we loved, the loveliest and the best
> That Time and Fate of all the Vintage prest,
> Have drunk their Cup a Round or two before,
> And one by one crept silently to Rest. (81–84)

Here, "Time and Fate" produce humanity as a "Vintage" which, in a bold doubling, humanity then drink from "their Cup." This figural collocation, being new in Browning's work, suggests the intervention of FitzGerald's text between Browning and his rereading of Isaiah.

A second figural collocation, this time not biblical in origin, also links the two poems. Khayyám plays constantly on the irresistible onrush of time and its disintegration for the perceiver into an ever-lengthening past, an evanescent present, and a doubtful future:

> Ah, my Beloved, fill the cup that clears
> TO-DAY of past Regrets and future Fears —
> To-morrow? — Why, To-morrow I may be
> Myself with Yesterday's Sev'n Thousand Years. (77–80)

In his introduction to the first edition of *The Rubáiyát,*[8] FitzGerald places this contrast at the centre of his reading of Khayyám,

> who, after vainly trying to unshackle his Steps from Destiny, and to catch some authentic glimpse of TO-MORROW, fell back upon TODAY (which has outlasted so many Tomorrows!) as the only Ground he got to stand on, however momentarily slipping from under his Feet. (xiii)

Ezra attacks his interlocutor's addiction to "This Present, thou, forsooth, wouldst fain arrest," arguing that "The Future I may face now I have proved the Past" (102). Browning has one earlier passage juxtaposing the past, present and future,[9] but during the twenty-nine years between Paracelsus and "Ezra" he avoided this three-way comparison.[10] It is striking that in turning to it here he employs a FitzGerald form of words to refute a FitzGerald form of argument of which there is no trace in his own earlier use of the figure.

If we take the two configurations together — potter-pot-wine and past-present-future — we have an ensemble that appears in no poem of Browning's before "Ezra" and only one poem after it. And that later example, "Jochanan Hakkadosh" from *Jocoseria* (1883), reworks the collocation in what constitutes a further response to *The Rubáiyát's* cynicism. "Jochanan Hakkadosh" concerns an imaginary Jewish Rabbi who, on the point of death, is awarded four extra spells of three months each from a lover, a warrior, a poet, and a statesman, in order to test the value of their respective ways of life and complete his own. None satisfies him, but because a child has secretly donated him three further months he lives on and dies in ecstacy having come to understand that it is from the after-life that life takes its meaning.

The process of life, while Jochanan doubts its value, is described as follows:

The Future — that's
Our destination, mists turn rainbows there,

Which sink to fog, confounded in the flats
O' the Present! Day's the song-time for the lark,
Night for her music boasts but owls and bats.

And what's the Past but night[?] (518–23)

Only upon enlightenment can he both fill out and modify this schema by achieving ''utter acquiescence in my past, / Present and future life'' (680–81). Similarly, where previously his life was described as ''that grand wine / Mighty as mellow'' (662–63), he finally makes a ''strange and new''

Discovery! — this life proves a wine-press — blends
Evil and good, both fruits of Paradise,
Into a novel drink which — who intends

To quaff, must bear a brain for ecstacies
Attempered (726–31)

From this vantage-point — he is as it were already in the after-life of which he speaks — life in time appears to be spent ''[s]triving at mastery'' on an earth where we ''bend above''

The spoiled clay potsherds, many a year of toil
Attests the potter tried his hand upon,
Till sudden he arose, wiped free from soil
His hand, cried ''so much for attempt — anon
Performance! Taught to mould the living vase,
What matter the cracked pitchers dead and gone?'' (765–71)

If anything, the reference to FitzGerald's poem is more explicit here than in ''Ezra,'' in that rather than simply opposing Isaiah to Jeremiah, Browning actually engages with FitzGerald's interpretation of the latter. As I have noted, FitzGerald takes the potter's shattering of his pot in Jeremiah as a sign of the irrationality and cruelty of God. Browning transforms this image into a picture of the individual's successive attempts to formulate their existence correctly, attempts which culminate in the ''performance'' of the perfect ''living vase'' in the afterlife. In ''Rabbi ben Ezra'' Browning had not engaged with this particular inflection of the potter-pot relation at all: its appearance in ''Jochanan Hakkadosh'' may register a new confidence that even FitzGerald's most threatening and persuasive image can be recuperated.[11]

3. Browning on FitzGerald

A SECOND, apparently quite separate interaction between Browning and FitzGerald took place at the end of Browning's life.[12] FitzGerald died in 1882. His collected works first appeared in 1889. Leafing through the volume containing his posthumous *Literary Remains* in July 1889, Browning stumbled upon a letter in which FitzGerald, writing in 1861, had expressed "relief" at the then-recent death of Elizabeth Barrett Browning (1: 280–81). Positively ill with distress and fury, Browning wrote a ferocious response in the form of a poem called "To Edward FitzGerald," which he sent to the *Athenaeum* next day: it appeared there on 13 July. Browning's family were embarrassed, his friends pained, his enemies gleeful. He was felt to have behaved improperly, even hysterically, one commentator comparing him to "a raving street-walker in Spitalfields" (Hawthorne 142). With the exception of Chesterton, early biographers either hushed up or explained away the episode,[13] and even he conceded its "indecent fury" (115).

I do not quote the poem itself because what interests me is not what it contains, but what it omits. It would be impossible to guess from it that FitzGerald had been the friend of Browning's friends Tennyson,[14] Thackeray, and Dante Rossetti, or that he was the translator/author of *The Rubáiyát of Omar Khayyám* or anything else. Browning certainly knew of the Tennyson connection: the terribly stilted tone of a letter congratulating Tennyson on his eightieth birthday a month later betrays his dread of having given offence.[15] But his concern in the poem and in letters of the time was to degrade not only that connection — he calls FitzGerald Tennyson's "adulatory lick-spittle" (*Letters* 312) — but all FitzGerald's other claims to notice. He is a "wretched Irish fribble and 'feather-head,' " a "scamp," (312) a "blackguard," (314), a "poor creature" (317) of such obscurity that "my wife never even heard of" (313) him, as Browning himself "never saw him" or so much as "heard of his name" until "a few years ago" (311). In other words, FitzGerald is a nobody who attracts attention by insulting his superiors.

Yet a rather different attitude coexists with these expressions of contempt. In one letter written at this time Browning describes FitzGerald as a "genius" and his translation of Omar Khayyám as "brilliant"; in another he admits that

> "contempt" is not exactly applicable to a man of such wide and high reputation as FitzGerald — whose opinion is likely to be of *real* influence just now — when a new edition is coming out, of the works he "thanks God are at an end." (*Letters* 314)

Here he acknowledges that however obscure FitzGerald was in his lifetime, he has achieved posthumously "such wide and high reputation" that his ridicule of Barrett Browning might even harm her reputation, and in particular compromise the prospects of the forthcoming "new edition" of her works. And there is more to come. On 13 July Browning will "not look at the book again" because "in all likelihood he has delivered himself of the usual impertinences about *me*" (*Letter* 312), yet on 17 July he admits: "I have inspected the book since: *my* name only occurs once in it — he calls me a 'great man' " (314; since the book is not indexed, only prolonged research could have yielded this information).[16] It seems almost as though Browning was as much concerned with his own relation to FitzGerald as with his wife's, and there is a curious parallelism in such phrasings as that she "never saw him (any more than did I) and never heard of his name — (as was only the case with me, a few years ago)," confirmed in the anacoluthon which Karlin notes at the end of the following passage:

> I should be sorry to even seem in the least moved by any other than contempt for the poor envious creature, and might wish I had let him alone, as the most dignified way: as it is, all I know is that the fellow insulted one unable to defend herself — who yet is able to express his loathing for such a scamp. (*Letters* 312)

Well, man and wife is one flesh, but this confusion of his wife's identity with his own, and the mental tendency it illustrates, complicate what Browning might be thought to mean when he calls FitzGerald "envious." If Barrett Browning only is involved, then FitzGerald might be thought to envy her her reputation at a time when he himself was quite unknown. But if Browning too is comprehended, what could FitzGerald envy in him? His reputation? Not in 1861. His marriage? Possibly, but FitzGerald himself married in middle life (disastrously, I should add: the marriage lasted only a few weeks), and Browning was always irritated by attempts to represent Barrett Browning as an angel and their marriage as made in heaven. Furthermore, things had changed by 1889. In admitting that " 'contempt' is not exactly applicable to a man of such wide and high reputation as FitzGerald — whose opinion is likely to be of *real* influence just now, of the works he 'Thanks God are at an end' " (*Letters* 314). Browning almost seems to envy FitzGerald for an imputed cultural power to repress, in the first instance, Barrett Browning's new edition, and by extension of the symbiosis of himself with Barrett Browning in Browning's mind, perhaps also the 1889 edition of his own works. FitzGerald, then, may be said to envy both Browning and Barrett Browning, but Browning on behalf of both reciprocally envies him.

4. A Bloomian Relationship

THE COMBINED DENIGRATION and dread which mark Browning's response to FitzGerald points towards a Bloomian reading of the relation between them which fits very neatly the intertexts between *The Rubáiyát,* "Rabbi ben Ezra," and "Jochanan Hakkadosh." The case for "Ezra" being influenced by *The Rubáiyát* always assumed that the relation between them was adversarial and thus in some sense Bloomian *avant la lettre*. In Bloomian terms, Browning's collocation of the tropes of wine and the potter-pot relation undertakes ''a corrective movement in his own poem, which implies that the precursor poem went accurately up to a certain point, but then should have swerved, precisely in the direction that the new poem moves'' (14). Browning, that is, accepts the image of the pot as an appropriate one for the human condition (''retain[ing] its terms''); but he ''means them in another sense,'' implying ''that the precursor poem went accurately up to a certain point, but then should have swerved, precisely in the direction that the new poem moves.'' FitzGerald's omission of the potter's wheel from his conceit is the specific issue. He thereby enables himself to ignore the process of the pot's production (conceive the pot as always already in its final shape), a process which Browning promotes to the forefront of his treatment by imagining life in time as God's progressive shaping of the pot, death as the moment of its completion, and the afterlife as its consummation in eschatological use. The secondary trope of wine and the reading of linear chronology are correspondingly also realigned.

Similarly, the intertexts between both poems and their biblical prototypes exemplify Bloomian Daemonisation, the trope by which ''the later poet opens himself to what he believes to be a power in the parent-poem that does not belong to the parent proper, but to a range of being just beyond that precursor'' (15). In this instance, Browning ''opens himself'' to a text of equal authority in the Judaic, the Christian, and the Muslim traditions, and therefore a common ancestor for Ezra, a Jew, Khayyám, a Muslim, and Browning as, at least in public, a Christian; with the implication that the non-Christian traditions of biblical scholarship have deformed the text which only Christian exegesis can restore to its pristine shape, positioning the Christian reading before the others, including the Judaic, its chronological predecessor — as Browning, and his poem, metaphysically predate FitzGerald, and his.

The evidence for this reading lies in Browning's infiltration of New Testament iconography into ''Rabbi ben Ezra.'' Isaiah is the text in the Old Testament most used in Christian exegesis as a prolepsis of the New, in particular through the reading of its ''suffering servant'' figure as a type of Christ, and Browning exploits this feature as a point of entry to New Testament revisions of the Old Testament imagery of wine. The most interesting of these are those which in the Synoptic Gospels surround the Last Supper, where the wine becomes that of the Communion:

> And he took the cup, and when he had given thanks, he gave it to them: and they all drank of it.
> And he said unto them, This is my blood of the new testament, which is shed for many.
> Verily I say unto you, I will drink no more of the fruit of the vine, until that day I drink it new in the kingdom of God. (Mark 14.23–25)

The word ''new'' occurs twice in this passage, shared between the ''testament'' and the ''wine''; Christ's postponement of his own next draught of wine turns that into a celebration which the festal imagery of ''Rabbi ben Ezra'' appropriately realises as a celebration of the perfection of man (and, at least in Luke, of the coming of ''the kingdom of God.'' In Matthew, the wine is to be drunk ''with you,'' i.e., the disciples, heightening the suggestion of a feast).[17] But that perfection, in its trope of wine, is textually intertwined with the ''new testament,'' the Christian revelation, a reading which Ezra, as a Jewish Rabbi, cannot allow. The historical Ezra's Commentary on Isaiah contains no trace of it: the ''suffering servant'' figure, in Christian typology a prolepsis of Christ, he identifies as ''[t]hat Israelite who is the servant of the Lord, or the whole nation of Israelites,''[18] and there is evidence of a not surprising hostility to Christian exegesis of the Old Testament. In ''Holy-Cross Day'' (1855) Browning had paraphrased the historical Ezra's ''song of death'' in terms which show that he knew that Ezra did not accept the divinity of Christ, though he is represented as willing to admit its possibility.[19] Ezra's vision in ''Rabbi ben Ezra'' uses elements of Isaiah into which Browning has smuggled the revisionary Christian reading. In this way, Ezra's rebuttal of the epicureanism of Omar Khayyám is itself subsumed and transcended by the Christian reading towards which he is shown unwittingly pointing.[20]

5. Revising Bloom: Precursors and Collaterals

MY ACCOUNT SO FAR assumes that Browning regarded FitzGerald as in some sense a precursor, that is, a threat to his own creative autonomy. But why should he? Bloom sees Browning as a ''Strong Poet,'' and by definition such a poet knows who amongst his predecessors are genuinely ''strong'' and worth confronting, and who are weak and of no account: it is not clear why Browning should have thought of the profoundly obscure FitzGerald as a ''father,'' especially when FitzGerald was in fact his contemporary,[21] whereas the Bloomian precursor is normally an earlier writer. But it seems a limitation that Bloom's schema affords a poet's contemporaries, his or her collaterals, so little significance. In this respect Bloom shadows one of his own precursors, T. S. Eliot, whose ''tradition'' in turn shadows the transhistorical classicism of Matthew Arnold: for all three, a patina of antiquity accompanied by incense of canonisation is essential to qualify a great poet to influence great successors. But as well as a reader of the classics, a poet is also a historical being, who responds to contemporary history as it goes by, and to contemporary writers as they write. Of Keats's ''To Autumn,'' for example, McGann rightly remarks: ''the poem's autumn is an historically specified fiction dialectically called into being by John Keats as an active response to, and alteration of, the events which marked the late summer and early fall of a particular year in a particular place'' (61). Similarly, a writer can hardly ignore those of their contemporaries whom s/he recognises as either competitors or allies, but will rather bond with them in a literary version of what sociologists call a social network, constituting the poem as, among other things, a "family discussion" or a "family quarrel" or both. The debate between Coleridge and Wordsworth about depression, its cause and cure, in "Dejection: an Ode" and "Ode: Intimations of Immortality," is negotiated through the shared phrase "There was a time" which denotes a private conversation between the writers as much as a public declaration of nostalgia.

But while McGann's New Historicist view is itself a necessary historical corrective to the idealisations of the Bloomian as of other neo-New-Critical schools, it need not negate them: a writer is also a transhistorical being insofar as he or she is conscious of various traditions which can be brought to bear on the contemporary stimulus to writing, and of specific earlier writers whom she or he wants in the literary network. The fact that the contemporary stimulus is so frequently allegorised or put into code in what is written, as Lovelace for example used the fable of the grasshopper to represent Charles I, attests the wish for a wider-angle lens through which to (re)view it.[22] All cultures seek to make sense of the contemporary by referring it to an established typology, which may be mythological or historical, but invariably characterises the present as the re-enactment of some or all of an already-completed action. McGann concedes the formalist characterisation of poetry as "a type of expression which forces its language to exhaust itself within the limits of the poetic experience as such" (21), and given that such closure is precisely what the present lacks, its achievement in the poem argues that the poem as a literary event can harmonise the encoded contemporary reference with the "timeless" recurrence of its archetype. And if the precursor at some level represents the poet's empirical father, the latter will also be projected into the contemporary events or persons the poet responds to, presenting the double face of a past and a present paradigm, as Kafka's *The Trial* responds both to *Bleak House* and to Kafka's father, Herman Kafka.

6. Revising Bloom: the Protean Precursor

ONE OF THE MOST fascinating dimensions which opens when history is introduced into the Bloomian account is the possibility that "precursors" are not fixed, but susceptible to historical change as more of their works appear and more about their empirical identity comes to light. I have documented one case of this: Browning's reconsideration of Wordsworth and Keats after reading *The Prelude* in 1850 and "The Fall of Hyperion" in 1856 and his subsequent refashioning of their identities in "Fifine at the Fair" (Woolford, "Browning Rethinks Romanticism"). I argued that Browning's early hostility to the Romantic poetics of dream or vision was modified by his reading of book 8 of *The Prelude* in the context of Keats's transformation of the alien, inhuman scale of "Hyperion" into the more humanly manageable dimensions of its dream-version, "The Fall."

In "Fifine," he incorporates allusions to these passages into the climactic dream-vision of the poem's speaker, Don Juan, indicating that these Romantic precursors had undergone revision in his mind after the appearance of their posthumous works. In the case of Browning and FitzGerald, the publishing history of *The Rubáiyát of Omar Khayyám* may equally have played a role in both establishing and then modifying the metaphysical picture of FitzGerald which Browning deduced from the poem.

I have noted that the first edition of *The Rubáiyát* was anonymous; in fact, FitzGerald never publicly acknowledged the poem in his lifetime and went to considerable lengths to conceal his authorship of it even from friends. So if Rossetti did show the poem to Browning in the 1860s, he was probably not in a position to name its author, or Browning to react to it in that knowledge. How would this influence his reading? Not knowing the identity of its translator, I take it that he would focus instead on Omar Khayyám himself. He could not have known how free FitzGerald's translation actually was, since he did not read Persian and (as far as I can establish) there had been no previous translation of Khayyám's quatrains into English, or any other language known to Browning.[23] So Browning could well have assumed that the formidable sceptical iconoclast who emerges from FitzGerald's translation was the real Khayyám, whose status as a leading scientist as well as poet redoubled his claim to be thought of as a precursor, a strong poet and worth taking on.

Browning's choice of speaker reflects the historical prestige of Khayyám. For Rabbi ben Ezra was like Khayyám a historical figure — Abraham Meir ben Ezra — and like him also a major one (he was a celebrated Jewish biblical scholar). Furthermore, his lifetime overlapped with Khayyám's. These facts make it both plausible that he would have resisted Khayyám's interpretation of the Bible by invoking Isaiah and possible that he might have addressed him directly in a poem (he was, like Khayyám, a poet as well as a scholar, and is rumoured to have visited Persia). In using him as a speaker, then, Browning could at once satisfy historical realism and recruit the Hebrew exegetical tradition in the person of one of its most celebrated representatives into his own response to *The Rubáiyát.*

But at some point Browning became aware of FitzGerald's identity as Khayyám's translator, as a letter to Anne Thackeray Ritchie of 20 July 1889 indicates. There Browning speaks of FitzGerald as "a man of genius I was desirous of knowing more closely than through his brilliant Omar translation" (Fuller and Hammersley 167). While it is not clear when he acquired this knowledge, it is tempting to speculate that it was in the early 1880s, and that "Jochanan Hakkadosh" and perhaps *Ferishtah's Fancies* show him revisiting *The Rubáiyát* from the point of view of this revelation. He could have learnt of FitzGerald's authorship from Whinfield's 1882 translation of Khayyám's quatrains: in his introduction Whinfield refers to "Mr FitzGerald's brilliant translation" (5), the phrase which Browning himself used in his letter to Ritchie, and Whinfield cites FitzGerald's notes to the quatrains in several of his own. And if he read on, Browning would have realised just how free the earlier translation had been. Whinfield makes it clear that FitzGerald's arrangement of Khayyám's quatrains, with their appearance of philosophical sequence, was actually imposed on what are in fact quite separate epigrams,[24] and the quatrains he translates which deal with the potter-pot relation all indicate that its primary application in the original was to reincarnation.[25] FitzGerald's invocation of Jeremiah in his translation of such quatrains would then appear to be his own daemonisation of the original.[26] Whinfield also differs from FitzGerald in his interpretation of Khayyám's overall philosophy. Where FitzGerald took Khayyám's wine for real wine and his philosophy for sceptical materialism, Whinfield interprets the first metaphorically (the "wine" of enlightenment) and the second as Súfic mysticism.[27] Browning probably already knew of this possibility, since the third edition of *The Rubáiyát,* which he possessed, includes a note quoted from the second edition (it is not in the first) in which FitzGerald refers to Nicolas's 1867 edition with the comment: "Mons. Nicolas . . . does not consider Omar to be the material Epicurean that I have literally taken him for, but a Mystic, shadowing the Deity under the figure of Wine, Wine-bearer, &c., as Háfiz is supposed to do; in short, a Súfi Poet like Háfiz and the rest" (xvii-xviii). FitzGerald vigorously disputes this as a general interpretation, while conceding that "No doubt many of these quatrains seem unaccountable unless mystically interpreted" (xx). He concludes with ironic agnosticism: "However, as there is some traditional presumption, and certainly the opinion of some learned men, in favour of Omar's being a Súfi — and even something of a Saint — those who please may so interpret his Wine and Cupbearer" (xxiv).

Both FitzGerald's identity as translator of *The Rubáiyát* and the controversy regarding the original meaning of the quatrains were certainly known to Browning by 1885, since a letter to him from Charles James Lyall dated 21 Jan. 1885 reveals both facts. The letter begins: "I am sending you with this a copy of the article I wrote in 1876 on FitzGerald's version of *Omar Khayyám,*" and goes into a detailed discussion of Khayyám's relation to Súfism, concluding: "I think he was more of a Súfi than he seems in a superficial view" (Baylor 103). The letter seems to be a response to a request from Browning; it certainly assumes that he knows about FitzGerald and Khayyám.

The possibility that FitzGerald had mistranslated his original, coupled with the discovery of his actual obscurity as a minor contemporary, would necessarily have altered his stature in Browning's eyes, and this transfiguration may explain what otherwise seems mysterious, Browning's recomposition of "Ezra" in "Jochanan Hakkadosh," and in particular his introduction of a passage which responds to FitzGerald's Jeremiah-based interpretation of Khayyám's potter-pot configuration. I have noted that this represents an advance on "Ezra," which had avoided this aspect of the image. The confidence to take it on in "Hakkadosh" would follow from the discovery of FitzGerald's identity and his bad faith towards the "real" Khayyám. For Whinfield's version presents an at least intermittently devout Khayyám, to whom Ezra's translocation of wine-drinking to the after-life (as distinct from FitzGerald's use of it for purely secular consolation) would be perfectly acceptable. In which case, the shattering of a pot could equally bear the positive interpretation assigned to it in "Jochanan Hakkadosh."

It is the knowledge, whenever acquired, of FitzGerald's identity, which, I believe, explains the complexity of his response to FitzGerald's *Remains* in 1889. I have noted the "contempt" which interlaces with his hostility and outrage towards FitzGerald at that point, and his allusions to FitzGerald's life and personality indicate that that contempt was based on some knowledge of his character as a man. At the same time, Browning's ferocity clearly has some basis in fear — fear that FitzGerald's opinion of Barrett Browning might harm her reputation and by extension his (as his search for unflattering allusions to himself in the *Remains* confirms.) And the source of that fear emerges inversely from his repeatedly-expressed wish that FitzGerald were "alive in the body — not, for the first time, alive in his words which only now go forth to the world" (*Letters* 317). To Ritchie he put it that FitzGerald is "alive again in his letters, complete in his hitherto unpublished works" (167). There is some irony in wishing FitzGerald alive when he had "thanked God" for Barrett Browning's death; but a deeper irony emerges from Browning's evident fear of "his words," the posthumous work which, as Browning angrily notes, was purchasing him so high a reputation. These represent another kind of life: the life, and the "complete [ness]," achieved by a writer in his works, a life which after empirical death renders him humanly invulnerable and poetically formidable — a precursor rather than a contemporary.

In this instance, then, we have a continuous modification and reformation of one poet's image in another's mind. The author of *The Rubáiyát* begins as a great Persian poet, who must be answered by an equally authoritative Jewish thinker. He then becomes (or rather to the first image a second is added) an obscure friend of Tennyson's and therefore a contemporary of Browning's own who has appropriated and distorted his precursor. But with the publication of his posthumous works his identity doubly alters: first, he is unmasked as a personal enemy, but at the same time he achieves the fame which makes that enmity formidable and threatening.

It is in this light that we should review the ending of "To Edward FitzGerald":

> . . . and were yourself alive, good Fitz,
> How return you thanks would task my wits:
> Kicking you seems the common lot of curs —

While more appropriate greeting lends you grace:
Surely to spit there glorifies your face —
    Spitting — from lips once sanctified by Hers.

Karlin acutely notes that "the poem rests on a rhetorical contradiction: that FitzGerald can be spoken to as if he were alive, though the content of what is said to him assumes that he is not"(31). He connects this prosopopeia to the fact that poetry was always for Browning resurrective,[28] and that as a result of Browning's exercise of this power, "FitzGerald is . . . resurrected in poetry to be (or rather not to be) kicked and spat on." Karlin is right here, and right to note how much more significant the poem becomes when thus integrated into Browning's overall aesthetic. What I would add to Karlin's account is to connect Browning's "resurrection" of FitzGerald with his earlier response to *The Rubáiyát,* a connection which in my view is essential to understanding the impulse behind "To Edward FitzGerald." Karlin sees it as a risk that the poem might "indeed, 'lend [FitzGerald] grace,' " but that I think is precisely the point. In a letter to his son, Browning explained: "I said a little of my mind and there it will remain — I expect as long as Fitzgerald's recorded 'relief' " (*Letters* 314). This indicates that Browning was indeed prepared to lend FitzGerald grace by immortalising him in verse, but the immortality involves decanonising him by dislodging him from the posthumous eminence accorded by his publications and substituting the image of him indulging a shameful private act of spite and "envy." Not to refer to FitzGerald's literary status implies that he has none. The rhetorical force of "To Edward FitzGerald" is to restore the author of the "brilliant Omar translation" to obscurity and to make his immortality dependent on Browning's own art.

NOTES

1. Text as in Woolford, Karlin and Phelan, which gives the first edition reading.
2. Here, as throughout, I quote the first edition text.
3. It is reasonably certain that Rossetti did possess and distribute copies of *The Rubáiyát* in the 1860s (see Lang 6: 187), and there is a tradition that Browning was one of the recipients, but I have been unable to trace its source. Browning was on visiting terms with Rossetti during this time, and in a letter to Monckton Milnes of 7 July 1863 mentions having "looked over" a poem of Swinburne's "a long while ago at Rossetti's," which suggests that Rossetti might also have shown him, and he read, *The Rubáiyát* during this time (DeVane and Knickerbocker 150). Alternatively, Rossetti or his brother William Michael might have read him the poem, a common practice of theirs, as when on 8 April 1850 William Michael records reading *Christmas Eve and Easter Day* aloud to a friend (Fredeman 69).
4. McAleer disputes the role of *The Rubáiyát* in "Ezra" on the ground that if the latter was, as McAleer argues, influenced by Arnold's "Empedocles on Etna," it could not at the same time have been influenced by *The Rubáiyát.* ("Empedocles and

Ezra'') This seems to me a weak argument, in that it assumes that plural influence is impossible, whereas in fact nothing is commoner. Browning did possess a copy of the third edition of *The Rubáiyát,* published in 1872. It was sent to him, presumably by a friend, who inscribed it ''R.B. from L.L.J. Sep. 1874.'' This volume, now in the Armstrong Browning Library of Baylor University, is of considerable interest. FitzGerald massively revised the first edition of *The Rubáiyát* for the second edition of 1868, and the third edition of 1872 again substantially differs from the second. In the copy of 1872 from Browning's library someone has emended all the third-edition readings back to their second-edition equivalents. Unfortunately, the handwriting is not obviously Browning's, and until this question is settled it is impossible to say more than that he owned and presumably read *The Rubáiyát* by 1874.

5. In fact he alludes to this passage in the notes to 1872 (34–35).
6. I have noted that they occur separately; they are never collocated.
7. A passage in *Christmas Eve* comes closest to Ezra's configuration:

> ''God who registers the cup
> ''Of mere cold water, for His sake
> ''To a disciple rendered up,
> ''Disdains not His own thirst to slake
> ''At the poorest love was ever offered:
> ''And because it was my heart I proffered,
> ''With true love trembling at the brim,
> ''He suffers me to follow Him
> ''For ever, my own way'' [.] (509–17)

Here as in ''Ezra'' God is imagined drinking the believer from a cup; the cup however seems to contain water, God has not explicitly made it, and it is not the composite product of life in time (in a simpler trope it represents ''my heart'' and that heart's contents, ''true love'').

8. This passage was removed from subsequent editions.

9\. Not so, dear child
> Of after-days, wilt thou reject the Past,
> Big with deep warnings of the proper tenure
> By which thou hast the earth: for thee the Present
> Shall have distinct and trembling beauty, seen
> Beside its shadow — whence, in strong relief,
> Its features shall stand out: nor yet on thee
> Shall burst the Future, as successive zones
> Of several wonder open on some spirit
> Flying secure and glad from heaven to heaven; (*Paracelsus* 5.815–23)

10. I should mention ''Popularity,'' which contains the words past, present and future: ''My poet holds the future fast, / Accepts the coming ages' duty, / Their present for this past'' (13–15). But ''present'' here means ''the present moment *of the future ages,*'' and at the end of the poem (characteristically) ''Hobbs, Nobbs, Stokes and Nokes combine / To paint the future from the past,'' eliding the present.
11. There are also biographical allusions to *The Rubáiyát* in both ''Jochanan Hakkadosh'' and the work immediately following it. Jochanan Hakkadosh like Rabbi ben Ezra is

a Jewish sage, but his utterance is set, like that of Omar Khayyám, in Persia ("Schipaz, on Bendimir, in Farzistan" 801). Browning's next work, *Ferishtah's Fancies,* begun immediately after FitzGerald's death and completed less than a year after the publication of "Jochanan Hakkadosh," is again set in Persia, but this time has for its protagonist a Persian sage, Ferishtah, who delivers his doctrine "'neath a rock / Or else a palm, by pleasant Nishapur." Naishapur's main claim to fame is that it was Omar Khayyám's birthplace.

12. The best account appears in Karlin.
13. See Karlin 29–30. Edward FitzGerald's most recent biographer, R. B. Martin, also neglects to mention the episode.
14. A reference to FitzGerald as "good Fitz" at 1. 7 probably derives from Tennyson's "To E. Fitzgerald" (1885), which begins: "Old Fitz, who from your suburb grange," but this is, to put it mildly, oblique.
15. To his son Pen he wrote: "I was dreadfully afraid that the letter might have been written to Tennyson" (*Letters* 312); to Tennyson: "Let me say I associate myself with the universal pride of our country in your glory. . . . I am and ever shall be, my dear Tennyson, admiringly and affectionately yours" (*Letters* 315). In another letter to Pen of 16 August Browning quotes the whole of Tennyson's gracious reply and goes on: "T.[ennyson] is not the man to sympathize with a poor creature like FitzGerald, whom I punished no more than he deserved" (*Letters 317).*
16. In a letter to Charles Eliot Norton of 15 Dec. 1878, apropos his translation of Aeschylus', *Agamemnon,* FitzGerald wrote: "So, at any rate, I have been the cause of waking up two great men (Browning and Kennedy) and a minor Third (I forget his name) to the Trial, if it were only for the purpose of extinguishing my rash attempt" (*Remains* 1: 432). He was referring to the fact that Browning's translation of the play appeared the year after his.
17. "The element in the Eucharist which was probably of greatest importance for Jesus and for the earliest Christian community was the conviction that the meal which Jesus was celebrating with his followers was a foretaste of the full fellowship to be experienced when the kingdom of God has come and all God's people are gathered into one" (Laymon 640–41). Fenton paraphrases verse 25: "May my death be the way in which God will begin his kingly role in the world; then, as at a banquet, I shall drink *new* wine with you, in *the new world"* (418: my italics).
18. Friedland 242. It is not necessary to claim that Browning knew this text, though he might have.
19. Ezra speaks of Christ in the following terms:

> "Thou! if thou was He, who at mid-watch came,
> By the starlight naming a dubious Name!
> And if we were too heavy with sleep — too rash
> With fear — O thou, if that martyr-gash
> Fell on thee coming to take thine own,
> And we gave the Cross, when we owed the Throne —
>
> "Thou art the Judge." (91–97)

20. This device, identified in Browning criticism with "Cleon," "Karshish" and "Imperante Caesar Natus Est . . . ," has as far as I know never previously been acknowledged for "Ezra."
21. FitzGerald was born in 1809 and was therefore three years older than Browning.

22. See Allen 80–92.
23. Browning might have come across Tassy during the late 1850s; it does contain a few prose translations.
24. Whinfield comments, ''all, or nearly all, his poems are entirely isolated in sense from those preceding and following'' (6).
25. Ah, potter, stay thine hand! With ruthless art
Put not to such base use man's mortal part;
See, thou art mangling on they cruel wheel
Feridun's fingers and Kai Khosru's heart. (225)

26. FitzGerald's translation policy, as stated for other translations, involved the utmost license with the original. Of his translation of Calderón, he remarked: ''I do not believe an exact translation of this poet can be very successful; retaining so much that, whether real or dramatic Spanish passion, is still bombast to English ears'' (vi). Similarly, he remarked in his preface to his translation of the *Agamemnon*:

I suppose that a literal version of this play, if possible, would scarce be intelligible. Even were the dialogue always clear, the lyric Choruses, which make up so large a part, are so dark and abrupt in themselves, and therefore so much the more mangled and tormented by copyist and commentator, that the most conscientious translator must not only jump at a meaning, but must bridge over a chasm. (ii–iii)

Browning's translation of the latter, published a year after FitzGerald's, and believed by FitzGerald to have been influenced by his (see *Remains* 1: 432), adopts precisely the opposite approach. The Calderón translation was attributed, the *Agamemnon* anonymous; Browning could easily have encountered both, and in the case of the *Agamemnon* learned of FitzGerald's identity as its translator: if so, both his sense of FitzGerald as a competitor holding opposite positions to his own, and his awareness of FitzGerald's license with Omar Khayyám would have been reinforced.

27. Thus the lines FitzGerald translates, ''A Muzzein from the Tower of Darkness cries / ''Fools! your Reward is neither Here nor There!' '' (24) Whinfield renders: ''But from behind the veil a voice proclaims, / ''Your road lies neither here nor there, O fools!'' (62), adding the gloss: ''The sense is that 'The Truth' is hidden alike from the popular theologian and from the philosopher, and is only revealed to the 'illuminated' mystic'' (88). The context in which FitzGerald places his version of these lines confirms that he interprets them nihilistically.
28. I have discussed this more fully in chapter 5 of *Browning the Revisionary.*

Works Cited

Allen, Don Cameron. *Image and Meaning: Metaphoric Traditions in Renaissance Poetry.* Baltimore: Johns Hopkins UP, 1960.

Bloom, Harold. *The Anxiety of Influence: A Theory of Poetry.* Oxford: Clarendon P, 1973.

Browning, Robert. ''Intimate Glimpses from Browning's Letter File.'' *The Baylor Bulletin* 37 (1934).

———. *Letters of Robert Browning Collected by Thomas J. Wise.* Ed. Thurman L. Hood. New Haven: Yale UP, 1933.

———. *The Poems of Browning 3.* Ed. John Woolford, D. R. Karlin, and J. P. Phelan. Harlow: Longman, forthcoming.

DeVane, William Clyde. *A Browning Handbook.* 2nd ed. New York: Appleton-Century-Crofts, 1955.

DeVane, William Clyde, and K. L. Knickerbocker, eds. *New Letters of Robert Browning,* London: John Murray, 1951.

Fenton, T. C. *St. Matthew.* Harmondsworth: Penguin Books, 1963.

FitzGerald, Edward. *Letters and Literary Remains.* Ed. W. Aldis Wright. 3 vols. London: Macmillan, 1889.

———. *The Rubáiyát of Omar Khayyám, Astronomer-Poet of Persia.* London: Bernard Quaritch, 1859.

———. *Six Dramas of Calderon freely translated by Edward FitzGerald.* London: William Pickering, 1853.

———. *Agamemnon: a Tragedy Taken from Aeschylus.* London: Bernard Quaritch, 1876.

Fredeman, W. E., ed. *The P. R. B. Journal: W. M. Rossetti's Diary of the Pre-Raphaelite Brotherhood.* Oxford: Clarendon P, 1975.

Friedland, M., ed. and trans. *The Commentary of Ibn Ezra on Isaiah.* London: N. Trübner for the Society of Hebrew Literature, 1873.

Fuller, H. T., and V. Hammersley. *Thackeray's Daughter.* Dublin, 1951.

Hawthorne, Julian. *Shapes that Pass: Memories of Old Days.* London: John Murray, 1928.

Karlin, Daniel. *Browning's Hatreds.* Oxford: Clarendon P, 1993.

Kelley, Philip, and B. Coley, eds. *The Browning Collections: A Reconstruction.* Winfield, Ks.: Armstrong Browning Library of Baylor University, The Browning Institute, Mansell Publishing, Wedgestone P, 1984.

Kelley, Philip, and R. Hudson, eds. *The Brownings' Correspondence: A Checklist.* Winfield, KS.: Wedgestone P, 1978.

Lang, Cecil Y., ed. *The Letters of Swinburne.* 6 vols. New Haven: Yale UP, 1962.

Laymon, Charles M. ed. *The Interpreter's One-Volume Commentary on the Bible.* Harmondsworth: Penguin, 1972.

McAleer, Edward C., ''Empedocles and Omar Khayyam, and Rabbi ben Ezra.'' *Tennessee Studies in Literature* 20 (1975) 76–84.

McAleer, Edward C., ed. *Learned Lady: Letters from Robert Browning to Mrs Thomas FitzGerald 1876–1889.* Cambridge: Harvard UP, 1966.

McGann, Jerome J. *The Beauty of Inflections: Literary Investigations in Historical Method and Theory.* Oxford: Clarendon P, 1988.

Sargent, F. L. *Omar and the Rabbi: FitzGerald's Translation of The Rubáiyát of Omar Khayyám and Browning's Rabbi ben Ezra,* Arranged in Dramatic Form by Frederick LeRoy Sargent. Harvard Cooperative Society, 1909.

Tassy, Garcin de. *Note sur les Rubaiyat de Omar Hhaiyam.* Paris, 1857.

Whinfield, E. H. *The Quatrains of Omar Khayyám,* Translated into English Verse. London: Trubner's Oriental Series, 1882.

Woolford, John. *Browning the Revisionary.* London: Macmillan, 1988.

———. ''Browning Rethinks Romanticism.'' *Essays in Criticism* 43 (1993) 211–27.

REVIEW ESSAYS

SELF STORIES

By Walter Kendrick

BIOGRAPHY: "The history of the lives of individual men, as a branch of literature," says the OED, citing John Dryden as the word's first user, in his *Life of Plutarch* (1683). Dryden, the OED surmises, was translating the Greek βιογραφια, which had been written as early as the sixth century, or else the Latin *biographia,* which came much later.

AUTOBIOGRAPHY: "The writing of one's own history; the story of one's life written by himself." The OED cites an anonymous book review of 1797 as this word's debut, though Robert Folkenflik, in his introduction to *The Culture of Autobiography,* credits Ann Yearsley's preface to her *Poems* (1786) with the first instance of "autobiographical" (1).

The words came late, but the things had evidently been in existence quite a while. Plutarch's first-century *Parallel Lives* certainly looks like biography; Augustine's *Confessions* (ca. 400) is in many ways still the autobiographer's paradigm. Autobiography languished through the Middle Ages but revived in the Renaissance with Montaigne's *Essays* (1580–95) and Cellini's *Autobiography* (written before 1574, first published in 1730). Biography never faded, at least if one counts the medieval *Legenda Aurea* and *Gesta Romanorum,* but biography, too, boomed in the Renaissance. Its English lineage includes Walton's brief lives of Donne, Herbert, and others, along with Aubrey's *Brief Lives* (completed by 1693, first published in 1813). But biography came of age only in the eighteenth century, with Johnson's *Lives of the English Poets* (1779–81) and Boswell's *Life of Johnson* (1791). Autobiography grew up at about the same time, with Rousseau's *Confessions* (1781–88) and Gibbon's posthumously published *Memoirs* (1796). Since the turn of the nineteenth century, both genres have burgeoned. And today most people think they know a "biography" or an "autobiography" when they see one.

Both traditions, however, have been assembled retrospectively, by sifting through the past in search of works that seem to resemble the modern, familiar forms. Until the late eighteenth century, those who wrote about their own or others' lives had no sense that they were contributing to a genre, and it would be a mistake to praise or blame them for flouting generic conventions. Fidelity to fact, for example, even the appearance of it, meant little to biographers before Johnson and Boswell; Plutarch blithely manufactured parallels when reality had neglected to provide them, and medieval saints' lives cared little for what we call truth. Nowadays, accuracy has become biography's hallmark, perhaps its fetish. It is difficult to see how the *Golden Legend* can have any bearing on a modern edifice like Michael Holroyd's four-volume biography of George Bernard Shaw (1988–92), which devotes three hundred pages to source notes alone.

Besides, it is definitive of both biography and autobiography that they deny belonging to genres at all. Generic conventions are the products of writing, not living, and all modern life stories claim to borrow their shape from their subjects, not from tradition. Most biographers obey the Red King's charge to the White Rabbit: "Begin at the beginning . . . and go on till you come to the end: then stop." It can be argued that the birth-growth-death structure is conventional, and therefore literary, if only because not all biographies conform to it. Peter Ackroyd's *Dickens* (1990), for instance, begins, "Charles Dickens was dead," a plan also followed by Denis Donoghue in his gratuitous *Walter Pater: Lover of Strange Souls* (1995). Yet these exceptions may merely prove the rule, since after unconventional beginnings they lapse into the year-by-year chronicle that mortality seems to dictate. Bookstores routinely shelve biographies and autobiographies in the nonfiction section, or else, if the subject is a novelist, after the novels, as a sort of appendix to them. And that is how literary critics tend to treat both genres, mining them for whatever facts they contain that may bear on a writer's fiction but seldom bestowing on biographies or autobiographies the attention that routinely goes to literature.

To judge from a few recent critical books, however, this habit may be changing. Some critics have been turning away from mere gauging of accuracy toward the consideration of biographies and autobiographies as literary in their own right. The development is tentative so far, and it remains fraught with difficulties. But the Victorian age is certainly the place to begin, because it was the first great age of both genres, exceeded in quantity if not quality only by our own.

In addition to the problems of fact and fiction that plague the entire biographical genre, Victorian biographies bear a special burden. We have not outgrown the scorn that Lytton Strachey expressed in the preface to *Eminent Victorians* (1918):

> Those two fat volumes, with which it is our custom to commemorate the dead — who does not know them, with their ill-digested masses of material, their slipshod style, their tone of tedious panegyric, their lamentable lack of selection, of detachment, of design? They are as familiar as the *cortège* of the undertaker, and wear the same air of slow, funereal barbarism. One is tempted to suppose, of some of them, that they were composed by that functionary, as the final item of his job. (vi–vii)

Strachey's condemnation of standard Victorian biography is a literary one, heavily inflected with Paterian aestheticism. Indeed, by likening the standard biographer to a "functionary" and his book to an "item of his job," Strachey drives the hapless Victorian biographer not only out of literature but altogether out of gentility, down to the level of hired help.

Strachey's brief lives of Cardinal Manning, Florence Nightingale, Thomas Arnold, and Charles Gordon made full use of his ponderous Victorian predecessors, but Strachey extracted only the most provocative material from those "ill-digested masses." He obeyed his own first rule for biographers, preserving "a becoming brevity — a brevity which excludes everything that is redundant and nothing that is significant" (vii). In the process, however, he produced a series of works — including his book-length studies, *Queen Victoria* (1920) and *Elizabeth and Essex* (1928) — that in retrospect have satisfied practically nobody. Elegantly structured and written, they mingle fact and conjecture too cavalierly to rank as authoritative biographies. At the same time, since they aspire to be read as nonfiction, their literary qualities have attracted little critical attention. With rare exceptions such as Perry Meisel's *The Myth of the Modern* (1987), which devotes half a chapter to actually reading Strachey, most critics have followed the lead of Michael Holroyd's *Lytton Strachey* (1967–68), treating these books as symptomatic of either their author or the society he lived in.

Although Strachey's feistily modern biographies have fallen between two stools and are threatened with oblivion in consequence, his dismissal of Victorian biography remains in force. A few specimens, like Elizabeth Gaskell's *Life of Charlotte Brontë* (1857) and J. W. Cross's *George Eliot's Life* (1885), are still read for the firsthand accounts they contain. But what is a belated reader or critic to make of encrusted slabs like John Robert Seeley's *Life and Times of Stein* (1879) or the moldy hack work of Macmillan's English Men of Letters series? In *Victorian Biography: Intellectuals and the Ordering of Discourse,* David Amigoni has found a thing to do with such lumber.

His book — which began as a Ph.D. thesis at Liverpool Polytechnic — might serve as a model of the ugliness that characterizes much of today's academic criticism. *Victorian Biography* is badly, sometimes ungrammatically written: Amigoni's verbs often disagree with their subjects, he consistently misuses "comprise" (to be fair, hardly anyone gets the word right these days), and jargon is mother's milk to him. He invokes the names of Michel Foucault and Mikhail Bakhtin superstitiously, as if simply writing them certified the soundness of his own arguments. Amigoni's prose teems with the speciously dramatic vocabulary of "challenge," "contest," and "transgression" (three of his favorite terms) that academic critics deploy in order to drape their work in an undeserved mantle of political engagement. On just one occasion, early in *Victorian Biography,* Amigoni expresses discontent with the "hard-line theoretical company" that would attack him for thinking "eclectically" (21) — that is, I suppose, for failing to line up as a doctrinaire Foucauldian or Bakhtinian. Amigoni's heresy seems slight; he confesses to having drawn as well on Louis Althusser and Antonio Gramsci, which does not strike me as a mortal sin. But then I am not obliged to take tea in the common room at Liverpool Polytechnic.

That said, I must add that Amigoni takes an important step toward placing Victorian biography, if not toward its criticism in a literary sense. Indeed, the crux of Amigoni's argument is that the late-Victorian ruling class — the upper-middle-class men who controlled the publishing industry — were at pains to distinguish biography as a discourse of truth, called history, from the discourse of imagination called literature. To some degree, *Victorian Biography* is an extended skirmish with Terry Eagleton's highly influential *Literary Theory: An Introduction* (1983), which proposed that "English" as an academic subject was the ruling class's response to a "dramatic crisis in mid-nineteenth-century ideology":

> As religion progressively ceases to provide the social "cement," affective values and basic mythologies by which a socially turbulent class-society can be welded together, "English" is constructed as a subject to carry this ideological burden from the Victorian period onwards. (23–24)

"Literature," in Eagleton's view, was an ideal diversion for the newly literate lower-middle class and for the increasing number of women who sought higher education:

> Since literature, as we know, deals in universal human values rather than in such historical trivia as civil wars, the oppression of women or the dispossession of the English peasantry, it could serve to place in cosmic perspective the petty demands of working people for decent living conditions or greater control over their own lives, and might even with luck come to render them oblivious of such issues in their high-minded contemplation of eternal truths and beauties. (25)

With luck, that is, the masses' new opiate might prove more soporific than their old one.

Sneering passages like this (written in the state-funded security of Wadham College, Oxford) established Eagleton as a founder of what Harold Bloom calls the School of Resentment, that sadly enormous cadre of contemporary academic critics who endeavor to thwart the Victorians by beating literature into a kit of tools for social activism. Amigoni counts among that revisionary company, but his approach is subtler than Eagleton's, and Amigoni does not sneer. He argues that, for many late-nineteenth-century pastors and masters, literature was hardly the sedative Eagleton took it to be. Indeed, because literature sprang from imagination and played fast and loose with fact, literature constituted "a sort of aberrant linguistic supplement, history's Other." Literature threatened to unleash "the dissident power of the heterogeneous cultural activity of reading itself —

a power which could misread or challenge claims that might be made about politics and the direction in which the nation should move.'' Literature therefore needed policing, and the coppers on this beat were history and biography:

> The discipline of history is the discourse in dominance within an ordering of discourse, but the biographer's voice also invokes other techniques of limitation to produce the effect of a publicly and politically acceptable form of rhetoric. These techniques of limitation ask readers to recognise certain forms of language which are external, practical and productively rhetorical in a controllable way. Implicitly, there also has to be an attempt to deal with the linguistic supplement which evades this discipline, and which has to be policed as ''literature,'' or a form of language which is effective but only in an ''imaginative'' or aesthetic sense. (118–19)

I warned you about Amigoni's prose.

Nevertheless, his point is a good one (and a nice riposte to Eagleton), even if all it shows is that Plato's mistrust of poets survived more than two millennia. The prejudice lives on in booksellers' apparently commonsensical distinction between nonfiction and fiction — disciplined discourse, that is, as opposed to the imaginative kind. Analyzing the stupefying works of J. R. Seeley, Amigoni examines how Seeley came to regard biography as ''the vehicle through which both specialist knowledge and expertise in legitimation could be demonstrated to a popular audience'' (97). The English Men of Letters series, launched in 1878 under the editorship of John Morley, also served a legitimizing function:

> Liberal intellectuals who wrote the biographies comprising [sic] ''English Men of Letters'' were most concerned to demonstrate the extent to which their subjects' writings anticipated or furthered the development of a master-narrative of positivist progress. While the ''literature'' that came about could be morally uplifting and mentally soothing it was not inevitably so, and the biographers who commented on the writings of ''English Men of Letters'' were ever vigilant against what they saw as deviant forms of ''literary'' rhetoric which threatened to subvert ''the historic idea.'' (137)

The idea that literature was ''the principal discipline promoting national salvation'' did not reach full flower until the Newbolt Report of 1921 (137); Eagleton and those who follow him are mistaken when they push that apotheosis back into the last quarter of the nineteenth century.

Stripped of its high-theoretical trappings, Amigoni's argument is a small one, yet it is not trivial. By challenging, if not wholly refuting, Eagleton's simplistic scenario, Amigoni contributes to a more complex understanding of the movements of power in late-Victorian culture. He does nothing, of course, so belletristic as actually to *read* the books on which he comments, except to find occasional remarks in them that support his thesis. Reading any text on its own terms is a retrograde project these days, and in any case those books are probably unreadable that way. The best thing to do with them, probably, is to treat them as counters in an old power game. The works that Strachey found repellent nearly eighty years ago have, to say the least, not aged well. Amigoni deserves credit for daring to tackle them at all.

Autobiography remains a much more congenial (and popular) field for criticism, no doubt because tiresome questions of truth bulk smaller there. It is expected that autobiographers bend the truth or simply lie, and biographers routinely comb through their subjects' self-writings, comparing them with other documents and noting discrepancies. Autobiographies are necessarily fictional to some degree; hence they attract criticism in a way that biographies do not. There is a fairly large archive of criticism that considers autobiography as a genre, sometimes denying its possibility (as Avrom Fleishman does in *Figures of Autobiography,* 1983), sometimes exploring the way this nongenre has formed a tradition (as Linda H. Peterson does in *Victorian Autobiography,* 1986). No autobiography, of course, is merely an imitation of any other. But, perhaps thanks to the limited number of shapes human life can take (and to the vast number of autobiographies the last two centuries have produced), critics tend to look for types and trends, either sorting their examples into categories or stringing them along chronologically. The result can be a kind of assembly-line criticism: autobiographies zip down the critical conveyor belt, and the reader, like Lucy in the candy factory, swallows as many as he can, letting the rest go by.

This is the method of Clinton Machann's *The Genre of Autobiography in Victorian Literature,* which in 165 pages covers eleven examples, from Newman's *Apologia* (1864) to Francis Galton's *Memories of My Life* (1908). In his introduction, Machann declares that his book has two aims: "to serve both advanced students and scholars as an introduction to Victorian autobiography" and to demonstrate that Victorian autobiography "can be profitably studied as a nonfiction genre" (1). Advanced students and scholars — if there is any difference between the two groups — might be grateful for brief accounts of Harriet Martineau's *Autobiography* (1877) and Herbert Spencer's *An Autobiography* (1904) that allow one to pretend some acquaintance with those Gobis of print without being compelled to traverse them. But Machann's equally speedy treatments of Newman, Mill, Trollope, Ruskin, and Gosse add little to the already substantial body of commentary on such juicier works. Quite unlike Amigoni, Machann is virtually theory-free and writes clear, plain English. Paddling the tepid shallows of *The Genre of Autobiography,* I nevertheless felt a yearning toward Amigoni's rougher waters, turbid though they are.

Machann spends most of his time on summary, but he makes sporadic gestures toward what Amigoni would call "theorizing" the works at hand, and these are occasionally thought-provoking. Machann's only theoretical guru is the French critic Philippe Lejeune, whose work is known in this country primarily through Paul John Eakin's anthology of excerpts, *On Autobiography* (1989); this translation appears also to be Machann's sole source. Machann relies on Lejeune's commonsensical definition of autobiography: ''Retrospective prose narrative written by a real person concerning his own existence, where the focus is his individual life, in particular the story of his personality'' (quoted in Machann 3; italicized in Lejeune 4). Hard-line theorists of an Amigonian strope would quarrel with just about every word of this. Machann accepts it without demur and is able to propose some useful qualifications.

Victorian autobiographers tend to consider themselves primarily as public beings; it is the rationale of their writing autobiographies in the first place, and they assume that their readers agree with them. Anthony Trollope went the furthest in this direction, remarking, for instance (much to the frustration of modern biographers): ''My marriage was like the marriage of other people, and of no special interest to any one except my wife and me'' (61). He even elevated this deliberate reticence into a principle: ''It will not, I trust, be supposed by any reader that I have intended this so-called autobiography to give a record of my inner life. No man ever did so truly — and no man ever will'' (314). Trollope's *Autobiography* exhibits in extreme form a pattern that Machann observes in his other subjects as well: once Trollope becomes a writer, his self-history becomes little more than ''the history of his publications'' (Machann 72).

This is, perhaps, no surprise from a group of professional writers, either proud (like Trollope) of their publishing success or touchy (like Spencer) about their books' commercial failure. The focus on publications is also, as Machann observes, a form of the ancient *res gestae,* which defined people according to ''their status in the public sphere'' (160). But this focus also ''creates enormous formal pressures'':

> Assuming that the autobiography will take its ultimate place on the bookshelf at the end of one's collected works, it must serve as a key to interpreting and evaluating the others, if not itself offering a culminating, definitive statement of life philosophy. . . . It is ironic that writers must give up their ideas and creations, must alienate them from themselves through publication before they can be said to own them, for ownership can only be validated in public, social terms through printing and the publication process. In terms of autobiography, this can be said about the very selfhood the author ''creates.'' (160–161)

Two pages from the end of *The Genre of Autobiography,* Machann tantalizingly remarks that, thanks to pressures of this kind, his subjects' ''personal myths'' can be reduced to ''relatively simple syntagms (sequences of life events or 'functions' that mediate between interior and outer development)'' (162). An intriguing claim, but Machann signs off soon after making it. If he had pursued this line of thought, *The Genre of Autobiography* might have been less disappointing.

Even as it stands, however, Machann's book is far ahead of John D. Barbour's *Versions of Deconversion: Autobiography and the Loss of Faith* (1994), which, astonishingly, remains as innocent of theory as if it had been written in 1954. Lucid, reader-friendly prose is a pleasant side effect of Barbour's critical atavism. But his native or deliberate naïveté also leads him to stretch his paradigm of "deconversion" — loss of faith, with or without the gaining of a new one — so far that it becomes virtually meaningless. In 216 pages, he aspires to comment not only on much of the received autobiographical tradition (Augustine, Newman, Ruskin, Gosse) but also on slave narratives, "Indian autobiographies" (85), recent "anticult literature" (174), and yet more recent "autobiographies that explicitly make issues of gender identity central to the account of deconversion" (186). Deaf to theory, Barbour hears the call of political correctness. It has not served him well.

Versions of Deconversion merits only brief mention here, because Barbour devotes less than a quarter of his book to Victorian autobiographies. But he does have some interesting comments to make on the ways in which nineteenth-century writers adopted Augustinian analogies and metaphors to describe deconversions that either were not specifically religious or did not precede reconversion to a new faith that the autobiographer regards as the true one. Only in the late nineteenth century, Barbour observes, did it become possible "to focus a narrative on deconversion itself, and to attempt to consider it in isolation from the autobiographer's faith at the time of writing" (16). This is the method, for instance, of Ruskin's *Praeterita* (1885–89) and Gosse's *Father and Son* (1907), which look back upon the rejection of parental Christianity without saying much about what sort of faith, if any, the autobiographer embraces now. Already in 1765, however, Rousseau had used "the traditional symbols and structure of spiritual autobiography to interpret changes without specific Christian content" (35). This method was employed by Carlyle in *Sartor Resartus* (1834) and John Stuart Mill in his *Autobiography* (1873); here, "loss of faith has become a metaphor for another kind of personal change" (41). To some extent, Barbour's argument merely rehashes M. H. Abrams's discussion of Romantic "crisis-autobiography" in *Natural Supernaturalism* (1971), but Barbour emphasizes the particular tropes that secular writers borrowed from a religious tradition. This is a useful line of inquiry; I wish Barbour had pursued it further, instead of spreading himself so thin.

A more sharply focused, altogether more intense approach is taken by Mary Jean Corbett in *Representing Femininity: Middle-Class Subjectivity in Victorian and Edwardian Women's Autobiographies.* Roping in a large number of texts — some familiar, some little-known, a few even written by men — Corbett seeks to place them in the context of their authors' experience as professional writers and members of the bourgeoisie. Like many other feminist critics, she is concerned with rescuing women's writings that criticism has neglected; she provides detailed discussions, for example, of autobiographies by actresses Fanny Kemble, Marie Bancroft, and Madge Kendal, as well as of Margaret Oliphant's

Autobiography (1899) and Mary (Mrs. Humphry) Ward's *A Writer's Recollections* (1918). But rescue is only a small part of Corbett's undertaking. Going out from the unsurprising observation that "the ideology of domestic femininity persistently shaped the written lives of Victorian and Edwardian women" (15), she notes how "men and women have been differently situated in relation to the public sphere of work and the public form of autobiography" (7). Baldly stated, this is no shocker either, but Corbett explores the difference in unexpectedly interesting ways.

She begins with a provocative analysis of how, at an accelerating pace from the mid-eighteenth century onward, literature became a commodity. The depersonalization of writing led to a new emphasis on the writer as a unique individual, which is reflected in Wordsworth's poetry from *Lyrical Ballads* through *The Prelude*:

> As literature itself becomes less a matter of the private circulation of manuscripts among equals and intimates and more an exchange of texts for money between parties with no extratextual knowledge of each other, self-representation becomes the linchpin between the anonymous writer and his writing. The presence of his signature, the narrative unfolding of his history, inscribes this text as belonging to Wordsworth, who becomes "knowable" to his readers and inseparable from this text as a function of that self-representation. Poems and prefaces thus contextualize the identity of their author so as to supply the biographical dimension, that necessary frame of reference, for the reading of the work. (40)

The rise of mass media provided "new possibilities for establishing what we might call a disembodied public identity, possibilities that may be open to women writers as much as to men" (41).

The same development also fostered the Victorian cult of the "man of genius," who is "wholly his own product, an individual whose native abilities alone enable him to succeed" (18). Women, however,

> have been dependent on fathers, brothers, husbands, lovers, and sons, and left impoverished when those supporting men died or disappeared. Marriage and motherhood have been made to seem the fitting destiny of every "normal" woman whether or not she is so inclined; women's access to education has been limited, women's political power appropriated. As a group — a multiple, diverse, irreducible group — women have not been historically self-determining or autonomous, but "relative creatures." (15)

As a result, when certain privileged women took advantage of their new opportunity to go public, they experienced "a specifically feminine anxiety . . . about public authorship," "a gendered discomfort with public exposure that professional literary men, always already members of a legitimate public body that has its 'home' in the public world, do not explicitly represent even if they may experience it" (58).

That last clause exemplifies the special virtue of *Representing Femininity,* Corbett's willingness to see men and women neither as creatures from different planets nor as eternal predators and prey but as history's dramatis personae. She is at her best when she explores the lamentable fact that writing women often allied themselves with their rulers, as Elizabeth Barrett Browning did in *Aurora Leigh* (1857):

> The poem and the poet look "transgressive," then, only if we have bought the idea that all women's speech is inherently liberatory, no matter what women have to say; yet knowing as we do that women *did* have voices in the nineteenth century must make us attentive to what they were saying and how what they said affected their ability to speak and to be heard. I find it crucial to remember here that women's speech, like women's silence, can also be a product of their ideological positioning; to assign a univocal meaning to either one — all speech is "good," all silence is "bad" — is to oversimplify the operations of both domination and resistance. (70)

Corbett goes on to examine how Irene Vanbrugh's *To Tell My Story* (1948), her recollections of sixty years as an actress, merely ratifies the system that gave her fame:

> The fierce individualism Vanbrugh's text demonstrates at its worst shows how in entering the professional work force, women may do little or nothing to change the structure itself: while she feels and represents the tension between the two selves, it never occurs to Vanbrugh — as indeed it does not to many women — that it is not only the self, but also and especially the structure that needs to be transformed. (149)

The ultimate aim of Corbett's own book is neither Victorian nor Edwardian but very much of the 1990s. Leading up to a discussion of suffragists' autobiographies, she pauses to characterize herself as "a white, heterosexual, working-class-identified feminist academic" (she is "self-consciously poststructuralist," too, as she has informed us in her introduction). Corbett goes on to admit that she wrote *Representing Femininity* "more to work through certain intellectual and political questions of my own, and of my generation perhaps, than to provide a 'true' narrative of a particular historical network of relations" (151). Such would-be engaging frankness — along with the vulgar habit of enclosing in quotation marks words that the writer wishes to disown while nevertheless using them — has recently become fashionable among academics. The purpose of such personal asides seems to be the encouragement of friendly rapport between writer and reader; it is an updated version of the old man-of-letters ploy that urged us to imagine ourselves all clubmen together, chatting about books over brandy and cigars.

Fashionableness permeates *The Culture of Autobiography: Constructions of Self-Representation,* but mainly in the form of culturally diverse subject matter, not rhetoric. Editor Robert Folkenflik has gathered together ten essays by a broad spectrum of scholars, from far-ranging theorists to specialists in eighteenth-century English painting, writings by and about Chicanos, and contemporary Pakistani travel narratives. *The Culture of Autobiography* originated in a conference at the University of California Humanities Research Institute in March 1990, but several of the essays are new to this volume, as is Folkenflik's valuable "Introduction: The Institution of Autobiography."

Relatively little in *The Culture of Autobiography* is apparently of specific interest to Victorianists. Only two of the essays — Linda H. Peterson's "Institutionalizing Women's Autobiography: Nineteenth-Century Editors and the Shaping of an Autobiographical Tradition" and Roger J. Porter's " 'In *me* the solitary sublimity': Posturing and the Collapse of Romantic Will in Benjamin Robert Haydon" — focus on Victorian subjects, and Haydon, who killed himself in 1846, really belonged to an earlier era. Peterson's essay features a discussion of *The Friends' Library,* a series of Quaker journals, memoirs, and more formal autobiographies published between 1837 and 1850, but some of the works in the series had been written as early as the seventeenth century. Her well-argued contention is that "Victorian women who wrote autobiography came to believe that they had inherited a domestic tradition from their female predecessors. In reality, they inherited it not so much from female predecessors as from male editors who transmitted to them their literary heritage" (94).

Peterson also examines the old texts themselves, interpreting them in ways that diverge from both Victorian and modern orthodoxy:

> The minimizing of romantic and domestic concerns in the spiritual autobiography — or, more specifically, in the autobiographical tradition that *The Friends' Library* reconstructs — should challenge the modern critical assumption that gender is always the operative force in self-writing. It would lead us to ask whether theory and criticism of women's autobiography proceeds most perceptively when it emphasizes sexual difference. (87)

Turning to another nineteenth-century series, *Autobiography: A Collection of the Most Instructive and Amusing Lives Ever Published,* launched in 1826, Peterson selects an eighteenth-century woman's autobiography to advance her argument. Colley Cibber's cross-dressing actress daughter published her *Narrative of the Life of Mrs. Charlotte Charke* in 1755; proto-Victorian editors John Hunt and Cowden Clarke reissued it in *Autobiography* in 1827. For Hunt and Clarke, Charke's life "traces a course of failure in virtually every feminine role: wife, daughter, sister, even actress" (98). But Peterson reads a different story: "Read apart from its editorial apparatus, Charke's *Life* challenges the notion of gender-specific patterns of autobiography. The content of the text focuses on acts of cross-dressing, both social and dramatic, thus arguing by example that autobiographical writing can be androgynous, if not genderless" (100).

Peterson's conclusion is ambitious:

> What Charke suggests is that critical reading proceed not from considerations of gender, but from concerns with genre. She pleads for a critical stance that nineteenth-century editors and readers were to ignore — indeed, that we in the twentieth century, with our interest in feminine, relational modes of self-conception, have tended to minimize. But there is good argument that we ought now to move beyond the critical practice of identifying only feminine, relational modes with "women's autobiography" and adopt a less restrictive approach to understanding what women have written — and will in the future write — as autobiography.
> (103).

Seen alongside Corbett's *Representing Feminimity*, Peterson's essay suggests a new turn, perhaps a new maturity, in feminist criticism, which is likely to continue among the most vigorous branches of literary study in all historical areas. Corbett and Peterson seem willing, however tentatively, to move beyond gender altogether, or at least to see gender as one among many social attributes rather than as the key to all mythologies. If this is a trend, the long-term result, of course, will be the end of "feminist" criticism, the absorption of gender into a multifaceted conception of human nature. A similar fate may await gay studies, as sexual preference, too, loses its sovereign status and comes to be seen as a variable, only partially definitive matter.

Taken together, the books I have considered here demonstrate that the study of biography and autobiography, in Victorian scholarship and elsewhere, has a long way to go before it establishes itself as a field in its own right, instead of merely an adjunct to criticism. For that reasons, if I were advising an aspiring graduate student on which field to enter, I would recommend biography and autobiography: for all the fine work that has been done there, much of the ground remains untilled, and the very existence of those genres is still in dispute. I can think of no more exciting venture for a scholar.

Fordham University

WORKS CONSIDERED

Amigoni, David. *Victorian Biography: Intellectuals and the Ordering of Discourse.* New York: St. Martin's, 1993.

Barbour, John D. *Versions of Deconversion: Autobiography and the Loss of Faith.* Charlottesville: UP of Virginia, 1994.

Corbett, Mary Jean. *Representing Femininity: Middle-Class Subjectivity in Victorian and Edwardian Women's Autobiographies. New York: Oxford UP, 1992.*

Eagleton, Terry. Literary Theory: An Introduction. Minneapolis: U of Minnesota P, 1983.

Folkenflik, Robert, ed. *The Culture of Autobiography: Constructions of Self-Representation.* Stanford: Standford UP, 1993.

Lejeune, Philippe. *On Autobiography.* Ed. Paul John Eakin. Trans. Kathleen Leary. Minneapolis: U of Minnesota P, 1989.

Machann, Clinton. *The Genre of Autobiography in Victorian Literature.* Ann Arbor: U of Michigan P, 1994.
Strachey, Lytton. *Eminent Victorians.* 1918. New York: Capricorn, 1963.
Trollope, Anthony. *An Autobiography.* 1883. Ed. Frederick Page. Oxford: Oxford UP, 1953.

RECENT WORK ON VICTORIAN GOTHIC AND SENSATION FICTION

By Tamar Heller

ANYONE FAMILIAR WITH the field of sensation fiction can recall, no doubt with glee, extravagant Victorian denunciations of the genre: "An appeal to the nerves rather than to the heart," "the cravings of a diseased appetite," "a pestilence so foul as to poison the very lifeblood of our nation." Such diatribes seem so quintessentially, stodgily "Victorian — whether we define "Victorian" as "repressed," or, in trendier post-Foucauldian fashion, as the habit of speaking obsessively about sex in order to contain it. Thus the critical tendency to see sensation fiction as a "subversion of orthodoxy" or a feminist "rebellion" against "the establishment" reinforces our own othering of the Victorians, a desire to read them as bifurcated beings split between respectable outsides and rebellious hidden identities (and thus, presumably, unlike our modern, well-integrated selves). Such a critical narrative reads those "tales of bigamy and seduction," as Margaret Oliphant called sensation fiction, as a literary id, a doppelgänger-genre unburying all its culture's sexual and social preoccupations in tales obsessed with the others of Victorian society — deviant women, criminals, the lower classes, homosexuals, racial and cultural outsiders.

I do not mean to invoke this reading of sensation fiction as subversion merely to dismiss it (after all, I have subscribed to it myself). Yet the best recent work on sensation fiction and its parent genre, the Gothic, which tends to be read in similar terms, complicates a reading of these narratives as in any simple sense countercultural. In an essay defining the genre, Patrick Brantlinger once asked, "What is sensational about the sensation novel?" It may be useful now to ask *how* sensational is the sensation novel, if by "sensational" we mean "subversive." If we are to read Gothic and sensation fiction as a rebellion against some monolithic Victorian establishment, we will want to be careful in defining both the subversion and the hegemony — and perhaps avoid so crisp an antithesis. It may well be more accurate, while acknowledging the ideological disruptiveness of these genres, to see them not so much apart from their culture as inextricably part of it, sites of contestation and negotiation of the debates surrounding gender, class, and national and sexual identities during the Victorian period. For, certainly, these genres often seem more clearly "about" ideology than others of the time; the degree to which Gothic and sensation fictions often overtly engage anxieties about sexuality, as well as their reflection of other contemporary issues such as urban crime, class unrest, and debates about women's role, makes them particularly fruitful testing ground for popular methodologies like feminism, Marxism, new historicism, and gay studies. In fact, the genuinely interdisciplinary nature of the most exciting recent work on these genres attests to the ongoing dialogue between Victorian literature and culture.

Victorian Gothic

BECAUSE GOTHIC HAS PROVED a compelling genre for women writers, feminist criticism has had a major impact on rediscovering and reevaluating Gothic texts. Indeed, not only has feminist criticism identified the tradition of women's writing it dubbed "female Gothic," but feminist critics themselves have often been inspired by the genre's carceral tropes, most famously in Gilbert and Gubar's analogy between the nineteenth-century woman writer and the Brontëan oppressed wife bursting out of her Gothic confinement. Feminist criticism of the Gothic, however, demonstrates both the strengths and weaknesses of reading the genre as an expression of feminine rebellion; while powerfully illuminating how Gothic reflects women's ambivalent relation to domesticity, feminist analysis tends — by no means inevitably — to be ahistorical, eliding the degree to which women invested in as well as protested dominant ideologies and thus obscuring the specificity of the genre's ideological messages.

A cluster of recent feminist books exemplifies such unevenness but also suggests promising new ways of reading Gothic and, in several cases, of extending a feminist perspective to the works of male writers. Eugenia C. DeLamotte's *Perils of the Night,* subtitled "a feminist study of nineteenth-century Gothic," ambitiously tackles male and female, British and American traditions to make some familiar points about women's anger at being "trapped in domestic space" (157). Although Victorianists will find readings of works such as *Jane Eyre* useful, the analysis here — which relies overmuch on abstract terms like "the self" — is neither particularly subtle nor original. A more sophisticated study is Susan Wolstenholme's *Gothic (Re)Visions,* a theoretical extravaganza of feminist, poststructuralist, psychoanalytic, and film theory which intriguingly argues that scenes of woman-as-spectacle in female Gothic provide a vehicle for women writers to "write their writing acts into their texts" (xiv) and thus address their problematic relation to linguistic authority. One difficulty with Wolstenholme's approach, however, is that it so expands the definition of Gothic as to make it, too vaguely, a trope for women's writing in general, while her psychoanalytic and deconstructive framework gives her little chance to historicize the tensions that women experienced in regard to literary voice. Kate Ellis's *The Contested Castle: Gothic Novels and the Subversion of Domestic Ideology* is more satisfying as an attempt to locate a dual literary and ideological origin for the genre by reading it (in versions by both male and female writers) as a critical response to the bourgeois domesticity emblematized by Milton's *Paradise Lost*; in the Gothic the ideal of home, Milton's site of salvation, is what is lost and becomes "the place from which some (usually 'fallen' men) are locked out, and others (usually 'innocent' women) are locked in" (ix). Although the ideological and literary-historical synthesis of Ellis's project is promising, her study, like DeLamotte's and Wolstenholme's, falters in its attempt to tackle too much material (in her last chapter, for instance, she seems uncertain whether to read Gothic as a radical reaction against domestic ideology or as an instrument of Foucauldian surveillance).

The most successful recent feminist reading of Gothic is Michelle Massé's *In The Name of Love: Women, Masochism, and the Gothic* — even if this success is due in part to the very narrowness with which she reads the genre as a series of changes rung on the scene of female masochism described by Freud in "A Child Is Being Beaten." Like Wolstenholme, Massé focuses on Gothic scopophilia, making Freud's figure of the woman who watches the father beat other women her image not only for the heroine of the Gothic text but its female readers and writers. Reflecting feminist-influenced trends in psychology, Massé defines female masochism not as a perverse love of pain but as a complex strategy for coping with the inequalities of domesticity. A problem with this theory is the underlying assumption, no matter how sympathetic, that women are masochists — an assumption with the unfortunate consequence, given feminist attempts to elevate the status of the Gothic, of associating it ever more firmly with depressed and neurotic women. Massé's readings of individual texts remain sophisticated and stimulating, even if the chapter on *Jane Eyre* — the one most useful to Victorianists — ignores the text's investment in domestic ideology by celebrating Jane as a liberal feminist heroine who distances herself with anachronistic thoroughness from gender oppression.

The recent feminist study that most specifically addresses Victorian Gothic is Alison Milbank's *Daughters of the House: Modes of the Gothic in Victorian Fiction,* which examines works by Dickens, Collins, Brontë, and Le Fanu. Pointing, like Ellis, to the Gothic obsession with houses, Milbank similarly claims that the genre develops out of differing male and female responses to domesticity: if women in Radcliffean Gothic try to escape claustrophobic homes, men in eighteenth-century male Gothic are house-breakers who attempt to "penetrate" and subjugate the female will (11). The inclusion of a chapter on Brontë is almost an anomaly in a study most provocative in its theory that nineteenth-century male writers are attracted not so much to the plots of female subjugation in earlier male Gothic as to the "maternal" Gothic tradition (201) and its representation of domesticity as carceral. In Victorian male Gothic, Milbank argues, not only the heroine but the male protagonist is a prisoner in the house (16). Such an argument has fascinating implications for the male writer's linguistic and social authority: imprisoned men are feminized, but women become jailors as well as fellow-prisoners. Milbank's ability to work out these implications is hampered by some problematic assumptions, the most troublesome signalled by the claim that she seeks to "find in seemingly conservative writers an unsettling and 'redemptive' dissatisfaction with the patriarchy they seem to defend" (2). Though the word "redemptive" is curiously unanchored in any context, Milbank implies that she is redeeming possibly offensive texts for the feminist reader, a project in which she appears to rely more on idiosyncratic responses to novels than on an analysis of their cultural context (she makes, for instance, the rather astonishing claim that Collins is more conservative in his portrayal of women than Dickens). Milbank is at her most insightful when she traces the thematics of houses in the work of that underread Victorian Gothicist, Sheridan Le Fanu, yet even here her inability to situate texts ideologically limits her interpretation. Reading *Uncle Silas* as a novel whose depiction of domesticity points "to a need to move beyond patriarchy to some new means of social organisation" (175), Milbank views the heroine's yearning for death at the novel's end as an image for "the transcendence of women, as they come to inherit the earth" (197). But for women to be linked with the spiritual realm *is* domestic ideology, not a movement against it; if Le Fanu represents domesticity as stifling, he also purposefully exiles his heroines from its ideal configuration — as in *Uncle Silas,* where Maud is stranded in a motherless household run by a decadent and abusive aristocrat. To see a negative portrait of the family as itself evidence of a "feminist hermeneutic" (18) overlooks the way in which many Victorian novelists, Le Fanu and Dickens among them, perform the ideological sleight of hand that Roland Barthes calls "Operation Margarine" — showing the problematic nature of an institution to suggest not that it be replaced but rather repaired.

Two studies on the Gothic that more successfully situate the genre in its culture are Ronald Thomas's *Dreams of Authority: Freud and the Fictions of the Unconscious* and Ian Duncan's *Modern Romance and Transformations of the Novel: The Gothic, Scott, Dickens.* Thomas's study, in fact, historicizes pyschoanalysis, a discourse often used to dehistoricize texts; his reading of dreams in Gothic and detective fiction, along with autobiographical novels, explains the influence of Victorian literature on Freud by seeing the narratives both of fiction and of psychoanalysis as stories that assuage the bourgeoisie's fears about the authority of their self-fashioning. Dreams that reflect cultural confusion become, through the ordering of narrative, "dreams of authority" rather than of social and psychic disintegration, although the potential for such disorder often threatens to undermine this ideological and formal closure. Such disordering potential, Thomas argues, is especially marked in detective fiction, which he sees as a literary version of social policing in an era of heightened anxiety about the costs of empire. Although Thomas could be more attentive to both gender and class as constituents of Victorian social identity, his fine analysis of such texts as *Frankenstein, Wuthering Heights,* and the Sherlock Holmes stories makes this book an important one for scholars of the Gothic.

Ian Duncan's *Modern Romance and Transformations of the Novel* locates elements of the Gothic in works not explicitly Gothic, addressing the ways in which nineteenth-century male writers respond to a feminine literary tradition. The response of Scott and Dickens to women writers is particularly complex because their appropriation of Gothic becomes a process of self-canonization and a celebration of the new bourgeois ethos that authorizes them as writers. Both of these projects rely on a clearly defined masculine identity undergirded by the ideology of the nation-state. In fact, what Scott and Dickens draw on in the Gothic, Duncan argues, is its construction of a "myth of national culture, of British historical identity" (23). Thus, Gothic's myth of origins, based on feudal ideals and folk culture, implies that bourgeois hegemony is the appropriate end of history; yet since the Gothic is also associated in its Radcliffean form with narratives of feeling and sensibility, it can aptly convey women's sense of dislocation and alienation from the bourgeois family romance. So subtle a theory of genre — arguing that on the one hand it encodes nationalist ideology while on the other enabling a disenfranchised group to express ambivalence and alienation — provides an appropriately flexible model for Duncan to address the question of how male authors revise the Gothic. As Duncan puts it, "Scott's novels rewrite the historical private subject as masculine in terms already feminine" (54). Scott's representation of a "dominant-class male subjectivity" is thus informed by the feminine "hesitancy" and "ambiguity" of female Gothic (54).

Duncan's study is marked by a sophisticated sense of how Gothic romance *reads* history, so that bourgeois domesticity and nationalism become "naturalized," logical ends; but, like Thomas, he also shows how the Gothic's "cultural uncanny" (9) fissures so robust an ideological and narrative telos. I might have wished Duncan to be even more attentive than he is to the historical formation of domestic ideology, and also to address more explicitly Dickens's modernization of Gothic (the book ends with a reading of *Dombey and Son* when some gesture toward the later career would be helpful). Yet in its theoretical synthesis, reworking Bloomian theories of literary influence through a sophisticated blend of formalist and historical methodologies, Duncan's work is theoretically original in a way welcome at a moment when even the most intelligent criticism can have a paint-by-numbers quality.

Another piece that similarly links the domestic and political agendas of Gothic is an excellent essay by Marjorie Howes, "Misalliance and Anglo-Irish Tradition in Le Fanu's *Uncle Silas,*" which addresses the pattern in Anglo-Irish literature of "encoding its discussions of tradition in representations of gender and sexual issues" (165). Expressing both Le Fanu's allegiance to the Protestant ascendancy and his sense of its genealogical instability through assimilation and miscegenation, the Gothic romance of *Uncle Silas* genders the theme of ethnic degeneration by linking Celts and nervous, hysterical women such as the novel's female narrator: "The self-accusatory narrative of a self-confessed hysteric has precisely the structure of the Anglo-Irish Gothic" (181). The best recent piece I know on Le Fanu, Howes's article should prove suggestive for further work linking gender and national ideologies in the Gothic.

The quality of Howes's article is the more welcome because there is so puzzlingly little on Le Fanu, one of the more versatile of nineteenth-century Gothicists, and one whose innovative synthesis of that genre with the historical novel makes him an ideal candidate for new historicizing approaches. Those working on this writer will want to consult the standard work, W. J. McCormack's *Sheridan Le Fanu and Victorian Ireland,* a critical biography that securely grounds the author in his cultural context. But scholars may also seek out such recent sources as Helen Stoddart's "'The Precautions of Nervous People Are Infectious': Sheridan Le Fanu's Symptomatic Gothic," a reading, influenced by Eve Sedgwick's work, of homosexuality and aristocratic decadence in Le Fanu's supernatural tales "Green Tea" and "Carmilla." For more on "Carmilla," Le Fanu's famous vampire tale, one must go back to William Veeder's "Carmilla: The Arts of Repression," or to Carol Senf's brief "Women and Power in 'Carmilla' " and relevant sections of her *The Vampire in Nineteenth-Century Literature.* My own essay, "The Vampire in the House: Hysteria, Female Knowledge, and Female Sexuality in Le Fanu's 'Carmilla,' " links the tale to nineteenth-century discussions of the hysterical woman.

One tendency suggested by the works I have mentioned so far is a movement away from the strict emphasis on female Gothic characteristic of earlier feminist criticism toward a retheorizing of male Gothic that attempts to account for the genre's relation to Victorian masculinities — the complex and changing definitions of gender and sexual identity for men during the nineteenth century. More work clearly needs to be done on this subject. One can go back to Eve Sedgwick's reading of the genre and homoeroticism in *Between Men* (1985) while a more recent effort to rethink male Gothic appears in Joseph Andriano's *Our Ladies of Darkness: Feminine Daemonology in Male Gothic Fiction.* Addressing the misogynistic fantasies rife in nineteenth-century male Gothicism, Andriano traces the presence of the "fiend in women's garments" in works by such authors as Lewis, Hawthorne, Stoker, and James. Yet Andriano's archetypal Jungianism is finally of little help in decoding the historical specificity of the sexism he examines, and which he comes uncomfortably close to reproducing by reading all women in the tales as simply anima-extensions of the male self.

Late Victorian Gothic is a particularly fruitful site for this project of retheorizing male Gothic, since during the fin-de-siècle the genre became at once more masculinized and medicalized — more securely the province of male writers and also marked by the professional language of medical discourses about female hysteria, homosexuality, and eugenicism. These issues continue to be explored, as does the relation of gender and sexuality to such other concerns as imperialism and modes of social regulation, including the creation of a criminal underclass.

One might at times get the impression that the field of late Victorian Gothic could be called Dracula Studies, so fashionable has that text become as a synecdoche for the period. Amid the welter of Transylvanian bibliography, I would point to several recent articles as representing promising new developments. Steven Arata, in "The Occidental Tourist: *Dracula* and the Anxiety of Reverse Colonization," connects Stoker's novel with the genre Patrick Brantlinger has called "imperial Gothic" — a Gothic that encodes anxieties about the decline of empire. Arata argues that by problematizing the boundaries between civilized and primitive on which the imperial project depended, Stoker "probes the heart of the culture's sense of itself, its ways of defining and distinguishing itself from other peoples, other cultures, in its hour of perceived decline" (628–29). The result is a striking generic transformation: the travel narrative, a Victorian genre that suggests mastery of the colonizer over the colonized, becomes gothicized as the boundary between explorer and primitive collapses. By drawing on fin-de-siècle discourses of eugenicism and science, Arata links his argument about imperialism to one about gender, arguing that the text reflects a fear of the enervation of Anglo-Saxon manhood by the virile racial Other and the fertile, rebellious women he seduces. Another recent article that considers Dracula in relation to discourses about the other — in this case the Jew — is Judith Halberstam's "Technologies of Monstrosity: Bram Stoker's *Dracula,*" which explores late Victorian parallels between representation of the Jew's body and that of the nervous degenerate. From this detailed analysis, Halberstam develops a more broad-ranging observation, useful for theories of the genre, about the "thrifty metaphoricity" of the Gothic and its ability to symbolize many types of Otherness (race, class, gender) by condensing "many monstrous traits into one body" (334). Meanwhile, arguing that consumption in the text figures economic as well as sexual preoccupations, Jennifer Wicke's "Vampiric Typewriting: *Dracula* and its Media" focuses on Stoker's representation of technology and mass culture, making the controversial if provocative point that Stoker's is the "first great modern novel in British literature" (469) because it prefigures modernist anxieties about the work of art in an age of mechanical reproduction.

The field of late Victorian Gothic, when not dominated by readings of *Dracula,* centers on the other famous male Gothic of the period, *Dr. Jekyll and Mr. Hyde.* William Veeder and David Hirsh's *Dr. Jekyll and Mr. Hyde after One Hundred Years* (1988) contains a useful selection of essays that look at the text from the vantage point of feminist, new historicist, and deconstructive criticisms and highlight such issues as homoeroticism, the text's self-reflexive narratives about writing, and the representation of male criminality. A strongly Foucauldian reading that situates *Jekyll and Hyde* against the backdrop of nineteenth-century criminological discourses appears in Marie Christine Leps's *Apprehending the Criminal: The Production of Deviance in Nineteenth-Century Discourse.* Finally, an article notable for *not* being either on *Dracula* or *Dr. Jekyll and Mr. Hyde* is Kelly Hurley's "The Inner Chambers of All Nameless Sin: *The Beetle,* Gothic Female Sexuality, and Oriental Barbarism." Hurley locates in Richard Marsh's 1897 novel *The Beetle* a "Victorian horror of female sexual appetite" and argues (in a theory applicable to the works of other Victorian writers) that in the Gothic an orientalized female sexuality becomes the ineffable gap, the "thing that one cannot name" (209). Hurley's argument reminds us that there are more than two late nineteenth-century Gothics — and thus suggests that we should not focus solely on such trendy texts as *Dracula,* but instead strive for a broader knowledge of the period.

Victorian Sensation Fiction

LIKE THOSE WORKING on Victorian Gothic, critics working on the Gothic subgenre of sensation fiction will find research on the historical referents of the narratives a necessity, especially given the insistent contextualizing at the basis of much recent criticism. In particular, the study of sensation fiction requires some knowledge of the Victorian city, that site to which crime, scandal, and sensation were literally and symbolically linked. The connection between the Victorian city and sensation fiction structures Thomas Boyle's *Black Swine in the Sewers of Hampstead* (1989), a pioneering foray into the coverage of urban crime in new print media, like newspapers, to suggest that sensationalism reflects cultural anxieties about social disintegration. A more scholarly look at the Victorian city and its influence on the "novel of urban mysteries" is Richard Maxwell's *The Mysteries of London and Paris,* which analyzes images of the city in the work of Victor Hugo, Eugene Sue, and Charles Dickens. Particularly useful for its reminder, so necessary for the insular field of English literature, that French novelists were influential in developing mystery fiction, Maxwell's book is steeped in literary history. At the same time, it is resolutely ahistorical in the sense associated with the new cultural criticism; Maxwell unproblematically reads novels as the romance-quest of a liberal male subject achieving transcendence of mystery through knowledge. Still, even the most committed Foucauldians — especially those working on Dickens — will find intriguing Maxwell's reading of the mystery novel's recurrent images of the city, such as crowds and labyrinths.

The most indispensable book on the Victorian city is Judith Walkowitz's *City of Dreadful Delight,* the most triumphant example I looked at of the intricate disciplinary crossover encouraged by the new cultural criticism — a distinguished work by an historian valuable to the literary scholar for its astute discussion of melodrama. Walkowitz's study concerns the spatial geographies that organized Victorian gender and class ideology and that divided men and women, middle-and working-class, into properly partitioned insides and outsides — a division disrupted by such late nineteenth-century trends as the growth of an urban working class, immigration, and the movement of women from private to public space. These days literary scholars often vaguely invoke the Foucauldian concept of power, but Walkowitz's reading of history vividly brings this notion to life, showing which groups were disempowered or empowered by late-nineteenth-century constructions of sexuality. Indeed Walkowitz's study — and this is where it is most useful for those working on sensational narratives — is notable for its sophisticated concept of ideological construction, or fictionality; as if inspired by Oscar Wilde's aphorism that life imitates art, she argues that Victorians employed melodramatic conventions to interpret and naturalize their experience. In analyzing these melodramatic conventions, Walkowitz is herself influenced by their structure, using London as the stage set for her retelling of a series of late nineteenth-century narratives of sexual and class danger, including the scandal surrounding Stead's publication of *The Maiden Tribute of Modern Babylon,* an attempt to confine a female spiritualist to an insane asylum, and the most famous Victorian sexual narrative of all, Jack the Ripper. The prostitute, so central a figure in recent Victorian criticism, is crucial to this analysis as a multivalent signifier for gender and class indeterminacy and for the New Woman (Walkowitz reminds us that middle-class women who ventured into the streets without a chaperone were often mistaken for streetwalkers). Anxieties about the autonomous female sexuality embodied by the prostitute inform the narrative emblematized by the media coverage of the Ripper murders, which reads women as temptresses who invite death through sexual transgressiveness while simultaneously desexualizing them by transforming them into victims of male violence. Another historical study of the same phenomenon is Angus McLaren's *A Prescription for Murder: The Victorian Serial Killings of Dr. Thomas Neill Cream,* which analyzes the Ripper-like case of a doctor — an abortionist, in fact — who poisoned prostitutes; the chapters on women, contraception, and eugenicism are a useful complement to Walkowitz's study for those interested in the historical dimensions of late Victorian gender ideology.

A treatment of sensation fiction that emphasizes the underlying ontological instability of the line separating the female criminal from the domestic woman is Anthea Trodd's lucid *Domestic Crime in the Victorian Novel.* As Trodd argues, in a formulation that resembles Walkowitz's, the sensation novel underscores Victorian anxieties about the permeability of the boundary between public and private worlds that was essential for maintaining bourgeois domesticity. By showing how commerce and crime could invade the sanctity of the middle-class home, the sensation novel points to tensions within domestic ideology, particularly in regard to the ''problematical relationship'' of the home and the ''cash nexus'' (2). Trodd's study is valuable not only for making a familiar point — that the angel in the house can, Lady Audley-like, secretly be a fiend — but for chapters on other topoi in sensation fiction, such as the ambiguous figure of the female servant, at once outsider and insider in the domestic realm, and a particularly illuminating chapter on the representation of women in courtrooms as witnesses or accused criminals — a theme that showcases the ''collision between femininity and the male institution of the law in Victorian Britain'' (132).

The imbrication of scandal and the feminine leads us to a recent survey of sensation fiction, Lyn Pykett's *The Improper Feminine: The Women's Sensation Novel and the New Woman Writing.* As her title indicates, Pykett does not limit herself to sensation writers, since she claims that both this genre and the new Woman novel of the 1890s engage the debate over how to define the ''true'' nature of woman that is central to the Victorian Woman Question controversy. The definition of the proper feminine in Victorian gender ideology, Pykett argues, ''*Implies* the improper feminine'' (16), the deviant sexual woman of sensation fiction; as she perceptively comments, one of the central paradoxes of the controversy over sensation fiction was its ''tendency to define the sensation novel as a form both characteristically feminine, and profoundly unfeminine, or even anti-feminine'' (33). By limiting her focus to women writers, Pykett tends to imply that the sensation novel was solely a form of *l'écriture féminine* (to which she likens it) rather than a reflection by both male and female writers of a pervasive cultural disquiet over such issues as female sexuality. Pykett's chapters are often brief, and her readings of novels such as *Lady Audley's Secret* and *East Lynne* are not fully developed. Nonetheless, the range of issues covered here, such as the rise of mass culture and the place of sensation fiction in an emerging canon, makes this a helpful survey for anyone working in the field; several of the insights Pykett imports from film and reader-response criticism, such as a discussion of the different subject positions available to the reader of sensation fiction, are particularly welcome. In a cogent reminder of the complexity of the genre, Pykett urges that we see sensation fiction ''not simply as either the transgressive or subversive field of the improper feminine, or the contained, conservative domain of the proper feminine'' but rather as ''a site in which the contradictions, anxieties, and opposing ideologies of Victorian culture converge and are put into play'' (50).

Nicholas Rance's *Wilkie Collins and Other Sensation Novelists: Walking the Moral Hospital* offers a survey of the genre with an emphasis diametrically opposed to Pykett's. While Pykett situates sensation fiction in the context of the Woman Question debates, Rance's analysis is class-based, portraying the genre as a critique of the discourse of entrepreneurial capitalism represented by Samuel Smiles's 1840s treatises on "self-help." Collins's version of sensation fiction, Rance argues, parodies the bourgeois ideal of upward mobility by exposing those who rise as duplicitous outcasts like Lady Audley or Magdalen Vanstone; these characters' transgression of class boundaries in turn points to the tension between two bourgeois ideals, a belief in social mobility on the one hand and in a providential order of society on the other. In positioning Collins, whom he sees as a critic of Victorian class hierarchies, in relation to other sensation writers, Rance distinguishes "radical" sensation fiction from the "conservative" version of Woods's *East Lynne.* Such a distinction, however, can be programmatic; for instance, Braddon's *Lady Audley's Secret,* which Rance calls a radical fiction, has the same double impulse both to excuse and to punish its duplicitous anti-heroine as Woods's supposedly conservative novel (not to mention Collins's *No Name).* And Rance overplays the centrality of Collins to the sensation school, making the female authors appear as acolytes of a male mentor rather than developers of the genre in their own right. At the same time, Rance's historicizing reading of ideology, particularly his stress on class unrest, makes a significant contribution to the study of sensation fiction, even if such an emphasis needs to be balanced with a sense of how a fairly liberal writer on class issues like Collins could be much more conservative and conflicted about gender.

The most satisfying integration of such class and gender issues among recent offerings appears in Ann Cvetcovich's *Mixed Feelings: Feminism, Mass Culture, and Victorian Sensationalism.* Cvetcovich's study, which centers on feeling of "the politics of affect" with which women are associated in domestic ideology, provides a timely corrective to the tendency to see sensation fiction as simply expressing subversive impulses. By thematizing feeling — as in *East Lynne,* where the narrative traces the heroine's suppressed mental agony — sensation fiction does provide an outlet for women's disquiet or "mixed feelings" about domesticity. Yet, as Cvetcovich sees it, focusing on feminine feeling does not radicalize sensation fiction so much as depoliticize it, reducing political and systemic problems to individual psychological crises. In face, by representing women as "mysterious and compelling" the sensation novel is often not subversive so much as diagnostic, its portrayal of the middle-class woman as "feeling subject" confirming the "importance of emotional expression" to bourgeois domesticity (7).

Cvetcovich's study, which contains chapters on Braddon's *Lady Audley's Secret,* Collins's *The Woman in White,* and Wood's *East Lynne,* has immense theoretical range and sophistication, integrating psychoanalytic, feminist, and new historicist theories with Marxism. Although one gap in the study of sensation fiction is the absence of a sustained attention to the rise of the sensation novel as a commodity, Cvetcovich's discussion of the sensation novel as mass culture adds an important dimension to understanding the economics of the genre. Moreover, Cvetcovich's book extends the traditional definition of sensationalism, containing illuminating readings of *Daniel Deronda* and, most provocatively, of Karl Marx's *Capital.* It is true that, like Alison Milbank, Cvetcovich subjects Victorian fiction to a contemporary radical litmus test it is scarcely likely to pass. But her book is easily the most theoretically stimulating of recent ones on sensation fiction and deserves to be influential.

In addition to these full-length studies of sensationalism, several other books contain noteworthy sections on the genre. An erudite chapter in Kate Flint's *The Woman Reader* situates the critical response to sensation fiction in light of anxieties about the ''proximity of sexuality and textuality for the woman reader'' (4). Flint addresses the ways in which sensation fiction was read, by its critics, as stimulating female sexuality and also explores the female reader's relation to the narratives. Helena Michie's incisive chapter on ''Sexual and Class Duplicity in Sensation Fiction'' in *Sororophobia* offers another argument about the ideological doubleness of sensation fiction. Targetting the sensation novel's obsession with ''female self-replication'' and fraudulence, Michie claims that the preoccupation with multiple feminine identities in sensation fiction reflects a characteristically Victorian ambivalence about women's duplicity, expressing both a conservative fear that women are not naturally angels and yet, in plots where one woman easily substitutes for another, a more radical critique of female economic and social disenfranchisement as well.

As such studies suggest, female sexuality — whose presence threatens to disrupt domestic ideology's construction of the maternal, spiritualized woman — is a crucial issue in recent analyses of sensation fiction, although its significance remains to be fully assessed. In a chapter on *Lady Audley's Secret* in *Fatal Women: Lesbian Sexuality and the Mark of Aggression,* Linda Hart approaches the sensation novel's depiction of female sexuality through an analysis of Victorian masculinity, arguing that the criminal woman must be marked off as deviant in order to transform male homosexual desire into heterosexual desire. Yet while this Sedgwickian reading sees the function of female sexuality as normalizing domestic ideology, Natalie Schroeder, in ''Feminine Sensationalism, Eroticism, and Self-Assertion: M. E. Braddon and Ouida,'' claims that in Braddon's work, as in that of her contemporary Ouida, female sexuality ''becomes a key element in determining feminine power and self-assertion'' (90). Schroeder's theory that female sexuality is a catalyst for female rebellion needs further nuance, however; both male and female sensation writers shared their culture's anxiety about the sexual woman, often to the extent of denying that even their deviant women were passionate. Gail Walker addresses this contradictory portrayal of female sexuality in ''The Sin of Isabel Vane,'' where she argues that in *East Lynne* female sexuality is so illicit that even the heroine's fall is desexualized (she runs off with her seducer in a fit of pique rather than of passion). In another view of Isabel's bestselling fall that focuses on the problematic of the Victorian mother's sexuality, E. Ann Kaplan's reading of ''maternal melodrama'' in *East Lynne* blends psychoanalytic and Marxist criticism to examine the "unconscious family romance . . . that structured cultural relations in the bourgeois imaginary" (86).

Wilkie Collins, who also created a number of transgressive and haunted female characters, has received more attention than either Braddon or Wood, a favoritism Lyn Pykett ascribes to his sex (198). Yet the fact that Collins's sex has affected his reevaluation is not due simply to the bias of present-day critics, but rather to the professional consequences of his masculinity in his own day — his status in the increasingly professionalized world of literature and his close relationship with its central figure during his generation, Charles Dickens. The persistent doubleness of Collins's position — as both important innovator and maverick, marginalized outcast — demonstrates how strange a business canonmaking and remaking can be. Perhaps Collins, denied at his death a monument in Westminster Abbey, has not yet quite made it into the pantheon of "Standard Literature" whose "composing influence" he derides in *The Moonstone.* Yet recent work on Collins also suggests that this marginality was self-consciously assumed, a pose as well as a reality — a status that makes him resemble his own play-acting sensation heroines. In this sense, Collins's career emblematizes, with greater clarity than that of any writer I have mentioned so far, the ideological contradictoriness of the genre he helped to develop: while he often was, as he loved to depict himself, a rebel against an oppressive establishment, he was also more firmly a part of conventional culture than he wished to admit.

The two recent, revisionary biographies on Collins by William Clarke and Catherine Peters suggest this doubleness, even if they do not fully explore its implications. Perhaps the crispest example of the "othering" of the Victorians I referred to at the beginning of this review, Clarke's *The Secret Life of Wilkie Collins* focuses not on the fiction but on the scandalous sexual life of the author (Clarke himself is a descendant of Collins's "morganatic" relationship with his working-class mistress Martha Rudd). A much more scholarly assessment is Catherine Peters's magisterial *The King of Inventors,* the best biography to date of Collins, which unearths much that has hitherto been buried about him with a detective-fever worthy of his novels. Particularly useful for its examination of Collins's relationships with other Victorians (whether his parents, melancholiac brother, or collaborator-friend Charles Dickens), *The King of Inventors* parallels Collins's preoccupation with "layered deceit" (151) in his novels with the tensions of his own secret life that made him an insider as well as an outsider in Victorian power structures. (For example, he could play the role of bohemian because of a social and gendered status that allowed him, unlike his mistresses or illegitimate children, also to assume the privilege of the respectable bachelor.) Those looking for an integration of a reading of the fiction with that of this complicated life will find Peters's insights a valuable improvement on the neglect or crude readings of Collins's work in earlier biographies. Yet, as a sketchy reading of that most important of his fictions about doubleness and outsiders,

The Moonstone, suggests, to explicate the tangled politics of otherness in Collins's work it is not enough to fall back on references to the writer's Jekyll-like private life. Rather, to illuminate the complex representation of power and identity in the novels requires more attention to Collins's ideological and cultural context — for instance, situating his portrayal of gender issues, which Peters does address, in the context of the Woman Question debates.

Those who wish a firmer sense of Collins's dialogue with his culture will need to refer back to Jenny Bourne Taylor's sophisticated *In the Secret Theatre of Home,* which, informed by feminist and new historicist methodologies, traces the influence of nineteenth-century psychology on the gender politics of Collins's fiction. Like Ronald Thomas, Taylor focuses on the shifty, unstable boundaries of identity during the Victorian period, paying particular attention to the female characters who manipulate, and are also manipulated by, the terms of bourgeois "moral management" that were so frequently reinforced by medical authority. Taylor's Foucauldian reading of both better- and lesser-known works of Collins is important and provocative, even if one quibble I have with her book is that it manages to lose all sight of the pleasure of Collins's narratives. The historicizing tendency of Taylor's criticism, especially when read in tandem with the incisive Marxism of Cvetcovich's approach to Collins, is a welcome antidote to the bland formalism of another recent book on Collins, Peter Thoms's *The Windings of the Labryrinth: Quest and Structure in the Major Novels of Wilkie Collins.* It is not that a formalist approach to Collins's work is inappropriate; indeed, Thoms's emphasis on the self-reflexive plots about writing in Collins's fiction is exciting. Focussing on the characters who, like Walter Hartright of *The Woman in White* and Franklin Blake in *The Moonstone,* are "surrogate writers," Thoms argues that storytelling, or "lifewriting" (16), is a "symbolic act of selfhood" (124) that allows characters to impose order on otherwise chaotic and oppressive events. Important as is such attention to issues of linguistic authority in Collins's multivoiced narratives, Thoms's analysis (unlike the more sophisticated examination of similar issues in Thomas's *Dreams of Authority*) is marred by an abstract set of terms — "selfhood," "human fate," "human family" — that do not allow him to examine the social factors that would complicate his readings of the transcendence of heroic male narrators. For instance, Magdalen Vanstone, of whose "moral laxity" (29) Thoms preachily disapproves, has considerably less chance as a woman to control the story of her life than Walter Hartright does.

Some of the most exciting recent work on Collins addresses his relation to discourses of race and imperialism. In an essay that complements his reading of the novel in *Dreams of Authority,* Ronald Thomas argues that in *The Moonstone* the political story of imperialism is reinscribed as a psychological narrative, a theory he extends to the representation of empire in the Sherlock Holmes stories. Two impressive articles on Collins and imperialism by Lillian Nayder represent a particularly timely theoretical direction. In "Agents of Empire in

The Woman in White,'' Nayder explores Collins's use of the ideologeme Stephen Arata has characterized as ''reverse colonization'' — a paradigm informed both by guilt about imperialism and a fear of the racial Other. The plot of *The Woman in White,* in which Austrian subjugation of Italy is condemned and yet the colonizing of Honduras shores up the class power of the hero, shows how in Collins's fiction ''resistance to dominant ideologies and . . . reinscription of them go hand in hand'' (6). Nayder's approach in this essay, as in her ''Robinson Crusoe and Friday in Victorian Britain: 'Discipline,' 'Dialogue,' and Collins's Critique of empire in *The Moonstone,*'' provides an important response to D. A. Miller's well-known argument about the ''monologic'' nature of Collins's multivoiced narratives. Distinguishing herself from this steel-trap Foucauldianism which, for all its sophistication, tends too crudely to reverse the terms of the sensation-fiction-as-subversion argument, Nayder urges us not to read Collins as just a mouthpiece of hegemony but instead to analyze more closely the ''cultural mediation'' and heteroglossia in his fiction — a direction which, as I have suggested, is fruitful for work in the field more generally.

By this time, it must be obvious that renewed interest in Gothic and sensation fiction has radically altered the shape of the Victorian canon. I have focused on secondary works, but the reevalutive efforts they represent have been both the outgrowth of and catalyst for the reissue of hitherto neglected texts: the Oxford World's Classics series, a useful barometer for such trends, has in recent years brought out scholarly editions of works by Collins, Braddon, and Le Fanu, and the publication of such Oxford anthologies as *The Oxford Book of Gothic Tales, Victorian Ghost Stories,* and *Victorian Tales of Mystery and Detection* similarly allows us to dispense with messy xeroxes, insuring through the indisputable authority of the textbook that we do not seem so weird when we teach ''weird'' Victorian fiction. These genres, then, whose history of marginality parallels the history of canon-formation — whose very existence points to the separation into high and low literature in the late nineteenth century — are ideal candidates for the cultural studies project of breaking down a hierarchical view of literature. And yet this process of remaking the canon raises its own set of concerns. In reevaluating Gothic and sensation fiction it may be best to avoid simply installing an alternative canon, with separate ghettoes for *Dracula* and *Woman in White* Studies, and instead work on uncovering a richer sense of a cultural and literary fabric (Ellen Wood and Mary Elizabeth Braddon wrote more than one novel, and other sensation writers like Charles Reade and Rhoda Broughton have scarcely received any attention). And — dare I suggest it in the wake of the O. J. Simpson murder case? — we may also want to use our knowledge of the ideological work of Victorian Gothicism to examine our own culture's fascination with the sensational, melodramatic, and morbid, an inquiry that would surely suggest we are not so post-Victorian as we like to think.

Postscript

IT IS SURELY NO SURPRISE that, since I wrote this review, there has been more work of note on Victorian Gothic and sensation fiction. Although I cannot do justice to all the new offerings, I would like to mention several because of their relevance to my earlier comments. In many ways Anne Williams's *Art of Darkness: A Poetics of Gothic* is the kind of synthesis I had been looking for in other feminist studies of the genre. While her psychoanalytic vocabulary has a familiar ring, Williams's is a more lucid and seamless feminist reading of anxieties about gender in both male and female Gothic than others I know, and provocative too in its use of a Kristevan language to explore feminine disruptions of the patriarchal family, or, as Williams puts it, "the revolutionary effects . . . of semiotic energies within the Symbolic" (175).

Susan David Bernstein's "Dirty Reading: Sensation Fiction, Women, and Primitivism" adds an important dimension to the study of sensation fiction and what Bernstein terms the "anxiety of assimilation," or fear of the loss of boundaries between genders and classes, found in Victorian responses to sensationalism. Likening reviewers' images of the all-devouring female readers of sensation fiction to anthropological discourses about the greed of "primitive" races, Bernstein locates a fundamental tension between the twin ideologies — capitalism and domesticity — that underlie Victorian culture. Although these ideologies are founded on containment — of female sexuality, of lower-class rebellion — the Victorian economy depended on its appeal to the potentially boundless desires of the female consumer. Bernstein argues that, in reviews of sensation fiction, its voracious villainesses as well as its greedy readers embody cultural anxieties about women whose monstrous appetite threatens to swallow the distinction between "civilized" and "savage." Such an argument underscores the importance of economic and material sources for the fear of Otherness in Victorian fiction, as does Stephen Arata's "The Sedulous Ape: Atavism, Professionalism, and Stevenson's *Jekyll and Hyde,*" which, in another look at the development of mass culture, examines Stevenson's negative response to the professionalization of literature and the widening divide between "high" and "low" genres.

Although the project of comparing Victorian obsessions and our contemporary lust for the sensational is far from complete, two books hot off the press as I write — Judith Halberstam's *Skin Shows: Gothic Horror and the Technology of Monsters* and Paula Marantz Cohen's Alfred Hitchcock: The Legacies of Victorianism — suggest new ways of examining the continuity between Victorian preoccupations with the Gothic and the formation of modern genres.

University of Louisville

WORKS CONSIDERED

Andriano, Joseph. *Our Ladies of Darkness: Female Daemonology in Male Gothic Fiction.* University Park, PA: Pennsylvania State UP, 1993.

Arata, Stephen D. "The Occidental Tourist: *Dracula* and the Anxiety of Reverse Colonization." *Victorian Studies* 33, 4 (Summer 1990): 621–45.

———. "The Sedulous Ape: Atavism, Professionalism, and Stevenson's *Jekyll and Hyde.*" *Criticism* 37, 2 (Spring 1995): 233–59.

Baldick, Chris, ed. *The Oxford Book of Gothic Tales.* Oxford: Oxford UP, 1992.

Bernstein, Susan David. "Dirty Reading: Sensation Fiction, Women, and Primitivism." *Criticism* 36, 2 (Spring 1994): 213–41.

Boyle, Thomas. *Black Swine in the Sewers of Hampstead: Beneath the Surface of Victorian Sensationalism.* New York: Viking-Penguin, 1989.

Brantlinger, Patrick. "What is 'Sensational' about the 'Sensation Novel'?" *Nineteenth-Century Fiction* 37, 1 (June 1982): 1–28.

Clarke, William M. *The Secret Life of Wilkie Collins.* London: Allison and Busby, 1988.

Cohen, Paula Marantz. *Alfred Hitchcock: The Legacies of Victorianism.* Lexington: U of Kentucky P, 1995.

Cox, Michael, ed. *Victorian Tales of Mystery and Detection: An Oxford Anthology.* Oxford: Oxford UP, 1992.

———, and R. A. Gilbert, eds. *Victorian Ghost Stories: An Oxford Anthology.* Oxford: Oxford UP, 1992.

Cvetcovich, Ann. *Mixed Feelings: Feminism, Mass Culture, and Victorian Sensationalism.* New Brunswick: Rutgers UP, 1992.

DeLamotte, Eugenia C. *Perils of the Night: A Feminist Study of Nineteenth-Century Gothic.* New York: Oxford UP, 1990.

Duncan, Ian. *Modern Romance and Transformations of the Novel: The Gothic, Scott, Dickens.* Cambridge: Cambridge UP, 1992.

Ellis, Kate Ferguson. *The Contested Castle: Gothic Novels and the Subversion of Domestic Ideology.* Urbana: U of Illinois P, 1989.

Flint, Kate. *The Woman Reader 1837–1914.* Oxford: Clarendon P, 1993.

Halberstam, Judith. *Skin Shows: Gothic Horror and the Technology of Monsters.* Durham: Duke UP, 1995.

Halberstam, Judith. "Technologies of Monstrosity: Bram Stoker's *Dracula.*" *Victorian Studies* 36, 3 (Spring 1993): 333–52.

Hart, Lynda. *Fatal Women: Lesbian Sexuality and the Mask of Aggression.* Princeton: Princeton UP, 1994.

Heller, Tamar. "The Vampire in the House: Hysteria, Female Sexuality, and Female Knowledge in Le Fanu's 'Carmilla.'" *The New Nineteenth Century: Feminist Readings of Underread Victorian Fiction.* Ed. Barbara Harman and Susan Meyer. New York: Garland P. 77–95.

Howes, Marjorie. "Misalliance and Anglo-Irish Tradition in Le Fanu's *Uncle Silas.*" *Nineteenth-Century Literature* 47, 2 (Sept. 1992): 164–86.

Hurley, Kelly. "The Inner Chambers of All Nameless Sin: *The Beetle*, Gothic Female Sexuality, and Oriental Barbarism." *Virgin Sexuality and Textuality in Victorian Literature.* Ed. Lloyd Davis. Albany: State U of New York P, 1993.

Kaplan, E. Ann. "The Maternal Melodrama: The Sacrifice Paradigm: Ellen Wood's *East Lynne* and its Play and Film Versions." *Motherhood and Representation: The Mother in Popular Culture and Melodrama.* London: Routledge, 1992.

Leps, Marie Christine. *Apprehending the Criminal: The Production of Deviance in Nineteenth-Century Discourse.* Durham: Duke UP, 1992.

Massé, Michelle A. *In the Name of Love: Women, Masochism, and the Gothic.* Ithaca: Cornell UP, 1992.

Maxwell, Richard. *The Mysteries of Paris and London.* Charlottesville: UP of Virginia, 1992.

McCormack, W. J. *Sheridan Le Fanu and Victorian Ireland.* Oxford: Clarendon P, 1980.

McLaren, Angus. *A Prescription for Murder: The Victorian Serial Killings of Dr. Thomas Neill Cream.* Chicago: U of Chicago P, 1993.

Michie, Helena. *Sororophobia: Differences Among Women in Literature and Culture.* New York: Oxford UP, 1992.

Milbank, Alison. *Daughters of the House: Modes of the Gothic in Victorian Fiction.* New York: St. Martin's, 1992.

Nayder, Lillian. "Agents of Empire in *The Woman in White.*" *The Victorian Newsletter* (Spring 1993): 1–7.

———. "Robinson Crusoe and Friday in Victorian Britain: 'Discipline,' 'Dialogue,' and Collins's Critique of Empire in *The Moonstone.*" *Dickens Studies Annual* 21 (1992): 213–31.

Peters, Catherine. *The King of Inventors: A Life of Wilkie Collins.* London: Secker and Warburg, 1991; Princeton: Princeton UP, 1993.

Pykett, Lyn. *The Improper Feminine: The Women's Sensation Novel and the New Woman Writing.* London: Routledge, 1992.

Rance, Nicholas. *Wilkie Collins and Other Sensation Novelists: Walking the Moral Hospital.* Rutherford NJ: Fairleigh Dickinson UP, 1991.

Schroeder, Natalie. "Feminine Sensationalism, Eroticism, and Self-Assertion: M. E. Braddon and Ouida." *Tulsa Studies in Women's Literature* 7, 1 (1988): 87–103.

Senf, Carol. *The Vampire in Nineteenth-Century Literature.* Bowling Green, OH: Bowling Green State U Popular P, 1988.

———. "Women and Power in 'Carmilla.'" *Gothic 2* (1987): 25–33.

Stoddart, Helen. "'The Precautions of Nervous People are Infectious': Sheridan Le Fanu's Symptometic Gothic." *Modern Language Review* 86 (Jan. 1991): 19–34.

Taylor, Jenny Bourne. *In the Secret Theatre of Home: Wilkie Collins, Sensation Narrative, and Nineteenth-Century Psychology.* London: Routledge, 1988.

Thomas, Ronald R. *Dreams of Authority: Freud and the Fictions of the Unconscious.* Ithaca: Cornell UP, 1990.

———. "Minding the Body Politic: The Romance of Science and the Revision of History in Victorian Detective Fiction." *Victorian Literature and Culture* 19 (1991): 233–54.

Thoms, Peter. *The Windings of the Labyrinth: Quest and Structure in the Major Novels of Wilkie Collins.* Athens: Ohio UP, 1992.

Trodd, Anthea. *Domestic Crime in the Victorian Novel.* New York: St. Martin's, 1989.

Veeder, William. "'Carmilla': The Arts of Repression." *Texas Studies in Literature and Language* 22 (1980): 197–223.

———, and David Hirsh, eds. *Dr. Jekyll and Mr. Hyde After One Hundred Years.* Chicago: U of Chicago P, 1988.

Walker, Gail. "The Sin of Isabel Vane: *East Lynne* and Victorian Sexuality." *Heroines of Popular Culture.* Ed. Pat Browne. Bowling Green, OH: Bowling Green State U Popular P, 1987. 23–34.

Walkowitz, Judith R. *City of Dreadful Delight: Narratives of Sexual Danger in Late-Victorian London.* Chicago: U of Chicago P, 1992.

Wicke, Jennifer. "Vampire Typewriting: *Dracula* and its Media." *ELH* 59 (1992): 467–93.

Williams, Anne. *Art of Darkness: A Poetics of the Gothic.* Chicago: U of Chicago P, 1995.

Wolstenholme, Susan. *Gothic (Re)Visions: Writing Women as Readers.* Albany: State U of New York P, 1993.

VICTORIAN DETECTIVE FICTION AND LEGITIMATE LITERATURE: RECENT DIRECTIONS IN THE CRITICISM

By Ronald R. Thomas

FROM ITS FIRST APPEARANCE — usually traced to Edgar Allan Poe in America and to Charles Dickens in England — critics have viewed detective fiction with a suspicious eye. Anthony Trollope condemned its unrealistic preoccupation with plots that were too complex and characters that were too simple. Mrs. Oliphant warned about the dangers of its implicit celebration of criminality and rebelliousness. Henry James regarded it and its twin, the sensation novel, as "not so much works of art as works of science." Indeed, some of the most ardent articulations of the aesthetic and moral attributes of high Victorian realism were occasioned by anxiety over the cheap effects and immense popularity of nineteenth-century detective and sensation fiction. Modern defenders as diverse as T. S. Eliot, Raymond Chandler, and Edmund Wilson countered such sentiments with their variously-pointed admirations for the form, while more recent critics have continued the debate over the moral and literary merit of detective fiction, its status as a literary genre, its ideological affiliations, and its evolution as a form of popular culture.

In spite of this cloud of contention — or perhaps in part because of it — contemporary critics repeatedly return to detective literature to illustrate new waves of critical methodology as they begin to come into fashion and establish themselves. In recent decades, detective stories have provided the demonstration pieces of choice for critics of popular culture, narrative theory, gender studies, Marxism, psychoanalysis, the new historicism, and cultural studies, to name a few. As Peter Brooks sees in the Holmes stories an allegory of plot revealing the double logic that drives all narratives, so Jacques Lacan sees in "The Purloined Letter" an allegory of the signifier that reveals the paradoxical logic of the text of the unconscious. Franco Moretti views the detective story as a contest between the individual and the social organism in which the ethic of bourgeois culture is erased from the consciousness of the masses. Michael Holquist reads it as the preeminent literary model for postmodernism's exposure of the subterfuge of order and the fundamental truth of chaos.

One positive outcome of all this critical attention has been to complicate what we mean by the term "detective fiction" and to release it from the exclusive domain of cultists and popular culturists. Without question, we owe a considerable debt to the pioneering criticism on detective fiction written from the perspective of popular culture and formula literature by figures like John G. Cawelti. This important work kept alive a tradition of taking detective fiction seriously and generated in its wake illuminating surveys of the genre by critics like Dennis Porter and Stephen Knight, both of whom offered impressive investigations of the relationship between the genre's broad ideological implications and its formal properties. In the 1980s, scholars went on to focus with more precision and specificity on the genre from other points of view, as manifested in the excellent collection of theoretically-oriented essays edited by Glenn W. Most and William W. Stowe in *The Poetics of Murder* and the distinguished group of essays collected by Umberto Eco and Thomas Sebeok that considered the genre in the light of the history of semiotics and logic.

Together with the rise of cultural studies, critical legal studies, law and literature programs, and the critique and expansion of the canon, work like this has accorded to detective and sensation fiction a more prestigious place in the house of "legitimate" literature. As a result, some of the most provocative current criticism on (especially) nineteenth-century detective fiction is appearing in work that is not concerned with offering another narrative of the genre's history, making a case for its distinctions as an identifiable form, or even setting it aside as a special category of literature. For the purposes of this review, I will examine a selection of these books and individual essays that unapologetically read detective texts alongside and in light of "legitimate" literary and cultural materials, treating them as equal participants in an emerging culture of knowledge and power in the nineteenth century. My survey of the subject is necessarily selective and largely appreciative in nature, therefore, focusing primarily on work that is not specifically "about" detective fiction and would not likely appear in a computer search run on the topic. One of the crucial underlying assumptions of this scholarship and my review of it, in fact, is that the classification and marginalization of popular forms like the detective story are effects of the culture of knowledge and power that produced them.

A logical point of departure from which to trace this trend is D. A. Miller's *The Novel and the Police,* a book that argues for the central importance of the detective's invisibility in the Victorian novel rather than his appearance in it. It is not that the detective isn't present in the novel, but that he is most present where he is least seen. In making a case for the "radical *entanglement* between the nature of the novel and the practice of the police" (2), Miller juxtaposes readings of what have come to be considered standard detective texts (like *The*

Moonstone or *Bleak House*) with a classic work of Victorian realism (*Barchester Towers*) and a central Victorian autobiographical novel (*David Copperfield*). Without dismissing the differences between such texts, Miller makes a compelling argument for their essential equivalence in deploying "representational technologies" that internalize in the novel-reading public (and more broadly in the nineteenth-century bourgeois self) the social practices of surveillance and regulation we associate with the detective police. In its form and its argument, Miller's book redefined the terms in which the Victorian novel was considered. It shifted the critical focus from analyzing the opposition between "high" Victorian realism on the one hand and the subversive "other Victorian" literary underworlds of gothic, detective, and sensation fiction on the other, to recognizing all these manifestations of the novel as continuous expressions — even agents — of a pervasive culture of social discipline.

If anything, detective novels like *Bleak House* and *The Moonstone* are given a privileged place in this analysis since they most conspicuously document the very process Miller investigates. The dual narrative structure and multi-plottedness of *Bleak House,* for example, dramatize the engendering of the desire for a detective plot to "make legible" the insoluble societal riddle of the Chancery plot and the unreadable personal identity of Esther Summerson's autobiography. Similarly, Miller reads the dismissal of Inspector Cuff in *The Moonstone* and his replacement by the improvised detective and narrative collaboration among Franklin Blake, Ezra Jennings, Gabriel Betteredge, and a host of others as demonstrating the appropriation by and distribution of policing power across the society and within the individual. As the title for Miller's *Moonstone* chapter suggests ("From *roman police* to *roman policier*"), this novel enacts in miniature the genre's general transformation from being something about detective work to being something that works like a detective. Rather than declaring detective fiction the illegitimate child of the realistic and the biographical novel, this analysis confers upon it the status of a dominant literary and cultural force that informs and secretly occupies those more traditionally revered forms.

In addition to reframing questions about the proper place of detective fiction in discussion of generic priority and influence in the nineteenth-century novel, Miller's book also furnished the genre with one of its most ambitious and productive applications of Foucauldian analysis. Virtually every subsequent critic of detective fiction has either elaborated on or taken issue with Miller's use of *Discipline and Punish* and his interpretation of the novel as an agent of essentially undifferentiated, monolithic, and irresistible normalizing power in the period. By shifting the terms of the debate about detective fiction and challenging its ghettoization as a subliterary genre, *The Novel and the Police* also succeeded in provoking considerable controversy on this point. Beyond that, the book helped to establish the detective novel as an important factor in the evolution of a repressive liberal culture in the nineteenth century and the modern bureaucratic state to which it gave rise — both of which were based on the invisible but pervasive deployment of discourses and practices of knowledge and control in such unexpected places as the novel.

One of the most impressive recent models for continuing and refining this project is Marie-Christine Leps's *Apprehending the Criminal: The Production of Deviance in Nineteenth-Century Discourse.* While Leps believes Miller's analysis of discursive networks posits too singular and monolithic an ideological force, and that he is too quick to dismiss the novel's capacities for resistance and transgression, she clearly is indebted to his work. Expanding what is essentially literary analysis in Miller, Leps examines the relation between the fictional and the factual discourses of detection and criminality in several other nineteenth-century disciplines. Leps brings together the Sherlock Holmes stories with works by Stevenson, Zola, and Bourget, and explains how such literary materials participated in the production and circulation of the ''truth'' about criminality that was being propounded in scientific research (such as Lombroso's *Criminal Man* or Charles Goring's *The English Convict*) and the popular press (such as the journalistic coverage of the Jack the Ripper murders). Leps takes up each of these discursive fields independently, investigating the cultural conditions that gave rise to them and their relation to the textual forms in which they became manifested.

What Leps discovers in combining these various fields of discourse is that the representation of the criminal in nineteenth-century culture demonstrates particularly well the way in which ''power is both the result and the support of a complex system of production and distribution of knowledge'' in a range of cultural institutions (such as literary entertainment, scientific theory, the operation and reform of the legal system, and the practice of the popular press). Within this process, detective fiction functions differently for Leps than it does for Miller since she allows literary discourse the capacity to critique the system in which it functions — at least to a limited degree. To illustrate, she interprets the ongoing debate about science and literature between Holmes and Watson in the Sherlock Holmes stories as at once an affirmation and a subversion of the absolute claims about the ''nature'' and ''truth'' of the criminal made by the other discursive regimes with which she is concerned.

The exploration of literary texts as transformative agents in the social ''production'' of truth continuous with a widespread culture of discipline is extended into a cogent cultural and narrative critique in Alexander Welsh's *Strong Representations: Narrative and Circumstantial Evidence in England. Strong Representations* is no more a book about detective fiction *per se* than *Apprehending the Criminal* is; indeed it is less so. But it shares the virtue of joining analysis of literary texts with other cultural materials — in this case, legal history and theory, scientific writing, texts on natural religion, and even nineteenth-century criticism of Shakespeare — to show how truth was being created and sustained for Victorians in a particular narrative form that included but was not restricted to detective stories.

Welsh argues persuasively that in the very decades when theorists and practitioners of the law were replacing the authority of verbal testimony with the more telling ''probative force'' of circumstantial evidence, a corresponding shift was taking place in the English novel. That shift can be detected in the ways in which ''the claim to represent reality in novels was expressed by their internal connectedness of circumstances'' rather than by the personal testimony of the fictional author or an elaborate frame of pretended documentation (like letters, memoirs, lost papers, and so forth, purporting to account for the real-life existence of the narrative they contained). When Welsh explains that by ''strong representations'' he refers to narratives of growing cultural authority across a range of disciplines ''that openly distrust direct testimony, insist on submitting witnesses to the test of corroborating circumstances, and claim to know many things without anyone's having seen them at all,'' he describes perfectly the role of the literary detective in the nineteenth century. Aptly, therefore, he incorporates compelling readings of the narrative structure of *The Moonstone* and the composition of *The Ring and the Book* in his analysis of a general transformation of the principles of evidence in the period. Like Miller and like Leps, without writing a book about detective fiction or even about ''literature'' narrowly defined, Welsh has offered a powerful argument for the centrality of the kind of writing we associate with the literary detective in the ordering and maintaining of Victorian culture.

John Kucich has provided an ingenious variation on this theme in another important book on Victorian culture. In *The Power of Lies: Transgression in Victorian Fiction,* Kucich is not so much interested in investigating how truth was produced for the Victorians as he is in determining who possessed the privilege of manipulating it. He is not concerned with the transgressions of criminals but with those of professionals, social initiates, aesthetes, and others who, through their ''dexterity with the truth,'' establish a position of social privilege *within* the ranks of the middle class. In a series of dazzling readings of Victorian novels informed by a nuanced understanding of the history of professionalism in the period, Kucich focuses on the intense power struggle that raged at the boundary between truth and deceit in the nineteenth century. His subtle readings of literary texts makes irresistible his argument that the much-vaunted valorization Victorians placed upon earnestness, truth-telling, and confession was complicated by an elaborately shifting and intensely contested terrain of justified lying.

Pairing writers of detective and sensation novels like Wilkie Collins and Ellen Wood with ''realistic'' novelists like Trollope and Gaskell, Kucich demonstrates how all these texts took part in the endorsement of a moral and epistemological sophistication that redefined stable moral categories without overthrowing the categories of truth and deceit — in acts like Walter Hartright's manipulation of the law and legal documents to establish the identity of Laura Fairlie and himself as her husband, for example. But this much sought-after "transgressive authority" was a privilege that could be earned only by some; it was valued as a form of social resistance for certain emerging classes and "ultimately laid a new foundation for middle-class aesthetic sophistication that would later support modernism's delicate appropriations of scientific and technical authority." To speak of the appropriations of scientific and technical authority, of course, is to invoke the authority best displayed by the literary detective in the nineteenth century; and while this figure is not the express subject of *The Power of Lies,* his presence haunts the argument throughout. In his nineteenth-century incarnation especially, the literary detective polices this transitional space between professional and non-professional discourses, and is specifically empowered to use whatever deceit and disguise might be necessary to deprive others of the power of their lies.

By recognizing detective fiction as one of several legitimate nineteenth-century novelistic forms, scholarship of this kind has fostered the integration of the literary detective into broad interdisciplinary discussions of the Victorian novel and the construction of Victorian culture. It reconfigures our understanding of Victorian realism as well as Victorian detection. This realignment is the subject of Martin Priestman's *Detective Fiction and Literature,* as the book's title suggests. In his consideration of classic detective texts from Poe, Collins, Doyle, and Chandler alongside work by the likes of Aristotle, Sophocles, and Henry James, Priestman explores the shifting boundary between popular and serious literature, arguing that a dialectical relation exists between the two in which each alternately scandalizes, appropriates, and domesticates the energies and techniques of the other. Together with studies like Richard Maxwell's *The Mysteries of Paris and London* and Anne Humpherys's "Generic Strands and Urban Twists: The Victorian Mysteries Novel," *Detective Fiction and Literature* reminds us that generic distinctions and cross-contaminations cannot be regarded as purely formal matters, but are themselves complex historical and sociological events.

This reinvigorated historicist approach to the genealogy of popular genres has been taken up by critics who have moved in new and more complex directions the treatment of detective fiction as an exceptional force in nineteenth-century literary and cultural history. Lawrence Rothfield's *Vital Signs: Medical Realism in Nineteenth-Century Fiction* is a good case in point. By linking a set of intelligent readings of classic texts in nineteenth-century realism (like *Middlemarch* and *Madame Bovary*) with an account of the history of professional medicine, Rothfield demonstrates the ways in which the epistemological orientation, discursive techniques, and professional exactitude of clinical medicine in the period gave rise to the narrative strategies and special authority of the realistic novel. He goes on to claim, however, that as clinical medicine came under attack from other sciences (such as microbiology, cell theory, and embryology), the accompanying epistemic shift was manifested in the development of quasi-realistic genres like detective fiction and naturalism, which staged their own critique of realism and led the way to modernism.

To make this point, Rothfield's chapter on Sherlock Holmes ("From Diagnosis to Deduction: Sherlock Holmes and the Perversion of Realism") argues that detective fiction diverges from realism's "medical" emphasis on the finality of the material self as a pathological "embodied person" in favor of a more "specialized" view of the subject as a collection of physiological material facts — what one might call the individuated body. While the style of Watson's narratives may resemble George Eliot's seeking out the truth about the embodied "person," Rothfield maintains, the methodology of Holmes's investigations has more in common with cubism's piecemeal decomposition and reconstruction of the individuated body's "identity." Detective fiction does not represent a complete break with realism, then, but a distortion or perversion of realistic modes, a shift that is made possible by the reconfiguration of the human sciences and the attendant subordination of the clinician's authority in the latter half of the nineteenth century.

The claim for detective fiction as a transitional narrative mode between nineteenth-century realism and high modernism is also posited in a pair of new books on detective fiction by Martin A. Kayman and Jon Thompson, respectively. Unlike the other work we have considered thus far, these books explicitly engage detective fiction as their primary subject. Like the others, however, they cannot accurately be regarded as "surveys" of the genre but are more properly understood as cultural criticism, distinctly interdisciplinary in their aims and methods. In *From Bow Street to Baker Street: Mystery, Detection and Narrative,* Kayman makes the case that detective narratives are properly read neither as mere puzzles nor as contributions to a repressive system of control. Rather, they are "symbolic and formal explorations in the representation of the mysterious territories of society and of the psyche which cannot be captured within the narrative strategies of literary realism, scientific positivism and contemporary legal structures." While Kayman concludes that detective fiction opposes rather than collaborates with the dominant discourses of the realist novel, science, and the law, he reaches this conclusion by first investigating the rise of the detective as a figure in legal history and then evaluates the cultural appropriation of the detective in the form of "detective literature."

Kayman argues that the classification of certain kinds of writing as detective literature in the nineteenth century emerged as a reaction on the part of the hegemonic force of nineteenth-century reformism. As the novel's claims to the status of serious literature began to depend more and more on the disavowal of its monstrous literary predecessors and the suppression of sensational subjects like monstrosity, insanity, and crime, writing that took up these subjects was subordinated and disregarded. Kayman maintains that these topics survive in what was condescendingly called "detective literature" as the residue of deep cultural "mysteries" that could not be assimilated by the reformist codes of moral management (law and medicine) and stood as a threat to those codes. Kayman reads Lady Audley's secret, for example — as he does Poe's purloined letter or Collins's moonstone — as a sensational signifier, an absence that generates nervous and discursive reactions in characters and readers alike, fracturing the cultural codes that sought to maintain order in the society. Running counter to conventional wisdom on the subject, Kayman argues that Sherlock Holmes cannot be regarded as the embodiment of these unsettling energies in nineteenth-century detection, but is their chief revisionist — a nostalgic and conservative figure rather than a forwarding-looking and subversive one. For Kayman, Holmes represents the final victory of a repressive model of mastery (represented by the dominant reformist discourses of realism, science, and the law against which the literary detective was established), just as Freud looks toward "a new, albeit persistently problematic, articulation of the subject in history and language."

Jon Thompson's *Fiction, Crime, and Empire: Clues to Modernity and Postmodernism* approaches the historical role of detective fiction from a different vantage point and arrives at rather different conclusions. Thompson considers British and American detective fiction — from Poe and Doyle to the present — as the "intrinsically" modernist literary expression of a capitalist and imperial culture dominated by the contradictory forces of constant renewal and disintegration. Defining modernism as "the institutionally and culturally dominant field of literary practices containing residual (realist) as well as emergent (postmodern) elements," Thompson traces out structural and empistemological similarities between detective literature, the modernist movement, and imperialist ideology. In each area, he finds some expression of the struggle between the oppressive hegemony of an elite culture against a suspect, subversive Other that threatens the dominant order either from within or from without. While Thompson's valiant effort to rescue detective fiction from disappearing into representation sometimes presents rather strained analogies between the detective story and modernity, he makes a strong case for the power of these narratives to intervene in history in ways that remain socially significant.

For all the accomplishment and range displayed in much of this scholarship, with one or two exceptions it deals only in glancing ways with the very complicated role of gender in "detective literature." That the authors considered so far are overwhelmingly men may or may not be significant; but the fact remains that women critics are still doing the best work on the genre from this perspective. One example is Virginia Morris's *Double Jeopardy: Women Who Kill in Victorian Fiction,* which offers a compelling historicist and interdisciplinary feminist critique of the characterization of a striking literary figure in Victorian fiction: the woman who kills. In her reading of central works by Dickens, Collins, Eliot,

Hardy, and Doyle against a background of nineteenth-century legal history and social attitudes toward women criminals, Morris examines the double bind of a certain class of Victorian women who were caught in the contradiction of being considered morally superior to men and yet inferior to them in every other way. Her study brings to light the dissonance between what was rather common in Victorian life but relatively rare in Victorian fiction — the woman driven to violence by systematic social oppression, offering that figure as a particularly productive site to explore the invention and enforcement of Victorian sexuality in literary texts.

These concerns are explored in more politically and theoretically sophisticated ways in two recent books on Victorian sensation fiction, one written by Ann Cvetkovich and the other by Tamar Heller. Since these works concern themselves directly with the relation between detective and sensation fiction, they contribute equally to the scholarship in both genres. Cvetkovich's *Mixed Feelings: Feminism, Mass Culture, and Victorian Sensationalism* analyzes the history of sensation, arguing that the link between sensational literature and bodily sensations is (like Victorian sexuality) a politically interested construction — a disciplinary apparatus with a traceable history. In her astute readings of the acts of detection in *Lady Audley's Secret* and *The Woman in White,* for example, Cvetkovich shows that the mad or hysterical woman is offered up in these texts as a scapegoat for the more general insanity manifested broadly across gender lines by middle-class consumer society. In like manner, the successful ''detection'' and identification of otherwise indistinguishable women in these plots turns out to rely upon the imposition of specific social determinations rather than the discovery of inherent or inborn qualities in them. In the brilliant conclusion to the book, Cvetkovich goes on to argue that the techniques of sensationalism were appropriated by writers of high culture like George Eliot to replicate rather than alter the structures of confinement for middle-class women, while Marx's critique of commodity fetishism in *Capital* may be read as appropriating these same techniques progressively, applying them to masculine subjects and domains as well as feminine.

Tamar Heller's *Dead Secrets: Wilkie Collins and the Female Gothic* considers the career of the single author most often identified with sensation fiction to explore the volatile boundaries of Victorian sexuality in light of the analogously unstable outlines of literary genres, social classes, and political ideologies in the period. Like the work of Cvetkovich, Heller's demonstrates that the terms of the ongoing debate over the distinctions between detective fiction, sensation fiction, Gothic, and realism are grounded in a network of social and political conditions, and that the gender affiliations commonly attributed to the readers and writers of these genres are consistent with the policing function of the novel in the nineteenth century, and with its often co-opted manifestations of resistance.

The field of vision for Victorian surveillance extended beyond the boundaries of England itself, of course. Aided by post-colonialist theory and new historicist methodologies, a number of recent journal articles on nineteenth-century detective texts have explored the dialectical relationship between narratives of policing at home and the policies of imperialism abroad. This is the subject of my own "Minding the Body Politic: The Romance of Science and the Revision of History in Victorian Detective Fiction," which takes as its point of departure the Indian Mutiny of 1857 and its reinscription in the detective plots of *The Moonstone* and *The Sign of Four.* I argue that England's imperial crimes and their attendant ideological embarrassments are displaced and transformed in these texts by the "scientific romance" of the detective, a romance that takes over the plots to relocate the signs and even the causes of political crimes in the criminal body. Ashish Roy's "The Fabulous Imperialist Semiotic of Wilkie Collins's *The Moonstone*" also reads Collins's novel as a fictionalization and justification of imperial history. Roy offers an intricate analysis of the text's narrative economy and its complex "semiotic repertoire," both of which entertain and then romance away the possibility of an imperial critique. Ian Duncan's ingenious "*The Moonstone,* the Victorian Novel, and Imperial Panic" provides the most sophisticated treatment of the issue. Duncan argues that by representing India as a kind of sublime, positive alterity which conquers English police skill in the plot, *The Moonstone* resists epistemological totalization or ideological closure on the imperial question. Neither a justification nor a critique of imperialism, as Duncan demonstrates, this detective novel offers instead a nightmare glimpse of the world economy of modernity, where the British themselves turn out to be the colonized subjects of empire, alienated from their own history and dominion.

The colonization of the English subject back home has been the subject of a number of recent essays centering on an analysis of the Sherlock Holmes stories. Since the present decade marks the centennial of the appearance of the best writing in the Holmes canon, it is to be expected that a great deal of scholarship will be generated around him and the literary genre often associated with him. Along with new editions of the "complete" Sherlock Holmes that continue to be produced (by Oxford in 1993, for example), accounts of the "real life" detecting of Arthur Conan Doyle, and photographic essays on Sherlock Holmes's London, some valuable collections of old and new critical essays on Doyle demonstrate the trends in approaching the genre we have been tracing out here (notably, John A. Hodgson's edition of *Sherlock Holmes: The Major Stories with Contemporary Critical Essays* and Harold Orel's *Critical Essays on Arthur Conan Doyle*).

Many of the most provocative recent articles on Holmes (some of which are reprinted in these volumes) reflect the enrichment by interdisciplinary approaches and extra-literary materials we have seen in the other critical work we have examined here. For example, Rosemary Jann's "Sherlock Holmes Codes the Social Body'' offers a sweeping survey of Holmes's deployment of nineteenth-century scientific typologies of the body to argue that the great detective's preference for physiological analysis was a manifestation of concerns over growing instabilities in the classification of class and gender at the turn of the century and was aimed at securing the conservative ideology in which Doyle was deeply invested. My essay, ''The Fingerprint of the Foreigner: Colonizing the Criminal Body in 1890s Detective Fiction and Criminal Anthropology,'' develops this line of argument by reading two Holmes stories together with Havelock Ellis's *The Criminal* and Francis Galton's *Finger Prints* to demonstrate how new scientific technologies for establishing personal identity were related to alterations in British national identity during the same period. An analogous case is made in even more specified terms by Audrey Jaffe in ''Detecting the Beggar: Arthur Conan Doyle, Henry Mayhew, and 'The Man with the Twisted Lip.' '' Jaffe reads this important Holmes story as the quintessential expression of capitalist society's paradoxical insistence upon the truth and the fiction of a singular and essential self. In a model for new historicist analysis, Jaffe argues that just as Mayhew's sociological project necessarily failed at reaching its goal of protecting middle-class identity by establishing and defining that of the poor beggar, Holmes's detective project at once assures his readers that false identities can be exposed and eliminated even as he implicates himself and us in the process of exchange that invents those alternate selves.

Since detective fiction itself — especially Victorian detective fiction — has gained a more legitimate literary status inside and outside the academy, some of the best scholarship in this area has, like D. A. Miller's police, been dispersed and disseminated in less visible ways into more rigorously interdisciplinary criticism of Victorian fiction and culture. Much of this work has deepened and complicated our understanding of the social and epistemological revolutions that shaped the nineteenth-century. It has also helped to explain how a world of DNA fingerprinting, satellite surveillance, and crime-scene computer simulation could become imaginable to us — and how important such representational technologies are to how we conceive of ourselves and how we are conceived by our society. The recent appearance of an interactive computer game called ''Sherlock Holmes, Consulting Detective'' (*Macworld* 1992) and an article on the great detective as the model successful business consultant published in the *Journal of Management Consulting* (1995) should clue us in to the fact that Victorian detection is still, indeed, an industry, and that it survives inside and outside the world of the text. These instances remind us as well that even in the computer age, we are still inclined to apprehend the literary detective — in whatever form he appears — in strictly Victorian terms.

Trinity College

WORKS CONSIDERED

Cawelti, John G. *Adventure, Mystery, and Romance: Formula Stories as Art and Popular Culture.* Chicago: U of Chicago P, 1976.

Cvetkovich, Ann. *Mixed Feelings: Feminism, Mass Culture, and Victorian Sensationalism.* New Brunswick: Rutgers U P, 1992.

Doyle, Arthur Conan. *Sherlock Holmes: The Major Stories with Contemporary Critical Essays.* Ed. John A. Hodgson. New York: St. Martin's, 1994.

Duncan, Ian. "*The Moonstone,* the Victorian Novel, and Imperial Panic," *MLQ* 55:3 (September 1994): 297–319.

Eco, Umberto and Thomas Sebeok, eds. *The Sign of Three: Dupin, Holmes, Peirce.* Bloomington: Indiana U P, 1983.

Heller, Tamar. *Dead Secrets: Wilkie Collins and the Female Gothic.* New Haven: Yale U P, 1992.

Humpherys, Anne. "Generic Strands and Urban Twists: The Victorian Mysteries Novel." *Victorian Studies* 34 (Summer 1991): 455–72.

Jaffe, Audrey. "Detecting the Beggar: Arthur Conan Doyle, Henry Mayhew, and 'The Man with the Twisted Lip,' " *Representations* 31 (Summer 1990): 96–117.

Jann, Rosemary. "Sherlock Holmes Codes the Social Body." *ELH* 57 (1990): 685–70.

Kayman, Martin A. *From Bow Street to Baker Street: Mystery, Detection, and Narrative.* New York: St. Martin's, 1992.

Knight, Stephen. *Form and Ideology in Detective Fiction.* London: Macmillan, 1980.

Kucich, John. *The Power of Lies: Transgression in Victorian Fiction.* Ithaca and London: Cornell U P, 1995.

Leps, Marie-Christine. *Apprehending the Criminal: The Production of Deviance in Nineteenth-Century Discourse.* Durham and London: Duke U P, 1992.

Maxwell, Richard. *The Mysteries of Paris and London.* Charlottesville and London: U P of Virginia, 1992.

Miller, D. A. *The Novel and the Police.* Berkeley: U of California P, 1988.

Morris, Virginia B. *Double Jeopardy: Women Who Kill in Victorian Fiction.* Lexington: U P of Kentucky, 1990.

Most, Glenn and William Stowe, eds. *The Poetics of Murder: Detective Fiction and Literary Theory.* New York: Harcourt, Brace, Jovanovich, 1983.

Orel, Harold, ed. *Critical Essays on Sir Arthur Conan Doyle.* New York: G. K. Hall, 1992.

Porter, Dennis. *The Pursuit of Crime: Art and Ideology in Detective Fiction.* New Haven: Yale UP, 1991.

Rothfield, Lawrence. *Vital Signs: Medical Realism in Nineteenth-Century Fiction.* Princeton: Princeton U P, 1992.

Roy, Ashish. "The Fabulous Imperialist Semiotic of Wilkie Collins's *The Moonstone,*" *New Literary History* 24 (Summer 1993): 657–81.

"Sherlock Holmes, Consulting Detective." *Macworld: The Macintosh Magazine* 9:8 (August 1992): 173.

Thomas, Ronald R. "The Fingerprint of the Foreigner: Colonizing the Criminal in 1890s Detective Fiction and Criminal Anthropology," *ELH* 61 (Fall, 1994): 653–81.

———. "Minding the Body Politic: The Romance of Science and the Revision of History in Victorian Detective Fiction," *Victorian Literature and Culture* 19 (1991): 233–54.

Thompson, Jon. *Fiction, Crime, and Empire: Clues to Modernity and Postmodernism.* Urbana and Chicago: U of Illinois P, 1993.

Webb, James R. "Sherlock Holmes on Consulting." *Journal of Management Consulting* 8:3 (1995): 34.

Welsh, Alexander. *Strong Representations: Narrative and Circumstantial Evidence in England.* Baltimore and London: Johns Hopkins U P, 1992.

HIT AND MYTH: NOTES ON A MODE IN LITERARY AND CULTURAL STUDIES

By Herbert F. Tucker

1

EACH OF THE BOOKS I have chosen for review concerns the vicissitudes of a *modern myth,* a term that seems self-contradictory but is actually no more than a paradox. Most of us, even us Victorianists who should know better, bring to the topic of mythology a set of thoroughly Victorian organicist prejudices. These add up, says Chris Baldick in my favorite book of the lot, to a "myth of myth," which holds that real myths, originating in the collective anonymity of oral tradition, may be ratified only in time's slow-chapped power, by gradual historical accretion. Yet consider a striking counterexample from our own day, the case of James Bond. In Agent 007, as Tony Bennett and Janet Woollacott tell it, we have a figure who attained world standing within a single generation. If Bennett and Woollacott are even half right, then under the supersaturated conditions of mass communication the distribution of a manufactured figure like Bond — and the random, mythically crucial process of his collective appropriation as common property — may take place on a drastically foreshortened time scale. That this acceleration of cultural mythopoeia was well underway in Britain by the second third of the nineteenth century is strongly suggested by the ensemble of titles here under review. The Victorian heirs of Vico and Herder might not think it possible, but the making of a modern mythology got into full swing right under their noses.

I cannot better the adroit discussion of this matter in Baldick's opening chapter; so I simply recommend it, framing things my own way instead with a two-step anecdote. Frame 1, 1984: A friend remarks to me late one afternoon, at an hour when our toddlers are receiving preschool indoctrination in the next room through the good graces of the Children's Television Workshop, that *Sesame Street* is providing the rising generation with just that common mythology which we have been taught the modern world distinctly lacks. I nod and ponder. Frame 2, 1992: I am sitting in the waiting room of an orthodontist; my toddler has become a teen, and the Vice Presidency of the United States has devolved on a man whose youth appeal, as events have made plain even to his sympathizers, outshines his fitness for world leadership. In a book of drawings on my lap the wicked humorist Callahan depicts the Vice President's mind by means of a pie graph, one vast slice of which bears the legend "Big Bird."[1]

Several of the scholars this review treats could no doubt make nice analytic work of the cartoonist's happy capture of the quality, and the media modality, of national life in the 90s. I bring it up, however, as evidence of the categorical validity of modern mythology as such. The fact that so many of us from so many backgrounds continue to live together in a society that is no less civil than it is depends on another fact. We hold in common certain typical figures: stories, scenarios, images usually converging on a person whose name everybody knows everybody knows. Such figures may invigorate the culture or they may deplete it; but they manifestly, relentlessly inflect its currencies. One or two of my authors discuss these figures under the sign of the "hero" or the "legend"; but *myth* remains the term of choice, preferred the more strongly the more rooted a scholar's concern with culture in a generally anthropological sense.

Solicit cultures and they present you with their myths; map a myth and you have x-rayed the culture it lives in. But where that culture is modern culture — the one that produces, among other things, anthropologically oriented scholarship on myth — myths start to display arresting peculiarities. One curious feature that distinguishes a modern myth from the traditionary myths of premodern societies is that the modern myth is very likely to have been *invented.* Not in the trivial sense that every existing thing originated somehow, but in a quite specific, often legally defended and bureaucratically registered sense, the bulk of the myths we hold by started out as *fictions*: textually situated characters made up by an author whom history vouches for and given to the world in a particular work that bears a date and, in every recent instance, a copyright to match.

When does such an authored fiction become a modern myth? Taken as a request for historical information, this is a question on which my double handful of titles preserve silence: the transformation is seldom pinpointed on the calendar, but is rather perceived to have occurred after a due interval of percolation and seasoning. Taken more generally, though, as an inquiry into enabling conditions, the question of origins elicits wide agreement. A modern myth is born, my authors concur, when it escapes its founding text, breaking out of individual proprietorship and into the cultural imaginary.[2] Launched into the sphere of common knowledge by an original work of extraordinary popularity and stamina, the modern myth attracts such recognition that the ur-work, while it does not fall away, becomes strictly speaking superfluous; becomes indeed a version, quaint and creaky, of the independently living thing it has brought into the world.

The once authored fiction attains and keeps mythic status through the self-propelling popular mechanics of fame in an era of mass publicity. Glistening with recognition, the modern myth infiltrates the cultural memory banks, where dwell the secular immortals. There it becomes available in a de facto public domain for appropriation by whoever wants it, and for purposes that may range from highbrow fiction through political cartooning to the selling of peanut butter.

The different uses to which a modern myth may be put make it a highly eligible index of divisions within the social formation it has fused with, and also of the formative changes that have constituted its history. So no wonder modern myths have attracted lots of scholarly attention during the ten years covered by our sample. At an epoch when literary studies have been conspicuously outward bound, compassing an expanded range of texts, genres, audience strata, and even material media, the renewed investigation of myth has offered the inquirer a whole menu of timely challenges. Here is an arena where textualism and contextualism both demand their due; where an acknowledged classic has made an incalculably diffusive difference in the wide world, yet where the "text" under study entails, if it does not in effect become, the mobile context out of which any given mythic instance is produced; where a history of mythic instances provides a capsule history of culture in convenient synecdoche; where the myth's transgressions of genre, medium, and national language reward advancing methods of interdisciplinary research; where the cells of deep structure may be unlocked by a new, anti-essentialist archaeology of vogues and surfaces. Undertaking to read the air we breathe, the analysis of a well-chosen myth puts cultural studies in a nutshell.

Above all, such study offers to combine glamour with safety. The proving ground of modern myth is the zone where, by definition, literature directly and conspicuously merges with popular culture — not because somebody says so but by universal agreement. What the last decade's most energetically prosecuted theories have announced in general about the social imbrication of literature emerges in myth studies as a matter of historical fact that calls for no fancy special pleading. The student of a modern myth's career therefore enjoys at one and the same time the prestige that now attaches to cultural studies, and the methodological security of what proves in practice to be a quite uncontroversial explanatory maneuver. Patiently tracking the thread which your topic has laid down before you, as a modern myth scholar you can hardly miss your way from the academic ivory tower into the marketplace of popular culture; yet if the weather should turn nasty your way back remains clearly marked too. At a time in literary studies when so many theories and approaches have been under construction that the critical air thickens with methodological dust, the hit-and-myth approach has clearly fortified the credibility of many a book project. It has also offered, to all but the most puritanically self-denying projectors (Rose,

Bennett and Woollacott), certain retrograde satisfactions involving a hermeneutic fusion between the critic's understanding and the original author's meaning.

2

Malory's King Arthur being a traditional legend and Marlowe's Doctor Faustus in some sort a real fifteenth-century man, the first English mythmaker in our special sense turns out to be Shakespeare. The honor is highly appropriate for a writer who has been accounted (most recently by Harold Bloom) *the* early modern creator of reflexive self-consciousness. For some ironic residue of self-reflexivity inhabits most instances of modern myth — as it does, needless to say, all contemporary studies of the subject. In *Shylock: A Legend and Its Legacy,* John Gross has written a strongly personal book that traces the familiar yet still breathtaking miracle whereby Shakespeare wrought a strong personality out of doubly unpropitious circumstances: in this case, the blunt Tudor caricature of the Jew, and the generic drive of comedy away from individuality into a bland economy of sameness. The emergence of personality also norms the history Gross narrates of Shylock's representations across 400 years and around the world. A raw clown in the seventeenth century and a sublime villain in the eighteenth, Shylock held on until, under Romanticism, Kean's sympathetic performance and Hazlitt's analytic vindication prepared the way that led through "the growth of nineteenth-century liberalism" (132) to Irving's portrayal of heroically dignified victimage.

Three centuries is a long wait for recognition, and yet Gross's metaphor of "growth" implies that it was just a matter of time before anglophone culture and its conditions of dramatic production caught up with the complexities of Shakespeare's script. This evolutionary, progressive understanding of mythic history merits emphasis here, since it represents one tendency to which the hit-and-myth approach is markedly liable. To be sure, Gross is not simply a Whig historian of the Shylock myth. He knows too much to fall into the Victorian error of identifying contemporary perspectives with the vantage of eternity, and (like all the authors here reviewed) he expressly disclaims the privilege of uttering the last word on his subject. And yet (like almost all the authors here reviewed) he does exercise something like that privilege by putting his own interpretation of Shylock last within the book, where it has the effect of a fifth-act anagnorisis. Gross also ballasts that interpretation with the weight of a fairly strict-constructionist intentionalism, pronouncing on what "Shylock is meant to be" (347): namely, a villain who is menacing, in ways firmly associated with traditional images of the Jewish usurer, yet who is redeemed into sympathy by the greatness with which he is imagined.

This happens to strike me too as the truth of the matter, but it is my duty here to call attention to the pattern of reinforcement whereby the modern-myth critic makes his truth tell. The rehearsal of Shylock versions from many periods and venues ultimately authorizes an identification of the critic with the bard, and of the myth's durable meaning (Shylock according to Gross) with its first written instantiation (Shylock according to Shakespeare). The proliferating afterlife of the myth ultimately realizes a guiding principle that was present from the beginning. In theory modern mythographers like Gross hold the authorized version to be inexhaustible.[3] But in practice they mostly invoke its authority for the perennial purpose of setting standards and inventorying failures. That clicking sound you hear as their books approach closure indicates that the interlocking system of literary interpretation and literary history still works.[4]

This maneuver is exceptionally overt in Gross, I suspect for two reasons. One of them has to do with the special conditions of dramatic art, which is intrinsically conservative just as the symphony and ballet are. Even the most radical production of *The Merchant of Venice* must orbit Shakespeare's script more closely than a discrete narrative version of a myth will do. (The same principle *a fortiori* distinguishes the books here reviewed from reception histories.) Indeed, insofar as any actor is *interpreting* Shylock, his performance falls short of the escape thrust that impels the modern myth into being. Shylock arrived at that mythic threshold only in the 1930s, at a point in the history of the West when sympathy or antipathy for the figure of the Jew became, inescapably, more than a theatrical pastime. The terrible surcharge which Shylock then acquired is the second reason I would adduce for the moral watch Gross keeps over his myth. His most powerful sequence juxtaposes the evenhanded Gielgud production (London, 1938) and the coolly disengaged scholarship of Mark Van Doren's *Shakespeare* (New York, 1939) with the contemporaneous reports of the Austrian *Anschluss,* for which Nazi productions of *The Merchant* during the thirties had at some level helped pave the way. With this failure of the humane imagination Gross rings down part 2 of the book ("Interpretations") and opens part 3 ("A Citizen of the World"): clearly the transition thus marked is also the transition from scripted fiction to myth. Shylock's mythic latency was suddenly precipitated out of Shakespeare by the abomination of the Holocaust, which imparted an ethical amplitude so great as to unfit him as anything *but* a myth, enlarged beyond the capacity of stage representation in our time.

If the moral commitment of this book occasionally distends its argument or obscures its scholarship, these are the defects of the real virtues that found it (uniquely on our list) a home with an American trade publisher. A more serious defect, however, is the largely blinkered vision with which Gross regards the part played in the Shylock mythology by economics. A curt late chapter on "Economic Man" establishes Gross's contempt for Marxism, and its vitriol helps one guess why the previous 300 pages have said so little about money. This bias has a particularly unfortunate effect on the account of nineteenth-century reactions to Western literature's most notorious moneylender. Some of the best nineteenth-century commentary Gross quotes suggests that Shylock served others than Marx (among them Byron and Ruskin) as a lightning rod for the mystique of capital in its superintendence of an ascendant credit empire. But Gross does not pursue these suggestions. Instead of sifting out economic implications from the racial remarks that have shadowed them throughout Shylock's history, Gross at every opportunity privileges the antisemitic over the anticapitalist alarm. Such priorities, as Ruskin once complained, have often been red herrings to distract and disable "wholesome indignation against usurers" (289). To the extent that Ruskin was right, Gross is wrong, in his contextual understanding of the Victorian *Merchant* and thus of an entire nineteenth-century movement of mind that wound the spring for Shylock's leap into mythology later on.

That said, give me Gross's myth of concern any day over the academic neutrality of its companion volume here, *Shakespeare's Caliban: A Cultural History.* The impersonal profile of this book may result from its collaborative authorship, by critic Alden Vaughan and historian Virginia Mason Vaughan. But its tone-death also illuminates a problem that potentially besets all studies of the hit-and-myth kind: information overload. Any claim to mythic status that is advanced on behalf of a fictional character rests perforce on a quantitative data base. Since ubiquity and universal recognition are beyond demonstration, myth scholars are tempted instead to invoke the arithmetical sublime, amassing and marshalling instances so as to persuade the reader that those instances are as good as innumerable. The risk in this, of course, is that the trees of evidence will obscure the forest of thesis. The synchronic context that lends pattern and point to a given episode in the myth's career, or the narrative argument which links episodes into a history, will be crowded out by ill coordinated examples. To this risk the Vaughans succumb pretty badly. *Shakespeare's Caliban* is too arbitrary an omnium-gatherum to be of much more than instrumental use as a hewer of wood and drawer of water for more powerfully theorized studies that may follow it.[5]

Not that no path of diachronic argument emerges, but you have to bushwhack in order to find it. Like Shylock, Caliban spent the seventeenth and much of the eighteenth century in grotesque disgrace, but Garrick's restoration of the original *Tempest* script signalled a revival of respect for Shakespeare that rubbed off on his creations (176). As Gross also demonstrates apropos Shylock, toward the turn of the nineteenth century actors found a tragic dimension in the monstrous outsider. In Caliban's case it remained for Romantic critics like Hazlitt to attach this tragic potential to revolutionary sympathies (104), and for visual artists like Robert Smirke to represent it in liberal images advocating indigene rights (233). By mid-century, abolitionist agitation and the shock waves of Darwinism sent Caliban over the top into myth, where he became variously available for Browning's dramatic monologue, Renan's dour essay on biological and political progress, and in our time Auden's lacerating soliloquy. It is the political valence of Caliban's servitude and resistance that has overshadowed twentieth-century appropriations: Americans took him over concurrently with the rise of U.S. imperialism (120–25); and postcolonialist writers have flung him in the face of oppression ever since, first as the brutal Yanqui and then as the unrepentant guerrilla.

This is an engaging and instructive story, but the reader has to piece it together with little help from the Vaughans. Their art history, intellectual history, stage history are herded into discrete chapters that discourage precisely the broader "cultural history" which their subtitle promises. Beyond that, the authors seem methodologically intimidated by the politics of their subject. They treat New Historicist readings at second hand and with kid gloves; the theme of Caliban's labor they leave nearly untouched. Time and again one feels the Vaughans drawing back from the large synthetic sweep, the bold gamble on a culturally significant resonance. Yet these are the ventures which studies of this kind must hazard if they are to overcome the drag of their own documentation and be more than *catalogues raisonnées.* The Vaughans' discussion of Caliban's presence in the film *Forbidden Planet* is admittedly venturesome and intriguing, but in just these respects it stands out from their book as a whole, which even in its film and television coverage most often feels derivative, hurried, or both. Thus *Shakespeare's Caliban* offers neither the provocation of a strong thesis (such as Green and Baldick propound), nor the informational convenience of tabular chronology and bibliography (schemes which free Davis and Rose to write as vividly as they do).

That both Shylock and Caliban rode to respectability around 1800 on the coattails of their increasingly revered creator seems more than merely coincidental. It seems especially so when we try to think of a modern myth that is not, like them, indelibly associated with an outstanding *character* (as against such authorless and many-heroed traditions as the matter of Troy, the Nibelungenlied, the Mahabharata).[6] Take as a hard case *A Christmas Carol,* the one modern myth on our list not explicitly named for a protagonist: even here Dickens's tale has been Scrooge's show almost from the first, with Bob Cratchit for visual relief and an obligatory sound bite from Tiny Tim. We may summon up Wonderland or Neverland, but only by calling first on Alice or Peter Pan. So it is with the Shakespearean myths. When Caliban grabs the microphone, Prospero looks bad, Ariel evaporates, and Miranda needs to be rescued all over again.[7]

And yet it is crucial to the mythmaking process that these subordinates should live on, in however vestigial a way, as significantly resisting others. For it seems that a culture embraces a myth when it has discerned there a social image of itself; and our sample inventory of myths the West has embraced since the turn of the nineteenth century suggests that those fictions which graduate to myth have imagined society in terms that oppose individual to collective values. Shylock and Caliban may owe their mythic longevity to their origin not in tragedy but comedy, a genre that locks into place an essentially antagonistic relation between the outsider victim and the insider establishment. By enforcing this relation structurally, instead of through the free moral struggle of a tragic hero, comedy paradoxically leaves its gagged victim the freer to find mythic expression elsewhere, in subsequent works. Thus the extroverted grotesques Shylock and Caliban have become modern myths, while the introverted Hamlet has not.[8] If Romeo and Juliet have broken genre ranks and made it into myth from tragedy, this may be due to the fatalistic way Shakespeare pits their isolated naivete against family and city. Their case seems an exception that proves the generic rule: abstraction from a hostile yet comedic social order becomes, in them alone among Shakespeare's tragic protagonists, an ideal to die for — and to live again by.

3

From Shakespeare to Ian Fleming, then, the evidence of our modern myths shows how the abstraction of the individual from society is a definitive fantasy among us, perhaps a necessary one. That this fantasy nevertheless always bears social meanings is the burden of Martin Green's fine essay *The Robinson Crusoe Story.* This book, while quite legible on its own, should ideally be read alongside the pathbreaking work Green has been doing for the last two decades on the role which adventure narrative plays in modern formations of sexuality and nationality. Green's important critical oeuvre deserves wider exposure and discussion than it has to my knowledge received; within the context it provides, some of what can seem digressive or sketchy in *The Robinson Crusoe Story* falls into place in a searching and, yes, ruggedly individualistic analysis that goes to the heart of the modern mythmaking enterprise.[9] Green handles the endemic coverage problem with a veteran's deftness, frankly acknowledging that the Crusoe tradition is alive in many genres and tongues, and that as yet no one has even catalogued the torrent of *Robinsonaden,* much less analyzed it. Green addresses his task instead by identifying a dozen successor texts to Defoe's, and devoting to each a meditative response that is founded on impressive historical learning and draws freely on dozens of other works in the tradition.

The resulting narrative runs as follows. Defoe's novel was always a hit, but the first step in its mythification was taken by eighteenth-century educational theorists, most importantly Rousseau. In selecting the shipwreck and island episodes as required reading for his *Emile,* Rousseau set the mythic parameters that were to matter to posterity. He also established the dialectically related categories — romantic and economic — in which the myth's commerce between individuality and society would be grasped. Crusoe as Romantic Man overcame the dualism of subject and object through a naturally developmental holism; Crusoe as Economic Man seized the world of objects for their immediate use value, deferring but never forgetting the exchange value they would eventually resume in the economized web of human relations. While the pedagogical function of the Crusoe myth never disappeared altogether, the variety of uses found for it during the nineteenth century makes it, in Green's hands, a virtual blueprint for stages in the phenomenon that contemporary pundits from all lands hailed as "the surge of Anglo-Saxon success" (206) and associated with Defoe's quintessential Englishman.

Early in the century a conservative Romantic organicism brought forth Johann David Wyss's *Swiss Family Robinson,* which performed the amazing cultural feat of making Crusoe's social bell jar the venue for a communitarianism rooted in family values. Green stumbles for once, I believe, in declaring Wyss's evangelicalism a brand new element (as if Bunyan had not been an indispensable resource for Defoe a century before). But Green shows very well how an unswerving patriarchy sustains the *Gemütlichkeit* of Wyss's work, while also acknowledging that the oddly diffracted circumstances of its publication made the *Swiss Family* from the first a multiple-versioned work well on the road to mythification.[10] Each of Green's four novelists from the middle of the century helped brick the wall of empire. Captain Marryat's *Masterman Ready* portended a siege mentality that was suitable for missionary and colonial outposts alike. Fenimore Cooper in *The Crater* put epic starch into the Crusoe tradition by introducing as a newly prominent motif the march of civilization under an elite leadership capable of holding the course against vulgar degeneracy. *The Coral Island* by R. M. Ballantyne, dividing its concerns between the sheer fun of boys' adventure and the administrative management of men, gave imaginative form to a primary Victorian dichotomy between work and leisure. Allied to these, Jules Verne's chief contribution to the myth was an updated stress on technology and on male bonding within the corps of Western engineers destined to implement it.

I have made the imperialist accretions of the Crusoe myth look more inevitably coordinated than Green's suppler chapters do, but my summary should illustrate the coherence of his demonstration that subliterary entertainment did important High Victorian cultural work. The next step in Green's demonstration is more intricate, and more problematic. At the acme of overt imperialism during the 1880s and 1890s, the most influential British *Robinsonaden* set about de-realizing the material conditions of expansion and conquest which had been staple topics since Defoe. Stevenson's *Treasure Island* aestheticized adventure, on the one hand, bearing boys'-book fun all the way back over the realist threshold into immaterial romance; on the other hand it replaced the evacuated materiality of the tale with a newly decadent mystique of evil. In Green's other major island escapade from the fin de siècle, *Peter Pan,* myth became not just an aestheticized entertainment but a knowing confection. Barrie's sly reduction of the Crusoe story carried fantasy to fairytale extremes, by arts of miniaturization which foregrounded not man's control over natural resources but the author's control over cultural ones. In the wake of the World Wars, the Robinson Crusoe story underwent ironic reductions symptomatic of recurrent crises in twentieth-century masculinity (Greene, Waugh, Michel Tournier, and best of all Golding's *Lord of the Flies*).

Still, it is the swath Crusoe cut across the nineteenth century that remains the heart of *The Robinson Crusoe Story,* and it prompts one further reflection here. Accounting for the century's late decadence elicits from Green a rhetoric of "subversiveness" (149) and "seduction" (157) that does not arise earlier in the book. Its appearance here seems due to a certain disappointment that the adventure story after Stevenson should have gone literary and begun trafficking with its sworn foe, the world of haute-culture and the academy. For Green's entire take on the adventure mode depends on a radical discrimination between it and literature as such. The two modes, he asserts, have been mutually exclusive for so long that intellectuals have signally failed to grasp in narratives of adventure the very imaginative forms which have done most to shape the modern world. A large and impressive claim, but one whose defense in 1990 probably necessitates a more comprehensive engagement than Green has thus far evinced with the more recent work of his comrades in "cultural studies" (12). For in this work the analytics of popular and of elite cultural forms have witnessed considerable rapprochement. To stay only with our authors here, there are tendencies in the books by Baldick, Rose, Bennett and Woollacott that erode Green's basic distinction between the high and low roads of culture. One could also dispute the point from a more conventional position in genre criticism: a close look at the overlap between adventure writing and romance might do much to complicate Green's literary sociology, on grounds of narrative form as well as of class and gender. Still, Green's ideas are important ones, and it will be to everyone's advantage that they should be ventilated and debated.

4

Nineteenth-century scholars can learn much from Crusoe, Caliban, and Shylock because the cultural installation of modern myths is primarily a nineteenth-century phenomenon. This may be why Romanticists and Victorianists have been quicker than others to generate hit-and-myth studies. In any case, our books on Frankenstein and on the Lady of Shalott have been out long enough to obviate extended notice here, and to permit reflection instead on the critical mode they represent. Within the hit-and-myth mode, *In Frankenstein's Shadow* by Chris Baldick seems to me the exemplary work to date. True, the extraordinary multivalence of the Frankenstein myth may have given Baldick a special boost, but by the same token the cultural power of this particular myth means that the competition is stiffer here than elsewhere. The Frankenstein materials are a multimedia labyrinth, and the critical works they have attracted are legion.[11] What makes

Baldick's work so impressive is the way he threads the labyrinth by holding fast to a dialectical notion of the relation between a myth and its instances.

The uncanny, polyvalent dynamic of the Frankenstein myth remains Baldick's unifying topic, but as he moves across the nineteenth century he remembers that like other myths this one lives only in its textually and contextually specific actualizations. He keeps at his disposal a sliding scale of emphases that are elicited as needed by historically changing pertinences in diverse genres: Shelley's Gothic novel and its science-fiction progeny, a host of plays and pamphlets and political cartoons, history (Carlyle), social science (Marx), and the differing realisms of Eliot and Zola. This flexibility lets Baldick pursue analogical hunches which can seem at first blush implausible but nearly always secure conviction. Furthermore, the sequence of strong local readings enacts a sustained demonstration of the Frankenstein myth's power to evoke shifting ideological complexes about control and revolt. Baldick succeeds, in a word, where both Gross and the Vaughans fall short: next to his flexibility, the former looks a bit stiff and cranky; where the latter suffer surfeit and indigestion, he assimilates and organizes. Sharing Green's capable sense of the reach and import of modern myth, in theoretical and generic terms Baldick is even more, well, adventurous. At the same time, *In Frankenstein's Shadow* does not induce the sense (not seldom oppressive in Bennett and Woollacott) that a myth is being analyzed in order to service a theory.

It is inevitably something of a comedown to move from the international electricity of Frankenstein to the insular handicraft of the Lady of Shalott, and from Baldick's triumphs to the comparative unsophistication of what are the earliest titles on our list: Jennifer Gribble's monograph and an exhibition catalogue consisting mainly of essays by graduate collaborators with George Landow at Brown a decade ago. No more than mythlet status may be claimed for Tennyson's Lady, not even here among Victorianist friends. But these two books make it plain that she does meet the basic criteria: her story does encapsulate pervasive conflicts concerning gender, class, and the instability of rival subcultural interests; and her representations do cross genre and media lines in ways that manifestly exceed her creator's purpose. In fact, the emancipation of the Lady of Shalott from Tennyson's influence is something that these books are if anything too ready to take for granted.

The Brown catalogue often treats images of the Lady as if she has a pedigree no different in kind from Arachne's or Guinevere's, and has as well a settled iconographic tradition sanctioning art-historical business as usual. Gribble likewise not only finds the Lady at large in the work of novelists from Charlotte Brontë to Henry James, but even goes on at one point (49–52) about Jane Austen, who died fifteen years before Tennyson's poem appeared. This anachronism implies that Gribble is not studying a modern myth in our sense of the term, but is at most comparing versions of an archetype (imprisoned damsel, mirror on the wall) — or at worst itemizing the inscriptions of patriarchy on heroines posed in domestic interiors. Here, and also in several of the essays on the exhibition at Brown, an exclusive interest in later reworkings forfeits those opportunities for critique that arise when the versions of a modern myth confront their original. Where Dickens's Dorrit and Eliot's Dorothea can subject Tennyson's Lady to "critique," but not vice versa, it seems the ironic astringencies of early Victorian Romanticism are being evaded for the sake of upbeat discoveries that with the proper attitude a beleaguered heroine can learn to regard "herself and the world she reflects more directly and openly" (105). Not in Tennyson she can't. The more clearly Gribble's reader recollects the austerity of the original poem, the more ruthlessly the myth her book flourishes exacts its revenge.

The most interesting survivals of the Lady of Shalott turn out to occur in visual images rather than novels, and at the level of aesthetic form rather than represented content. This seems an appropriate development for a modern myth first given to the world in verse, and not in prose of such questionable shape as Defoe's and Shelley's. It may be that the relative elaborateness of poetry deters the cultural seizure of what can seem perfectly wrought already: formal polish in an initiating fiction may actually stunt mythic growth. At all events Tennyson's Lady, being herself a visual artist split by incompatible allegiances to art and to reality, enjoyed her most vivid Victorian afterlife in nonliterary media. This may be why Gribble's most memorable comparatist insight involves a painting (Hunt's "Awakened Conscience"), and why the most provocative essays from *Ladies of Shalott* prove to be those centering on painterly techniques that parallel Tennyson's in verse. Analyzing the famous images Holman Hunt made of the Lady, Marc Rolnik and Timothy Rodgers draw attention to formal features in the division and texture of the picture plane. These, while no doubt derived as the authors say from Dutch or Pre-Raphaelite masters, may also owe a thing or two to Tennyson's asymmetrical proportioning of the stanza and his neutrally flat management of images.

"My dear Hunt," the poet grumbled, "I never said that the young woman's hair was flying all over the shop." To which the painter replied, with mythmaker's license: "No, but you never said it wasn't" (Gribble 2). Extrapolation and its lucrative henchman sequelization have been the more ordinary methods of survival among modern myths: witness *Shylock's Revenge, Son of Frankenstein,* the naked opportunism of the next James Bond movie. It is worth remarking that the Victorian visual appropriation of the Lady of Shalott proceeded by *interpolation* instead: a weaving of detail into the spaces left by the original text.[12] Tennyson's successors filled out his poem by means of an embroidery that not only was quite Lady-like but in some respects was foreordained by the poem's staging of perception and reception as problems in optics. The precision with which its best illustrators seized on the crises of seeing that are represented within "The Lady of Shalott" suggests that these are the places where its mythic soul lay. Hunt bred his myth out of the artistic producer's dilemma (the Lady caught between mirror and window), D. G. Rossetti his out of the equal and opposite dilemma of the artistic consumer (Lancelot conning the Lady's corpse as aesthetic object). Both artists found, between the lines as it were, mythic gaps within the original text where Tennyson had figured, for those with eyes to see it, the price of fame under the conditions of an art given over to the market — which is to say, the conditions of modern myth itself.

5

What is true of the mythlet Lady of Shalott seems no less true of her more robust Victorian peers. Superstars like Ebenezer Scrooge, Alice in Wonderland, and Peter Pan (stars, too, of the second magnitude like the Pied Piper, Heathcliff, and Mr. Kurtz) were first introduced to the world in narratives incorporating overtures that appear, in retrospect at least, to foretell their imminent mythification. Maybe a built-in logic of this prophetic sort animates modern myths right across the board. But there is special reason to seek such a logic in myths whose ur-texts appeared after 1800. For, from that time forward, the dissemination of enlightened ideas about culture and history made it an increasingly important part of a modern education to understand the role played in culture by the evolutionary transmission of legendary ballads and tales — and, for that matter, the classics and indeed the very scriptures. Some grasp of the life and death cycle of a society's traditions became indispensable equipment for living in an era that knew itself to *be* an era, and whose public discourse about culture was successively dominated by Carlyle's expostulations over the fortunes of the "Mythus," Max Müller's lectures on solar mythology, and the comparatist anthropology of Tylor, Frazer, and others. Such being the knowledge that made the Victorians modern, the most culturally ambitious popular authors capitalized on it by putting a steady flow of candidate myths up for collective adoption. And they made sure to equip these candidates with suggestions, if not outright instructions, for their own reproduction.

Paul Davis makes this point right away in *The Lives and Times of Ebenezer Scrooge*: "Rather than beginning as an oral story that was later written down, the *Carol* was written to be retold" (3). More is meant here by "retold" than the familiar scenario of hearthside reading, or the author's public performances, or even the nearly instantaneous machinery of appropriation whereby Dickens's text was fully pirated within three weeks of publication and, within three more, translated to several metropolitan and provincial stages. The spectacular explosion of *A Christmas Carol* into its fissioning versions forms the larger subject of Davis's book, which arranges these versions into the sort of sequential history we have been considering already. From the standpoint of the modern mythography analyst, though, the most intriguing moments of *The Lives and Times* are those that give insight into features of the original text which facilitated so extraordinary a cultural destiny, by anticipating it as a matter of narrative form.

Davis distinguishes between "the *Carol*" (Dickens's 1843 fictional text) and "The Carol" (the myth it has effectively become) — a useful distinction, if one that can be carried too far. "The Carol is the sum of all its versions, of all its revisions, parodies, and piracies"; Davis accordingly "recognizes all the versions of the Carol as manifestations of an ongoing myth in the consciousness of the industrial era" (5). *All* the versions? Not today, thanks. When modern mythographers take to this hyperbolically totalizing way of explaining their work, start sniffing for incense, but don't take them at their word.[13] The principle of universal inclusion would if acted on make hit-and-myth books intolerably boring. In fact, we may be grateful that Davis like others has seen the practical wisdom of arguing by historical synecdoche. Neither the lavish dispersal of fourscore illustrations across his book, nor a discursive breeziness that is as apt to ruffle as to soothe, seriously distracts attention from a firm argument that moves in roughly twenty-year increments through phases in the Carol's development.

Davis links his several phases to definitive period crises. These are in every case clichés of social and intellectual history, but they serve as a background to Davis's real business, which is to find out what succeeding festive generations, and the customized Carol they made for themselves, can tell us about each other. The undercurrent theme of the Carol within Dickens's lifetime was ambivalence over urbanization, while in the 1860s and 1870s it turned to the struggle of faith with doubt. During the decades before the Great War the tale of Scrooge first became a children's classic; thereafter transatlantic users reclaimed it as an economic parable with which to diagnose the Depression: in Britain this meant indulging fantasies of plenty, in America prescribing a nostrum that mingled charity with gumption. The heady 1960s left social determinants behind for the sake of psychedelitherapeutic approaches to Scrooge's hangups, but by the mean 1980s the old man was back out on the streets confronting ills that were all too Dickensian. Davis conducts this sweeping panorama in a lively and amiable fashion, chapter by chapter, with side trips into such unexpected places as Browning's *Christmas-Eve,* a Doonesbury strip spoofing George Will, and Capra's *It's a Wonderful Life,* of which he offers a particularly full and discerning interpretation.

Yet the chapters taken together resemble a pageant more than a connected narrative, and in this respect the book is cumulatively disappointing. The transitional writing is nugatory, and by and large each chapter works the same tactic: label the epoch in question with an uncontroversial theme culled from received historical ideas, match it with elements from leading representations of the Carol, and admire the fit. Negative evidence that might disconfirm or complicate received ideas, and evidentiary lacunae indicating dormancy or atrophy in aspects of the myth, get next to no play. Confronting an admittedly overwhelming wealth of material, Davis has avoided information overload by electing to see just one thing at a time, one aspect of *A Christmas Carol* per chapter. This is an understandable strategy, but as a modern mythographer Davis has to pay for it twice.

It costs him, first, much of the historical complexity that a different approach might find in that "consciousness of the industrial era" he intends to illuminate. *The Lives and Times* become just that: plural, protean, capricious, without more than a hint of how, say, religious motives for charity might tangle with socioeconomic motives, or how either one might incite or engross the other through reciprocal causation and effect. As a kind of festive Foucauldianism, Davis's division of his subject into brief epistemes not only suspends the question of change; it suffers a second loss by forestalling any full or consistent engagement with Dickens. It is seldom clear which themes of the Carol were present in the original *Carol,* or what happens when the proportional emphases among Dickens's themes are altered, or even how one might go about deciding such questions. The radical peculiarity of modern myths, after all, is that with them we retain the ur-text. Here that ur-text remains present as *A Christmas Carol* Past: a standard to measure posterity by; or, conversely, a treasure to be inventoried afresh through a look at what has come of it. The march Davis leads across a century and a half leaves one little wiser about this entire aspect of the subject.

What Davis does show, to his credit, is in how apparently concerted a way Dickens's *Carol,* if it did not predict in detail the Carol which the years have made of it, nevertheless took pains to ensure that a Carol of some sort there would be. Like many a modern myth, and not by accident, *A Christmas Carol* is a ghost story, with a troop of spirits prominently including the narrator "standing in the spirit at your elbow," in the crepuscular, desacralized yet still ritual time which made Victorian Christmas cheer so creepy (63–64). The conspicuous invitation to revenance and reenactment thus issued by the narrative frame gets further exercise, Davis observes, in Scrooge's heavily ritualized dream sequences, and also in the typological relations that obtain between the Cratchit family and the Holy Family, between Scrooge and Tiny Tim as types of the Christ child (78–79). In consequence of these multiple structural reinforcements, "the therapeutic effect of the story does not derive from the dream itself but from its telling" (206). Because what the Carol most deeply desires is "to transcend the contradiction of innocence and experience" — the contradiction, we might say, between *living* a myth and *knowing* it — the all-reconciling Carol becomes "the means to achieve simultaneously a fresh experience and a retelling" (209). These are fine remarks on Dickens, and splendidly germane to the general operation of those manufactured legends which the Victorians embraced as classics. Modern myth in its nineteenth-century incarnations, like its first avatar the Ancient Mariner, convokes and instructs by its very form an audience who will thrill to have heard it already, once upon a time.[14]

6

That an ambitious modern text should formulate the recipe for its own reception is the most durably interesting proposition behind the title Jacqueline Rose gave her landmark study ten years ago: *The Case of Peter Pan.* The way Rose reads the outward wrappings and trappings of Barrie's premeditated classic — its strange "case" or cultural integument — remains a triumph of historically situated media analysis that is well worth returning to in the 1990s, and the Pennsylvania press is to be congratulated on its capture and paperback reissue. The years have been less kind, though, to another sense for Rose's "case": the sense which casts the cultural-studies exponent as social case worker. With a hairtrigger feel for scandal, and little patience with the creative imagination, Rose "exposes," "dismantles," and "demystifies" as nothing less than child abuse the projection of adult fears and fantasies onto a literature ostensibly for children; and the stridently whistle-blowing rhetoric of the book now seems the most dated thing about it.[15] Quizzing what her subtitle denounces as *The Impossibility of Children's Fiction,* Rose scorns any adult's pretensions to speak "*for* children" (9). Yet her case study, in its advocacy aspect, surely does aspire to speak *for* the child; and it does so to best effect, curiously, when Rose approaches her material *as* the child, looking at the Peter Pan phenomenon's cloudy textuality and posing some devastatingly naive questions about what is, and is not, there for all to see.

"The question of how things are done, as well as for whom, and by whom, they are produced, the question which the child first asks when confronted with the family drama" (34): here is what Rose most wants to know about the family romance or drama of culture, and her interrogations yield a three-ply result. As a matter of historical fact, she shows how complicit Barrie's work was from the beginning with Edwardian financial and educational institutions already in the ascendant at the fin de siècle. *Peter Pan* caught, then famously accelerated, late-Victorian movements that put childhood up for sale as both a target and a spur to consumer desires. *En revanche,* this nearly instant myth played a signal role in ongoing classist debates about paideia, democracy, and the centrality of children's stories to the educational process.[16] The Peter Pan myth discharged these institutional functions, Rose demonstrates at a second level, by means of a campaign that was bent on disclaiming them — a campaign sanctioned by Barrie's several scripts and books, but effectively conducted in his name by a squadron of publicists and experts sworn to uphold the white magic of the myth's integrity and innocence. What made this defense utterly fantastic was the actual disarray of the texts it was based on, for *Peter Pan* rapidly accumulated a primary bibliography so chaotic that as a "literary object" it can hardly be said to exist at all (143). As with many a myth before it (traditional or modern), the faux integrity that *Peter Pan's* adorers claimed for it was a consensually enforced construct. Coming along very late in the game, Barrie possessed the special distinction — we might call it genius, though Rose would not — of reducing the mythmaking process to its essentials. He saw how to jump-start the social enginery of appropriative remembering, by unfixing *Peter Pan* textually from the beginning. Planting Babel, he sowed textual indeterminacy at, and as, the very origin of myth.

While Rose provides an abidingly valuable account of this complex bibliography, the one text on which she spends most time is not Barrie's 1904 play (withheld from print until 1928) but the long-delayed, quickly-overshadowed narrative that he published in 1911 as Peter and Wendy. This children's novel is a tale for kids, yes, but one whose ironic manner is pitched so consistently to the adult reader over their shoulders that its habitual wink gets hard to tell from a tic. At her third and inmost stage of inquiry into "how things are done," Rose demonstrates how Barrie broke all the rules, flouted the orthodoxy that was even then arraying itself about the Peter Pan myth, and in the incorrigibly mixed address of his narrative trampled down the cordon sanitaire demarcating juvenile from adult spheres. "A travesty" (83); "an attack, or at least an affront" (86): such descriptions of *Peter and Wendy* are certainly accurate, yet all Rose does with them is pillory the author as a bungler or bully. It never occurs to her to credit Barrie with an ironic take on the conditions under which created myths get on in the modern world. Why not read the shocks of the text as the shock tactics of an artist ambivalent about the idealization of children which was going on all around him, and was hailing him as its prophet into the bargain? What if Barrie was already aware, in his own time and place, of precisely what Rose calls the "impossibility" of children's fiction?

With the benefit of a decade of Bakhtinian discourse analytics, or indeed of the better works reviewed here (like Green's chapter on *Peter Pan*), more might now be done with the disjunctions of perspective that Rose has discerned in Barrie's narrative and dramaturgy. Domesticity versus adventure, childhood versus adulthood: these are the major dichotomies with which the Peter Pan myth has to do. They sustain the thematics of the Nursery/Neverland plot frame and inhabit the doublings and forkings among major characters. And it is across the dialectical irresolution of these forces, their "impossibility," that the myth's modern ironies must keep winking, if the show is to go on. A myth of any provenance survives thanks to the conflicts which it contains without solving — and which, if solved, would cease to call for its services. But mythic modes of conflict containment vary historically. If nineteenth-century myths from Frankenstein to Dracula absorbed and expressed their energizing conflicts within the mechanics of narrative transmission, and twentieth-century myths put their tensions into forms of irony, then the case of Peter Pan is admirably transitional. Its child and adult perspectives make mouths at each other incessantly; it ironizes home with empire, and vice versa, at a pace worthy of Conrad, Kipling, and Wells. At the same time, though, there is a boundary drawn around all this twentieth-century mischief by the indubitable Victorian privilege that *Peter Pan* gives to the telling and hearing of stories per se.

"Barrie had the power which is much greater than that of story-telling of compelling successive generations to invent his story afresh, to tell it to themselves and in their own terms" (110). This quotation comes from Rose's book, but Rose is herself quoting a *TLS* leading article fifty years old, published on the occasion of Barrie's death in 1937. If a contemporary journalist could theorize the cultural power of myth so confidently, then Barrie — like Dickens and Tennyson, if not Mary Shelley — had no choice but to honor that power by giving it pride of place within his fiction. Rose is finally right to declare that "the only meaning of *Peter Pan* is the eternal sameness with which it (or he) recurs" (x), and also to surmise that it is the work of such repetition "above all to ward off something with which it is impossible to deal" (38). Just so: the repetition that makes myth is society's stutter, an impediment in the *langue* that is culture. But what was that forfended "something," that impediment at the threshold of our century? For Rose it remains (in 1992 as in 1984) an anxiety of adulteration, an unspeakable cultural misgiving lest every grownup imagination should turn out to be just a child's mind whose molestation we agree to overlook. Our survey here of modern mythography, however, proposes that the repetition-compelling impediment may be an anxiety of a different order: an anxiety of anthropology, a metacultural dread. What if every myth we can recall should turn out to be just a fiction whose molestation we agree to overlook? That is the malaise to which the grim bogey of the modern gives shape, as we connive at the aggrandizement of yesterday's fictions into tomorrow's myths. And the other figure, the grey blur loitering a little further off, the one who won't meet our gaze? That's the bogey of the postmodern, biding its time until the malaise of metaculture ceases to hurt and nobody thinks too much about myths any more.

University of Virginia

NOTES

1. John Callahan, *Do What He Says! He's Crazy!* (New York: Morrow, 1992), 82.
2. Attempts at artificial insemination of a myth are not unknown. See, for example, *Raymond Chandler's Philip Marlowe: A Centennial Celebration* (New York: Knopf, 1988), for which editor Byron Preiss solicited from a range of writers new detective stories starring a gumshoe who, despite a degree of celebrity and even the help of Humphrey Bogart, cannot I think be said to have made the break into myth. (Bennett and Woollacott 14 compare Marlowe with James Bond on this score.)
3. The interpreters of myth have frequent recourse to the sublime rhetorics of infinity and obscurity. For Denis de Rougemont myth "sums up an infinite number of more

or less analogous situations'' (Gribble 3). Rose calls it the ''bearer and veil for a hidden history'' (xvii), Green ''a coded message from the culture,'' often diplomatically obscured (*Dreams of Adventure* [cited below] 55).

4. The privilege of last word on Shakespeare is also reserved by the Vaughans and by Martin Scofield, *The Ghosts of Hamlet* (Cambridge: Cambridge U P, 1980). Works in our mode on Shakespeare's greatest contemporary, Cervantes, follow much the same pattern: see Anthony Close, *The Romantic Approach to ''Don Quixote''* (Cambridge: Cambridge U P, 1978); R. M. Flores, *Sancho Panza Through Three Hundred Seventy-five Years* (Newark, Delaware: Hispanic Monographs, 1982); Eric J. Ziolkowski, *The Sanctification of Don Quixote* (University Park: Pennsylvania State U P, 1991). The fantasy dimension that lurks within this closed hermeneutic system emerges in Erica Jong's 1987 novel *Serenissima,* where the heroine becomes Shakespeare's lover and inspires *The Merchant of Venice.*
5. Can this possibly be a fate reserved for studies devoted to servant figures? It dooms Flores's book on Sancho Panza as well as the Vaughans'; maybe Leporello is part of the problem with J. W. Smeed's desultory *Don Juan: Variations on a Theme* (London and New York: Routledge, 1990). Prospective students of Figaro and Jeeves take note.
6. Modern myths make it part of their regular business to put traditional myths in their place. Not only do *Don Quixote* and *A Christmas Carol* implicitly stand in for the Gospel (Davis, Ziolkowski); there often takes place a literal framing of traditional myth. Witness the subtitle of Shelley's novel *(The Modern Prometheus)*; or the way Holman Hunt surrounds his Lady of Shalott with iconic miniaturizations from Christian scripture and allegory. The fate of modern myths, of course, includes subjection to exactly the same treatment by later fictions: young Ebenezer Scrooge devours *Robinson Crusoe* in Christmas Past; *Peter Pan* is read aloud during an episode from Spielberg's *E. T.* Perhaps ambivalence about the modern displacement of oral traditions is responsible for a related urge to identify the myth with the author. Cervantes *was* Don Quixote; George du Maurier suffered the fate of his own Trilby at the hands of that insatiable Svengali the public; Crusoe merged with Defoe, Fleming with Bond. Such widespread fancies may bespeak a residual oral fixation within the modern mind, a compensatory need to exalt the storyteller as the spirit-medium through whom myth came and dwelt among us.
7. Thus *Shakespeare's Caliban* 171. In a study contemporaneous with the Vaughans', however, Elaine Showalter argues for a renewed Miranda tradition in modern women's writing: see *Sister's Choice* (Oxford: Clarendon, 1991).
8. See Scofield, *The Ghosts of Hamlet*; Paul A. Cantor, *Hamlet* (Cambridge: Cambridge U P, 1989).
9. Green's related work includes *Dreams of Adventure, Deeds of Empire* (New York: Basic Books, 1979); *The Great American Adventure* (Boston: Beacon P, 1984); *Seven Types of Adventure Tale* (College Park: Pennsylvania State U P, 1991); *The Adventurous Male* (College Park: Pennsylvania State U P, 1993). It is a sign of Green's comparative isolation from other cultural-studies work that his Crusoe book nowhere cites Patrick Brantlinger's report from the field in *Crusoe's Footprints* (New York: Routledge, 1990).
10. The emancipation of a myth through variant and even pirated versions of its founding text — witness Quixote, Crusoe, Scrooge, Peter Pan — constitutes a fascinating subtopic, the proper pursuit of which would lead across a spectrum of issues ranging from type fonts to copyrights. If we let ourselves enter here the immense Sherlock Holmes hoard, we should never get back again; but the proprietary interest which

Conan Doyle's estate holds to this day in Sherlock Holmes is a salutary reminder that a modern myth can be simultaneously a household name and an assignable heirloom. For an exemplary look at technical and bibliographical aspects of modern mythmaking — at how microvariant casualties of the printshop must inevitably accompany, and in their way affect, a myth's macrocultural explosion — see Donald A. Redmond, *Sherlock Holmes Among the Pirates* (Westport: Greenwood P, 1990). The symbiosis of mythic dissemination with human error finds a perfect emblem in Sidney Harold Meteyard's handsome Tennysonian gouache, which blazons in the best period calligraphy the immortal culinary misspelling ''The Lady of Shallot'' (*Ladies* 10).

11. Donald F. Glut, *The Frankenstein Catalogue* (Jefferson, N. C., and London: McFarland, 1984), described and indexed 2666 entries, and that was a decade ago.
12. One outstanding example of an interpolation's complete merger with a developing myth is the idyllic waterside scene involving Frankenstein's Creature, a little girl, and some flowers. This scene is nowhere in Mary Shelley but has now become a fixture, thanks to Boris Karloff; ditto the gadgetry in Dr. Frankenstein's lab and the bolt through the neck. Such additions often prove susceptible of analysis along structuralist lines as recombinations of materials already there in the original — one way modern myths, like other forms of folklore, contrive to govern their own replication.
13. See also Bennett and Woollacott's profession of allegiance to ''the total range of cultural and ideological traffic'' (259); even Baldick, while he does not pursue this utopian methodology, commits himself to it in theory.
14. On the textual logic of self-fulfillment in the publication and reception histories of Coleridge's poem, see Jerome J. McGann, ''The Meaning of the Ancient Mariner,'' in *Spirits of Fire,* ed. G. A. Rosso and Daniel P. Watkins (London and Toronto: Associated University Presses, 1990), 208–39. While the invented myth and the authored scripture exhibit a good deal of functional overlap within modern culture, there are also significant differences between them as regards access and stability. Entrusted to the keeping of initiates, the secular ''sacred book'' is harder to get at than the myth; elaborate protocols, likewise, make it harder to change. And ''The Rime of the Ancient Mariner,'' as Harold Bloom has remarked, is a poem remarkably barren of *poetic* successors other than Wilde's *Ballad of Reading Gaol.*
15. Rose may by now have been as much. Her new preface of 1992 (''The Return of Peter Pan''), while it reviews supervening scholarship and new productions in theater and film, seems most attentive to current events with more front-page potential: the fortunes of the Great Ormond Street Hospital for Sick Children (Barrie's legatee for royalties until 1987), and the great leap in public knowledge concerning children's sexual abuse. In keeping with the increasingly direct engagement of recent cultural studies with contemporary politics, Rose's rapprochement between Barrie's Britain and Thatcher's in one sense affirms the pertinence of her 1984 analysis. In another sense, of course, the mere mention of such hot topics has a way of putting on ice the abstractly ideological concerns that simmer and hiss through the unrevised chapters themselves.
16. Not only does the theme of education, as a plot matter, preoccupy modern myths from Caliban to Peter Pan; but the educational function of modern myths is partly responsible for the juvenile reduction they have all undergone at some point in the last hundred years. In reopening the question of how myth relates to education — which is what ''culture'' primarily meant in the nineteenth century — Rose performs an essential service. Her scholarship on nineteenth-century education, however, is

partial; a more flexible and historically trustworthy account is Juliet Dusinberre's in *Alice to the Lighthouse: Children's Books and Radical Experiments in Art* (New York: St. Martin's, 1987).

WORKS CONSIDERED

Baldick, Chris. *In Frankenstein's Shadow: Myth, Monstrosity, and Nineteenth-Century Writing*. Oxford: Clarendon P, 1987.

Bennett, Tony and Janet Woollacott. *Bond and Beyond: The Political Career of a Popular Hero*. London: Macmillan, 1987.

Davis, Paul. *The Lives and Times of Ebenezer Scrooge*. New Haven and London: Yale U P, 1990.

Green, Martin. *The Robinson Crusoe Story*. University Park and London: Pennsylvania State U P, 1990.

Gribble, Jennifer. *The Lady of Shalott in the Victorian Novel*. London and Basingstoke: Macmillan, 1983.

Gross, John. *Shylock: A Legend and Its Legacy*. New York: Simon and Schuster, 1992.

Landow, George P. et al. *Ladies of Shalott: A Victorian Masterpiece and Its Contexts*. Providence: Brown U P, 1985.

Rose, Jacqueline. *The Case of Peter Pan, or The Impossibility of Children's Fiction*, 1984. Rev. ed. Philadelphia: U of Pennsylvania P, 1992.

Vaughan, Alden T. and Virginia Mason Vaughan. *Shakespeare's Caliban: A Cultural History*. Cambridge: Cambridge U P, 1991.

VICTORIAN SUBJECTS: AESTHETICISM AND DECONSTRUCTION

By E. Warwick Slinn

FOR STUDENTS OF LITERATURE and culture, subjectivity is always an issue. It now seems axiomatic in modern criticism that the means by which we understand texts and the texts we feel we understand are intertwined, so that when we examine an author's expression or argument, we are led inevitably to relativize our own speaking position, at once to constitute and incorporate our position as subject. Even the very notion of subjectivity emerges not just from what we know, but from the means by which it is known — from the discourses and ideologies which produce and affect our perceptions and understanding. We might say, then, with Richard Machin and Christopher Norris, that knowledge, understanding and personal identity exist in "a disconcertingly fine balance" (*Post-Structuralist Readings of English Poetry* [1987] 6). We belong, thus, to a complicity of knowing and subjecting (being subject, being subjected) from which the cultural critic cannot escape.

One of the obvious challenges of existing in this subject–focussed network is to historicism. W. David Shaw, for example, formulates the question which he says is raised by my recent book, *The Discourse of Self in Victorian Poetry* (1991): "Can the scholar's historical faith in an objectively existing past be reconciled with the critic's saving faith in an idea that transforms our understanding of that past?" (*MLQ* 55: 3). Professor Shaw wishes to answer in the affirmative, but, notwithstanding the way his image of liturgical credence certainly acknowledges a commitment of subjectivity, the complicity of knowledge and identity leads me to suggest that reconciliation is not the appropriate question, since the two concepts which Shaw places in opposition (historical objectivity and conceptual transformation) are always already hopelessly intertwined.

I speak, if somewhat glibly, in terms of the double action of the post-structuralist subject, who in writing is being written, and the double action of the cultural critic, who in reconstituting the past critiques it in the same interpretative act.

At the same time I do not mean to deny the array of questions surrounding these models of subject-action, questions about the relationship between literary interpretation and historical or political understanding, about the nature of literary knowledge and the role of the acting critic. They are obviously important questions for the current emphasis on contextualizing literary study, and, further to my purpose here, they underline the topicality of recent books by J. Hillis Miller and Jonathan Loesberg. Each book in its own way revisits debates from the 1980s in order to remind cultural critics of the nineties that the tenets of deconstruction and aestheticism, and what has been called rhetorical criticism (the rigorous analysis of semiotic processes), do not, as some have suggested, evade political or historical realities.

Hillis Miller's book focuses more directly on the nexus of the subject. As a collection of earlier published essays, *Victorian Subjects* provides in part an opportunity to reflect on the prolific and outstanding contribution to Victorian studies of this major critic, but it also confronts us with both the nodes of subjectivity in reading Victorian literature and the paradoxical nature of a critical reading which is disruptive while it is constitutive.

Miller uses ''subjects'' in three senses: (1) topics, (2) subjectivities or consciousness, and (3) subjects of the Queen (subject to reigning ideologies). He intends each sense to focus a double strand of critical reproduction and critical displacement, with a consequent challenge to conceptual homogeneity. The first sense, for example, questions presuppositions about a homogeneity of the age, and the second questions whether individual subjectivity can be taken for granted as a starting place for literary analysis. The self as subject, he says, has no independent substance; it is ''a virtuality constantly being transformed by its relations to . . . others'' (viii). Both issues should now be incontrovertible, superfluous even, although items by *NYRB* reviewers such as Denis Donoghue might still suggest otherwise.

More provocative is Miller's third sense of being subject, where he challenges the mimetic view that each author is merely the representative of a pre-existing ideology. Works do not enter history as ''mere reflections of what was already there, but function creatively, performatively.'' In other words, Victorian writers, as subjects of the age, were not only subjected to Victorian ideological forces; they also ''reworked and transformed'' those forces (ix). Entirely apposite to postmodernist debate about the possibility of art intervening within hegemonic structures, this model of authorial double action, of transforming ideology in the act of being constructed by it, makes history and textual representation coincident, where all texts are simultaneously in and out of their historical moment.

Also provocative is Miller's claim to a ''co-presence'' throughout the essays of both the ''reliving from within of ideological formations'' and the ''critique of ideology by way of rhetorical criticism'' (viii). What is claimed is a double action of reenactment and critique which is analogous to the authorial double action of reflection and transformation, though the balance for the critic is perhaps a precarious affair, an "uneasy co-presence," varying presumably in its critical efficacy at different moments in his writing history.

The first essay, however, "The Creation of the Self in Gerard Manley Hopkins," is quite astonishing in that it shows Miller in 1955 already foregrounding the presence of documents (poems, fragments, letters, notebooks, papers, lecture notes, commentaries, sermons), as well as exploring the relationship between verbalization and subjectivity — specifically the transformation of perception, through verbalization, into "the very substance of thought, and . . . into the very substance of Hopkins himself" (1). It is too easy of course to observe from forty years on that "substance" remains a covert and unexplained metaphor here, masquerading as a literalism. It is more useful to observe the seeds for a deconstructive reading of the self which comes later, where the self is the process of interweaving discursive strands, perceived indeed as a constructed verbalization which is at once literal and figurative. Certainly some of the earlier criticism shows what still needed to be done. In this same essay on Hopkins, for example, there lurks an unresolved issue about the relationship between perception and representation: "words can imitate things" and yet "to name a thing is to perceive it." But how is the representation to be distinguished from the real thing when the thing "is only perceived when it is . . . named" (13)? Word and referent coalesce here, requiring that revision of conventional mimesis which Miller later develops in "Nature and the Linguistic Moment."

In this later essay Miller picks up the conflict in Hopkins's work between its theology and its linguistic underthought. Along with other features of Victorian literature, where nature becomes transmuted into a set of figurative signs rather than providing sources of meaning and value, this conflict leads Miller to discern a strand of Victorian writing which focuses on words themselves. Victorian writers are committed to versions of conventional mimesis, but they also develop versions of what Miller calls the linguistic moment: "the moment when language as such, the means of representation in literature, becomes problematic, something to be interrogated, explored, or thematized in itself" (211). Eventually expanded into a book, *The Linguistic Moment: From Wordsworth to Stevens* (1985), this concept remains one of Miller's most useful contributions to Victorian studies. Such "moments" involve recognition of the irreducibly figurative nature of language (language as constitutive, not just as referential) and the rejection of a unitary origin of meaning. The interaction of this sense of figuration (which may exist on three planes: nature itself, the relationship between sign and referent, and the relation of sign to sign) with the function of conventional mimesis (the exact reproduction of appearances; an appeal to truth as correspondence between things and their copies; reference to a deity as guarantee of that truth; the notion of art as revelation), or what Miller has also described as the interaction of two mutually contradictory and yet mutually supporting systems, remains an aspect of Victorian writing which seems to me relatively unexplored. The potentially apolitical effect of this apparent abstraction probably makes the concept unappealing in current criticism, but the linguistic moment is not a moment outside time and if it functions to render problematic the historical as well as the linguistic, that is not to be ahistorical. Attention to this interaction, for instance, particularly when combined with Miller's claims about the copresence of hegemonic and subversive meanings in the same texts, should provide a focus for textual analyses which are politically consequential as well as discursively rigorous.

The premise that the battle among forms of belief in nineteenth-century writing is not just fought between individuals and sects, but within individuals and within individual texts, is introduced in "Theology and Logology in Victorian Literature." Each text, Miller argues, may contain a "submerged counterpoint to its manifest meaning," with the consequence that a counter-culture may be found within expressions of the official culture, effectively "a subversion not from the outside but from within" (281). All distinguished Victorian texts may contain both their manifest religious position and an opposing position. By 1979, then, Miller was arguing for approaches to Victorian literature and culture which were "not governed by disabling presuppositions about the way texts have meaning" — by which he meant the notion of meaning as singular, verifiable, and unambiguous. In every "important" Victorian writer, he suggests, "some version of Christian-Platonic metaphysics is co-present with its undermining deconstruction" (281).

There is a provocation here for the problematic relationship between canonical literature and more broadly inclusive cultural studies: only "important" writers are able to combine the system and its subversion. If Miller is right to suggest that only writers who have not thought out their premises far enough do not subvert themselves (281), then studies of popular culture which include "unimportant" writers should not be surprised to find only corroboration for hegemonic structures. At the same time there is a further question to be asked about conscious intention. Were the "important" writers being honest to the subtlety of their thought, as Miller implies, or were they simply conforming to the dialogical requirements of discourse?

Miller goes on in the same essay to make what are now two commonly understood points from post-structuralist theory: that the counter-culture has only instruments drawn from the official culture with which to attack, and that any cultural expression, such as a literary text, contains an "irreducible plurality" of meanings (287). He then confronts the historical problem of subject-centered knowledge and understanding: from where does such plurality emerge — authorial confusion, historical accident, or critical ingenuity?

He argues that the plurality of meanings arises not from confused authors or overcomplicating readers, but from the necessity of all texts to depend on terms and patterns in the finite reservoir of Western languages. "The counter-culture has always been present within the official culture, waiting to be brought out into the open in new ways by the George Eliots, Swinburnes, and Wildes of each new generation" (287). The copresence of orthodoxy and subversion emerges, therefore, from a textual plurality whose existence depends upon the interdependent action of discourse (the reservoir) and author (the writing subject). Such pluralistic and subject-centered discursiveness also requires the dissolution of history as a series of self-enclosed epochs. We can certainly distinguish between texts, persons, countries, epochs. Concepts of difference remain. But to the concept of difference in history must be added the notion of repetition. Hence the elements from the past which are present in Victorian texts (figures of speech, myths, concepts) "contain within themselves the genetic possibility of both thought and underthought, both cultures and counter-cultures, in inexhaustible, though not unbounded, permutation" (288). I find this model of historicism persuasive. The balancing of repetition and difference accounts for the contextual specificity of otherwise historically contradictory readings; it explains the emergence and re-emergence of conceptual propositions either before or after certain temporally defined moments; it allows for conceptual transformation according to the particularity of historical circumstances; it accommodates the way historical meaning tends to be both old and new at the same time — always repeated and yet different with each repetition. And the analogy from genetic theory accounts for a process of displayed double action: both genetic inheritance (established discursive structures and connotations) and environmental intervention (the self as agent).

Even so, the problematical performance of the reader remains, that network of subjective transformation with which I began. These essays, and others variously on money, comedy, realism, form, ethics, and truth, "sketch the outlines of ideological assumptions in the Victorian period" (vii), but they also probe the critical enactment which produces that outline. As we know, Professor Miller usually emphasizes the act of reading as a critically constitutive act, a performative use of language which is the means by which critical and textual meaning is produced. In the preface to this volume, however, he also refers to "discoveries" of reading, and a question arises about a potential contradiction between the metaphor of discovery and the metaphor of performance. As he says in an essay on *Sartor Resartus*, "a performative creates rather than discovers" (315).

The relationship between discovery and performance is perhaps best illustrated in Miller's last essay, where he shows that what Nietzsche called Carlyle's dishonesty against himself is an undecidability intrinsic to Carlyle's doctrine. Miller uses the distinction between constative and performative speech acts to show the impossibility of deciding whether Carlyle's utterance of the "Everlasting Yea" is constative (based on prior knowledge of his vocation) or performative (based not on prior knowledge but on an action or gesture, where action precedes conviction and knowledge). Constative statements correspond to mimetic representations, recording an act of knowledge which is judged by its truth of correspondence; such knowledge exists prior to the statement and is therefore available for discovery in the representation. Performative statements, however, make something happen; they do not correspond to anything already there and they are not the result of an act of knowledge (315). Miller exposes here the way literary discourse is often unclear about distinctions between discoverable (already existing) or enacted (performatively created) knowledge. Literature allows contradictory readings (in this case the views of Emerson and Nietzsche about Carlyle) to be correct, or rather both and neither. Further he shows how this undecidability emerges from the very nature of Carlyle's enterprise, so that the uncertainty is not merely arbitrary, but intrinsic to the aims and methods of this particular (and historical) text.

If it is in the nature of literary discourse to foreground a double action of substantive and performative utterance, where knowledge which precedes speech coincides with knowledge which is created by that speech, then the critical act itself is an inseparable part of this structure of understanding. There is knowledge and meaning already embedded in the text, enabling the critic to make constative statements, but that knowledge has to be performed in order to be known, since critical statements about the text are never the same as what is exactly in the text (otherwise critical activity would be doomed to mere replication). Miller's statements about Carlyle's Yea are not found in Carlyle's text. Without Miller's statements of explanation, we may not have observed this degree of uncertainty, so that in a real sense the notion of Carlyle's undecidability does not exist outside Miller's performative critical utterance. And yet Miller's statements are verifiable against the text and as such they are also constative. Thus critical utterance is at once constative and performative, both an act of discovery and an act of constitution. Miller's metaphor of discovery does not cancel his metaphor of performance.

At the same time the question of verifiability is fraught, since literary meaning may often involve the uniqueness of a phrase or figure which will not easily allow any variant or version to replace it while retaining the exactness of its meaning (particularly if that exactness is a plurality). If, for example, as Miller observes about Carlyle's use of the term, a symbol is "a form of catachresis" (that is, neither figurative nor literal), "it is the only possible expression of what it says and therefore may not be compared to any alternative form of expression, either figurative or literal" (312). Writing in its performative function may thus evoke the presence of what exists in no other form; in certain use of symbols, there is no other name but the symbolic one, and, again, no referent against which to measure its meaning (see also Miller's "postface" in *The Linguistic Moment*). We are faced, therefore, with this peculiar feature of literary discourse that its foregrounding of special phrases, of the uniqueness of particular verbal flourishes, emphasizes propositions (a meaning, a concept) which do not otherwise exist. For the cultural and historical critic, there ensues the problem of how to relate this proffering of the unique in all its complexity to the abstractions of the general, without which the unique tends not to make much sense. Here surely is the act of critical contextualizing which is necessary to all meaning and yet which immediately engages contingency, transformation, and difference — the complicity of knowing and being subject.

Literary evidence, then, usually consists of analysis of unique events, of samples which are not examples of anything other than themselves, and yet critics claim implicitly their representative status. As Miller notes, much literary criticism depends upon the model of synecdoche, upon the assumption that an example does indeed represent the whole, but, as he asks, how can we decide, "without analyzing all the parts in detail, that a given example is in fact typical" (202)? Literary knowledge is based "on the extremely problematic assumption of the validity of synecdoche" (203), on the particularity of the unique example and how that unique particular partakes of the cultural universal. When literary studies wishes to become cultural studies, it has to find a way of representing the truth of that universal without reducing to travesty the complexity of the unique which is at once its manifestation and its validation. There is, I suspect, a great deal at stake here. If no reading is politically neutral and all readings are in some measure radically specific, in what sense can readings establish their function as exemplar? If, for instance, a cultural critic responds to this dilemma by reducing the element of radically specific analysis and attempting instead to incorporate a multitude of "examples" from a multitude of "sources" (varying discursive forms), such evidence and argument is even more open to a deconstructive analysis which would point out the consequences of repression, exclusion or dubious typicality. If, alternatively, we simply acceded to the impossibility of truth claims and taught only a chosen ideology, we would be behaving no more intelligently (or morally) than inquisitors who burnt witches at the stake in the belief that they were saving victims and behaving with political (or theological) correctness.

Rather than establishing univocal cultural truths, literary texts, upon detailed scrutiny, tend more often to offer a multivocal intertextuality, a plurality of signification, where the hegemony would usually prefer singularity and order. Miller's form of criticism retains a strong concern with radically specific analysis, precisely in order to demonstrate this failure of distinctions to cohere within texts and in order to indicate thereby the powerful potential for complex texts to embody a cultural critique. He continually points to moments where literature evinces a form of cultural dissolution, moments where the unique "example" of what is otherwise nonexistent exposes the false boundaries of hegemonic meaning and authority.

As I have been arguing and as Miller's essays illustrate, this possibility for art to subvert the hegemony requires a critical performative for its recognition. At the same time, the critic's act is crucially a double act of repetition and difference. The performative redisplays the textual critique, but the element of difference also provides a gap, what Miller calls an "ironic displacement through citational miming," which becomes itself "an implicit critique" (viii). Hence the critical performative establishes in turn its own combination of uniqueness and typicality, enacting the further repetition of an undecidable constative-performative.

Given, then, a genetic model for historicism, the possibilities for a critique are always potentially present in literary discourse. If the copresence of the hegemonic and the subversive is part of historical reality, an ever-present potential as Miller claims, a reading which combines discovery and performance is nevertheless required in order to realize that copresence, and herein lies the significance of Miller's rhetorical method: its combination of miming and displacement. It is in the very constitutive nature of his performative action, that he makes his contribution as a cultural critic. The repetition of literary and historical texts through interpretative reenactment is not merely a formalist exercise, as some have claimed. Attention to linguistic and rhetorical function renders interpretation necessarily formalist, but it can be, at the same time, through exploiting the gap of ironic displacement which reenactment requires, a means of writing political and cultural criticism.

Victorian Subjects shows Miller's growing realization about the semiotic aspects of identification, processes which he earlier took for granted. Aware from the outset of potential contradictions in Victorian texts and of the possibilities for discursive plurality, he demonstrates a strong sense of the coextensive relationship between earlier assumptions about consciousness and the more rhetorically based methods of deconstructive reading. Above all, these essays remind us that excessive demand for political relevance or historical contextualizing may sometimes risk a repression of the presence of intralinguistic as well as mimetic practice in historical (Victorian) texts.

My emphasis on the relationship between rhetorical analysis and cultural criticism in Miller's book is intended to act also as a covert discussion of the political function of deconstruction, the topic of a recent book by Jonathan Loesberg, *Aestheticism and Deconstruction: Pater, Derrida, and de Man.* Loesberg's interest in the relationship between philosophy and aesthetic form focuses on Pater's impressionism and on the deconstruction of Derrida and de Man. The book is important generally for debate about the continuing role of deconstruction in the context of cultural criticism; and it is important particularly to Victorian scholars for its argument that Walter Pater is directly relevant to contemporary literary theory. Such a claim appears to be part of a broader contemporary development which is reconsidering the relevance of nineteenth-century decadence and aestheticism: see, for example, Jonathan Dollimore in *Sexual Dissidence* (1991), or Richard Shusterman in *After the Future: Postmodern Times and Places*, edited by Gary Shapiro (1990).

Accepting the common charge against deconstruction that it supports aestheticism, Loesberg seeks to reverse the terms of that charge. He argues that deconstructive aestheticism does not at all advocate escape into an unreal realm of art separate from social or historical effect. On the contrary, ''aestheticism has always operated as a central mode both of engaging in and of interpreting philosophy, history, and politics'' (4), and it is rather the critics of aestheticism themselves who assume ''a constitutive alterity between the aesthetic and the real'' (9). This argument enables us to observe an irony in the movement from, say, Northrop Frye's ''polemical introduction,'' which announced a plan of defining the study of literature as its own subject, to cultural materialism, which urges the demise of any attempt of literary study to define itself as its own thing. Loesberg's point is that the rejection of attempts to separate literary artifacts from historical or political contexts is already theorized by what new historicists and cultural critics often think they are refuting — deconstruction and aestheticism.

The initial responses to Pater established the main charges against aestheticism: it is not historical because its formalism detaches art from its contexts; it is not moral because it affirms pleasurable sensation as the only value; and it is politically passive because it contends that political commitment is delusory and that only the moment counts. Recent criticisms of deconstruction are simply variations of the same three claims: ahistoricism, relativism, and political quietism. The common ground to these charges is a belief that art and literature are distinctively separate from discourses concerned with truth and that aestheticism therefore seeks ''a position outside the effects of history and politics'' (5). Loesberg's contention is that Pater and deconstruction confront precisely this common ground, refuting its assumptions.

Pater's philosophical critique, Loesberg argues, emerges from a connection of art for art's sake with philosophical empiricism, which grounds all knowledge in sensations. But the existence of sensations depends on their difference, on the change, or friction, between one sensation and the next. Consequently, because art formally embodies friction — differences between sensations — it is not an escape from reality, but is precisely a founding mode of knowledge. The presence of friction embeds a contradictory abstraction within the tangibility of sensation, and Pater transfers this recognition of a foundational necessity for abstraction at the very moment of sensation (the source of all perception) onto all other forms of interpretation and knowledge. Aestheticism, therefore, is as fundamental a mode of social interpretation as other forms of philosophical and historical theory. Further, aesthetic sensation embodies the meeting place between the philosophical and the historical, and that form of sensation is employed in Pater's own aesthetic form, the narrative of *The Renaissance*, thus re-enacting in his own criticism that connection of philosophical abstraction with historical particularity which is the founding act of human perception and knowledge.

Loesberg explains a subtle, yet crucial paradox about Pater's use of the notorious phrase, art for art's sake: "the value of art is instrumental, but only to the extent that it cannot be perceived instrumentally" (12). Art is valuable, that is, because it provides a "quickened sense of life," as do political and religious enthusiasms, but the paradox is that art has this value more potently precisely because it cannot be used for political or religious purposes (not experienced instrumentally), but only for its own sake, as an aesthetic experience. The point has to do with the question which Pater raises about teleological structures: the goal in art is experience itself, not the attainment of some specific religious, political, or historical purpose. Art for art's sake does not, therefore, "refer to the content of art but to the way in which art is experienced" (13).

Loesberg acknowledges that Pater's method is neither self-evident nor coincident (17), and a great deal rests on his reading of the famous Conclusion to *The Renaissance*. I suspect that his claims rely more upon an act of Miller's critical performative than he might care to admit. Still, I find the performance persuasive, particularly the argument that Pater desires an ideal form within sensation: that is, Pater wants to combine the flux of experience, gaining as many pulsations as possible in life from that experience, with a position from which to enjoy that flux, a position which transcends flux while remaining a part of it (this conflicting desire explains the differences between those critics who stress his idealism and those who stress his empiricism). His desire both to observe flux as abstract necessity and to experience it from within reproduces the implicit contradiction in empiricism's founding definitions. With the sensation which is also an abstract form (sensation as the irreducible minimum of reality depends for its identity, to mark its existence, upon change and therefore upon its "own absence"), Pater "marks the necessary and contradictory idealism within empiricism"(20).

Pater shows that sensation carries within itself a necessity for reflection and analysis which empiricism classes as secondary and which it can neither accommodate nor expel. Thus, like Derrida after him, he seeks to "place within foundations precisely what those foundations must exclude in order to maintain a theoretical consistency" (23). Aesthetic experience, in drawing attention to the act of sensation, is thus a form of "embodied epistemology" because it recreates "the reflexiveness of the paradoxical, founding sensation" (24), and art for art's sake means "the aesthetic perception of perception" (25). Far from being an escape from chaos into pure form, Pater's art was an engagement with reality: "the solidity of aesthetic perception never transcends its immersion in sensational friction" (26).

Aesthetic experience, then, is the meeting point between empirical sensation and idealist abstraction, and what lies behind these arguments is post-Kantian recognition of aesthetic experience as a test case where conceptual abstraction and sensory perception meet and circumscribe each other, preventing rationality, for instance, from losing itself in pure metaphysics. What also ensues is the political significance of aesthetic form, whether or not aesthetic ideology evades cultural politics. Much of Paul de Man's work, for example, was devoted to showing how aesthetics had been kidnapped by a conservative (Romantic, humanist, idealist) ideology, where art eases the move from a simplified (phenomenalist) theory of perception to a simplified (organicist) notion of society and politics (Machin and Norris 13–14). Loesberg's reading of Pater, Derrida, and de Man argues that they all resist this conservative ideology, maintaining an interrelationship between politics, philosophy, and aesthetics.

Loesberg is very good on common misreadings of Derrida: Derrida does not question philosophical foundations in order to make truth or meaning disappear, but in order "to call into question the validity of the arbitrary exclusionary maneuvers that moments of foundational definition seem to necessitate"(76); Derrida does not come down on the side of freeplay, but denies the possibility of choice between freeplay and centralized meaning (91). Loesberg also provides an excellent account of why Derrida says that *différance* is neither a word nor a concept (83–84). More important, however, is his explanation of Derrida's attack on foundational philosophy. Just as Pater showed that sensation in empiricism needed its excluded opposite, abstract form, so Derrida shows that "a foundational abstraction, the structure of reference, depended on a material entity that it also excluded" (85). In particular he targets Husserl's moment of pure perception or unmediated consciousness. Whereas Husserl's transcendental subject attempts to exclude any material or external intervention, Derrida argues that the subject's apprehension of itself within consciousness is always at least partly linguistic (87). For Derrida there is always language's externality, even when speaking and hearing are internalized. As for Pater, Derrida does not deny specific forms of knowledge or meaning or truth, but he connects the attempt to ground systems of knowledge with "a contradictory exclusion of some form of nonknowledge" (89). It is this concern with the act of exclusion itself which leads him to value literary language precisely because it identifies the activity of representation; it foregrounds its own acts of reference and it reenacts the foundational problems it seeks to analyze (99–100).

Similar points emerge from the discussion of de Man, leading Loesberg to refute those critics of deconstruction who believe that literature has "an irrevocable inside" distinct from "an inescapable outside" that is known variously as "history, political activity, ideological hegemony, empirical or transcendental truth" (122). Pater, Derrida, and de Man deny the existence of any extra-aesthetic category; they deny that the aesthetic excludes an outside, or must be broken out of into the real. They do not reduce history to philosophy or philosophy to history, but void the question of priority. The accusation that there is nothing outside language is itself based on logocentric assumptions that "art and language stand in opposition to direct discourse and represented reality" (122), and once this opposition is removed deconstruction's textual analysis takes on a new edge, albeit an edge which combines the mutually contradictory forces of historicism and an abstracting philosophy.

In the last chapter, "Aesthetic Analysis and Political Critique," Loesberg writes more provocatively in his resistance to treating deconstruction as a knowledge which founds a method for encompassing politics. He outlines, for instance, what he regards as two inaccurate versions of deconstruction that attempt to apply it to political ends. The first is the hope that deconstruction will provide a way out from political, institutional, and conventional constraints (161). But Derrida does not look for a discourse outside politics. He looks for a discourse "that recognizes the absence of any position of external neutrality from which to make political judgments" (163). The second is the proposition that "deconstruction itself is a powerful method of exhibiting the inbuilt prejudices, biases, and injustices of ruling concepts of thought" (163). But, while deconstruction provides a way of exposing the internal incoherence of political structures, it does not provide a means of preferring one structure over another. Furthermore, a deconstructive approach is often not needed when ordinary logic will suffice equally well, and sceptical analysis of an institutional system does not guarantee any positive change in that system (165). Loesberg suggests that critics who argue for the political value of deconstruction, such as Michael Ryan and Christopher Norris, seem to fear that unless deconstruction is seen as a powerful critique from outside structures of power, its process will become merely an aesthetic spectacle (166). Loesberg's response, his main point throughout, is that "aestheticization does not create an artificial spectacle opposed to a consequential, material reality" (166). All Derrida claims is the absence of neutrality and thus the possibility of analyzing how policing works.

The absence of neutrality may seem a somewhat weak political claim, but Loesberg argues a more subtle point: "deconstruction becomes an effective political critique at the moment that it recognizes the system in which it is enclosed as artificial, but it remains effective only as long as it accepts that enclosure" (166). The political relevance, then, of deconstruction lies in retaining consciousness of self-referentiality, in exploiting the very point which detractors have used against deconstruction, that it contradicts itself. For Loesberg this means accepting deconstruction as "an act of self-resistance," a form of resistance which might even entail "resistance to the assumptions behind one's own reformist discourse, without abandoning the acts of reform themselves" (167). The standard deconstructionist position has always been that it is not possible to step outside a discursive system in order to dismantle or critique it, and for many this proposition of enclosed textuality has meant the impossibility of political intervention or effectiveness. But Loesberg's point is that political realization is achieved at the moment when analysis leads to the recognition that what appeared to be separate or transcendental knowledge produced by that analysis was actually part of the system it was supposed to be analyzing (167). Political effectiveness is thus located at the point of recognizing a hitherto unseen limit to one's own discourse, particularly when that discourse was thought to be in some way transcendent. While this resistance is simply a version of the radical scepticism with which deconstruction has always been associated, as evinced by de Man's continual argument against the systematization of the reading activity and therefore against enshrining nihilism or any other fixed position (175), Loesberg's concern is to emphasize its positive features, its inclusive rather than repressive qualities.

Aware that "self-resistance" might sound suspiciously quietist, he uses Pater's review of Mrs. Humphry Ward's novel *Robert Elsmere* to illustrate the difference between self-resistance and a quietist cooperation with a ruling authority. Pater refuses to choose between negative sceptics, who cannot be sure the sacred story is true and promptly leave the Church, like Robert Elsmere, when they belatedly come to doubt its historical truth, and positive sceptics, who cannot be sure the story is false and stay within the Church in a state of philosophical uncertainty. Religion, for Pater, comprises both believers and sceptics, making Elsmere's act one of "partial and exclusive dogmaticism" (171). Dogmatic thinkers of either color, whether believers or doubters, exclude an aspect of reality which they cannot accommodate. Pater's refusal to doubt either the truth or the falseness of Christianity could appear quietest, but his position "has more the character of self-resistance than of critique from the outside." In other words, Pater looks to the limits in all positions, including his own, but with an attitude of inclusiveness; he does not resist agnosticism as such, but rather the moment when agnosticism, seeking to assert its own power, "insists on its own exclusions" (171). The importance of self-resistance, therefore, resides in its opposition to attempts by scepticism, or any other critical discourse, to transform itself into another controlling force.

So deconstruction cannot be used to critique authoritarian concepts from the outside, and if concepts are foundational, deconstruction will not do away with them. On the other hand, while a foundational discourse will not disappear, its claims are radically questioned. Loesberg's version of deconstructionist scepticism, his concept of self-resistance, is more than self-abnegation when placed within an institutional structure, since the deconstruction of a conceptual foundation allows the involvement of previously excluded positions. While, to use his example, feminist arguments about noncanonical issues within canon formation do not produce reasons for alternative canons, they do break a canon's exclusionary power, opening the possibility of other voices (184).

For Loesberg the philosophical argument is clear: "whereas neither aestheticism nor deconstruction can engage in the kind of refutation of institutional or oppressive forces from the outside that critics sometimes want from literary criticism, the philosophical and political environment created by their open-ended inclusion from within is not very hospitable to those forces'' (185). Ultimately not a great deal is claimed here (simply that deconstruction has tended to work in alliance with reformist movements rather than against them), and it is perhaps disappointing that Loesberg does not more directly confront the current difficulty of finding our way among conflicting discourses. Deconstruction shows there are no reliable or consistent grounds for any foundational system, but that means there is no reliable way of testing the value or validity of claims made under the heading, say, of political correctness. Even to propose that validity should be tested could be rejected as ideologically suspect. If there is no way of refuting ideologies from without, how can any reliable choice be made between cultural forces, or how can excessive moral or political demands be distinguished from reasonable ones? Are the categories of ''excessive'' and ''reasonable'' themselves suspect — on what grounds? Loesberg's covert answer, his version of Derrida's ''constant vigilance,'' should not be easily dismissed. Self-resistance and its policy of inclusiveness at least has the merit of resisting all attempts to flaunt or reclaim power while not relinquishing at all the need for social reform. Perhaps self-resistance may, after all, remain the only coherent or intellectually honest response in the face of so many conflicting political demands. It may also allow the argument within teaching institutions that ideologically based courses (effectively all courses) should directly and self-consciously incorporate self-resistance into their teaching content. At that point, deconstruction would certainly become politically consequential.

What Loesberg says about ''self''-resistance returns us to the divisive, often contradictory, perceptions which constitute human subjectivity. For both Miller and Loesberg, it is still a value of literary discourse that it foregrounds these foundational processes, and students of Victorian poetry will readily identify texts which illustrate the point: the lyrical/narrative opposition in *Amours de Voyage*, the sensation/concept division in ''Dover Beach,'' the spirit/matter fusion in ''The Windhover,'' or the tension between materiality of form and histrionic conceptualizing in Robert Browning's monologues. One of the challenges for literary/cultural critics, perhaps, in the rush to restore literary texts to their political contexts, is not to allow political questions to elude the subjective and textual processes of their production, not, in other words, to forget Foucault's point that all is already interpretation. Cultural criticism still needs, I suggest, to examine what Loesberg calls embodied epistemology, not in terms of dualistic, post-Cartesian, subject-object distinctions, but in terms of the dialectical and dialogical complexity of literary representation, where texts both reenact foundational problems and foreground their own acts of reference, both reflect denomination and denominate reflection.

Massey University (New Zealand)

WORKS CONSIDERED

Loesberg, Jonathan. *Aestheticism and Deconstruction: Pater, Derrida, and de Man.* Princeton: Princeton UP, 1991.
Miller, J. Hillis. *Victorian Subjects*. Durham: Duke UP, 1991.

"THAT AIN'T NO LADY TRAVELER . . . IT'S A DISCURSIVE SUBJECT": MAPPING AND RE-MAPPING VICTORIAN WOMEN'S TRAVEL WRITING

By Catherine Barnes Stevenson

BEFORE THE LATE 1970S, women's travel writing was virtually *terra incognita* — its reaches uncharted, its contours unmapped, its strategic importance unknown. With the exception of Paul Fussell's elegant study of British literary traveling, *Abroad* (1980), travel writing itself was a form of literary production still largely untheorized. Then in the 1980s literary explorers, schooled in feminist acts of recovery and in gynocriticism, opened the territory of women's travel writing to popular audiences, surveying its dimensions and charting preliminary routes. They discovered "lost" texts, unearthed the buried lives of remarkable women, tried to locate travelers within personal, cultural, and even political nexuses. In keeping with the spirit of the times, they focused on the achievements of these women worthies, documented the personal and rhetorical postures dictated by Victorian gender roles, and searched for commonalities in literary techniques or psychological dynamics.

Recently, armed with post-colonial theory, cultural studies and a heightened sense of what James Clifford calls the "predicament of culture," a second wave of explorers has ventured into a newly problematized territory. Scholars now interrogate the conventions of travel literature as they relate not only to issues of literary representation but also to imperial discourse and the construction of "the self" and "the other." They unpack the cultural baggage that women travelers carried with them. They investigate the intersecting and competing imperatives of gender, race, and imperial privilege as these played themselves out in the women's travels and writings. Although there is still much territorial mapping to be done (as evident in the work of Billie Melman on women's writing about the "Orient"), many recent scholars eschew biography and geography to focus on the traveler's ''subject position'' in relation to the institutions and ideologies of her home culture.

Opposing itself to earlier ''celebratory'' and ''estheticist'' traditions of studying travel writing, Mary Louise Pratt's landmark *Imperial Eyes* presents itself as a ''critique of ideology'' (4), specifically of the way that European travel writing about non-European parts of the world ''produced'' that world for its readers and engendered in a metropolitan audience imaginative investment in European ''expansionist enterprises.'' With considerable wit, agility, and a commitment to a ''dialectical'' approach, *Imperial Eyes* examines the ''conventions of representation'' in a wide variety of travel writing over two centuries: eighteenth-century naturalists' accounts of Southern Africa, ''sentimental'' travel accounts from the Caribbean and West Africa (1780–1840), ''discursive reinventions'' of South America (1800–1840), Victorian writers in Central Africa (1860–1900), and finally postcolonial travelers of the 1960s and eighties. By elucidating the intersections of travel writing with other forms of expression, particularly natural history and sentimental literature, Pratt is able to offer a highly useful contextualization of the literature of travel within its historical, cultural, intellectual, and literary milieu.

Because of its facility with the discourses of both literary criticism and ethnography, *Imperial Eyes* has given the field of travel writing a new vocabulary for discussing cultural encounters and their representations. Pratt's contributions to the lexicon include the following. The **contact zone**: those ''social spaces where disparate cultures meet, clash, and grapple with each other'' (4); it stresses the ''interactive, improvisational dimensions of colonial encounters,'' the way that ''subjects are constituted in and by their relations to each other'' (7). **Transculturation**: an ethnographic term that describes how subordinated or marginal groups select and use materials transmitted from the dominant culture (6); Pratt also uses this term to suggest the ways in which metropolitan European culture was constructed from the outside. **Anti-conquest**: those strategies of innocence adopted by the male European bourgeois subject to distinguish himself from the imperial conqueror while at the same time asserting hegemony through his imperial gaze (7). **Auto-ethnography**: the colonized subject's self-representations which ''engage with the colonizer's own terms'' (7).

Although women's travel writing is referenced in several different contexts here, I want to focus on the most extended discussion of the gender differences in travel accounts, the chapter entitled ''Reinventing America II: The Capitalist Vanguard and the *Exploratrices Sociales*.'' Here two traditions in early nineteenth-century travel accounts of South America are elucidated, each of them distinct from the earlier accounts of explorers or naturalists. The first — a male, heroic mode — represents travel in a ''goal-oriented rhetoric of conquest and achievement'' and allegorizes the journey through ''the lust for progress'' (148). The ideological work of this kind of writing was to invent a ''backward and neglected'' America, full of unclean and indolent peasants, a land very much in need of capitalist investment and ''rationalized exploitation.'' The second tradition emerges in Flora Tristan's *Peregrinations of a Pariah* (1837) and Maria Callcott Graham's *Voyage to Brazil and Journal of a Residence in Chile* (1824). In contrast to the linear narrative pattern of the capitalist vanguard, these works are centripetally structured around the woman's place of residence in the city. Where the capitalist vanguard desires to collect and possess the surrounding world, these women travelers strive to possess themselves and a ''room of their own,'' while at the same time registering (to a higher degree than their male counterparts) the social and political realities of colonial life. These women's narratives enact the search for ''self-realization and social harmony'' (168); in fact, each constructs ''feminotopias,'' idealized worlds of autonomy, empowerment, and pleasure for women. In reinventing America in their writings, these women were, in fact, reinventing themselves.

Pratt's focus on women travelers' personal liberation through their travel writing allies her with the work of the first generation of students of women's writing, as does her identification of gender-based differences in the meaning of and representation of the travels. An earlier generation of commentators saw in the travelers' personal growth and social awakening a transformative force that changed their understanding of their place in their own culture, their subsequent actions, even their political and social attitudes. This tradition is continued by two of the books discussed here — Frawley and Melman. However, another school of contemporary scholars represents women travel writers as enmeshed in incompatible ideologies, not so much speaking of their experiences as being spoken by contradictory discourses.

Perhaps the most extreme version of the latter approach appears in Sara Mills's *Discourses of Difference*. Writing only about women who traveled to countries that were under British economic, religious, or political control (but mysteriously omitting India), Mills positions three Victorian women's texts in both colonial and discursive frameworks. Her thesis is that women's involvement with colonialism and their representations of that involvement differ from men's because of the pull of two discursive pressures: the power of patriarchy, ''which acted upon them as middle-class women'' and the power of colonialism, ''which acted upon them in relation to the people in the countries they describe in their books.'' The ''convergence and conflict of these two power systems . . . determines the style and content of women's travel writing'' (180). By creating a deterministic, binary system, *Discourses of Difference* oversimplifies the complex range of discursive models which women travelers employed in their writings: for example, little attention is paid to literary discourse, or the discourses of science, ethnography, religion, and women's rights. The result is a cartoon-like flattening of texts along two dimensions only.

Like other commentators on women's travel writing, Mills looks for gender-based differences; her approach, however, is general and theoretical, not specific in its analysis of the effect of destination, mode of travel, or period of travel. Women's texts, she argues, share a sense of "personal involvement and relationships with" the people among whom they traveled and possess "less authoritarian" narrative stances than those of their male counterparts. Because of their indeterminate position between discourses, women travelers produce "counter-hegemonic voices" in their writings through humor, self-deprecation, statements of affiliation, and descriptions of relationships (22). "Whereas men could describe their travel as individuals and as representatives of the colonial power, women could only travel and write as gendered individuals with clearly delineated roles" (103). That reductive "only" points to the missing element in this analysis: an understanding of the dynamic forces that operate even within those gendered roles — the way, as Susan Blake shows in "A Woman's Trek: What Difference does Gender Make?" (*Western Women and Imperialism*), that race, gender, and class intersect and modify each other in women's travel writing.

Discourses of Difference proposes to study an important, under-investigated topic: the production and reception of women's travel writing. Relying on Foucault, it analyzes the constraints on the production of women's travel writing, sometimes covering old ground in a new theoretical wagon, sometimes discovering some unexplored patches. To find a voice to accommodate gender norms even when their behaviors challenged these, women travel writers employed both the conventions of colonial writing (the male adventure hero/protagonist, the construction of the colonized "other,") and the conventions of women's writing (eschewing topics that women were not allowed to talk about, employing the discourse of femininity in their focus on the personal and domestic). Within the framework of production and reception theory, Mills asks a set of useful questions: how did these texts manage to get published? why were they read? how were they were read? Unfortunately, the answers are not sought through close analysis of the institutions of reviewing, sales practices, negotiation with publishers, or women's attempts to market their works. Instead, Mills's text focuses on the way in which cultural assumptions about women's writing — particularly the autobiographical imperative, the distrust of women's veracity, and the concern with the exceptional nature of the woman traveler — shaped the reading of these works.

The second half of the book considers three "case studies" — Alexandra David-Neel, Mary Kingsley, and Nina Mazuchelli. The aim is to produce a "symptomatic reading" of one text by each of these writers in order to exhibit the contradictions inherent in the power relations within colonialist discourse and to demonstrate how any discursive position is called into question by other elements in the text. Autobiographical readings are shunned since a "coherent self, in textual terms, is impossible'' (37). By focusing on the discursive frameworks, *Discourses of Difference* claims to present new ways of understanding the texts of women travel writers; instead it offers a kind of re-categorization of some familiar concepts about women's writing. Thus, David-Neel's *My Journey to Lhasa* (1827) is seen in terms of its reception by male critics as ''exaggerated.'' The complex, wonderful, frustrating *Travels in West Africa* (1897) by Mary Kingsley becomes simply an example of the contradictory clashes of colonialism and feminine ideology — an ultimately unstable text that is *neither* fully colonial, nor feminine, nor feminist. Finally, Nina Mazuchelli's *The Indian Alps and How We Crossed Them* (1876) is seen to inscribe the discourses of femininity and colonialism, although the narrator's behavior transgresses the norms of female conduct; the text thus exemplifies ''the clashes and reinforcements of these discourses'' (194). The reader is left agreeing with the author's assessment of the results of her methodology: ''The reading which is produced is more unwieldy . . . and ultimately it is more difficult to make generalizations about the text'' (195). Perhaps the readings might have been less unwieldy if, instead of employing a binary model, Mills had developed a fuller sense of the ''interdiscursiveness'' of these texts, as articulated by Dave Morley: ''Both the text and the subject are constituted in the space of the interdiscursive; and both are traversed and intersected by contradictory discourses — contradictions which arise not only from the subject positions which these different discourses propose, but also from the conjuncture and institutional site in which they are articulated and transformed'' (''Texts, Readers, Subjects'' 171).

A more sophisticated application of cultural studies theory to women's travel writing, one much closer to Morley's notion of the ''interdiscursive,'' is Alison Blunt's *Travel, Gender, and Imperialism: Mary Kingsley and West Africa.* Like Mills, Blunt eschews ''any realist claim to biographical authenticity and/or authority'' in her investigation of the ''subject positionality'' of Mary Kingsley. Specifically, she examines the construction of Kingsley's subjectivity by herself and others along the lines of gender, race, class — at home and abroad (4). With great dexterity and a real appreciation of the fluidity of these discursive categories, *Travel, Gender, and Imperialism* examines the ways in which imperialism, the sex-gender system, the discourses of race and class produced both the texts of and the public persona of ''Mary Kingsley.''

In an opening discussion of travel as metaphor, Blunt examines a dynamic which underlies much of her analysis: ''travel . . . involves the familiarization or domestication of the unfamiliar at the same time as the defamiliarization of the familiar or domestic'' (19). It both offers and contains the possibility of transgression. Travel writing itself is the construction of spatial and textual difference; imperial travel writing, the instantiation of ''mythological otherness'' (30). By studying Kingsley, whose many personae were spatially and temporally distinct, this book proposes to ''give voice to those marginalized by such totalizations while at the same time revealing their ambivalence rather than fixity'' (37).

Clearly, "ambivalence" is privileged by the post-modern critic much as irony and paradox were by the new critic.

Because of its specificity, its theoretical sophistication, and its willingness to admit that a private life exists and has some importance, however, Blunt's analysis is neither reductive nor tedious. For example, by focusing on Kingsley's "gendered subjectivity" both at home and abroad, Blunt is able to frame some of the puzzling doubleness of *Travels in West Africa* and *West African Studies* (1897). Kingsley's desire to participate in the masculine tradition of trade and exploration aligned her, it is argued, with imperial authority and its construction of racial difference; this conflicts with her feminine self-consciousness, which is a source of both personal and national identity. Blunt offers a provocative formulation to help explain the ambivalences in attitude and the shifting gender identities of Kingsley the traveler: "During travel racial superiority came to supersede gender inferiority"(105). As a result, Kingsley regarded African women with a privileged male gaze, feeling no special gender bond with them while she regarded African men in terms of race. Although this blanket statement over-simplifies Kingsley's complicated attitude toward African women, Blunt goes on to acknowledge "the tensions and contradictions" in Kingsley's writing that arose from the clash of gender-based self-conceptions (105). Kingsley was liberated by travel, Blunt argues, because she was able to "identify with imperial power and authority" while at the same time maintaining her sense of "otherness" through an intact gendered subjectivity.

In a sense the book's most valuable and original contributions appear in its final chapters, "Return: Reconstituting Home" and "Institutional Responses to Women Travel Writers." Here Kingsley's marginality as a woman is shown to undergird the reception of her travels, her writings, and her political activities. Using readers' responses found in reviews and obituaries, Blunt demonstrates how the identities that Kingsley constructed on her travels were reconstructed at home. The largely favorable reviews of *Travels In West Africa* focused on the novelty of the woman traveler and on her femininity — her clothes, the dangers she encountered, her eccentricity. The mixed critical reviews of the more scientific *West African Studies*, on the other hand, highlighted the work's "chatty" feminine style and the book's intellectual content — but not her political proposals. Kingsley's relationship to the institutions that shaped policy and regulated knowledge was marginal, yet through her voluminous private correspondence, often with other women, she established a position of public political influence without violating her allegiance to the lady's proper sphere.

Also greatly concerned with the woman traveler's construction of a professional identity at home is Maria Frawley's *A Wider Range: Travel Writing by Women in Victorian England*. This work undertakes the ambitious project of describing "the major forms of Victorian women's travel writing," of correlating those forms to geographical regions, and of demonstrating "how decisions about the travel account's form and the . . . choice of region relate finally to questions of and choices about professional identity'' (36). The material is organized according to the intersection of geography (Italy, the Middle East, America) and the traveler's ''mode'' of self-presentation (the ''adventuress'' versus the art historian or the sociologist). The result is a hybrid structure in which the focus shifts from the range of writing produced *about* a region to individual women writers who sought a specific professional identity through their travel writing. Thus the opening chapter on Italy as it was written by women travelers gives way to discussion of two women who made their reputations as writers about art history. America as a destination yields to a focus on women as sociologists; the chapter on the Middle East is essentially an examination of Harriet Martineau's and Frances Power Cobbe's attempts to write a kind of history in which the traveler is an active ''witness'' of the past who recreates it for her readers (138). The middle chapter is not destination-specific but mode-specific, for it considers ''Victorian Adventuresses'' — that is, any woman who traveled to remote, exotic locales.

Following a long line of feminist critics, Frawley argues that travel enabled women to ''reimagine and rework'' gender differences, simultaneously to maintain distance from and proximity to their home culture, to experiment with identities. More than this, travel gave them what Bourdieu called ''symbolic capital'' that empowered them to speak on social, intellectual, and political issues and to compete in the Victorian marketplace of ideas. *A Wider Range* offers some valuable new insights into the way that travel writing enabled women to construct professional identities and to garner cultural authority, although it does not fully examine the institutional barriers to their complete acceptance as professionals. Drawing on Tuchman and Fortin's sociological work on Victorian authorship in *Edging Women Out*, Frawley situates travel writing as a ''mixed specialty,'' and thus a ''politically expedient'' form of writing for women who wanted to break into the ''high prestige'' areas of non-fictional scholarly and critical writing.

The strength of Frawley's method is evident in the first two chapters on Italy: ''Into the Temple of Taste'' and ''The Professionalization of Taste: Art Historians Abroad.'' Positioning women's writing within the context of the hundreds of accounts of journeys to this cultural mecca, Frawley considers those which achieved the status of ''cultural commodities,'' that is, those that were ''published, reviewed, compared in the press to male-authored accounts'' (47). The writings of Mary Shelley, Frances Trollope, Frances Elliott, and Vernon Lee provide evidence that women who wrote about Italy attempted to straddle the camps of tourist and traveler, combining the tourist's acts of obeisance to prescribed spots with the traveler's more personal engagement with lesser known attractions. (In the wake of James Buzard's masterful work on the evolution and cultural valences of these terms in *The Beaten Track*, one longs for a fuller discussion of the implications of the posture of "the tourist" or "the traveler" for women.) In the attempt to rise above the status of "mere tourist" to more professional heights, these travelers "introduced into their commentaries the problematic discourse so often linked . . . with the idea of middle-class women's work" (Frawley 51). Although tourism was permissible as a lady's leisure activity, writing about one's travels, especially from a position of authority or expertise, challenged the ideology of separate spheres. So women travel writers adopted strategies that enabled them to find "authentic" authorial positions without directly challenging cultural definitions of appropriate roles. In their search for an "authentic Italy," these women "discovered an uncultivated Italy, one offering more potential for vision" (70). In striking contrast to the writers on South America that Pratt discusses, these women de-materialized the country, describing a landscape divorced from the specifics of history and politics, "one perhaps more fanciful and, in a sense, more exotic that those of their male counterparts" (70).

A subgroup of the female writers on Italy used their experiences as travelers to cultivate "professional identities" as art historians, identities that ultimately subsumed their personae as travelers. Their works strained beyond the limits of traditional travel writing by blending travel, art history, and criticism. Focusing on the lives and works of Anna Jameson and Elizabeth Rigby Eastlake, Frawley charts the evolution of each woman's sense of "authenticity and authority," the gender ideologies that shaped their definitions of themselves, and, most interestingly, the development of a professional community of women in the arts in Victorian Britain. Jameson's work gives evidence of an evolving sense of herself as an art historian and a feminist; in fact Frawley privileges a reading of *The Diary of an Ennuyée* as a "primer for beginning art historians." Because of her feminism, Jameson was able to bridge the gap between her identities at home and abroad, to be both a professional and a woman. On the other hand, the influential Lady Eastlake began as a travel writer, moved into the world of male discourse in her essays for the *Quarterly Review*, and married into a position of privilege. In Frawley's estimate she struggled with the contradictory status of the woman writer, desiring to gain legitimacy for her intellectual work yet to remain within the appropriately female sphere. Her solution was to garner authority for her work by minimizing gender issues and foregrounding class. By making class the "ultimate determinant of authority," she was able to negotiate the tensions between being a proper lady and a woman art critic.

One of the most tantalizing aspects of this chapter is its reflection on the intellectual community among women art historians and the cultural role of the museum in women's lives. Travel was the entree to the world of art but the real making of the art historian, Frawley argues, happened at home in museums and through interaction with other intellectual women. The museum, though clearly a professional site for art historians, was also a socially acceptable venue for spending leisure time; a safe place in which women could negotiate the ideological contradictions of their social position. I would like to have seen a more consistent and complete discussion of the woman writer's attempt to locate herself within various personal and institutional spaces that would allow her to develop a professional identity — something along the lines of Billie Melman's discussion of Amelia Edwards's position in the academic disciplines of Egyptology and archaeology or Alison Blunt's analysis of Kingsley's ethnographic and political contributions.

In *A Wider Range* destination is seen to determine literary and professional destiny; thus, women who journeyed to remote locales, which they mythologised as repositories of "the primitive," are treated here as "Adventuresses" whose works manifest similar attitudes and similar narrative strategies. The argument falters here, possibly because of the range of kinds of writing and of locales grouped together — Africa, Patagonia, the South Seas, Egypt. As a group, Victorian adventuresses are said to draw on two powerful male models — the military man and the intrepid explorer — in constructing identities that express the "aggressive side of their national identity" and demonstrate through their physical adventures that they could compete with men (108). Frawley ignores the ironizing of the role of the great male adventurer in the works of several adventuresses. Somehow, the book's focus on women's attempt to construct professional identities based on travel experiences seems to slip in this chapter: Mary Kingsley's struggles to be taken seriously as an ethnographer and her extensive involvement with colonial politics are dismissed in one paragraph. No mention is made of Florence Dixie's role as a war correspondent or of her later attempt to influence the political fate of the Zulu nation.

Instead, Frawley dwells on the anomalous sexual position that the adventuress occupied on returning home. She argues, not completely convincingly in the light of Alison Blunt's work, that women travelers were presented by the press as aggressively sexualized and thus demonized figures. To deflect this response, they adopted strategies of accommodation by domesticating their adventures or by adopting the pose of the ethnographer gathering data. Lumping together a wide range of women's responses to indigenous peoples, Frawley argues that "adventuresses" inspected the "natives" from a distance as scientific specimens: "Representing the peoples she [sic] encountered as either radically different — or worse, entirely absent — allowed some women travelers to preserve contrasts that made traveling new, exciting, strange, and appealing" (124). Such a generalization is painfully inadequate in accounting for the complex emotional bond forged by Dixie and Kingsley with the African peoples or Lucie Duff Gordon with the Egyptians. Frawley goes on to argue that many adventuresses, like Kingsley, construct their identities in relation to Nature, "endow[ing] the landscape with the capacity for powerful feeling and expression that they wouldn't let themselves see in the natives" (125). Again this generalization seems to flatten out the complex literary strategies that women travelers employ in describing the landscape — strategies that arise from a range of ideologies. In the end all that can be asserted about these adventurous women is that they helped to redefine the market for learned works and "could not help but have influence on opinion at home" (130). This reader, at least, was left clamoring for more specific and nuanced analyses.

If Frawley's treatment of the "Victorian adventuress" is flawed because of its attempt to lump into one category women who traveled to a range of different locales, Billie Melman's *Women's Orients* concentrates on a single loosely defined, but nonetheless circumscribed geographical location, "the Orient." She surveys two centuries of women's writing about the region with an eye to the difference that gender made in women's relations to the Orient, in their mode of travel and of writing. So as to attend to the "plurality of voices and idioms, reflecting the proliferation . . . of experiences of individuals and groups, of gender and class" (315), Melman organizes the writings into genres: Harem Literature, which focuses on the domestic; Evangelical Ethnography, a new brand of vocational literature; and autobiographical travel narratives by individuals — Harriet Martineau, Amelia Edwards — and by that "orientalist couple," the Blunts. She alternates between chapters that locate "themes, key words, and formulaic representations" (21) in groups of writers and those that focus on individuals. This "prosopography" of women's travel writing places the travelers within their cultural and literary contexts. To do so, it surveys 187 travel accounts written by women, compiles biographies of 53% of the writers, analyzes the lives along various matrices, and investigates the literary conventions found in the writings.

Although this organization sometimes produces needless repetition from chapter to chapter, it also allows the author to cover in rich detail an array of fascinating topics and to attend to the *heteroglossia* that she encounters. As part of the strategy of domesticating the Orient, Melman argues, Victorian women travel writers surfeited readers with details of Oriental women's lives, dwelling particularly on their physical features, food, hygiene, costume (including the tropes of dress and undress), and their domestic and child care arrangements. These writers also desexualized the Orient. The veil, a symbol of women's sexual liberty for Augustan writers like Mary Wortley-Montagu and Elizabeth Craven, was figured by their Victorian successors as "a trope for female virtue and respectability" (11). Similarly, the harem was represented as a bourgeois home, not as a place of sexual license.

Unlike these secular travelers, the evangelical writers featured in the second section of *Women's Orients* represented the *haremlik* as a locus of impurity, the manifestation of a patriarchal construct. Unlike Frawley, who assumes that destination determines form and attitude, Melman documents how the ideological framework of the journey structures perception. She offers a detailed portrait of female missionaries to the Middle East, documenting their numbers, the range and kind of their activities, and the leitmotifs of their writings. Throughout she points to the importance of the evangelical construction of gender; by figuring the Christian home as the woman's sphere and womankind as inherently spiritual, the agent of moral reform, evangelicalism opened the way for women to assume the role of professional missionaries. Not surprisingly, these missionary writers domesticated Palestine and "feminized" the landscape by associating it specifically with "religious experiences that are perceived as generically female as well as with women's history as it is revealed in sacred texts" (193). In fiction and travel writing, evangelical women represented themselves as "mothers" to their Jewish "daughters" (Melman observes that Muslim women and their culture were invariably excluded from Evangelical writings). When they confronted the Middle Eastern landscape, they "tamed the exotically oriental, by locating landscape and people in a conceptual and ideological framework familiar to the Christian West" (219). Of special interest is the discussion of how pictorial imagery, particularly that derived from Holman Hunt's "The Scapegoat," and Biblical typology, particularly that derived from the Naomi-Ruth story, shaped verbal landscape painting in several of these travel works.

Like Maria Frawley, Melman in her final section examines the intersection of autobiography and professional authority in travel writing and the development of stylistic techniques to represent experience. Identifying Harriet Martineau's *Eastern Life* as "the first feminine travelogue proper [about the Middle East] that is not an account of a pilgrimage" (253), Melman attests to the shaping force of the autobiographical instinct and Martineau's "notion of history" (236). Rather tartly, Melman argues for the derivative nature of Martineau's ideas (particularly the influence of Unitarian Biblical interpretation, higher criticism, and the antiquarian *récits de voyage),* the influence of her ideology of history on her representation of landscape, and the role of her inflated self-esteem in shaping the narrative. Amelia Edwards, one of the first female "Orientalists" and the author of *A Thousand Miles Up the Nile* (1889), receives a more sympathetic treatment in a chapter that discusses the evolution of archaeology and Egyptology as disciplines, Edwards's intellectual and structural position in these developing fields, and her rhetorical strategies in representing Egypt. Defeminizing her traveler/narrator and distancing herself from the peoples of contemporary Egypt (particularly the women and children), the narrator of *A Thousand Miles* presents a detailed, "scientific" account of the archaeological riches of Egypt which attempts a photographic description of objects, in a style virtually devoid of metaphor. Particularly concerned with the status of Egyptian women in history, Edwards parallels their legal and social position to that of contemporary British women, aiming to evoke a "retrospectival envy" in her Victorian female audience.

Arguing that "domestic politics shaped the rhetoric of domesticity which characterizes the co-produced accounts of travel" (277), Melman turns her attention finally to the writings of "orientalist couples," particularly Anne and Wilfrid Blunt. In this case, the complex politics of the Blunt family encompassed the traditional rhetoric of female submission on Anne's part, the affirmation of separate spheres (in *Bedouin Tribes*, 1878, Anne described life in the desert, Wilfrid added the "serious" informative chapters at the end), and a growing dissonance between the two in religious beliefs. Having investigated the "primary sources" used in the construction of the narrative of *Pilgrimage to Nejd* (1881) — Anne's travel journals, Wilfrid's travel journals, and Anne's more private pocket diaries — Melman concludes that this volume, although "edited" by Wilfrid Blunt, is decidedly Anne's allegorical account of her spiritual pilgrimage. Unlike the narratives produced by the romantic male travelers who preceded her (Burton and Palgrave), Anne's travelogue creates a self-effacing narrative persona while affirming the order and design she finds in the landscape of central Arabia that they had found so "wild."

Women travelers' relationship to the people among whom they travel seems a particularly vexed question in these works: Alison Blunt argues that a traveler like Mary Kingsley distances herself from African women; however, Melman contends, despite the example of Amelia Edwards, that in general nineteenth-century women travelers to the Orient locate "the similarities between western and exotic familial structures . . . [and] note the sameness of womankind, regardless of culture, class or ethnicity" (309). Although she argues for the emergence of an empathetic connection between women travelers and Oriental peoples, Melman does admit that "cultural smugness and ethnocentrism" were also probable outcomes of such encounters, especially among liberal feminists or reformers.

The five books under consideration here concur that no single meta-narrative can account for women travelers' representations of the other or themselves; no single model can capture the complex encoding of experiences for diverse audiences. Moreover, despite wide differences in the theoretical frameworks which inform these texts, they share a surprising number of common concerns. For instance, all of them argue for a "difference" in women's writing, even though they disagree on its determining causes: women's position as gendered subjects? or their exclusion from professional authority? or the material conditions of their journeys? or their ability to experience empathy with the people among whom they travel? or their individual values and experiences? All of these critical works find manifestations of difference in women's writing, whether in narrative paradigms, descriptive conventions, the "gazes" they employ, or the "counter-hegemonic" voices they record. Several find "ambivalence" and instability at the heart of women's travel writing. All are interested in the cultural status of travel writing itself and the extent to which the writer's gender shaped the way that the text was consumed. Finally, even in the face of profound shifts in critical consciousness over the last decade, all of the critics except Sara Mills, still circle around the central feminist insight of the criticism of the 1980s: the ways in which the experience of travel both catalyzed and symbolized Victorian women's redefinition of their private selves and their social/professional personae.

University of Hartford

WORKS CONSIDERED

Blunt, Alison. *Travel, Gender, and Imperialism: Mary Kingsley and West Africa.* New York and London: Guilford, 1994.

Buzard, James. *The Beaten Track: European Tourism, Literature, and the Ways to Culture, 1800–1918.* Oxford and New York: Clarendon, 1993.

Chaudhuri, Nupur and Margaret Strobel, eds. *Western Women and Imperialism: Complicity and Resistance.* Bloomington and Indianapolis: Indiana UP, 1992.

Frawley, Maria H. *A Wider Range: Travel Writing by Women in Victorian England.* London and Toronto: Associated University Presses, 1994.

Melman, Billie. *Women's Orients: English Women and the Middle East, 1718–1918.* Ann Arbor, Michigan: U of Michigan P, 1992.

Mills, Sara. *Discourses of Difference: An Analysis of Women's Travel Writing and Colonialism.* London and New York: Routledge, 1991.

Morley, Dave. "Texts, Readers, Subjects." *Culture, Media, Language.* Ed. Stuart Hall, Dorothy Hobson, Andrew Lowe and Paul Willis. London: Unwin Hyman, 1980. 163–176.

Pratt, Mary Louise. *Imperial Eyes: Travel Writing and Transculturation.* London and New York: Routledge, 1992.

ROBERT AND ELIZABETH BARRETT BROWNING: AN ANNOTATED BIBLIOGRAPHY FOR 1993

By Sandra M. Donaldson

The following abbreviations appear in this year's bibliography:

DAI	*Dissertation Abstracts International*
TLS	*Times Literary Supplement*
VLC	*Victorian Literature and Culture*
VP	*Victorian Poetry*
VS	*Victorian Studies*

An asterisk* indicates that we have not seen the item. Cross references with citation numbers between 51 and 70 followed by a colon (e.g., C68:) refer to William S. Peterson's *Robert and Elizabeth Barrett Browning: An Annotated Bibliography, 1951–1970* (New York: Browning Institute, 1974); higher numbers refer to *Robert Browning: A Bibliography 1830–1950*, compiled by L. N. Broughton, C. S. Northup, and Robert Pearsall (Ithaca: Cornell UP, 1953).

Readers are encouraged to send offprints to Sandra Donaldson, Department of English, Box 7209, University of North Dakota, Grand Forks ND 58202. I especially need articles that have appeared in less familiar journals.

I would like to thank Dominic Bisignano for help with translations from the Italian.

A. Primary Works

A93: 1.* Browning, Elizabeth Barrett. *Elizabeth Barrett Browning: Selected Poems*. Bloomsbury Poetry Classics. New York: St. Martin's, 1993.

A93: 2.* Browning, Elizabeth Barrett, and Robert Browning. *Robert and Elizabeth Browning*. Decorative Arts Books, Poets Series. Jarrold, 1993. 146 pp.

A93: 3.* Browning, Robert. *My Last Duchess and Other Poems*. Thrift Edition. New York: Dover, 1993. 128 pp.

A93: 4.* Browning, Robert. *The Pied Piper of Hamelin*. Illus. André Amstutz. London: Orchard P, 1993. 32 pp. ¶Rev. by Jeff Hynds, *Books for Keeps* 80 (May 1993): 37; Teresa Scragg, *School Librarian* 41.3 (August 1993): 106–07.

A93: 5. Day, Aidan, ed. and introduction. *Robert Browning: Selected Poetry and Prose*. [See A91: 3.] ¶Rev. by Chris Jones, *Notes and Queries* 40 (March 1993): 113–14; Peter Morgan, *English Studies* 74.2 (April 1993): 192–93.

A93: 6. Dunn, Douglas, ed. and introduction. *The Essential Browning*. The Essential Poets series. New York: Ecco P, 1990. 181 pp.

A93: 7. Jack, Ian, Rowena Fowler, and Margaret Smith, eds. *Bells and Pomegranates, VII–VIII*. Volume 4 of *The Poetical Works of Robert Browning*. [See A91: 5.] ¶Rev. by Peter Morgan, *English Studies* 74.2 (April 1993): 192–93.

A93: 8. Kelley, Philip, and Scott Lewis, eds. *The Brownings' Correspondence*, Volumes 9 & 10. [See A91: 8 & A92: 12.] ¶Rev. by Ian Jack, *TLS* 7 May 1993: 12.

A93: 9. Kelley, Philip, and Scott Lewis, eds. *The Brownings' Correspondence, Volume 11: July 1845–January 1846*. Winfield, KS: Wedgestone P, 1993. xiv + 422 pp.

A93: 10. McSweeney, Kerry, ed. Introduction and notes to *Elizabeth Barrett Browning: Aurora Leigh*. World Classics series. Oxford: Oxford UP, 1993. xliv + 361 pp. ¶Rev. by Andrew Motion, *Observer* 2 May 1993: 58.

A93: 11. Reynolds, Margaret, ed. Introduction and notes to *Aurora Leigh, by Elizabeth Barrett Browning*. [See A92: 16.] ¶Rev. by Deirdre David, *VP* 31.4 (Winter 1993): 435–38; Corinne Bieman Davies, *Dalhousie Review* 73 (Spring 1993): 124–26; Daniel Karlin, *TLS* 15 January 1993: 24.

A93: 12. Woolford, John, and Daniel Karlin, eds. *The Poems of Browning*, Volumes 1 & 2. [See A91: 10 & 11.] ¶Rev. by Philip Drew, *Review of English Studies* 44 (August 1993): 439–40; Chris Jones, *Notes and Queries* 40 (March 1993): 113–14.

B. Reference and Bibliographical Works and Exhibitions

B93: 1. Cohen, Edward H., ed. "Victorian Bibliography for 1993." *VS* 36.4 (Summer 1993): 729–30.

B93: 2. Donaldson, Sandra. *Elizabeth Barrett Browning: An Annotated Bibliography of the Commentary and Criticism, 1826–1990.* New York: G. K. Hall, 1993. xiv + 642 pp. ¶Rev. by J. R. Luttrell, *Choice* 31 (November 1993): 428.

B93: 3. Donaldson, Sandra M. "Robert and Elizabeth Barrett Browning: An Annotated Bibliography for 1990." *VLC* 20 (1992): 407–23.

B93: 4. Maynard, John. "Guide to the Year's Work in Victorian Poetry: 1991 and 1992: Robert Browning." *VP* 31.3 (Autumn 1993): 280–93.

B93: 5. Mermin, Dorothy. "Guide to the Year's Work in Victorian Poetry: 1991 and 1992: Elizabeth Barrett Browning." *VP* 31.3 (Autumn 1993): 275–80.

B93: 6.* Shroyer, Richard J., and Thomas J. Collins. *A Concordance to the Poems and Plays of Robert Browning.* 7 vols. New York: AMS P, 1993.

C. Biography, Criticism, and Miscellaneous

C93: 1. Anderson, Amanda. "Reproduced in Finer Motions: Encountering the Fallen in Barrett Browning's *Aurora Leigh.*" *Tainted Souls and Painted Faces: The Rhetoric of Fallenness in Victorian Culture.* Ithaca: Cornell UP, 1993. 167–97. [See C90: 1.] ¶Interrogates the cultural belief that women's sexual experience outside marriage necessarily "produced a predictable and accelerated decline," looking at how Marian in EBB's *Aurora Leigh* "effectively appropriates the power of self-expression and self-definition" as EBB attempts "to reconcile literary work and transformative social action." EBB revises "the distorting relation to the other that typifies Victorian inscriptions of impure femininity," but "Aurora's concept of intersubjectivity remains restrictively dyadic and hence cannot generate a larger understanding of social plurality and social hierarchy." Mentions RB's "Porphyria's Lover" as well.

C93: 2. Ash, Timothy Garton. "International Books of the Year." *TLS* 3 December 1993: 13. ¶Cites as his favorite a 1949 edition of *Poems of Robert Browning.*

C93: 3. Bancroft, RoseLee. "The Victorian Concept of the Italian Renaissance in Browning, Ruskin, Eliot, and Pater." *DAI* 54.1 (July 1993): 184A–85A.

C93: 4. Berggren, Kerstin. "En episod från Napoleonkrigen." Trans. Gunnar Mascoll Silfverstolpe. *Studiekamraten* 74.2–3 (1992): 44–45. ¶In Swedish. Includes translation of RB's "Incident of the French Camp."

C93: 5. Cervo, Nathan A. " 'Cool, I' Faith' and 'A Pan's Face': The Social Unity of Shepherd and Flock in Browning's 'Bishop Blougram's Apology'."

English Language Notes 30.4 (June 1993): 48–52. ¶Provides a reading of two phrases from RB's poem, seeing the Bishop's words as pastoral.

C93: 6. Chandran, K. Narayana. "Echoes of 'Abt Vogler' in *The Cantos*: 74, 81." *English Language Notes* 30.4 (June 1993): 59–61. ¶Suggests that sections ix and x of "Abt Vogler," among others, are echoed in two of Ezra Pound's *Pisan Cantos* (74 and 81), embodying the ideas of "time's wreckage, and the good that survives it."

C93: 7. Collins, John. *The Two Forgers: A Biography of Henry Buxton Forman and Thomas James Wise*. New Castle, DE: Oak Knoll Books, 1992. xiii + 317 pp. ¶Revisits the question of who created unauthorized editions of various authors' works, the most famous of which is EBB's *Sonnets from the Portuguese.* Both Wise and Forman are implicated, and works by both EBB and RB were involved. Rev. by W. Baker, *Choice* 29 (July/August 1992): 1663–64; Sidney E. Berger, *Libraries and Culture* 28.2 (Spring 1993): 210–14; *Book Collector* 41 (1992): 525–26; Arthur Freeman, *TLS* 12 June 1992: 24; *Papers of the Bibliographical Society of America* 86 (1992): 483–84; John Sutherland, *London Review of Books* 15.1 (7 January 1993): 16–17.

C93: 8. Corbett, Mary Jean. *Representing Femininity: Middle-Class Subjectivity in Victorian and Edwardian Women's Autobiographies.* New York and Oxford: Oxford UP, 1992. 252 pp., passim. ¶Includes a discussion of EBB's *Aurora Leigh* as an effort "to counter the professional's prohibition against female labor and to rewrite Wordsworth's narrative of poetic development," substituting "a vision of interdependence." The poem points out the cost of Romantic isolation and individualism for men and women both. Yet, finally, in her "underlying adherence to the ideologies she presumably contests," EBB looks transgressive only "if we have bought the idea that all women's speech is inherently liberatory, no matter what women have to say." She also reproduces "elitist norms of literary values," privileging poetry over prose.

C93: 9. DeLuise, Dolores, with Michael Timko. "Becoming the Poet: The Feminine Poet-Speaker in the Work of Elizabeth Barrett Browning." *Virginal Sexuality and Textuality in Victorian Literature*, ed. Lloyd Davis. Albany: State U of New York P, 1993. 87–103. ¶Explores the development of EBB's virgin texts to her texts of experience, a shift from male to female. Her early poems figured the creative poet as a male lover initiated "into a type of sexual experience that becomes explicitly female." In "Lady Geraldine's Courtship," "the speaker is a male poet-genius, the 'lady' of the poem is not fully identified with her author, nor is the poem written from Lady Geraldine's point of view. In the *Sonnets*, the poet is a male poet-genius, and the speaker and 'lady' are female and closely identified with the author. In *Aurora Leigh*, all these roles become one: the speaker and lady are female and are closely identified with the author, who is the poet-genius.''

C93: 10. Dessommes, Nancy B. ''Browning's 'Soliloquy of the Spanish Cloister'.'' *Explicator* 52.1 (Fall 1993): 34–36. ¶Considers the pact with Satan that the speaker in RB's ''Soliloquy of the Spanish Cloister'' intends to make in order to damn Brother Lawrence, and then to break.

C93: 11. Dooley, Allan C. *Author and Printer in Victorian England*. Charlottesville and London: UP of Virginia, 1992. xii + 192 pp., passim. ¶Charts typical patterns of book production and textual change in nineteenth-century Britain, using RB's career as a major example. Examination of his practice with regard to punctuation, revision, use of proofs, and other involvement in production — especially regarding the 1863 and 1865 *Poetical Works* with Chapman and Hall and a new edition with Smith Elder in 1868 — shows how he asserted and maintained textual control.

C93: 12. Falk, Alice. '' 'It Is To the Greeks that We Turn': Greek and Women Writers.'' *DAI* 53.9 (March 1993): 3221A. ¶Includes EBB.

C93: 13. Faurot, Margaret. '' 'Bishop Blougram's Apology': The Making of the Poet-Shepherd.'' *VP* 31.1 (Spring 1993): 1–18. ¶Reads RB's poem in the light of the Higher Criticism, arguing that RB ''queries the claims of poetry to supply the place of a diminished religion.'' The Bishop engages in a ''dialectic of self-discovery'' that leads to an art of belief, bringing ''art and faith into unified being.''

C93: 14. Fay, Elizabeth A. ''Romantic Men, Victorian Women: The Nightingale Talks Back.'' *Studies in Romanticism* 32.2 (Summer 1993): 211–24. ¶Traces a line of conversation in 19th century poetry that became inverted, silencing female voices. RB's dramatic monologues and EBB's *Aurora Leigh* ''dramatize and attempt to come to terms with'' this silencing. Her *Sonnets from the Portuguese* ''define her as a poet of love'' writing from the empowering stance of troubadour. Her ''Bianca Among the Nightingales,'' however, is ''a balladic monologue'' depicting a deserted woman sentenced to silence who descends into madness, ''an echoing of the very form her husband so inscribed with women's deaths.'' ''None of these resolutions courts dialogue.''

C93: 15. Gibson, Mary Ellis, ed. *Critical Essays on Robert Browning*. [See C92: 23.] ¶Rev. by *Nineteenth-Century Literature* 47.4 (March 1993): 530.

C93: 16. Gosse, Edmund. "Robert Browning 1812–1889." *Portraits from Life*, ed. Ann Thwaite. Aldershott: Scolar, 1991. 43–48. [See C1383 & 1385.] ¶Reprints Gosse's memorial to RB from the *New Review* in 1890, included as "Personal Impressions" in his book, *Robert Browning: Personalia* (1890).

C93: 17. Haddon, Celia. *Faithful to the End: An Illustrated Anthology about Dogs and Their Owners*. London: Headline; New York: Thomas Dunne, St. Martin's, 1991. 12–13, 41, 52. ¶Cites EBB and her dog, Flush, under friendship, cleverness, and family tension, quoting from letters and quoting "Flush or Faunus."

C93: 18. Harvey, A. D. "The Saga of Nationalism." *Times Higher Education Supplement* 28 May 1993: 19. ¶Examines the "idea of a great epic poem as the foundation of a nationalist literature," mentioning RB's *The Ring and the Book* as an experiment with the long form that was not traditional.

C93: 19. Hawthorne, Mark D. "Allusions to Robert Browning in Jerzy Kosinski's *The Hermit of 69th Street*." *Notes on Contemporary Literature* 23.4 (Sept. 1993): 3–5. ¶Notes references to RB's *The Ring and the Book*, "Childe Roland to the Dark Tower Came," *Sordello*, and *Pauline*.

C93: 20. Houston, Gail Turley. "Gender Construction and the *Kunstlerroman: David Copperfield* and *Aurora Leigh*." *Philological Quarterly* 72.2 (Spring 1993): 213–36. ¶Uses EBB's *Aurora Leigh* to interrogate the claims of the Kunstlerroman's "double vision of the author as typical but also as special creation and creator [, an idea] . . . grounded in the notion that the artist is male." Comparing EBB's poem with Dickens's novel "provides an important strategy for studying Victorian gender construction vis-à-vis the construction of the self as artist within the constraints of a market system." Specifically, EBB's poem "replaces the phallic gesture of the male-authored *Kunstlerroman*'s assumption of manhood with the abundant, erect, tangible female breast, which, instead of reiterating the old flaccid dead mythologies, engenders a new metaphor for woman as writer."

C93: 21. Hudson, Gertrude Reese. *Robert Browning's Literary Life: From First Work to Masterpiece*. Austin, TX: Eakin, 1992. xxi + 638 pp. ¶Studies 280 reviews as well as other materials from the period 1833–70 in order to map the reception of his works and also to correct misconceptions. He was grateful for "helpful reviews" and attempted to "provide guidance for his readers." Early critical coolness gave way to a "slow and steady acclimatization to the original qualities of Browning's poetry and the arrival at a revised notion of the function of poetry." Includes a bibliography of reviews from the period.

C93: 22. Ingersoll, Earl G. ''Autumn Songs: Robert Browning's 'Andrea del Sarto' in Context.'' *Durham University Journal* 54.1 (January 1993): 75–79. ¶Examines RB's poem in the context of the Romantic myth of autumn and its later use by Joyce in ''A Little Cloud.'' The ''waning of the year at close of day'' evokes decadence and belatedness, melancholy, and self pity in Andrea, and also in Joyce's Chandler.

C93: 23. Kahn, Jacqueline Sue. ''Women's Associations in Victorian Literature and Culture: Friendship, Rivalry, and Alternative Alliances in the Third Sphere.'' *DAI* 54.5 (November 1993): 1811A. ¶Includes EBB.

C93: 24. Karlin, Daniel. *Browning's Hatreds.* Oxford: Clarendon; New York: Oxford UP, 1993. 272 pp. ¶Examines instances of hatred and hating, which are associated with conflict and aggression, in RB's work. He believed that ''struggle is the condition of existence,'' especially the dialectical struggle between love and hate. Topics considered are personal emotion, intellectual opposition, creativity, popularity, righteous hatred, physical and sexual violence; these may be seen in characters, landscape, and plot.

C93: 25. Keats, Patrick H. ''Chesterton, Browning, and the Decadents.'' *Chesterton Review* 19.2 (May 1993): 175–91. ¶Explores reasons for Chesterton's affinity for RB, seen especially in his 1903 biography. Chesterton defends RB against the charge of obscurity, depicting him ''as a democrat, a liberal and, in most respects, a conventional and ordinary man.'' RB combined ''a fundamental personal humility with a large and eclectic knowledge of out-of-the-way things.'' Chesterton sees RB as a love poet rather than a philosopher. His use of the grotesque is distinguished from the Decadents' use of it by his optimism and clear-mindednsess, in contrast to their nihilism and skepticism.

C93: 26. Kennedy, Richard S. *Robert Browning's ''Asolando'': The Indian Summer of a Poet.* Columbia and London: U of Missouri P. xii + 152 pp. ¶Attends to the poems in RB's final volume, *Asolando*, as ''a poetic resurgence,'' seeing them as representative of RB's ''ideas and practices during his long career.'' Thirteen poems are reprinted. Originally presented at the New York Browning Society in 1990.

C93: 27. Kienitz, Gail Marie. ''The Efficacy of Ambiguity: A Study of Browning's Reception.'' *DAI* 53.11 (May 1993): 3920A. [See C92: 36.]

C93: 28. Lampedusa, Giuseppe Tomasi di. ''Further Reflections on English Literature: Browning & Other Victorians.'' *New Criterion* 12.2 (October 1993): 30. ¶Observes that reading RB is worthwhile, despite the obscurity in his poetry.

C93: 29. Lassandro Rocci, Giuliana. "Elisabeth Barret Browning." *Esperienze Letterarie: Rivista Trimestrale* 18.2 (April–June 1993): 73–76. ¶In Italian. Traces aspects of feminine sensibility, especially love and pity for the oppressed, in "Lady Geraldine's Courtship," which combines "ideals of Christian liberty with social equality," and "The Cry of the Children," in which EBB denounces "the inhuman conditions of boys and girls forced to work." *Aurora Leigh* "reveals her vast social and cultural interests," and *Sonnets from the Portuguese* "mirrors and reflects her passionate story of love."

C93: 30. Leighton, Angela. *Victorian Women Poets: Writing Against the Heart.* [See C92: 43.] ¶Rev. by Gillian Beer, *TLS* 13 November 1992: 24; J. A. V. Chapple, *Victorian Review* 19.1 (Summer 1993): 77–80; V. L. Radley, *Choice* 30 (March 1993): 1149–50; *Virginia Quarterly Review* 69.2 (Spring 1993): 48–50.

C93: 31. Lewis, Scott. "Eton Assumes Guardianship of Casa Guidi." *Through Casa Guidi Windows* 10 (Autumn 1993): 1. ¶Announces transfer of ownership of the Brownings' home in Florence from the Browning Institute to Eton College.

C93: 32. Lewis, Scott. "Eton College — New Custodian of Casa Guidi." *Through Casa Guidi Windows* 10 (Autumn 1993): 2. ¶Profiles Eton College and its Barrett and Browning family associations, as well as related additions to the College's library.

C93: 33. Loeffelholz, Mary. *Dickinson and the Boundaries of Feminist Theory.* Urbana: U of Illinois P, 1991. viii + 179 pp., passim. ¶Compares Emily Dickinson's poetry and that of EBB in terms of Lacanian psychoanalytic theory. Dickinson rejects the "unifying apocalyptic" vision of *Aurora Leigh* and exorcises its "terrifying mother figure"; EBB's poem, however, as "an inaugural text of women's literary tradition" is "richly, fruitfully contradictory." In "The Poet's Vow" EBB, like Dickinson later, revises and reverses "the male topos" of a "father text, Wordsworth's 'Lucy' poems." Rev. by Angela Leighton, *TLS* 3 July 1992: 29; Elizabeth A. Petrino, *Tulsa Studies in Women's Literature* 12.2 (Fall 1993): 361–63; Karen Sánchez-Eppler, *American Literature* 64.3 (September 1992): 607–08.

C93: 34. Loucks, James F. "Browning's 'An Epistle . . . of Karshish'." *Explicator* 52.1 (Fall 1993): 30–33. ¶Cites epistolary conventions to argue against Altick's suggestion that St. Paul is a "hovering presence" in RB's "An Epistle . . . of Karshish." Rather, both St. Paul and the fictive Karshish emulated "a pre-existing epistolary style."

C93: 35. "Margaret Keep Collection Attracts Researchers." *Armstrong Browning Library Newsletter* 39 (Fall 1993): 3. ¶Lists items obtained by the ABL that were owned by RB's friend, Margaret ("Magari") Keep.

C93: 36. Maxwell, Catherine. "Browning's 'Porphyria's Lover'." *Explicator* 52.1 (Fall 1993): 27–30. ¶Offers *Othello* and *The Winter's Tale* as additional underlying texts for the story of the murderous male in RB's "Porphyria's Lover." These "revisionary allusions" portray his behavior as rational, but "founded on dangerously idealized notions of love and an endorsement of male self-determination at the expense of female autonomy."

C93: 37. Maxwell, Catherine. "Browning's Pygmalion and The Revenge of Galatea." *English Literary History* 60.4 (Winter 1993): 989–1013. ¶Suggests Ovid's story is "a larger mythic influence" in RB's poems than that of Andromeda's rescue by Perseus because it reveals the misogyny of masculine possession. His male speakers "desire feminine simulacra, static art-objects," but by presenting these desires equivocally he "shows us their fatuity." In his portraits, RB examines the way "creativity is characterized by a continuing process of construction and dissolution."

C93: 38. Maxwell, Catherine. "Robert Browning and Frederic Leighton: 'Che farò senza Euridice?' " *Review of English Studies* 44 (August 1993): 362–72. ¶Explores references in RB's "Eurydice to Orpheus" and Leighton's paintings on the subject in 1855–56 and 1864, and Greek themes in their work generally, to elaborate aspects of their friendship. The "mythic theme of the resurrected wife" absorbed both Leighton and RB and involved music as well, especially Gluck's operas.

C93: 39. Mermin, Dorothy. *Godiva's Ride: Women of Letters in England, 1830–1880.* Bloomington: Indiana UP, 1993. xix + 181 pp., passim. ¶Views the legend of Lady Godiva, whose "powerlessness is her power, her nakedness her shield," as an image for Victorian women writers for gendered action which is both enabling and contradictory. EBB's early public display — her poetic action — similarly had political motivation. Writing in a context of religious belief, women's "ambition turned to altruism, and the eroticism and vulnerability that went with self-exposure became signs of chastity and modes of power." Discussion includes considerations of "Beth," *Sonnets from the Portuguese*, and *Aurora Leigh*; other authors considered include the Brontë sisters, George Eliot, Harriet Martineau, Anna Jameson, Elizabeth Gaskell, Margaret Oliphant, and Christina Rossetti.

C93: 40. Millgate, Michael. "Robert and Pen Browning." *Testamentary Acts: Browning, Tennyson, James, Hardy.* [See C92: 54.] ¶Rev. by W. Eugene Davis,

English Literature in Transition 36.3 (1993): 360–63; Douglas Hewitt, *Notes and Queries* 40 (September 1993): 412–13; Philip Horne, *Nineteenth-Century Literature* 48.2 (September 1993): 261–64; Lawrence Poston, *VS* 37.1 (Autumn 1993): 152–53; H. J. Rosengarten, *University of Toronto Quarterly* 63.1 (Fall 1993): 172–74; John Schad, *Times Higher Education Supplement* 2 April 1993: 22; M. Timko, *Choice* 30 (January 1993): 795.

C93: 41. Monteiro, George. ''The Seahorse in *A Streetcar Named Desire*.'' *Notes on Contemporary Literature* 23.3 (May 1993): 9. ¶Suggests that Blanche Dubois's selection of a seahorse pin in Tennessee Williams's play evokes the image of taming in RB's ''My Last Duchess.'' She is broken by both Stanley and the doctor who comes at the end to take her to an asylum.

C93: 42. Nolan, Edward F. ''Browning's 'Rabbi Ben Ezra,' Lines 124–25.'' *Explicator* 51.2 (Winter 1993): 90. ¶Contends that editors' suggestion that readers supply ''whom'' after ''I'' in 124 and after ''they'' in 125 of RB's ''Rabbi Ben Ezra'' is incorrect. Rather, these lines should be read as written, seeing the ''the world arraigned'' and ''my soul disdained'' as nominative absolutes.

C93: 43. O'Neill, Patricia. ''*Paracelsus* and the Authority of Science in Browning's Career.'' *VLC* 20 (1992): 293–310. ¶Locates *Paracelsus* as a pre-Darwinian and post-Romantic poem embodying RB's appreciation of ''the importance of science as a cognitive and communal process rather than as a body of knowledge produced from a fixed or exclusive standpoint.'' The poem demonstrates ''how a literary work can mediate ideological conflicts,'' conflicts which he explored throughout his career.

C93: 44. Petch, Simon. ''Law, Narrative, and Anonymity in Browning's *The Ring and the Book*.'' *VLC* 20 (1992): 311–33. ¶Examines the dynamic of narrative in the plotting of *The Ring and the Book*, focusing on its three anonymous books (II–IV) and two anonymous pamphlets in RB's source. The books' variant plots, semi-official discourse, and stock stories constitute the social relationships of the poem. Through the poem ''a legal code speaks to a social world,'' revealing that the law is ''a species of narrative and dramatic poetry.''

C93: 45. Pettit, Alexander. ''Place, Time, and Parody in *The Ring and the Book*.'' *VP* 31.1 (Spring 1993): 95–106. ¶Argues that Caponsacchi and Guido both ''are dislocated geographically and temporally.'' This disjunction of character and context makes them ''representatives of exhausted cultural and literary traditions.'' The poem is a ''parody of characters who act in ignorance of the cultural requirements of genre'': they are anachronistic and equally absurd.

C93: 46. Philipose, Lily. ''The Gospel of the Hearth: Domestic Evangelical Literature in Victorian England.'' *DAI* 54.1 (July 1993): 190A. ¶Includes EBB.

C93: 47. Ryals, Clyde de L. *The Life of Robert Browning: A Critical Biography.* Oxford and Cambridge, MA: Blackwell, 1993. xi + 291 pp. ¶Sees RB's poetry as having ''both biographical presence and biographical absence,'' a paradox ''essential to his self-fashioning.'' His theatrical metaphors and the religious metaphors of immanence, transcendence, and incarnation are most apparent in his idea of the person. Rev. by S. C. Dillon, *Choice* 31 (Nov. 1993): 456.

C93: 48. St. George, E. A. W. *Browning and Conversation.* London: Macmillan, 1993. vii + 235 pp. [See C91: 73.] ¶Suggests ways of reading RB's later long poems: in the context of Victorian expectations about conversation; in the context of his own manner of talk; relating conversational style and narrative in *Red Cotton Night-cap Country*; examining dialogue in *The Inn Album*; considering his responses to critics in *Pacchiarotto*, some *Dramatic Idyls, Jocoseria,* and *Ferishtah's Fancies*; and seeing RB ''at his most talkatively self conscious'' in *Parleyings With Certain People of Importance in Their Day.*

C93: 49. Schoffman, Nachum. *There is No ''Truer Truth'': The Musical Aspect of Browning's Poetry.* [See C91: 74.] ¶Rev. by Leslie White, *Analytical and Enumerative Bibliography* 6 (1992): 251–53; Matthew Wilson, *Notes* 49.3 (March 1993): 1056–58.

C93: 50. Srebrnik, Patricia Thomas. '' 'The Central Truth': Phallogocentrism in *Aurora Leigh.*'' *Victorian Newsletter* 84 (Fall 1993): 9–11. ¶Explores EBB's failure ''to deconstruct the Symbolic or revise the Imaginary'' articulated early in *Aurora Leigh* in the image of the palimpsest. ''By repudiating her love for Marian, by failing to imagine a female God[, and] . . . by affirming her belief in a God who guarantees the masculine Symbolic / Imaginary,'' Aurora capitulates to the power of phallogocentric discourse and inscribes her art in the old logic.

C93: 51. Stainton, Leslie. ''Love Among the Ruins.'' *Michigan Alumnus* Jan./Feb. 1993: 24–30. ¶Describes a visit to the Brownings' home in Florence, recounting the story of their courtship and marriage, their life and work at Casa Guidi, the auction of their possessions, and the history of the building itself.

C93: 52. Starzyk, Lawrence J. *The Dialogue of the Mind with Itself.* Calgary: U of Calgary P, 1992. 162 pp., passim. ¶Revises and expands C90: 89.

C93: 53. Stone, Marjorie. ''A Cinderella Among the Muses: Barrett Browning and the Ballad Tradition.'' *VLC* 21 (1993): 233–68. ¶Examines EBB's ''The

Poet's Vow'' and ''The Romaunt of the Page'' and others as examples of her revising the ballad tradition. ''Vow'' critiques Wordsworth's *Lyrical Ballads*, and ''The Romaunt'' addresses Bishop Percy's ballads. Her ballads were popular, and the genre was appealing because of ''its energy, its frank physicality, its elemental passions, its strong heroines, and its sinewy narrative conflicts.'' These features ''allowed her to circumvent the passionless purity conventionally ascribed to the middle-class Victorian woman.''

C93: 54.* Timko, Michael. *Robert Browning and Magari, A Faint Show of Bigamy?* Waco, TX: Armstrong Browning Library, 1993. 40 pp. ¶Examines RB's friendship with Margaret Keep during the last three years of his life.

C93: 55. ''A Touch of the Poets in Ann Arbor.'' *Michigan Alumnus* Jan./Feb. 1993: 30–31. ¶Describes Peter Heydon's association with the Browning Institute and his collection of manuscripts, first editions, and related items, such as the poets' writing tables.

C93: 56. Tucker, Herbert F. ''Representation and Repristination: Virginity in *The Ring and the Book*.'' *Virginal Sexuality and Textuality in Victorian Literature*, ed. Lloyd Davis. Albany: State U of New York P, 1993. 67–86. ¶Observes that truth is the ''leading topic'' of RB's *The Ring and the Book* ''and virginity its leading trope'' because images of virginity ''structure both the historical action of Browning's epic — a mythos of draconian oppression, virginal distress, and heroic rescue — and its hermeneutic activity of getting at the truth about that historical-mythical action.'' RB as well as his ''two maiden principals Caponsacchi and Pompilia . . . repeatedly express in images of virginity their cognate fidelities to the love of truth and the truth of love; and the paradoxes entailed by the imagination of virginity enforce a recognition of the inevitably constructed nature of the faiths they espouse.''

C93: 57. Vaughan, Alden T., and Virginia Mason Vaughan. *Shakespeare's Caliban: A Cultural History*. Cambridge: Cambridge UP, 1991. xxviii + 290 pp., passim. ¶Notes that RB's Caliban may reflect Victorian pessimism, but he is ''more human, thoughtful, and sympathetic than the monster of the eighteenth century.'' Rev. by Christine Dymkowski, *Modern Language Review* 88.4 (October 1993): 939–40.

C93: 58. Walsh, Cheryl. ''The Voices in Karshish: A Bakhtinian Reading of Robert Browning's 'Epistle'.'' *VP* 31.3 (Autumn 1993): 213–26. ¶Relates Bakhtin's concept of regenerative ambivalence to RB's use of irony and incongruity in ''An Epistle . . . of Karshish,'' considering especially its Christian aspect, the apparent degradation of Christ. The story of Lazarus ''reiterates on more than one level the ancient death and regeneration theme of the carnival,'' and the dialogic operates in the poem's two voices, that of the physician and a more speculative voice.

C93: 59. Ward, John Powell. *The English Line: Poetry of the Unpoetic from Wordsworth to Larkin.* London: Macmillan, 1991. 217 pp., passim. ¶Briefly considers both EBB and RB in relation to the line of poetry characterized by brooding subjectivity and ordinary language, regarding her ''The Lost Bower'' as a woman poet's subversion of the male cast to English poetry, and placing his poetry in contrast to this line. Rev. by Michael Walters, *TLS* 21 February 1992: 21.

C93: 60. Welsh, Alexander. *Strong Representations: Narrative and Circumstantial Evidence in England.* [See C92: 100.] ¶Rev. by Lenora P. Ledwon, *Nineteenth-Century Contexts* 17.1 (1993): 106–09; Michael Levenson, *VS* 36.4 (Summer 1993): 485–86; John E. Loftis, *Rocky Mountain Review* 47 (1993): 115–17; Merritt Moseley, *Sewanee Review* 101.1 (Winter 1993): xxxi-xxxiv; Mark A. Weinstein, *South Atlantic Review* 58.2 (1993): 162–64.

C93: 61. Woolford, John. ''Browning Rethinks Romanticism.'' *Essays in Criticism* 43.3 (July 1993): 211–27. ¶Argues that because RB destroyed drafts of his work, successive workings out of an idea may be observed in published poems, and earlier works ''may become subjectively alienated.'' In *Sordello* (1840) he rejects Romanticism, and in *Fifine* (1872) he ''rejects his own rejection.'' Wordsworth's *The Prelude* (1850), with its ''empiricist meliorism,'' was more consistent with RB's views than Keats's radical equivocation ''over the ontological value of dream and imagination,'' renewing ''his own Romanticism.'' In *Fifine* the ''dream is now the poetry, and its vagaries the responsibility of the transforming imagination, here rehabilitated in Browning's aesthetic for the first time since Sordello's attack on it.''

C93: 62. Woudhuysen, H. R. ''Sales of Books and Manuscripts.'' *TLS* 11 December 1992: 193. ¶Notes upcoming sale of a 1908 edition of ''Browning's Love Poems'' inscribed by D. H. Lawrence to Margaret Brinton.

BIBLIOGRAPHY INDEX

INDEX

Page numbers in **bold face** refer to illustrations